W9-BBB-229

A SURVEY OF
ARAB–ISRAELI
RELATIONS

A SURVEY OF ARAB–ISRAELI RELATIONS

SECOND EDITION

Europa Publications
Taylor & Francis Group

LONDON AND NEW YORK

First Edition 2002
Second Edition 2004

© **Europa Publications Limited 2004**
11 New Fetter Lane, London EC4P 4EE, United Kingdom
(A member of the Taylor & Francis Group)

ISBN   1-85743-261-4

Editor: Cathy Hartley
Contributor: Paul Cossali
Proof reading: Simon Chapman

Chronology data manipulation and data base design: Bibliocraft

Typeset by Bibliocraft, Dundee
Printed and bound in Great Britain by Antony Rowe Ltd, Chippenham, Wiltshire

Foreword

This is the second edition of *A Survey of Arab–Israeli Relations*, one of Europa's range of international reference books, which documents the principal events in one of the most intractable and long-running international disputes in the contemporary world. The book aims to provide a comprehensive and impartial review of the events that have shaped the Arab–Israeli dispute in the period between the end of the British Mandate in Palestine and the present. Europa's standing as a current-affairs publisher throughout this period enables it to provide a unique record of the region's events.

The five sections comprising this book aim to approach the issues in such a way as to present the reader with more than one perspective on a particular topic. A chronology of the period gives a record of events with an important bearing on the subject matter. The second section contains two essays: Arab–Israeli Relations 1947–67, and Arab–Israeli Relations since 1967, an essay compiled over time by a number of academics and writers on Middle Eastern affairs; these essays detail events since 1947 in a more analytical context. The third part, Documents on Palestine, reproduces the texts of a number of letters, treaties and agreements that have arisen from the Arab–Israeli dispute, and illustrates a number of these with maps. Fourthly, a series of profiles of the most prominent political figures in Arab–Israeli relations in the period concerned permits the reader to understand the personalities involved. Lastly, a bibliography provides further reading on the subject and closely related topics.

At a time when the prospect of a durable peace in the region appears more remote than for some years, and references are frequently made to earlier events in the history of Arab–Israeli Relations, it is hoped that this book will prove a significant and impartial addition to the body of published material on the subject.

April 2004

Acknowledgements

The editors gratefully acknowledge the interest, co-operation and advice of all who have contributed to this volume. In particular we would like to thank the Foundation for Middle East Peace (cartographer Jan de Jong) for use of the map on p. 403 and the Israeli embassy in London for the maps on p. 341.

Contents

List of Maps

Abbreviations

Adm.	Admiral
a.m.	*ante meridiem* (before noon)
Brig.	Brigadier
c.	*circa*
Cdre	Commodore
CIA	Central Intelligence Agency
Col	Colonel
Dr	Doctor
EC	European Communities
EEC	European Economic Community
EU	European Union
etc.	et cetera
GCC	Gulf Co-operation Council
Gen.	General
HM	His (or Her) Majesty
IDF	Israeli Defence Force
kg	kilogram(s)
km	kilometre(s)
Lt	Lieutenant
m.	million
Maj.	Major
Mgr	Monsignor
NATO	North Atlantic Treaty Organization
OIC	Organization of the Islamic Conference
PA	Palestinian (National) Authority
PFLP	Popular Front for the Liberation of Palestine
PLC	Palestinian Legislative Council
PLO	Palestine Liberation Organization
PNA	Palestinian National Authority
PRC	Popular Resistance Committee
Prof.	Professor
SLA	South Lebanon Army
St	Saint
UK	United Kingdom
UN	United Nations
UNHCR	United Nations High Commissioner for Refugees
US	United States
USA	United States of America
USS	United States Ship
USSR	Union of Soviet Socialist Republics
WZO	World Zionist Organization

A Chronology of Arab–Israeli Relations since 1947

1946–47: The territory of Palestine, administered under a Mandate by the United Kingdom since 1920 (the terms of the Mandate having been approved by the League of Nations, the precursor organization to the UN, in 1922) witnessed intercommunal violence between Arab and Jewish groups.

April 1946: A joint British-US Committee of Inquiry recommended the admission into Palestine of some 100,000 European Jewish refugees, the lifting of restrictions on Jewish purchases of land within the Mandated territory and the eventual creation of a binational state with the UN as guarantor.

2 April 1947: The United Kingdom referred its Palestinian Mandate to the UN.

15 May 1947: The UN General Assembly voted to create a Special Committee on Palestine (UNSCOP), which subsequently recommended the partition of Palestine into two states.

18 July 1947: British forces intercepted the *Exodus*, a ship carrying some 4,500 European Jewish refugees to Palestine and forced the refugees to return to France.

31 August 1947: The UN General Assembly proposed two plans concerning the future of Palestine: a majority plan for the partition of the territory into two states, one Jewish and one Arab, with economic union; and a minority plan for a federal state.

29 November 1947: The UN General Assembly adopted the majority plan for Palestine.

13 May 1948: A provisional Israeli Government was formed in Tel-Aviv, with David Ben-Gurion as Prime Minister.

14 May 1948: The British Mandate for Palestine was terminated. The State of Israel was officially declared in Palestine by the Jewish authorities; it was granted immediate recognition by the USA and the USSR.

15 May 1948: Troops of the Transjordanian Army, the Arab Legion, Egypt, Iraq, Lebanon and Syria attacked Israel.

20 May 1948: The UN appointed Count Folke Bernadotte of Wisborg to mediate between Israel and the Arab States.

28 May 1948: The Israeli Defence Force (IDF) was created.

June 1948: A brief cease-fire between Israel and the Arab states was brokered by Bernadotte; a second such truce was arranged the following month.

September 1948: An Arab government was formed in Palestine at Gaza under Egyptian tutelage.

17 September 1948: Bernadotte was assassinated by Jewish agents.

14 October 1948: Egyptian and Israeli armed forces renewed hostilities in the Negev desert.

22 October 1948: Egypt and Israel agreed to observe a cease-fire ordered by the UN Security Council in the Negev desert area. By this time the IDF had made considerable territorial gains in the Negev and adjacent areas.

29 November 1948: The provisional Government of Israel formally applied for membership of the UN.

December 1948: King Abdullah ibn Hussein al Hashimi of Transjordan (renamed Jordan in June 1949) was proclaimed King of All Palestine at Jericho.

1949: Following the establishment of the State of Israel, and during the subsequent Arab–Israeli wars, thousands of Palestinians fled to Lebanon and were housed in refugee camps in the south of the country.

13 January 1949: Egypt and Israel concluded an armistice agreement.

25 January 1949: Legislative elections were held in Israel. The centre-left Mapai movement emerged as the strongest force in the resulting coalition administration.

24 February 1949: Egypt and Israel signed another armistice agreement.

3 April 1949: Israel and Jordan signed an armistice; the territory on the west bank of the River Jordan (West Bank) and Eastern Jerusalem were incorporated under Jordanian rule.

20 July 1949: Israel and Syria signed an armistice agreement.

5 December 1949: The Israeli parliament, the Knesset, unanimously adopted a resolution which declared Jerusalem to be an integral part of Israel.

10 December 1949: The UN General Assembly unanimously adopted a resolution seeking the internationalization of Jerusalem and surrounding areas.

26 December 1949: The Knesset was convened in Jerusalem.

23 January 1950: The Knesset adopted a resolution declaring Jerusalem to be the capital of the State of Israel.

April 1950: In accordance with Arab League policy, Jordan agreed to refrain from the annexation of Palestinian territory and from entering into negotiations with Israel.

1 April 1950: The Council of the League of Arab States (Arab League), meeting in Cairo, Egypt, unanimously adopted a resolution which stated, among other things, that 'No Arab State has the right to negotiate separate peace treaties or any political, military or economic agreement with Israel, or the right to ratify any such agreement'.

24 April 1950: Abdullah formally annexed Arab Palestine; the annexation was recognized by the United Kingdom but condemned by the Arab League.

14 June 1950: The Israeli Government paid the UN a sum in excess of US $50,000 in reparation for the assassination of Count Folke Bernadotte in 1948.

July 1950: The Knesset adopted the Law of Return, which gave every Jew the right of immigration into Israel.

September 1950: The Knesset established a Development Authority to be charged with the disposal of property formerly owned by Arabs or controlled by the British mandatory authority. The Development Authority would enjoy the sole right of disposal, but it was stipulated that almost all of the land in question must be sold to the Jewish National Fund, which would not be permitted to resell it.

14 July 1952: The Knesset adopted a nationality and citizenship law, with retroactive effect from 14 May 1948, stipulating that all Jews resident in Israel on 14 July 1952 would automatically acquire Israeli citizenship, whether they were nationals of other countries or not; that Jewish immigrants arriving in Israel after that date would automatically acquire citizenship; that Arabs and other non-Jews were eligible for Israeli citizenship provided they were citizens of Palestine during the period of the British Mandate, were legally resident in Israel, and that their names were included in the population register on 1 March 1952.

early 1954: The Jordanian Government rejected a US-sponsored scheme for the distribution of water taken from the River Jordan among Iraq, Israel, Jordan and Syria because it necessitated co-operation with, and therefore recognition of, the State of Israel.

10 July 1953: Israel announced that its Ministry of Foreign Affairs would be relocated from Tel-Aviv to Jerusalem.

14–15 October 1953: Israeli armed forces launched an attack on the Jordanian village of Qibya in retaliation for recent Jordanian raids on Israeli villages in the area.

2 December 1953: The USSR recognized Jerusalem as the capital of Israel, despite Arab protests.

17 March 1954: An Israeli bus was ambushed by unidentified Arab assailants at Scorpion's Pass in the Negev desert; 11 civilians were killed. Israel accused Jordan of responsibility for the attack. Despite Jordan's denial, Israel subsequently withdrew from the Israeli-Jordanian Mixed Armistice Commission.

25 September 1954: Israel appealed to the Arab states for a peaceful settlement of their disputes.

28 September 1954: An Israeli freighter, the *Bat Galim*, was seized by Egyptian authorities when it attempted to pass through the Suez Canal.

28 February 1955: Egyptian and Israeli armed forces engaged in hostilities near Gaza.

29 March 1955: The UN Security Council unanimously adopted a resolution in which it described the fighting in Gaza on 28 February as a violation by Israel of its obligations under the general armistice agreement and the UN Charter.

3

18 September 1955: The Israeli Prime Minister, Moshe Sharett, urged the Western powers to supply arms to Israel.

11–12 December 1955: Israeli armed forces attacked Syrian positions north of Lake Tiberias.

29 December 1955: Israel announced its intention to propose that a peace conference with Egypt should be held under the terms of the Egyptian-Israeli armistice agreement.

5 April 1956: Exchanges of artillery fire took place between Egyptian and Israeli armed forces in the Gaza area.

12 April 1956: The Israeli Government gave an assurance to the UN Secretary-General that Israel fully and unconditionally accepted the armistice agreement previously concluded with Egypt.

3 May 1956: The Israeli Prime Minister, Ben-Gurion, gave assurances regarding Israel's observation of the armistice agreements with Jordan, Lebanon and Syria.

26 July 1956: The Egyptian President, Col Gamel Abd an-Nasser, announced that the Suez Canal Company had been nationalized; British and French forces subsequently began to plan military action, with the assent of Israel, aimed at preventing the nationalization.

29 October 1956: Israeli armed forces attacked Egyptian positions in the Sinai peninsula.

30 October 1956: France and the United Kingdom issued 12-hour ultimatums to Egypt and Israel to cease hostilities and withdraw their forces from the immediate vicinity of the Suez Canal and requested the Egyptian Government to allow Anglo-French forces to occupy positions at three points on the canal. Following Egypt's refusal to accept this condition, the two European states began military action the following day.

1 November 1956: The Egyptian garrison in Gaza surrendered to Israeli armed forces.

2 November 1956: Israel took control of almost all of the Sinai peninsula.

6 November 1956: A cease-fire halted an advance by British, French and Israeli armed forces on Egypt. The Suez Canal was eventually reopened, under Egyptian state control, in March 1957.

9 November 1956: The Israeli Prime Minister announced that Israel would withdraw its forces from the Sinai peninsula after an international force had taken up positions in the Suez Canal area.

19 January 1957: The UN General Assembly adopted a resolution expressing its concern at Israel's failure to comply with resolutions adopted in November 1956 regarding its withdrawal to the 1949 armistice lines in respect of the Gaza Strip and the Gulf of Aqaba.

22 January 1957: Israeli armed forces completed their withdrawal from most of the Sinai peninsula.

23 January 1957: Ben-Gurion stated that Israel required UN guarantees regarding freedom of navigation in the Gulf of Aqaba and the non-resumption of Palestinian guerrilla raids in the Gaza Strip before it would withdraw its armed forces from those areas.

2–3 February 1957: The UN General Assembly deplored Israel's failure to withdraw its armed forces (in the Gulf of Aqaba and the Gaza Strip) behind the armistice demarcation lines of 1949, and recognized that the 'scrupulous maintenance of the armistice agreement requires the placing of the UN Emergency Force on the Egyptian-Israeli armistice demarcation line'.

3 February 1957: Israel reiterated its refusal to comply with UN General Assembly resolutions of November 1956 in respect of the Gaza Strip and the Gulf of Aqaba without UN guarantees, as detailed above.

6–8 March 1957: Israeli armed forces withdrew from the Gaza Strip and the west coast of the Gulf of Aqaba.

November 1957: Egypt and Syria condemned Jordan's relations with the USA and accused it of entering into covert negotiations with Israel.

13 July 1958: An agreement on compensation for parties adversely affected by the nationalization of the Suez Canal was signed.

19 July 1958: A defence pact between Iraq and the United Arab Republic (UAR) was announced.

21 May 1959: The UAR prevented a Danish freighter from carrying Israeli cargo through the Suez Canal.

24 July 1960: The UAR suspended diplomatic relations with Iran in response to that country's recognition of Israel.

28 September 1960: Following a *coup d'état* in Syria, the new regime announced the country's withdrawal from the UAR, an action accepted by President Nasser some days later

1964: The Palestine Liberation Organization (PLO) was formed to co-ordinate the activities of various Palestinian political and military groups; its activities were initially concentrated in southern Lebanon, where many displaced Palestinians lived in refugee camps and sites for the training of guerrillas had been established.

13–16 January 1964: An Arab League conference was held in Cairo to discuss Israeli plans for the diversion of the River Jordan.

6 March 1965: President Bourguiba of Tunisia proposed the Arab recognition of Israel, on the terms of the 1947 UN resolution.

4 November 1966: A mutual-defence agreement was signed by Syria and the UAR.

13 November 1966: Israeli forces raided the Jordanian village of Samu; attacks on Israel by groups based in its neighbouring Arab states had increased in frequency throughout the mid-1960s. The raid, which was subsequently condemned by the UN Security Council, increased pressure on King Hussein of Jordan to resume his support for the PLO, withdrawn in July; when the king refused, the PLO urged Arabs to overthrow him.

7 April 1967: Fighting occurred between Israeli and Syrian forces on the countries' border.

14 May 1967: The Israeli Prime Minister, Levi Eshkol, stated that an Israeli–Syrian war was inevitable if incursions into Israel by Syrian guerrillas continued.

18 May 1967: The UAR officially requested that the UN force be withdrawn from the area of its border with Israel.

23 May 1967: The UAR imposed a blockade on Israeli shipping in the Straits of Tiran.

30 May 1967: Jordan and the UAR signed a mutual-defence pact.

5 June 1967: A period of military tensions between Israel and its neighbouring Arab countries was ended when Israel attacked the air bases of Jordan, Syria and the UAR. The Arab countries' air forces were severely damaged, and Israel was swiftly able to capture territory from each of the Arab combatants (notably the West Bank and Old Jerusalem from Jordan, the Golan Heights from Syria and the Sinai peninsula from the UAR).

6 June 1967: The United Kingdom and the USA were accused by President Nasser of the UAR and King Hussein of Jordan of military collusion with Israel; 10 Arab states imposed an embargo on petroleum supplies to the two countries. Diplomatic relations with the USA were suspended by Algeria, Iraq, Sudan, Syria, the UAR and Yemen; Iraq, Syria and the UAR terminated relations with the United Kingdom.

10 June 1967: Syria and the UAR signed a cease-fire with Israel, as Jordan had done some days earlier, thus concluding the conflict, which came to be known as the 'Six-Day War'; Israel retained the territories it had gained in the conflict.

29–31 August 1967: At a conference of Arab heads of state in Khartoum, Sudan, the petroleum-producing states agreed a substantial aid programme for Jordan and the UAR; Syria, which did not send a delegation to the conference, was excluded from the agreement.

21 October 1967: The Israeli destroyer *Eilat* was sunk off Sinai, with many casualties, by UAR warships.

25 October 1967: Israeli shelling at Suez succeeded in disabling the UAR's principal petroleum refineries for several months.

22 November 1967: The UN Security Council adopted Resolution 242, which urged the withdrawal of Israeli forces from the Occupied Territories, the acknowledgement by all countries in the region of the others' sovereignty, a solution to the problem of Palestinian refugees and advocated a negotiated settlement to the region's disputes. The Resolution became the basis of international efforts to agree a settlement to the Israeli-Palestinian question.

22 November 1967: Gunnar Jarring was appointed UN Special Representative to mediate between Israel and the Arab states.

1968: Yasser Arafat, the leader of the al-Fatah movement, became Chairman of the PLO.

21 March 1968: Israeli forces attacked the Jordanian village of Karameh, claimed to be the headquarters of the al-Fatah guerrilla organization.

5 June 1968: Israeli forces bombarded the Jordanian village of Irbid as a reprisal for what it termed an 'incessant artillery barrage' by groups based in the area against Israeli settlements.

4 November 1968: Extensive fighting took place between the Jordanian army and Palestinian guerrilla forces.

22 November 1968: A car filled with explosives by Arab guerrillas exploded in a Jerusalem market, killing 13.

26 December 1968: An Israeli passenger aircraft was the subject of a machine-gun attack by Arab guerrillas at an airport in Greece.

28 December 1968: Israeli commandos raided the airport of the Lebanese capital, Beirut, destroying 13 Arab aircraft.

31 December 1968: The UN Security Council unanimously condemned the Israeli raid on Beirut.

April 1969: Fierce fighting between Israeli and UAR forces occurred throughout the month in the Suez Canal area.

21 August 1969: Fire caused severe damage to the Al-Aqsa mosque in Jerusalem.

9 September 1969: The Israeli army launched a major raid on the UAR.

9 December 1969: The USA's 10-point peace plan for the Middle East was publicly announced.

January 1970: Israeli aircraft bombarded a number of targets in the UAR, including some in the Cairo area.

12 February 1970: An Israeli air raid on a scrap-metal processing plant in Egypt killed a reported 70 civilians.

1 May 1970: Israel claimed that Soviet pilots were flying operational missions from bases in the UAR.

23 July 1970: President Nasser unconditionally accepted US proposals for a cease-fire with Israel.

8 August 1970: A cease-fire between Israel and its Arab neighbours came into effect, on Israel's post-1967 frontiers.

9 August 1970: The Central Committee for Palestinian Resistance announced its rejection of US peace proposals for the Middle East.

31 August 1970: The Arab 'Eastern Front' against Israel was split into separate national fronts.

6–13 September 1970: Arab-Israeli peace talks were held in New York (USA); Israel withdrew.

16–27 September 1970: Exceptionally fierce fighting between the army and Palestinian commandos led to an agreement being signed by King Hussein and the leader of the PLO, Yasser Arafat; despite the signature of a further accord in October, civil war in Jordan continued.

14 January 1971: A new agreement was reached between the Jordanian Government and Palestinian guerrillas after continuing fighting between the two sides.

29 January 1971: The flow of petroleum through the Syrian section of the US-owned Trans-Arabian Pipeline (Tapline) resumed after Syria allowed repairs to be made; a section of the pipeline near the Syrian border with Israel had been damaged in early 1970, causing the flow of petroleum to be discontinued.

7 March 1971: The President of the UAR, Anwar Sadat, announced that the cease-fire with Israel would not be renewed.

28 March 1971: The Libyan leader, Col Muammar al-Qaddafi, urged Jordanians to overthrow King Hussein.

1–8 May 1971: The US Secretary of State, William Rogers, visited Israel, Jordan, Lebanon, Saudi Arabia and the UAR to discuss plans for reopening the Suez Canal, which had been closed since the Six-Day War.

3 June 1971: Palestinian guerrilla movements, including al-Fatah, advocated that King Hussein be overthrown.

13–16 June 1971: The Jordanian army attacked Palestinian guerrilla positions; Iraq and Syria closed their borders with Jordan in protest, and Algeria suspended relations; at the conclusion of the operations, King Hussein declared the guerrilla problem to be 'solved'.

11–13 August 1971: Altercations occurred on the border between Jordan and Syria; Syria suspended diplomatic relations the following day.

13 January 1972: President Sadat stated that a plan for action against Israel by the end of 1971 had been abandoned owing to the conflict between India and Pakistan.

25 January 1972: Student riots in favour of military action against Israel took place in Cairo; President Sadat met the student leaders and stated that a decision on such action had already been made.

24–28 February 1972: Israel attacked targets in Lebanon.

8 May 1972: Members of an Islamist group seized a Belgian passenger aircraft and ordered it to be flown to Israel, where the passengers were held hostage—Israeli commandos subsequently freed the hostages and killed or captured the suspected hijackers.

21–23 June 1972: Israeli forces carried out further attacks on Lebanon; 36 civilians and 30 guerrillas were reported to have been killed and 80 civilians and 50 guerrillas wounded; five Syrian army officers were taken captive.

5 September 1972: Eleven Israeli athletes were abducted and killed by Arab activists at the Olympic Games in Munich, Germany.

8 September 1972: The Israeli air force bombarded sites believed to be guerrilla bases in Lebanon and Syria; further raids were carried out on 15 October.

19–20 September 1972: A letter-bomb killed an Israeli diplomat in London; 17 other letter-bombs addressed to Israelis were discovered elsewhere in the world.

9 November 1972: Israeli and Syrian fighter aircraft were involved in aerial combat over the Golan Heights.

8 December 1972: The UN General Assembly advocated prompt implementation of UN Security Council Resolution 242, adopted in 1967.

28–29 December 1972: The Israeli embassy in Bangkok, Thailand was occupied by four armed members of the Palestinian Black September Organization.

13 February 1973: Abu Daoud and other Palestinian guerrillas were arrested for subversive activities in Jordan.

21 February 1973: A Libyan passenger aircraft was shot down by Israeli fighters over the Sinai desert; 108 people on board were killed.

27 February 1973: Israeli commandos conducted a raid into Lebanon against Palestinian Arab guerrilla-training bases.

9 April 1973: Arab guerrillas made unsuccessful attempts to kill the Israeli Ambassador in Nicosia, Cyprus.

10 April 1973: Israeli troops in civilian dress killed three Palestinian Arab guerrilla leaders in Beirut.

September 1973: King Faisal of Saudi Arabia mediated a reconciliation in the dispute between King Hussein of Jordan and the Egyptian and Syrian leaders.

6 October 1973: Egyptian armed forces crossed the Suez Canal into the Sinai desert to begin an offensive against Israel; Syrian armed forces began a simultaneous attack against Israel through the Golan Heights; these hostilities became known as the 'Yom Kippur War', after the Jewish religious festival during which the offensives began.

10 October 1973: Palestinian guerrillas used southern Lebanon as a base from which to launch attacks on Israel; the region was the victim of several Israeli reprisals.

16 October 1973: Having halted the initial surprise advance by the Arab armies, Israeli forces made an incursion west of the Suez Canal to attack Egyptian positions there; an attack on Egyptian forces in Sinai began the following day.

22 October 1973: Egypt and Israel agreed to a cease-fire, but were unable to maintain the truce. A renewed, UN-monitored cease-fire was agreed two days later, and Israel signed a cease-fire with Syria on 26 October.

November 1973: Following the declaration of a cease-fire, Jordanian officials attended a peace conference in Algiers, Algeria, during which they demanded that Israel evacuate territory gained in 1967 which the Arab forces had failed to regain during the conflict.

1 December 1973: Ben-Gurion died.

21 December 1973: A peace conference was convened in Geneva, Switzerland, under UN auspices. Egypt, Israel, Jordan, the USA and the USSR participated; Syria declined its invitation.

18 January 1974: Egypt and Israel signed an agreement for the disengagement of forces on the Suez-Sinai front—the agreement had been negotiated in part by the US Secretary of State, Dr Henry Kissinger, and was ratified by the Knesset on 22 January.

March 1974: Abu Dhabi, Algeria, Bahrain, Egypt, Kuwait and Saudi Arabia agreed to lift the embargo on petroleum supplies to the USA imposed in 1973 in response to US support for Israel; shipments to the Netherlands were resumed in July.

30 May 1974: Israel and Syria signed a disengagement agreement.

September 1974: Following the agreement made by Egypt, Syria and the PLO, which identified the PLO as the sole legitimate representative of the Palestinian people, Jordan announced its intention to boycott any further Arab-Israeli peace talks.

October 1974: At a 'summit' meeting of the Arab League in Rabat, Morocco, the members' unanimously resolved to recognize the PLO as the sole legitimate representative of Palestinians, with the right to establish national authority over any liberated Palestinian territory; King Hussein of Jordan was reported to have supported the resolution with reluctance.

13–23 January 1975: Israeli forces made an incursion into southern Lebanon.

10–15 February 1975: Kissinger visited the Middle East with the aim of securing the basis for agreement between Egypt and Israel on a further disengagement of forces in the Suez-Sinai sector; he repeated his visit in March.

August 1975: A Supreme Command Council, directed by King Hussein of Jordan and President Hafiz al-Assad of Syria, was established to co-ordinate political and military action against Israel.

1 September 1975: Egypt and Israel signed a further limited agreement on military disengagement in the Sinai peninsula.

22 February 1976: The implementation of the second Egyptian-Israeli disengagement agreement of 1975 was completed.

29 February 1976: The Israeli Cabinet's approval of a plan to expropriate Arab land in Galilee provoked a general strike by Israeli Arabs and widespread disturbances.

12 April 1976: Municipal elections were held in 24 towns in the Israeli-occupied West Bank.

27 June 1976: An Air France passenger aircraft was hijacked *en route* from Tel-Aviv to Paris, France, by the 'Che Guevara' cell of the Popular Front for the Liberation of Palestine (PFLP); the aircraft was redirected to Entebbe, Uganda.

3–4 July 1976: Israeli troops mounted a successful operation to rescue the passengers held captive by PFLP hijackers at Entebbe.

November 1976: The PLO was recognized by the UN and granted observer status.

11 November 1976: The UN Security Council issued a consensus statement deploring Israeli attempts to modify the demographic nature of the Occupied Territories through the establishment of Jewish settlements there.

21 November 1976: Syrian military deployment in southern Lebanon provoked fears of a confrontation between Israel and Syria.

29–30 December 1976: Sadat made new proposals as part of an attempt to revive the Geneva Middle East peace conference. The proposals urged the USA to apply pressure on Israel to accept a settlement based on UN Security Council Resolution 242.

8 March 1977: The Israeli Prime Minister, Itzhak Rabin, stated that Israel would not participate in a renewed Geneva Middle East peace conference which included the PLO.

July 1977: The Presidents of Egypt and the USA and King Hussein of Jordan discussed the possibility of a link between Jordan and a future Palestinian entity; the concept was condemned by the PLO.

19–20 July 1977: The new Israeli Prime Minister, Menachem Begin, of the Likud bloc, made procedural proposals with regard to a renewed Geneva Middle East peace conference.

12 September 1977: The USA stated publicly, for the first time, that a settlement of the Palestinian question was vital to the success of a renewed Geneva Middle East peace conference.

25 September 1977: The Israeli Cabinet accepted that a unified Arab delegation to a renewed Geneva Middle East peace conference should include a Palestinian component. However, it insisted that Palestinian representatives should be attached to the Jordanian component of such a delegation and should not be members of the PLO.

18–20 November 1977: President Sadat visited Israel. Addressing the Knesset, he accepted the existence of Israel, but stated that peace in the Middle East depended on Israel's withdrawal from occupied Arab territory and on recognition of Palestinian rights.

14 December 1977: A preparatory conference aiming to facilitate the resumption of the Geneva Middle East peace conference commenced in Cairo.

25 December 1977: Begin made an official visit to Egypt, the first such visit by an Israeli Prime Minister. During the visit he detailed new Israeli proposals regarding Sinai, the West Bank and Gaza Strip.

28 December 1977: The Knesset approved a 26-point government plan regarding the restoration of Egyptian sovereignty in the Sinai peninsula, and for the West Bank and Gaza Strip.

11–13 January 1978: The Egyptian-Israeli military committee met for the first time in Cairo.

11 March 1978: PLO guerrillas attacked numerous Israeli targets.

14–15 March 1978: Israel invaded southern Lebanon with the declared aim of eradicating Palestinian guerrilla bases there.

19 March 1978: The UN Security Council adopted Resolution 425, in which it urged 'strict respect for the territorial integrity, sovereignty and political independence of Lebanon within its internationally recognized boundaries'; sought the immediate cessation of Israeli 'military action against Lebanese territorial integrity' and the immediate withdrawal of Israeli forces from all Lebanese territory; and decided 'to establish immediately under its authority a United Nations Interim Force for Southern Lebanon (UNIFIL) for the purpose of confirming the withdrawal of Israeli forces, restoring international peace and security and assisting the Government of Lebanon in ensuring the return of its effective authority in the area'.

23 March 1978: Israel indicated that it would co-operate fully with the UN over southern Lebanon.

11 April 1978: Israel implemented a partial withdrawal of its armed forces from southern Lebanon.

21 May 1978: Israel announced that it would withdraw all of its armed forces from southern Lebanon by 13 June, provided that Palestinian guerrillas were not permitted to return there; that no further attacks against Israel took place; and that the security of southern Lebanon's inhabitants was guaranteed.

13 June 1978: The withdrawal of Israeli armed forces from southern Lebanon was completed. Final positions were, however, transferred to the Lebanese Christian militia.

18 June 1978: The Israeli Cabinet approved a statement in which Israel agreed that five years after the application of 'administrative autonomy' in the West Bank and Gaza Strip negotiations would commence on 'the nature of the future relations between the parties'.

September 1978: The Jordanian Government refused to participate in the US-sponsored Camp David peace negotiations with Israel.

17 September 1978: Following negotiations at the US President's residence at Camp David, Maryland, Begin and Sadat signed two agreements: 'A Framework for Peace in the Middle East' and 'A Framework for the Conclusion of a Peace Treaty between Egypt and Israel'.

28 September 1978: The Israeli Knesset approved the Camp David Agreements.

12 October 1978: Negotiations commenced between Egypt and Israel on the text of a formal peace treaty in the context of the Camp David Agreements.

27 October 1978: Begin and Sadat were awarded the Nobel Peace Prize.

November 1978: Jordan accepted a grant of US $1.25m. from Iraq to attend a conference of the Arab League regarding the situation in Israel.

17 December 1978: The formal deadline for the conclusion of a peace treaty between Egypt and Israel passed, without agreement.

March 1979: The Israeli agriculture minister, Ariel Sharon, stated that the Palestinians should take control of Jordan and establish a government there.

26 March 1979: Egypt and Israel signed a peace treaty, by which Israel agreed to return Sinai to Egypt, while retaining control of the Gaza Strip.

April 1979: Both Egypt and Israel ratified the peace treaty agreed the previous month.

7 May 1979: In a speech to the Knesset, Begin offered to engage in peace negotiations with Lebanon.

25 May 1979: Israeli, Egyptian and US negotiating teams commenced talks on Palestinian autonomy.

27 June 1979: Israeli and Syrian fighter aircraft engaged in hostilities over southern Lebanon.

10 August 1979: The US President, Jimmy Carter, denied that the USA supported the creation of an independent Palestinian state and declared that the USA would not negotiate with the PLO unless it accepted UN Security Council Resolution 242.

26 August 1979: The UN brokered a cease-fire between Israeli and Palestinian forces after an intensification in hostilities between them throughout the month in southern Lebanon.

29–30 August 1979: The UN Security Council held an extraordinary session to address the deteriorating security situation in southern Lebanon.

25 September 1979: The USA announced that it would attempt to mediate a solution to the crisis in Lebanon and envisaged the holding of an international peace conference in which both Israel and the PLO, among others, would participate.

21 October 1979: Moshe Dayan resigned as Israel's Minister of Foreign Affairs in protest at the Government's perceived inflexibility with regard to negotiations with Egypt and the USA on Palestinian autonomy in the West Bank and Gaza Strip.

21 October 1979: The first phase of Israeli military withdrawal from the Sinai peninsula was completed.

26 January 1980: Egypt and Israel formally established diplomatic relations.

7 February 1980: Begin warned that Israel would not remain passive in the event of attacks on the Christian minorities in Lebanon.

30 July 1980: The Knesset adopted legislation declaring a unified Jerusalem to be the capital and an integral part of Israel.

20 August 1980: The UN Security Council adopted a resolution urging all states with diplomatic missions in Jerusalem to withdraw them.

26–30 October 1980: President Itzhak Navon made first official visit by an Israeli head of state to Egypt.

7 June 1981: Israel attacked and destroyed a nuclear reactor close to the Iraqi capital, Baghdad.

24 July 1981: The US envoy to the Middle East, Philip Habib, arranged a cease-fire between the Syrian and Israeli forces in Lebanon.

14 December 1981: Israeli 'law, jurisdiction and administration' was extended to the Golan Heights, an action widely interpreted as annexation.

25 April 1982: Israel completed its military withdrawal from the Sinai peninsula.

6 June 1982: Israel launched 'Operation Peace for Galilee', an armed incursion into Lebanon.

July–August 1982: The Israeli forces subjected west Beirut to persistent bombardment.

1 September 1982: The US President, Ronald Reagan, announced that while the USA would not accept the establishment of a Palestinian state, it would support the granting of some autonomy to the West Bank Palestinians, in association with Jordan; the policy became known as the 'Reagan Plan'.

6–9 September 1982: Arab leaders meeting in Fez, Morocco, adopted a Middle East peace plan (the 'Fez plan') that envisaged, among other things, the establishment of an independent Palestinian state.

15 September 1982: Israeli armed forces occupied positions around Palestinian refugee camps in Muslim areas of west Beirut.

17 September 1982: An estimated 2,000 Palestinian refugees at the Sabra and Chatila camps were massacred, apparently by Lebanese Christian Phalangists.

28 September 1982: The Israeli Government initiated a full judicial inquiry into the massacres at Sabra and Chatila.

November 1982: The Jordanian Government and the PLO agreed to create a Higher Jordanian-Palestinian Committee, jointly chaired by the Prime Minister, Mudar Badran, and Arafat.

December 1982: Jordan and the USA held discussions on the 'Reagan Plan'.

28 December 1982: Direct talks began between Israel and Lebanon on the withdrawal of foreign forces from Lebanon.

1983: Opposition to the 'Reagan Plan' from Palestinians, Arab states and elements within Israel ensured it could not be implemented.

8 February 1983: The Israeli Supreme Court concluded that Lebanese Phalangist militiamen were responsible for the Sabra and Chatila massacres, but also that Israel's political and military leaders bore indirect responsibility through negligence.

22 February 1983: The USA announced that it would guarantee the security of Israel's northern border after the withdrawal of Israeli armed forces from Lebanon.

April 1983: Jordan announced that it would not support the 'Reagan Plan'.

10 April 1983: The Israeli Ministry of Agriculture announced plans to increase the number of settlements in the occupied West Bank from 108 to 165 in 1983–87.

24 April 1983: Arafat and King Hussein of Jordan failed to establish a joint negotiating position based on a compromise between the Reagan and Fez peace proposals.

May 1983: Relations between Arab states and the USA were strained when the US Senate sanctioned the sale of military aircraft to Israel.

17 May 1983: Israel, Lebanon and the USA signed an agreement providing, among other things, for the withdrawal of Israeli armed forces from Lebanon and the termination of the state of war between Israel and Lebanon. The Israeli Government, however, did not consider itself bound to the agreement unless Syrian troops also withdrew.

July 1983: Israel began to redeploy its troops; by the end of the year the number of its soldiers in Lebanon had been reduced from 30,000 to 10,000.

July 1983: At a meeting of the UN Security Council, the USA vetoed a draft resolution submitted by Jordan, which proclaimed Israeli settlement of the West Bank to be illegal.

28 August–7 September 1983: The 'International Conference on the Question of Palestine' was organized by the UN in Geneva.

4 September 1983: Israel redeployed its forces in Lebanon south of Beirut along the Awali river.

30 May 1984: The UN Security Council voted unanimously to prolong the mandate of its peace-keeping force in the Golan Heights, for an additional six months.

September 1984: Jordan re-established diplomatic relations with Egypt.

October 1984: The Jordanian Government rejected an Israeli offer of direct peace negotiations; King Hussein suggested instead a conference attended by delegations from all the states in the region.

November 1984: The Lebanese Government met Israeli representatives to discuss the withdrawal of the IDF from the south. The two sides failed to agree on the role of the UNIFIL and the Lebanese army in the patrolling of the evacuated area.

22 November 1984: At the 17th session of the Palestine National Council, King Hussein of Jordan proposed that the PLO and Jordan should pursue a peace initiative based on UN Security Council Resolution 242 of 1967.

14 January 1985: The Israeli Cabinet voted in favour of a unilateral withdrawal from Lebanon; the withdrawal began in February.

23 February 1985: King Hussein and Arafat announced the co-operation of the Jordanian Government and the PLO in a joint peace initiative. It was agreed that any peace proposals should be discussed by the five permanent member countries of the UN Security Council and all parties concerned in the conflict. The Palestinian people would exercise the right to self-determination in the context of a proposed confederate state of Jordan and Palestine.

March 1985: President Muhammad Hosni Mubarak of Egypt proposed negotiations between Egypt, the USA and a joint Jordanian-Palestinian delegation; the PLO rejected the proposal, however, claiming that it deviated from its accord with Jordan.

3 March 1985: Israeli forces began to withdraw from the Beka'a valley. Shi'ite guerrillas attacked the retreating troops; this prompted a programme of retaliation by the Israeli army against the Shi'ite communities.

May 1985: King Hussein proposed a four-stage plan for Middle East peace negotiations, consisting of separate meetings between the USA and a Jordanian-Palestinian delegation, in addition to wider discussions involving the UN Security Council.

10 June 1985: The withdrawal of IDF forces from Lebanon was officially completed; however some units remained to support the Israeli proxy South Lebanon Army (SLA).

10 June 1985: The Israeli Prime Minister, Shimon Peres, suggested that Israel and Jordan should engage in direct peace negotiations. Proposing a five-year timetable, he advocated the formation of a joint Jordanian-Palestinian-Israeli committee to draft an agenda for a peace conference.

14 June 1985: Two Shi'ite Muslims, allegedly members of Hezbollah (Party of God), hijacked a passenger aircraft flying between Greece and Italy. The hijackers forced the aircraft to fly to Beirut and Algiers twice, releasing some 100 hostages in the process.

17 June 1985: The hijacked aircraft was forced to land in Beirut for a third time; Nabih Berri, the hijackers' spokesman, announced that the remaining passengers, who were mostly US citizens, had been taken to secret locations in the city where they would be detained until 766 Lebanese nationals held in Israeli prisons were released. Israel refused and the US Government threatened to impose sanctions on Lebanon. Following the intervention of President Assad, the prisoners were eventually set free at the end of the month.

16 July 1985: Israel rejected as unacceptable seven Palestinians proposed as potential nominees for a Palestinian component of a joint Jordanian-Palestinian delegation to peace talks.

October 1985: The Israeli press published a secret government document, which suggested the establishment of an interim Israeli-Jordanian condominium of the West Bank, granting a degree of Palestinian autonomy and gave details of an Israeli-Jordanian mutual agreement on the need for a forum for peace talks.

1 October 1985: Israeli aircraft bombarded the PLO headquarters in Tunis, Tunisia.

17 October 1985: Peres informed President Reagan that he was prepared to participate, without preconditions, in negotiations with Jordan, and to consider 'territorial compromises'.

19 February 1986: Following Arafat's refusal to accept resolutions of the UN Security Council as the foundation for peace negotiations, King Hussein suspended relations with the PLO and repudiated the Amman agreement.

August 1986: The Jordanian Government announced the introduction of a five-year development programme for the West Bank and the Gaza Strip; the project was to cost US \$1,300m. and was supported by the Israeli Government.

11 September 1986: President Mubarak of Egypt and Peres met in Egypt to discuss ways of reviving the Middle East peace process.

5 October 1986: A British newspaper, *The Sunday Times*, claimed that Israel had amassed an arsenal of nuclear weapons in the Negev desert. Mordechai Vanunu, a former employee of the Israeli Atomic Energy Commission and the 'source' of the story, was subsequently abducted and taken to Israel by agents of the external security force, Mossad.

20 October 1986: Itzhak Shamir replaced Peres as Prime Minister of Israel.

April 1987: King Hussein and the Israeli Minister of Foreign Affairs, Peres, agreed to proposals for a peace conference involving all parties concerned, under the auspices of the UN.

May 1987: At the conclusion of a series of secret negotiations with King Hussein, Peres claimed that enough progress had been made regarding the issue of Palestinian representation at peace negotiations to seek the consent of Egypt, Jordan and the USA to convene an international conference.

December 1987: An *intifada* (uprising) occurred among the Palestinians on the West Bank in opposition to Israeli rule and the policies of King Hussein.

22 December 1987: The UN Security Council adopted Resolution 605, condemning Israel's violent methods of suppressing Palestinian demonstrations.

5 January 1988: The UN Security Council adopted Resolution 607, urging Israel to comply with the International Red Cross's fourth Geneva Convention of 1949 concerning the treatment of civilians in wartime. The Resolution was supported by the USA, voting in favour of the censure of Israel for the first time since 1981.

February 1988: The US Secretary of State, George Shultz, devised a new peace initiative. The 'Shultz Plan' provided for an international conference to be attended by all parties involved in the Arab-Israeli conflict and the permanent members of the UN Security Council, in addition to separate talks between Israel and each of its Arab neighbours. Shultz also recommended a three-year transitional period of autonomy for the 1.5m. Palestinians in the West Bank and Gaza Strip territories.

10 March 1988: The European Parliament condemned 'the instances of torture, arbitrary arrest, reprisals, expulsions, and all acts of violence committed by the Israeli army against the Palestinian population'.

16 April 1988: Khalil al-Wazir ('Abu Jihad'), the PLO deputy leader and commander of the Palestine Liberation Army (PLA), was assassinated by Israeli agents in Tunis.

June 1988: At a meeting of the Arab League in Algiers, King Hussein expressed Jordan's unconditional support for the PLO as representatives of the Palestinians and relinquished its claim to the West Bank.

July 1988: King Hussein cancelled the West Bank development plan and severed all Jordan's legal and administrative ties with the West Bank, renouncing the Jordanian claim to the West Bank and East Jerusalem.

15 November 1988: The PLO declared an independent Palestinian State and endorsed UN Security Council Resolutions 242 and 338, thereby implicitly recognizing Israel's right to exist.

14 December 1988: Arafat presented a three-point peace initiative to the UN General Assembly.

7 February 1989: The US State Department criticized a 'substantial increase of human rights violations' by Israel against the Palestinian population of the West Bank and the Gaza Strip.

22 February 1989: The Soviet Minister of Foreign Affairs, Eduard Shevardnadze, met separately with his Israeli counterpart, Moshe Arens, and with Arafat, in Cairo.

26 February 1989: Israel agreed to return an area of the Red Sea town of Taba to Egyptian control.

14 May 1989: The Israeli Cabinet approved Shamir's proposal that Palestinian elections should be held in the Occupied Territories; the proposal was subsequently approved by the Knesset.

22 May 1989: The US Secretary of State, James Baker, urged the Israeli Government to abandon its 'unrealistic vision of a 'Greater Israel', while urging the Palestinians to abandon violence and concentrate their efforts on diplomacy.

23 July 1989: Attempts by the Minister of Trade and Industry, Ariel Sharon, and other Cabinet ministers to amend Shamir's proposal for Palestinian elections were unsuccessful.

15 September 1989: President Mubarak of Egypt proposed a 10-point plan aiming to revive Israeli-Palestinian peace negotiations.

14 January 1990: The Israeli Prime Minister, Shamir, claimed that the Occupied Territories would be used to settle Jewish immigrants from the USSR.

11 April 1990: Jewish settlers occupied the St John's Hospice in Jerusalem.

20 May 1990: Widespread rioting occurred in the Gaza Strip, following the murder of a number of Palestinian civilians by an Israeli civilian.

21 May 1990: The PLO urged the USA to defend the Palestinian people.

25–26 May 1990: The UN Security Council convened in Geneva to discuss the Palestinian question.

28–30 May 1990: An emergency Arab League 'summit' meeting was held in Baghdad to discuss the increased emigration of Soviet Jews to Israel, and their potential settlement in the Occupied Territories.

30 May 1990: The Palestine Liberation Front launched a seaborne attack on Israeli beaches.

20 June 1990: The USA suspended its dialogue with the PLO.

8 October 1990: Israeli security forces killed 21 Palestinians during unrest in Jerusalem; the action was subsequently condemned by the UN Security Council.

24 October 1990: Israel banned all movement in or out of the Occupied Territories amid increasing tension between Jewish and Arab communities.

4 November 1990: The Israeli Cabinet rejected proposals made by the UN Secretary-General for the protection of Palestinians living in the Occupied Territories.

20 December 1990: The UN Security Council adopted Resolution 681, condemning Israeli conduct in the Occupied Territories.

17 January 1991: Iraq, which was being attacked by a multinational force in response to its annexation of Kuwait, commenced attacks with *Scud* missiles against Israeli and Saudi Arabian targets.

19 January 1991: King Hussein stated that Jordan would defend its airspace in the event of any incursion by the Israeli air force.

20 February 1991: The US Secretary of State signed a guarantee for a US $400m. loan to Israel for the purpose of housing immigrants.

6 March 1991: The US President, George Bush, identified the resolution of the Arab-Israeli conflict as one of his administration's principal aims in the period following the Iraqi conflict.

7–14 March 1991: The US Secretary of State visited Egypt, Israel, Kuwait, Saudi Arabia and Syria.

31 March 1991: The Israeli Cabinet introduced new measures to combat the Palestinian *intifada*.

16 April 1991: The first new Israeli settlement in the West Bank for two years was established.

22 May 1991: The US Secretary of State identified Israel's policy of establishing settlements in the Occupied Territories as the biggest obstacle to US efforts to achieve a Middle Eastern peace settlement.

14 July 1991: Syria agreed to participate in direct negotiations with Israel at a regional Middle East peace conference.

29–31 July 1991: The Israeli Minister of Foreign Affairs, David Levy, visited Egypt for talks with his Egyptian counterpart and with President Mubarak.

31 July 1991: The Presidents of the USA and the USSR announced that they would co-sponsor a regional Middle East peace conference which they scheduled to take place in October 1991.

23 September 1991: Arafat stated the PLO's commitment to the success of the proposed regional Middle East peace conference.

29 September 1991: The Palestinian National Council (PNC) approved Palestinian participation in the proposed regional Middle East peace conference.

7 October 1991: The Prime Minister announced that any proposals involving the exchange of land for peace at the forthcoming Middle East peace conference would be rejected; he subsequently announced that he would lead the Israeli delegation to the conference himself.

13 October 1991: King Hussein announced Jordan's unconditional acceptance of the terms for participation in a regional Middle East peace conference to be held in Madrid, Spain.

30 October 1991: The Middle East peace conference commenced in Madrid, attended by representatives from Egypt, Israel, Lebanon and Syria, in addition to a joint Palestinian-Jordanian delegation.

3 November 1991: The first sessions of bilateral talks between Arab and Israeli delegations took place within the framework of the Middle East peace conference.

10 December 1991: A second round of bilateral negotiations between Israeli and Arab delegations commenced in the US capital, Washington, DC; a third round took place there in January 1992.

16 February 1992: Sheikh Abbas Moussawi, Secretary-General of Lebanese Hezbollah, was killed in an attack by the Israeli air force.

24 February 1992: A fourth round of bilateral negotiations between Israeli and Arab delegations commenced in Washington, DC; the same city hosted further rounds in April, August and October and November.

11 May 1992: Multilateral negotiations between Israeli and Arab delegations resumed in various locations.

21 July 1992: The Israeli Prime Minister, Itzhak Rabin, visited Egypt.

16 December 1992: The Israeli Cabinet approved a mass deportation of alleged Palestinian supporters of the Islamic Resistance Movement (Hamas) from Israel to Lebanon.

17 December 1992: Arab delegations withdrew from the eighth round of bilateral negotiations with Israel.

11–12 January 1993: The foreign ministers of the Arab League member states met in Cairo to discuss the deportation of Palestinians from Israel to Lebanon.

28 January 1993: The Israeli High Court ruled that deportation of Palestinians to Lebanon in December 1992 had been lawful; the following week the Government offered to allow 101 of the deportees to return.

11 April 1993: Israel announced the indefinite 'closure' of the Occupied Territories.

27 April 1993: A ninth round of bilateral negotiations between Israeli and Arab delegations commenced in Washington, DC; a 10th round began in June.

25 July 1993: Israeli armed forces initiated intense air and artillery attacks against Hezbollah fighters and Palestinian guerrillas in southern Lebanon.

15 August 1993: Palestinian deportees in southern Lebanon approved an offer by the Israeli Government permitting their staged return to Israel by December 1993.

30 August 1993: A secretly negotiated draft peace agreement between Israel and the PLO was announced; the negotiations had taken place in the Norwegian capital, Oslo.

13 September 1993: The Declaration of Principles on Palestinian Self-Rule in the Occupied Territories (known informally as the Oslo Agreement) was signed by Israel and the PLO in Washington, DC. Israel and the PLO formally recognized each other.

15 September 1993: Israel and Jordan agreed an agenda for future bilateral negotiations between their respective delegations to the Middle East peace conference.

12 October 1993: The PLO Central Council approved the Declaration of Principles signed with Israel in September.

13 October 1993: Israeli and Palestinian negotiators commenced talks in Taba, Egypt.

24 November 1993: Imad Akel, a commander of Qassem (the military wing of Hamas), was shot dead by Israeli forces.

10 December 1993: Hanan Ashrawi resigned as spokeswoman of the Palestinian delegation to the Middle East peace talks.

13 December 1993: By this date, Israeli forces should have begun to withdraw from the Gaza Strip and the Jericho area under the terms of the Declaration of Principles on Palestinian Self-Rule; however, a failure to agree on security arrangements for border crossings led to the process being delayed.

January 1994: Jordan and the PLO signed an agreement on economic co-operation and the co-ordination of financial policy in the Occupied Territories.

16 January 1994: The US President, Bill Clinton, met President Assad to discuss the Middle East peace process; the two leaders met again in October.

22–29 January 1994: The 12th round of bilateral negotiations in the Middle East peace process commenced in Washington, DC.

25 February 1994: The PLO and other Arab delegations withdrew from the Middle East peace negotiations, following the murder of some 30 worshippers at a mosque in Hebron by an Israeli civilian.

27 February 1994: Lebanon and Syria withdrew from the Middle East peace process.

18 March 1994: The UN Security Council adopted a resolution condemning the killings in Hebron.

29 April 1994: Israel and the PLO signed an economic agreement, concerning the relations between Israel and the autonomous Palestinian entity in the five-year period prior to self-rule.

4 May 1994: Israel and the PLO signed an agreement providing for Palestinian Self-Rule in the Gaza Strip and Jericho; Israel was to withdraw its forces from the areas, and a Palestinian National Authority (PNA) would assume the powers of the Israeli military governments (with the exceptions of external security and foreign affairs). Elections to the PNC, which had been scheduled to take place in July, were postponed until October.

13 May 1994: The Israeli armed forces completed their withdrawal from the Gaza Strip.

26–28 May 1994: The newly-appointed PNA met for first time in Tunis.

1 June 1994: Israeli forces launched a major attack on a Hezbollah training camp in Lebanon.

26 June 1994: The PNA met in Gaza for the first time.

1 July 1994: Arafat arrived in the Gaza Strip.

25 July 1994: Israel and Jordan signed a joint declaration formally ending the state of war between them.

1 September 1994: Morocco announced its decision to open a liaison office in the Israeli city of Tel-Aviv.

30 September 1994: The Gulf Co-operation Council ended its secondary and tertiary trade boycott of Israel.

20 October 1994: Following an attack in Tel-Aviv by a suicide bomber representing Hamas, Israel temporarily closed its borders with the West Bank and Gaza Strip.

26 October 1994: Israel and Jordan signed a comprehensive peace treaty.

10 November 1994: King Hussein of Jordan made his first public visit to Israel.

18 November 1994: Twelve people were killed in clashes between Palestinian police and supporters of Hamas and Islamic Jihad in Gaza.

22 January 1995: The Islamic Jihad movement claimed responsibility for bomb attacks in Netanya, which killed 21 people.

9 February 1995: Israeli armed forces completed their withdrawal from Jordanian territory.

14 March 1995: The US Secretary of State, Warren Christopher, announced that peace negotiations between Israel and Syria were to resume.

24 May 1995: Israel and Syria concluded a 'framework understanding' on security arrangements in the disputed Golan Heights.

27–29 June 1995: Israeli and Syrian Chiefs of Staff met in Washington, DC.

28 September 1995: The Israeli-Palestinian Interim Peace Agreement on the West Bank and Gaza Strip was signed; the accord (known informally as the Taba Agreement or 'Oslo II') provided for elections to an 82-member Palestinian Council, and for a Palestinian Executive President, in addition to the progressive withdrawal of Israeli forces from West Bank towns and the release of Palestinian prisoners.

10 October 1995: The President of Syria, Hafiz al-Assad, stated that Syria would not conclude a peace agreement with Israel which did not meet all of its aspirations.

11 October 1995: The first Palestinian prisoners to be released under the Second Israeli-Palestinian Interim Peace Agreement were freed.

25 October 1995: The PNA took control of the West Bank town of Jenin; Israeli forces completed their withdrawal from the town in November, and from five other towns in December.

4 November 1995: Rabin was assassinated by a Jewish student opposed to the peace process. Peres was appointed acting Prime Minster and was subsequently invited (with the approval of Likud) to form a new administration.

27–29 December 1995: Peace negotiations between Israel and Syria resumed.

5 January 1996: Yahya Ayyash, a leading figure in the Hamas movement, was killed in Gaza; the group alleged that Israeli agents were responsible.

20 January 1996: Palestinian presidential and legislative elections took place. In the presidential election, Arafat received 88.1% of the votes cast and was duly elected; Fatah won 54 of the 88 elective seats in the Palestinian Legislative Council (PLC—one seat was reserved for the President, *ex officio*).

25 February–4 March 1996: Suicide-bomb attacks were carried out in Jerusalem and in several other cities.

7 March 1996: The inaugural session of the PLC opened in Gaza City.

13 March 1996: A 'Peacemakers summit meeting' was convened in Sharm esh-Sheikh, Egypt; Lebanon and Syria boycotted the meeting.

11 April 1996: Israel launched a campaign of aerial and artillery bombardment of Hezbollah targets in southern Lebanon (known as 'Operation Grapes of Wrath'), with the stated aim of preventing rocket attacks on northern Israeli towns.

18 April 1996: More than 100 Lebanese civilians were killed in an attack by Israeli armed forces on a UN base at Qana; Israel claimed the base had been attacked in error.

24 April 1996: The PNC voted in favour of amending the Palestinian Covenant and elected a new Executive Committee.

27 April 1996: A cease-fire between Israel and Lebanese Hezbollah came into force.

5–6 May 1996: Israeli and Palestinian delegations commenced 'final status' negotiations.

29 May 1996: Binyamin Netanyahu, the leader of Likud, was elected Prime Minister of Israel.

21–23 June 1996: An Arab 'summit' meeting was held in Cairo in response to Likud's victory in the Israeli elections.

2 August 1996: Israel relaxed restrictions on the expansion of Jewish settlements in the West Bank and Gaza Strip.

29 August 1996: A Palestinian general strike was organized in the West Bank and Gaza Strip.

25 September 1996: Violent disturbances occurred in the West Bank and Gaza Strip after the Israeli Government opened a tunnel close to al-Aqsa mosque.

15 October 1996: King Hussein visited the West Bank for the first time since 1967.

31 December 1996: A bomb exploded on a bus in Damascus; Syria held Israel responsible for the attack.

17 January 1997: The redeployment of Israeli troops in Hebron began.

16 February 1997: The Israeli Minister of Foreign Affairs, David Levy, and the chief Palestinian negotiator, Mahmoud Abbas, attended the first session of renewed bilateral negotiations.

26 February 1997: The construction of 6,500 new homes for Jewish settlers at Har Homa, in East Jerusalem, was approved; despite condemnation of the decision by Palestinian groups and Arab governments, construction commenced in March.

7 March 1997: The PNA rejected the Israeli government interpretation of the terms agreed for future troop deployment in the Occupied Territories.

7 March 1997: A UN Security Council resolution to halt the Har Homa development in East Jerusalem was vetoed by the USA.

18 March 1997: Construction of new Jewish homes at Har Homa, East Jerusalem, commenced.

21 March 1997: A proposed UN Security Council resolution to halt the Har Homa development was vetoed by the USA for a second time.

21 March 1997: A suicide-bomb attack carried out in Tel-Aviv by a member of Hamas resulted in the deaths of three Israelis and injuries to at least 40 others; Israel closed the West Bank and Gaza Strip in response.

29 April 1997: The Israeli Government announced that it would allow 55,000 Palestinian workers to enter Israel from 30 April.

6 May 1997: The PNA announced new legislation sentencing to death Palestinians found guilty of selling land to Jewish settlers.

15 June 1997: The US House of Representatives recognized Jerusalem as the undivided capital of Israel.

22 July 1997: Levy and Arafat met in Brussels, Belgium, for preliminary discussions concerning the peace process.

28 July 1997: Israeli and Palestinian officials announced that peace talks were to be resumed in early August.

30 July 1997: An attack by two Palestinian suicide bombers resulted in the deaths of 14 Israelis in Jerusalem; in response Israel closed the West Bank and Gaza Strip and withheld the payment of some US $50m. in tax revenues owed to the PNA.

18 August 1997: One-third of the PNA funds being withheld by the Israeli Government was released.

1 September 1997: The West Bank and Gaza Strip were reopened by Israel.

5 September 1997: Twelve Israeli soldiers were killed by Lebanese armed forces while attempting to enter a Lebanese village known to be inhabited by Hezbollah members.

14 September 1997: The Israeli Government released 50% of the PNA funds withheld since 30 July and relaxed restrictions on the movement of Palestinians in the Occupied Territories.

15 September 1997: Netanyahu vetoed an Israeli housing project in East Jerusalem which had been anticipated to cause disruption to the peace process.

25 September 1997: The leader of the Palestinian Hamas group, Khalid Meshaal, was the subject of a failed assassination attempt by Israeli agents in Amman; diplomatic activity to preserve cordial relations between Israel and Jordan ensued.

1 October 1997: A number of Arab prisoners, including Sheikh Ahmad Yassin—one of the founders of Hamas—were released from Israeli prisons, reportedly in exchange for the return of two Israeli secret-service agents who had been detained in Jordan following the attempted assassination of Meshaal.

8 October 1997: Arafat and Netanyahu had their first direct discussions for eight months at the Erez check-point between Israel and the Gaza Strip.

16–18 November 1997: The Fourth Middle East and North Africa (MENA) economic conference was convened in Doha, Qatar; the event was the subject of a widespread Arab boycott, owing to the participation of an Israeli delegation.

30 November 1997: The Israeli Cabinet agreed, in principle, to a partial withdrawal from the West Bank, but did not agree the timing or scale of such a withdrawal; the Government also undertook to create a team of Ministers to decide which areas of the West Bank should be permanently retained by Israel.

20 January 1998: During a visit to the USA Netanyahu held talks with US President Clinton, at which he reportedly rejected US proposals for a second-stage redeployment of forces from 10%–15% of West Bank territory, proposing instead redeployment from no more than 9.5% of the territory.

31 January 1998: The US Secretary of State, Madeleine Albright, visited the Middle East region and held talks with Netanyahu and Arafat; the effort failed to restart the peace process.

16 February 1998: The commission of investigation into the Israeli military intelligence agency's alleged involvement in the attempted assassination of the Hamas official Khalid Meshaal in September 1997 published its report; Netanyahu was absolved of responsibility for the operation. Maj.-Gen. Danny Yatou, the head of the agency (known as Mossad), who had been severely criticized in the report, resigned and was replaced by Ephraim Halevy.

15–18 March 1998: The British Secretary of State for Foreign and Commonwealth Affairs, Robin Cook, visited the Middle East on a tour intended to raise the profile of the European Union (EU) in the peace process. During his time in the region, Cook made a controversial visit to the Har Homa settlement.

29 March 1998: The discovery in the West Bank of the body of Muhiad-Din Sharif, a leader of the armed wing of Hamas, led to fears of reprisal attacks against Israel; however, Hamas members were later arrested for the murder, which was reportedly the result of an internal power struggle.

1 April 1998: Israel's 'inner' Security Cabinet voted unanimously to accept UN Security Council Resolution 425 (adopted in March 1978) and withdraw from southern Lebanon, conditional upon Lebanese guarantees of the security of Israel's northern border. Lebanon continued to assert that Resolution 425 required an unconditional withdrawal from its territory, and refused to accede to Israel's terms for departure.

16–21 April 1998: The British Prime Minister, Tony Blair, undertook a tour of the Middle East region during which he invited Arafat and Netanyahu to attend a 'summit' for peace in the British capital, London, in early May. During his visit Blair signed an EU-Palestinian security agreement.

4–5 May 1998: Albright, held separate talks with Netanyahu and Arafat, in London. No significant progress was made and although both parties were invited to Washington, DC, for further talks, Netanyahu declined to attend since the talks were made conditional on Israeli support for a US plan for a 13.1% redeployment in the West Bank.

26 May 1998: Serious clashes erupted in East Jerusalem after a Jewish settler organization began construction work on a religious settlement on disputed territory in the Arab quarter of the city.

21 June 1998: The Israeli Cabinet approved a draft plan to widen Jerusalem's municipal boundaries; the decision was condemned by the Palestinians, the Arab states and the international community.

7 July 1998: The UN voted to upgrade the status of the PLO at the UN, despite objections from Israel and the USA, to allow the organization greater participation.

19–22 July 1998: Israeli and Palestinian negotiators held their first direct peace talks for some 16 months; however, the talks failed to secure agreement on redeployment.

22 July 1998: Syria condemned Israeli legislation stating that any withdrawal from the Golan Heights would require the approval of the legislature and of the electorate in a referendum.

22 July 1998: The Knesset gave preliminary approval to a bill which required a majority vote in the Knesset and a referendum to be held prior to allowing an Israeli withdrawal from either the Golan Heights or any part of Jerusalem; this action was condemned by Syria.

28 September 1998: At a US-mediated meeting in Washington, DC, the Israeli and Palestinian leaders agreed to attend a tripartite peace 'summit' in the USA in mid-October 1998; in an address to the UN General Assembly, Netanyahu had previously stated that a unilateral declaration of an independent Palestinian state would occasion the end of the peace process.

15 October 1998: US-brokered talks between Netanyahu and Arafat opened in the Wye Plantation, Maryland, USA.

23 October 1998: Following nine days of negotiations Arafat and Netanyahu signed the Wye River Memorandum in the presence of President Clinton and King Hussein; the agreement outlined a three-month timetable for the implementation of the 1995 Interim Agreement and facilitated the beginning of the 'final status' talks. The Wye River Memorandum was the first development in Israeli-Palestinian relations for some 19 months.

20 November 1998: Israel implemented the first stage of troop redeployment from the West Bank and released 250 Palestinian prisoners, as agreed under the Wye River Memorandum.

24 November 1998: Arafat formally opened Gaza International Airport.

12–15 December 1998: President Clinton visited the Palestinian territories; violent clashes between Palestinian demonstrators and Israeli security forces in the West Bank and Gaza preceded the visit.

14 December 1998: The PLC reconfirmed, in a session attended by President Clinton, the deletion of those articles of the Palestinian National Charter (PLO Covenant) deemed to be anti-Israeli.

15 December 1998: A 'summit' meeting was held between President Clinton, Netanyahu and Arafat at the Erez check-point; Netanyahu announced that Israel would not proceed with the second troop redeployment prescribed by the Wye River Memorandum—Arafat demanded that no further Jewish settlements be constructed in disputed territory and refused to exclude the possibility of a unilateral declaration of Palestinian statehood.

20 December 1998: The Israeli Cabinet voted to suspend the implementation of Wye River Memorandum.

1 January 1999: The Security Cabinet voted to respond to future Hezbollah offensives by targeting infrastructure in central and northern Lebanon.

18 February 1999: Israeli forces annexed the Lebanese village of Arnoun, on the edge of the Israeli 'security zone'; Arnoun was subsequently liberated by thousands of Lebanese students.

28 February 1999: The Commander of the Israeli army's liaison unit with its client SLA, Brig.-Gen. Erez Gerstein, was killed in a Hezbollah ambush in southern Lebanon—the most senior Israeli officer to be killed there since the 1982 invasion; Israel responded with series of air raids against Hezbollah targets in southern Lebanon.

26 March 1999: EU leaders, meeting in Berlin, Germany, issued the 'Berlin Declaration', which urged Israel to conclude 'final status' negotiations with the PNA within one year.

14–15 April 1999: Israeli forces reannexed the Lebanese village of Arnoun.

29 April 1999: The PLO Central Council announced the postponement of any unilateral declaration of Palestinian statehood until after the Israeli general election; violent protests against the decision occurred in the West Bank, Gaza and East Jerusalem.

4 May 1999: The 'Oslo interim period', as outlined in the Interim Agreement signed by Israel and the PNA on 28 September 1995, ended.

17 May 1999: Ehud Barak, of the Labour Party, won the Israeli prime-ministerial election.

1–3 June 1999: The Israeli-supported SLA completed a unilateral withdrawal from the enclave of Jezzine, in the north-east of Lebanon's 'security zone'.

3 June 1999: Palestinians in the West Bank declared a 'day of rage' against the continuing expansion of Israeli settlements.

24–25 June 1999: The outgoing Israeli administration initiated a series of aerial attacks on infrastructure targets in central and southern Lebanon, the heaviest raids since 'Operation Grapes of Wrath' in 1996; at least eight civilians were killed and as many as 70 were injured.

9 July 1999: Barak began a series of 'summit' meetings with Arab and other world leaders; the first was with the Egyptian President, Mubarak.

11 July 1999: Barak and Arafat held their first direct discussions at the Erez check-point.

20 July 1999: Syria declared a cease-fire with Israel.

1 August 1999: Talks between Israeli and Palestinian delegations collapsed after Arafat rejected Barak's proposal to delay implementation of the Wye River Memorandum and to combine further Israeli troop withdrawals from the West Bank with 'final status' negotiations.

25 August 1999: Security forces closed the offices of Hamas in Amman; Meshaal's home was raided and a number of leading Hamas activists arrested.

4 September 1999: Israel and the PNA signed the 'Wye Two' agreement in the Egyptian resort of Sharm esh-Sheikh, detailing a revised timetable for out-standing provisions of the original Wye River Memorandum.

9 September 1999: Israel released 199 Palestinian prisoners, as agreed under 'Wye Two'.

10 September 1999: Israel transferred a further 7% of West Bank territory to Palestinian self-rule.

22 September 1999: Three Hamas leaders, including Meshaal, were detained by Jordanian security forces on their arrival at Amman airport; they faced charges of organizing illegal political activities and involvement in terrorism.

2 November 1999: Barak and Arafat held discussions in Oslo, while attending a ceremony marking the fourth anniversary of the assassination of Itzhak Rabin.

8 November 1999: Israeli and Palestinian negotiators began talks on 'final status' issues in the West Bank town of Ramallah.

21 November 1999: Jordan expelled Meshaal and other senior members of Hamas to Qatar.

15–16 December 1999: Following an agreement reached earlier in the month to resume peace talks suspended since 1996, Barak and the Syrian Minister of Foreign Affairs, Farouk ash-Shara', met in Washington, DC, for talks hosted by President Clinton.

21 December 1999: Arafat and Barak met for talks in Ramallah—the first occasion on which an Israeli premier had attended peace talks in Palestinian-controlled territory.

3–9 January 2000: Israeli-Syrian peace talks at Shepherdstown, West Virginia, USA, attended by the Israeli Prime Minister and Syrian Minister of Foreign Affairs, proved inconclusive. A further round of talks, scheduled for 19 January, was subsequently postponed indefinitely.

17 January 2000: At a meeting in Tel-Aviv between Barak and Arafat, the Israeli premier required flexibility in respect of deadlines for troop redeployments and for reaching agreement on 'final status' issues.

3 February 2000: Talks in Gaza between Arafat and Barak ended in acrimony, following disagreement over the third Israeli troop redeployment.

7 February 2000: Israel launched a series of bombing raids on Hezbollah positions and infrastructure targets in Lebanon, in reprisal for the deaths of Israeli military and SLA personnel in assaults at the end of January.

13 February 2000: The deadline expired for agreement on a framework agreement on permanent status (FAPS) by Israel and the PNA, as stipulated in the 1999 Sharm esh-Sheikh agreement.

5 March 2000: Israel declared that it would unilaterally withdraw from southern Lebanon by 7 July.

9 March 2000: Meeting at Sharm esh-Sheikh for talks hosted by President Mubarak, Arafat and Barak agreed a formula for the resumption of peace talks.

21 March 2000: Israeli troops completed the final phase of the second-stage redeployment, as agreed in the 1998 Wye River Memorandum. Israeli and Palestinian negotiators resumed 'final status' negotiations in Washington, DC.

26 March 2000: A 'summit' meeting in Geneva between President Assad and President Clinton failed to find a formula for the resumption of negotiations on the Israeli-Syrian track of the peace process.

13 April 2000: Israel announced an end to the suspension of settlement construction in the Golan Heights.

30 April 2000: Palestinian negotiators withdrew from 'final status' negotiations in Eilat, in protest at Israeli proposals to expand the settlement of Ma'aleh Edomin.

7 May 2000: Arafat and Barak met in Ramallah for 'crisis' talks, mediated by US special envoy Dennis Ross, ahead of the impending expiry of the extended deadline of 13 May for agreement on FAPS.

15–18 May 2000: A Palestinian 'day of rage', declared in commemoration of the 52nd anniversary of the declaration of the State of Israel, resulted in violent confrontations with Israeli security forces throughout the West Bank and Gaza; at least six Palestinians were killed, and several hundred injured.

24 May 2000: The accelerated Israeli withdrawal from southern Lebanon was completed, several weeks ahead of the original deadline, after Hezbollah forces and civilian supporters overran positions abandoned by the Israeli proxy SLA.

10 June 2000: President Assad died. An emergency session of the Syrian People's Assembly approved a constitutional amendment lowering the minimum age of eligibility for a presidential candidate from 40 years to 34— the age of the late President's second son, Bashar, who was eventually elected to succeed him.

11–25 July 2000: Arafat and Barak attended a peace meeting at Camp David, in the presence of President Clinton; negotiations failed to achieve agreement on the issue of the status of Jerusalem.

6 September 2000: President Clinton held separate meetings with Arafat and Barak in New York, where the leaders were to attend the UN 'millennium summit'.

10 September 2000: Following a two-day meeting in Gaza, the PNC adopted a recommendation by Arafat to delay the unilateral declaration of a Palestinian state on 13 September, upon the expiry of the deadline for the conclusion of permanent status negotiations.

19 September 2000: Israel cancelled a scheduled round of talks with Palestinian negotiators in Jerusalem, citing the Palestinians' failure to resolve the impasse in the peace process.

25 September 2000: Barak and Arafat met at the Israeli premier's home for their first peace talks since the Camp David 'summit' in July, amid reported preparations by negotiators from both sides for further talks in the USA.

28 September 2000: The Israeli Likud leader, Ariel Sharon, visited the disputed sacred site known as Temple Mount by the Jews and Haram ash-Sharif by Muslims; this provoked violent protests throughout the West Bank and the Gaza Strip.

5 October 2000: Barak left US-sponsored peace talks in France early and announced that he would not be attending further discussions in Egypt.

6 October 2000: Israeli police stormed the compound of the al-Aqsa mosque in Jerusalem in order to apprehend a group of Palestinian youths who had attacked them several hours previously; the action provoked violent protests among Palestinians and Israeli Arabs throughout the country and was condemned by the international community.

7 October 2000: Barak announced that Arafat must suppress the violence in East Jerusalem, Gaza and the West Bank—which had become known as the Al-Aqsa *intifada*—within 48 hours, otherwise the armed forces would intensify offensives against Palestinian targets. The UN Security Council issued a resolution condemning Israel's excessive use of force against Palestinians.

7 October 2000: In protest at the detention of Palestinian and Lebanese prisoners held by the Israeli authorities, Hezbollah guerrillas captured three Israeli soldiers in the disputed Shebaa Farms area near the Syrian border.

9 October 2000: The Iraqi Government called for a *jihad* (holy war) to liberate Palestine and announced that it would donate US $5m. to the cause.

11–12 October 2000: The UN Secretary-General, Kofi Annan, visited Beirut in an attempt to negotiate the release of the Israeli soldiers detained at the Shebaa Farms.

12 October 2000: Israel criticized the Palestinian authorities for releasing significant numbers of Hamas prisoners. On the same day, Palestinian demonstrators stormed a police station in Ramallah and killed two members of the Israeli security forces detained there; Israel subsequently launched a rocket attack on the building.

16–17 October 2000: At a UN-mediated summit meeting led by President Clinton in Sharm esh-Sheikh, Israel agreed with the Palestinians to end the violence, and establish a mission to investigate its causes, to end the closure of Palestinian-controlled areas and redeploy troops stationed there and to reopen Gaza airport. Barak also demanded that Arafat re-arrest 65 Islamist militants whom the PNA had freed earlier in the month.

18 October 2000: Barak and Arafat met to discuss the implementation of the peace agreement; the following day Israeli troops began to withdraw from their positions in the West Bank and Gaza. The Karni border crossing to the Gaza Strip was also reopened after its closure during unrest two weeks previously.

19 October 2000: At a meeting of Arab foreign ministers in Cairo, Syria urged an end to the normalization of relations with Israel.

21–22 October 2000: At a meeting in Cairo, Arab leaders determined that Israel bore full responsibility for the recent violence. In the ensuing weeks Morocco, Oman and Tunisia terminated diplomatic ties with Israel, followed by Egypt and Qatar in November.

22 October 2000: Israel announced that it was taking a formal pause from the peace process owing to renewed Palestinian violence; Israeli troops had shot dead nine Palestinians since the implementation of the cease-fire agreement.

24 October 2000: An anti-Israeli demonstration took place near the Israeli border; the participants demanded that Palestinian refugees in Jordan be allowed to return to their homes.

26 October 2000: Islamic Jihad carried out a suicide-bomb attack on an Israeli security post in Gaza.

29 October 2000: Israel sent tanks and armoured vehicles into the Gaza Strip to open the road to the Jewish settlement of Netzarim; one Palestinian was killed and several others wounded in the operation.

1 November 2000: Peres, the Israeli Minister of Regional Co-operation, held crisis talks with Arafat in Gaza; truce agreements made at the meeting collapsed the following day when two Israelis were killed in a car bomb attack perpetrated by Islamic Jihad.

16 November 2000: Hezbollah perpetrated a further bomb attack in Shebaa Farms, in which two Israeli soldiers were injured; one soldier was killed and a further two injured in another bomb attack in the area later in the month.

17 November 2000: The Israeli Government imposed an economic blockade of the West Bank and Gaza.

20 November 2000: A bomb exploded near an Israeli school bus in the Gaza Strip, killing two adults and injuring a further nine adults and children. In retaliation, the Israeli forces shelled the Palestinian security forces and the Fatah party buildings, killing four Fatah officials.

28 November 2000: Barak announced that prime-ministerial elections would take place in February 2001. The following day Sharon announced his candidacy.

29 November 2000: Russia mediated a further round of peace talks between the Israelis and Palestinians. Barak announced that Israel would withdraw its armed forces from the West Bank, on condition that the PNA would agree to postpone any discussion of remaining 'final status' issues; this was rejected by the PNA.

7 December 2000: A court in Nablus convicted a man of collaborating with the Israeli secret services in the assassination of a Hamas commander and sentenced him to death. Later in the month, two more alleged collaborators were assassinated.

11 December 2000: An inquiry was begun into the recent violence by an international delegation, led by a former US Senator, George Mitchell.

27 December 2000: US-mediated peace talks collapsed following further explosions in the Gaza Strip and Tel-Aviv. President Clinton was believed to have proposed the creation of a Palestinian state, including the Gaza Strip and 95% of the West Bank, on the condition that the PNA relinquish their demand that Palestinian refugees be allowed to return to the areas they left in 1948. The plan was rejected by the Palestinians.

30 December 2000: The Democratic Front for the Liberation of Palestine called on Arafat to issue weapons to all Palestinians, following the wounding of one of its leaders in an Israeli gun attack.

31 December 2000: Israeli forces shot five Palestinians, including a 10 year-old boy. The Palestinians retaliated with three bomb attacks in the Israeli town of Netanya, injuring more than 40 people.

31 December 2000: The leader of the extremist Jewish settler movement Kahane Chai, Binyamin Kahane, was shot dead. On the same day, a senior Fatah official was killed in the West Bank.

5–16 January 2001: US-mediated talks resumed; however, they ended shortly after the killing of a Jewish settler in the Gaza Strip; revenge attacks by Jewish settler extremists on Palestinians ensued.

21 January 2001: The Israeli Government announced that it would boycott the inquiry led by Mitchell, after the commission visited Temple Mount/Haram ash-Sharif without permission from the Israeli authorities. The commission was subsequently suspended.

21 January 2001: Peace talks took place in Taba, Egypt; proceedings were soon suspended, however, after Israeli civilians were killed in a gun attack in the West Bank, for which Hamas later claimed responsibility.

5 February 2001: Following criticism from the UN, Israel agreed to demolish a security barrier which it had constructed inside Lebanese territory evacuated by Israeli troops eight months previously.

6 February 2001: Sharon won the prime-ministerial election, receiving 62.4% of the votes cast; 62.3% of those eligible to vote participated. Following his defeat, Barak resigned as leader of the Labour Party and announced his retirement from political life.

6 February 2001: There were violent demonstrations in the West Bank and Gaza following the election of Sharon as Prime Minister in Israel; it was widely believed that he was responsible for the massacre of Palestinian refugees in Lebanese camps in 1982 and it was his visit to Temple Mount/Haram ash-Sharif that was widely held responsible among Palestinians for the unrest in 2000–01.

8 February 2001: Following the election of Sharon as the Prime Minister of Israel, who had indicated in his campaign that he would seek to reconcile his country with Syria, Assad emphasised that the Government would only consider peace negotiations if Israel withdrew from the Golan Heights.

19–20 March 2001: As Sharon visited Washington, DC, for talks with the newly inaugurated US President, George W. Bush, Palestinian guerrillas shot dead a Jewish settler on the West Bank; in Gaza, Israeli troops injured a Palestinian spokeswoman, Dr Hanan Ashrawi, and four children.

27–28 March 2001: Amman hosted a 'summit' meeting of Arab leaders, which was also attended by the UN Secretary-General. The leaders pledged more financial support for the Palestinians, but failed to agree common policies regarding sanctions on Iraq and the reconciliation of Iraq and Kuwait.

5 April 2001: The Israeli Supreme Court rejected a petition from the ultra-nationalist Temple Mount Faithful to be allowed to celebrate Passover at Temple Mount. The court ruled that such an event could lead to Palestinian rioting.

15 April 2001: Israel carried out air raids on a Syrian air base in eastern Lebanon; three Syrian soldiers were killed.

24 April 2001: The Israeli authorities closed off all access to and from the West Bank and the Gaza Strip, ostensibly to protect Israel from potential Palestinian attacks during independence celebrations.

28–29 April 2001: Peres held discussions with President Mubarak of Egypt regarding a joint Egyptian-Jordanian peace plan; the proposals suggested that the Israelis and Palestinians should maintain a month-long truce, followed by talks on a future peace deal. At the conclusion of the negotiations, Peres announced that the border restrictions on the Palestinian territories would be relaxed.

30 April 2001: Peres met the UN Secretary-General, to discuss the peace plan; he suggested that the truce period should be extended before peace talks commenced; in the subsequent days he discussed the Egyptian-Jordanian peace proposals with President Bush and the US Secretary of State, Colin Powell.

3 May 2001: President Assad visited Spain for discussions with senior government officials regarding greater EU participation in the Middle East peace process; it was Assad's first visit to a Western country since taking office.

6 May 2001: King Abdullah and the Egyptian President, Mubarak, discussed their joint proposal for peace negotiations to end the Arab–Israeli conflict. The two countries urged Israel to withdraw from reoccupied territory in the Palestinian Autonomous Areas and proposed the imposition of restrictions on construction in the territories and the renewal of peace negotiations. The following day, King Abdullah travelled to France to discuss the proposals with that country's President, Jacques Chirac, and its Prime Minister, Lionel Jospin.

10 May 2001: The Israeli armed forces carried out missile attacks on the headquarters of the Palestinian police buildings and the Fatah headquarters in Gaza city.

16 May 2001: Israeli helicopter gunships carried out further attacks on security-force buildings, killing 12 Palestinian police officers.

16 May 2001: The Secretary-General of the PLO, Mahoud Abbas, met the US Secretary of State, Colin Powell. During talks regarding the peace process, Abbas asked the US Government to formally endorse the findings of Mitchell's inquiry.

16 May 2001: Helicopter gunships carried out further attacks on Palestinian security force buildings.

18 May 2001: Peres declared that Israel would be prepared to stop any further seizures of land around the Palestinian territories.

19 May 2001: Following a suicide-bomb attack on an Israeli shopping centre by Islamist militants, Israel launched rocket attacks on the towns of Tulkarm and Jenin, in which three people were wounded.

21 May 2001: Israel carried out air raids on what it believed to be a Palestinian mortar factory in Jabilya, outside Gaza city. Israeli tanks also moved into the town of Qarara.

22 May 2001: The report of the international inquiry into the causes of the recent Arab-Israeli violence was published; the Mitchell Report emphasized that Jewish settlement expansion was the main obstacle to peace and recommended that it be halted; it also called for an immediate cease-fire in preparation for peace negotiations. In a change of policy, the Israeli Government refused to halt Jewish settlement programmes but declared a unilateral cease-fire.

24 May 2001: The Israeli air force shot down a Lebanese civilian light aircraft near the Israeli town of Netanya, killing the pilot. Israel claimed that the pilot had failed to respond to warnings; Lebanon accused the Israeli forces of forcing the pilot to fly into Israeli airspace.

25 May 2001: Sharon stated that Israel would maintain its unilateral cease-fire for several more days, despite further suicide-bomb attacks.

26 May 2001: At an emergency meeting of the foreign ministers of the OIC, Arafat accused the UN Security Council of failing to adequately protect the Palestinians.

27 May 2001: Following a meeting with the new US envoy to the region, William Burns, the Israeli Government proposed a return to co-operation with the Palestinians. As the discussions were taking place, two bomb attacks were carried out in Jerusalem by the PFLP.

1 June 2001: A total of 18 Israelis were killed and more than 100 injured during a Palestinian suicide-bomb attack on a night-club in Tel-Aviv. Arafat denounced the attack and advocated an immediate cease-fire; numerous armed Palestinian groups rejected the demand.

6 June 2001: Some 20,000 Israeli settlers demonstrated in Jerusalem, demanding that the Government end its unilateral cease-fire.

12 June 2001: The Israeli Government made a cease-fire agreement with the Palestinians, which was to come into effect the following day, in a series of meetings mediated by the US CIA Director, George Tenet. The Israeli defence minister announced that the blockade of Palestinian towns would cease and that the armed forces would be deployed.

14–30 June 2001: The Jordanian authorities detained a Qatar Airways aircraft carrying the exiled Hamas activist, Ibrahim Gosheh, at Amman airport. Gosheh was denied entry to Jordan and the aircraft refused permission to leave unless Gosheh was on board. The Palestinian activist was eventually granted entry to Jordan; Qatar Airways subsequently announced that it would take legal action against the Jordanian Government for its conduct during the incident.

19–20 June 2001: Continuing bomb attacks on Israeli targets by Palestinians prompted the Government to reconsider the cease-fire; however, it decided to maintain its position.

28 June 2001: The UN envoy to Beirut announced that Israel had agreed to cease military flights over Lebanon; this was later denied by Israel.

29 June 2001: Hezbollah guerrillas fired mortars on Israeli positions in the Shebaa Farms area. Israeli forces retaliated with attacks on the town of Kfor Shouba. The following week, the UN Security Council expressed its concern over the escalating violence in the region.

1 July 2001: Following Hezbollah mortar attacks on Israeli positions, Israel launched air raids on a Syrian military radar station in Lebanon, wounding three people.

2 July 2001: Following Israeli air-raids on Hamas targets, during which three Palestinians were killed, Islamic militants detonated two car bombs in the town of Yehud, near Tel-Aviv.

4 July 2001: The Israeli Government gave the army permission to use more force against the Palestinians, effectively ending the cease-fire.

10 July 2001: The Israeli security forces demolished 17 Palestinian houses in the Gaza Strip; a gun battle between the Palestinians and the security forces ensued.

11 July 2001: The UN admitted that a video recording which showed fake UN vehicles and uniforms believed to have been used by Hezbollah during its kidnapping of Israeli soldiers in October 2000 had been made by a member of UNIFIL. The UN Secretary-General ruled that an edited version of the recording could be shown to the Israeli Government and ordered an investigation into the handling of the evidence by the UN.

13 July 2001: Following allegations apparently made by an unidentified peace-keeper in an Israeli newspaper, the UN announced a further investigation into whether its troops had collaborated with Hezbollah in the capture of the Israeli soldiers.

19 July 2001: President Mubarak of Egypt stated that he did not believe that any further progress towards peace would be made while the incumbent Israeli Government remained in power.

29 July 2001: Palestinians attempted to stop a group of messianic Jews from placing a symbolic cornerstone in the Temple Mount/Haram ash-Sharif complex; police stormed the al-Aqsa mosque to end the violence and several Israelis and Palestinians were injured. The Palestinians dispersed after the intervention of the Israeli Arab politician, Ahmed Tibi.

31 July 2001: Israeli armed forces launched an offensive on the Hamas headquarters in Nablus; among at least eight Palestinians killed were two Hamas leaders allegedly implicated in the night-club bombing in Tel-Aviv in June. Eight Palestinians had been killed in a number of separate incidents the previous day.

9 August 2001: At least 15 Israelis were killed in a suicide bombing, for which Hamas claimed responsibility, on a restaurant in central Jerusalem.

10 August 2001: Israeli security personnel occupied and closed Orient House, the *de facto* headquarters of the PNA in East Jerusalem. The seizure was condemned by many Western Governments as an unnecessary provocation.

14 August 2001: Israeli forces entered the Palestinian-controlled town of Jenin, destroying PNA offices, in reprisal for a suicide bombing by Islamic Jihad in Haifa, in which some 20 Israelis had been injured.

27 August 2001: Abu Ali Moustafa, the leader of the PFLP, was assassinated in Ramallah by Israeli security forces.

9 September 2001: Following a series of incursions into Palestinian-controlled territory by the IDF, Hamas and Islamic Jihad carried out a series of bombings and gun attacks. The Israeli Government dismissed the Palestinian Authority's condemnation of the attacks.

11–17 September 2001: Israeli forces attacked the Palestinian town of Jenin, overcoming resistance from the Palestinian security forces and destroying all their bases in the town. A number of other incursions into Palestinian territory followed, as did increased Palestinian unrest. Sharon claimed that Arafat was equivalent to Osama bin Laden, the dissident Islamist believed to be responsible for terrorist attacks on the USA on 11 September.

17 September 2001: Arafat urged Palestinians to observe a cease-fire. Despite a consequent decrease in Palestinian armed activity, Sharon refused to allow Peres to meet the PNA Chairman.

26 September 2001: Peres met Arafat; the two men agreed a cease-fire, although this truce lasted less than a day, as Palestinian guerrillas attacked an IDF post and Israeli forces raided the town of Rafah in response.

4 October 2001: President Bush announced that he favoured the eventual creation of a 'viable Palestinian state'.

8 October 2001: Following the beginning of US military action against Osama bin Laden and the Taliban regime in Afghanistan, student demonstrations in Gaza were violently suppressed by Palestinian security forces, and several protesters were killed.

17 October 2001: The Israeli Minister of Tourism, Rehavam Ze'evi, a member of an extreme right-wing party, was assassinated in a hotel in Jerusalem. The PFLP claimed responsibility for the attack, in retaliation for the assassination of Abu Ali Mustafa. Sharon, referring to the attacks on the USA, claimed that Ze'evi's murder was 'Israel's own Twin Towers', and urged the PNA to detain and surrender those it considered to be responsible, or risk being considered a terrorist organization.

18–22 October 2001: Israeli forces entered a number of Palestinian-controlled towns, amid further resistance. In Bethlehem alone, 14 Palestinians were killed.

22 October 2001: The US State Department urged Israel to withdraw its forces from Palestinian areas.

28 October 2001: The withdrawal of IDF troops from Beit Jala and Bethlehem was announced. On the same day, four Israelis were killed by Islamic Jihad.

3 November 2001: The Gaza Strip's Security Chief, Muhammad Dahlan, tendered his resignation in protest at Arafat's policies towards demonstrators and those accused by Israel of attacks on its citizens. He was subsequently persuaded to withdraw his resignation.

4 November 2001: Israel announced that the incursions into Palestinian towns had achieved their objectives, and that a phased withdrawal would begin.

5 November 2001: Arafat and Peres met informally.

19 November 2001: The US Secretary of State, Colin Powell, announced the appointment of Gen. (retd) Anthony Zinni to the post of US envoy to the region. Powell affirmed US support for a lasting peace in the region, and urged an immediate end to violence.

23 November 2001: Mahmud Abu Hanud, a senior figure in the military command of Hamas, and two of his bodyguards were killed by an Israeli missile. Hamas threatened retaliatory attacks.

1–2 December 2001: Hamas agents carried out suicide bombings in Jerusalem and Haifa, killing a total of 25 Israelis.

3 December 2001: Sharon stated that he attributed to Arafat sole responsibility for the prevailing atmosphere of violence. On the same day, Israeli forces initiated an assault on the infrastructure of the Palestinian territories and that of the PNA itself—aircraft bombarded and destroyed Arafat's helicopter fleet and a number of fuel depots, while the runway at Gaza's airport was rendered unusable. Arafat, who had moved to Ramallah to avoid the attacks on Gaza, was effectively isolated in his compound there—the IDF stated that he would not be permitted to leave the town until the arrest of a list of named activists wanted by Israel in connection with attacks on its territory.

6 December 2001: The Egyptian Minister of Foreign Affairs, Ahmed Maher, travelled to Israel to attempt to negotiate an end to Arafat's isolation in Ramallah, without success.

11 December 2001: A convoy of settlers in the West Bank was ambushed by Palestinian gunmen, believed to have links with Arafat's Fatah movement; 10 settlers were killed. In the previous week some 100 Islamist militants had been detained by the Palestinian security forces, although some of those on the Israeli list had not been arrested, or had been swiftly released, and Israel and the USA considered the action insufficient—IDF incursions into Palestinian territory resumed.

12 December 2001: Sharon termed Arafat 'irrelevant' to the peace process, again attributing responsibility for the actions of Islamist extremists directly to him.

13 December 2001: The USA vetoed a draft resolution of the UN Security Council, condemning all violence in the Israeli-Palestinian conflict, claiming that the text would have had the effect of isolating Israel.

16 December 2001: Arafat demanded a 'complete cessation of military activities', reiterating his condemnation of suicide-bomb attacks and ordering the closure of a number of organizations with Islamist links. Hamas and Islamic Jihad condemned the speech, claiming it amounted to appeasement of Israel, although they were reported to have agreed to suspend armed operations inside Israel.

24 December 2001: Israeli forces refused to release Arafat from Ramallah in order that he might travel to Christmas celebrations in Bethlehem.

30 December 2001: An IDF incursion in Gaza resulted in the deaths of six Palestinians.

3 January 2002: The *Karine A*, a freighter carrying significant amounts of armaments, was detained in the Red Sea by the Israeli navy. The Israeli Government claimed that the arms had originated in Iran, and were destined for the PA. Both Palestinian and Iranian officials denied involvement. The US Administration eventually agreed that there appeared to have been Palestinian involvement. Although it initially expressed reservations about Israel's claim that there was evidence of links with Iran and Hezbollah, later in the month it accepted that there may have been such a connection.

6 January 2002: Zinni met Israeli and Palestinian security officials, detailing the confidence-building measures necessary before the proposals made by Mitchell and Tenet could be implemented.

12 January 2002: Two of the PA officials suspected by Israel of involvement in the *Karine A* affair were arrested by the PA police. On the same day the Israeli navy attacked a port in the Gaza Strip. On the previous day the IDF had made an incursion into the Rafah refugee camp, demolishing a number of houses and shops—this was widely considered to be a response to a number of attacks claimed by Hamas.

14 January 2002: Following the assassination of a local leader of the al-Aqsa Martyrs brigade in Tulkarm, the Palestinian paramilitary groups announced that they considered the cease-fire over. An upsurge in violence followed from both sides, and continued throughout January and February.

1 February 2002: Sharon was widely criticized after an Israeli newspaper quoted him as saying that he regretted that Israeli forces had not killed Arafat during the conflict in Lebanon in 1982.

5 February 2002: The EU's High Representative for the Common Foreign and Security Policy, Javier Solana, stated that investigations appeared to suggest a link between Iran and the PA in the *Karine A* affair.

12 February 2002: EU foreign ministers published a series of proposals for the advancement of the peace process—Israel and the USA refused to support them, while the Palestinians expressed 'serious reservations'.

17 February 2002: The *New York Times* published details of a peace plan put forward by the Crown Prince of Saudi Arabia, Abdullah Ibn Abd as-Sa'ud. The proposals, which were officially announced by the Saudi Arabian Government later in the month, involved the recognition of Israel within its pre-1967 borders by Arab states, the establishment of a Palestinian state and the division of Jerusalem.

22 February 2002: In a televised address, Sharon announced that he remained committed to fighting Palestinian terrorism, stating that he would order further incursions into refugee camps if it was suspected that terrorists were being harboured there.

28 February 2002: Amid continuing attacks on Israeli targets, IDF forces entered the refugee camps at Balata and Jenin, killing an estimated 30 residents. Palestinian militant groups claimed that this provoked a number of attacks on Israeli targets in subsequent days, most notably a suicide bombing in an orthodox Jewish district of Jerusalem on 2 March, in which nine people, including four children, were killed.

3 March 2002: The Israeli Security Cabinet decided to escalate its military response to the Palestinian attacks on its citizens. Several incursions into the West Bank and Gaza were made in the following days. On 4 March a senior Hamas figure survived an assassination attempt.

10 March 2002: Following a suicide bombing in a café in Jerusalem, in which 22 people were killed, Israeli forces attacked Arafat's presidential compound in Gaza. Reports from both sides stated that the compound had been completely destroyed.

12 March 2002: In what was described as Israel's biggest military operation since the invasion of Lebanon in 1982, an estimated 20,000 troops, supported by tanks, artillery and air strikes, entered PA areas in the West Bank and Gaza. Palestinian forces were unable to defend key targets, and a number of towns, including Ramallah, were reoccupied. The EU and Annan denounced the operation, claiming that it used excessive force. The UN Security Council passed Resolution 1397 that evening, reaffirming the international commitment to an end to violence and a peaceful solution to the conflict. The resolution was notable for being sponsored by the USA, its first involvement in a resolution on the Middle East since the mid-1970s.

14 March 2002: Zinni arrived in the region to attempt to negotiate a calming of the recent escalation in violence; the following week the US Vice-President, Dick Cheney, visited the region at the end of a tour of Arab nations aimed at gaining support for military intervention in Iraq. The US Administration expressed concern at the scale of Israel's attacks.

15 March 2002: IDF forces withdrew from Ramallah, in what the Israeli Government described as a 'goodwill gesture'. Reciprocal attacks continued, however—it was estimated that more than 300 Palestinians were killed in March, and suicide bombings occurred throughout Israel.

27 March 2002: An Arab League summit meeting, at which the Saudi peace plan was discussed, was marred by boycotts and withdrawals at various stages by numerous delegations, including those of Egypt and Jordan. The plan was generally welcomed, although the force of any of the decisions made was questionable, given the scant participation. On the same day a suicide bombing in Netanya, claimed by Hamas, resulted in 29 deaths.

29 March 2002: Sharon announced that Israel was at war; a few hours earlier the IDF had re-entered Ramallah and, amid severe fighting, attacked Arafat's compound, in what was described as 'Operation Defensive Shield'. It subsequently emerged that Sharon had intended to arrest and expel Arafat, but had decided to leave him surrounded following representations from the USA and other international officials. In the subsequent days Israeli forces occupied towns throughout the West Bank. During an attack on Bethlehem, some 100 Palestinian fighters sought refuge in the Christian Church of the Nativity—the IDF laid siege to the building.

30 March 2002: The UN Security Council endorsed Resolution 1402, which condemned the recent increase in violence, urged all sides to return to peaceful means of argument, and demanded that Israel withdraw from towns in the PA areas.

3 April 2002: Israeli forces entered Nablus, the West Bank's largest town, and the Jenin refugee camp. By this time, of the territory's major population centres, only Jericho and Hebron remained under PA control. While the policy was popular within Israel, international criticism was fierce, with demonstrations taking place throughout the Arab world.

7 April 2002: Following a number of increasingly stern criticisms of 'Operation Defensive Shield' by members of his Administration, President Bush demanded that Israel retreat from Palestinian areas 'without delay', and announced that Powell would visit the Middle East to attempt to negotiate a cease-fire. Sharon replied by stating that the operation would continue until the 'terrorist infrastructure' of the Palestinians had been dismantled. US criticism of the action increased in intensity in subsequent days.

9 April 2002: Amid Palestinian allegations of war crimes and human-rights abuses by the IDF in Jenin, a number of ambushes in the town resulted in the deaths of 13 soldiers.

11 April 2002: Powell arrived in Israel. By this time, Israeli forces had withdrawn from a number of Palestinian towns, although the sieges in Ramallah and Bethlehem continued, and international attention was focusing on the IDF action in Jenin.

13 April 2002: Arafat issued a statement condemning the numerous suicide attacks against Israeli targets; Powell agreed to visit the PA leader the following day.

15 April 2002: The UN Human Rights Commission accused Israel of 'gross violations of humanitarian law' in the West Bank.

17 April 2002: Having secured from Sharon a commitment to only a partial withdrawal, and from the PA no meaningful cease-fire proposal, Powell left the region.

18 April 2002: Israeli forces withdrew from the town of Jenin and from part of the refugee camp. A UN envoy who arrived several hours later stated that the conditions there were 'horrific beyond belief', and qualified Israel's refusal to allow humanitarian aid into the camp as 'morally repugnant'. Palestinian groups alleged that IDF forces had massacred civilians in the camp, a claim denied by Israel. On the same day Annan proposed that the UN Security Council send an armed force to restore peace in the area. The Council subsequently voted to send a fact-finding mission to Jenin, rather than the full investigation demanded by many Arab countries.

19 April 2002: The UN Security Council adopted Resolution 1405, which qualified the humanitarian situation in Jenin, and for the Palestinians in general, as 'dire', and urged all parties to support the fact-finding mission initiated by Annan.

20 April 2002: Israel announced the withdrawal of its forces from most of Ramallah, but stated that they would remain in place around Arafat's residence and the Church of the Nativity in Bethlehem. On the same day the US Assistant Secretary for Near Eastern Affairs, William Burns, visited the refugee camp at Jenin, describing the incidents there as 'a tragedy for thousands of innocent Palestinian people'.

24 April 2002: President Mubarak made an untypically fierce condemnation of Israel, accusing the country of 'state terrorism' in its treatment of the Palestinians.

25 April 2002: Four men were convicted in a Palestinian security court of involvement in the murder of the Israeli tourism minister, Rehavam Ze'evi, in October 2001, and were sentenced to between one and 18 years' imprisonment. Israel rejected the convictions, insisting that the men be extradited, and indicating that the siege of Arafat's compound in Ramallah might end were this to happen.

27 April 2002: At a meeting with President Bush in Texas, Crown Prince Abdullah of Saudi Arabia made new peace proposals, while criticizing continued US support for Israel.

28 April 2002: Following a week of negotiations, the Israeli Government announced that it would not participate in the UN fact-finding mission to Jenin. It criticized the composition of the mission and its remit, and claimed that it intended to 'smear' Israel. The mission was abandoned with reluctance by the UN the next day, to be replaced by a report compiled by the organization's local officials.

29 April 2002: Following mediation by US officials, Israeli forces agreed to withdraw from the area surrounding Arafat's compound in Ramallah, in return for the transfer to international custody of those wanted in connection with the murder of Ze'evi. President Bush stated that Arafat should now show 'leadership' and take action against terrorist groups.

2 May 2002: Arafat emerged from his compound at Ramallah.

5 May 2002: An agreement to end the siege of the Church of the Nativity, mediated by US and British delegations, was reached 'in principle'. A number of fighters had left the church in the previous days.

7 May 2002: A suicide bombing, the first since 12 April, killed 16 people in Rishon Letzion. Israeli forces mustered in response, and fears of new incursions into Gaza and the West Bank were raised, but no offensive occurred.

8 May 2002: Sharon visited President Bush in Washington, DC. At a press conference, Bush stated that he believed the PA to be in need of complete reform, and that Arafat had failed the Palestinian people.

10 May 2002: The siege at the Church of the Nativity ended. Of the Palestinian militants involved, 26 were sent to Gaza, while 13, described by Israel as 'high-level terrorists', were deported to Cyprus, pending transfer to other EU countries. Israel withdrew its forces immediately after the departure of the last of the 39 from its territory.

13 May 2002: Despite the opposition of Sharon, Likud adopted a resolution stating that it would never accept a Palestinian state in the West Bank and Gaza. On the same day, Arafat left Ramallah for the first time since his release, and toured towns in the West Bank.

16 May 2002: Following an announcement by Arafat of plans to reform the PA's institutions, Sharon, in contravention of his party's position adopted earlier in the week, stated that the eventual establishment of a Palestinian state was likely. On the same day IDF troops made new raids on Ramallah and Nablus.

23 May 2002: Arafat announced that presidential and parliamentary elections would be held in early 2003.

25 May 2002: After a number of suicide bombings in previous days, Israeli troops entered Qalqilya—in the remaining days of the month incursions were also made into Bethlehem and a number of other West Bank towns.

30 May 2002: Arafat met Burns in Ramallah. On the same day, he was reported to have signed the Basic Law of the PA, something he had hitherto refused to do.

3 June 2002: The director of the CIA, George Tenet, arrived in Jerusalem, as the USA attempted to intensify its efforts to achieve a viable peace agreement. He met Sharon, before travelling to Ramallah the following day to meet Arafat.

5 June 2002: Sharon announced his support for a plan to construct a 'security fence' along the border between pre-1967 Israel and the West Bank, roughly between Qalqilya and Jenin. Later that day, a car bomb exploded next to a bus carrying Israeli soldiers and companions in Megiddo, near the route of the proposed fence. A total of 17 people, including the driver of the car, were killed. Israeli forces responded by re-entering Jenin.

6 June 2002: Israeli forces again attacked Arafat's compound in Ramallah, withdrawing after a six-hour offensive. Arafat termed the action to be 'racism and fascism'.

8–9 June 2002: President Mubarak visited President Bush, presenting new proposals for peace, and urging him to endorse a timetable for the establishment of a Palestinian state. Bush declined, but stated that he supported the eventual establishment of such a state, while reiterating his demands that the PA be reformed and improve its anti-terrorism measures. Sharon later praised Bush for his rejection of a timetable, stating that no such plan could be implemented until Palestinians decisively rejected terrorism.

9 June 2002: Arafat reorganized his Government, eliminating 11 ministries, reallocating several of the remaining portfolios and streamlining the PA's security structure. The new Cabinet was unable to attend its initial meeting, however, as Israeli forces made another incursion into Ramallah, again surrounding Arafat's compound.

10 June 2002: Sharon met President Bush. In a statement viewed as his strongest support thus far of the Israeli position regarding Arafat, Bush stated that he believed there to be no 'partner for peace' among the Palestinian leadership.

16 June 2002: Construction of the security fence on the West Bank border began amid international condemnation. Arafat denounced the barrier as 'racist'.

18 June 2002: A new wave of violence began—two suicide bombings killed a total of 26 people. Arafat condemned the bombings and appealed for no further such attacks to be made.

20 June 2002: Amid increasing violence, Sharon announced the beginning of 'Operation Determined Path', whose primary aim was the reoccupation of any territory necessary in order for Israel's security criteria to be met. Most of the major towns in the West Bank were reoccupied.

24 June 2002: In a statement of his Middle East policy, President Bush urged restraint from all sides in the conflict, and reiterated his support for the establishment of a Palestinian state, albeit on a 'provisional' basis. He went on to make his heaviest criticism of Arafat yet, stating that the Palestinians should elect new leaders who were not 'compromised by terror'. The speech was widely criticized in the Arab press as representing open support for Israel, while many other international observers considered the remarks excessive. However, certain Arab governments stated that the new policy was the only chance for peace, and welcomed much of its content.

26 June 2002: Israel announced that 20 illegal settlements in the West Bank would be demolished. On the same day President Bush suggested that his Administration would consider sanctions against the PA if new leaders were not elected.

30 June 2002: Construction of a new security fence, in Jerusalem, began. On the same day Israeli forces effected a 'targeted killing' against a Hamas military leader.

1 July 2002: Powell announced that the US Administration would no longer deal with Arafat.

8 July 2002: Peres met the PA Minister of Finance, Salam Fayed, in the first ministerial contact between the two Governments since before the April incursions. A further round of discussions scheduled for 13 July was postponed after Israel claimed it needed more preparation time.

15 July 2002: Talks between Israeli and Egyptian delegations were reported to have made progress on several issues, but none on the principal matter of difference—that of Arafat's future.

17 July 2002: A meeting of the Quartet group (comprising the EU, the USA, Russia and the UN) revealed that none of the other three members supported the US Administration's policy on the Middle East, particularly its insistence that Arafat be removed from power. On the same day Arafat announced that he would seek election to the PA presidency in the elections scheduled for early 2003.

19 July 2002: Following two suicide attacks in the previous week, the Israeli authorities arrested 21 male relatives of the bombers and proposed to expel them from the West Bank to Gaza.

21 July 2002: Peres and Saeb Erekat met to discuss humanitarian issues.

23 July 2002: Israeli aircraft attacked a residential building in Gaza City. The leader of the military wing of Hamas, Sheikh Salah Shihada, the target of the attack, was among 15 people killed. Sharon claimed that the attack was a great success, although the USA, the EU, the UN and many governments condemned it, particularly as it had resulted in the deaths of eight children. A new cycle of Palestinian attacks and Israeli military responses began following the attack, lasting into mid-August.

1 August 2002: The UN report into the events in Jenin earlier in the year was released. It concluded that Palestinian claims of a massacre were unsupported by any evidence, and that the number of people killed in the incursion was 52—the total reported by the IDF at the conclusion of the operation. The findings were praised by Israel and condemned by the PA.

5 August 2002: Amid continuing violence, Israel announced a total ban on travel by Palestinians in much of the West Bank. That evening the UN General Assembly passed a resolution urging Israel's withdrawal from PA territory.

8 August 2002: A Palestinian delegation, led by Arafat, met with Powell.

12 August 2002: A meeting of the various Palestinian militant factions drafted proposals aimed at limiting the scope of attacks on Israelis, most notably the ending of any attacks targeting civilians. Hamas rejected the proposal, which foundered as a result, and withdrew from the talks two days later.

19 August 2002: Israel agreed to withdraw its forces from Gaza and Bethlehem, in return for increased PA efforts to reduce suicide bombings—the first withdrawals were completed the same day. The Palestinian militant factions rejected the deal, however.

28 August 2002: Israel cancelled further troop withdrawals and withdrew from scheduled talks following continued violence in Gaza. On the same day the Israeli Government announced that it had foiled an attempt to smuggle weapons into Gaza by sea.

2 September 2002: Israel announced that it would hold an inquiry into the conduct of IDF units in Palestinian towns in the previous weeks. Some 40 Palestinians, including 10 children, had been killed amid reports of IDF brutality.

3 September 2002: The Israeli Supreme Court upheld government plans to expel the families of a number of suicide bombers from the West Bank to Gaza. The inquiry was concluded several days later, and found that no improper conduct had occurred.

9 September 2002: The PLC met in Ramallah, amid growing opposition to Arafat and to his government, after a number of ministers were accused of corruption. Arafat criticized Israeli military attacks, and urged an end to suicide bombings. He stated that elections would be held in January 2003, but not while Israeli forces occupied or besieged Palestinian towns.

11 September 2002: The PA Government resigned.

17 September 2002: The Quartet announced that they intended to 're-launch' the Middle East peace process. To that end, Annan stated, they had drafted a series of general principles, known as a 'roadmap', which would be developed into concrete proposals in the subsequent months.

19 September 2002: Following two suicide bombings in the previous days, the IDF attacked Arafat's compound, forcing him to move, accompanied by several hundred security personnel, from his office into a more easily protected area. Nearly all the compound apart from this 'inner sanctum' was destroyed. The IDF action was criticized in a UN Security Council resolution and the USA, which abstained in the vote, urged Israel to abandon the operation. Meanwhile, interventions in other Palestinian areas, particularly in Gaza, continued.

29 September 2002: With most of the buildings in Arafat's compound in ruins, the Israeli forces withdrew from the site, but remained stationed nearby.

1 October 2002: As several of the security personnel who accompanied Arafat during the siege left the compound, a small Israeli force returned to the site, reportedly with the aim of preventing any identifiable militants from escaping.

3 October 2002: The US Congress approved legislation urging the transfer of the US embassy in Israel from Tel-Aviv to Jerusalem, and recognizing the latter city as its nation's capital. Numerous Arab states protested at the perceived violation of stated positions on the future of Jerusalem. President Bush said that the legislation was unhelpful and beyond the remit of Congress, and stated that his policy on the matter had not changed. The PLC immediately drafted legislation declaring Jerusalem to be the capital of a future Palestinian state.

6 October 2002: Israel again raided targets in Gaza, causing 17 deaths.

16 October 2002: Sharon met Bush in Washington, DC. It is believed that certain details of the 'roadmap' proposals were presented at the meeting. While Sharon stated that he considered the current US Administration to be the most helpful to Israel in recent history, it emerged that the USA intended to make more public criticism of Israel at appropriate times, as it attempted to build a coalition of nations supporting military action in Iraq.

21 October 2002: Following the explosion of a car bomb next to a bus in Hadera, in which 15 people were killed, Israel announced that, while it would respond, it would do so with precision in order to aid the USA's coalition-building.

30 October 2002: The Labour Party withdrew from the Israeli governing coalition, in protest at poor economic conditions. Sharon was unable to form a new administration, and thus announced that legislative and prime-ministerial elections would be held in early 2003. Eventually, he appointed an interim administration, in which Netanyahu was given the foreign affairs portfolio.

13 November 2002: Netanyahu announced that he would seek to expel Arafat from Israel and the PA-controlled areas if elected Prime Minister.

14 November 2002: Leaders of Fatah and Hamas met, the first such encounter for several years. It was reported that a strategy for the Israeli electoral campaign was agreed.

15 November 2002: Palestinian gunmen ambushed a group of Israeli settlers in Hebron, killing 12. The IDF entered the city in response, taking control of large areas.

16 November 2002: President Mubarak announced that Israel should be placed under the same international pressure as Iraq with regard to the possession of weapons of mass destruction.

19 November 2002: Islamic Jihad claimed responsibility for the Hebron ambush. The USA immediately demanded that Syria close the organization's office in Damascus—Syria refused.

21 November 2002: Amid the most severe escalation in violence for several months, a further suicide bombing in Jerusalem led to another occupation of Bethlehem. On the same day, the Secretary-General of the PLO, Mahmud Abbas (also known as 'Abu Mazen') stated that the *intifada* had been damaged by the actions of paramilitary groups.

23 November 2002: Following an attack on an Israeli military boat, the waters off the coast of Gaza were closed to all Palestinian vessels.

28 November 2002: Sharon defeated Netanyahu in the contest to be Likud's candidate for the premiership (Labour had previously elected a moderate general, Amram Mitzna). On the same day an Israeli-owned hotel in the holiday resort of Mombasa (Kenya) was bombed, resulting in 15 deaths, and two missiles narrowly missed an Israeli passenger aircraft leaving the same resort. The involvement of al-Qa'ida was immediately suspected.

2 December 2002: Israeli forces were criticized after a warehouse holding UN food aid was destroyed. The IDF stated that wanted Palestinian militants were also in the building, and that it did not know that the food was being stored there.

15 December 2002: Arafat announced his rejection of messages of support from al-Qa'ida, stating that Osama bin Laden was not interested in the Palestinians, only in exploiting Muslim sympathy with their plight to attract support for his own aims.

17 December 2002: The British Government invited numerous Palestinian figures to a conference on reform of the PA in January 2003. The conference, and the invitations, were criticized by Israel.

21 December 2002: The USA vetoed a proposed UN Security Council resolution condemning Israel for causing the deaths of the UN workers killed in the attack on the food warehouse. In the previous week, Syria had voted against a resolution condemning the Mombasa attacks, claiming that Israel could never be portrayed as a victim while occupying Palestinian territory.

22 December 2002: Arafat announced that the elections to the PLC scheduled for January would be delayed until the IDF had withdrawn from all Palestinian areas. Israel claimed that this was a means of retaining power, and stated that any progress in the peace process depended on Arafat's departure from office.

29 December 2002: Amid another upsurge in violence, Sharon again defended his policy of 'targeted killings' of selected Palestinian militants.

6 January 2003: Following two suicide-bombings in Tel-Aviv the previous day, in which 23 people, many of them migrant workers, were killed, the Israeli Government informed the PNA that two of its ministers, who were scheduled to travel to London for discussions on reform of the Authority, would not be permitted to leave the Palestinian territories. On the same day it was announced that the IDF would intensify its operations against suspected leaders of Palestinian paramilitary organizations.

14 January 2003: The London Conference took place as scheduled; the Palestinian ministers participated via video link.

28 January 2003: Likud and other right-of-centre parties performed strongly in Israeli parliamentary elections, while Labour and Meretz suffered declines in support. It appeared likely that a coalition would be formed involving Likud and a number of other right-wing parties.

29 January 2003: Sharon rejected Arafat's message of congratulation, and his offer to resume negotiations.

February 2003: As delegations from the PA and numerous Palestinian factions held negotiations in Cairo, aimed at achieving a viable cease-fire, violence again increased, with numerous suicide bombings and armed Israeli incursions.

Hamas agreed to a cease-fire on condition that the IDF abandon its programme of 'targeted killings' against its leaders. The Israeli Government rejected the proposal.

14 February 2003: Arafat agreed 'in principle' to the creation of a new government structure in the PNA, including the post of prime minister, in which significant executive powers would be vested.

27 February 2003: Following the conclusion of extensive coalition negotiations, the Knesset approved a new Government, again led by Sharon. The coalition contained members of the National Religious Party, the National Union Party and Shinui. Netanyahu was appointed Minister of Finance—although this was seen by many as a less prestigious position than his previous foreign affairs portfolio, Sharon stated that the country's economy was the new administration's primary concern. Netanyahu's predecessor as Minister of Finance, Silvan Shalom, was appointed Minister of Foreign Affairs. Despite his new Government being widely perceived as one of the most right-wing in Israel's history, Sharon insisted that he was ready to make 'painful concessions' for peace.

8 March 2003: The PLO's Central Council approved Arafat's nomination of Mahmud Abbas, the Organization's deputy leader, as the candidate for the post of prime minister, should the PLC approve changes to the PA's government structure.

10 March 2003: The PLC approved the proposed changes to the structure of the PA's government, and confirmed Abbas as Prime Minister-designate. Israel and the international community appeared relatively satisfied with the events, although concern was expressed that the delineation of powers in the new structure left security and foreign relations within the remit of the presidency.

14 March 2003: Reiterating his Administration's refusal to work with Arafat, President Bush announced that he would permit the publication of the so-called 'roadmap' as soon as a Prime Minister 'with genuine authority' was appointed by the PNA.

19 March 2003: Abbas agreed to accept the post of Prime Minister, and began the task of forming a Government.

22 March 2003: It was reported that the formation of the new PA Government was being delayed by a disagreement between Abbas and Arafat. The latter objected to the nomination of Muhammad Dahlan as Minister of Internal Affairs, claiming that the constitutional division of powers gave him control over security policy and, therefore, the appointment of the relevant ministers. The international community urged Arafat to accept Dahlan—Powell claimed that if Abbas was not allowed to choose the identity of his entire cabinet, the opportunity to move towards peace would be lost.

23 March 2003: Following intensive negotiations, and pressure from various Arab and European Governments, Arafat relented, and allowed Dahlan to be appointed Minister of State for Security, reporting directly to Abbas, who would assume the internal affairs portfolio in addition to his duties as Prime Minister. A number of other ministries were allocated to supporters of Arafat.

26 March 2003: Following the initiation of the US/UK-led military action against Iraq, the British Prime Minister, Tony Blair, stated that he was committed to bringing the Israeli–Palestinian peace process to the forefront of the US Administration's foreign policy.

23 April 2003: Abbas and Arafat appeared together in public, ending rumours of a permanent rift caused by the dispute over government appointments.

29 April 2003: The new PA Government, led by Abbas, was approved by the PLC.

30 April 2003: The roadmap proposals were presented to the Israeli and Palestinian Governments (see Documents on Palestine, p. 437). It emerged that both sides had a number of reservations with the text as drafted.

11 May 2003: At a meeting in Jericho, Abbas informed Powell that the PA would accept the roadmap proposals as they were drafted. On the same day Sharon announced that the Israeli Government considered the document unacceptable, citing particular concerns about conditionality and disarmament, and stating that Israel would not recognize any Palestinian state until the Palestinians renounced their insistence on the 'right of return'.

13 May 2003: Powell visited the Syrian President, Bashar al-Assad, in Damascus, urging full Syrian participation in the roadmap, the closure of any terrorist organizations operating in Syria and the withdrawal of troops from Lebanon.

14 May 2003: Powell visited Lebanon, demanding the dissolution of Hezbollah and the deployment of the Lebanese military to protect the country's border with Israel.

18 May 2003: As specified in the roadmap, negotiations between senior government delegations from Israel and the PA were held, including a meeting between Abbas and Sharon. Shortly after the talks concluded a suicide bomber attacked a bus in Jerusalem, resulting in seven deaths—Israel responded by stating that foreign officials who met with Arafat would not be welcome in Israel.

24 May 2003: The Israeli Cabinet narrowly endorsed the country's participation in the roadmap process. The previous day Sharon had secured a commitment from the US Administration to address Israel's list of specific concerns regarding the document's content.

27 May 2003: Sharon stated that he considered the 'occupation' of Palestinian areas to be bad for Israelis and Palestinians, and for their economies, and stated that he could contemplate an eventual withdrawal. This was considered a major softening of his position.

30 May 2003: Following talks between Abbas and Sharon, Israel agreed to release a number of Palestinian prisoners and lift restrictions on Palestinians' movement.

4 June 2003: Abbas, Bush and Sharon held talks at a 'summit' meeting in Jordan. Both Middle Eastern leaders expressed their support for the roadmap proposals, despite domestic criticism.

6 June 2003: Hamas suspended all contact with Abbas, claiming that his actions at the summit amounted to surrender—several other militant organizations followed suit.

10 June 2003: Israeli military teams began dismantling certain settlements, in accordance with the roadmap, amid stern protests. On the same day, a number of 'targeted killings' were attempted, including an unsuccessful one on the political leader of Hamas, Abd al-Aziz ar-Rantisi.

17 June 2003: The Knesset again supported Sharon's actions with regard to the roadmap.

21 June 2003: A senior Hamas commander in Hebron was killed in an Israeli military operation. The move provoked some criticism from the USA, especially as it believed it had convinced Israel to agree to suspend its policy of attacking individual senior Palestinian militants, in the hope that peace talks might begin.

29 June 2003: Following a visit to both Israelis and Palestinians by the US National Security Adviser, Condoleezza Rice, a number of paramilitary groups, including Fatah, Hamas and Islamic Jihad, agreed to a three-month suspension of attacks against Israeli targets. Israel announced that it would ignore the truce until it appeared to be working, but authorized the withdrawal of its forces from certain areas of Gaza, as specified in the roadmap.

9 July 2003: Hamas stated that it did not believe that Israel was releasing Palestinian prisoners quickly enough, and criticized Abbas for allowing the situation to persist. Abbas responded by threatening to resign.

28 July 2003: Some 500 Palestinian prisoners, including more than 200 members of Islamist paramilitary groups, were released from Israeli detention. A further, smaller release took place in mid-August.

August 2003: The security barrier in the West Bank once again became the focus of international protests, with many governments and organizations claiming that it must be dismantled if the peace process were to have any chance of succeeding. Responding to US criticism of the barrier, Sharon stated that it was considered necessary for Israel's security.

18 August 2003: Talks aimed at agreeing a permanent Israeli withdrawal from Jericho, Qalqilya, Ramallah and Tulkarm ended in failure.

20 August 2003: Negotiations were suspended following a bus bombing in Jerusalem, which killed 20 Israelis.

1 September 2003: The Israeli Government announced the suspension of all contacts with the PA.

4 September 2003: Following a speech at a public meeting in Ramallah, Abbas was attacked by members of Fatah loyal to Arafat. He was uninjured.

6 September 2003: Abbas resigned the post of Prime Minister, stating as his primary reason the lack of progress towards the implementation of the roadmap. He held the Israeli Government responsible, and claimed that the Quartet, and particularly the USA, were not doing enough to ensure Israel's full participation. However, he also made a reference to domestic strife—widely interpreted as an allusion to his numerous disagreements with President Arafat, the most persistent and serious of which had concerned the control over the PA's security forces. A number of other ministers, including Dahlan, also resigned.

7 September 2003: It emerged that the spiritual leader of Hamas, Sheikh Ahmad Yassin, had survived a 'targeted killing' attempt the previous day. His warning that Israel would pay 'a heavy price' was widely interpreted as meaning the definitive end of the recent cease-fire.

10 September 2003: The Speaker of the PLC, Ahmed Quray (also known as 'Abu Ala'), accepted Arafat's offer to assume the post of Prime Minister, and began attempts to form an emergency Government.

12 September 2003: Amid increasing violence, Israel announced that it intended to remove Arafat from the West Bank. The announcement was criticized by the international community, including the USA.

16 September 2003: The USA vetoed a draft Security Council resolution, sponsored by Syria, condemning Israel for revealing its intention to 'remove' Arafat from its territory, and demanding that he should not be harmed. Arab governments responded with fierce criticism, claiming that the USA was effectively giving Israel permission to kill Arafat.

30 September 2003: A report by the UNHCR's *rapporteur* stated that the presence of the security barrier in the West Bank amounted to an 'unlawful annexation' of territory. Israel dismissed the report. A draft Security Council condemning the 'Wall' was vetoed by the USA in mid-October.

4 October 2003: A total of 19 Israelis were killed when a female suicide bomber attacked a café in Haifa. Quray and Arafat both condemned the act—their condemnations were dismissed by Israel.

5 October 2003: Israeli aircraft bombed a military facility in central Syria, claiming that it was used for the training of members of Islamic Jihad. Syria denied this and expressed its outrage at the attack on its territory. The USA, which had previously accused Syria of sponsoring terrorism, refused to condemn the Israeli action. Violence erupted in the Occupied Territories, particularly in Gaza, in response.

14 October 2003: Israel ordered the expulsion of a further 15 detainees from the West Bank to Gaza.

21 October 2003: Following major air-raids on targets in Gaza, in which at least 10 people were killed, a number of Israeli ministers, mostly from the Shinui party, criticized the action.

11 November 2003: A further UN report suggested that the security barrier was causing hardship to the Palestinians living in its vicinity. Again, the report was rejected by the Israeli Government.

12 November 2003: The new PA Government was confirmed. The majority of its positions went to apparent Arafat loyalists, amid suspicion that Quray, like Abbas before him, was frustrated at Arafat's reluctance to allow the Prime Minister to select the Cabinet.

28 November 2003: Powell met the authors of a new, unofficial peace plan, known as the Geneva Accord. The plan offered little that was new, but its authors, a former senior negotiator from each side, claimed that it represented the best hope for resuming progress towards peace. The Israeli Government dismissed the plan, as did the Palestinian paramilitary organizations.

30 November 2003: Israel rejected Palestinian demands that construction of the security barrier cease if peace talks were to resume.

8 December 2003: After several days of intensive negotiations, representatives of the various Palestinian factions left Cairo having failed to agree terms for a new cease-fire.

18 December 2003: Following a number of increasingly 'dovish' statements by ministers and military figures in previous weeks, Sharon announced that he was prepared to take unilateral action to secure peace, with or without Palestinian participation, should the roadmap fail. The actions, which he stated would include dismantling settlements, would, he said, be aimed solely at making Israel safer, and would represent a 'disengagement' from the conflict. The speech drew a mixed reaction from international observers; domestically, nearly all parties criticized the plans, claiming that they amounted to a rapid abandonment of established Israeli policy.

Arab–Israeli Relations 1947–67

PAUL COSSALI

By the beginning of 1947 it was evident the British mandatory authorities in Palestine were failing to prevent sectarian conflict sliding into civil war. Attempts to enforce restrictions on Jewish immigration, in line with promises given to the Arabs in the White Paper of 1939, had led militant Zionist organizations to lead a campaign of violence against British interests, with the aim of making the mandate unworkable. The political leadership of the Zionist movement applied pressure itself, lobbying extensively to allow free immigration to Palestine and the realization of its goal of a Jewish homeland in the Middle East. With the full horrors of the Nazi holocaust so recently revealed, public opinion in the West was highly sympathetic to the Zionist cause. US President Harry Truman was a crucial and powerful ally. Washington's pressure on London to allow Jewish refugees into Palestine was instrumental in the British Government's decision in spring 1947 to refer the question of the future of Palestine to the UN.

In April 1947 the UN General Assembly established a special commission (UNSCOP) to report on the situation in Palestine. In August UNSCOP presented minority and majority proposals. The former suggested a federal solution to the Palestine problem, while the latter proposed the partition of the country into Arab and Jewish states with the Jerusalem district becoming a *corpus seperatum* administered by the UN. Both plans envisaged the termination of the Mandate. Under the partition proposals the Jews, who comprised one-third of the population and owned less than 6% of the land, were to gain 60% of the country. Zionist organizations viewed partition as the realization of their goal of a Jewish homeland and gave it their enthusiastic backing. Palestine's Arabs were joined by the rest of the Arab world in voicing their bitter opposition. Partition, particularly along the territorial lines put forward by UNSCOP, was viewed as lacking legal or moral justification. An attempt to challenge the UN's competence to recommend partition through recourse to the International Court of Justice was rejected. During the autumn of 1947 the US administration its full diplomatic support to the partition proposals, with the result that in critical UN vote (Resolution 181) on 29 November, the General Assembly by 33 votes to 13, with 10 abstentions, to approve the division of Palestine mo. less in accordance with the UNSCOP recommendations. The impact of the U e, and the concomitant United Kingdom decision to terminate its Manda May 1948, resulted in an intensification of the conflict between Jewish and Arab communities. More than ever before, control of the land became the focus of the military efforts of both sides. The struggle, however, would prove to be an unequal one. The Jews boasted well armed and highly motivated militias for which the poorly equipped Arab forces were no match. In the period between the partition resolution and the end of the Mandate Jewish forces not only consolidated control over their own districts, but also seized substantial territory assigned to the putative Arab state. The extent to which Jewish fighters carried out planned and deliberate expulsions of the Arab populations in the areas they occupied would become an enduring point of controversy. What is not in dispute is that many thousands of Arabs fled their homes in the fighting and that atrocities committed against Arab civilians, most infamously the Deir Yassin massacre of April 1948, contributed to the scale of the exodus.

At the termination of the Mandate on 14 May 1948 the Jewish authorities in Palestine declared the creation of the State of Israel and set up a provisional government with Ben Gurion as Prime Minister. The USA granted immediate recognition to the Jewish state and the USSR did so shortly afterwards. Israel's Arab neighbours, Egypt, Syria, Lebanon and Transjordan (known as Jordan from 1949) sent a combined force of 20,000 troops in a failed attempt to overthrow the new state. In the fighting Israel's armed forces, bolstered by shipments of weapons from Czechoslovakia, were able to seize additional Arab lands. A UN-brokered cease-fire came into effect in July 1948 and armistice agreements were signed between Israel and its neighbours in 1949. At the end of formal hostilities the Jewish state occupied nearly 80% of historic Palestine. Refugees and Egyptian troops remained in a small strip of land around the coastal town of Gaza, while Jordan retained control of the West Bank of the River Jordan, including East Jerusalem. Some 750,000 Palestinian Arabs had fled their homes as a result of the conflict, while approximately 150,000 had remained in territory claimed by the new State of Israel. In December 1948 the UN General Assembly passed Resolution 194 which called for the refugees to be allowed to return to their homes or to receive compensation if they chose not to. Israel refused to comply. In the years following statehood, the Israeli authorities destroyed the overwhelming majority, more than 380, of former Arab villages.

In approaches towards Israel, the Arab League endeavoured to maintain a united front around the core principles of non-negotiation, the inviolability of Palestinian territory and a refusal to accept the situation of Palestinian refugees as permanent. The Jordanian regime proved the least willing to abide with the League's resolutions on the Palestine question. It took steps to settle refugees and in 1950, following favourable election results in Arab Palestine, the Kingdom formally annexed the West Bank. Rumours that Jordan was engaged in secret talks with Israel also circulated widely. In July 1951 Palestinian extremists were responsible for the assassination of King Abdullah of Jordan in Jerusalem.

The Israeli state underwent rapid and impressive development in the 1950s, its economy boosted by war reparations from West Germany and the arrival of hundreds of thousands of new immigrants. Many of the new arrivals were Arab-speaking Jews, some expelled from their countries of birth and others no longer comfortable with the virulently anti-Israeli (and often anti-Jewish) feeling that swept across North Africa and the Middle East in the wake of events in Palestine. Indeed, the implacable hostility of its Arab neighbours ensured that military imperatives defined the political thinking of successive Israeli administrations. Defence spending consumed a huge proportion of the national budget. Not that Arab rhetoric was matched by battlefield capability. In the early 1950s Israeli settlements were subjected to frequent cross-border raids. While these led to some loss of life—175 soldiers and civilians were reportedly killed between 1949 and 1953—many infiltrators were unarmed refugees and those who did carry weapons, the self-styled *fedayeen*, were too few in number to pose an existential threat. Nevertheless, Israeli defence chiefs adopted a policy of retaliatory and often disproportionate deterrence. On several occasions during the early and mid-1950s Israel was censured by the UN Security Council for attacking neighbouring civilian and military targets.

The objective threat to Israel increased with the military coup in Egypt, which brought the Arab nationalist regime of Col Gamal abd an-Nasser to power in 1954. It was Nasser's view that achieving military parity with Israel should be the strategic goal of the Arab world in its confrontation with Israel and he embarked on an ambitious programme of arms procurement from the USSR and Eastern Europe. Nasser's pledge to regain Palestine for the Arabs, his increasing ties with Moscow and the July 1956 nationalization of the Suez Canal (an Anglo-French concern) would lead Britain and France to conspire with Israel to topple the Egyptian President. On 29 October 1956 Israeli forces invaded the Sinai peninsular and the Egyptian-administered Gaza Strip and rapidly advanced to the banks of the Suez Canal. London and Paris issued an ultimatum to Egypt and Israel to withdraw their troops to 10 miles from the canal. Nasser's refusal to withdraw from his own territory while Israeli tanks were in control of most of the Sinai had been anticipated in London and Paris and became the *causus belli* they had sought. Anglo-French forces invaded the Port Said area on 5 November after bombing Egyptian airfields and other targets. Condemnation in the UN and opposition from Washington—which, although opposed to Nasser's policies, regarded developments in Egypt as dangerously destabilizing—delivered a commitment by the invading parties to withdraw from Egyptian territories. By the end of the year British and French troops had left Egypt. The Israelis evacuated most of the Sinai but it was not until March 1957 that they agreed to withdraw from Gaza and Sinai's eastern coastal fringe. A UN Emergency Force (UNEF) was positioned along the Egyptian-Israeli border to monitor the cease-fire arrangements.

The Suez crisis had a profound impact on geopolitical realities in the Middle East. It confirmed Nasser as the populist leader of the Arab world and ensured that the new Arab nationalism would have at its heart a belief in Western collusion with Zionism to thwart Arab independence. The USSR would in turn see Arab nationalism's antagonism towards the West as a useful vehicle for advancing Soviet influence in an area of prime strategic importance. As a consequence, the Arab–Israeli conflict would be increasingly orientated along the fault lines of the Cold War, with the flow of US and French arms and aid to Israel being more than matched by shipments from the Soviet bloc to Egypt and Syria. Suez had also been disastrous for both the French and the British Governments, severely denting their credibility in the region and effectively ending any possibility of a European counterweight to US influence in the Middle East.

Nowhere in the Arab world was Nasser's standing higher in the aftermath of Suez than among the Palestinians. His avowed commitment to reclaiming Palestine on the foundations of Arab unity was warmly received by a people lacking faith in either their own powers to effect change or in the commitment of the international community to address their dispossession. However, although

Nasser successfully enhanced Egypt's military potential, attempts to bring about political union in the Arab world were to prove fruitless. The union of Egypt and Syria in the United Arab Republic was short-lived and was dissolved in 1961, mainly as a result of petty national jealousies. Elsewhere, Egypt's sponsorship of movements and organizations sharing its pan-Arabist outlook brought its government into conflict with the conservative regimes of the Arabian peninsula. Rather than forging unity in the Arab world, Nasser's efforts largely served to illuminate its divisions and rivalries.

By the beginning of the 1960s, Palestinian loyalty to Nasserism had been reduced by these failures. The development of a more distinctive Palestinian national identity, coupled with Palestinian agitation for greater political autonomy, had also begun to unsettle Arab states, Egypt included. In 1963 the Council of the Arab League responded to the gathering unrest by agreeing to sponsor the creation of a nominally independent political body for the Palestinians. The following year the Palestine Liberation Organization (PLO) was inaugurated in Jerusalem. Provision was also made for the establishment of a military wing, to be known as the Palestine Liberation Army (PLA). Egypt gave its consent for the PLO to recruit and organize military training in the Gaza Strip, but here, as elsewhere among the front-line states, the PLO's freedom of action was constrained. This was particularly true in Jordan. Having broken with the Arab consensus to consolidate his rule over the West Bank and assimilate its Palestinian population, King Hussein of Jordan was, unsurprisingly, hostile to the PLO. Even so, the semi-clandestine Palestinian groups that emerged in the early 1960s viewed the PLO as little more than a tool of the Arab regimes and initially remained aloof. The most significant of these was the Palestine National Liberation Movement, known as al-Fatah (a reverse of the Arab acronym meaning Conquest) and founded *inter alia* by a young engineer called Yasser Arafat.

Attacks on Israel by Palestinian guerrillas operating from Syrian and Jordanian territory increased sharply from 1965. These were met by retaliatory strikes by Israeli forces, heightening regional tensions. In April 1967 fighting broke out along the Israeli-Syrian border, during which six Syrian fighter jets were shot down. The following month the Israeli Prime Minister, Lev Eshkol, warned Syria that failure to curb cross-border raids would result in serious reprisals. Egypt's President responded to this threat against his closest Arab ally by massing troops in the eastern Sinai and ordering UNEF to leave Egyptian territory. Nasser also alleged, falsely, that Israeli forces were gathering on the Syrian border in preparation for an immediate attack. On 23 May there was a further escalation in the crisis with Egypt's closure of the Straits of Tiran to Israeli shipping, effectively blockading the Red Sea port of Eilat. As the prospect of war in the region loomed larger, Egypt and Jordan put aside their mutual animosity and concluded a mutual-defence agreement. Iraq joined the pact immediately afterwards. Convinced that war with the Arabs was now inevitable, Israel launched pre-emptive strikes in the early hours of 5 June, destroying the bulk of the Egyptian, Jordanian and Syrian air forces on the ground. With total air superiority, Israeli ground troops were able to advance rapidly. By the time the warring parties had agreed to UN calls for a cease-fire on 10 June, Israeli forces had occupied the Syrian Golan Heights, the Egyptian Sinai and the two remaining areas of historic Palestine, the Gaza Strip and the West Bank (including Arab East Jerusalem).

Arab–Israeli Relations since 1967

The early months of 1967 saw the escalation of existing tensions in the Middle East. The Israeli policy of raiding sites in its neighbouring countries suspected of being bases for attacks on Israel had developed throughout the 1960s, and gained most international attention when Israeli forces destroyed the Jordanian village of Samu, near Hebron on the West Bank of the River Jordan, in November 1966. The raid, ostensibly against a number of camps of the Palestine Liberation Organization (PLO) said to be in the settlement, was condemned by Resolution 228 of the UN Security Council. Discontent within Arab countries at their governments' policies towards Israel increased, as opposition groups, most notably those active in Jordan, claimed that the attitudes amounted to appeasement.

A series of clashes on the Israeli-Syrian border in January–April 1967 increased tension on Israel's northern borders, and Egyptian and Israeli troop manoeuvres near the countries' mutual border extended this concern to Israel's south. The UN force present on the armistice demarcation line between Egypt and Israel reported increased threat from both countries' troops. In May the Egyptian President, Col Gamal abd an-Nasser, made a formal request to the UN that its force be withdrawn from the demarcation-line zone. Fearing for their troops' safety amid the escalating Israeli–Egyptian tensions, the UN withdrew, removing the physical obstacle to direct confrontation. President Nasser subsequently ordered that his forces blockade the Straits of Tiran, the entrance to the Gulf of Aqaba, which provided Israeli shipping's only route to the Indian Ocean. As the prospect of war became increasingly likely, Egypt and Jordan signed a mutual-defence agreement on 30 May. Iraq subsequently became a party to the agreement, although Syria refused, ostensibly owing to fears of Egyptian military dominance in the event of any conflict with Israel.

On 5 June 1967 Israel chose to pre-empt any action on the part of its Arab neighbours by attacking the air bases of Egypt, Jordan and Syria. All three air forces were virtually destroyed and, with aerial supremacy assured, Israel was able to advance into each of the three countries and swiftly gained substantial amounts of territory. On 7 June, with its forces unable to defend the country, Jordan signed a cease-fire with Israel, under the terms of which Israel remained in control of the territory it had gained from Jordan during the brief conflict, namely the West Bank and Old Jerusalem. Three days later, Egypt and Syria were forced to replicate this action, ceding control of the Sinai peninsula and the Golan Heights, respectively.

---

* Based on an original article by MICHAEL ADAMS with subsequent additions by DAVID GILMOUR, PAUL HARPER, STEVEN SHERMAN and the editorial staff.

Israel's decisive victory over the Arab states in what became known as the Six-Day War raised hopes that at last it would be possible to reach a definitive settlement of the Arab–Israeli conflict. Instead, it soon became apparent that the dispute had merely been complicated by the occupation of further Arab territory, the displacement of still more refugees and an aggravation of the sense of grievance felt by the Palestinians and now shared more widely than ever in the rest of the Arab world.

Once a cease-fire was in operation in June 1967, the UN Security Council's next step was to pass a resolution (No. 237, of 14 June 1967), urging Israel to facilitate the return of the new refugees who had fled (and were still fleeing) from the areas occupied by Israel during the war. The resolution also demanded that Israel ensure the safety, welfare and security of the inhabitants of the 'Occupied Areas'.

An emergency meeting of the UN General Assembly reiterated on 4 July 1967 the Security Council's statements regarding the refugees and on the same day it declared 'invalid' the Israeli annexation of the Arab sector of Jerusalem; however, the Assembly failed to produce an agreed resolution for a settlement.

The deadlock became total when an Arab summit conference, held in Khartoum, Sudan, between 29 August–3 September 1967, confirmed earlier decisions not to negotiate directly with Israel, not to accord it recognition and not to sign a peace treaty. The Israeli Government, for its part, announced its refusal to undertake any but direct negotiations; if no such negotiations developed, Israeli forces would maintain their occupation of the Arab territories conquered during the war.

RESOLUTION 242

In late 1967 the UN Security Council considered a number of draft resolutions which failed to gain approval, either because (according to supporters of the Arabs) they condoned the acquisition or occupation of territory by military force, or because (according to supporters of Israel) they contained no adequate guarantee of Israel's security. Finally, on 22 November 1967, the Security Council unanimously adopted Resolution 242 (see Documents on Palestine, p. 332), which was to be the basis of all peace initiatives during the next five years and which remains an important element in attempts to resolve the Palestinian question. By emphasizing the illegitimacy of the acquisition of territory by war, the resolution satisfied the demand of the Arabs and their supporter, the USSR, for an Israeli withdrawal. At the same time, by being less than categorical about the extent of that withdrawal, it was acceptable to Israel and its supporter, the USA. All the subsequent arguments which developed centred on the question of whether Israel, in return for a definitive peace treaty, should have the right to retain parts of the Arab territories occupied during the war.

PALESTINIAN RESISTANCE

In the immediate aftermath of the fighting, despite the Israeli Prime Minister's declaration on the eve of the war that Israel had no intention of annexing 'even one foot of Arab territory', the Israeli Knesset had legislated the 'reunification' of Jerusalem, which in fact amounted to the annexation of the Arab sector of the city. This appeared to confirm Arab allegations of Israeli expansionism, and greatly encouraged the rise of a Palestinian resistance movement, already stimulated by the impotence of the Arab governments and the humiliation which the war had brought on the Arab world. When Israel began, as early as September 1967, to establish Jewish settlements in the Occupied Territories, support for the resistance movement became widespread in the Arab world. It was reinforced when Israel, after agreeing to allow the return of refugees (who were still streaming eastward), closed the border again after only 14,000 of the 150,000 who had filed applications with the Red Cross had been allowed to re-enter Palestine.

Thus, the situation was deteriorating even before Dr Gunnar Jarring, whom the UN Secretary-General had appointed as his Special Representative in accordance with Resolution 242, travelled to the Middle East at the end of 1967. During the first half of 1968 there were increasingly frequent breaches of the cease-fire along the Suez Canal (which remained blocked to traffic), while Palestinian guerrilla raids prompted costly Israeli reprisals in the Jordan valley. In July 1968, guerrillas of the Popular Front for the Liberation of Palestine (PFLP) carried out the first hijack operation in the Middle East, diverting an Israeli airliner to Algiers.

LEBANESE INVOLVEMENT

Israel, while not rejecting Resolution 242, stated that it could not be a substitute for specific agreements between the parties. When the UN General Assembly met in late 1968, Israel put forward a nine-point plan for a Middle East settlement which made no mention of withdrawal, but rather of 'a boundary settlement compatible with the security of Israel and the honour of the Arab states'. This produced no response from the Arab governments, which were shocked when President Lyndon B. Johnson, at the height of a US election campaign, announced that the USA was considering the sale of *Phantom* aircraft to Israel. A month later Richard Nixon was elected as President Johnson's successor. The sale of 50 *Phantoms* to Israel was confirmed at the end of December and marked an important stage in the escalation of the arms race in the Middle East.

The day after the sale of the *Phantoms* was announced, Israeli commandos raided Beirut airport, in reprisal for an Arab guerrilla attack on an Israeli airliner in Athens, and destroyed 13 aircraft. This incident brought Lebanon directly into the Arab–Israeli confrontation. After the UN Security Council had unanimously condemned Israel for the raid, the Soviet Government took up an earlier French proposal for talks involving those two countries, the United Kingdom and the USA to obtain agreement between the major powers over the implementation of Resolution 242.

At the beginning of February 1969, President Nasser declared his willingness to enter into direct negotiations once Israeli forces had withdrawn from Arab territory. Levi Eshkol, the Prime Minister of Israel, stated his readiness to meet President Nasser and declared that Israel was prepared to be flexible about all the Occupied Territories except Jerusalem and the Golan Heights (captured from Syria in 1967). But, as the year progressed, sporadic fighting continued along both the Suez Canal and the Jordan fronts, until in July President Nasser publicly gave up hope of a peaceful settlement, forecasting that a long 'war of attrition' would be necessary to dislodge Israel from the Occupied Territories.

THE ROGERS PLAN

The quadripartite talks were suspended while Soviet and US representatives met separately. There was optimism when it appeared that a formula had been found for 'Rhodes-style' negotiations (after the talks conducted in Rhodes which led to the armistice agreements between Israel and the Arab states in 1949), but an Israeli suggestion that this would amount to direct negotiations prompted the Arabs to reject the formula. Instead, on 9 December 1969, the US Secretary of State, William Rogers, produced a set of proposals which came to be known as the Rogers Plan. This was an attempt to steer a middle course between the Arab view, that the Security Council Resolution should be implemented *in toto* and did not require negotiation, and the Israeli preference for direct negotiations which would decide where the new borders should be drawn. The most important aspect of the plan was that it made clear the US view that there should only be minor modifications of the pre-June 1967 boundaries. This ensured Israeli hostility to the plan, since, despite the insistence of the Israeli Minister of Foreign Affairs, Abba Eban, that 'everything is negotiable', it had now become clear that his Cabinet colleagues were deeply divided on this crucial question.

In January 1970 Israel initiated a series of bombing raids (using the new US *Phantom* aircraft) on targets inside Egypt. Gen. Moshe Dayan, Israel's Minister of Defence, announced at the beginning of February that the Israeli bombing attacks had three aims: to force Egypt to respect the cease-fire along the Suez Canal front, to prevent Egyptian preparations for a new war and to weaken the Egyptian regime. In practice, the raids had three results: they strengthened Egyptian support for President Nasser, they damaged Israel's international reputation and they provoked the USSR into providing further assistance to Egypt.

International concern over these developments led to a renewal of diplomatic efforts. Israel's requests for more *Phantoms* in early 1970 were not granted and it appeared that the immediate US objectives were to renew the cease-fire and to extract from the Israeli Government an undertaking to withdraw from the greater part of the Occupied Territories as part of an overall peace settlement. Israel made no public commitment to withdrawal, but its response in private was sufficiently encouraging for Rogers to relaunch his proposals, with the backing of the four major powers. In a speech on 23 July 1970 President Nasser announced Egypt's acceptance of the US proposal for a renewal of the cease-fire, followed by negotiations through Dr Jarring for the implementation of Resolution 242. A week later the Israeli Government, after receiving assurances on the future supply of arms from the USA, also agreed to the US proposal, with the provisos that Israel would never return to the pre-war boundaries and that none of its troops would be withdrawn from the cease-fire lines until a binding peace agreement had been signed.

The renewed cease-fire along the Suez Canal front came into operation on the night of 7/8 August 1970. It was to last 90 days, during which the two sides were to engage in indirect negotiations through Dr Jarring. However, after a single meeting with Dr Jarring in New York, the Israeli representative was recalled and the Israeli Government protested that the cease-fire had been violated by the movement of Soviet missiles behind the Egyptian lines. Negotiations had not been renewed when a serious crisis in Jordan distracted the attention of all the parties concerned.

KING HUSSEIN AND THE PALESTINE GUERRILLAS

On 6 September 1970 Palestinian guerrillas of the PFLP hijacked two airliners and diverted them to a desert airfield near Zerqa, in Jordan. A third airliner was taken to Cairo and destroyed there. Three days later a fourth aircraft was hijacked and joined the two in Jordan, where the guerrillas demanded the release of a substantial number of Palestinians held prisoner in Israel, in exchange for some 300 hostages.

This episode proved the last straw for the Jordanian Government. During the previous two years, as the strength of the guerrilla movement increased, it had faced a dilemma. By allowing the guerrillas freedom of movement in Jordan, it had invited (and would continue to invite) retaliation from Israel in the form of ground and air raids which had depopulated the East Bank of the Jordan and caused severe casualties. If, however, the Government tried to control or suppress the activities of the guerrillas, it faced the possibility of civil war in Jordan.

The Palestine resistance movement, whose declared objective was the recon-stitution in Palestine of a democratic state open to Jews and Arabs alike, opposed the idea of a political settlement with Israel implying the recognition and perpetuation of a Zionist state. King Hussein had accepted the Rogers Plan and was thus committed to the principle of a political settlement. So long as this was not in prospect, it had been possible for the King and the guerrillas to pursue their diverse objectives without coming into open conflict, but as soon as such a settlement became a serious possibility the uneasy coexistence between them was threatened. On several occasions in 1969 and 1970 the Jordanian Government and the guerrillas had come close to a confrontation, and after the renewal of the cease-fire in August 1970 and the acceptance by the Jordanian Government of the Rogers Plan, a clash became inevitable.

On 16 September King Hussein appointed a military Government in Jordan which the next day set about the liquidation of the resistance movement. After 10 days of heavy fighting in Amman, mediation efforts by other Arab governments, and in particular by President Nasser, brought about a truce, which was signed in Cairo on 27 September. On the following day the Egyptian leader suffered a heart attack and died soon after.

PRESIDENT SADAT AND THE CEASE-FIRE

There was both surprise and relief when the new President of Egypt, Anwar Sadat, showed himself willing to take up the pursuit of a settlement. He agreed to renew the cease-fire for 90 days and, after intensive consultations between Israeli and US leaders and the extension of US credits worth $500m., Israel agreed to return to the Jarring talks. As the cease-fire was expiring on 5 February 1971, President Sadat once more agreed to its renewal, for 30 days, proposing that Israel should begin to withdraw its forces from the east bank of the canal, which Egypt would then be able to clear for navigation.

On 8 February Dr Jarring wrote to the Governments of Israel and Egypt, expressing his optimism about the desire of both parties for a settlement and inviting each of them to give firm commitments which would resolve the central deadlock. Israel, he suggested, should agree on certain stated conditions (providing guarantees for security and freedom of navigation) to withdraw to the international boundary between Egypt and the Palestine of the British Mandate. Egypt should give a parallel undertaking to conclude a peace agreement explicitly ending the state of belligerence and recognizing Israel's right to exist in peace and security. In other words, both parties were asked formally to accept the principal obligations imposed on them by Resolution 242.

The Egyptian reply gave the undertaking called for by Dr Jarring, provided that Israel did the same and agreed to withdraw its forces to the international border. Israel's reply stated firmly that, while it would be prepared to withdraw its forces to 'secure, recognized and agreed boundaries to be established in the peace agreement', it would in no circumstances withdraw to the pre-June 1967 lines. This embarrassed the US Government, which had first withheld and then granted military and economic assistance to Israel, in the attempt to persuade the Israeli Government to accept only 'minor rectifications' of the armistice lines. The USA made one further attempt when Rogers urged Israel to accept international guarantees in place of territorial gains, adding that security did not 'necessarily require additions of territory' and that in the US view 'the 1967 boundary should be the boundary between Israel and Egypt'.

PROPOSAL FOR A 'PARTIAL SETTLEMENT'

The US Government adopted instead President Sadat's suggestion of an Israeli withdrawal for some distance into Sinai to allow the reopening of the Suez Canal. However, the new proposal for a partial settlement quickly became bogged down in arguments over the extent of the Israeli withdrawal and whether it should be seen as the first step to complete withdrawal. The arguments continued through most of 1971 until the proposal was finally dropped by the USA in November.

In December the UN General Assembly, in a resolution reaffirming the 'inadmissibility of the acquisition of territory by war' and calling for an Israeli withdrawal, also urged Israel to 'respond favourably' to the proposals made by Dr Jarring in February. Only seven states, including Israel, voted against the resolution and the USA, which had always voted in support of Israel on territorial questions, abstained, reflecting its view that Israel should withdraw from almost all of the Occupied Territories. The year ended with President Sadat in a dangerously weakened position. He had taken considerable risks in pursuit of a political settlement and had promised the Egyptian people that 1971 would be the 'year of decision'. He blamed the lack of progress on US 'political manoeuvring', and when 1972 (a US presidential election year) began with the US Government promising Israel a further 42 *Phantom* and 90 *Skyhawk* aircraft, it seemed unlikely that a fresh US suggestion of indirect talks between Israel and Egypt in New York would be fruitful.

In February 1972 Israel launched a large-scale incursion into Lebanon, stating that its aim was the elimination of guerrilla bases near Israel's northern border. In June a further Israeli raid on Lebanon was condemned by the Security Council after more than 70 civilians had been killed or wounded.

In July 1972 President Sadat unexpectedly requested the withdrawal from Egypt of the Soviet advisers engaged in the reorganization of Egypt's defence system. This was interpreted as a final appeal to the US Government to bring pressure to bear on Israel to accept a settlement involving an Israeli withdrawal from Sinai.

In Europe, however, a reappraisal of Middle Eastern policy was taking place. This found expression in the annual Middle East debate in the General Assembly of the UN, when all the members of the European Community (EC), except Denmark, followed the lead of France and the United Kingdom in voting for a resolution strongly critical of Israel. (The USA again abstained.)

TERRORISM AND COUNTER-TERRORISM IN THE MIDDLE EAST

The cease-fire along the Suez Canal was maintained, but along the northern borders of Israel and Israeli-held territory there was a renewal of violence in the second half of 1972, accompanied by a mounting series of terrorist attacks by both Israelis and Palestinians in various parts of the world. In mid-1972 a number of Palestinian leaders were killed or seriously injured by explosive devices sent to them in Beirut. In September, during the Olympic Games in Munich, Palestinian guerrillas captured 11 Israeli athletes and held them hostage in an attempt to obtain the release of Palestinians held captive in Israel. West German police, after promising the Palestinian captors safe conduct out of Germany, opened fire on them at Munich airport, whereupon the guerrillas killed the hostages and were themselves either killed or captured.

The Munich attack was followed by Israeli ground and air raids into Lebanon, which the Israeli Government held responsible for the activities of guerrillas whose bases (since their expulsion from Jordan in 1970 and 1971) were in the refugee camps of Beirut and elsewhere in Lebanon. Letter bombs were subsequently posted to Israeli representatives in various countries and representatives of the PLO were attacked in Rome, Stockholm, Paris and Nicosia.

At the beginning of 1973 Hafez Ismail (President Sadat's political adviser), King Hussein of Jordan and Golda Meir (the Israeli Prime Minister) visited Washington, DC for talks with US President Nixon. However, the frail hopes aroused by this were dashed when an Israeli attack on guerrilla installations in a refugee camp in northern Lebanon was followed within 24 hours by the shooting down by Israeli fighters of a Libyan airliner which had strayed over occupied Sinai. The two incidents provoked an unprecedented wave of criticism of Israel on the eve of Meir's arrival in Washington.

STALEMATE

In the second half of 1973, the Arab–Israeli conflict appeared to be further from resolution than ever. Israel, confident that its military supremacy over the Arabs had increased, remained in control of all the territories it had occupied in 1967 and had established in these territories some 50 civilian and paramilitary settlements. The Egyptian and Jordanian Governments—though not yet the Syrian—had long since modified their earlier refusal to negotiate a settlement and had indicated their willingness to recognize the State of Israel; but they still refused to envisage a peace settlement which did not provide for the return of all the Occupied Territories. The UN, despite the passage every year of resolutions demanding an Israeli withdrawal, found all its efforts to devise a settlement blocked by Israel's refusal to relinquish its 1967 conquests.

More than ever, the key to the situation rested in the hands of the USA, which found itself isolated in support of Israel while becoming increasingly dependent on petroleum produced by the Arab states. The USA's allies, for whom dependence on Arab petroleum was already a fact, were increasingly impatient with the US Government's Middle East policy, which seemed to be aimed at maintaining Israel's overall supremacy without seeking any concessions from the Israeli Government over the Occupied Territories. The isolation of the USA was emphasized in the Security Council in the summer of 1973, when it vetoed a resolution put forward by eight non-aligned members, which was strongly critical of Israel's continued occupation of Arab territory. All the other Council members except the People's Republic of China, which abstained, voted affirmatively.

RENEWAL OF THE WAR

A surprise attack was launched on two fronts by the Egyptian and Syrian forces on 6 October 1973. Unusual activity behind the lines had been observed by Israeli and US intelligence agencies west of the Suez Canal and east of the cease-fire line on the Golan Heights; but Israel was convinced that the Egyptian army was incapable of the elaborate operation required to cross the canal and breach the chain of Israeli fortifications, known as the Bar-Lev line, on the east bank. This element of surprise won for the Egyptian and Syrian forces a substantial initial advantage on both fronts. This was enhanced by the fact that 6 October was Yom Kippur, the Day of Atonement in the Jewish calendar, when all public services were suspended, making it unusually difficult for the Israelis rapidly to mobilize its forces. By midnight on the first day of the war, 400 Egyptian tanks had crossed the canal, the Bar-Lev line had been outflanked and a massive Syrian tank attack beyond the Golan Heights had only been stemmed by rearguard action by greatly outnumbered Israeli armour, aided by air-strikes.

During the next three weeks (despite the declaration of a UN-sponsored cease-fire on 22 October), the Syrian forces were driven back beyond the old cease-fire line and counter-attacking Israeli forces effected a westward crossing of the Suez Canal. At the end of the war, the military advantage lay with Israel, which had occupied a further area of Syrian territory and was threatening Damascus, while its units west of the canal had isolated an Egyptian army in Suez. However, largely as a result of the intervention of the Arab petroleum-producing states, the political objectives of the Arabs had been achieved and the whole context of the confrontation decisively altered.

By making unexpectedly efficient use of new weapons, the Arab armies demonstrated that since 1967 they had significantly narrowed the (military) technological gap between themselves and Israel. They had exposed the fallacy on which Israeli strategy had been based since the Six-Day War: that the control of wide buffer zones (the territories occupied since 1967), together with the military supremacy of which it felt assured, rendered Israel immune to Arab attack. This assumption had encouraged the Israeli leaders to disregard the mounting pressure of world opinion calling for an Israeli withdrawal as the essential condition of a negotiated settlement with the Arabs.

THE PETROLEUM FACTOR

Soon after the outbreak of the war, there were calls within the Arab world to deny Middle East petroleum to the supporters of Israel. In October 1973 a meeting in Kuwait of representatives of the Arab petroleum producers resulted in an agreement to reduce output, while Abu Dhabi took the lead in halting exports to the USA. In adopting and then intensifying these measures, the Arab petroleum-producing states displayed unexpected unity. This had an evident effect on the governments of Western Europe, conscious of their dependence on the free flow of petroleum from the Middle East. On 6 November the nine member states of the EC endorsed a statement advocating an Israeli withdrawal from the territories occupied in 1967 and asserting that, while all states in the Middle East should enjoy the right to secure boundaries, the legitimate rights of the Palestinians should be taken into account in any settlement (see Documents on Palestine, p. 340). Israel accused the Europeans of giving in to Arab 'black-mail', but for several years the Europeans had been dissociating themselves from US policy and registering their growing impatience with Israel's intransigence.

US INITIATIVE

A peace conference was convened in Geneva, Switzerland, on 21 December 1973, under UN auspices, and attended by delegations from Egypt, Israel, Jordan, the USA and the USSR. Although little was agreed at the conference, a process of dialogue, in which the USA was the principal interlocutor, emerged.

The USA, which alone possessed the influence that could induce Israel to withdraw—and which now found itself inconvenienced much more by the petroleum embargo than it had anticipated—accepted its responsibility to bring about a settlement. The US Secretary of State, Dr Henry Kissinger, now embarked on a dramatic series of visits to Middle Eastern capitals, from which emerged disengagement agreements between Egypt and Israel (signed on 18 January 1974) and between Syria and Israel (signed on 30 May 1974). In mid-June 1974 President Nixon, whose domestic position had become danger-ously insecure after the Watergate scandal, embarked on a triumphant tour of the Middle East, forecasting a new era of co-operation between the USA and the Arab world, while reassuring Israel of continuing US support. This US initiative was generally well received, except by some Israelis who foresaw mounting pressure on Israel to make concessions inconsistent with its security, and by the extreme wing of the Palestinian resistance movement, which engaged in a series of terrorist attacks on targets in northern Israel in an effort to frustrate a settlement which did not guarantee Palestine's total liberation. Otherwise, President Nixon's visit revealed a strong desire on the part of the Arab governments to restore friendly relations with the USA. Diplomatic relations between Syria and the USA were re-established and the embargo on the export of Arab petroleum to the USA was lifted.

CHANGE IN THE BALANCE OF POWER

This reconciliation was one of the most striking results of the October War; it was a reminder of the greatly increased influence of the Arab states so long as they continued to act in concert. Conversely, Israel's international position had been much weakened by the failure of its pre-war policies and by the revelation of the extent to which the rest of the world was dependent on Arab goodwill. The Government headed by Golda Meir was widely blamed both for provoking the October War by its policy of 'creeping annexation' and for being caught unawares when the war came. After winning a narrow victory in a general election at the end of 1973, Meir finally abandoned the attempt to rebuild her coalition in April 1974. She was succeeded as leader of the Labour Party and Prime Minister by Gen. Itzhak Rabin, who had been Chief of Staff at the time of the 1967 war and later Israeli Ambassador in Washington, DC. In the Arab world, the effect of the war was to strengthen the position of the regimes in Cairo and Damascus and to give new authority to King Faisal of Saudi Arabia, whose control of the greatest share of the petroleum reserves of the Middle East made him a dominant figure in Arab politics. The fact that the disengagement agreements involved small but significant Israeli withdrawals from Arab territory gave satisfaction throughout the Arab world, but the central problem of the future of the Palestinians remained unsolved. The difficulty of finding a solution acceptable both to Israel and to the PLO (which the Arab governments, meeting in Algiers in November 1973, had recognized as 'the sole legitimate representative of the Palestinian people') posed a continuing threat to the stability of the disengagement agreements of 1974.

Despite the new unity of the Arab world, the movement towards a settlement in the Middle East lost momentum during the second half of 1974 and a further outbreak of war seemed imminent at times. The disengagement agreements were honoured and UN forces were inserted between the combatants in Sinai and on the Golan front, but Syria and Israel exchanged mutual recriminations over the ill-treatment of prisoners and the destruction of the Syrian town of Quneitra by the Israeli forces on the eve of their withdrawal.

While the optimism generated by the disengagement agreements gave way to stalemate between the Arab governments and Israel, the Palestinians' central role in the conflict was strikingly endorsed. On 21 September 1974, the UN General Assembly voted to include 'the Palestine Question' on its agenda for the first time since the establishment of the State of Israel in 1948. (Only four Governments opposed this decision: Israel, the USA, the Dominican Republic and Bolivia.) On 14 October the General Assembly invited the PLO to take part in the debate and a month later the Chairman of the PLO, Yasser Arafat, outlined to the Assembly the PLO's design for a 'democratic, secular state' in Palestine in which Jews and Arabs would coexist on terms of equality, specifying that 'all Jews now living in Palestine who choose to live with us there in peace and without discrimination' were included in this design. At the end of October a meeting of Arab heads of state in Rabat reiterated that the PLO was the 'sole legitimate representative of the Palestinian people', with the right to speak for the Palestinians at any future Middle East peace talks and to establish an independent national authority in any part of Palestine liberated from Israeli occupation.

These decisions greatly strengthened the hand of the Palestinians and the PLO. However, they also deepened the impasse over a settlement because the Israeli Government refused to have any dealings with the PLO, dismissing it as a terrorist organization. The PLO's position was also complicated by internal divisions over its ultimate objective. Although Yasser Arafat at the UN had spoken only of the PLO's goal of a unitary Palestine (which would mean the elimination of the State of Israel), he was under pressure from the Arab governments to accept the limited objective of a Palestinian state on the West Bank and the Gaza Strip, which could only be envisaged in the context of the recognition of Israel within its pre-1967 borders. A majority within the PLO appeared at the end of 1974 to be moving towards acceptance of this formula, but the minority rejected any thought of compromising the long-term goal of the total liberation of Palestine. This 'rejectionist front', with the backing of the Governments of Iraq and Libya, made it difficult for the PLO openly to align itself with those Arab governments (notably Egypt) which were prepared to exchange recognition of Israel for withdrawal from the territories occupied in 1967, including Arab Jerusalem, and the creation of a Palestinian state on the West Bank.

This was in effect the pattern for a settlement which had been envisaged in the Security Council's Resolution 242 and which had provided the basis for all the international initiatives undertaken between 1967 and 1973. These initiatives had failed because Israel, before October 1973, had felt confident of its ability to retain control of at least substantial parts of the Occupied Territories. The October War, by undermining this confidence, had highlighted Israel's dependence on US support; moreover, the initial efforts of Dr Kissinger immediately after the war had encouraged the Arabs to believe that US influence would at last be used to promote a settlement based on Israel's withdrawal.

ARAB IMPATIENCE

The Arab-US reconciliation, in which President Sadat had taken the lead and to which he totally committed himself during 1974, had failed by the end of the year to produce any results beyond the initial disengagement agreements. Apart from the tiny areas of territory conceded by Israel under those agreements, the Israeli occupation was maintained in Sinai, the Golan Heights (including the plateau up to the outskirts of Quneitra), the West Bank (including the Old City of Jerusalem) and the Gaza Strip, with no relaxation of the ban on political activity by the Arab population and other repressive measures. None of the Jewish settlements, of which about 50 had been established in the Occupied Territories before October 1973, had been given up; indeed the Israeli Government, under pressure from the right-wing opposition and the religious parties in the Knesset, continued to announce plans to extend Jewish settlement.

These developments caused growing impatience in the Arab world. When Dr Kissinger returned to the Middle East in March 1975 in an attempt to further the process of disengagement between Israel and Egypt, it was widely assumed that he had obtained prior assurances from both sides. However, after two weeks of intensive 'shuttle diplomacy' he had to admit failure when Israel refused to withdraw from the Mitla and Giddi passes in Sinai and from the petroleum-exploration site at Abu Rudeis, without an explicit assurance of future non-aggression from President Sadat. The latter was clearly unrealistic, since it would have confirmed Arab suspicions that Egypt was prepared to abandon its allies for a separate peace with Israel. There was therefore little surprise when Dr Kissinger (and later President Gerald Ford) blamed Israeli obstinacy for the failure of the negotiations and announced that the USA would embark on a 'reassessment' of its Middle East policy. This was held to mean that Israel's latest request for increased military and economic aid from the USA would not be granted until Israel showed a more conciliatory attitude.

The breakdown of Dr Kissinger's mission coincided with the assassination in Riyadh of King Faisal of Saudi Arabia, whose prestige and authority had been greatly increased by his support for the Arab war effort during and after the October War. In May 1975 the Syrian Government unexpectedly agreed to renew for a further six months the mandate of the UN force separating the two sides on the Golan front, and on 5 June the Egyptian Government reopened the Suez Canal, eight years to the day after the outbreak of the war which had led to its closure in 1967.

FURTHER DISENGAGEMENT IN SINAI

On 21 August 1975 Dr Kissinger flew to Israel to promote a second disengagement agreement between Israel and Egypt. After two weeks of intensive negotiations he persuaded the countries' delegations to accept an agreement which was signed in Geneva, Switzerland, on 4 September (see Documents on Palestine, p. 344). The new agreement provided for an Israeli withdrawal from the strategic Mitla and Giddi passes and the return to Egypt of Abu Rudeis, on which Israel had depended for some 50% of its petroleum supplies since 1967. As in the first disengagement agreement, a UN buffer zone was established separating the Egyptian and Israeli forces. The most important new element was the provision for five electronic listening posts in this zone, of which one was to be manned by Egyptians, one by Israelis and the other three by a team of 200 US civilians who would monitor troop movements both east and west of the passes. Both sides undertook to respect the cease-fire and to resolve the conflict between them by peaceful means. Non-military cargoes in ships sailing to or from Israel were to be allowed through the Suez Canal and the agreement was to remain in force 'until superseded by a new agreement'.

The conclusion of this second agreement was considered a triumph for US diplomacy and it had significant effects on Egypt's relations with its Arab allies. Only Saudi Arabia, Sudan and (with reservations) Kuwait expressed approval of the agreement, which was criticized—most vehemently by Syria and the PLO—as a surrender to US and Israeli interests. The united Arab front presented during the October War was now seriously disrupted.

The agreement marked a further stage in the US-Egyptian *rapprochement* and the estrangement between Egypt and its former ally, the USSR. In October 1975 President Sadat made an official visit to Washington, DC, while his repeated criticisms of the USSR led to a steady deterioration of relations culminating in Egypt's abrogation of the Soviet-Egyptian Treaty of Friendship in March 1976.

Syria now assumed the leadership of the Arab cause. President Hafiz al-Assad found his position in the Arab world greatly strengthened and even succeeded in restoring close relations with King Hussein of Jordan, establishing a joint Syrian-Jordanian Command Council. In October 1975 he visited Moscow for talks with President Nikolai Podgornii and other Soviet leaders and gained a promise of further arms supplies to counter the deliveries reaching Israel from the USA. At the end of November Syria's already considerable prestige as the most consistent defender of the rights of the Palestinians was enhanced when

President Assad agreed to renew the mandate of the UN Disengagement Observer Force (UNDOF) on the Golan Heights, extracting in return a promise that the Security Council would hold a special debate on the Palestine question in January 1976, with the participation of the PLO.

PLO'S STANDING ENHANCED

This debate further strengthened the international position of the PLO. In November 1975 the UN General Assembly had adopted three resolutions concerning Palestine. The first had established a 20-nation committee to work out plans for the implementation of the Palestinian right 'to self-determination and national independence', the second invited the PLO to take part in all future UN debates on the Middle East, and the third denounced Zionism as 'a form of racism and racial discrimination'. (The last of these provoked an international storm of criticism in which the importance of the other two resolutions was widely overlooked.) A month later a US veto saved Israel from censure by the Security Council for a series of air raids on targets in Lebanon in which 75 people were killed. When the Security Council debated the Palestine question in January 1976, the USA again used its veto to prevent the adoption of a resolution affirming the Palestinians' right to establish a state of their own and calling for an Israeli withdrawal from all the territories occupied since June 1967.

In January 1976 Western press reports suggested that US officials were in secret contact with Palestinian representatives, and the impression that a major change in US policy was in the offing was reinforced in March when the UN Security Council debated the question of Israeli policies in the Occupied Territories. Although the USA again exercised its veto to defeat a resolution, on Israel's behalf, its delegate strongly condemned Israel's establishment of 'illegal' settlements in Jerusalem and other occupied areas.

Israel's persistence in establishing these settlements was a major factor in provoking serious rioting all over the occupied West Bank and in Gaza during mid-1976. The riots had a decisive effect on the outcome of municipal elections organized by the Israeli occupation authorities in the West Bank in April. Instead of producing, as the Israeli authorities had hoped, 'moderate' Palestinian leaders who would accept a measure of autonomy under continuing Israeli occupation, the elections demonstrated the strength of Palestinian nationalism and widespread support for the PLO.

CIVIL WAR IN LEBANON

The disunity in the Arab camp was highlighted by events in Lebanon, where armed clashes between Palestinian guerrillas and Christian militiamen in April 1975 led to a civil war which threatened to destroy the Lebanese state and almost provoked another Arab–Israeli confrontation. Attempts at mediation by the Arab League and by French and US emissaries failed to reconcile the warring parties, which, in turn, were supported by rival Arab interests. In January 1976, after nine months of heavy fighting, in which Palestinian guerrillas were drawn into a leftist alliance against the defenders of the conservative Christian establishment, the Syrian Government employed Syrian-based units of the PLA to impose a cease-fire which was to be followed by a reform of the Lebanese political system. However, the cease-fire broke down in March, when Christian extremists, supporting President Sulayman Franjiya, prevaricated over the implementation of the reform programme and the Druze leader of the leftist alliance tried to force the President's resignation.

Faced with a victory for the leftists and their Palestinian allies, which might provoke an Israeli military intervention in southern Lebanon, Syria used its influence to restrain the leftists, sending Syrian troops across the border at the end of May 1976, with tacit US approval. At the same time President Assad renewed the mandate of the UN force on the Golan front for a further six months.

In late 1976 the obstacles which had prevented any movement towards an Arab-Israeli settlement were removed. After repeated failures on the part of the Arab League to play an effective mediating role in Lebanon, determined efforts by the Saudi Arabian and Kuwaiti Governments brought about a restricted Arab summit meeting in Riyadh in October, at which the leaders of Egypt, Syria, Lebanon and the PLO agreed to the terms of a cease-fire. These were confirmed at a further meeting in Cairo on 26 October, and provided for the creation of a substantial Arab peace-keeping force which, within a month, had halted the savage fighting in Beirut, reopened the Beirut–Damascus road and occupied the main towns in the north and south of the country.

NEW ADMINISTRATION IN WASHINGTON

In the USA the President-elect, Jimmy Carter, had indicated his intention to take early action over the Middle East. Once more Israel found itself under pressure both from the Arabs and from the USA. On 11 November 1976 the USA approved a unanimous 'consensus statement' by the Security Council that 'strongly deplored' Israel's actions in establishing settlements in the Occupied Territories and attempting to alter the demographic balance in Jerusalem. On 19 November the US Ambassador to Israel, addressing the annual convention of B'nai B'rith in Jerusalem, stated that 'unless Israel's professed willingness to return occupied territory is seen as more than mere rhetoric, the vicious circle of mutual mistrust cannot be broken'. On 24 November the USA joined 117 other nations in voting in the UN General Assembly (against the opposition of Israel and Costa Rica) to deplore Israel's refusal to allow the return of the Palestinian refugees who had left their homes in 1967.

In the occupied West Bank there was intermittent unrest throughout 1976. Demonstrations in Nablus, Ramallah and the Old City of Jerusalem in May and June were suppressed by the Israeli security forces with exceptional violence. In October there were serious riots in Hebron over the respective rights of Jews and Arabs to pray in the mosque built over the Tombs of the Patriarchs. Israel's occupation policy was again condemned by the UN General Assembly on 20 December, following the publication of a report by the UN Special Committee for the Investigation of Israeli Practices in the Occupied Territories. The UN Human Rights Commission expressed 'grave concern' over the deteriorating situation in the Occupied Territories, and unanimously urged the Government of Israel to adhere to the terms of the Fourth Geneva Convention in its treatment of civilians.

Conscious of the growing tension in the Middle East and of the steadily increasing dependence of the Western world on Arab petroleum, the new US

Administration moved swiftly to revive the Arab-Israeli peace process. In February 1997 President Carter dispatched the US Secretary of State, Cyrus Vance, on a tour of the Middle East and invited Israeli and Arab leaders to visit him in Washington, DC. During an interim period and as the prelude to a final peace agreement, the US President indicated that arrangements might be made to extend Israel's defence capability beyond its eventual legal frontiers. A week later President Carter stated, unexpectedly, that the final element in an Arab-Israeli settlement should be the creation of a 'homeland' for the dispossessed Palestinians.

ISRAELI GOVERNMENT RESIGNS

The renewed emphasis on the Palestinian aspect of the problem was not welcomed by Israel. The governing coalition was already under considerable internal pressure as a result of the difficult economic situation and the failure to devise any constructive policy for achieving peace with the Arabs; in addition, it had been undermined by a series of scandals involving leading figures in the Labour Party, which had dominated every government since the creation of the state. The most crucial issue facing the Government concerned the Occupied Territories and, in particular, the extent to which it should allow—or could control—Jewish settlement on the West Bank. The right-wing Likud coalition opposed any withdrawal from the West Bank, and Rabin's Cabinet was divided on the issue; following a dispute with one of his coalition partners, Rabin announced the Government's resignation. A general election was fixed for 17 May 1977.

ARAB GOVERNMENTS AND THE PLO

Once they had achieved a reconciliation between themselves and put an end to the war in Lebanon in late 1976, the Arab governments enlisted the help of the new US Administration in working towards a peace settlement with Israel. Their common position was that the Geneva Conference should be reconvened, with the Palestinians participating, and that an overall settlement should be negotiated on the basis of an Israeli withdrawal to the 1967 borders and the establishment of a Palestinian state on the West Bank and the Gaza Strip. However, the PLO refused to renounce its objective of a unitary, 'secular, democratic state' in the whole of Palestine (which would replace the existing State of Israel), although PLO spokesmen did indicate their willingness to establish a state 'on any part of Palestine' from which Israel would withdraw.

Since Israel refused either to entertain the idea of an independent Palestinian state or to negotiate under any circumstances with the PLO (whether or not the PLO agreed to recognize the State of Israel), no accommodation appeared possible unless the US Government brought pressure to bear on Israel. This the Carter Administration was reluctant to do, given the proximity of the Israeli general election, although there were indications that the USA was in contact with the PLO in an effort to persuade the Palestinians to modify their attitude.

RIGHT-WING VICTORY IN ISRAEL

The prospects for a negotiated Arab-Israeli settlement received a severe setback in May 1977, when the elections in Israel resulted in an unexpected victory for the right-wing Likud grouping. The elections were fought mainly on domestic issues and the defeat of the ruling Labour Party was widely attributed to discontent over the economy and the series of scandals involving senior figures in the former administration. Likud, led by Menachem Begin (who, prior to 1948, had been the leader of the insurgent organization, Irgun Zvai Leumi), was committed to maintaining Israeli rule over the whole of the occupied West Bank, on the grounds that it constituted part of Israel's divinely-ordained inheritance.

Faced with this challenge, President Carter invited the new Prime Minister of Israel to Washington, DC, and took steps to restate his own view of the prerequisites for a peace settlement in the Middle East and to obtain the acceptance of these by the USA's allies in Europe. A statement published at the end of June by the State Department reaffirmed US adherence to Resolution 242, stressing that a settlement had to involve Israeli withdrawal 'on all three fronts of the Middle East'—that is, Sinai, Golan, and West Bank/Gaza—and reiterating President Carter's belief in 'the need for a homeland for the Palestinians, whose exact nature should be negotiated between the parties'.

The theme of a Palestinian 'homeland' was taken up at a meeting of the heads of government of the EC in London. In a declaration published on 29 June 1977, the leaders of the nine members restated 'their view that a peace settlement should be based on Security Council Resolutions 242 and 338', adding that a solution to the Middle East conflict would be possible 'only if the legitimate right of the Palestinian people to give expression to its national identity is translated into fact, which would take into account the need for a homeland for the Palestinians'. The Declaration also stated that representatives of 'the Palestinian people' must be included in peace negotiations.

When Begin arrived in Washington, DC, in July 1977, he achieved an unexpected success with the US public, but it became clear that no serious attempt had been made in his talks with President Carter to examine the basic conditions for a peace settlement. The US Administration was now intent on securing Palestinian participation in any peace negotiations, to which the Israeli Government was strenuously opposed. In the course of a tour of Middle Eastern capitals in August, the US Secretary of State, Cyrus Vance, was informed by the Saudi Arabian Government that the PLO would accept Resolution 242 if it were amended to include provision for Palestinian self-determination—this provided a moment of optimism in which Carter spoke of the possibility that acceptance by the PLO of Resolution 242 might open the way to PLO participation in a reconvened Geneva peace conference. However, Vance's visit ended discouragingly in Israel, where Begin's Government refused categorically to negotiate under any circumstances with the PLO or to consider the idea of a Palestinian 'homeland'. In any case, the PLO, sceptical about the terms of the proposed bargain, finally refused to amend its stance over Resolution 242 without firm assurances that it would receive in return something more substantial.

Within days of Vance's departure, Israel announced that social services in the fields of education, health and welfare were to be extended to the Arab population of the West Bank and the Gaza Strip, which was widely interpreted as a step towards the annexation of these areas. This, and the decision to authorize three new Jewish settlements on the West Bank, caused an immediate consolidation of the PLO attitude and complicated still further the task of the USA in bringing Israel and the Arabs—including, if possible, the Palestinians—to the negotiating table.

When the Israeli foreign minister, Moshe Dayan, travelled to Washington, DC. in September 1977, he took with him draft proposals for a territorial settlement which envisaged the maintenance of the Israeli occupation throughout the West Bank and the Gaza Strip. These proposals expressed the continuing resolve of the Begin Government not to agree to any step that could lead to the creation of an independent Palestinian state. The USA, by contrast, was apprehensive that anything which appeared to extinguish all hope of that ill-defined Palestinian 'homeland' would not merely ensure the continuation of Palestinian resistance but would also alienate those Arab governments on whose goodwill the USA was increasingly dependent.

In late September 1977 there was a fresh outbreak of fighting in southern Lebanon, with Israeli troops openly intervening across the border in support of right-wing forces and against the Palestinians. This prompted a US initiative, reluctantly accepted by the Israeli Government, to include Palestinian representatives in a joint Arab delegation to the peace conference in Geneva. Dayan emphasized that this did not mean that Israel was ready to abandon its attitude towards the PLO or its rejection of a Palestinian state. A joint Soviet-US statement published on 1 October advocated a Middle East settlement that would ensure 'the legitimate rights of the Palestinians'. The use for the first time of this phrase by the US Government alarmed Israel and was taken by the Arabs as an indication that President Carter was prepared for the confrontation that had long been threatening with the Israeli Government and its powerful supporters in the USA. However, the prospect raised by the joint statement that the two superpowers were prepared to collaborate again made a renewal of the Geneva conference more likely and encouraged diplomatic activity, with even the PLO expressing its qualified acceptance of the Soviet-US statement as the basis for a reconvened peace conference.

PRESIDENT SADAT'S VISIT TO JERUSALEM

On 9 November 1977, in the course of a speech to the Egyptian parliament in which he expressed impatience with the numerous debates over procedural questions, President Sadat stated that he would be willing to travel to Jerusalem and to the Knesset itself to negotiate with Israel. Despite widely expressed scepticism, the suggestion was immediately taken up by the Israeli Prime Minister and pursued through intermediaries in the US embassies in Cairo, Beirut and Jerusalem. Resisting a rising tide of Arab disapproval, and despite the last-minute resignation of the Egyptian Minister of Foreign Affairs, President Sadat flew to Jerusalem on 19 November, and the next day made a dramatic appeal for peace in the Knesset and before the television cameras of the world.

This unexpected initiative was greeted with enthusiasm in the West, where it was regarded as a constructive departure from the sterile attitudes of the past, and with incredulous delight by Israel, which glimpsed the prospect of an end to its dangerous isolation. Among the Arabs, however, while there were scattered expressions of approval and optimism, the general reaction of furious resentment created a state of unparalleled disunity, making it harder than ever to achieve a common platform on which to negotiate with Israel.

Nor did the euphoria which surrounded President Sadat in Jerusalem long survive his return to Cairo. It soon became apparent that his Israeli hosts had assumed—like his Arab critics—that President Sadat had despaired of achieving an overall settlement and had set himself the more limited objective of an Egyptian-Israeli peace treaty. The Israeli leaders were ready to withdraw from almost all Egyptian territory, but they were not prepared to meet Sadat's other demands for a complete withdrawal from all Arab territory occupied in 1967 and recognition of the Palestinian right to self-determination.

Serious negotiations were postponed until 25 December 1977; Begin flew to Ismailia for a summit meeting with President Sadat, at which the Israeli Prime Minister produced a set of proposals for the future of Sinai, the West Bank and the Gaza Strip. On the crucial question of the future of the Palestinians, Begin offered only a limited form of self-rule for the population of the West Bank and the Gaza Strip, with Israel remaining in control of 'security and public order'. This was criticized in the Arab world as being merely a formula for the maintenance of the Israeli occupation.

President Sadat's position was made more difficult by a statement from US President Carter apparently approving the Begin proposal for Palestinian 'self-rule'. When Carter, in an evident attempt to repair the damage, altered the schedule of a foreign tour in order to meet Sadat at Aswan, he took the opportunity to reiterate the need to recognize 'the legitimate rights of the Palestinian people' and to enable the Palestinians 'to participate in the determination of their own future'. Elsewhere in the Arab world, however, cynicism about an overall Arab-Israeli settlement was deepened by mistrust of Sadat's motives and by the apparent inconsistency of US policy.

The Ismailia summit meeting produced a commitment to bilateral talks on political and military questions affecting a settlement. The military talks opened in Cairo on 11 January 1978 and were at once complicated by a dispute over Israeli settlements in Sinai, which had been criticized as illegal by the International Commission of Jurists. This criticism was echoed by President Carter a week later and when the political talks opened in Jerusalem on 16 January they were interrupted after only 24 hours when President Sadat recalled the Egyptian delegation, stating that in view of Israel's insistence on retaining the settlements he saw no hope of reaching agreement.

ISRAELI INVASION OF SOUTH LEBANON

A visit by Menachem Begin to Washington, DC, in March 1978 was delayed for a week after a terrorist raid near Tel-Aviv by Palestinian guerrillas operating from southern Lebanon, in which 36 Israelis were killed. Israel undertook a major cross-border attack into southern Lebanon, initially to destroy Palestinian guerrilla bases and establish a security belt along the Lebanese side of the frontier. After the USA hurriedly introduced a resolution in the UN Security Council calling for an Israeli withdrawal to be supervised by a UN force, the Israeli forces advanced further, and by the time a cease-fire finally came into effect on 20 March they were in occupation of the whole of south Lebanon as far as the Litani river, with the exception of the port of Tyre.

The Israeli invasion, which was accompanied by heavy and indiscriminate land, sea and air bombardments, provoked world-wide denunciation, especially as it became clear that an estimated 1,000 Lebanese civilians had been killed, in addition to some 200 guerrillas, and more than 200,000 refugees had been driven from their homes. When Begin finally met President Carter on 20 March 1978, the differences between them over the basic prerequisites of a Middle East peace settlement led to a confrontation which was barely masked by diplomatic protocol. Begin returned from Washington to face a threat to his leadership in Israel, where there was dissension within the Cabinet.

There was friction over the role of the UN Interim Force in Lebanon (UNIFIL), whose mandate was to supervise the withdrawal of the Israeli army from southern Lebanon and to restore the authority of the Lebanese Government. Israel carried out a partial withdrawal at the end of April 1978, but insisted that it would maintain an armed presence in Lebanon until the UN force could ensure the security of northern Israel against attacks by Palestinian guerrillas. The PLO, determined not to relinquish its last area of operations, promised to co-operate with UNIFIL.

In May 1978 Begin again visited Washington, DC, where President Carter assured him that 'we will never waver in our absolute commitment to Israel's security'. However, two weeks later the US Senate authorized the sale of advanced fighter aircraft to Saudi Arabia. This decision clearly reflected US impatience with Begin's stand on peace negotiations, and the importance the USA attached to retaining the friendship of Saudi Arabia, the leading petroleum producer in the Middle East.

When Israel withdrew the last of its forces from south Lebanon on 13 June 1978, it refused to transfer control of their positions to UNIFIL, leaving them under the command of Lebanese Christian militia units which had been collaborating with Israel against the Lebanese Government. This contributed to a crisis in Beirut at the beginning of July, when the Syrian-dominated Arab peace-keeping force attempted to impose its authority on the right-wing Christian militias.

The US Government, alarmed at the prospect of renewed Israeli intervention and of the final breakdown of the peace initiative launched by President Sadat in November 1977, exerted its influence to restrain both sides in Lebanon and persuaded the Israeli and Egyptian Governments to send their ministers of foreign affairs to a meeting in the United Kingdom, which took place at Leeds Castle in July 1978. When this meeting failed to narrow the gap between the two sides, President Sadat announced that he would not engage in further negotiations with Israel unless the Israeli Government changed its position. Faced with a deteriorating situation, President Carter took the unexpected step of inviting the Egyptian and Israeli leaders to meet him at his Camp David residence at the beginning of September 1978.

THE CAMP DAVID SUMMIT AND REACTIONS

The Camp David meeting, which lasted for 12 days and appeared more than once to be on the point of breaking down, ended on 17 September 1978, when

President Carter made a triumphant appearance on television to announce that Begin and President Sadat had signed two documents which together provided a framework for peace in the Middle East (see Documents on Palestine, p. 345). One of these dealt with the bilateral problems between Egypt and Israel, which the two leaders undertook to resolve by concluding within three months a peace treaty providing for an Israeli withdrawal from Sinai and the establishment of normal relations between the two countries. The other dealt with the wider question of the future of the West Bank and Gaza and provided for the election of a self-governing Palestinian authority to replace the existing Israeli military Government; once the authority was in being, there should be a transitional period of not more than five years during which the inhabitants of the West Bank and Gaza would exercise autonomy; and finally, 'as soon as possible, but not later than the third year after the beginning of the transitional period', there should be negotiations to determine the final status of the West Bank and Gaza and to conclude a peace treaty between Israel and Jordan.

The Camp David agreements were greeted with a mixed reception by the participants. President Carter's own standing was greatly enhanced in the USA, where it was felt that his daring personal diplomacy had forced the Israeli and Egyptian leaders to make concessions. In Israel the agreements were greeted with more cautious approval, in the belief that Begin had realized Israel's long-standing ambition to conclude a separate peace with Egypt without making any substantive concessions over Israel's right to maintain control of the West Bank and Gaza. In the Arab world, however, the agreements were regarded as proof that President Sadat had abandoned the Palestinians and his Arab allies. Even the Government of Saudi Arabia commented that the Camp David agreements constituted 'an unacceptable formula for a definitive peace', while the resignation of the Egyptian Minister of Foreign Affairs (who was at Camp David with President Sadat) showed that not even Egyptian opinion was wholeheartedly in favour of the Camp David formula.

The controversy within the Arab world centred on whether or not the agreements offered any real promise of eventual self-determination for the Palestinians. The advocates of the Camp David 'framework for peace' argued that if the Palestinians co-operated in the arrangements for a transitional period of self-rule they would set in motion a process which would be irreversible; that the end result of this process would be an independent Palestinian state; and that, if the Palestinians refused to co-operate, they would provide Israel with an excuse to perpetuate its occupation of the West Bank and Gaza. Critics argued that it was futile for Egypt to negotiate on behalf of the Palestinians over an issue on which the Palestinians themselves had not been consulted; that the arrangements for Palestinian autonomy outlined at Camp David were so imprecise as to be useless; that in any case Israel would hold a power of veto over their implementation and over the eventual future of the West Bank; and that Israel had no intention of ending its occupation or of allowing any development which might lead to Palestinian independence.

The last of these arguments was given greater credence in the immediate aftermath of the Camp David meeting by the actions of Begin. On his return to Israel, he declared emphatically in the Knesset that Israel would not 'under any conditions or in any circumstances' allow the establishment of an independent Palestinian state, and that Israel would continue to create new settlements on the

West Bank and would expect to maintain an armed presence there even after the end of the five-year transitional period.

ARAB OPPOSITION INTENSIFIES

In the circumstances it was not surprising that Cyrus Vance, whom President Carter dispatched to the Middle East to enlist Arab support for the Camp David agreements, met with a frosty reception. The Governments of Jordan (whose co-operation would be necessary if the provisions for the West Bank were to be put into effect) and of Saudi Arabia (whose influence was important in shaping Arab opinion) both expressed serious reservations, while the more radical Arab governments, led by Syria acting in co-operation with the PLO, declared their rejection of the agreements.

So strong were the feelings aroused in the Arab world that they led to a reconciliation between the rival Baathist Governments of Iraq and Syria, and to a summit conference of all the Arab states (apart from Egypt) in Baghdad, Iraq, at the beginning of November 1978 to consider means of preventing the implementation of the Camp David agreements. After a fiery debate in which various proposals were aired for isolating Egypt and denying it economic aid, the Arab leaders agreed, at the insistence of Saudi Arabia, to delay implementation until Egypt had signed a peace treaty with Israel, thus allowing President Sadat the opportunity to reconsider a policy which would leave him totally dependent on the support of the USA. Further decisions by Israel to proceed with its settlements in the West Bank led President Sadat to press for a revision of the Camp David agreements in order to link the provisions concerning the future of the West Bank more closely to those for a bilateral peace treaty between Egypt and Israel. In addition, President Sadat demanded that a specific timetable be adopted for the introduction of autonomy in the West Bank. This brought the peace-making process once again to a standstill, and the target date of 18 December (by which time the two sides had agreed at Camp David to sign a peace treaty) passed with the outstanding issues unresolved.

REVOLUTION IN IRAN

The disintegration of the Shah's regime in Iran at the end of 1978 had important repercussions throughout the Middle East. The suspension of petroleum exports from Iran, as a result of industrial action, threatened an international energy crisis and cut off the most important source of Israel's petroleum supplies. It also became clear, even before the Shah went into exile on 15 January 1979, that whatever government might succeed him would give strong backing to the Palestinians.

These developments gave added urgency to the US desire to achieve at least a partial Arab-Israeli settlement, but reinforced the positions of all the possible participants. Israel insisted on an Egyptian undertaking in the draft peace treaty to guarantee it access to petroleum from Sinai after its evacuation of the peninsula. For President Sadat it became more necessary than ever to obtain some concession over the West Bank. Without such a concession it was less likely that Saudi Arabia or Jordan—let alone the other Arab states—would moderate their opposition to the Camp David peace formula.

PRESIDENT CARTER VISITS THE MIDDLE EAST

When a further ministerial meeting in Washington, DC, between Egypt and Israel failed to remove the remaining obstacles to an agreement, President Carter flew to the Middle East on 7 March 1979 in a final effort to persuade Egypt and Israel to sign the long-deferred peace treaty. Carter returned to Washington to announce that 'we have now defined the major components of a peace treaty'; but before the treaty could be signed there were further acrimonious arguments about Israeli settlements on the West Bank, while opposition to the peace treaty on the part of even the most moderate Arab governments emphasized the isolation of Egypt.

ARAB BOYCOTT OF EGYPT

The attitude of Saudi Arabia was crucial, and the euphoria in the USA over the signing of the peace treaty—which finally took place in Washington, DC, on 26 March 1979 (see Documents on Palestine, p. 349)—was dispelled when Saudi Arabia demonstrated its opposition by attending a meeting of the Arab League in Baghdad at which a decision was taken to impose a political and economic boycott against Egypt. Arab ambassadors were recalled from Cairo, economic aid to Egypt was suspended and it was announced that the headquarters of the Arab League would be transferred from Cairo to Tunis. In agreeing to these measures and in subsequently severing diplomatic relations with Egypt, the Government of Saudi Arabia in effect chose to maintain solidarity with the rest of the Arab world at the expense of an open breach with the USA.

Arab opposition to the peace treaty focused on its failure to make any clear provision for Palestinian self-determination. President Sadat maintained that the treaty was the first step towards a comprehensive settlement which would restore Palestinian rights; but to the other Arabs it appeared to be a separate peace between Egypt and Israel which would restore Sinai to Egypt but would leave Israel in control of the rest of the Occupied Territories. That this was also the view of the Israeli Government seemed to be confirmed when Begin, in a broadcast on Israel's Independence Day, reiterated that no border would ever again be drawn through 'the land of Israel' and that 'we shall never withdraw from the Golan Heights'.

THE AUTONOMY TALKS

Soon after the signing of the Egyptian-Israeli peace treaty the two countries began negotiations on the question of autonomy for the Palestinians in the Occupied Territories. The principal issue on which the two sides differed was the establishment of Israeli settlements in the Occupied Territories, which Begin insisted were in no way contrary to the Camp David accords. When the Israeli Minister in Charge of Settlements, Ariel Sharon, announced plans at the end of May 1979 to build new settlements on the West Bank and in the Gaza Strip, the Egyptian Prime Minister, Mustapha Khalil, warned Israel that this would jeopardize the peace process. Shortly afterwards, on 12 June, the second round of talks ended with the two sides unable to agree on even the first principles of the autonomy plan.

On 4 September 1979 President Sadat went to Haifa for new talks with Begin, and announced that he was 'determined to spread the umbrella of peace to include the Palestinian people'. Bilateral agreements were made on the issues of border patrols, petroleum sales from Egypt to Israel, and the return of the Santa Caterina monastery to Egypt, but no progress was registered on the autonomy question. The two countries drifted still further apart a week later when the Israeli Government withdrew its ban on the purchase by Israeli citizens of Arab land in the Occupied Territories, an action immediately condemned by the US Government.

ISRAEL'S INTERNAL DISPUTES
In Israel, a parliamentary committee in July 1979 approved plans to build 13 new settlements in the Occupied Territories during the forthcoming 12 months, despite demonstrations organized by the opposition movement, Peace Now. However, the Israeli Supreme Court ruled that the Elon Moreh settlement near Nablus was illegal. The ruling denied that the settlement served a necessary military function and ordered the expropriated land to be restored to its Arab owners. At the end of October an extremist nationalist party, Tehiya, was founded, its principal objective being the construction of Jewish settlements throughout the West Bank.

PALESTINIAN DIPLOMATIC GAINS
In mid-1979 there was speculation that the USA was making overtures to the PLO in order to bring it into the peace process. Although this was repeatedly denied by President Carter, the US Ambassador to the UN, Andrew Young, met the PLO observer, Zehdi Labib Terzi, in September. After strong protests by Israel, Young resigned, declaring that the USA's refusal to talk to the PLO was ridiculous.

Meanwhile, the PLO was making significant diplomatic progress in Western Europe. In July 1979 Arafat had talks with Chancellor Bruno Kreisky of Austria and in September he was officially received by King Juan Carlos of Spain and his Prime Minister, Adolfo Suárez. At the UN General Assembly meeting later in the month, the Irish Minister of Foreign Affairs, Michael O'Kennedy, speaking on behalf of the EC, voiced strong criticism of current Israeli policy and mentioned, for the first time, the role of the PLO. In the same debate the British Foreign Secretary, Lord Carrington, called for an end to Israel's policy of settlement in the Occupied Territories and for a reversal of the decision to allow Israeli citizens to buy land there. In November the PLO was accorded 'political recognition' by the Italian Government and at the same time Arafat was received by the President and Prime Minister of Portugal. In addition, the PLO's spokesman on foreign affairs, Farouk Kaddoumi, held talks with the foreign ministers of Belgium, Greece and Italy.

UNREST IN THE WEST BANK
While Egypt and Israel made little progress on the autonomy question, the Palestinian population of the West Bank grew increasingly restless and frustrated. In February 1980 a new crisis arose when the Israeli Cabinet decided in

principle to allow Jews to settle in the town of Hebron. This action was widely condemned in Israel and abroad and led to increased tension throughout the West Bank. Riots and demonstrations took place in a number of towns and in April a group of Jewish extremists mounted attacks in Ramallah. On 1 May a Palestinian youth was shot dead by an Israeli officer in Anabta, and the following day PLO guerrillas struck in Hebron and killed six Jewish settlers. The Israeli authorities reacted by destroying a number of houses near the scene of the ambush and deporting the mayors of Hebron and Halhul and the Qadi (religious leader) of Hebron.

NO PROGRESS TOWARDS REAL PEACE

The seizure of US embassy officials in Iran and the Soviet invasion of Afghanistan at the end of 1979 diverted international attention from the Arab–Israeli conflict and the USA concentrated its attention on the recovery of the hostages in Tehran. On 1 March 1980, however, the UN Security Council unanimously adopted a resolution (465—see Documents on Palestine, p. 353) calling upon Israel to 'dismantle the existing settlements' and 'to cease, on an urgent basis, the establishment, construction and planning' of new ones. Two days later President Carter astonished the international community by retracting the affirmative US vote and announcing that it had been a mistake. The US vote, he stated, had been 'approved with the understanding that all references to Jerusalem would be deleted', and he added: 'While our opposition to the establishment of the Israeli settlements is long-standing and well known ... the call for dismantling was neither proper nor practical.' This retraction was widely seen as a surrender to the Zionist lobby by a US President needing votes in an election year.

As the autonomy negotiations showed little sign of progress, the EC sought new ways to break the deadlock. One idea was the suggestion that Resolution 242 should be amended to include a reference to the right of self-determination for the Palestinians. In February 1980, during a visit to Bahrain, the Irish Minister of Foreign Affairs recognized the PLO and called for the establishment of a Palestinian state. In the course of an important tour of the Middle East in the following month, President Valéry Giscard d'Estaing of France supported the principle of self-determination for the Palestinians and spoke of the need to include the PLO in peace negotiations. In April the PLO's diplomatic success in Europe continued when Chancellor Kreisky of Austria officially recognized the PLO as the representative of the Palestinian people.

The USA made it clear that it disapproved of European attempts to intervene in the peace process. In March 1980 President Carter, under attack from the other presidential candidates for his inept handling of the Security Council vote, decided to make yet another attempt to mediate between Israel and Egypt. Although the two countries had exchanged ambassadors and some successes had been achieved in bilateral relations, their positions on the autonomy issue were as far apart as ever. Determined to make some progress before 26 May (the target date for the completion of the autonomy talks), President Carter invited Sadat and Begin to visit him separately in Washington, DC, during April. Nothing was achieved and at the beginning of May President Sadat announced that Egypt was suspending its participation in the negotiations indefinitely.

THE EUROPEAN INITIATIVE

Despite the opposition of Israel, Egypt and the USA, the EC countries finally produced their Middle East statement at a meeting in Venice, Italy, on 13 June 1980 (see Documents on Palestine, p. 355). After criticism from the new US Secretary of State, Edmund Muskie, and a warning from President Carter that the USA would not hesitate to use its veto in the Security Council, the EC abandoned any attempt to introduce a resolution on Palestinian rights at the UN. However, it did go further than ever before in its support of Palestinian aspirations.

In the Venice statement, the EC declared, for the first time collectively, that the Palestinian people must be allowed 'to exercise fully its right to self-determination', and called for the PLO 'to be associated with the negotiations'. It also repeated its condemnations of Israeli settlements and any attempt to change the status of Jerusalem. Finally, the EC announced its intention of consulting all the parties concerned, in order to determine the form of a European initiative.

EGYPTIAN–ISRAELI RELATIONS

The negotiations over Palestinian autonomy, which President Sadat had postponed in May 1980, were reopened in Washington, DC, in July. However, the parties' positions were as firmly entrenched as ever, and there was speculation that President Sadat had decided to resume the talks only in order to increase the chances of President Carter's re-election in the forthcoming US elections.

Meanwhile the so-called 'normalization' of relations between Egypt and Israel was moving forward at a slow pace. Although both countries had established embassies in each other's capitals and there were regular air flights between the two, other agreements were taking a long time to implement.

WEST BANK NATIONALISM

Only a month after the mayors of Hebron and Halhul had been deported by the Israeli authorities, Jewish extremists placed bombs in the cars of three other West Bank mayors. Two of them were severely injured, including Bassam Shaka, the Mayor of Nablus. The attacks revealed the existence of a militant underground movement among Jewish settlers in the West Bank, which, in the ensuing weeks, issued death threats to Arabs and moderate Israelis, including Knesset members and prominent journalists. Tension increased as leading Palestinians, including Mayor Shaka, accused the Israeli Government of having links with the extremists. The Government's failure to investigate the crime properly, and the allegation that the head of the Shin Bet (Israel's internal security and intelligence service) had resigned because Begin had refused to allow him to carry out an investigation of members of Gush Emunim (the main West Bank settlement organization), added substance to these suspicions.

PARTY RIVALRY IN ISRAEL

Opinion polls in Israel had long been predicting a disastrous defeat for Begin's Government at the next general election, which had to be held before November 1981. Likud's unpopularity stemmed largely from its failure to solve the country's economic problems but during the early months of 1981 attention in Israel and abroad was focused on Likud and Labour's conflicting policies towards the Occupied Territories.

For electoral and other reasons, the Labour Party refused to define its policy towards the West Bank but it emphasized that it did not plan to annex the area. The Labour leader, Shimon Peres, seemed to favour the so-called 'Jordanian option', involving the return of the populated areas to Jordan but the retention of the Jordan valley and various blocks of settlements. Although King Hussein of Jordan repeatedly declared that no such option existed and that he was not empowered to speak for the Palestinians, Labour politicians continued to think in terms of a partition of the West Bank.

The Likud Government was determined to make it impossible to implement this policy. In the months before the election, which was to be held in June 1981, the Likud coalition authorized a vast new settlement programme which an incoming Labour government would be unable to dismantle.

REAGAN ELECTED IN THE USA

The election of Ronald Reagan as President of the USA in 1980 was greeted enthusiastically in Israel but caused dismay in the Arab world. During the campaign Reagan had made pro-Israeli statements that seemed excessive even for a US presidential candidate and his early appointments reflected the influence of his team of Zionist advisers. Nearly all of the Reagan appointees shared the feelings of the new Secretary of State, Alexander Haig, and the National Security Adviser, Richard Allen, who judged the Arab–Israeli conflict not on its own terms but in the context of the East–West confrontation. Dismay in the Arab world was increased by the new President's apparent ignorance of the issues; in an interview soon after taking office, Reagan declared that the Israeli settlements were 'not illegal', thereby contradicting what had long been official US policy.

The US Administration soon made it clear that it regarded the European initiative as a hindrance to its own efforts in the Middle East. The USA's main preoccupation was not with the Palestinian question, but with the threat which it believed the USSR posed to the oil-rich Gulf. To counter this threat, the USA created a rapid-deployment force able to intervene where necessary in the Gulf area. Although the Gulf Arabs denied the existence of a Soviet threat and declared their opposition to such a force, the USA proceeded with its plans to establish bases in Oman, Somalia and Kenya. In April 1981 Haig visited Egypt, Israel, Jordan and Saudi Arabia, intent on convincing the conservative Arab regimes of the Soviet threat. Both Jordan and Saudi Arabia, two of the USA's closest allies in the Arab world, showed themselves to be highly sceptical about the Reagan Administration's new priorities, while Syria, the PLO and other forces in the region were even more critical of US policies.

FIGHTING ESCALATES IN LEBANON

At the beginning of March 1981 the Syrian and Lebanese Governments agreed to send regular units of the Lebanese army to join UNIFIL forces in southern Lebanon. This move was opposed by the Israeli-backed Lebanese rebel leader, Maj. Saad Haddad, whose troops subsequently opened fire on UNIFIL positions. It was in response to this action and to attempts by the Phalangist

Christian militia to strengthen its positions around the Lebanese town of Zahle that Syrian troops of the Arab Deterrent Force moved against the Maronite Christian positions in central Lebanon.

In early April 1981 Lebanon experienced its most serious fighting since the end of the civil war in 1976. The battles around Zahle were followed by fighting in Beirut and Baalbek and in the south between Haddad's forces and the Palestinians. After a truce during the week before Easter, Israel launched a series of attacks against the south. Renewed fighting broke out between Syrian forces and the Phalangists on 27 April and the following day the Israeli air force shot down two Syrian helicopters. In response to this attack Syria deployed a number of SAM-6 anti-aircraft missiles to defend its positions in the Beka'a valley.

THE SYRIAN MISSILE CRISIS

Although the Syrian missiles were stationed deep inside Lebanon, far from the Israeli border, and fulfilled a defensive function, Begin demanded their withdrawal because they limited Israel's ability to fly over its northern neighbour. Philip Habib, the US Special Envoy to the Middle East, made a series of visits to Jerusalem and Damascus during May 1981 in an attempt to draft a compromise formula to persuade Saudi Arabia to encourage Syria to modify its position. Instead, Saudi Arabia opened a round of inter-Arab negotiations aimed at reaching agreement on the main points of a comprehensive Lebanese settlement, which would then make it easier to solve the crisis caused by the missiles. The settlement envisaged was to be based on the conclusions of the Beiteddine conference of 1978 with provisions for the future relations between the Lebanese factions, between Syria and Lebanon, and between the Palestinians and the Lebanese Government. Meanwhile, inter-Arab relations, which had deteriorated since the beginning of the Iran–Iraq War, improved, and at a meeting of Arab ministers of foreign affairs in Tunis on 23 May, Syria received the almost unanimous backing of the Arab world.

Hopes that Syria might accept a formula offered by the USA were frustrated by a new wave of Israeli attacks on Lebanon and by the further demands of Begin, who insisted on the removal of anti-aircraft missiles inside Lebanon and a Syrian guarantee that Israeli aircraft would not be targeted while they were 'patrolling' Lebanon. In June 1981 Begin warned that, if the USA failed to arrange the withdrawal of the missiles through diplomacy, Israel would remove them by force.

ISRAEL ATTACKS IRAQ

On 7 June 1981, with the Syrian missile crisis still unresolved, Israel bombed and destroyed the nuclear plant near the Iraqi capital, Baghdad. Begin immediately claimed that the attack was justified on the grounds of self-defence, as Iraq would soon have had the capacity to produce nuclear bombs. However, the International Atomic Energy Agency (IAEA) in Vienna, which had recently inspected the plant, said that Iraq would not have had the means to make nuclear weapons for many years, a view supported by the Congressional Research Service in Washington, DC. The IAEA pointed out that Iraq, unlike Israel, was a signatory of the Nuclear Non-Proliferation Treaty and that it had co-operated with the Agency over safeguards.

The raid was criticized by governments all over the world, while in the UN Security Council, the United Kingdom and France demanded a 'firm resolution' condemning Israel. Even the Israeli opposition leader, Shimon Peres, accused Begin of 'acting out of electoral considerations which ignore the national interest'. President Reagan responded by suspending the delivery of four F-16 aircraft to Israel until the US Congress had decided whether or not Israel had violated an agreement whereby US weapons were sold on condition they were not used in 'an act of aggression against any other state'. Nevertheless, the President made it clear where his sympathies lay when he stated that Israel had 'reason for concern' about Iraq's nuclear capacity.

BEGIN RETAINS POWER

The Israeli general election, which took place on 30 June 1981, was the most violent in the country's history. The campaign was characterized by the Prime Minister's demagogic performances in front of huge crowds and by the physical attacks of his Likud supporters against members and property of the opposition Labour Party. Begin's aggressive foreign policy obscured his Government's failures in tackling domestic problems and, in the election, the Labour Party failed to gain the predicted huge victory. The results showed the two main parties to be evenly balanced, but it was soon clear that the Prime Minister would remain in power if he could persuade the various religious parties to join him in a coalition. This he achieved and the new Cabinet that emerged was more homogeneous and uncompromising than its predecessor. The most significant appointment was that of Ariel Sharon, one of Israel's leading 'hawks', to the defence ministry.

Ten days after the election, Israel launched a series of air strikes against Palestinian targets in southern Lebanon. Guerrillas belonging to the PLO retaliated with rocket and artillery attacks against settlements in Galilee, and Israel, in turn, responded with further air strikes and with raids by sea-borne commandos. This time the targets included urban areas and in one strike against Beirut on 17 July more than 150 people were killed and 600 wounded. The international community was shocked by the action and the USA reacted by again suspending the delivery of F-16 aircraft to Israel and by making intensive attempts to bring about a cease-fire. While Philip Habib was attempting to persuade Israel to accept a truce, Saudi Arabia was putting similar pressure on the Palestinians. A cease-fire finally came into effect on 24 July.

THE DEATH OF SADAT

In August 1981 President Sadat visited Washington, DC, for the first time since the election of President Reagan. Although the USA did not accept his suggestion that it should negotiate with the PLO, the visit was considered to be a diplomatic success. Yet, for all his popularity in the West, Sadat faced major problems inside Egypt.

During the summer there had been serious clashes between Copts and Islamist fundamentalists, and at the beginning of September some 1,700 people were arrested, a number of newspapers closed and several foreign journalists expelled. Among those arrested were a large number of the President's political opponents who were neither Copts nor Islamists, which suggested that Sadat was using the religious clashes as a pretext to purge the opposition. A month after the arrests, however, President Sadat was assassinated by Islamist extremists at a military parade in Cairo. The large Western attendance at his funeral, which included three former US Presidents, presented a stark contrast to the lack of grief in evidence on the streets of the capital and indicated how much Sadat's popularity in his own country had declined as a result of his pro-Western stance on foreign policy.

EUROPE AND THE FAHD PLAN

The major diplomatic initiative of the second half of 1981 came from Saudi Arabia. The so-called 'Fahd Plan' was put forward by Crown Prince Fahd (see Documents on Palestine, p. 357). Although the USA reacted cautiously to the plan, European ministers of foreign affairs described it as 'extremely positive' and particularly welcomed Point Seven which, by guaranteeing 'the right of all states in the region to live in peace', indicated that Saudi Arabia was prepared to recognize Israel in return for a complete withdrawal from the Occupied Territories and the establishment of an independent Palestinian state.

Although Begin described the Fahd Plan as a recipe for the destruction of Israel, the Europeans were quick to note its similarities to their own Venice Declaration of June 1980. By the end of the year, however, both plans had been virtually abandoned. Europe's initiative was wrecked when the French Minister of Foreign Affairs, Claude Cheysson, dissociated his Government from it during a visit to Israel and the Saudi plan collapsed at the end of November. Since its publication in August no member of the Arab League, apart from Libya, had rejected the Fahd Plan outright and even the PLO Chairman, Yasser Arafat, had expressed approval. The Saudi delegation went to the first Fez Arab summit in November confident, therefore, that it could win broad support for its proposals. However, a number of Arab states, led by Syria, were opposed to the plan, not so much for its content as for its timing. At Fez the opposition hardened and, rather than allow the summit to degenerate into a lengthy public quarrel, King Hassan of Morocco closed the meeting after only a few hours.

THE GOLAN ANNEXATION

In December 1981, while international attention was concentrated on the crisis in Poland, the Israeli Government decided to annex the Syrian Golan Heights. Overruling the more cautious minority in his Cabinet, on 14 December Begin pushed through the Knesset a bill which extended Israeli laws, jurisdiction and administration to the territory Israel had occupied since 1967. The UN Security Council unanimously condemned the action and instructed Israel to rescind its decision within two weeks. When the Israeli Government refused to comply, the Security Council reconvened at the beginning of January 1982 in order to study what measures should be taken against Israel. Syria advocated a resolution calling for mandatory sanctions under Chapter Seven of the UN Charter but, in an attempt to attract wider international support, Jordan introduced a milder resolution calling merely for voluntary sanctions against Israel. Even this was too harsh in the opinion of the USA, which vetoed the resolution, although at the same time stressing its opposition to the annexation.

THE USA WITHOUT A POLICY

After more than a year in office, the Reagan Administration, which had been lukewarm to the Fahd Plan and hostile to the European initiative, had still not made any proposals of its own. While ostensibly working towards a resumption of the autonomy talks between Egypt and Israel, and hoping that the Israeli withdrawal from Sinai in April 1982 would take place smoothly, the US Administration's main concern remained the so-called 'Soviet threat'. It was primarily for strategic reasons that the USA made its two most important moves in the autumn of 1981: the sale of sophisticated radar aircraft (AWACS) to Saudi Arabia, which was endorsed by Congress after strong opposition from the Zionist lobby in October, and the signing of a 'memorandum of understanding' on defence co-operation with Israel on 30 November. However, this last agreement was suspended by the USA a fortnight later to show its disapproval of Israel's annexation of the Golan Heights; Begin reacted by verbally attacking the USA and repudiating the memorandum altogether.

ISRAEL WITHDRAWS FROM SINAI

Although President Mubarak of Egypt indicated soon after he succeeded Sadat that he wanted to improve his country's relations with the rest of the Arab world, it was clear that his immediate goal was the return of the last third of Sinai, which Israel was due to hand back in April 1982. Consequently, he was anxious to avoid any action which might offer Israel a pretext to continue the occupation. Within Israel there was much apprehension over the evacuation of Sinai and fears that it might lead to violence among the Jewish population.

In March, after several months of hesitation, the Government finally ordered the army to move into the Yamit area and evict illegal settlers who had recently entered it. The withdrawal took place as scheduled on 25 April 1982 and, in order not to antagonize Israel, Egypt recovered the key areas of Rafah and Sharm esh-Sheikh with as little ceremony as possible.

THE WEST BANK REVOLTS

For several months Israel had been attempting to create an 'alternative' leadership among the inhabitants of the West Bank which would collaborate in imposing some form of limited autonomy on the Palestinians. With financial aid and military protection from Israel, a small number of 'village leagues' were established in a move to counter the radical nationalism of the urban leadership. Although the attempt was largely unsuccessful, it did provoke several of the West Bank's more radical mayors into refusing to collaborate with the Israeli administration. In response, on 18 March 1982, the occupation authorities dismissed the Mayor of al-Bireh, Ibrahim Tawil, as well as the town's council.

The dismissals caused a three-day strike in East Jerusalem and the rest of the West Bank, which was later extended as a result of the harsh manner in which the Israeli army dealt with Palestinian demonstrators. Rioting took place in most West Bank towns and spread to the Gaza Strip. A week after the action taken against the al-Bireh town council, Israel issued summary dismissal orders against the Mayor of Ramallah, Karim Khalaf, and the Mayor of Nablus,

Bassam Shaka. These dismissals provoked two weeks of the worst rioting the West Bank had yet seen, in which several Palestinians were killed.

ISRAEL'S 1982 INVASION OF LEBANON

The cease-fire on the Israel-Lebanon border, which had been arranged by Philip Habib in July 1981, held for less than a year. In May 1982 the Israeli air force struck at Palestinian positions inside Lebanon and PLO guerrillas retaliated by shelling Galilee. On 4 June, anti-PLO Arab gunmen shot and wounded the Israeli Ambassador to the United Kingdom, Shlomo Argov, and Israeli aircraft bombed targets in southern Lebanon and west Beirut. The PLO's subsequent bombardment of northern Israel—which did not result in loss of life—was the official pretext for an invasion the Israelis entitled 'Operation Peace for Galilee'. However, Gen. Sharon subsequently revealed that he had been planning the operation since becoming Minister of Defence in July 1981 and he had even visited Beirut secretly in January 1982, in preparation.

On 6 June 1982 the Israeli army, numbering some 30,000, brushed aside the UN forces in southern Lebanon and attacked Palestinian positions around Beaufort Castle and along the coast road to Tyre. While Israel's air force, with naval support, bombed Beirut and other towns, infantry units were landed along the Lebanese coast. The Israelis captured Nabatiyah, Tyre, Sidon and Damour after massive bombardments which resulted in severe damage and several thousand civilian casualties. By 10 June Israeli troops had reached positions overlooking Beirut.

Syria, which had maintained some 30,000 troops in Lebanon since its inter-vention in 1976, tried to avoid being drawn into the war but on the fourth day of the invasion its forces clashed with the advancing Israelis. Although the battles on the ground never became as serious as in the 1973 war, Syria committed its air force against the Israelis and suffered a heavy defeat. On 11 June 1982, under diplomatic pressure from the USA, Israel agreed to a cease-fire with Syria. However, fighting continued between Palestinian guerrillas and Israeli forces. During the siege of Beirut Sharon announced that the PLO should be expelled from the country and, if possible, destroyed altogether. As for Lebanon, Sharon's intention was to expel the Syrian troops from Beirut and the centre of the country and to install a client regime drawn from the right-wing Phalangist Party.

THE SIEGE OF BEIRUT

The siege of Lebanon's capital began a week after the invasion and lasted almost two months. It was bombed almost continuously from land, sea and air from 13 June 1982 to 12 August. When the siege had ended two Lebanese newspapers, quoting government sources, calculated that since the beginning of the invasion 18,000 people had been killed and 30,000 wounded. About 85% of the casualties were civilians.

Israel's terms for ending the siege were that PLO forces in Beirut, numbering some 9,000 combatants, should surrender or leave the country, along with those Syrian troops still in the city, otherwise the Israeli army would force its way into Beirut and forcibly expel them. While US officials tried to negotiate an agree-ment with the PLO, the Israeli armed forces continued to bombard the city. They also cut off water and electricity supplies to west Beirut and prevented food and medical supplies from reaching its beleaguered population. Finally the PLO agreed to leave and on 21 August 1982 its guerrillas began their evacuation. By the end of the month the last Palestinian units had left the city that had been their headquarters since the Jordanian civil war 12 years earlier. Israel had achieved one of its principal objectives. A second goal was attained almost immediately when, on 23 August, the Lebanese National Assembly was persuaded to choose the right-wing, pro-Israeli, Phalangist commander, Bachir Gemayel, as the new President of Lebanon.

THE SABRA/CHATILA MASSACRE

The agreement governing the evacuation of the PLO from Beirut provided for the deployment of a multinational force to supervise the Palestinian withdrawal and to protect the inhabitants of Muslim west Beirut. On 25 August 1982 this force, composed of French, Italian and US soldiers, disembarked at Beirut. Only two weeks later, they began to withdraw, a fortnight earlier than provided for in the agreement.

On 14 September 1982 Gemayel was killed by a bomb explosion at the Phalangist Party headquarters and a few hours later, in contravention of the evacuation agreement, the Israeli army moved into west Beirut. The day after the assassination Israeli officers held a meeting with local Phalangist commanders in which they agreed to help a force of Phalangist militiamen 'clean up' the Palestinian refugee camps of Sabra and Chatila. On the evening of 16 September the Phalangists entered the camps and began a massacre which resulted in the deaths of as many as 2,000 refugees.

The outrage which the atrocity caused throughout the world eventually forced the Israeli Prime Minister to order an inquiry. In its report published in February 1983, the Israeli Commission of Inquiry criticized a number of leading Israelis, including Begin, Sharon, the Minister of Foreign Affairs, Shamir, as well as high-ranking army officers, such as the Chief of Staff, Eitan. Sharon was considered principally responsible for planning the operation; he resigned as Minister of Defence, although Begin allowed him to remain in the Cabinet as a minister without portfolio.

TWO PEACE PLANS

On 1 September 1982 President Reagan announced a new plan to settle the Arab–Israeli conflict (see Documents on Palestine, p. 357). It was widely considered to be the work of the new Secretary of State, George Shultz, and it represented a significant change in US policy. While the Camp David accords had been ambiguous about the future of the territories occupied by Israel since 1967, the Reagan Plan envisaged their restoration to the Arabs. Nevertheless, at the same time the USA reaffirmed its opposition to the creation of a Palestinian state and proposed 'self-government in association with Jordan'.

The Reagan Plan was rejected by the Israeli Government, which immediately embarked on a new and more intensive programme of building settlements on the West Bank. A week after the announcement of the Reagan Plan, the Arab states, meeting again in Fez, countered with their own proposals (see Documents on Palestine, p. 357), which were almost identical to the Fahd Plan of the year before and called for the creation of a Palestinian state in the Occupied Territories. Point Seven of the proposals, which urged 'the United Nations Security Council to provide guarantees for peace between all states of the region . . .', implicitly recognized Israel's right to exist.

At the end of October 1982 King Hassan of Morocco led a delegation of Arab ministers of foreign affairs to Washington, DC, to explain their proposals to President Reagan. Although the US and Arab plans both envisaged the restoration of Arab rule over the Occupied Territories, they differed over the issue of who exactly would govern them. The crucial figure in the US strategy was King Hussein of Jordan, who visited Washington in December. Hussein was prepared to negotiate with the USA on the basis of the Reagan Plan only if he received a mandate to do so from the Palestinians. In January 1983 the King held talks with the PLO leader, Yasser Arafat, aimed at establishing a joint Jordanian-Palestinian position, and the following month the Palestinian National Council (PNC) debated the matter in Algiers.

Although it was clear that Arafat and the Palestinian moderates were anxious to give Hussein the mandate he required, there was strong opposition from some sections of the PNC, particularly from those groups backed by Syria. The PNC duly endorsed the Fez proposals and criticized the Reagan Plan without rejecting it outright. Although Arafat failed to achieve his objectives, discussions between Jordan and the PLO continued until King Hussein brought them to an end in April.

AMERICAN DIPLOMATIC EFFORTS

On 24 April 1983 George Shultz began a visit to the Middle East, shortly after a bomb attack, apparently carried out by an unknown Shi'ite group, had destroyed the US embassy in Beirut and left a large number of dead, including 17 US citizens. After a series of consultations with Arab and Israeli leaders, Shultz was able to persuade the Lebanese and Israeli Governments to sign an agreement on 17 May providing for the withdrawal of Israeli troops from Lebanon. Although Israel did not succeed in securing some of the ambitious security demands it had been making earlier, the agreement did provide for the establishment of joint Israeli-Lebanese patrols operating inside the Lebanese border.

The Israeli Government had made clear at the time that any agreement to withdraw its troops from southern Lebanon was conditional on a commitment by Syria simultaneously to withdraw its army from the Beka'a valley. The Syrian Government, however, which had recently entered into a closer alliance with the USSR, quickly denounced an agreement that seemed to benefit only the USA and its allies, Israel and the Lebanese Government of Amin Gemayel (the brother of the late President-elect). Negotiations had neglected consideration of an Israeli withdrawal from the Syrian Golan Heights and the Occupied Territories of Palestine and President Assad, therefore, adopted an intransigent attitude. As an indication of Syrian policy, Assad supported a revolt by Palestinian dissidents inside Fatah (the militant Palestine National Liberation Movement) who were opposed to Arafat's moderate, diplomatic approach. With the help of the Syrian army, the Fatah rebels under their extremist commander, Abu Musa, captured Palestinian loyalist positions in the Beka'a valley and in June Assad expelled Arafat from Syria.

The Israeli Government, meanwhile, was refusing to withdraw its army from Lebanon without a simultaneous reciprocation by Syria—yet it was reluctant to leave its troops in occupation of so much Lebanese territory because of the toll being taken on them in attacks by Lebanese and Palestinian guerrillas. In Israel, demonstrations were held to demand the immediate withdrawal of Israeli troops. A year after the invasion the Government admitted that 500 soldiers had been killed in Lebanon and people began to question whether the war's objectives could justify such losses. It was in this atmosphere that the Israeli Government began to discuss proposals for a limited withdrawal to the Awali river, north of Sidon.

THE ISRAELI WITHDRAWAL FROM BEIRUT

Escalating factional violence in Lebanon during the summer of 1983 underlined the impracticability of both Israel's and the USA's plans for that country. A principal aim of Israel's invasion—the establishment of a strong central government closely allied to Israel—had clearly been abandoned when on 20 July the Israeli Cabinet decided, unilaterally, to withdraw its forces behind the more easily defensible line of the Awali river. Simultaneously, a visit to Washington, DC, by President Gemayel left the US Administration with few illusions that the 17 May Lebanon/Israel agreement, which it had brokered, would ever be ratified, far less implemented. The sense of failure provoked the replacement of Habib as Middle East special envoy by Robert McFarlane, and the announcement by Begin, on 28 August, of his intention to resign as Prime Minister. The situation in Lebanon deteriorated further (on 23 July the Druze leader Walid Joumblatt had announced the formation of a pro-Syrian coalition, the National Salvation Front, in opposition to the Gemayel Government). Any hope that without external support Gemayel's authority could be extended beyond the capital itself was extinguished following Israel's sudden withdrawal to the Awali on 4 September, which precipitated a war between the Druze and the right-wing Christian forces. With Syrian logistical support, the Druze quickly gained the ascendancy; their advance was impeded only at Souk el-Gharb, a strategic mountain town overlooking Beirut, at which point the USA took the decision to intervene directly in the conflict with shelling by its offshore fleet of Druze- and Syrian-controlled territory.

AMERICAN INVOLVEMENT

The increasing US involvement in the Lebanese conflict, with the concomitant danger of 'superpower' confrontation, alarmed not only the USA's European partners in the UNIFIL multinational force (MNF) but all levels of opinion in the USA itself, which was for the first time paying the price in American lives for its Middle East policy. The longer-term worry was that such involvement would destroy US credibility as the broker of a wider settlement of the Arab–Israeli conflict. On 26 July 1983 masked gunmen killed 3 Palestinian students and wounded 38 others in an attack on Hebron University. Then, on 2 August the USA vetoed a UN Security Council resolution declaring the West Bank settlements illegal and condemning the violence against Palestinian civilians. Although, on 27 August, President Reagan declared the establishment of new Israeli settlements in the Occupied Territories to be 'an obstacle to peace', two days later the USA boycotted the UN International Conference on the Palestinian Question in Geneva, Switzerland, which was attended by 137 states, including its NATO allies in Europe.

BEGIN'S RESIGNATION

Any hopes that the resignation of Begin as Prime Minister on 30 August 1983 heralded a change in Israeli policies were banished when the Herut Party chose the even more uncompromising Minister of Foreign Affairs, Itzhak Shamir, to be his successor as leader of the party. Shamir, a veteran of the Jewish underground group, Lehi, had allegedly given the order for the assassination of UN mediator Count Folke Bernadotte in 1948, and had opposed the Camp David accords. Begin withheld his formal resignation until 15 September, giving Shamir time to form a viable Likud coalition. Sure of a narrow majority in the Knesset, Shamir was asked to form a government on 21 September.

THE INFLUENCE OF SYRIA

If Lebanon was the key to progress towards a wider settlement, it appeared to many observers that President Reagan believed that the civil war there could be settled in President Gemayel's favour through the exercise of US military might. This was despite efforts in the US Congress to invoke the 1973 War Powers Act requiring presidential consultations with Congress if US forces abroad faced 'imminent hostilities'. The impossibility of a force of 1,600 marines with naval support sustaining the authority of Gemayel's Government, whose pleas to Israel for help against the Druze offensive had been dismissed, became increasingly clear in the aftermath of the fragile cease-fire agreed on 25 September 1983 through Saudi Arabian mediation. The terms of the cease-fire provided for a dialogue of national reconciliation with Syrian participation, in recognition of Syria's effective power of veto over decisions relating to the future of Lebanon.

There were signs too that Syria was seeking to extend its control over another key area of the Middle East conflict. On 29 July 1983 Arafat declared that Syrian and Libyan troops were involved in continuing clashes between pro- and anti-Arafat Palestinian factions in the Beka'a valley. Prolonged meetings of the PLO's Executive Committee and Central Council in Tunis in early August were unable to heal the rift in Palestinian ranks. Arafat managed to retain the loyalty, or at least the neutrality, of the more radical groupings, such as the PFLP, led by George Habash, and the Democratic Front for the Liberation of Palestine (DFLP), led by Naif Hawatmeh, but was obliged in return to submit to the Central Council's denunciation of the Reagan Plan, something which the last PNC meeting had carefully avoided. The remaining pro-Arafat forces in Syrian-controlled northern Lebanon were steadily losing ground, and Arafat seemed to have decided to make his last stand with them when in mid-September he returned to the loyalist stronghold in the northern Lebanese port of Tripoli. This soon came under siege from Syrian and Palestinian forces.

With Syria dominating events in Lebanon and with the pro-Syrian Fatah dissidents led by Abu Musa apparently poised to inherit Arafat's leadership of the PLO, it seemed that any solution of the crisis must be acceptable in Damascus. The US Administration was forced belatedly to recognize Syria's influence and negotiations were initiated by McFarlane through the Saudi

Arabian Ambassador to the USA, Prince Bandar ibn Sultan. Much to the consternation of its European allies, however, the USA appeared unwilling to alter its perception of the conflict in Lebanon in terms of a Soviet threat to its interests in the region, a view in which it was encouraged by Syria's acquisition of Soviet long-range SS-21 missiles in early October 1983. There was, equally, no hint of US readiness to put pressure on Israel over the issues necessary for Syrian acceptance of a peace settlement: Israeli withdrawal from southern Lebanon and, crucially, the inclusion of the Syrian Golan Heights, annexed by Israel in 1981, in any talks aimed at a wider settlement. Israel, in turn, applied its own leverage, threatening to close the bridges over the Awali river, now Lebanon's *de facto* line of partition. President Reagan's domestic position improved some-what on 30 September with a Senate vote approving the deployment of US forces in Beirut for a further 18 months, but the precarious position of these forces made their withdrawal imperative before the 1984 presidential election campaign began in earnest.

SUICIDE BOMBINGS IN LEBANON

All the Reagan Administration's calculations were overturned on 23 October 1983 when simultaneous suicide-bomb attacks destroyed the headquarters of the French and US contingents of the MNF in Beirut, killing 241 US marines and 58 French soldiers. Two extremist Shi'ite groups thought to have had links with a detachment of Iranian revolutionary guards stationed in Baalbek in eastern Lebanon claimed responsibility for the atrocities. Responsibility for the attacks, initially ascribed by the USA to Iran, was widened to include Syria and the USSR, all of which vigorously denied any involvement. Although President Reagan was quick to reaffirm America's commitment to maintaining the marines in Lebanon—a determination echoed at a meeting of the ministers of foreign affairs of all four countries contributing to the MNF in Paris on 27 October—domestic opposition to his Middle East policy inevitably increased. In the case of the attack on the French forces, there was reason to believe it was linked with France's support for Iraq in the Iran–Iraq War; in the case of the USA the marines' deaths could not help but be attributed to its decision to intervene, as it appeared, directly on the side of Lebanon's Christian President against the largely Muslim opposition, and to the antipathy which US support for Israel had provoked among the Arabs at large. Israel's distancing itself from the US involvement in Lebanon, as reaction to the bombings emerged, was evidence of its sensitivity to the charge that by invading Lebanon it had set in motion the chain of events leading to the disaster. US resentment was evinced by the rejection of Israel's offer to help in treating the victims of the attack. Ten days before the Beirut attacks Israel had disclosed secret US plans to arm and equip a Jordanian military force for possible intervention in a Gulf crisis. The disclosure led to the Senate Appropriations Committee vetoing the proposal on 2 November and gravely damaged the US-Jordanian dialogue, which had been focused on King Hussein's willingness to revive talks with the Palestinians on the basis of the Reagan Plan.

The USA forged closer links with Israel after a bomb attack on Israel's military headquarters in Tyre which killed 60 people, including 32 Palestinians and Lebanese held captive there. Israeli aircraft immediately bombed

Palestinian and Druze positions in the Chouf, and a 72-hour blockade of the occupied south was imposed. The USA seemed to be convinced by the Israeli Minister of Defence, Moshe Arens, that US reverses in Lebanon were due to lack of co-ordination with Israeli forces there and it decided on a policy of 'strategic co-operation' with Israel. Syria, which Israel publicly held ultimately responsible for the Tyre attack, warned of 'aggressive US and Israeli intentions' and ordered a general mobilization of its forces on 7 November.

THE LEBANESE NATIONAL RECONCILIATION CONFERENCE

Despite the relative success of the organizers of the national reconciliation conference—which was convened in Geneva, Switzerland, at the beginning of November 1983—in persuading the protagonists, including the Syrian Minister of Foreign Affairs, Abd al-Halim Khaddam, to participate, Lebanon's internal strife persisted. The demand by Syria and its allies in the National Salvation Front for the abrogation of the 17 May agreement with Israel had prompted a compromise proposal whereby President Gemayel was to seek a substitute arrangement with the USA for securing Israeli withdrawal. The new US strategy (which coincided with the appointment on 3 November of a new Special Envoy for the Middle East, Donald Rumsfeld) of ever closer identification of its interests with those of Israel dictated the joint US-Israeli refusal to reconsider the unratified accord. President Gemayel's Christian constituency retained sufficient faith in US support and in the possibility of further Israeli military intervention on its side to resist changes to its constitutional privileges, and internal reconciliation made no progress. That US and Israeli strategies were coinciding more and more was demonstrated by a massive increase in US military aid to Israel, and, in Lebanon, by further Israeli air raids on Syrian-controlled territory and a direct US–Syrian clash on 4 December in which two US aircraft were shot down.

ARAFAT'S DEPARTURE FROM TRIPOLI

The prestige which Syrian President Assad won in the Arab world as a result of his policy of confrontation with the USA was enhanced by Arab dismay at the US-Israeli accord. President Mubarak of Egypt, the USA's closest ally in the Arab world, described the accord as catastrophic and King Hussein of Jordan considered it a reward for Israeli intransigence. President Assad's apparent propaganda success in defying the USA was partly vitiated, however, by the assault against forces loyal to Arafat in Tripoli, which by the end of November 1983 had claimed at least 500 lives. His evident determination to prevent Arafat from leaving the country alive was conditioned by the knowledge that, liberated from the influence of extremist dissidents backed by Syria, the PLO Chairman would be in a position to attempt to forge a joint Jordanian-Palestinian alliance based on the Reagan Plan, a move repeatedly advocated by King Hussein. Although the PLO dissidents had initially attracted considerable sympathy, their collaboration with Syria against the loyalists swung opinion behind Arafat, especially in the Occupied Territories, and the struggle was increasingly seen as one for PLO independence from external control. Arafat's standing was enhanced on 24 November when six Israeli prisoners held by his forces in

Tripoli were exchanged for 4,800 Palestinians and Lebanese imprisoned by Israel in southern Lebanon. Support for Arafat from many quarters, including the USSR, but especially from the Arab Gulf states, helped to secure a Saudi/Syrian-sponsored agreement to end the fighting on 24 November, in accordance with which Arafat and his supporters were to withdraw from Lebanon within two weeks. The UN Security Council agreed on 4 December to grant the ships evacuating Arafat's 4,000 supporters the protection of the UN flag, but naval attacks on Tripoli by Israel, and its refusal to guarantee the evacuation fleet safe passage, delayed its departure until 20 December.

ISRAEL'S DOMESTIC PROBLEMS

Israeli bombing raids continued against what were termed terrorist bases in Syrian-controlled Lebanon, inflicting heavy civilian casualties. Losses were also mounting from almost daily guerrilla attacks on Israeli forces in occupied southern Lebanon, where the overwhelmingly Shi'ite population had built up an increasingly effective military resistance movement. In addition, Israel was experiencing an economic crisis and record rates of inflation, which threatened the new Government of Itzhak Shamir. Huge debts had brought the country to the verge of bankruptcy and forced the new Minister of Finance, Yigal Cohen-Orgad, to devalue the shekel, impose drastic restrictions on subsidies to basic commodities and draft an austerity package which included reductions in the hitherto sacred areas of defence and settlement. This, in turn, further endangered the ruling coalition's narrow majority in the Knesset, as the religious parties threatened to withdraw their support if the rapid colonization of the Occupied Territories was not sustained.

ARAFAT'S DIPLOMATIC INITIATIVES

On leaving Tripoli Arafat travelled to Egypt for a meeting with President Mubarak, becoming the first prominent Arab leader to visit that country since the signing of the Camp David accords. However, Egypt's continued commitment to the treaty was emphasized immediately after the meeting by the visit of a senior Egyptian official to Israel, the first of its kind since the 1982 invasion of Lebanon. Nevertheless, Arafat's visit was followed by the signing of an Egyptian-Jordanian trade protocol, a visit to Cairo by the Saudi Prince Talal ibn Abd al-Aziz, and, on 19 January 1984, by the decision of the OIC to readmit Egypt to its ranks. The *de facto* ending of the Arab boycott of Egypt could, it was felt, provide the bridge for possible Arab-Israeli negotiations and the emergence of a moderate Arab alignment between Egypt, Jordan, the PLO and possibly Iraq. Syria, Libya and the PLO's left-wing factions vehemently denounced the *rapprochement* with Egypt and the burgeoning Jordan-PLO relationship. Although Shamir also denounced the Arafat-Mubarak meeting as a 'severe blow to the peace process', the US Administration welcomed it as a boost for the Reagan Plan.

In a move which was interpreted as preparing the constitutional ground for a joint Palestinian-Jordanian initiative, King Hussein decided on 5 January 1984 to reconvene the Jordanian Parliament (its representation theoretically divided between the East and the (occupied) West Banks of the Jordan), which had been suspended since 1974 (when the Rabat Arab summit accorded the PLO the status of sole representative of the Palestinian people), and had not actually convened since 1967.

DISQUIET AT THE USA'S ROLE IN LEBANON

The Reagan Administration in the USA refused to acknowledge the untenability of the position of US forces in Lebanon, despite warnings from US marine commanders in Beirut, mounting dissent on Capitol Hill, and public disquiet among the USA's European partners in the MNF, who in January 1984 announced partial withdrawals of their contingents. The difference between US and European perceptions of the Arab–Israeli conflict was illustrated on 11 January when the British Foreign Secretary, Sir Geoffrey Howe, advocated a radical change in Israeli policies and urged Israel to negotiate with the PLO. The influence of the 1984 US presidential election campaign was already evident in dissuading the Reagan Administration from responding to the Arab peace initiative. A formal request from Egypt that 160 members of the PNC from the Occupied Territories be allowed to attend a proposed session of the Jordanian Parliament, aimed at securing a mandate for Arafat's progress towards a joint position with Jordan, was rejected by Israel, with no sign of US opposition.

THE WITHDRAWAL OF THE MULTINATIONAL FORCE FROM BEIRUT

Meanwhile, US naval bombardments of anti-Gemayel forces in the hills over-looking Beirut prompted renewed attacks on the US contingent of the MNF. At the beginning of February more than 200 people died in three days of continuous heavy fighting, the Lebanese Government resigned, and the Lebanese army disintegrated along sectarian lines. Druze militiamen from the mountains linked up with their Shi'ite allies in the southern suburbs of Beirut on 15 February 1984. The USA still refused to consider the one thing that might have halted the onslaught against Gemayel—the abrogation of the 17 May agreement—but it had clearly lost all control of events. Despite public avowals of support for the Gemayel Government and promises to keep US forces in the country, the decision had already been taken to 'redeploy' the marines even before President Reagan announced their withdrawal on 7 February. The next day the United Kingdom announced and completed the withdrawal of its token contribution to the MNF, followed by the Italian force on 20 February. The last US marines were evacuated from Beirut on 26 February, to be followed by the French in March, leaving the western sector of the city, as in the days before the Israeli invasion, under the control of Muslim and left-wing militias. On 5 March, bowing to Syrian influence, President Gemayel abrogated the 17 May Lebanon-Israel agreement in return for guarantees of internal security from President Assad.

THE CONSEQUENCES OF ISRAEL'S INVASION

The failure of Israel's 1982 invasion now became fully apparent. Far from securing a 'client regime' in Beirut, it had brought about the defeat of Israel's Christian allies, who had been forced to retreat into their traditional enclaves in east Beirut and around Jounieh. Abandoned by the USA, and with little prospect of further military support from Israel, there seemed little alternative to cantonization or a power-sharing deal with the Muslim majority. Meanwhile, the enormous cost of the Lebanese campaign in lives and resources appeared to have undermined Israel's security, rather than consolidate it. The death of the pro-Israeli militia commander, Maj. Sa'ad Haddad, on 15 January 1984, further disappointed Israel's hopes of creating a security zone along the Lebanese side of its northern border, and despite the setbacks suffered by the PLO in Lebanon, armed attacks against Israelis in Israel continued. In addition, the growth and increasing sophistication of a Jewish anti-Arab terrorist underground was both embarrassing the Government and threatening a backlash throughout the Arab and Muslim world. The Karp report, drawn up by a Ministry of Justice commission in May 1982, but suppressed until 8 February 1984, detailed the Government's failures to curb Jewish terrorism against Arab civilians. At the end of April Israeli security services finally acted, arresting some 30 people suspected of planting bombs on Arab buses. By that time the defection of the small Tami party from the ruling Likud coalition had led to the defeat of the Government in a vote to dissolve the Knesset and hold early elections, which were subsequently scheduled for 23 July. The lengthy trial of members of the Jewish terrorist underground, arrested in April, distracted attention from the election campaign, especially after it became known that some of the suspects, who were mainly Gush Emunim settlers but also included two army officers, had confessed to the 1980 assassination attempts on three Palestinian mayors in the West Bank and the previous year's attack on the Islamic college in Hebron. Their stated aim was to force a mass exodus of Palestinians from the Occupied Territories. The Government's own attitude toward the underground movement was called into question by a statement by a cabinet minister, Yuval Ne'eman, of the Tehiya party, who cited the bombing of the Palestinian mayors as having 'effectively paralysed the leading agitators' in the West Bank.

Abroad, Lebanon remained a cause for concern. On 4 April 1984, a new commander, ex-Lebanese army Col Antoine Lahad, was installed at the head of the militia in southern Lebanon, formerly led by Maj. Haddad, which Israel had reinforced and renamed the 'South Lebanon Army' (SLA). Israel's strategy was to remain in occupation of southern Lebanon until the SLA was capable of maintaining control there. However, neither Israel nor its surrogate force seemed capable of preventing a growing number of guerrilla attacks against the occupying army.

LEBANON'S GOVERNMENT OF NATIONAL RECONCILIATION

In Beirut, a new Government of national unity installed at the end of April 1984 had resolved to secure Israel's complete and unconditional withdrawal. Comprising a delicate balance of Christians and Muslims achieved after a year's painstaking mediation on the part of Syria, the new Lebanese Cabinet included the Shi'ite leader Nabih Berri—an indication both of the increasing influence of the Shi'ites and of how far the balance of power had shifted in favour of Lebanon's non-Christian communities (although Amin Gemayel retained the presidency). Berri, leader of the Shi'ite Amal movement, which was spearheading the resistance to Israel in the south, joined the Government on the condition that he be made minister for the south, and his appointment signalled the first test of President Gemayel's pledge of 'support for the national resistance' given at the reconvened national reconciliation conference in Lausanne, Switzerland, in March. The new Prime Minister, Rashid Karami, a Sunni Muslim, confirmed the Government's intentions on 3 June by calling for the removal of Israel's 'liaison office' at Dbayye, in the Christian enclave north of Beirut. Israel's Likud Government was adamant that it would not leave southern Lebanon in the control of a Syrian-influenced government in Beirut. The USA was unwilling to mediate between Lebanon and Israel to secure a withdrawal, even assuming that its participation would have been countenanced by Syria. On 10 June, during a tour of the Middle East, the UN Secretary-General, Javier Pérez de Cuéllar, quashed Israeli hopes that UN forces could act as a buffer north of Israel's lines, on the grounds that this would reinforce Lebanon's *de facto* partition. Israel, in turn, rejected the suggestion that UNIFIL could police Israel's northern border and ensure its security after an Israeli withdrawal. By the second anniversary of the invasion, the war in Lebanon had cost almost 600 Israeli lives, with 3,049 wounded—more than the total number of military and civilian casualties in the Six-Day War of 1967.

ISRAEL'S INCONCLUSIVE GENERAL ELECTION

In his election manifesto, Shimon Peres, who had been unanimously re-adopted on 12 April 1984 as leader of the Labour Party, pledged to bring Israel's troops home within 'three to six' months of gaining power, and this appeared to be a crucial factor in his party's favour. However, the immediate concern of the Israeli voter as the election approached was the economy. With inflation reaching 15% a month, a balance-of-payments deficit of US $5,000m., foreign debt of $23,000m. and a chronic shortage of foreign-currency reserves, Israel was on the verge of bankruptcy—the occupation of Lebanon alone was costing the country an estimated $1m. a day.

At the election on 23 July 1984, the major party groupings, Likud and the Labour Alignment, each secured just over one-third of the Knesset's 120 seats. The balance of power lay once again with the minority parties, which won the remaining 35 seats. The result confirmed the trend towards polarization in Israeli politics: the extreme right-wing Tehiya party increased its representation from three to five seats, and was joined on the far right by two members of the religious-nationalist Morasha party, which drew its support from the Gush Emunim movement, and by Rabbi Meir Kahane of the Kach party, who had campaigned on an openly racist platform. At the other political pole, Reserve Gen. Matti Peled and Muhammad Mv'ari were elected as representatives of a newly formed Arab-Jewish coalition, the Progressive List for Peace, which called for dialogue with the PLO and the establishment of an independent Palestinian state in the Occupied Territories. The impasse was resolved when Labour leader Peres was entrusted with forming the new Government after the factions in the political centre, Yahad and the National Religious Party, agreed to lend their support to Labour on condition that Peres form a 'national unity' government with Likud. On 30 August Labour and Likud agreed to such an arrangement, with Peres as Prime Minister and Shamir as Minister of Foreign Affairs, their posts to be exchanged every two years. On 13 September the Knesset approved a bi-partisan Cabinet, completing the political rehabilitation of Sharon, who was appointed Minister of Industry and Trade.

SYRIAN INFLUENCE IN LEBANON

In Lebanon, Syria was exercising unprecedented control over the Government in Beirut. On 18 June 1984 President Assad succeeded in sponsoring a Christian-Muslim power-sharing agreement, which included the implementation of a balanced security plan throughout Beirut, where local militias were to be disbanded and the port and airport reopened. The plan was executed on 4 July, the army taking over positions in the city from the militias, including the hitherto intransigent Lebanese Forces (LF, the military wing of the Christian Phalangist Party), within hours. However, despite Syria's efforts, plans to extend the Lebanese army's deployment throughout the rest of the country made no headway, and renewed sectarian clashes threatened to reverse the progress that had been made, exposing Syria's inability to control its Druze and Shi'ite allies. Israel demonstrated its determination to thwart Syria's designs in Lebanon by a series of air raids on Druze- and Syrian-controlled areas and, on 10 September, an armoured column was deployed north of its lines on the Awali river into the Kharroub region to support Christian militias under attack from the Druze.

MOVES TOWARDS AN ISRAELI WITHDRAWAL FROM LEBANON

The new Government in Israel gave the first public indication that Israel had lost the political struggle for Lebanon; the hitherto rigid insistence on a simultaneous withdrawal of Syrian troops from the country was abandoned, and the Minister of Foreign Affairs, Shamir, stated that Israel wanted the USA to mediate with Syria on a procedure for Israeli withdrawal. The US Assistant Secretary of State for Near East Affairs, Richard Murphy, visited Lebanon, Syria and Israel in September 1984, holding two rounds of talks with President Assad in Damascus, the first such US-Syrian contact and the first display of active US diplomacy in the region since the withdrawal of US forces from Beirut in February. Murphy followed in the footsteps of the UN Assistant Secretary-General, Brian Urquhart, who returned assured by all parties of their desire for UNIFIL to play a larger part in any settlement. However, Israel insisted that, though a withdrawal of forces need not be simultaneous, it should not be unilateral. Nevertheless, talks began under UN auspices on 8 November, at UNIFIL's headquarters in the Israeli-Lebanese border town of Naqoura, between military delegations from Israel and Lebanon, within the framework of the 1949 Armistice Commission.

DIPLOMATIC INITIATIVES ON PALESTINE

The new Israeli Government had also to contend with the nascent Arab 'peace alliance' between Arafat's wing of the PLO, Jordan and Egypt. Egypt's credibility in the Arab world and non-aligned movement was strengthened by its decision to restore full diplomatic relations with the USSR. However, it was

King Hussein's surprising decision on 25 September 1984 to restore diplomatic ties with Egypt which first raised the possibility of talks between the new Israeli Government and a joint Jordanian-PLO delegation supported by Egypt. Arafat had been preoccupied by a long and difficult struggle to win the agreement of the various PLO factions to convene the PNC, which Arafat hoped would supply the Palestinian consensus for a joint peace strategy with Jordan. Amid signs of a thaw in relations between Syria and Arafat's mainstream PLO, and after mediation efforts by the USSR, the People's Democratic Republic of Yemen and Algeria, leaders of Fatah and the quadripartite Damascus-based Democratic Alliance, including the PFLP and the DFLP, met in Algiers on 18 April. Subsequently it was declared that the PFLP and DFLP had abandoned their opposition both to Arafat's leadership and to the dialogue with Jordan. Syria, however, remained opposed to any Damascus-based group attending a PNC meeting, and warned that those who did attend would not be allowed to return to Syria. The stalemate was finally broken on 14 October at a meeting in Tunis of the PLO Executive Committee, Fatah's Central Council and about 80 representatives of other Palestinian organizations, at which it was declared that the PNC must be convened before the end of November, and that 'the minority must accept the decision of the majority'. The 17th session of the PNC was duly scheduled for 22 November in Amman, Jordan. On 9 October President Mubarak visited the Jordanian capital, where a joint Egyptian-Jordanian strategy on Palestine was announced. Israel welcomed the new Egyptian-Jordanian relationship as helpful to peace, but Egypt, while welcoming the inauguration of Peres as Israel's Prime Minister, made it clear that its primary commitment was to the Arab world, and that it stood by its conditions for normalizing the frosty relations between them that had prevailed since Israel's invasion of Lebanon: namely, the initiation of steps to gain the confidence of the Palestinians living in areas under Israeli occupation, and talks on the disputed border strip of Taba on the Red Sea, which Israel continued to occupy after vacating Sinai in 1982. For his part, King Hussein dismissed speculation that a US-sponsored peace initiative along the lines of Camp David was in prospect when, on 10 October, he denounced Peres' proposal for direct negotiations between Jordan and Israel, explicitly excluding Palestinian involvement, as 'subterfuge and deception'.

REAGAN IS RETURNED TO THE WHITE HOUSE

In the USA the Administration concentrated on advancing the US-Israel strategic relationship. An unprecedented military exchange agreement between the countries' air forces was announced in early September 1984, and, during a visit to Israel in mid-October by the US Defense Secretary, Caspar Weinberger, details were released of the transfer of hitherto restricted US technology crucial to the development of Israel's *Lavi* fighter aircraft. To help Israel address its economic crisis the US also consented to transfer the whole of its $1,200m. annual civilian aid grant immediately, rather than in instalments.

As far as the Arab world was concerned, the US Administration appeared to be retreating into a defensive posture, as evinced by 'anti-terrorist' legislation drafted by the State Department in April 1984. It was indisputable that the Reagan Administration had attracted an unprecedented degree of hostility in the Middle East. Threats of violence against and kidnappings of US citizens had led on 28 May to the recall of marines to protect the US embassy in Beirut. Nevertheless, on 20 September a suicide-bomb attack, responsibility for which was claimed by the Shi'ite Islamic Jihad (Holy War) organization, killed more than 20 people and accelerated the steady exodus of US diplomats, journalists and relief workers from Lebanon. Although, as a result of the intervention in Lebanon, more US citizens had been killed in international conflict than at any time since the Viet Nam War, seemingly no blame was attached to President Reagan, who was re-elected by a massive majority on 5 November.

FAILURE OF TALKS ON ISRAELI WITHDRAWAL

At the talks in Naqoura on Israel's withdrawal from Lebanon, Lebanon's demands included an unconditional Israeli withdrawal, the abolition of the SLA and US $10,000m. in war reparations. Israel responded by threatening to withdraw unilaterally, without making provision for local security. The talks made little progress, with Syria evidently refusing to give Israel any assurance of its security once its forces had withdrawn. The pressure was, nevertheless, increasing on Israel to withdraw. Guerrilla attacks on the IDF continued during the negotiations, and both the troops and the Israeli public were becoming increasingly frustrated at the high casualty toll. On 8 January 1985 Israel announced its withdrawal from the Naqoura talks; a week later the Israeli Cabinet approved a three-phase unilateral withdrawal from Lebanon, which, Prime Minister Peres pledged, would be completed by July. Israel remained committed to intervening in Lebanon if it perceived a threat to its security, and to aiding 'friendly' militias and maintaining a security zone patrolled by the SLA on the Lebanese side of the border.

JORDANIAN-PALESTINIAN PARTNERSHIP

Matters elsewhere looked more promising in the wake of Arafat's success at the PNC meeting in Amman in late November 1984. Although the PFLP and DFLP did not attend, they undertook not to approve the formation of an alternative organization, and the PLO succeeded in demonstrating its independence from Syria. In his address to the PNC, King Hussein laid down the guide-lines for a new Arab approach to the peace process, consisting of a joint Jordanian-PLO initiative, based on UN Resolution 242 and the right of the Palestinian people to self-determination, in accordance with the principle of an exchange of territory for peace with Israel. The PNC, however, reiterated its rejection of Resolution 242, which refers to the Palestinians only as refugees, implicitly denying their right to self-determination and recognizing the State of Israel. Israel, which had always prohibited Palestinians living in areas under its occupation from attending the PNC, ignored King Hussein's proposals; nor did it respond to a statement by the Egyptian Minister of State for Foreign Affairs, Boutros Boutros-Ghali, expressing Egypt's willingness to back a new initiative in which Jordan and a delegation of West Bank and Gaza Palestinians would enter peace talks with Israel under a mandate from the PLO. In this, however, Egypt was not supported by either Jordan or the Palestinians, who made it clear that the PLO should be a full partner in any future peace negotiations. PLO-Jordanian relations were strengthened by a series of meetings between King Hussein and Arafat, culminating on 11 February 1985 in the signing in Amman of a PLO-Jordanian accord, which provided for Palestinian self-determination within the framework of a Jordanian-Palestinian confederation and for peace negotiations between all parties to the conflict, including the PLO, and the five permanent members of the UN Security Council. Israel promptly rejected the agreement.

The Amman agreement, which attracted strong opposition from Syria and Arafat's PLO opponents and was clearly a source of contention within the PLO Executive Committee itself, illustrated the urgency with which King Hussein and Arafat viewed the need to salvage the Occupied Territories for a future Palestinian homeland before Jewish settlement established a *de facto* extension of Israel. Despite pledges from the new Israeli Government to raise the quality of life for the Palestinians in the Occupied Territories, violence against the Arab population there persisted. Nor did the Labour component of the Government of national unity seem able or willing to halt the continued seizure of Palestinian land for Israeli settlement. On 10 February 1985 a study by the US-financed West Bank Data Project found that, as of 1 January 1985, there were 42,500 Israeli settlers living on the occupied West Bank, double the figure of just two years earlier.

ISRAEL'S ECONOMIC CRISIS

The decision to spend more on colonizing the Occupied Territories drew protests from Israelis alarmed by the rapidly increasing rate of inflation and, for the first time in the country's history, widespread unemployment. A wages and prices 'freeze' agreed on 2 November 1984 between the Government and trade unions and employers temporarily checked the rise in inflation, but did not address the deep-rooted crisis in the economy. The Israeli shekel, having fallen to less than one five-hundredth of its 1977 value, was replaced for most practical purposes by the US dollar. An Israeli economic delegation travelled to Washington, DC, at the end of December to request US $4,100m. in aid in 1986, an increase of $1,500m. on the 1985 total approved by the US Congress just three months previously. Initially, the US Government insisted that any increase in aid should be conditional on the introduction of more rigorous measures to tackle the crisis. On 17 January Israel and the USA finalized a free-trade agreement, and on 30 January President Reagan agreed to increase US military aid to Israel by $400m. to $1,800m. for the 1986 fiscal year. The same day, the Administration bowed to pressure from the pro-Israel lobby and delivered what appeared to be a deliberate snub to Saudi Arabia, its most important Arab ally. Less than two weeks before King Fahd was to pay a state visit to Washington, DC, it was announced that the sale of 40 F-15 fighter bombers to Saudi Arabia had been postponed pending a review of US arms sales to the Middle East. King Fahd's appeal to the USA to revive the peace process was made in Washington on the same day (11 February) that Arafat and King Hussein signed the Amman agreement, but the USA continued to insist that the PLO explicitly accept UN Resolution 242 to secure participation in negotiations. The Arab initiative was complicated shortly afterwards when President Mubarak launched proposals for direct talks between Israel and a Jordanian-Palestinian delegation, following preliminary discussions between the latter and the USA, a suggestion which clearly went beyond anything envisaged by King Hussein and Arafat. Mubarak's move, which drew sharp opposition from Syria and many Palestinians, as well as from the USSR, was cautiously welcomed by Peres, who stated on 25 February that Israel would be willing to meet such a delegation provided it did not contain PLO members.

ISRAEL'S WITHDRAWAL FROM LEBANON

The first phase of Israel's withdrawal plan, the evacuation of the western seaboard from the Awali to the Litani, was accomplished peacefully in February 1985. Almost immediately, however, Shi'ite guerrillas stepped up their attacks. Israel launched a policy of 'Iron Fist' reprisal against villages suspected of harbouring guerrillas, storming scores of townships, killing and wounding their inhabitants, destroying houses and confining hundreds of men to prison camps. The IDF clashed with UNIFIL forces protesting against the destruction of Shi'ite homes, and on 12 March the USA vetoed a UN Security Council resolution, proposed by Lebanon, which condemned Israel's behaviour in southern Lebanon.

Israel's reprisal tactics did not have the desired effect: UN figures showed that in the first month in which the 'Iron Fist' policy operated, attacks on the IDF in Lebanon actually doubled. On 17 March 1985 Peres announced that the with-drawal was to be accelerated and completed in 8–10 weeks. In late March elements of the LF, determined to salvage what they could from the retreat and the increasingly pro-Syrian policies pursued by the Gemayel Government, staged a revolt. Fighting in the capital and in the south between the Lebanese army and the Christian rebels soon degenerated into a general conflict between Christians and Muslims, which was accompanied by a fresh Israeli campaign against Shi'ite villages in the occupied southern area. Israeli–Shi'ite antagonism was exacerbated by the news that, in contravention of the Geneva Convention, Israel had secretly transferred more than 1,000 Lebanese Shi'ite detainees to Israel, where the army Chief of Staff, Gen. Moshe Levi, said they would remain imprisoned until 'the security situation improved'. The second phase of Israel's withdrawal (from the central and eastern sectors of southern Lebanon) was completed during April, as the sectarian fighting north of its lines intensified. Druze and Muslim militias took control of the main Sidon–Beirut highway on 28 April, overrunning many Christian villages whose inhabitants fled in their thousands towards the new Israeli lines. Israel, which at the beginning of May began fortifying its international border with Lebanon, clearly indicated that it would not intervene again to help the beleaguered Christians.

THE SUPPRESSION OF THE PLO IN BEIRUT

Meanwhile, in Beirut, Syria's two main militia allies in Lebanon, the Druze and the Shi'ite Amal, unleashed a violent *putsch* against the Sunni Murabitoun militia. The Sunni Prime Minister, Rashid Karami, resigned in protest on 17 April 1985 but was persuaded to remain in office. Significantly, the

Murabitoun were the only force in Lebanon still supportive of Yasser Arafat's PLO. The determination of Syria and its Lebanese allies to prevent the resurgence of pro-Arafat Palestinian forces in Lebanon after the Israeli withdrawal was ruthlessly demonstrated when troops of the Shi'ite Amal movement attacked the Palestinian refugee camps in Beirut on 20 May. The savagery of the assault, in which several hundred Palestinians were killed, led the hitherto pro-Syrian Palestinian factions in the camps to join forces with pro-Arafat fighters. As the third anniversary of Israel's invasion approached it appeared that a *pax Syriana* could be established in Lebanon after Israel had withdrawn if Syria could control its Lebanese allies and prevent the country dividing along sectarian lines into religious cantons.

ISRAEL'S CONTINUED REFUSAL TO NEGOTIATE WITH THE PALESTINIANS

On the wider front, the refusal of Israel and the USA to deal directly with the PLO remained the single greatest obstacle to all negotiations, including those on the basis of 'territory for peace' involving Israel, the Palestinians, Jordan and Egypt, proposed by King Hussein and President Mubarak. However, on 5 April 1985 the US Administration finally took a more active role, scheduling visits to the Middle East by Murphy in April and Shultz in May. Neither succeeded in resolving the central issue of Palestinian representation at peace talks, despite reports that, while in Jordan, Shultz had been presented with a list of Palestinians who were not PLO members for possible inclusion in a joint Jordanian-Palestinian delegation. Shultz was denied the economic pressure, which he could have brought to bear on Israel over the issue of Palestinian representation, when the US Administration finally decided to recommend to Congress, shortly before he left Washington, DC, that Israel receive the additional US $1,500m. in emergency aid which it had requested. Israel's position hardened on 12 May when it announced that members of the PNC were also unacceptable as negotiating partners.

On 20 May 1985 three Israeli prisoners of war who had been held since the invasion of Lebanon by the hardline PFLP General Command, led by Ahmad Jibril, were exchanged for 1,150 Palestinians detained in Israel. The release of the Palestinian prisoners, some of them convicted terrorists, proved highly controversial in Israel, generating intense pressure on the Government to release Jews convicted of, or awaiting trial for, terrorist offences against Arabs. In an attempt to lend momentum to the peace initiative launched by the Jordan-PLO agreement, King Hussein travelled to Washington, DC, at the end of May 1985 to establish some form of international framework for his proposals. Radical quarters of the Arab world had already accused Jordan of seeking a separate deal with Israel, and King Hussein was clearly anxious to avoid the ostracism suffered by Egypt as a result of the Camp David treaty, preferring an international conference co-sponsored by both superpowers. By far the greatest obstacle to talks remained the issue of Palestinian representation. It was not until July that the PLO submitted to Jordan a list of names of 22 leading Palestinians for inclusion in a joint Jordanian-Palestinian delegation to meet US officials prior to the opening of wider negotiations involving Israel. Israel rejected the list (with two exceptions), calling for 'authentic Palestinian representatives' from the Occupied Territories, who had no direct links with the PLO.

ISRAEL COMPLETES ITS WITHDRAWAL

Israel announced the completion of its withdrawal from Lebanon on 10 June 1985, but its retention of an 8–10 km-wide 'security zone' along the border inside Lebanon, policed by the Israeli-sponsored SLA and supported by smaller numbers of Israeli troops, proved a constant source of friction with UNIFIL, to the north.

Syria succeeded in sponsoring a cease-fire of sorts on 31 May 1985 in the battle for control of the Palestinian refugee camps in Beirut, after Shi'ite Amal militiamen had failed to subdue stubborn Palestinian resistance, but there was no foreseeable end to the sectarian violence. The rise of Lebanon's Shi'ite factions in particular (supported by Iran in certain cases), with their associated underground guerrilla groups, compounded the descent into anarchy, which extreme Islamic and anti-Western groups began increasingly to exploit. On 11 June a Jordanian airliner with 65 passengers on board was diverted by Shi'ites to Beirut, where the hostages were later released and the plane destroyed. Less than 48 hours later a US TWA airliner carrying 153 passengers including 43 US citizens, was also hijacked, and flown between Beirut and Algiers (where 100 hostages were released) before landing for the third time in Beirut on 16 June. The USA responded with a build-up of naval forces off Lebanon, but the dispersal of the hostages in Shi'ite-controlled west Beirut precluded any US attempt to free them by force, putting pressure instead on Israel to accede to the hijackers' demands and release over 700 Lebanese Shi'ites being held in Israel. The intervention of President Assad of Syria resulted in the US hostages being freed unharmed (with the exception of one who had been killed when the plane was first seized) on 30 June. In return Israel released its Shi'ite prisoners in stages to avoid the impression of a surrender to terrorism. For the USA, the TWA hijacking was instrumental in diverting attention from a Middle East peace settlement to the immediate problem of combating terrorism.

Further Arab–Israeli violence on the occupied West Bank also threatened the prospects for negotiations. After the killing of two Israeli teachers, and of an occupation official, reprisal actions by Jewish settler groups were accompanied by additional security measures, including curfews, the closure of universities and newspapers, and detention without trial. Palestinians were also deported (a total of 26 in 1985)—a practice which Israel had discontinued in 1980 after widespread international criticism. The result was an escalation of violence by Arabs and Jews throughout August and September 1985, at the end of which regular army troops were sent into occupied areas. The harassment of Palestinians by both the Israeli army and settler vigilantes was widespread, and there were signs that the Israeli coalition Government's right-wing Likud component was exploiting the unrest to sabotage the prospect of talks with a joint Jordanian-Palestinian delegation. Blaming PLO 'command centres' in Jordan for co-ordinating Palestinian resistance in the Occupied Territories, the Likud leader and Minister of Foreign Affairs, Shamir, urged that Israel suspend diplomatic contacts so long as the PLO was allowed to maintain 'forward headquarters' on Jordanian soil. The future of the proposed talks was already in serious doubt after the failure of Murphy to meet members of a Jordanian-Palestinian delegation during his tour of the Middle East in mid-August 1985.

Jordan was increasingly fearful of isolation within the Arab world, a fear heightened by the refusal of the Arab summit held in Casablanca, Morocco, on 7 August 1985 to endorse the aims of the Jordanian-Palestinian accord. This fear was somewhat allayed by the US decision, prior to King Hussein's visit to Washington, DC, on 30 September 1985, to submit to Congress a US $1,900m. arms deal with Jordan despite intense opposition to it from the Zionist lobby. Moreover, although US opposition to a meeting with PLO or PLO-associated Palestinians was as firm as ever, Jordanian hopes of progress were boosted in late September when the British Prime Minister, Margaret Thatcher, following her visits to Amman and Cairo, invited a Palestinian-Jordanian delegation (including two members of the PLO Executive Committee) to London for talks with the British Foreign Secretary. Nevertheless, King Hussein was clearly insuring against the initiative's failure when, before leaving for the USA, he sanctioned the initial approaches in a *rapprochement* between Jordan and its main opponent in the Arab world, Syria.

ESCALATION OF VIOLENCE

On 1 October 1985, three days after King Hussein had arrived in the USA to address the UN General Assembly with an appeal for Arab–Israeli peace, Israeli jets bombed the PLO's headquarters in Tunis, killing 75 people, in retaliation for the killing of three Israelis by the PLO's élite Force 17 in Cyprus. The Israeli raid was condemned by the UN and by European leaders, but support for it from the White House as a 'legitimate response' to terrorism was a serious blow to US–Arab relations and to the USA's credibility as a peace-broker. Despite Jordanian and PLO pledges of continued commitment to the peace process, Arab anger over the affair clearly led to increased violence in the Israeli-occupied territories. On 7 October, four Palestinians succeeded in hijacking an Italian cruise liner, the *Achille Lauro*, with over 400 passengers and crew on board. The action was condemned by the PLO, which swiftly persuaded the hijackers to surrender themselves to the Egyptian authorities, but not before one passenger, an elderly American Jew, had been murdered. Egypt had agreed with the PLO that the hijackers would be flown to PLO headquarters in Tunis to stand trial, but the Egyptian airliner carrying them was intercepted *en route* by US fighter-planes and forced to land at a NATO base in Sicily. The US plan to take the hijackers, who were accompanied by the alleged mastermind of the operation, the leader of the Palestine Liberation Front, Muhammad Abu al-Abbas, to the USA for trial was thwarted by Italy, which prevented the Americans from taking custody of the Palestinians and subsequently allowed Abu al-Abbas to leave the country on the grounds that he had not been actively involved in the hijack.

The political repercussions of the *Achille Lauro* affair set back the prospect of peace talks. In US and Israeli eyes, it further justified the exclusion of the PLO from the peace process for as long as it was involved in terrorism. On 21 October 1985 Jordan signed a three-point agreement with Syria which included a pledge not to seek a separate peace with Israel and was regarded as a clear move away from the peace process based on Jordan's collaboration with Arafat, towards whom Syria and the Damascus-based PLO factions remained hostile.

With no progress being made in the peace process, attention focused on the summit meeting between President Reagan and the Soviet leader, Mikhail Gorbachev, on 19 November 1985 in Geneva. There was speculation that a new approach based on US-Soviet co-operation might result, but the summit meeting passed with no sign of any agreement on the Middle East, and the prospect of an international conference began to recede. One reason was the PLO's continued refusal to accede to the USA's precondition that it accept UN Resolution 242, renounce terrorism and recognize Israel. Jordanian impatience with the PLO mounted, as the reconciliation between King Hussein and President Assad proceeded apace; on 10 November King Hussein issued a statement accepting responsibility for the long period of poor relations with Syria and pledging an end to the activities of anti-Syrian elements based in Jordan. Syria did not conceal its view that the *rapprochement*, which continued with a meeting in Damascus between King Hussein and President Assad on 30–31 December, foreshadowed the end of the Jordan-PLO agreement. Arafat, despite warm support from Egypt during a visit to Cairo in mid-November, in the course of which the PLO leader renounced terrorist violence outside the Occupied Territories and against civilians, was becoming increasingly isolated. His position and the credibility of the PLO as a participant in peace talks was not improved by simultaneous terrorist attacks by Palestinians at Rome and Vienna airports on 27 December which killed 19 people (including five US citizens) and injured more than 100. Yet in the aftermath of the atrocities the US Administration, and the Government of Israel, whose El Al airline facilities had been the target of the attacks, for the first time made a distinction between the PLO, led by Arafat, and the dissident PLO splinter group (the Fatah Revolutionary Council), led by Abu Nidal, which was widely held to be responsible for the attacks. US and Israeli anger, and the threat of military retaliation, was directed almost exclusively toward Abu Nidal's alleged sponsor and protector, Libya, despite the more prominent links between the Abu Nidal group and Syria. The US Sixth Fleet was deployed off the Libyan coast, and on 7 January 1986 a package of anti-Libyan political and economic sanctions was announced by President Reagan, though European Governments refused to adopt them.

JORDAN RENOUNCES ITS AGREEMENT WITH THE PLO

During the first few weeks of 1986 it became clear that there was little prospect of progress in the Jordan-PLO peace initiative. A 12-day session of talks in January between King Hussein and Arafat, who travelled to Amman to reply to 'final' US terms for Palestinian participation in peace negotiations, collapsed without agreement. Although these terms represented a concession on the long-established US-Israeli position in that they entailed an invitation to the PLO to attend an international peace conference in return for the organization's acceptance of Resolution 242, this the PLO refused to do, unless the USA first recognized the Palestinian right to self-determination. No sooner had the Jordanian-Palestinian talks ended than the US Administration notified King Hussein that it was postponing indefinitely its request to Congress to sell advanced weaponry to Jordan, a sale which President Reagan had earlier said was 'essential to create the conditions for a lasting Middle East peace'. The Jordanian-PLO peace initiative was formally dissolved on 19 February, when

King Hussein announced the end of political collaboration with the PLO leadership, intimating that he would now seek a new partner in peace moves in the form of alternative representatives of the Palestinians. The principal reason given by King Hussein for the schism was the PLO's preoccupation with Palestinian self-determination at the expense of the 'liberation of the land' and its refusal to accept Resolution 242. The immediate effect was to raise Arafat's standing among the considerable body of Palestinians who had suspected him of giving up the Palestinians' 'last card', by acknowledging Resolution 242, with its implicit recognition of Israel, in return for vague US promises of participation in peace talks. King Hussein's chances of finding alternative Palestinian representatives, who would have the backing of the majority of Palestinians and the Arab world at large, seemed slight.

THE TABA ISSUE

Israel's reaction to the collapse of the Jordan-PLO initiative was one of relief at avoiding a US-PLO dialogue and with it the threat of a split in the Government between the Labour bloc and the Likud faction, which was militantly opposed to any form of territorial concession. The fragile Israeli coalition Government had already been seriously threatened by the issue of Taba, the tiny coastal enclave claimed by both Egypt and Israel and outwardly the principal cause of the discord between the two, which had begun with the 1982 Israeli invasion of Lebanon. Peres, keen to improve relations with Egypt, was in favour of acceding to Egypt's demand to submit the issue to international arbitration, a course bitterly opposed by the Likud leader, Shamir, a veteran critic of the Camp David treaty. Israel's overtures to Egypt were, however, undermined by its bombing of Tunis on 1 October, which President Mubarak denounced as a 'fatal blow' to peace; five days later seven Israeli tourists, including four children, were killed by an Egyptian policeman in Sinai. Israeli-Egyptian contacts resumed in December, and on 14 January 1986 Peres succeeded in obtaining Likud's approval to submit the Taba issue to arbitration. In return Egypt agreed to a series of measures to improve bilateral relations, including the return of Egypt's Ambassador to Tel-Aviv. However, the expected improvement quickly became bogged down in low-level talks and Peres' hopes of a summit meeting with President Mubarak were not realized.

US-ISRAELI TIES

During his visit to Washington, DC, in early April 1986 Peres proposed that the USA should support a 'Marshall Plan' (such as was employed to assist European recovery after World War II) for the Middle East—a US $20,000m.–$30,000m. development fund, primarily designed to help Arab states affected by the sharp drop in the price of petroleum. The proposal was welcomed by US officials as worthy of serious consideration, despite the unlikelihood that Arab states would co-operate in any plan involving Israel while the latter was in occupation of Arab territory. The positive US response to Peres' proposals underlined the strength of the US-Israeli alliance, despite two developments which were outwardly damaging to the relationship. First, on 24 November 1985 a US naval intelligence officer, Jonathan Pollard, was arrested by the US Federal Bureau of Investigations and charged with supplying classified documents to Israel. Then, in April 1986, a licensed Israeli arms dealer, retired Gen. Avraham Baram, was indicted in the USA for his part in a conspiracy to smuggle $2,500m. worth of advanced US weaponry, including tanks, missiles and fighter aircraft, to Iran. The indictment listed, among the items in the attempted sale, $800m.-worth of arms that had been delivered to Israel as part of the US military aid programme.

On 17 January 1986 the USA invoked its veto in the UN Security Council to prevent the adoption of a resolution deploring Israel's behaviour in southern Lebanon, where the presence of Israeli troops remained a source of conflict. On 30 January the USA vetoed a draft resolution, which had won the support of all Council members with the exception of Thailand, condemning Israel's actions over Islamic holy places in Jerusalem, where religious extremists had provoked Palestinian rioting by attempting to establish a Jewish foothold in the compound of the al-Aqsa mosque.

Peres was keen to gain credit for some progress in Arab–Israeli relations before surrendering power to Shamir under the terms of their power-sharing agreement. With Egypt proving unco-operative, and King Hussein ignoring repeated Israeli appeals to proceed to peace talks independently of the PLO, in February 1986 Peres resorted to the idea of 'imposing' a limited autonomy on the Palestinian inhabitants of the Occupied Territories. As with similar attempts in the past, the 'unilateral autonomy' plan quickly foundered in the face of Palestinian opposition that united pro-Jordanian and pro-PLO leaders in the West Bank, who refused to countenance anything short of an end to Israeli occupation.

SYRIA REARMED

The dashing of peace prospects was followed by rising tension between Israel and Syria, which had been re-equipped militarily by the USSR to the point where its forces threatened Israel's long-standing military supremacy. On 19 November 1985 the Israeli air force had shot down two Syrian *MiG* fighters, reportedly in Syrian airspace. In response, Syria deployed SAM missiles in eastern Lebanon, a move denounced by Israel as a threat to its reconnaissance flights over that country. Its own threat to destroy the missile sites provoked a crisis which could have escalated into armed conflict, and which was only defused by US mediation. The underlying tension between the two countries remained and President Assad made a defiant speech reasserting Syria's determination to recover the Golan Heights 'annexed' to Israel in 1981. In turn, Israeli military analysts began to discuss the possibility of a pre-emptive Israeli attack to prevent Syria achieving military parity with Israel. In mid-April the Syrian Government accused Israel of responsibility for a series of terrorist bomb attacks inside Syria, which claimed many lives, while Israel charged Syria with sponsoring Arab terrorism in Europe.

THE USA CLASHES WITH LIBYA

US mediation in the Middle East was effectively ruled out by the Reagan Administration's preoccupation with combating terrorism, at the expense of tackling the fundamental causes of regional violence and instability. This narrowly-focused policy led to a military exchange between the USA and

Libya, whose alleged sponsorship of international terrorism was apparently regarded by US policy-makers as the root cause of Middle East tension. On 24 March 1986, after *SAM-5* missiles had been fired at US aircraft, fighters from the US Sixth Fleet in the Mediterranean sank four Libyan patrol vessels in the Gulf of Sirte and destroyed shore-based missile and radar facilities near the town of Sirte. The pretext for the incident was a US challenge to Libya's claim that the entire Gulf constituted Libyan territorial waters. Two weeks later a bomb exploded at a nightclub in West Berlin, Germany, frequented by US servicemen, killing two people and injuring more than 200, in what the US Administration claimed was a Libyan-sponsored attack. In response US aircraft, including US Air Force bombers based in the United Kingdom, carried out air raids on Tripoli and Benghazi, which resulted in many civilian casualties, including family members of the Libyan leader, Col Muammar al-Qaddafi. The confrontation destroyed what little credibility the USA retained as a potential mediator in the Middle East conflict and many feared that, far from preventing terrorism, the US action would encourage it.

THE VANUNU AFFAIR

The international media focused on Israel's nuclear weapons capability with the arrival in London, in October 1986, of Mordechai Vanunu, a former employee at the so-called 'textile factory' at Dimona in the Negev Desert in southern Israel. Vanunu claimed that he had worked as a technician at Dimona and that Israel had succeeded in developing thermonuclear weapons, and was stockpiling them there. The true nature of the Dimona plant had long been common knowledge in the West, in spite of official Israeli denials, yet the Israeli Government's first reaction to Vanunu's 'defection' was to prohibit Israeli papers from reporting the affair. Subsequently, Vanunu was lured to Rome by a female agent of Mossad, the Israeli external security service, which then abducted him to Israel to stand trial for treason.

SUPPORT FOR AN INTERNATIONAL PEACE CONFERENCE

Hopes of a revival in the peace process had been rekindled on 12 September 1986 when Peres, only a month before the scheduled transfer of power to coalition partner Shamir, met President Mubarak in Alexandria. In a two-day summit, staged with the US and Israeli media very much in mind, the two leaders agreed, in principle, on the formation of a preparatory committee for an international conference to discuss the Arab–Israeli conflict. Such a conference, they agreed, should include the five permanent members of the UN Security Council, but the thorny issue of Arab, and particularly Palestinian, representation was left untouched. Support for an international conference grew to include King Hussein and the ministers of foreign affairs of the EC; the fact that clear backing, at least in principle, for such a conference had also been forthcoming from the USSR and the PLO, was a sign of both the range of possible delegates envisaged by the various parties concerned, and of how far the project was from becoming a reality since the two main protagonists, Israel and the PLO, were no nearer the required goal of mutual recognition.

SHAMIR ASSUMES THE PREMIERSHIP OF ISRAEL

In Israel, the major obstacle to an international conference was the assumption of power, on 16 October 1986, of Shamir, in accordance with the rotation agreement of September 1984 between the two main parties. Shamir unequivocally opposed such a conference. Peres, however, who became Minister of Foreign Affairs, made it quite clear that he had no intention of relinquishing the conference idea, and continued to promote it, causing great embarrassment to Shamir. Indeed, Peres travelled to Egypt on 22 February 1987 to meet President Mubarak, and both leaders made repeated visits to Washington, DC, to secure the support of the US Administration. The coalition Government appeared to be about to disintegrate on a number of occasions, but Peres failed to secure the necessary support in the Knesset for his Labour bloc to carry a motion of 'no confidence' in the Government, which would have precipitated a general election. From Peres' point of view, however, the danger inherent in forcing a general election was that it might leave Likud in a position to form a coalition which excluded Labour.

THE 'IRANGATE' SCANDAL

Having already seen its standing in the region plummet after a series of foreign-policy miscalculations, the final blow to the USA's credibility in Arab opinion came with the revelation, in November 1986, in the Lebanese magazine *Ash-Shira'*, of secret arms deals between Iran and the USA. The progressively more damaging disclosures which followed the publication of the article seriously undermined President Reagan's domestic popularity. It transpired that the arms contracts were brokered by Israeli arms merchants acting with the backing of the Israeli intelligence services and Government. From the perspective of links between Iran and Israel, the deal was not very unusual, Israel having been a major source of arms for Iran since the 1950s. On the other hand, the active part played by the USA, through its National Security Agency and with the clear knowledge and connivance of both President Reagan and many of his senior aides, was a stark contradiction of the USA's stated policy of not negotiating with regimes it held responsible for international terrorism. Israel originally convinced the USA of the desirability of the arms sales by claiming that they would help to bring about the release of a number of Western hostages held by Iranian-backed groups in Lebanon. An additional incentive was that the profits from the transaction could be used to circumvent US Congressional restrictions on aiding the Contra guerrillas who were waging, by their own admission, a campaign of terror against the legitimate, but socialist, Government of Nicaragua.

The USA's traditional allies in the Arab world were dismayed by this further demonstration of the way in which supporters of Israel seemed to be able to sway US foreign policy so easily, even against the USA's own stated interests. Israel's success in persuading the USA to sell to Iran the very weapons systems that it had only recently refused to sell to Jordan, a staunch ally, made the Arab states' sense of betrayal even more acute.

DEVELOPMENTS IN THE OCCUPIED TERRITORIES

In the Occupied Territories the cycle of repression and protest continued. The appointment by the Israeli military authorities of Arab mayors in three West

Bank towns was interpreted as part of a policy to isolate the PLO in the territories by fostering a more moderate Palestinian constituency and an alternative, 'acceptable', Palestinian leadership, and coincided with Jordanian efforts to the same end. These included the announcement in August 1986 of a five-year development plan for the West Bank and the Gaza Strip involving projected expenditure of US $1,300m. This apparent coincidence of interests resulted in the arrest and deportation of Akram Haniya, editor of the Jerusalem daily newspaper, *Ash-Sha'ab*. This action was regarded as a submission to Jordanian wishes—Haniya's hostility to Israel was no more threatening than that of any other newspaper editor in the Occupied Territories, but his aversion to King Hussein's plans in the West Bank clearly irritated the Jordanian authorities. This episode was the prelude to a series of demonstrations by Palestinians and arrests by the military authorities, interspersed with acts of violence against Palestinian communities by Israeli settlers. December began with a number of clashes between the Israeli army and Palestinian demonstrators, the worst occurring at Bir Zeit University, where two students were shot dead. The subsequent closure of Bir Zeit, as well as an-Najah University in Nablus, brought no reduction in the level of Palestinian protests or in the consequent level of Israeli reprisals.

THE 'WAR OF THE CAMPS' SPREADS IN LEBANON

Lebanon continued to stumble from crisis to crisis in the second half of 1986. With sporadic fighting in the south between Israel's proxy SLA and the various Lebanese, mainly Shi'ite, forces opposing it, elements of the Maronite Lebanese Forces (LF) militia, opposed to President Gemayel, attempted a *coup d'état* in east Beirut, which would have succeeded, but for the intervention of the Lebanese army. The failure of the coup was a blow to Syria's plans for a reconciliation of the many opposing forces in the country, for the Maronite forces loyal to President Gemayel remained the major obstacle to a Syrian-brokered peace plan. In the south violent clashes flared up between Amal and PLO forces in and around Tyre and Sidon. Paralleled by the so-called 'war of the camps' in south Beirut, these clashes, which ushered in a prolonged period of conflict between the two forces, were a clear indication of the extent to which armed Palestinians from various PLO factions had re-established themselves in Lebanon, particularly in the Palestinian refugee camps. To Syria, this PLO revival, particularly in the number of fighters loyal to Arafat, was another challenge to their hegemony over the country and to their bid to create an alternative PLO, independent of Arafat. Amal, as Syria's closest ally in Lebanon, was the only Lebanese militia involved in this conflict, and Damascus relied on its ability to crush the resurgence of Palestinian military strength. Another source of concern for Syria was that pro- and anti-Arafat fighters made common cause in the defence of the camps, and their shared resentment of the Syrian role in suppressing the PLO threatened to cause a reconciliation. By December, with over 500 dead, there was no sign of any respite in the fighting in Tyre, Sidon and Beirut. The refugee camps at the core of the conflict were besieged, with essential supplies from outside effectively cut off.

THE WAVE OF ABDUCTIONS IN LEBANON

It was not until January 1987, however, that the Western news media turned its attention back to Lebanon, with the return to Beirut on 12 January of Terry Waite, the special envoy of the Archbishop of Canterbury (the Primate of the Church of England). The purpose of Waite's mission, against which he was strongly warned by both the British Ambassador to Lebanon and the Archbishop himself, was to negotiate the release of the 20 remaining Western hostages being held in Beirut. The abduction of foreigners had begun in Beirut in early 1984, and by the time of Waite's second visit more than 60 such abductions had taken place, several of the hostages having been killed by their captors. No reliable figures are available for the numbers of Lebanese who had been abducted, many never to be seen again, since the civil war began. Waite himself disappeared on 21 January 1987 and remained in captivity until the end of 1991. Shi'a Muslims in the pay of Iran were believed to be responsible for his abduction.

Waite's disappearance, which was followed three days later by that of three US lecturers from the Beirut University College, provoked a strong response from the USA, whose Sixth Fleet was increasing its strength off the Lebanese coast. This deployment was backed up by calls for Westerners remaining in west Beirut to leave, as well as by strong criticism of the Iranian Government, which many held to be ultimately responsible for the abductions. Significantly, however, the group which held the three lecturers called itself 'Islamic Jihad for the Liberation of Palestine', and made its hostages' safe return dependent on Israel's release of 400 Arab prisoners. Whatever the true identity and motivation of the kidnappers, they drew attention to Israel's role in the Lebanese crisis, to the complexity of the problems affecting the Middle East, and to the need to address the fundamental problem of Palestine, as a precondition of a wider settlement.

Israel's involvement in Lebanon was by no means confined to the security zone that it had established to the north of its northern border, policed by the SLA with support from Israeli troops. Israeli air raids on Palestinian targets around Tyre and Sidon continued, and were usually claimed to be retaliation for mortar and *Katyusha* rocket attacks from south Lebanon into Galilee. On 2 January 1987 Israel intercepted a passenger ferry bound for the Maronite port of Jounieh from Larnaca, in Cyprus, accusing the LF of allowing PLO fighters to use the ferry to reach Lebanon and the Palestinian camps. This was neither the first time that Israel had impounded a Cyprus–Lebanon ferry, nor the first evidence of clandestine collaboration between Fatah and the Maronites loyal to President Gemayel. The Maronite leadership, presumably seeing little immediate prospect of relief from its traditional ally, Israel, sought instead to strengthen anti-Syrian forces in west Beirut.

SYRIAN TROOPS ASSERT THEIR AUTHORITY IN BEIRUT

Throughout January 1987, however, it became clear, as the 'war of the camps' continued, that the pro-Syrian nexus of Muslim forces in west Beirut was about to crumble. The Druze militia, the Sunni-dominated Parti Socialiste Progressiste (PSP) militia and the Shi'ite-dominated Hezbollah and Lebanese Communist Party militias had never shared Amal's enthusiasm for fighting the Palestinians. On several occasions the PSP had sent supplies into the camps and actively supported the besieged Palestinians. As a result, in February, open fighting broke out in Shi'ite areas between Amal and the Communists, supported by the PSP. Amal suffered a heavy defeat and this, coupled with increasingly heavy casualties sustained in the siege of Shatila and Bourj el-Barajneh, threatened Syria's position of influence in west Beirut, raising the prospect of an alliance of PLO and leftist forces in control of the city. With Western media attention arousing widespread international sympathy for the plight of the besieged Palestinians, President Assad decided to act. On 22 February some 4,000 Syrian troops occupied west Beirut, put an end to the clashes between the rival militias and lifted the siege of the Palestinian camps in Beirut, though Syrian influence failed permanently to relieve those in the south of Lebanon, and Syrian troops stopped short of precipitating a confrontation with Hezbollah by entering the Shi'a-dominated southern suburbs of Beirut.

PLO REUNIFICATION

The 'war of the camps' in Beirut resulted in another serious blow to President Assad's regional plans. Faced with Amal's onslaught and besieged in poorly fortified refugee camps, the disparate factions of the PLO had no choice but to unite on the ground in order to protect the Palestinian population whose defence was their ultimate *raison d'être* in Lebanon. After months of mediation by Algeria, Libya and, perhaps most significantly, the USSR, factions representing the majority of the PLO were finally brought together in March 1987. The principal rebel groups, the DFLP, the Palestine Communist Party (PCP), the two wings of the Palestine Liberation Front and the largest left-wing group, the PFLP, agreed to attend a session of the PNC, after agreement on key issues had been reached with Arafat. The PLO's reunification at the 18th session of the PNC in Algiers from 20–25 April appeared to signal an end to the post-1982 alignments within the movement. Resolutions adopted by the PNC confirmed the agreements between the factions made prior to the session. Under the agreements, Arafat undertook to abrogate the Amman accord between Jordan and the PLO and to downgrade co-operation with Egypt until that country formally rejected the Camp David agreements with Israel (the PFLP had initially demanded the immediate severing of links with Egypt); while the left-wing factions (principally the PFLP and the DFLP) endorsed Arafat's continued leadership of the movement, effectively emasculating the Syrian-backed Palestine National Salvation Front, based in Damascus.

The reunification caused genuine celebration among the Palestinians under Israeli rule, whose attempts at resistance had been severely limited by years of factional wrangling. It alienated the Arab front-line states, Jordan, Egypt and Syria, each of whom saw their future ability to manipulate the PLO seriously undermined. The Israeli leadership was evidently dismayed at the PNC's failure to relapse into internal division but, with the PLO thus isolated from the most important Arab states, Peres was able to predict a decline in its relevance to a solution of the Middle East conflict. Indeed, as far as the much-vaunted idea of a Middle East peace conference was concerned, the reunification of the PLO, which urged the rejection of the USA's terms for negotiation, specifically Resolution 242, if taken in isolation, underlined the problem of accommodating the PLO at such a conference. However, the PNC explicitly supported the idea of a conference, with the PLO as the sole representative of the Palestinians, a suggestion which remained unacceptable to Israel.

POLITICAL DEADLOCK IN ISRAEL

Frustration at Palestinian unity was reinforced by the bitter impasse within Israeli politics. The Labour-Likud coalition Government of national unity had only managed to survive thus far because each party feared the consequences of fresh elections. Despite indications of a significant lead for Labour in opinion polls in early 1987, the party was unable to rally enough support in the divided Knesset to be sure of winning a vote to dissolve parliament and force new elections. With the political parties divided on the fundamental issue of peace moves, polarization within Israeli society over the same issue was increasing. While Labour supporters became more and more frustrated with Shamir's dogged refusal in mid-1987 even to contemplate the possibility of an international conference, the Right grew increasingly contemptuous of what it saw as pandering to the Arabs with talk of 'land for peace'. Peres' visit to Washington, DC, in May confirmed the isolation of his Likud rival in the international arena. Peres' opinion of the form which a peace conference should take was given strong backing by George Shultz, who, however, was unwilling to bring pressure to bear on the Israeli Prime Minister to take a more flexible line.

September 1987 brought a direct attack on the PLO's status in the USA. Bowing to congressional pressure, the US State Department arrogated to itself the right to close the PLO's observer mission at the UN, in New York, and the Palestine Information Office in Washington, in spite of objections from US human rights groups protesting against what they believed to be a denial of freedom of speech. The move came as a surprise to US allies in Europe, who saw it as counterproductive to a proposed peace conference. With increased diplomatic activity by the USSR, which led to an improvement in Soviet relations with Israel, the proposed international conference was beginning to gather renewed support. The crucial obstacle remained the position of Shamir's Likud party, which remained firmly opposed to any form of conference conducted on the basis of an exchange of land for peace, and had not even conceded the notion of a conference with superpower or UN Security Council participation, whatever the terms of negotiation. With Shultz's visit to Moscow in October expected to cover the Middle East, it was widely hoped that he might bring some pressure to bear on Shamir during a brief visit to Israel. In the event, however, his views failed to make any impression on Shamir. Besides, the USA's Middle East preoccupations were, at this time, focused on developments in the conflict between Iran and Iraq, with the Arab–Israeli conflict of secondary importance.

ARAB PRIORITIES

Such preoccupations were also troubling the Arab states themselves. The Arab League summit meeting in Amman, in November 1987, had been convened primarily to consider the conflict between Iran and Iraq, and the Palestine issue had been moved well down the agenda. Faced with the deepening involvement of Kuwait and Saudi Arabia in the war, it was hoped that the Amman summit would unite the Arab nations against Iran. In fact, the summit was the first such gathering not to give the Palestine issue priority. Although the PLO's status as sole Palestinian representative was upheld, in spite of Syrian efforts to undermine it, it was only entrusted with joint responsibility, with Jordan and Syria, for drafting the meeting's Palestine resolution. With peace moves baulked and Israel seemingly entrenched in the Occupied Territories, there appeared to be little to distract Arab attention from Iran's perceived belligerence.

THE PALESTINIAN UPRISING

The events of the second week of December 1987 in the Gaza Strip and the West Bank took the international community by surprise. Thirteen Palestinian civilians were killed, 50 wounded and several hundred arrested in the most serious and sustained clashes between Palestinian youths and the Israeli army for many years. These confrontations proved to be the beginning of what has become known as the *intifada* (uprising), a mass Palestinian demonstration against Israeli rule, which surprised none more than the Palestinians themselves by continuing into the 1990s. A number of factors clearly played a part in creating the conditions that led to a revolt on such a scale.

Ten days of serious clashes took place in Gaza in October 1987, in which seven supporters of a resistance group new to the Occupied Territories, calling itself 'Islamic Jihad', were killed by the security forces. The very emergence of a radical fundamentalist group in Palestine was significant in itself; three of those killed had escaped from prison and returned to lead attacks on the Israeli forces and thereby greatly enhanced their popularity. As a result of this, the demonstrations which followed their deaths were particularly ferocious, but Israel was able eventually to restore order in the Strip. Indeed, the level of repression in the Occupied Territories was at its highest for many years: a large number of Palestinians had been 'administratively' detained (i.e. without trial) during 1987, and deportations, house demolitions, and other repressive measures were beginning to try the Palestinians' collective patience. The Amman summit itself was, doubtless, another factor in driving the Palestinians to revolt. At the time it was being held, widespread demonstrations were taking place in the Occupied Territories to protest at Arafat's cold reception in the Jordanian capital. The heavy-handed Israeli response provoked further clashes.

The spark that actually ignited the *intifada*, however, appears to have been a traffic accident. On 8 December 1987 an Israeli army lorry crashed into a car queuing at the road-block on the Gaza Strip's northern frontier, crushing four Palestinians to death. Few people believed it was an accident, and the Gaza Strip erupted in violent demonstrations. Quickly spreading to Nablus, the West Bank's largest town, the scale of the uprising caught the Israeli authorities quite unprepared. A panicked Israeli response—shooting on sight, harassing Muslim worshippers, attacking hospital patients and staff—was probably crucial in establishing and then maintaining the uprising's momentum. By the end of 1987, 28 Palestinians had been killed, the great majority in the Gaza Strip.

INTERNATIONAL REACTION TO THE INTIFADA

By mid-January 1988 it had become clear that what was under way in the Occupied Territories was a mass popular revolt. The Israeli authorities had adopted a series of severely repressive measures (including curfews and travel bans), none of which had brought the recalcitrant Palestinians to heel. One of the uprising's most notable achievements in its earlier stages was to attract international press, particularly television, coverage which was unprecedentedly hostile to Israel. Western TV viewers were shown footage of Israeli troops firing live bullets and tear gas at Palestinian demonstrators; most spectacularly on 15 January, when the security forces invaded the precincts of the al-Aqsa mosque in Jerusalem, and attacked worshippers. Israel's attempts to restrict press access to areas of unrest merely provoked media fury, attracting further criticism from the Western press, which previously had generally been sympathetic towards Israel. Other Israeli countermeasures included the imposition of a curfew in towns, villages and refugee camps, which caused serious absenteeism of Palestinian workers from their jobs in Israel (an estimated 120,000 Palestinians from the Occupied Territories worked in Israel), adding economic hardship to Israel's difficulties. But the most disturbing aspect of the *intifada*, from Israel's viewpoint, was the emergence, as early as January 1988, of an underground leadership (the Unified National Leadership of the Uprising—UNLU). The UNLU was composed of representatives of the various PLO factions and co-ordinated strikes and demonstrations. It issued regular, serialized communiqués which detailed day-to-day protest activities.

Lacking a coherent strategy in response to the uprising, Israel attempted various ways of undermining it. Apart from shooting at demonstrators (46 had been shot dead by 15 January 1988), mass arrests and other collective punishments, nine Palestinians were served with deportation orders on 3 January (in the face of international opposition), and a concerted campaign against the Palestinian press was launched, including the arrest and detention of many journalists, the closure of newspapers and press bureaux, and the imposition of stricter-than-usual military censorship.

Faced with mounting international censure over the high number of Palestinian casualties, the Israeli Minister of Defence, Rabin, issued new instructions to his troops in the Territories at the end of January 1988. Firing live ammunition at demonstrators was to be superseded by the widespread use of CS tear-gas and indiscriminate, pre-emptive, beatings. The spate of savage assaults by club-wielding Israeli soldiers on unarmed Palestinians recorded by television cameras were merely part of a campaign that lasted three weeks.

Israel's reputation was suffering particular damage in the USA, most significantly among the American Jewish community, its staunchest and most crucial source of support. Shocked by extensive TV coverage of violent scenes, American Jewish leaders began to voice the community's discontent to their Israeli counterparts and to the US Government. The Reagan Administration was further spurred to action by the visit of President Mubarak to Washington, DC, at the end of January. Mubarak emphasized the need for the USA to re-engage itself in the peace process. As a result, the USA prepared for a foreign-policy initiative in an area from which it would normally have remained aloof at the start of an election year. Philip Habib was reappointed Special Envoy and dispatched to Amman on 30 January to seek consultation with King Hussein.

The Arabs too were by now keenly aware of the *intifada*. An extraordinary meeting of Arab ministers of foreign affairs in Tunis, in January 1988, effectively reversed the previous deprioritization of the Palestine question, returning it to the top of the Arab world's agenda. Such was the response to the uprising in the Occupied Territories that a special fund was established, under PLO supervision, to which member states of the Arab League were to be obliged to contribute to 'ensure the continuation of the uprising'. EC Commissioner Claude Cheysson publicly condemned Israel's actions as 'shameful' and called for its 'evacuation' of the Occupied Territories. The incoming Chairman of the EC Council of Ministers, the West German Minister of Foreign Affairs, Hans-Dietrich Genscher, caused further embarrassment to Israel by stating his intention to make the Middle East the priority of his foreign policy during his six-month tenure. He made clear, with full EC support, his intention to seek a role for Europe in promoting plans for an international peace conference under UN auspices.

THE SHULTZ PLAN

Genscher's initiative (which led him to undertake visits to various regional capitals) was, however, overshadowed by that of his US counterpart, George Shultz, who made his first visit of 1988 to the Middle East on 25 February, impelled not so much by an overriding desire to settle the region's problems as equitably as possible (his record in office contained no previous diplomatic successes of any note, relating to the Arab–Israeli conflict), as by pressure from within the USA, particularly the Jewish community, to do something to relieve the pressure on Israel which the *intifada* had created. His plan was outlined by Richard Murphy, now the US Under-Secretary of State for Near Eastern and South Asian Affairs, on a preliminary visit to the region between 5 and 11 February. The plan proposed: a six-month period of negotiations, beginning on 1 May 1988, on the basis of UN Security Council Resolutions 242 and 338, between Israel and a joint Jordanian-Palestinian delegation, to determine a form of interim autonomy for the Occupied Territories, which would last for three years pending a permanent negotiated settlement; the provision in the interim agreement for an Israeli military withdrawal from the West Bank, and for municipal elections of Palestinian officials to be held during 1989; and negotiations on a final settlement, to be started by the end of 1988; both sets of negotiations to run concurrently with an international conference, involving the five permanent members of the UN Security Council and all other parties to the conflict, proceeding on the basis of UN Security Council Resolutions 242 and 338, but having no power to impose a settlement or veto any agreement reached in the separate Israeli-Jordanian-Palestinian negotiations (see Documents on Palestine, p. 360). The plan was fatally flawed. Some form of interim arrangement would clearly be a requirement of any peace plan, but the absence of PLO representation and the 'toothless' nature of the international conference would not endear Shultz's proposals to Arab governments, and the Israeli obstacle was well known. The time-scale for the plan's operation was an indication of the importance the USA attached to the peace process. However, another fundamental obstacle to the plan's acceptance was the Reagan Administration's lack of credibility in the Arab world. In the Arab view, the USA had done little or nothing in recent years to bring pressure to bear on Israel to reconsider its stance on peace negotiations—was it prepared to act differently now?

When Shultz visited the Middle East at the end of February 1988 to consult regional leaders, Israel's response to his plan, or, rather, the divided response of its two main leaders, was all too predictable: general endorsement, after some initial reservations, from Peres; outright rejection, after initial, hesitant interest, from Shamir. For the latter, the US plan had 'no prospect of implementation'; if Shultz advocated it too forcefully, Shamir believed, the Israeli Government would fall, and, given the new political climate engendered by the Palestinian uprising, Likud would win a majority of Knesset seats at the ensuing election. Egypt and Syria stopped short of an outright rejection of the plan, but Syria, in particular, gave no cause to suggest that it would in any way support its implementation. Jordan pronounced itself sceptical that Israel would relinquish control over the Territories and reiterated its opposition to 'partial or interim solutions', although it welcomed the USA's acceptance on 1 March of the concept of the Palestinians' 'legitimate rights'. The UNLU interpreted the Shultz plan as an attempt to abort the uprising and halt the political momentum it was generating world-wide in favour of Palestinian national rights. The PLO rejected the plan outright, as it made no provision for the creation of a Palestinian state and did not recognize the PLO's right to be involved in the peace negotiations. So, when Shultz returned to the USA, following another visit to the region at the beginning of March, it was with virtually nothing to show for his peace initiative. In his absence US TV cameras had continued to record Israel's repressive measures to suppress the uprising and the climate of sympathy for the Palestinians had not faded.

THE INTIFADA CONTINUES

In the Territories themselves, there had been no slackening in the intensity of the *intifada*. A total of 76 Palestinians had been shot dead by the end of February 1988; others were beaten to death or killed by exposure to CS tear-gas. Fifteen were victims of the gas (over 80 aborted pregnancies were also attributed to the exposure of the mothers to the gas) following its use in confined spaces (narrow alleyways or even inside people's homes), in contravention of the manufacturer's recommendations. (The chemical was sold, and is used elsewhere, as a means of crowd dispersal in open areas. At the beginning of May the manufacturers eventually agreed to ban its sale to Israel.) Meanwhile, arrests, beatings, press restrictions, deportations, prolonged curfews, the forced opening of shops (closed according to strike instructions issued by the Palestinian underground leadership), and the closure of schools and colleges, all continued to be employed by the Israeli authorities to contain the uprising.

NEW LEADERSHIP IN THE OCCUPIED TERRITORIES

In response, the Palestinians used a surprise weapon: unity. After its apparently spontaneous beginnings, it became clear to the Israeli authorities that the uprising was being carefully orchestrated. The degree of cohesion and co-ordination this gave to the various components of Palestinian society was unprecedented in its recent history. The solidarity engendered among Palestinians was the key factor in making the uprising viable on a prolonged basis. With clear support from Palestinians and Arabs inside pre-1967 Israel, and from many groups and individuals on the left of Israeli politics, the uprising had already made an indelible mark on Israeli society by March 1988.

Palestinian politics were also greatly affected. That the uprising was a spontaneous expression of popular frustration with Israel's rule and of the solidarity between Palestinian Christians and Muslims against Israel's oppression was undeniable, but it marked a new departure in that the PLO leadership outside the Occupied Territories was not instrumental in organizing and sustaining it. After initial reports of differences between the PLO in Tunis and the underground leadership in the Territories, a working relationship between the two was quickly established, principally to ensure the passage of funds from outside into the Territories, but also to co-ordinate, as far as possible, the political strategy of the PLO as a whole. (The new leadership in the Territories was unequivocal in its allegiance to the PLO.)

At the end of March 1988 the Israeli authorities intensified their crackdown on the rebellion. Telephone links between the Occupied Territories and the outside world were severed; restrictions were placed on movement between districts within the Territories, and between the Territories and Israel and Jordan; a 24-hour curfew was imposed on the entire Gaza Strip for three successive days. The restrictions, which were primarily intended to prevent a massive Palestinian demonstration planned for Land Day on 30 March (commemorating the killing in 1976 of six Israeli Arabs demonstrating against Israeli land seizures), also included the suspension of fuel supplies and severe restrictions on press and media access. The arrest and detention without trial of suspected leaders became more common. However, these measures only hardened Palestinian resolve. Local committees organized the distribution of food, fuel and other resources (as they also supervised strikes and the closure of shops, which the Israeli authorities attempted to keep open by force, to preserve an appearance of normality), as well as taking responsibility for security after a mass resignation of Palestinian policemen, who had been threatened with reprisals for co-operating with the occupying power. Solidarity between Palestinian communities on both sides of the pre-1967 frontier was, if anything, strengthened.

With battle-lines thus, uncompromisingly, drawn, Shultz returned to the Middle East in mid-April 1988. However, his efforts were obstructed by Shamir's obstinacy, and hamstrung by his own unwillingness to bring pressure to bear on the Israeli Prime Minister. Despite a loss of interest in the Western media, engendered chiefly by the restrictions Israel had imposed on reporting in the Occupied Territories, the *intifada* continued. Shootings, beatings, tear-gassing and other less 'telegenic' acts of violence remained the Israeli authorities' most visible means of combating the uprising. In addition, universities and schools were closed for four months, from April until the end of July; petrol supplies were periodically suspended; there were weeks of continuous night-time curfew throughout the Gaza Strip, and thousands of Palestinians were detained, many without trial, for six months, under martial law. By the end of July more than 290 Palestinians had been killed in the uprising and 28 deported. Fundamental changes had taken place in Palestinian society since the *intifada* began; old class divisions had begun to disintegrate, as the West Bank's urban élite found itself as dependent on home-produced food as the poorest peasant families. In such a climate, Israeli repression alone could not break the popular will to continue the uprising, which was now a central fact in the life of every Palestinian in the Occupied Territories, and a rallying point for Palestinians throughout the diaspora.

THE ASSASSINATION OF 'ABU JIHAD'

On 16 April 1988, in Tunis, an Israeli assassination squad killed Khalil al-Wazir (alias 'Abu Jihad'), Arafat's deputy as commander of the PLA. In the wave of ensuing demonstrations in the Occupied Territories, 16 Palestinians were killed in a single day. The assassination prompted a *rapprochement* between Arafat and President Assad, who had been at odds since 'Abu Musa', an al-Fatah dissident, led a Syrian-backed revolt in Lebanon against Arafat's leadership of the PLO in 1983. On 25 April 1988 Arafat and President Assad met in Damascus, where 'Abu Jihad' was buried, to discuss their differences. It was Arafat's first visit to Syria since his expulsion in June 1983. However, any prospect of a further improvement in relations was nullified by the renewal, in May 1988, of attempts by Syrian-backed PLO guerrillas, led by 'Abu Musa', to drive Arafat loyalists out of the Palestinian refugee camps in Beirut.

At the beginning of June 1988 an extraordinary summit meeting of the Arab League was held in Algiers to discuss the *intifada* and Middle East peace moves. The final communiqué of the summit, endorsed by all 21 League members, effectively rejected the Shultz Plan by demanding PLO participation in the proposed international peace conference and insisting on the Palestinians' right to self-determination and the establishment of an independent Palestinian state in the Occupied Territories (i.e. the principles of the 1982 Fez Plan). The summit hailed the 'heroic' Palestinian uprising and pledged all necessary assistance (including an unspecified amount of financial aid) to sustain it.

JORDAN SEVERS TIES WITH THE WEST BANK

On 28 July 1988 Jordan cancelled a US $1,300m. five-year development plan for the Occupied Territories, which had been launched in November 1986 but had failed to attract sufficient foreign funds. Then, two days later, King Hussein severed Jordan's 'administrative and legal links' with the West Bank, dissolving the House of Representatives (the lower house of the Jordanian National Assembly), where West Bank Palestinians occupied 30 of the 60 seats. The King explained that his actions were taken in accordance with the wishes of the PLO and the Arab League, as expressed in the resolutions of the Rabat summit of 1974, which recognized the PLO as the sole legitimate representative of the Palestinian people and which advocated the establishment of an independent Palestinian state in the West Bank, and in the peace plan proposed at the Fez summit of 1982. Commentators were quick to point out that King Hussein stopped short of actually repealing the annexation of the West Bank, which would have constituted a formal and irrevocable abrogation of Jordan's 38-year old ties with the region, while the dissolution of the House of Representatives would have little effect, as the Jordanian legislature had exerted little practical influence over affairs in the West Bank since the Israeli occupation in 1967.

King Hussein's decision to reduce Jordan's links with the West Bank was interpreted as partly a response to the Palestinian *intifada*, which had encouraged support among Palestinians for an independent Palestinian state, and partly as an attempt to persuade the PLO to accept responsibility for the Palestinian people and the peace process. It was suggested, however, that King Hussein considered the PLO constitutionally incapable of making the concessions necessary to the progress towards peace, and that the necessity of involving Jordan in any settlement would inevitably become apparent. In the short term, however, the effect of Jordan's actions was to strengthen the position of the Likud bloc (which had always ridiculed the Labour party's support for a Jordanian-Palestinian federation in the West Bank) in the period preceding the Israeli general election in November 1988. They also isolated the USA, whose peace initiatives, because they would not countenance negotiations involving the PLO, depended on Jordan's acting as interlocutor and forming part of a delegation representative of the Palestinians in any future peace talks.

To the PLO, King Hussein's move represented a considerable challenge. The Occupied Territories, with the exception of East Jerusalem, were now claimed *de jure* by no state as part of its sovereign territory, providing the PLO with an historic opportunity to assert sovereignty over a specific area. The PLO immediately began to make preparations regarding the issues of a provisional government and Palestinian statehood to be included on the agenda at the next session of the PNC in the autumn of 1988. In the Occupied Territories themselves, Jordan's severing of its ties with the West Bank was widely applauded. Communiqué No. 24 of the UNLU described the move as the *intifada's* 'greatest accomplishment'.

With Jordan's disengagement leaving the PLO the exclusive voice of Palestinian national aspirations, Arafat began to seek diplomatic support for a 'two-state' solution to the Arab–Israeli conflict. Addressing the European Parliament in Strasbourg, France, on 12 September 1988, he sought the EC's active endorsement for the PLO's strategy. In his speech, he made a number of new concessions, stating that the PLO was ready to negotiate with Israel at an international peace conference on the basis of the UN Security Council's Resolutions 242 and 338, and to seek 'reciprocal recognition', whereby, in return for Israeli recognition of an independent Palestinian state, the PLO would accept Israel's right to security. Arafat also repeated his declaration, made in Cairo in 1985, which eschewed armed action outside the Occupied Territories. Armed struggle within the Territories remained, Arafat said, a justifiable option for the Palestinians, although firearms were only used in isolated instances.

POPULAR COMMITTEES OUTLAWED

However, the general tactic of demonstrations and stone-throwing continued unabated, as did the Israeli authorities' counter-measures. Widespread demonstrations in Gaza on 14 August 1988 led to the imposition of a curfew throughout the Strip, and the protests spread to the West Bank during the following week. Here the two most immediate grievances were the deaths, by shooting, of two Palestinian political prisoners, and the deportation orders served on 25 activists on 17 August. The deportation orders provoked a spontaneous appeal for a three-day general strike in Nablus, Ramallah and Bethlehem. A military order (issued on the same day), outlawing the 'popular committees' (*lijan ash-sha'biya*), was of more far-reaching significance. Membership of the committees was declared to be an imprisonable offence, thus providing Israel with 'a more convenient legal means to deal with the institutionalization of the uprising', according to the Israeli Minister of Defence, Rabin. The popular committees had been established at a very early stage of the uprising to organize day-to-day activities, such as the distribution of food and other supplies, agriculture, medical care, education and security. When the committees were forced underground, it became more difficult both for them to function and for the authorities to monitor and suppress their activities. The Israeli intelligence services therefore increased their efforts to infiltrate Palestinian organizations, while the Palestinians, in turn, intensified their campaign of exposing, and often executing, people known to have collaborated with the Israeli authorities.

THE EFFECT OF THE INTIFADA ON PLO POLICY

Mass popular participation in 'grass-roots' organizations in the West Bank and Gaza had a major impact on PLO policy. The growth of the popular committees and the gradual, although partial, abrogation by Israeli state institutions of their role in the Territories encouraged Palestinian intellectuals to formulate ideas for the establishment of a provisional government for an independent Palestinian state. Despite the occupation, many national institutions had been established over the years, and, with the widening participation in the management of Palestinian society that was brought about by the *intifada*, they suggested the model for the structure of such a government. From a series of meetings of the Executive Committee of the PLO in August and September 1988, there emerged two basic proposals for debate at the meeting of the PNC in Algiers in November. The first was for the declaration of an independent state in the West Bank and Gaza, and advocated the establishment of a provisional government. The second recommended that the Occupied Territories be placed under the trusteeship of the UN, pending a settlement of the conflict.

DECLARATION OF PALESTINIAN INDEPENDENCE

The 19th session of the PNC, held in Algeria on 12–15 November 1988, brought together all the major factions of the PLO, including those based in Damascus. As expected, the PNC unilaterally declared the establishment of the independent State of Palestine, with its capital at Jerusalem. The UN General Assembly's Resolution 181 (see Documents on Palestine, p. 330) had provided the principle for Palestinian statehood in 1947, proposing the partition of Palestine into two states with defined borders. However, the declaration of independence left open the question of the new state's territory. The state was declared to be established, 'relying on the authority bestowed by international legitimacy as embodied in the resolutions of the United Nations since 1947', no mention being made of the specific details of any particular resolution, other than the principle of partition (and, thereby, a Palestinian state) in Resolution 181.

The UN General Assembly's Resolution 181 stipulated specific borders for two states in Palestine, while the UN Security Council's Resolution 242 of 1967 urged Israel to withdraw from territories occupied in the 1967 war. The borders that had been established by the 1948–49 Armistice Agreements between Israel, Egypt, Jordan, Lebanon and Syria, since they were 'dictated exclusively by military and not political considerations', gave Israel no technical right, under international law, to territories other than those designated by Resolution 181, which it had occupied in the hostilities of 1947–48. According to a strict interpretation of the international legal status of the former British Mandated

Territory of Palestine, the declaration of an independent Palestinian state could have made reference to a specific territory, and many delegates representing the Occupied Territories at the PNC's 19th session urged such a move, and the creation of a provisional government. Prior to the meeting, however, there had been considerable disagreement within the PLO regarding the composition of such a government, and it was decided to refer the matter back to the Executive Committee for further consideration. The Executive Committee, it was decided, would function as an *ad hoc* government.

ACCEPTANCE OF RESOLUTION 242

Another source of controversy was the question of the UN Security Council's Resolution 242. For many years, the USA, supported by Israel, had demanded that the PLO should accept its provisions. However, since this Resolution sought 'respect for the sovereignty, territorial integrity and political independence of every state in the area', such a concession would amount to recognition of the State of Israel. As the Fez Arab summit proposal of 1982, endorsed by the PLO, explicitly recognized Israel's existence, the PLO had already effectively recognized Israel. It had, furthermore, repeatedly stated its acceptance of all the pertinent UN resolutions. At the 19th session of the PNC in Algiers, Arafat and others within Fatah wanted to accept Resolution 242 'in isolation', in order to appease and encourage the USA. However, left-wing factions within the wider Palestinian movement, as well as many Fatah cadres, forced the leadership to adopt a compromise formula: the PLO's acceptance of Resolution 242 was, in conjunction with Palestinian rights of self-determination and to international legality on the basis of UN resolutions, to provide the basis of an international peace conference. In a press conference at the end of the PNC session, Arafat was explicit: he sought acceptance of UN Security Council Resolution 242 as a mandate 'to actively pursue peace', and challenged the USA to respond to the PLO's overtures.

RESPONSES TO THE DECLARATION OF INDEPENDENCE

By the time that the 19th session of the PNC took place, the Israeli general election had resulted in a narrow victory (but not a clear parliamentary majority) for Shamir's Likud party, while, in the USA, a Republican President had again been returned to power and the Democrats retained control of Congress. Shamir dismissed the results of the 19th PNC session as 'tactical moves devoid of any importance'. The response of the outgoing US Administration was more damaging. Invited to address the UN General Assembly in New York in December 1988, Arafat and his aides had to obtain visas to enter the USA. On the personal instructions of George Shultz, the visas were denied. Elsewhere in the world, however, the PNC's declaration of independence encountered more favourable responses. By the time that Shultz had banned Arafat from entering the USA, more than 60 states, including two permanent members of the UN Security Council (China and the USSR), had recognized the State of Palestine. Although the 12 members of the EC had not recognized the new state, they welcomed the decisions of the 19th PNC session as a 'positive step forward', and continued, with the backing of the USSR, to support the PLO's appeal for the convening of an international peace conference.

ARAFAT ADDRESSES THE UN GENERAL ASSEMBLY

Arafat eventually addressed the UN General Assembly on 13 December 1988, the meeting having been relocated to Geneva, Switzerland, where he made a number of historic concessions. Inviting the 'leaders of Israel' to join him in reaching a peace agreement, Arafat presented the General Assembly with a three-point programme, the main proposals of which were that the UN Secretary-General should establish a preparatory committee for an international peace conference; that the Occupied Territories should be brought under the temporary supervision of UN forces, which would oversee Israel's withdrawal; and that there should be a comprehensive settlement, among the parties concerned, including Israel, at an international peace conference to be held on the basis of UN Security Council Resolutions 242 and 338. In his address, Arafat explicitly recognized Israel and rejected 'terrorism', as the USA had demanded.

Shamir dismissed Arafat's address as a 'public relations exercise'. Its impact on the attitude of the USA towards the PLO was, nevertheless, alarming enough to persuade Shamir to disregard most of his party's differences with the Israeli Labour Party and to establish a new coalition government of national unity.

US RECOGNITION OF THE PLO

Although he found his Government almost completely isolated (in particular among its European allies) over its decision to ban Arafat from entering the USA, Shultz still refused to acknowledge that Arafat had conceded anything previously demanded of him by the USA. Following Arafat's address in Geneva, it required hours of intense Swedish diplomacy to detail the concessions asked of the PLO in words which the USA would find unambiguous. Even then, it took pressure from the incoming Administration of President-elect George Bush to convince Shultz. On 16 December 1988 the US Ambassador to Tunisia, Robert Pelletreau, held talks lasting 90 minutes with two representatives of the PLO. The USA had finally recognized the PLO. At the meeting, it was agreed that the dialogue should be maintained, and a second session of talks was planned for 20 January 1989. The PLO thus achieved its most important diplomatic breakthrough, although it did not necessarily expect any concrete advances in the peace process to follow quickly.

THE FIRST YEAR OF THE INTIFADA

In the Occupied Territories, the outcome of the 19th session of the PNC was greeted with widespread jubilation, and the declaration of independence was regarded as the greatest achievement of the *intifada*. The opening of a dialogue between the PLO and the USA was also widely perceived as a victory for the uprising, although many in the Occupied Territories feared that Arafat had conceded too much in return for too few guarantees. By the end of 1988, with more than 300 Palestinians shot dead and another 100 killed by other means in the first year of the uprising, a widespread pessimism had developed among the population of the Territories.

Apart from momentary lulls, there was no relaxation of the uprising. Palestinian protesters were still able to surprise the Israeli authorities by means of an underground network. Furthermore, despite the emergence of an autonomous Islamist fundamentalist group in Gaza (the Islamic Resistance Movement, allied to the Muslim Brotherhood and known by its Arab acronym, Hamas), both the UNLU and the people at large had managed to maintain unity of action and purpose. Israel's only real resort remained brute force.

The use of pre-emptive beatings to suppress the uprising, espoused by Rabin in early 1988, gave way to the more widespread use of plastic and rubber bullets, many of which also contained lead, and which, contrary to official guide-lines, were often discharged at very close range. On 18 December violent demonstrations erupted in Nablus after troops opened fire on a funeral procession, killing two people. The Israeli authorities reacted severely and a further eight Palestinians were killed, and a curfew was imposed on the city for six consecutive days. By 16 January 1989 a total of 31 Palestinians had been killed, and more than 1,000 wounded, in confrontations with troops, as the indiscriminate firing of 'non-lethal' ammunition into crowds of demonstrators became commonplace. A further alarming development was the emergence of Israeli 'death-squads' which sought out, and attempted to liquidate, leaders of the uprising.

ISRAEL'S DIPLOMATIC INITIATIVE

Meanwhile, there were signs that Israel was preparing to announce a diplomatic initiative. Pressure from the USA and Europe, from both governments and Jewish communities, for Israel to redeem its image, together with condemnations of the high number of casualties, led to rumours that Shamir intended to reveal the initiative when he made his first visit to Washington, DC, since the election of President Bush.

However, even after the dialogue between the USA and the PLO had begun, and most Arab states had expressed support for Arafat's strategy, Shamir could still say, in January 1989, that 'nothing has changed' and that the 'Arab intention is the same: the destruction of Israel'. It was surprising, therefore, to learn that discussions had been taking place between Israeli officials and a prominent Jerusalem Palestinian, Faisal Husseini, the head of the Arab Studies Centre in Jerusalem, since the beginning of 1989. Despite this diplomatic initiative, there was no sign of an end to Israel's use of brutal methods to suppress the uprising. Indeed, discussions of Israeli concessions caused further problems for Palestinian communities in the form of attacks by Israeli settlers in the West Bank and Gaza. The death of a West Bank settler in February 1989 provoked a series of revenge attacks on the town of Qalqilya and a raid on the village of Burin, near Nablus. It was alleged in the Knesset that a well-armed settlers' militia was operating in the West Bank. Further serious disturbances occurred in Rafah and Nablus at the end of February.

THE USSR ENDORSES THE PLO'S PROPOSALS

Diplomatic initiatives from the USA were slow to develop. A tour of the Middle East by the Soviet Minister of Foreign Affairs, Eduard Shevardnadze, in February 1989 emphasized the USA's inactivity, as he demonstrated, by his talks in Syria, Jordan, Egypt, Iran and Iraq, that the USSR was the only superpower able to talk freely to all parties to the Middle East conflict. With the exception of Israel's Likud party, all concerned agreed with Shevardnadze's proposal for the convening of an international peace conference.

THE USA CLARIFIES ITS POSITION

Despite a visit to Washington, DC, by the Israeli Minister of Foreign Affairs, Moshe Arens, in early March 1989, it became clear, when the dialogue between the USA and the PLO resumed, that the USA now accepted that the PLO was the only negotiating partner qualified to represent the Palestinians. However, several serious points of contention remained, in particular the purpose of the dialogue itself, which the PLO regarded as a prelude to wider negotiations and, eventually, an international peace conference. The USA rejected this notion.

During Arens' visit to Washington, the US Government hinted that Israel might eventually have to negotiate with the PLO, and pressure on Israel to formulate peace plans intensified. By the time that Prime Minister Shamir met President Bush in Washington on 6 April 1989, the details of his peace plan were widely known. Based largely on the proposals that Minister of Defence Rabin had presented, the plan offered 'free and democratic' elections in the Occupied Territories in return for the ending of the *intifada*. The elections, according to Shamir's plan, would produce a delegation to conduct negotiations with Israel for a permanent settlement. The USA gave its cautious approval to the plan, while Palestinians, both inside and outside the Territories, sought more specific details and attached a number of conditions to their acceptance of it. Israeli right-wing parties condemned the proposals and demanded a firmer suppression of the *intifada*.

THE VIOLENCE ESCALATES

April 1989 was one of the *intifada's* bloodiest months, with the death toll since the outbreak of the uprising surpassing 500. The worst atrocity of the uprising to date occurred on 7 April at the village of Nahalin, near Bethlehem. Members of the Israeli border police entered the village early in the morning and attacked people leaving a mosque, killing five and injuring more than 50. Violence in Gaza on 22–23 April left a further two people dead and 87 injured.

In Gaza, following violent disturbances during the Islamic festival of Id al-Fitr, three Palestinians were shot dead, and more than 400 wounded, as troops fired 'plastic' bullets and canisters of CS tear-gas into crowds. On 8 May 1989 the territory was sealed off, with border crossings closed and telephone connections severed. An indefinite curfew was imposed, which continued until the end of the month, when the Israeli authorities began to issue identity cards to all Gazans with a record of political activity, effectively denying them entry into Israel.

PALESTINIANS' RESPONSE TO ISRAEL'S PLAN
FOR PEACE

These tougher measures were in accordance with Minister of Defence Rabin's warning, issued on 15 May 1989, when he threatened Palestinians with greater repression if they did not accept the Israeli Government's peace proposals. However, the leadership of the *intifada* and of the PLO in Tunis remained adamant that certain conditions must be satisfied before the plans could be accepted, although they did not reject the proposals outright. Full details of the Israeli peace plan were disclosed after its approval by the Knesset on 14 May.

The plan was similar to the Camp David proposals in many respects. Its failure to clarify either who would be eligible to be a candidate or to vote in the proposed elections or the status of the residents of East Jerusalem; its reiteration of Israel's opposition to the creation of a Palestinian state and its proviso that no change in the status of the Territories could take place without the consent of the Israeli Government, all fell short of what was acceptable not only to the Palestinians and the USSR, but also to the EC states. However, the plan made too many concessions for right-wing opinion in Israel, and its announcement provoked threats by settlers to establish their own independent state on the West Bank if Israel ever agreed to relinquish the territory.

PRESSURE ON ISRAEL INCREASES

In early May 1989 Arafat was invited by President Franççois Mitterrand of France to make an official visit to Paris. The visit was a great success, especially after Arafat declared that the Palestinian National Charter (or PLO Covenant— see Documents on Palestine, p. 333) had been superseded by the resolutions of the Algiers session of the PNC in November 1988. Israel was sufficiently disturbed by the success of Arafat's visit to Paris for Shamir to begin a European tour two weeks later, fearing, perhaps, that the PLO's publicity exercise might be repeated in other European capitals.

The USA was also beginning to give the Israeli Government cause for alarm. Shamir's visit to Washington, DC, had coincided with that of Egypt's President Mubarak, to whom President Bush had confided that the US Government shared Egypt's aim of ending Israel's occupation of the West Bank and Gaza. A warning by the USA that the time had come for Israel to renounce the idea of maintaining its control over the Territories, and the USA's description of the vision of a Greater Israel as 'unrealistic', caused further anxiety. The USA seemed to be gradually distancing itself from the policy of almost unquestioned support for Israel which had characterized President Reagan's term of office. In July 1989, however, in order to appease critics of Israel's peace initiative within the Likud, Shamir agreed to a resolution which added four principles to the original plan. These clarified four areas of the initiative which had deliberately been left ambiguous to avoid alienating the USA and the PLO from the outset. They stipulated that residents of East Jerusalem would not be permitted to participate in the proposed elections in the West Bank and in Gaza; that violent attacks by Palestinians must cease before elections could be held in the Occupied Territories; that Jewish settlement should continue in the Territories and that foreign sovereignty should not be conceded in any part of Israel; and that the establish- ment of a Palestinian state west of the River Jordan was out of the question, as were negotiations with the PLO. In response, the leadership of Israel's Labour Party recommended that the Party should withdraw from the coalition Government. At the end of July, however, it was reported that the Israeli Cabinet had voted in favour of endorsing the peace plan in its original form.

The *intifada* continued unabated throughout the summer of 1989. On 19 June the deportation of a further eight Palestinians was ordered, giving rise to more street protests, and in August the newly appointed commander of Israeli forces in the West Bank, Itzhak Mordechai, issued an order permitting troops to open fire on Palestinians who wore face masks during demonstrations. An increase in raids on Palestinian villages by the IDF, together with the deliberate targeting of organizers of the popular committees, contributed to a rising casualty toll.

In Gaza, meanwhile, a fierce battle of wills developed between the local population and the Israeli authorities over the introduction of new identity cards. The Israelis stipulated that possession of a new, computer-readable, magnetic identity card was necessary for all those travelling outside of the Gaza Strip. However, such cards would only be issued to those Palestinians who acquired security clearance and who could prove they were up-to-date with payment of taxes. As the majority of Gazans earned their living inside Israel, the Israeli authorities hoped that economic pressure would force them to accept the new identity cards. The popular committees responded by urging a boycott of the new identity cards, which were confiscated as soon as they were issued. By mid-July 1989 so few Gazans were reporting for work in Israel that employers pressurized the IDF into allowing some Gazans to leave the Gaza Strip without identity cards. However, fearing the financial hardships of a prolonged boycott, the UNLU eventually abandoned it.

Acts of communal resistance persisted in the West Bank. In Beit Sahur, a small Christian town near Bethlehem, residents had observed a total boycott of tax payments ever since the UNLU had first called for payments to the civil administration to be withheld. A six-week campaign to break the boycott was launched by the Israeli authorities in 1989. It began with arrests, the imposition of lengthy curfews and the cutting of electricity and telephone lines, and ended with the blockading of the town and the confiscation of property in lieu of payment.

Despite the defiance in Beit Sahour and the struggle against the new identity cards in Gaza, there were signs that a combination of exhaustion and frustration at the lack of political return was fostering extremism. At the end of June 1989 a US aid worker was the victim of an unprecedented abduction in Gaza and two weeks later 14 people were killed when a young Palestinian seized control of an Israeli bus in which they were travelling and sent it crashing down a ravine.

MUBARAK'S ATTEMPT TO RESTART THE PEACE PROCESS

In mid-September 1989 President Mubarak of Egypt attempted to restart the peace process by asking the Israeli Government to clarify 10 points concerning the procedure and substance of Shamir's peace plan. Mubarak sought commitment to the principle of exchanging land for peace and the participation of the residents of East Jerusalem in the plan's proposed election. At the same time, Mubarak offered to convene an early meeting of Israeli and Palestinian delegations to discuss the details of the election. The US Government had been privy to Mubarak's proposals since mid-July, but had cautioned against making them public in the hope that the Israeli Government would be able to sustain what was, after all, its own peace initiative. The fact that President Bush had now permitted Mubarak to announce an initiative of his own revealed the US Administration's ebbing faith in the Israeli Government.

The reaction of the Israeli Government to Mubarak's initiative was divided. Peres voiced his support, while Shamir stated his opposition and spoke of the need 'to fight off grave threats'. No formal rejection was sent to Cairo, but the

Israeli Prime Minister was clearly irritated by the Egyptian Government's attempt to usurp his peace initiative. Both Mubarak and the US Secretary of State, James Baker, anxious not to further alienate Shamir, insisted that the Egyptian proposal was merely a supplement to his plan, not a replacement. By mid-October, however, it was clear that the USA was failing to persuade Likud to embrace the revised peace proposals. Shamir and Arens did not regard Mubarak's 10 points as a basis for negotiations, nor would they agree to talks with a Palestinian delegation which had any connection whatsoever with the PLO. In a final attempt to keep the peace initiative alive, Baker put forward five proposals (the 'Baker plan') which aimed to remove Israeli objections. Essentially, Baker proposed that acceptance of Mubarak's 10 points should not be a precondition for participation in the Cairo talks and that the composition of the Palestinian delegation should be decided by the Governments of Israel, the USA and Egypt.

PLO'S FORMAL RESPONSE TO THE 'SHAMIR PLAN'

The 'Shamir plan' and the subsequent attempts to modify it aroused little enthusiasm in Palestinians or the PLO, who were convinced that Shamir had only conceived his peace initiative as a concession to the USA, and in order to pressurize the Palestinians. Moreover, the PLO believed that Mubarak's clarifications of the 'Shamir plan' still fell short of its own minimum negotiating position. At a meeting of the PLO's central council in Baghdad, Iraq, in October 1989, the PLO stated that the negotiating team should be selected by the PLO and should comprise Palestinians from both inside the Occupied Territories and the Palestinian diaspora; and that the dialogue should be attended by the five permanent members of the UN Security Council and should constitute the preliminary stage in the convening of an international peace conference.

Although the gulf between the 'Baker plan' and the PLO's response appeared to be unbridgeable, the PLO was not keen to be seen to officially abandon a peace initiative which was being promoted by the USA. Privately, however, PLO officials complained that the USA was ignoring the need for the PLO to play a role in the peace process while, at the same time, seeking its support for the same process. The USA's insistence that its endorsement of the peace process should be private rather than public so as not to deter Israel was also criticized by the PLO.

EXECUTION OF COLLABORATORS

Within the Occupied Territories opposition to the Baker proposals was widespread and was expressed in the underground communiqués of the UNLU. However, during the latter half of 1989 another issue drew the attention of the international media. The execution of Palestinians suspected of collaborating with the Israeli security forces had been accepted as necessary by most Palestinians, especially after it emerged that Israel had organized 'hit squads' of its own. During the second half of 1989, however, there was a dramatic increase in the killing of collaborators. Palestinian leaders began to fear that unless the killing was checked it might legitimize the use of violence to resolve factional disputes; they also recognized that the death of Palestinians at the hands of other Palestinians was a public-relations disaster.

By the beginning of October 1989 the UNLU was urging the popular committees to show maximum restraint in their dealings with suspected collaborators. The activities of vigilante groups, such as the Red Eagles and the Black Panthers, were ultimately halted by the Israeli authorities. However, the widespread mourning and disturbances following the deaths of their members demonstrated to the UNLU and to the PLO that as the *intifada* approached the end of its second year, the political stalemate inside the Territories and the diplomatic impasse outside was strengthening the hand of radicals.

DIVISIONS WITHIN THE ISRAELI GOVERNMENT

There were few signs from Israel that the 'Baker plan' was improving the prospect of an Israeli-Palestinian dialogue in Cairo. Peres had signalled Labour's readiness to talk to a Palestinian delegation composed of deportees living outside the Occupied Territories as well as pro-PLO personalities from within the Territories. For Shamir, this was tantamount to talking to the PLO itself and he warned that Israel would boycott any talks with a delegation endorsed by the PLO. Moreover, in what amounted to a significant retreat from the terms of the original 'Shamir plan', the Israeli leadership demanded a guarantee that at any future meeting discussion would be confined to electoral procedure and would not address the question of a final settlement. In a visit to Washington, DC, in November 1989, Shamir failed to gain assurances on these questions, but did not face any real pressure from the US Government. In a private meeting with Shamir, President Bush reportedly criticized Israel's handling of the *intifada*, while Baker urged Israel to show greater flexibility towards the peace process. Shortly before Shamir's visit, however, the USA had once again vetoed a UN Security Council resolution criticizing Israeli policy in the West Bank and in Gaza, and at the end of the visit Shamir was confident enough to declare that 'tensions had been relieved' by his trip.

In a letter to President Bush, Arafat stated that Israeli intransigence was convincing Palestinians that Israel was not serious in its quest for peace and 'creating an atmosphere that rouses the radicals against the moderates'. The USA did not reply to the letter and, in a further rebuff, announced that it would withhold funds to the UN's Food and Agriculture Organization if it co-operated with the PLO over agricultural development in the Occupied Territories.

Divisions in the Israeli Cabinet intensified in 1990. After returning from a visit to Cairo at the end of January, Peres announced that he had the support of Rabin for withdrawing from the Government if there was no progress on the issue of the Israeli-Palestinian dialogue. Shamir also faced pressure from right-wing elements within Likud. At a meeting of Likud's central committee on 7 February 1990, the Minister of Trade, Sharon, the populist leader of the 'rejectionists', announced his resignation from the Cabinet. Sharon's resignation was ostensibly prompted by disagreement with Shamir over the 'Baker plan', but in reality it amounted to a thinly-veiled bid for the party leadership. While Shamir managed to retain the support of the majority of Likud members within the Knesset, the attempted *putsch* weakened his authority. It was followed, a few days later, by the decision of Itzhak Modai to withdraw his Liberal faction from Likud. On 21 February, with Shamir barely recovered from the dissent in his own ranks, Peres announced that he would give him two weeks to respond positively to the 'Baker plan' before withdrawing the Labour Party from the coalition. Moreover, the USA declared that further dilatory tactics by Israel might lead it to abandon the Middle East peace process altogether.

COLLAPSE OF THE COALITION

On 10 March 1990 Labour ministers walked out of a cabinet meeting after Shamir had refused to allow a vote on a proposal regarding the Cairo talks. Three days later, after Labour had stated its intention to vote with the opposition in favour of a 'no-confidence' motion against the Government, Shamir dismissed Peres from the Cabinet. The remaining Labour ministers immediately submitted their own resignations. In the ensuing 'no-confidence' debate, the small religious party, Shas, abstained, causing the collapse of the coalition. Israel's President, Chaim Herzog, granted Peres two weeks to form a Labour-led administration. Meanwhile, Shamir would continue as interim Prime Minister.

PROGRESS OF THE INTIFADA

The publication on 21 February 1990 of the US State Department's Country Reports on human rights indicated that, despite the lower profile of the Palestinian *intifada* in 1989, its second year had been as bloody and intense as its first. The US report claimed that 304 Palestinians had been killed by Israeli soldiers and settlers in the year under review, while a further 128 suspected Palestinian collaborators had been killed by other Palestinians and 13 Israelis had died in *intifada* incidents. Up to 20,000 Palestinians had been wounded, 26 deported and 164 homes demolished or partially sealed. At the beginning of 1990 9,138 Palestinians, more than 2% of the adult male population, were being detained, more than 1,200 without charge or trial. The Palestinian universities remained closed throughout 1989 and the schools for many months.

Throughout 1989 the UNLU coalition had maintained an operational unity, although factional tension was increasing. Disputes concerned the PLO's pursuit of a diplomatic solution to the Middle East conflict and the short-term tactics of the *intifada*. In general, the PCP was prepared to give qualified support to Fatah, and sought to maintain the momentum of the *intifada*. The traditionally radical PFLP put the least faith in talks and moderation, and, unlike the PCP, favoured the steady escalation of strikes, street confrontations and civil disobedience. The DFLP occupied a position between that of the PCP and that of the PFLP. In the first quarter of 1990 disagreements between DFLP 'hardliners', led by Naif Hawatmeh, and a more pragmatic faction led by Yasser Abd ar-Rabbuh, caused a serious rift in the party.

Relations within the Occupied Territories between the UNLU and Hamas remained strained, although in some areas a *modus vivendi* was achieved. Gaza remained the stronghold of Hamas and of the more militant Islamic Jihad organization. The latter enjoyed a revival in 1989, having been weakened by arrests and deportations in 1988. It remained strongly opposed to the PLO's diplomacy.

EMIGRATION OF SOVIET JEWS TO ISRAEL

Following the USSR's relaxation of restrictions on Jewish emigration in 1989, a reported upsurge of anti-semitism in the Russian Republic and the USA's decision to reduce the number of visas it issued to Soviet Jews, 1990 offered the prospect of a huge increase in the emigration of Soviet Jews to Israel. Shamir claimed that up to 1m. Soviet emigrants might settle in Israel. More realistic estimates put the number at 150,000, but, whatever the figure, an influx of immigrants was regarded as a fillip for the Israeli right. Increased immigration helped counter the demographic argument used by those Israelis who favoured a withdrawal from the Occupied Territories and argued for increased 'colonization' of the West Bank and Gaza. Shamir commented on 14 January 1990, 'We will need a lot of room to absorb everyone and every immigrant will go where he wants ... for a big immigration we will need a big and strong state'.

In Arab capitals and in the Occupied Territories the prospect of mass Jewish emigration to Israel, together with Shamir's statement, caused grave concern. King Hussein expressed a fear that the settlement of Jewish immigrants in the West Bank would presage the 'transfer' of the indigenous population to the East Bank, thus transforming the Hashemite Kingdom into a Palestinian state. Similar concern was expressed by the Arab League, which decided to send a high-level delegation to the superpowers and to the EC in order to discuss ways of reducing the flow of emigrants to Israel. Arafat conceded the right of Israel to accept Jewish refugees, but stated the PLO's opposition to the use of immigrants to perpetuate the occupation of the West Bank and Gaza. Within the Occupied Territories the UNLU urged the convening of an Arab summit meeting to debate the issue.

There was no clear evidence that Israel's Ministry of Immigrant Absorption was directing Soviet Jews to settle in the West Bank and in Gaza and only a small number were said to be considering making a home there. However, Israeli officials stated repeatedly that they would not discourage the new immigrants from settling in Judaea, Samaria and Gaza. Many of the new arrivals were already being directed to housing in occupied East Jerusalem. This caused considerable anger in the USA, from which Israel had requested an extra US $400m. to facilitate the absorption of Jewish immigrants, at a time when Israeli intransigence over the peace process was straining US–Israeli relations. In a noticeable departure from the policy of the Reagan Administrations, President Bush stated his Administration's strong opposition not only to the settlement of Jews in the West Bank and in Gaza, but also in East Jerusalem. This pronouncement on what Israel regarded as its 'undivided and eternal' capital would certainly have provoked an acrimonious confrontation, had it not been for the collapse of the Likud-Labour coalition in March. A few weeks earlier, the leader of the Republican Party in the US Senate, Robert Dole, had attacked another 'sacred cow' of US–Israeli relations by suggesting that the USA's aid programme to eastern Europe should be financed by a 5% cut in aid to the five principal recipients of US aid, of which Israel was the major beneficiary.

LABOUR'S FAILURE TO FORM A NEW GOVERNMENT

By mid-April 1990 Peres' attempts to form a new government had failed, despite the Labour leader's determination to persuade the orthodox religious parties to lend their support to a new, Labour-dominated coalition. As the chance to form a new government passed back to Shamir, the Minister of Defence in the former Government, Rabin, was reported to be considering challenging Peres for the leadership of the Labour Party. Meanwhile, both Peres' and Shamir's unseemly attempts to gain the support of the religious parties with lavish offers of cash and cabinet posts had prompted widespread disaffection among Israelis. On 7 April some 100,000 people gathered in Tel-Aviv to call for an end to such political 'horsetrading' and for the reform of the country's electoral system.

FURTHER ESCALATION OF VIOLENCE

Soviet immigration, and the continuing controversy over Israeli settlement policy, was continuing to raise tension in the Occupied Territories. On 9 March 1990 violent protests against the settlement of Soviet Jews in East Jerusalem led to the killing of two young Palestinians. One month later attempts by a nationalist-religious group to settle in the Christian quarter of Jerusalem's Old City provoked violent confrontations with Israel's security forces. Palestinian anger was deepened by revelations that the Israeli Government had funded the settlers' fraudulent purchase of a building belonging to the Greek Orthodox Church.

By May 1990 the situation in the Occupied Territories was extremely volatile. On 20 May a uniformed Israeli approached a group of Palestinians congregating at a roadside labour market in Rishon le Zion. After checking their identity cards, he opened fire with an automatic rifle, killing eight of them and wounding 10 more. Demonstrations erupted and attempts at suppression by the army were ignored. By the end of that week more than 20 Palestinians had been killed and, for only the second time since December 1987, Arab-populated regions inside Israel witnessed events of the *intifada*.

Following international criticism of Israel's response to the demonstrations, the US Government stated that it would consider an Arab-sponsored move to send UN observers to the Occupied Territories. At a specially convened session of the UN Security Council in Geneva, Switzerland, Arafat accused Israel of attempted 'genocide' in the Occupied Territories. While no agreement was reached to send the UN observers to the Territories, Israel was now arguably more isolated than at any other time in its 42-year history. Further, and more predictable, pressure came from the Arab summit meeting held in Baghdad, Iraq, at the end of May 1990 to discuss Soviet Jewish immigration to Israel and Western hostility to Iraq's reported attempts to develop a nuclear capability. The Iraqi leader, Saddam Hussain, reiterated his threat to unleash a chemical attack on Israel if it attacked Iraqi nuclear sites. The Jordanian delegation suggested that Israel was trying to engineer a war with Jordan as a means of expelling the Palestinian population from the West Bank. The USA was also criticized for its support of Israel and a pledge was made to honour a two-year-old promise of the Arab states to 'fund the *intifada*' at a rate of US $40m. per month.

NEW COALITION FORMED

The new Israeli coalition Government (an alliance of the Likud and small, right-wing religious groupings formed in early June 1990) was regarded as the least conciliatory in recent Israeli history, and unlikely to further the peace process. Rather, its very survival was dependent on its ability to appease those within the

Knesset who sought to prevent any future dialogue between Israel and the Palestinians. A further obstacle to the peace process was the decision of the USA on 20 June to suspend its dialogue with the PLO after the PLO had failed satisfactorily to condemn an abortive attempt by the PLF (led by Muhammad Abbas—'Abu Abbas', a member of the PLO's Executive Committee) to land guerrillas on Israel's Mediterranean coast in May. At the same time, in a formal letter to Shamir, President Bush questioned the commitment of the new Israeli Government to the revival of the Middle East peace process. The first talks between representatives of the USA and the new Israeli Government were held in late July 1990.

IRAQ INVADES KUWAIT

Iraq's invasion of Kuwait in August 1990 was not regarded with the same sense of outrage in the Arab world as it was in the West. Although few Arabs condoned Iraq's occupation of Kuwait, there were many who admired the Iraqi President, Saddam Hussain. At a time of considerable disillusion with Western attitudes towards the emigration of Soviet Jews to Israel, and with the US Administration's decision to terminate its dialogue with the PLO, the militant rhetoric of the Iraqi leader and his promises to use Iraq's formidable military strength to confront Israeli expansionism had been favourably received by the Arab masses. Kuwait, on the other hand, was resented both for its prosperity and for its pro-Western outlook. As Arab heads of state tried unsuccessfully to mediate between Iraq and Kuwait, two developments attracted popular support for Iraq. The first was Saddam Hussain's attempt to link Iraq's withdrawal from Kuwait to that of Israel from the Occupied Territories. The second was the decision of the USA to dispatch a large military force to the Gulf region in order, initially, to defend Saudi Arabia. What had begun as an act of aggression by one Arab state against another was now perceived by many Arabs as a confrontation between the forces of Arab nationalism and Western imperialism.

Many Palestinians, in particular, shared this perception. That the USA should act so swiftly to deter territorial conquest in Kuwait when it had effectively sustained such conquest in the areas occupied by Israel since 1967 was taken by Palestinians as proof of the West's hypocrisy and hostility to their cause. Saddam Hussain was swiftly championed as a saviour in the style of Nasser. By mid-August large pro-Iraqi demonstrations were taking place throughout the Occupied Territories and Jordan, and in the countries of the Maghreb.

THE POSITION OF THE PLO

The position of the PLO was far from clear at the outset of the new crisis in the Gulf. Privately, its leadership was said to be dismayed by the Iraqi invasion of Kuwait because it deflected attention from the *intifada* and created further divisions in the Arab world. However, the PLO's wish to broker an Arab solution to the crisis, together with its traditionally close ties to Iraq, made it reluctant to condemn the invasion. At the chaotic Arab summit meeting convened in Cairo on 10 August 1990 the PLO condemned Iraq's annexation of Kuwait, but abstained in the vote on whether to deploy a pan-Arab military force in Saudi Arabia. Furthermore, the PLO joined Algeria, Jordan, Tunisia and Yemen in denouncing the proposed deployment of US armed forces in the Gulf region.

On 19 August 1990 the PLO confirmed its opposition to the invasion of Kuwait in its first official statement on the crisis in the Gulf. Together with Jordan and Libya, it continued to attempt to act as a mediator, but with the US success in building an anti-Iraq coalition rapidly polarizing the Arab states, there was no sign of the consensus that was needed to make their proposals feasible. Instead, the concept of linkage of the Gulf conflict with the Palestinian question, popular support for Iraq and distrust of the USA all dictated that the PLO should align itself with Iraq. At the end of August 1990 Arafat issued a joint statement with the Iraqi leader in Baghdad, proclaiming that the Palestinians and the Iraqis were united in a common struggle against Israeli occupation and US military intervention in the Gulf. The political risks of such a firm alliance with Iraq were immense, but PLO officials argued that, given the mood of their constituency, they had no other option. Inside the Occupied Territories a special UNLU communiqué condemned the deployment of the US-led multinational force in Saudi Arabia and elsewhere in the Gulf region. It also upheld the rights of peoples to self-determination, but noticeably refrained from demanding Iraq's withdrawal from Kuwait.

The PLO's partisanship earned it the opprobrium of the West and alienated its principal financial supporters, Saudi Arabia and the Gulf states. Jordan, Sudan and Yemen, whose Governments were most hostile to Western military involvement in the Middle East, similarly had to endure the full weight of US and conservative Arab displeasure. Jordan, traditionally pro-Western and in the process of democratization, was subjected to particular criticism for having allowed a meeting of Arab nationalist and left-wing political parties to take place in Amman in mid-November 1990.

ISRAEL AS BENEFICIARY

Israel was one of the principal beneficiaries of the events which followed the invasion of Kuwait. It had until recently been internationally isolated for its procrastination over the peace process and the repression in the Occupied Territories; the Gulf crisis offered it the prospect of rehabilitation. Israeli leaders lost no time in restating their old claim that it was the lack of democracy in the Arab world, not Israel's occupation of Arab territory, which was the principal cause of instability in the region. The PLO's stance on the Iraqi invasion, they argued, conclusively validated their refusal to negotiate with it. Equally, the vociferous support in the West Bank and Gaza for Saddam Hussain confirmed Israel's wisdom in treading the path of diplomacy with caution, and maintaining its opposition to a Palestinian state.

Moreover, in President Bush's attempt to persuade Arab and majority Muslim states to participate in 'Operation Desert Shield', the codename for the deployment of the multinational force in Saudi Arabia, Israel also saw scope for political gain. The Israeli Prime Minister, Shamir, understood that Israeli military action against Iraq, like its attack in 1981 on Iraq's nuclear reactor, would be disastrous for the USA: it would spell the end of Arab involvement in the multinational force, a political if not a military prerequisite for its success, and would also threaten a wider conflagration in the Middle East. Israel hinted that its restraint would be conditional upon its receiving certain guarantees from the USA: of increased military and economic aid, and of an easing of pressure with regard to the peace process. Israel's Minister of Defence, Arens, also made it clear that, from an Israeli point of view, the only acceptable conclusion to the crisis would be one that included the dismantling of the Iraqi military machine.

THE PRICE OF ISRAEL'S SUPPORT FOR THE USA

Just as the USA had to pay for Israel's passivity, so it had to offer inducements for Arab governments to participate in the multinational force. The Gulf states, potentially vulnerable to further Iraqi aggression, needed little persuasion to do so. Egypt, Morocco and Syria were also in favour of deploying armed forces in Saudi Arabia, the Governments of Egypt and Syria being deeply mistrustful of Baathist Iraq. However, it was the prospect of economic aid and of influence in any post-crisis settlement which ultimately persuaded them to dispatch troops to fight alongside Americans against fellow Arabs. President Assad, a longstanding radical, and hence the most unlikely of the coalition partners, certainly expected the crisis to be followed by moves to end the Israeli occupation of Arab, including Syrian, territory. President Mubarak, who was anxious to see his country reinstated as the *primus inter pares* of the Arab world, aired the same concerns in discussions with his US and European counterparts.

The burden of conflicting expectations from Israel and the Arab states placed the USA in a delicate position. President Bush and his Secretary of State, Baker, had to avoid any linkage of the crisis in the Gulf with the Arab–Israeli conflict since this would effectively reward Saddam Hussain and displease Israel. At the same time, they had to reassure the Arab world. Speaking in September 1990, President Bush agreed that sooner rather than later the Arab–Israeli conflict had to be resolved. Nevertheless, he dismissed the possibility of an international conference on the issue in the near future. The EC states were more sensitive to Arab charges of hypocrisy over tackling the problems of the Middle East and hence to an implicit linkage of the occupation of Kuwait with other outstanding issues. During an emergency debate on the Gulf crisis in the British Parliament at the end of August 1990, members of all political parties spoke of the urgent need for a swift conclusion of the crisis, to be followed by the resolution of the Palestine problem. In an address to the UN General Assembly on 24 August, President Mitterrand of France proposed a timetable for the settlement of all the Middle East's problems. This would begin with an Iraqi declaration of intention to withdraw from Kuwait, but would also include direct dialogue between the concerned parties on the issues of Palestine, Lebanon and Israel's security. Moreover, at a meeting of EC ministers of foreign affairs in Paris in mid-September, the President of the EC Commission, Jacques Delors, warned Israel that once the Gulf crisis was over it would have to accept 'the legitimate rights of the Palestinians'. In addition, the Italian Minister of Foreign Affairs, Gianni de Michelis, who was acting as chairman of EC foreign-policy meetings, informed his Israeli counterpart, the newly appointed David Levy, that the Palestinians had a right to their own state.

EVENTS IN THE OCCUPIED TERRITORIES

Meanwhile, the Palestinian *intifada* continued, albeit with less intensity. Exhaustion, and the adoption of new tactics by Israel's Ministry of Defence (now led by Arens), contributed to the decrease in activity. Arens believed that intensive policing of population centres was largely counter-productive. Instead, he instructed the IDF to reduce its presence in the towns and villages of the West Bank and Gaza, and to redeploy troops on highways and at major road intersections. Fewer clashes and fewer Palestinian casualties resulted, but arrests and collective punishments continued. Palestinians were encouraged by Saddam Hussain's rhetoric, but the economic repercussions of the Gulf crisis were very damaging. Many Palestinian families relied on remittances from relatives working in Kuwait, and the loss of this income at a time when the population was already suffering economically caused severe hardship. Factionalism was another source of concern for the Palestinian leadership. In September 1990 fierce disputes in Gaza and some towns of the West Bank, between the nationalists of Fatah and the fundamentalists of Hamas, led to ugly street brawls and at least one death. Divisions within the DFLP also resulted in a *de facto* split, prompting a struggle for the control of its various front organizations, such as trade unions, women's committees and press offices.

Yet even while international attention was firmly fixed on the huge military deployment in the Gulf, events in the Occupied Territories continued to remind the world of the unresolved issue of Palestine. On 8 October 1990 at least 17 Palestinians were shot dead in the Old City of Jerusalem when a large crowd, protesting at an attempt by an extremist Israeli group to lay the symbolic cornerstone of the Third Temple on the Temple Mount, was indiscriminately fired on by Israeli security forces. News of the killings at Islam's third holiest shrine immediately precipitated a wave of protests which claimed a further three lives and left many injured. It was the bloodiest day yet of the *intifada*. Palestinian leaders in the Occupied Territories responded to the killings with an emotional appeal to the UN Security Council: 'We do not understand how oil in the Gulf can be more highly prized by you than Palestinian blood . . .' they wrote; 'we do not understand how the Security Council can ignore our pleas for protection when it is prepared to send troops to the Gulf region'. Moreover, the UNLU issued its most uncompromising communiqué so far, calling for a week of mourning and declaring that 'every soldier setting foot on the land of Palestine is a fair target to be liquidated'. Anxious to avoid charges of hypocrisy at such a sensitive time in Arab–US relations, the USA submitted a draft resolution to the UN Security Council condemning the Temple Mount killings. It also supported the decision of the UN Secretary-General to dispatch an investigative mission to Jerusalem. Although this fell short of the PLO's demand for UN protection for the population of the Occupied Territories, the USA's censure of Israel at the UN Security Council was significant for being the first vote of its kind for eight years. Predictably, Israel denounced the UN vote, and its decision to send a fact-finding mission to the Occupied Territories, as interference in its internal affairs. It declared that the UN representatives would only be admitted as 'tourists'. In an interview with the Israeli daily newspaper, *Ma'ariv*, Shamir castigated both President Bush and Baker for 'messing with Israel'. What they failed to understand, opined Shamir, 'is that Israel is Washington's only reliable ally'. The Arab League's own deliberations in Tunis on the Temple Mount killings ended in acrimony and confirmed the rift provoked by the Gulf crisis. A resolution which condemned the killings, but was also sharply critical of US bias towards Israel, was defeated by 11 votes to 10. In what was effectively a vote on the US military presence in the Gulf, only Morocco, facing mounting domestic criticism for having agreed to participate in the multinational force, confounded expectations by voting with the anti-US faction.

The killings of 8 October 1990 were followed by a spate of attacks by Palestinians on Israeli civilians and soldiers. The worst incidents occurred on 21 October, when three people were stabbed to death by a lone Palestinian in West Jerusalem, and at the beginning of December, when a series of attacks in Tel-Aviv claimed four lives and left several people injured. A number of Palestinians died in anti-Arab protests following the stabbings, and also in the violence precipitated by the assassination, in New York, of Rabbi Meir Kahane, the leader of the neo-fascist Kach movement. Nearly all the attacks by Palestinians were the work of individuals acting on their own initiative, although Hamas did claim responsibility for some of the murders in Tel-Aviv, and Islamic Jihad gave its complete support to a 'revolution of knives'. The PLO factions were more ambivalent in their attitude towards the stabbings: Faisal Husseini denied that the stabbing of Israeli civilians had been sanctioned by the leadership of the *intifada*; the UNLU spoke only of the need to employ 'all forms of resistance'; and graffiti praising the use of knives was signed by both Fatah and the PFLP. Shortly after the incident on 21 October, the Israeli Ministry of Defence ordered all Palestinians from the Occupied Territories working in Israel to return to their homes. The borders were sealed for four days, after which Arens declared an intention to reduce the number of Palestinians working inside the 'Green Line' and to bar altogether those with a record of activism. The announcement was welcomed by some Palestinians as a further step towards redefining the 'Green Line'.

UN SECURITY COUNCIL RESOLUTION 678

The passing of UN Security Council Resolution 678 on 29 November 1990, which effectively authorized the use of military force against Iraq if it had not withdrawn from Kuwait by 15 January 1991, considerably increased tension in the region. In Israel the authorities completed the distribution of gas masks to the civilian population and issued instructions on civil defence against attacks with chemical weapons. Only belatedly did they decide to provide masks to limited areas of the West Bank. Iraq and Israel continued to exchange threats, while Jordanians and Palestinians expressed fears that Israel might use the pretext of military conflict in the Gulf to drive Palestinians from the West Bank into Jordan. Palestinian support for Saddam Hussain remained high during the weeks preceding the UN deadline for Iraq's withdrawal from Kuwait, while the PLO's relations with the USA's Arab allies continued to deteriorate. The leader of the PLF, 'Abu Abbas', warned that his organization would strike against Western targets if hostilities erupted. In mid-December Israel's Prime Minister travelled to Washington, DC, for his first meeting with the US President in more than a year. The proximity of the deadline set by UN Resolution 678 ensured that the encounter was cordial, despite a strong undercurrent of mutual distrust. Shamir sought and received assurances that the Gulf crisis would not be resolved at Israel's expense. However, no promises were made on the question of aid for the settlement of the 200,000 Soviet Jews who had emigrated to Israel during 1990, or on the sale of arms by the USA to Arab participants in the multinational force.

There was a resurgence of the *intifada* at the beginning of 1991. Seven Palestinians were killed in protests linked to the anniversary, on 1 January 1991, of the founding of Arafat's Fatah organization. On 6 January Saddam Hussein declared that the impending military conflict would be a 'battle for the sake of Palestine'. After the failure of meetings in Geneva, Switzerland, on 9 January between the Iraqi Minister of Foreign Affairs, Tareq Aziz, and the US Secretary of State, war was generally accepted as inevitable.

IRAQ ATTACKS ISRAEL

On 19 January 1991, less than three days after the multinational force had begun a massive aerial bombardment of Iraq, Iraq launched an attack on Israel, firing adapted *Scud* missiles against Tel-Aviv and Haifa. The missiles were fitted with conventional, rather than chemical warheads, and although damage to buildings was considerable, casualties were light. Further attacks with *Scud* missiles on the nights of 20 and 22 January provoked panic, but resulted in only two deaths. The attacks drew immediate demands for retaliation from some senior Israeli military figures and politicians, but both the USA and the European members of the multinational force vigorously urged Israel to exercise restraint. Their concerns were obvious: while Arab states in the force had indicated that they would not be opposed to Israel taking appropriate and proportionate defensive action against an Iraqi attack, Syria and Egypt had made it quite clear that they could not remain aligned against Iraq if Israel were to attack it. Furthermore, Jordan had warned Israel that it would be forced to respond if there was any violation of its airspace. The US Administration backed its calls for restraint with an urgent airlift of *Patriot* anti-missile batteries to Tel-Aviv, and undertook to make the destruction of Iraq's mobile missile launchers a military priority. To be courted so attentively by the West after such a long period of soured relations was an agreeable novelty for Israel, and not one it had much incentive to jeopardize. Given the intensity of the bombing of Iraq, Israel's leaders were aware that any Israeli contribution to the campaign would be militarily insignificant as well as potentially catastrophic in political terms. Moreover, the Israeli Government knew that as long as the casualties from the *Scud* attacks remained minimal and chemical warheads were not employed, domestic pressure for retaliation would be containable. Shamir consequently assured the USA that there would be no unilateral retaliation by Israel. Immediate benefits were reaped from the policy of restraint: the USA indicated that it would provide funding for the development of Israel's anti-ballistic missile project, hitherto in some financial difficulty, while Germany promised up to US $1,000m. in military and economic aid. However, just as important for Israel's leaders was the wave of international sympathy for Israel which the Iraqi attacks provoked.

THE CONSEQUENCES OF IRAQ'S DEFEAT FOR THE PLO

Palestinians of the West Bank and Gaza endured a strict curfew for most of the duration of the war in the Gulf. The UNLU and Hamas instructed their supporters not to clash with the Israeli army during the curfew in order to avoid reprisals. Nevertheless, a number of people were shot and killed for curfew violations. The economic impact of the curfew was severe. According to Palestinian economists, losses to the local economy ranged between US $150m.–$200m., equivalent to approximately 8% of the gross domestic product (GDP) of the Occupied Territories.

The decisive defeat of Iraq by the multinational force in February 1991 left the PLO demoralized and in its most vulnerable state for several years. As expected, the GCC countries suspended their funding to the PLO, thereby raising the prospect of financial crisis. It was also made clear in the USA and the Gulf that the best chance of improving relations lay in a change in the PLO leadership. Overtures were made by Saudi Arabia and other GCC member states to anti-Arafat Palestinian groups based in Damascus, but, given the political radicalism and the small following of these factions, it was difficult to imagine what Saudi Arabia hoped to achieve. Within the PLO itself there were a number of senior figures, for the most part identified with the conservative wing of Fatah, who had voiced criticism of the Organization's support for Iraq and who could have formed the nucleus of a leadership acceptable to both Saudi Arabia and the USA. Yet the fact that the PLO had enjoyed overwhelming support among Palestinians for its stance on the Gulf crisis proved an important antidote to US and Arab hostility. The EC adopted a more pragmatic approach towards the PLO. At the conclusion of hostilities with Iraq it agreed to 'freeze' contacts at ministerial level. By the end of April 1991, however, the French Minister of Foreign Affairs, Roland Dumas, had met Arafat in Tripoli.

BAKER VISITS THE MIDDLE EAST

The Israeli Government drew comfort from the PLO's isolation, but was wary of the political pressures that might accompany the post-war search for a resolution of the Arab–Israeli conflict. As expected, Baker undertook several tours of the Middle East in the weeks following the end of the war. He hoped to persuade Israel and the Arab states which had participated in the multinational force to move towards mutual recognition, and to win support for a regional peace conference, to be sponsored by the USA and the USSR. It soon became clear, however, that these propositions were not acceptable to either side. Although Levy indicated that Israel would give its approval to such a regional conference if it led directly to bilateral talks, and conceded that issues like the status of the Golan Heights could be negotiated, these were not views shared by Shamir and most of his colleagues within the Likud. Rebuking Levy, Shamir stated his opposition to Soviet involvement in the Middle East peace process. He also opposed negotiating the future of the Golan Heights or making goodwill gestures to the Palestinian population of the West Bank and Gaza, as urged by Baker, as long as the *intifada* continued. After the US Secretary of State had held talks with leading pro-PLO figures in East Jerusalem, Shamir warned that Israel did not consider any of them to be suitable partners for negotiation.

Israel's Arab neighbours expressed their own reservations about Baker's proposals. After lengthy talks with Baker in Damascus, Syrian officials reaffirmed that Syria would only attend a peace conference held under UN sponsorship and based on the implementation of UN Security Council

Resolutions 242 and 338. Jordan and the PLO indicated that they were in full agreement with Syria. The PLO also voiced its suspicions that the concept of a regional conference had been promoted with the intention of normalizing Arab–Israeli relations and of avoiding the issue of Palestinian national rights. The PLO was relieved by the reluctance of the GCC states to open a dialogue with Israel. At the end of May 1991 PLO representatives made a rare visit to Damascus in order to discuss their common position with Syria on the peace process. Syrian officials also urged the PLO to readmit pro-Syrian Palestinian groups, including Fatah rebels from the 1983 revolt and the PFLP-GC, into the Organization.

Baker was reluctant to apportion blame for the lack of progress in his peace mission. However, the continued settlement of Soviet Jewish immigrants in the Occupied Territories angered the US Secretary of State enough for him to testify: 'I don't think there is any bigger obstacle to peace than the settlement activity that not only continues unabated but at an enhanced pace'. Further US pressure on Israel, regarded by much of the international community as essential if the opportunity for a peace agreement in the Middle East was not to be missed, did not materialize. Continued US arms supplies to Israel and the Gulf states, together with promises that the USA would guarantee Israel's regional military superiority, appeared to contradict President Bush's stated goal of working towards disarmament in the region, and heightened Arab cynicism about the US President's much-vaunted 'new world order'.

WORSENING CONDITIONS IN THE OCCUPIED TERRITORIES

There was little optimism in the Occupied Territories following the defeat of Iraq. After the lifting of the curfew many Palestinians discovered that they had lost their jobs in Israel to Soviet immigrants. Another series of knife attacks, including the killing of four women at a bus stop in Jerusalem in March 1991, prompted the Israeli authorities to impose further travel and employment restrictions. Only Palestinians with the requisite permits were allowed to enter Israel, including East Jerusalem. Those Palestinians fortunate enough to be issued with work permits had to be transported in buses to and from work by their employers. Those found working without permits faced fines or imprisonment. The result was soaring unemployment in the West Bank and in Gaza and the effective division of the West Bank into northern and southern zones. Concerns over the economic situation and continued Israeli settlement were raised in meetings with the US Secretary of State. There was debate within the Occupied Territories as to whether these meetings were appropriate, and the Palestinians who did meet Baker only did so after they had received the formal authorization of the PLO. Nevertheless, the US Administration's refusal to hold direct talks with the PLO led the Organization's Communist and PFLP affiliates to boycott the meetings.

Adding to Palestinian gloom was uncertainty over the direction of the *intifada*. The killing and intimidation of Palestinians by other Palestinians, increasing criminal activity and further outbreaks of violence between followers of Hamas and the PLO factions were causing much public alarm. Several articles appeared in the Arab press in the first half of 1991, urging an end to the killing of suspected collaborators and a complete reappraisal of *intifada* tactics.

Palestinian activists subsequently announced that the scale and frequency of strikes and demonstrations would be reduced, and efforts made to control the masked fugitives responsible for most of the *intifada's* excesses. The use of firearms against military targets was widely predicted. Calls were made for greater democracy within the PLO, including elections to the PNC. Senior Communist Party officials also challenged the Palestinian leadership over its uncritical support for Iraq during the Gulf War and for having unrealistically raised Palestinian expectations of an Iraqi victory.

THE SYRIAN-LEBANESE TREATY

In May 1991 the Lebanese and Syrian Presidents signed a treaty of 'fraternity, co-operation and friendship', confirming Syria's dominant role in the affairs of its neighbour. Israel condemned the treaty as tantamount to a Syrian takeover of Lebanon and as a threat to its security. On 3 June the Israeli air force launched its heaviest raids on Lebanon since 1982. At least 20 people were killed and many injured in a series of attacks on Palestinian and Lebanese militia targets in the south of the country.

NEGOTIATIONS WITH SYRIA

Meanwhile, PLO forces grouped around the Lebanese port of Sidon fell victim to the Lebanese Government's plan to disarm the country's militias and deploy the Lebanese army nationally. The attempts of PLO leaders to persuade the Lebanese Government that their forces should be exempt from the disarmament process, or at least that the process should be delayed until the rights of the country's Palestinian population had been formally safeguarded, were ignored. At the beginning of July 1991, in a brief but bloody battle, units of the Lebanese army expelled PLO fighters from positions above Sidon. The defeated Palestinians withdrew to the refugee camps and were subsequently forced to give an undertaking to surrender their heavy weaponry. The circumstances surrounding the PLO's loss of its sole military stronghold in Lebanon fuelled speculation that Syria, deprived of its Soviet sponsor, had reached an understanding with the USA whereby the latter would tolerate Syria's control over Lebanese affairs in return for President Assad's backing for the Bush Administration's Middle East peace plans. Palestinians expressed suspicions that Syria and the USA had been conspiring to ensure that the PLO remained militarily weakened and diplomatically isolated.

The extent to which the end of the Cold War had pushed Syria to revise its foreign policy was underlined in dramatic fashion in mid-July 1991. During Baker's fifth peace mission to the Middle East, it was announced that President Assad had acceded to US and Israeli conditions for the convening of a Middle East peace conference. Abandoning his long-held insistence that any conference on the Arab–Israeli dispute should have the coercive weight of the UN behind it, Assad gave his consent to a more symbolic gathering. Although based on UN Resolutions 242 and 338, this would only feature the UN in the role of an observer and would pave the way for direct negotiations between Israel and its Arab adversaries. Assad agreed to a joint Soviet-US chairing of the proposed conference with EC observers also present.

TOWARDS A PEACE CONFERENCE

The Syrian *volte face* was swiftly followed by Egyptian, Jordanian and Lebanese acceptance of the USA's proposals. Baker also received the backing of the G-7 nations meeting in London, United Kingdom, and, more significantly, of Saudi Arabia. Saudi Arabia also gave its support to an Egyptian proposal that the Arab states should end their trade boycott of Israel in return for a 'freeze' on new settlements in the Occupied Territories, a gambit that Israel declined. Indeed, despite a *de facto* Arab capitulation to Shamir's conditions, the Israeli Government's attitude to the progress engineered by Baker was far from generous. The Israeli Cabinet endorsed Shamir's acceptance of the Baker conference proposals, but with the proviso that Israel hold a veto over the composition of any Palestinian negotiating team. Even this, however, failed to satisfy three right-wing members of the Cabinet, including Sharon, who voted against Israel's acceptance of the Baker formula. Moreover, in a pointed snub to both Arab states and the USA, which were hoping for a goodwill gesture from Israel in return for Arab flexibility, a new West Bank settlement was inaugurated less than two days after the cabinet meeting.

At the heart of Palestinian uncertainty over the proposed conference lay the issues of representation and settlement. It was accepted that the PLO would not participate officially and that Palestinians might have to be represented as part of a joint team with Jordan, but the threat of an Israeli veto of a Palestinian delegation that included East Jerusalem residents led those Palestinians who had met with Baker to warn that they might not get popular backing for their attendance. They also demanded that the USA should apply pressure on Israel to halt settlement during negotiations, and that a letter of assurance be drafted on such issues as the USA's interpretation of UN resolutions and its commitment to mandatory international arbitration in the event of a deadlock in negotiations. Some PLO factions, notably the PFLP and the DFLP faction loyal to Naif Hawatmeh, rejected Palestinian participation outright. The PFLP issued a communiqué within the Occupied Territories calling the conference 'a conspiracy aimed at bypassing the PLO and Palestinian rights'. The fundamentalists of Hamas were even more forthright in their opposition, condemning the Baker proposals as a 'conference for selling land' and threatening any would-be participants. However, the two leading Palestinian participants in the Baker talks, Faisal Husseini and Hanan Ashrawi, made it clear that it would be the PLO which ultimately decided whether the Palestinians were represented at the conference.

It was clearly dangerous for the PLO to exclude itself from a process that might offer an opportunity to end the occupation of the West Bank and Gaza. However, the PLO was concerned that by giving approval to the peace conference it might be abdicating its role as the Palestinians' sole representative. There was also the sobering realization that the Organization could no longer rely on the support of Arab states for its own negotiating positions and that there was a real danger that a normalization of Arab–Israeli relations could be achieved without addressing the fundamentals of the Palestinian problem. Initiatives by the PLO, supported by Jordan, to organize a meeting with Arab front-line states in order to co-ordinate negotiating positions in the run-up to the conference, were rejected by Egypt and Syria.

At the end of August 1991 the PLO held a meeting in London, attended by a number of Palestinian personalities from the Occupied Territories, to set guidelines for the letter of assurances from the USA that would facilitate Palestinian participation in the planned conference. The letter that Baker did finally present to Ashrawi in Amman did not fulfil all the Palestinian criteria for attending the conference, not least because Baker refused to contradict assurances he had already given to Israel. Arafat described the letter as 'a positive step, but one which fell short', referring to the fact that while Baker had clarified the US interpretations of the relevant UN Resolutions and the status of East Jerusalem, which agreed with that of the Arabs, there was no mention of the USA's commitment to Palestinian self-determination nor any proposals for a resolution of the Jerusalem issue. Nor was there any suggestion that Baker would demand a 'freeze' on settlements in the Occupied Territories or allow the PLO to formally nominate the Palestinian delegation. Arafat allowed the PNC meeting in September to debate the question of Palestinian involvement in the peace conference. The Council's resolutions reiterated Palestinian commitment to the principle of autonomy, but such was the pressure on the PLO—from the USA and the Arab states—to support the US proposals that by the end of September 1991 it was clear that the Palestinians would be sending representatives, albeit on terms that were far from satisfactory. Jordan, with which the Palestinians were now certain to form a joint delegation, had assured the PLO leader that it would fight for Palestinian objectives, but had also stressed that it would attend the conference whether these were achieved or not. Moreover, the failure in the USSR of an attempted coup, which had been welcomed by some prominent Palestinians, removed any hopes that the USSR would counteract US authority in the Middle East.

SUSPENSION OF LOAN GUARANTEES

Israel, meanwhile, was engaged in its own battle of wills with the Bush Administration. The Likud Government had sought US \$10,000m. in loan guarantees from the USA in order to help the settlement of immigrants from the USSR. However, in the prelude to the peace conference the combination of Bush's displeasure at the continuing settlement, and a desire not to offend Arab sensibilities, led the US President to ask Israel for a four-month delay in its formal submission for the loan guarantees. Bush also warned that if the loan request was approved by the US Congress, he would impose his veto. Shamir accepted the challenge and set Israel's formidable lobbying machine in motion. However, opinion polls in the USA suggested that an overwhelming majority of the public supported the Government's position and this was reflected in congressional support for the President's stance. It was the first time since the Suez crisis that a US Administration had made aid conditional on Israeli policy.

THE MADRID CONFERENCE

The peace conference, to be held in Madrid, Spain, on 30 October 1991 (see Documents on Palestine, p. 368), was preceded by a series of inter-Arab meetings. Denied the Arab summit he had originally proposed, Arafat was nevertheless invited to talks in Cairo, Amman and Damascus—his first visit to the Syrian capital for eight years—where he was assured that there would be no

Arab concessions until the question of territory was resolved. Faced with Israel's insistence that residents of East Jerusalem be barred from the Palestinian negotiating team, the PLO offered a compromise whereby the Palestinian delegation should include an advisory body made up largely of East Jerusalem residents. The USA supported this proposal, recognizing the advisers as an official part of the Palestinian delegation. Dr Haider Abdel Shafei, veteran chief of the Gaza Red Crescent Society, was named head of the negotiating team and Hanan Ashrawi was to be chief spokesperson. Faisal Husseini was in overall charge of the delegation which included supporters of Fatah, the Abd ar-Rabbuh faction of the DFLP, and the PCP as well as several independents. Shamir decided to head Israel's team himself, intimating that he did not trust the Minister of Foreign Affairs, Levy, with such an important mission.

As Israel had never before attended a peace conference with its Arab neighbours, including the Palestinians, the Madrid conference generated intense media interest. In spite of the precedent, however, no real progress was made. During the three-day plenary session the Israeli delegation offered no prospect of an Israeli withdrawal from the Occupied Territories, while Arab ministers of foreign affairs and Palestinians stated that there could be no peace without territorial compromise. Exchanges between Syria and Israel were particularly hostile and rapidly degenerated into mutual invective. Predictably, their first round of bilateral talks, which followed the plenary sessions, swiftly reached an impasse; Syria's Minister of Foreign Affairs left Madrid repeating that Syria would not attend the proposed multilateral negotiations on regional issues until Israel committed itself to territorial concessions. Israel's talks with the other Arab delegations were more cordial but scarcely more productive. On the two principal issues of discussion, a venue and an agenda for the second round of talks, there was no agreement. Israeli officials demanded that the negotiations be held in the Middle East to emphasize the regional rather than the international nature of the process, and, for the opposite reason, the Arab states and the Palestinians insisted on a European venue. Only the Palestinian delegation had cause for satisfaction after the Madrid conference. It had won an early procedural victory by gaining the same (45-minute) period in which to make its representations as the other Arab delegations, and enjoyed public-relations successes with eloquent and dignified articulations of the Palestinian case. Madrid was also significant for the Palestinian acceptance that self-determination should follow a period of autonomy in the Occupied Territories. However, the presence in Madrid of a high-level PLO delegation left little doubt that the Palestinian team was in close contact with the PLO.

The impression that the Palestinians had successfully exploited the opportunities afforded by the Madrid conference was reflected in several peace marches in the Occupied Territories. Some were tolerated by the Israeli army, but others ended in confrontation; a 15-year-old from Hebron became the 1,000th casualty of the *intifada* when he was shot dead during a demonstration in support of the conference. However, the strong support for a general strike called by Hamas and the Popular and Democratic Fronts to protest against the conference underlined the strength of the radical opinion opposed to Palestinian participation in the peace talks. Meanwhile, in southern Lebanon there were Israeli and SLA air strikes and artillery bombardments of Shi'ite and Palestinian positions, ostensibly in revenge for successful Palestinian and Hezbollah ambushes.

THE WASHINGTON CONFERENCE

The failure of the Arabs and Israelis to agree a venue or agenda for the next session of bilateral talks prompted Baker to issue invitations for negotiations in Washington, DC, on 4 December 1991. A set of US guide-lines suggesting how each delegation might conduct its negotiations was included with the invitations. However, while these efforts to maintain momentum in the peace process were largely welcomed by the Arab side, they were coolly received in Israel. Shamir announced that the Israeli delegation would not be travelling to Washington until five days after the scheduled opening of the talks. US disappointment was contrasted with satisfaction from Israeli government hardliners who applauded the 'revolt against American compulsion' and urged Shamir to take further steps to disrupt the peace process.

Israel's decision was interpreted in the Occupied Territories, as in the rest of the Arab world, as evidence of Shamir's contempt for the peace process. On the West Bank and in Gaza, it became increasingly difficult to convince the growing number of sceptics that there was any value in pursuing negotiations with an intransigent Israel. A decision by the USA to refuse visas to several senior PLO figures who had played a covert role in Madrid further eroded Palestinian goodwill. Arafat tried to mobilize Arab support for a delayed attendance at the talks in solidarity with the PLO, but he was informed that the Arabs in general and the Palestinians in particular could not afford to be seen to disrupt the peace process. In the end the Palestinian delegation registered its disapproval by delaying its flight to Washington by 12 hours.

Israel's absence from the first days of the talks meant that the Arab delegations had to sit opposite empty chairs in the conference rooms. When the Israeli delegation did arrive, they immediately attempted to undermine the Palestinian status as a delegation in their own right in Madrid by refusing to negotiate on Palestinian issues with a team that did not come under Jordanian auspices. As a result, most of the time allocated for Israeli-Palestinian and Israeli-Jordanian talks was spent on procedural issues. The questions of a 'freeze' on settlements in the Occupied Territories, interpretations of UN Resolutions and the nature of interim autonomy in the Occupied Territories were barely discussed. Israeli talks with Syrian and Lebanese delegations also achieved very little. Israel's refusal to accept that Resolution 242 compelled it to withdraw from occupied Arab territories continued to infuriate Syria. Lebanese-Israeli talks were less disorderly but threatened to founder on the Lebanese insistence that Resolution 425, demanding an Israeli withdrawal from Lebanese territory, was non-negotiable, and Israeli determination that it be discussed as part of the peace process. With little prospect of a solution to the impasse, the Arab delegation signalled that there was need of some form of US intervention. However, Baker had indicated that the USA would be adopting a 'hands-off' approach, commenting that the USA could not want peace more than the concerned parties themselves. For the Arabs this was tantamount to a surrender to Israeli obstructionism. 'If the Americans want us to talk to Israel without them . . . well, we have done', commented one Arab delegate, 'Without US intervention, however, they should have known success would be a long shot'. In New York, meanwhile, the UN General Assembly voted over-whelmingly to repeal its 1975 Resolution equating Zionism with racism. Several Arab states refused to participate in the vote.

EVENTS IN THE OCCUPIED TERRITORIES

Palestinian frustration was exacerbated by the accelerated settlement pro-gramme in the Occupied Territories. Indeed 1991 had been the most vigorous year for the building of settlements in nearly 25 years of occupation. Under the supervision of the Ministry of Housing, work had begun on 13,500 housing units in the Occupied Territories, excluding East Jerusalem, a 65% increase over all the units established in the previous 23 years. It was also reported that 13% of immigrants from the former USSR were being settled on occupied Arab lands, boosting the Israeli population in the territories to over 200,000. While the Washington talks were in progress a leaked report revealed that government approval had been given for a massive programme of Jewish colonization of Arab neighbourhoods in East Jerusalem. This was confirmed in mid-December, when a combined force of settlers and Israeli police took over several houses in the Silwan district of the city, evicting Palestinian families in the process. 'The Israelis are destroying the ground under our feet', commented Faisal Husseini on the effects of the settlement policy on his efforts to build support for the peace process. Israel's decision in early January 1992 to deport a further 12 Palestinians (reportedly in retaliation for the killing of a Jewish settler in Gaza) and to establish a settlers' civil guard in the West Bank and in Gaza, was further evidence that the Shamir Government was attempting to provoke the Palestinians to withdraw from the peace talks, or, at least, to widen the rift between opponents and supporters of negotiation.

Clashes between Fatah and Hamas activists in Gaza and the West Bank became increasingly common as the *intifada* entered its fifth year. Despite appeals from PLO figures and community leaders for an end to the killing of collabora-tors, suspected informers were stabbed and shot almost every day. In the refugee camps of Gaza and the nationalist strongholds of the West Bank the knives and axes once carried in ceremonial fashion by masked activists were being replaced by pistols and automatic rifles. As predicted, there was an increase in armed attacks on settlers and soldiers at the beginning of 1992. In the most serious incident, in mid-February, three soldiers were bludgeoned to death in a raid on an army camp just inside the 'Green Line'. Meanwhile, Israel's Ministry of Defence relied more heavily on the activities of undercover units to combat the *intifada*. An upsurge in what witnesses described as summary executions of Palestinian activists led journalists and human rights organizations to accuse Israel of operating Latin American-style death squads in the Occupied Territories.

Following the deportation orders in January 1992, the Palestinians decided to postpone the sending of a delegation to the next round of bilateral talks in Washington, DC. The other Arab delegations subsequently agreed to follow the Palestinian lead. The deportations also seemed to draw a more conciliatory line from the Bush Administration; visas, which had been refused to PLO members the previous month, were now granted. When the negotiations began on 16 January, Israel dropped its earlier objections to separate Palestinian repre-sentation, but refused to address the principal items on the Arab agenda, namely the interpretation of Resolution 242, borders, and settlements. The Palestinian delegation was told that the issue of settlements had no bearing on the autonomy details and could only be discussed when the final status of the territories had been decided. Arab frustration was compounded by the premature departure of the Israeli delegation. Israel's steadfast avoidance and obstruction of substantive negotiations created profound disillusion in Palestinian ranks; many believed that it was only to avoid alienating the USA while the question of loan guarantees was in the balance that Israel remained at the conference table. It was also recognized that President Bush was unlikely to pressurize Israel into breaking the deadlock with an election due in November.

TALKS IN MOSCOW

The prospect of a negotiated settlement receded further in January 1992 when the far-right Moledet and Tehiya parties resigned from the Israeli Government in protest at discussion of Palestinian autonomy in the Occupied Territories. This left the Shamir Government without a majority in the Knesset and made an early election inevitable. Nevertheless, multilateral regional talks opened in Moscow at the end of January. With inter-Arab relations still strained in the wake of the 1991 Gulf War, it came as little surprise that they failed to agree on a coherent policy. Eleven states attended, a sufficient number for Israel to claim a diplomatic breakthrough, while Syria and Lebanon stuck to their earlier promise to observe a boycott of regional talks until progress had been made in the bilateral negotiations. The PLO, concerned at Arab disarray but determined to use the multilateral session to highlight the issue of Palestinian representation, sent a delegation composed of personalities from the West Bank and Gaza, Jerusalem and the diaspora. While conceding that representatives from the diaspora and Jerusalem could be included in some of the working groups that the conference was to establish—on the refugee problem for example—the USA only issued invitations to the plenary session to Palestinian delegates from Gaza and the West Bank. Believing that they had already made too many concessions, especially on the issue of representation, the Palestinian delegation refused to attend the talks. Baker voiced his disappointment at the Palestinian decision and promised that diaspora Palestinians could be included in two of the five working groups scheduled to meet in the spring. The Palestinians had demanded free representation on all five, but could take some solace in the fact that their fears of Israeli and Arab participants taking steps towards normalizing relations were unfounded.

ESCALATION OF HOSTILITIES IN LEBANON

On 16 February 1992 the leader of the Lebanese Hezbollah, Sheikh Abbas Moussawi, was killed in an Israeli helicopter attack on his motorcade in southern Lebanon. Moussawi's wife, child and several bodyguards also died. Many observers were puzzled by the assassination; for all its anti-Israeli rhetoric Hezbollah had never launched attacks against targets inside Israel, nor had there been a noticeable increase in raids on the IDF or its SLA allies in the Israeli security zone prior to the killing. One SLA spokesman even described Hezbollah as 'militarily insignificant'. Moreover, the killing halted negotiations to exchange Lebanese and Palestinian prisoners in return for news of Israeli servicemen missing in Lebanon. It also provoked an escalation of warfare in the south. Hezbollah rocket attacks on northern Israel were followed by heavy Israeli shelling of Shi'ite villages. Syria eventually persuaded Hezbollah to halt its salvoes, which led the organization to search for other means of retaliation.

On 9 March Israel's chief security officer in the Turkish capital, Ankara, was assassinated, and on 17 March a massive car-bomb destroyed the Israeli embassy in Buenos Aires, Argentina, killing 30 people. Responsibility for both attacks was claimed by Islamic Jihad.

The situation in Lebanon deepened the pessimism surrounding the peace process. The Israeli delegation arrived in Washington, DC, for the fourth round of bilateral talks in an unforgiving mood. At the end of February 1992 Baker had finally ended speculation over Israel's request for US $10,000m. in loan guarantees, telling Congress that they would not be granted unless there was a halt to new settlement activity in the Occupied Territories, a condition that Shamir had already rejected.

BILATERAL TALKS IN WASHINGTON

Negotiations over the form of Palestinian autonomy within the Occupied Territories confirmed the extent of the gulf between Israel and Arab–Palestinian aspirations. The Israeli delegates outlined a proposal which would maintain Israeli control over land, and guarantee the right of unlimited settlement and full responsibility for public order. There was no mention of elections with the implication that the limited administrative powers devolved to the Palestinians would be executed by official appointees. This contrasted with the Palestinian plan for a Palestinian interim self-governing authority along with the election of a legislative assembly, a halt to all settlement, a transfer of judicial and administrative power and the phased withdrawal of Israeli forces leading to Palestinian self-determination throughout the Occupied Territories. A US State Department spokesman described both positions as 'maximalist', but went on to criticize the Palestinians for trying to pre-empt the negotiations by declaring sovereignty as their goal. Although this criticism reflected the USA's long-standing opposition to a Palestinian nation, it was interpreted as an attempt to counterbalance the refusal to grant Israel's loan guarantees. Israel's outright rejection of territorial compromises left negotiations with Syria and Jordan in stalemate. Attempting to negotiate with Israel, stated a Syrian spokeswoman, was 'an exercise in futility'.

REACTIONS IN THE OCCUPIED TERRITORIES AND ISRAEL

Within the Occupied Territories there was further opposition to continued Palestinian involvement in the peace process. The PCP, renamed the Palestinian People's Party (PPP), had initially supported the Washington talks, but withdrew its backing during the fourth round after the Palestinian delegation had agreed to negotiate on the issue of autonomy without having secured Israel's prior agreement to a settlement 'freeze'. Yet more evidence of public opinion turning against the talks came in the elections to the Ramallah Chamber of Commerce in early March 1992. Hamas supporters won a clear majority of seats despite the fact that Ramallah had a sizeable Christian majority and had long been considered as the stronghold of liberal, secular nationalism.

Party manoeuvring and infighting were also in evidence in Israel in the prelude to the general election. In February 1992 Peres was deposed as the leader of the Labour Party by his more 'hawkish', but equally veteran colleague, Rabin, whose reputation as a 'hardliner' on defence and security was widely regarded as a boost to the Labour Party's battle to win voters from Likud. Their fortunes were further enhanced by rifts within the Likud ranks. In a speech broadcast live on Israeli television, the Minister of Foreign Affairs, Levy, angered by what he claimed was a plot against his supporters during internal party elections, accused Likud of being 'racist'. Although he was dissuaded from resigning, Levy's vitriolic attack on his own party undoubtedly contributed to steady Labour gains in the opinion polls. Meanwhile, three parties of the centre-left, the Civil Rights and Peace Movement, Shinui and Mapam, decided to merge their lists to form a new electoral bloc, Meretz.

The fifth round of the bilateral talks was held in Washington, DC, at the end of April 1992, but was largely overshadowed by the Israeli election campaign. As predicted, the Israeli delegation arrived in Washington with a plan for phased municipal elections in the West Bank and in Gaza. The Palestinian delegation offered to consider the proposal, but reiterated its commitment to a nationally-elected legislative assembly. Hanan Ashrawi later described municipal elections as 'a dead-end'. There was also a suspicion among Palestinians that the Israeli offer was a Likud public relations exercise designed to win the moderate vote. Interestingly, those Palestinian factions which had raised the strongest objections to the autonomy negotiations—Hamas, the PFLP and DFLP—argued that municipal elections were a better option precisely because they did not commit Palestinians to the autonomy plan. Following its gains in the Ramallah Chamber of Commerce election, Hamas also viewed municipal elections as a welcome test of strength against a divided nationalist bloc. However, in elections to the Nablus Chamber of Commerce in mid-May, the nationalist bloc, standing as the National Muslim Coalition, won nine of the 12 seats contested.

There was an increase of violence associated with the *intifada* in the weeks leading up to the election. Four Palestinians were shot dead and 80 injured in Rafah on 7 April 1992 and several were killed in armed clashes during May. There was also an increase in the death-toll during demonstrations. The killing of an Israeli girl in a Tel-Aviv suburb at the end of May by a lone Palestinian was the catalyst for several nights of anti-Arab rioting and for a government decision to further restrict the movement of Gazans into Israel; unemployment rates in some parts of the Gaza Strip were reported to exceed 50%. The stabbing of an Israeli settler in Gaza shortly afterwards was followed by wide-scale destruction of Palestinian crops and property.

In mid-June 1992 members of the Palestinian negotiating team travelled to Amman for a televised meeting with Arafat. Israeli government ministers condemned the meeting and demanded the arrest of the participants on their return. The USA made clear its firm opposition to such measures, leaving Israel's Minister of Police to make the somewhat empty threat of calling in the Palestinians concerned for questioning.

ELECTION VICTORY FOR LABOUR

A combination of public discontent over the economy, the state of relations with the USA, the plight of Russian immigrants and the lack of progress in the peace process, made Labour gains in the Israeli elections on 23 June 1992 inevitable. However, the extent of the Labour majority over Likud, 44 seats to 32, exceeded most expectations. Meretz became the third largest party in the new Knesset with 12 seats, while the right-wing Tzomet Party, headed by the fiercely anti-clerical Rafael Eitan, made an unexpectedly strong showing and won eight seats. The right-wing Tehiya Party failed to win any seats. There was a slight drop in support for the orthodox religious parties and the Arab-dominated lists.

As expected, Meretz entered into partnership with Labour. The inclusion of the Sephardi Orthodox party, Shas, gave Rabin an overall majority, but an attempt to increase his majority and broaden his constituency by recruiting Tzomet into the coalition came to nothing. Former Labour leader Peres was appointed Minister of Foreign Affairs in the new Government, while Rabin retained the defence portfolio.

INITIAL REACTIONS TO RABIN

The USA and the EC, in the belief that only a Labour victory could keep the peace process alive, warmly welcomed the outcome of the election. The defeat of Shamir and Likud was also greeted with relief in the Arab capitals where the attitude towards the new Israeli Government was one of official caution and unofficial optimism. The reaction of Palestinians was more equivocal. Those who had supported the peace negotiations saw Rabin's election as a positive development. However, left-wing and Islamist factions feared that a Labour government would pave the way for an agreement on the autonomy proposals they so bitterly opposed. Relations between Fatah and Hamas supporters in particular grew more volatile following the election and, in July 1992, the Occupied Territories witnessed the worst round of internecine fighting in many years. Several people had been killed and scores injured in gun battles and street confrontations before an uneasy truce was brokered.

Rabin's initial comments on the peace process did little to reassure Palestinians. He stated that he would be willing to travel to any Arab capital to pursue peace negotiations, but stopped short of instituting the settlement 'freeze' the Palestinians had demanded. He promised a halt to the building of 'non-political' settlements, but insisted that all existing contracts would be honoured. This was positive enough for Egypt's President Mubarak to issue an invitation to Rabin to visit Cairo—the first such visit by an Israeli Prime Minister for six years—and for the USA to intimate that it might release at least part of the US $10,000m. in loan guarantees that Israel had requested. In mid-July 1992 Baker began another round of 'shuttle' diplomacy in the Middle East in an effort to reactivate the peace process. In the wake of the Baker mission, Arab leaders, including the PLO, met in Damascus with Palestinians from the Occupied Territories in order to co-ordinate policy before a possible renewal of bilateral talks.

In mid-August Rabin travelled to the USA for a visit intended to restore US–Israeli relations to their traditional amicability after the frostiness of the Bush-Shamir years. The Israeli Prime Minister left Washington, DC, with pledges of further military aid and assurances of Israel's enhanced strategic importance to the USA in the post-Cold War era. For his part, Rabin promised that the coming round of bilateral talks would achieve progress on substantive issues.

OPTIMISM AND DISAPPOINTMENT

Rabin's optimistic approach to the peace process was not shared by the Palestinians. There was disappointment that the new Israeli Government had refrained from implementing a complete 'freeze' on settlement in the Occupied Territories, and dismay at the USA's readiness to grant the US $10,000m. in loan guarantees without such a policy change. Moreover, the goodwill measures that the Labour Government had announced prior to the resumption of negotiations—the rescinding of deportation orders against 11 Palestinians, the release of a small number of political prisoners and the reopening of some of the roads sealed during the *intifada*—were considered to be little more than political cosmetics. Government spokesmen in Jordan and Syria also expressed concern at the repercussions that the rapidly improved US–Israeli relations would have on the USA's supposed impartiality as co-sponsor of the peace process.

Despite Arab reservations, Israel's continued intimations that there was a real prospect of a breakthrough in the stalled peace process ensured that the mood before the sixth round of bilateral talks began in Washington, DC, was more sanguine than for some time. Delegates spoke of a 'positive new tone' and a constructive informality that previous encounters had lacked. However, by the end of the fourth week, the longest round of bilateral talks to date, the Arab parties described the negotiations as 'deadlocked'. Syria's chief negotiator accused Rabin's Government of exhibiting 'exactly the same attitude and policy as Shamir'. His comments were provoked by Israel's insistence that Syria should commit itself to a full, normal peace with Israel before the issue of withdrawal from the Golan Heights could be discussed. The Palestinian delegation expressed similar frustration with its Israeli counterpart on the 'land for peace' issue. While the Palestinians insisted that the entire peace process—including discussions on Palestinian autonomy—should be guided by Resolution 242, the Israelis argued that UN resolutions were only applicable to negotiations on the ultimate status of occupied Arab land. Hanan Ashrawi, the chief Palestinian spokesperson, told journalists that Israel was still adhering to the notion of 'autonomy for the people but not the land'.

PEACE TALKS FOUNDER

The failure of the sixth round to produce tangible results strengthened the hand of Palestinian groups opposed to the peace process. Meeting in Damascus in mid-September 1992, 10 Palestinian organizations, four from within the PLO and six from outside, signed a memorandum urging a withdrawal from the Madrid process. A strike organized by the 10 factions was widely observed in the Occupied Territories and caused clashes between Fatah and Hamas supporters. However, while pressure from the rejectionist group narrowed Arafat's field of manoeuvre and reflected the substantial opposition to further Palestinian involvement in the Washington talks, other developments encouraged the Palestinians to remain engaged. Israel's Minister of Justice announced his intention to repeal legislation outlawing contact between Israelis and Palestinians and the PLO, and economic controls were eased in order to allow a less restricted flow of capital to the Occupied Territories. One of the quietest periods in the *intifada* finally came to an end in mid-October when a hunger strike by Palestinian prisoners in Israeli prisons prompted a series of violent protests in the Occupied Territories and an increase in Palestinian deaths and injuries.

A meeting of the PLO's Central Committee was called by Arafat in October 1992 in order to obtain official approval for Palestinian participation in the seventh round of peace talks in Washington, DC. Arafat achieved a minor victory in persuading the PFLP and DFLP to attend the meeting, although both factions refused to vote on the issue of participation and were bitter critics of the Palestinian negotiating position. Their opposition was intensified by reports that Israel was considering an exchange of land in return for peace with Syria. At a meeting of Arab foreign ministers in Amman, Jordan, in mid-October Syria refused to give assurances to its Jordanian and Palestinian colleagues that it would not conclude a separate Israeli-Syrian peace treaty, arguing that progress in the Israeli-Palestinian talks could take years. An angry Arafat cancelled a scheduled visit to Damascus.

The Israeli delegation travelled to Washington for the seventh round of bilateral talks buoyed by the USA's formal approval of the release of $10,000m. in loan guarantees, and with an apparent willingness to discuss 'withdrawal in the Golan' with its Syrian counterpart. However, the proximity of the US presidential election and an expected change to an unambiguously pro-Israeli administration ensured that the negotiations would be cautious. The Israeli-Lebanese dialogue was given a particular poignancy by artillery duels between the IDF and Hezbollah fighters that were prompted by the deaths of five Israeli soldiers in a land-mine explosion. Israel used the pretext of the fighting to attempt to persuade Lebanon to agree to the establishment of a joint military commission in the south of the country. Lebanon interpreted the offer as a ploy to legitimize Israel's occupation of the south and insisted that there could be no peace without a full Israeli withdrawal. After the Israeli delegation accused its Lebanese counterpart of 'abdicating responsibility to terrorists' and warned that they 'could make normal life impossible' for Lebanon, the Lebanese delegation walked out of the talks. The Israeli-Palestinian dialogue again foundered on disagreement over the applicability of UN resolutions to the interim negotiations on Palestinian autonomy in the Occupied Territories. A total impasse was only averted by Palestinian consent to a series of 'informal' talks on the substance of interim Palestinian autonomy. The Palestinian delegation was at pains to stress the exploratory nature of the talks for fear of being seen to give assent to discussions on the technicalities of autonomy before the broader political principles governing interim and final-phase negotiations had been established. Israel's talks with Syria also disappointed. The Israeli delegation had come to Washington prepared to discuss territorial compromise in the Golan, but it rapidly became obvious that it would only commit itself to discussing a limited withdrawal. Talks with Syria were further soured by Israel's repetition of its earlier call that Syria should not hold out for a comprehensive resolution of Arab–Israeli disputes but should 'stand on its own'. Only in the talks between Israel and Jordan was there a modicum of success, with both parties agreeing on a provisional agenda for the next round of talks.

CLINTON ADMINISTRATION TAKES OVER IN USA

The seventh round of bilateral talks coincided with the victory of the Democratic candidate, William Jefferson (Bill) Clinton, in the 1992 US presidential election. The outgoing Bush Administration was eager to bequeath a viable Middle East peace process to the new Administration and dutifully suggested a resumption of talks in December. Not surprisingly, however, there was little enthusiasm for a further round of negotiations before the formal inauguration of the new US President. The Palestinians, under mounting pressure from a sceptical constituency to protest at the lack of progress in, and general media indifference to, the peace process, were the most reluctant to attend. However, with the Arab states committed to returning to Washington, the Palestinians were left to register their disenchantment by sending a delegation of only four to deal with Israel's controversial proposals for Palestinian 'interim self-government'. The draft model for Palestinian autonomy envisaged a stratified system of authority in the Occupied Territories (excluding East Jerusalem); Israeli jurisdiction would be maintained over Israeli settlements, public lands would come under joint Palestinian-Israeli jurisdiction, and an Israeli-supervised Palestinian authority (whose composition and competence were to be negotiated) would govern private Palestinian lands and municipalities. While the Palestinian delegation was not in a position to reject the Israeli proposals outright, it argued that they would lead to the creation of a Palestinian 'Bantustan'.

The inconclusive eighth round of Washington talks coincided with the fifth anniversary of the *intifada*. The character of the Palestinian uprising had changed considerably since its beginnings in Gaza. The popular committees that had served as the *intifada's* original dynamo had long since fallen victim to Israeli repression and factional infighting. The UNLU itself existed largely in name only and its bi-weekly communiqués no longer set the tone or tenor of resistance. Instead, the activities of small armed groups had come to be viewed as the principal focus of the uprising. Many of these owed only nominal allegiance to identifiable political factions and some of their more dubious activities, especially the settling of political scores in the guise of eliminating collaborators, had led to heated debate and calls for the young gunmen to be restrained. However, with scant prospect of a breakthrough in the Washington talks, there was undeniable political capital to be made out of successful armed attacks against Israeli targets. Hamas, as self-appointed inheritor of the radical Palestinian mantle and an uncompromising opponent of the peace process, was the best placed, politically and militarily, to exploit the armed option. Bolstered by generous financial backing from Iran (which reportedly paid a bonus for every Israeli soldier killed), Hamas fighters embarked on a spectacular series of military operations. During two weeks in December four Israeli soldiers were killed in Hamas ambushes in Gaza and Hebron, and another was kidnapped inside Israel and later murdered (the IDF lost a further soldier to an Islamic Jihad gunman near Jenin in the same week).

DEPORTATION OF ALLEGED ISLAMIST ACTIVISTS

Rabin promised radical steps to counter the Islamist movement's military successes. On 16 and 17 December 1992 1,600 alleged Hamas and Islamic Jihad activists were detained by the Israeli security forces. Some 413 of those arrested were subsequently transported to the Lebanese border and, with the approval of Israel's Supreme Court, expelled through Israel's security zone into south Lebanon. The Lebanese Government refused to accept the deportees, a stance which the Arab world unanimously applauded, leaving the displaced Palestinians to establish a makeshift refugee camp on a barren mountainside wedged between the IDF and Lebanese army front lines. Although Rabin explained that the deportees would be eligible to return to their homes after a two-year period, the mass expulsions elicited a chorus of international condemnation. The UN Security Council, affirming the inadmissibility of deportations under the Fourth Geneva Convention, unanimously passed Resolution 799 demanding the immediate safe return of the expelled Palestinians. UN Secretary-General Boutros Boutros-Ghali also warned Israel that he might ask the Security Council to take further measures if it did not comply with the UN Resolution. In the Occupied Territories, and particularly in Gaza, where the majority of the deportees originated, Rabin's action provoked another surge of violent street protests—six demonstrators were killed in Khan Yunis on 21 December alone.

The mainstream PLO appeared to benefit from the political and diplomatic repercussions of the deportations. Firstly, it was believed that the PLO would be able to extract significant concessions from Israel and the USA before sanctioning a Palestinian return to the negotiating table; secondly, in the opinion of some observers, Rabin's demonization of Hamas was effectively paving the way for a future Israeli-PLO dialogue; and thirdly, the December events provided Arafat with an opportunity to manage his troublesome opposition. In reluctant admission of the PLO Chairman's stewardship of the Palestinian cause in times of crisis, Hamas and the Damascus-based 'rejectionists' accepted invitations to a series of talks in Tunis. Although no real concessions were made by either side, with Arafat ignoring calls for a Palestinian withdrawal from the peace process, Hamas representatives agreed to work towards ending sectarian conflict and to co-ordinate activities with Fatah inside and outside the Occupied Territories. Hamas later signalled a significant revision of its maximalist position of settling for nothing less than an Islamic state in all of historical Palestine, by dropping objections to an independent state in part of Palestine.

US ATTEMPTS TO SAVE PEACE PROCESS

The deportations were a clear embarrassment for the new Clinton Administration. With the PLO and the Arab states urging the imposition of sanctions on Israel for non-compliance with Resolution 799, Clinton and the US Secretary of State, Warren Christopher, persuaded Israel to take steps to assuage international unease over the expulsions. The Rabin Government subsequently announced that the expulsions had been an 'exceptional' measure and that the Palestinians would be allowed to return home before the end of 1993. It added that 101 of the deportees would be allowed back to the Occupied Territories immediately (this was rejected by the deportees' spokesman). Armed with the Israeli concessions, the USA embarked on a vigorous diplomatic campaign to persuade the six 'third world' members of the UN Security Council to abandon their support for sanctions against Israel. The USA argued that Israel had moved towards compliance with Resolution 799 and that the imposition of sanctions would irreparably damage the fragile peace process. Madeleine Albright, the new US Ambassador to the UN, also warned that the USA would veto any move to impose sanctions. By 12 February 1993 the USA's heavy-handed diplomacy had borne fruit. The President of the UN Security Council issued a statement to the effect that there was to be no further debate on Resolution 799. He urged all parties 'to reinvigorate the Middle East peace process'. The UN decision caused glee in the Rabin Government, but confirmed the deep-seated Arab and Palestinian belief that Israel was immune to international law.

CHRISTOPHER TOURS MIDDLE EAST

In mid-February 1993 Christopher made a tour of the Middle East with the primary intention of enticing the Palestinians and the front-line Arab states to resume talks in Washington, DC. Syria and Lebanon were the easiest targets, since they had already indicated that they were prepared to separate the deportation issue from the peace process. However, President Assad went some way towards allaying Palestinian fears by stressing, in his talks with Christopher, that a separate Syrian-Israeli peace was impossible without a resolution of the Palestinian issue. Jordan proved to be less amenable to Christopher's urgings. It had said that it would not accept an invitation to Washington as long as the deportation issue was outstanding. This was not repeated by King Hussein in his talks with Christopher, but the Jordanian monarch left the US Secretary of State in no doubt that it would be almost impossible for a Jordanian delegation to attend the next round of talks if the Palestinians did not do so. It was clear, therefore, that the success or failure of the Christopher mission depended on the outcome of his meetings with the Palestinian peace team in Jerusalem. Initial reports suggested that progress had been made, and a six-point plan, designed to address Palestinian grievances, was agreed by the two sides. The outcome was a further letter of US assurances to the Palestinians. The Administration reiterated its commitment to Resolutions 242 and 338, stated its willingness to participate as a full partner in the peace talks, expressed opposition to deportation and settlement and affirmed its readiness to stand by assurances given by the previous Administration with regard to the peace process (most crucially the acknowledgement that East Jerusalem was occupied territory). Christopher also told the Palestinians that Israel would not resort to deportations in the future. However, while the Secretary of State flew back to the USA, the Palestinians waited in vain for a positive Israeli response to the six points and a statement of principle on deportations. Instead, the Israeli media announced that the Palestinians would be attending the ninth round of talks on 20 April. Angered by subsequent US inaction and complaining bitterly that it was being taken for granted, the PLO ordered the Palestinian delegates to refuse an invitation to the talks. 'If Israel cannot comply with the six points,' commented one PLO official, 'then we cannot participate in the next round.'

PALESTINIANS RELUCTANTLY RETURN TO TALKS

The PLO's refusal to accept an invitation to the talks led to a series of inconclusive inter-Arab meetings and the postponement, at the end of March 1993, of any decision on whether to attend until further talks had been held with the US Administration. Privately the Palestinians had by now resigned them-selves to the resumption of negotiations before the return of the deportees, but they insisted that they could not resume talks without major Israeli concessions on the issue of the deportations. The USA and Egypt's President Mubarak subsequently urged Rabin to adopt some confidence-building measures to facilitate Arab participation. The result was a declaration by Rabin that mass deportation was not government policy and a promise to allow the return of a small number of Palestinians expelled since 1967. In a departure from the Israeli Government's previously-held policy of refusing to allow Palestinians from East Jerusalem to participate in the negotiations, Rabin also announced that it no longer objected to Faisal Husseini becoming the official leader of the Palestinian delegation. This last point was regarded by some Palestinians, not least by Husseini himself, as an important gain and a sufficient concession for the Palestinian delegation to attend talks in Washington, DC. However, for the majority of Palestinians, including delegation leader Haider Abdel Shafei, who had given an undertaking in his native Gaza that there would be no return to the talks while the deportees languished on a Lebanese hillside, Israel's concessions and the USA's promise to play a full and active role in the talks still fell short of the minimum required to enable them to return to Washington.

RENEWED VIOLENCE IN THE WEST BANK AND GAZA

Public opinion in the Occupied Territories remained firmly opposed to a retreat from commitments made to the deportees and had hardened as repression escalated in the West Bank and Gaza. Since the deportations there had been a dramatic increase in violent incidents in Gaza and the West Bank, with Palestinian deaths and injuries equalling those of the *intifada's* bloodiest months. The death of children had reached alarmingly high levels, as had summary executions of Palestinian fugitives by Israeli undercover units. Scores of homes were also being destroyed as the IDF adopted the controversial new tactic of targeting houses suspected of harbouring wanted Palestinians with rocket fire. Yet the militarization of occupation policy failed, as had mass expulsions, to halt anti-Israeli violence. Instead, the frequency of attacks and demonstrations in the Gaza Strip led some Israeli military figures to conclude that Gaza had been 'lost'. Each Israeli casualty drew appeals for stiffer policies to be applied in the Territories. Following the killing of two secondary school students in Jerusalem in March, Rabin ordered the closure of the Occupied Territories. Such a measure had been employed many times during the *intifada* but this time, Rabin stated, the West Bank and Gaza would be sealed for an indefinite period. Tens of thousands of Palestinians lost their livelihoods as a result. Pressure from Israeli employers eventually persuaded the Government to issue work permits for a few thousand Palestinians, but this still left many areas of Gaza and the West Bank in the grip of an economic catastrophe.

Against this background the PLO faced unenviable choices. Domestic ani-mosity to the Middle East peace process was counterbalanced by pressure from the USA, the EC and Arab states for the PLO to resume talks. Syria paid official lip-service to Resolution 799, but it was eager to capitalize on its improving relations with the USA and sensed that there might be some movement on the Golan issue. Saudi Arabia also made it clear to the cash-starved PLO that restored relations and future funding would be contingent on Palestinian attendance at the ninth round of bilateral talks. Despite huge misgivings and against a chorus of protest from the Occupied Territories, Arafat finally consented to Palestinian participation in the ninth round, stating that 'We go to the negotiations because if we do not have a place on the political map we will not have a place on the geographical map either'. Another member of the PLO's old guard, Farouk Kaddoumi, called attendance 'the lesser of two evils'. The Palestinian peace delegates, who remained strongly opposed to Palestinian attendance at the talks, had to be ordered back to Washington, DC. Hamas called the PLO's decision an act of 'treason' and severed contact with the Organization. A protest strike called by opposition factions shut down the Occupied Territories and precipitated a further round of bloody demonstrations.

Palestinian disarray immediately before the ninth round of bilateral talks fuelled Israeli intransigence. No promises were given on the return of the deportees, Rabin maintained his refusal to acknowledge that the West Bank and Gaza were 'Occupied Territories', in accordance with UN Security Council Resolution 242, and, despite the inclusion of Husseini in the Palestinian delegation, its Israeli counterpart continued to insist that East Jerusalem was not on the agenda. When, during the last days of negotiations, the USA submitted a draft proposal of principles in an attempt to prevent a stalemate and honour its earlier promise of playing a more active role in the negotiations, the Palestinian delegates complained that it was almost a carbon copy of Israeli positions. Further evidence of the USA's tilt towards Israel came in the testimony of the Assistant Secretary of State, Edward Djerejian, to a US Congress foreign affairs sub-committee on the Middle East, in which he voiced no objections to the use of the unfrozen US $10,000m. in loan guarantees to finance 'natural growth' of existing settlements in the Occupied Territories. A disgruntled Abdel Shafei concluded at the end of the ninth round of bilateral talks that nothing had been accomplished. He said that the delegation would not return for further talks unless the PLO Chairman convened a session of either the PNC or the PLO's Central Council to assess the situation. This brought a sharp rejoinder from Husseini who said that the decision on whether to attend further talks rested with the PLO leadership. Rifts within Palestinian ranks grew wider with the resignation of the PNC's veteran speaker in protest at the direction of the peace process. 'Tragedies are befalling the Palestinian people', he stated in his resignation address, 'and I do not want to be blamed for it'. There was little progress in the other bilateral talks. A claim by Israel's Minister of Foreign Affairs, Peres, that the Jordanian and Israeli delegations were on the brink of agreement was angrily denied by Jordan.

SOMBRE MOOD AT 10TH ROUND OPENING

The 10th round of bilateral negotiations opened in mid-June 1993 in quiet, almost ritualistic fashion and without Arab preconditions or expectations. Several Palestinian delegates, including Abdel Shafei, did not attend the talks but refrained from announcing an official boycott. The sense of Palestinian demoralization was deepened by comments made by the PLO Chairman to an Israeli newspaper to the effect that if Israel agreed to withdraw from Gaza and parts of the West Bank it would be proof of its implementation of Resolution

242. Arafat's statement was cited as evidence of the PLO leadership's abandonment of principle and absence of policy and led to calls for a complete re-evaluation of the Palestinian negotiating strategy. In a thinly-veiled attack on the PLO leader, Abdel Shafei also pleaded for democratization of the Organization. There was no progress in Washington, DC, to provide relief for the beleaguered Chairman. US efforts to produce a joint Israeli-Palestinian declaration of principles eventually led to the issuing of a draft proposal designed to constitute the new terms of reference for the peace talks. For the Palestinians the US document was an unacceptable departure from the assurances upon which their participation in the peace process was premised; firstly, because the USA insinuated that both Israel and the Palestinians had claims to sovereignty over the West Bank and Gaza; and secondly, because the issue of East Jerusalem was excluded from negotiations on interim self-government arrangements. The US proposals, Palestinian leaders agreed, were not even suitable as a starting point. Speculation that there might be progress between Israel and Syria was scotched after Rabin, under pressure from right-wing Jewish settlers, rejected a Syrian offer of a 'total' peace in exchange for a 'total' withdrawal from the Golan Heights.

'OPERATION ACCOUNTABILITY'

At the end of July 1993, following the killing of seven Israeli soldiers in south Lebanon by Hezbollah fighters, the IDF launched its severest bombardment of Lebanese territory since 1982. More than 55 villages were heavily damaged, 130 people, mainly civilians, were killed and 300,000 Lebanese fled north during the week-long assault. Hezbollah responded by firing salvoes of *Katyusha* rockets into northern Israel. These reportedly caused little damage and resulted in few casualties. Rabin code-named the IDF's action 'Operation Accountability' and stated that its purpose was to create a refugee crisis in Lebanon and thus pressurize Lebanon and Syria into taking action against Hezbollah. The deliberate targeting of civilians provoked harsh international condemnation. Boutros-Ghali declared it 'deplorable that any government would consciously adopt policies that would lead to the creation of a new flow of refugees and displaced persons', sentiments that were echoed by Arab states and the European Union (EU—formerly EC). Fears that the fighting would deal a fatal blow to the faltering peace process prompted Syria and the USA to mediate an end to the hostilities and to arrange what was termed an 'understanding' between Israel and Hezbollah whereby the IDF would refrain from attacking civilian targets as long as Hezbollah fighters confined their military operations to Lebanese territory. Israel declared its attack on south Lebanon a success, but it quickly became evident that Hezbollah had not been entirely subdued by the IDF. Less than three weeks after the Israeli bombardment, nine Israeli soldiers were killed in two ambushes carried out by Hezbollah fighters in Israel's security zone. Significantly, Israeli reprisals were confined to limited air strikes on Hezbollah bases in the Beka'a valley.

THE OSLO ACCORDS

Throughout the summer of 1993 the political and financial crisis within the PLO deepened. Two prominent members of the PLO Executive Committee resigned before the beginning of the 11th round of bilateral talks in protest at Arafat's negotiating strategy; the resignation of Husseini, Saeb Erekat and Ashrawi from the Palestinian delegation was only averted by the PLO's acceptance of their demands for greater democratization of the decision-making process. Rumours of corruption and mismanagement of the Organization's finances caused further erosion of support for Arafat's leadership, as did the growing chorus of dissent from the Damascus-based Palestinian groups, independents and erstwhile Fatah supporters. With the prospect of the PLO's disintegration seeming ever more likely, a dramatic development at the end of August injected sudden energy into the peace process and promised to shift Arab–Israeli relations onto a more positive footing. It emerged that Israel and the PLO had been engaged in secret negotiations in the Norwegian capital, Oslo, and had reached agreement on mutual recognition and a plan for staged Palestinian autonomy in the West Bank and the Gaza Strip. The precise details of the autonomy agreement were purposefully vague, but according to initial press reports the key components of the 'Oslo Accords' were said to include an early withdrawal of Israeli forces from Gaza and the Jericho area; the redeployment of Israeli troops in other areas of the West Bank; the gradual transfer of power from the civil administration to a Palestinian authority; the creation of a Palestinian police force; and the election of a Palestinian Council. Permanent status negotiations were to begin within two years of the Israeli withdrawal from Gaza and Jericho, be concluded within five years and would address such issues as Jerusalem, borders, settlement, co-operation, security and refugees. The reaction of the Arab world to the nascent PLO-Israeli agreement was decidedly mixed, not least amongst Palestinians themselves. Arafat managed to secure majority support for the Accords from the Fatah Central Committee, but failed to persuade three of the movement's co-founders, Farouk Kaddoumi and Khalid and Hani Hassan, to give their backing. Hamas and the Damascus-based Palestinian groups denounced the agreement as a betrayal, an interpretation that was shared by the majority of Palestinian refugees in Lebanon who staged protest marches and decked their camps with the black flags of mourning. The prominent Palestinian writer, Edward Said, scorned the agreement for transforming the PLO from a national liberation movement into a municipal council. Within the Occupied Territories, many ordinary Palestinians, no doubt swayed by the attrition of the *intifada* years, expressed guarded approval of the plan. Nevertheless, there was widespread concern among activists of all persuasions that the agreement represented a capitulation to Israeli demands and a dangerous journey into the unknown. Crucially, however, there was a strong consensus against the use of violence to settle inter-Palestinian differences. Gaining the support of the Arab world was as important for Arafat as winning over his domestic constituency and to this end the PLO Chairman embarked on a hurried tour of regional capitals at the beginning of September. President Mubarak predictably gave full support to the agreement, while Egyptian officials let it be known that they had played a seminal role in securing the two sides' agreement. King Hussein of Jordan initially displayed considerable pique at the failure of the PLO to consult him over the details of its talks in Oslo, and the Jordanian press expressed official disquiet at a 'separate' Israeli-Palestinian peace. However, given the USA's endorsement of the Oslo Accords and Jordan's traditional, if cautious, advocacy of Arab-Israeli peace, it came as little surprise that Jordan soon expressed support for the PLO Chairman. On 4 September King Hussein told a press conference that the Oslo Accords were 'part of a process leading to the implementation of [Security Council Resolution] 242 ... so I will emphasize our full support.' A day later the foreign ministers of the GCC member states gave their qualified support to what was described as 'a first step towards the liberation of all occupied land, including Jerusalem'. President Assad proved to be far less amenable to the new developments. At various times during the peace process Syria had been accused of negotiating a separate peace deal with Israel regarding the Golan Heights. Revelations that the PLO was on the verge of concluding its own agreement with Israel prompted the government-controlled media in Syria to issue lengthy commentaries denouncing disunity within Arab ranks. During six hours of talks in Damascus, Arafat failed to persuade the Syrian President to endorse the Oslo Accords. President Assad stressed that he believed the PLO's action had made the achievement of an Israeli withdrawal from the Golan Heights and southern Lebanon more difficult. These fears were shared by the Lebanese Prime Minster, Rafik Hariri, who was even more outspoken in his objections to the Israel-PLO deal. Addressing concerns that the Accords effectively froze the position of Palestinian refugees in Lebanon, he announced that 'under no circumstances whatsoever' would Palestinians be allowed to settle permanently in Lebanon.

The Israeli Cabinet unanimously approved the Oslo Accords on 30 August 1993 and early opinion polls suggested that there was a significant majority in the country in favour of the agreement. As government officials were quick to explain, there was little in the substance of the Oslo Accords to cause alarm in Israel. Withdrawal from the chaos of the Gaza Strip was broadly popular and dialogue with the PLO had become far more acceptable to the national psyche since the growth of Islamist fundamentalism. For the more 'hawkish' and sceptical sectors of the Israeli population there was solace in the fact that, under the terms of the agreement, security for the West Bank and Gaza would remain an Israeli responsibility, and that the short-term future of Israeli settlements was assured. Agreement with the Palestinians also offered the prospect of an end to the Arab economic boycott of Israel and of normalized relations with the Arab world. The Likud opposition was largely unimpressed by Labour's arguments, however. It accused Rabin and Peres of laying the cornerstone of a Palestinian state and stated that if Likud came to power it would refuse to honour the agreement. Representatives of the settler movement and of the extreme right-wing vowed to resort to civil disobedience in order to prevent the implementation of the Accords.

THE DECLARATION OF PRINCIPLES

The official signing of the Israeli-PLO Declaration of Principles took place on 13 September 1993 (see Documents on Palestine, p. 369) on the White House lawn in Washington, DC. In front of 3,000 international guests Rabin declared: 'We the soldiers who have returned from the battle stained with blood, we who have fought against you the Palestinians, we say to you today in a loud and clear voice: "Enough blood and tears! Enough!".' For his part, Arafat pleaded for 'courage and determination to continue the course of building coexistence and peace between us', and added, 'Our people do not consider the exercising of our right to self-determination could violate the rights of their neighbours or infringe on their security.' Significantly, however, it was Peres and the PLO spokesman on foreign policy, Mahmud Abbas, who actually signed the Declaration documents. The ceremony was concluded by an embarrassed, but highly symbolic handshake between Arafat and Rabin. Support for the Oslo Accords had grown steadily in the Occupied Territories in the two weeks since the PLO-Israeli agreement had been made public and the day of the signing was marked by massive celebrations throughout the West Bank and the Gaza Strip. Detecting the shift, and fearful of its marginalization, Hamas revealed once again its pragmatic streak. While stressing its continued opposition to the Accords, it acknowledged that a new reality had been created which it would be foolish for it to ignore. It also agreed with Fatah that their respective demonstrations in favour of and in opposition to the Accords should be allowed to pass without interference. Contrary to the fears of Palestinians, there were few reports of clashes between the two sides. Nevertheless, on the eve of the Washington ceremony Hamas sent a warning signal to the PLO and Israel when its gunmen ambushed and killed three Israeli soldiers on the edge of Gaza City; while in Beirut eight people were killed when units of the Lebanese army fired on a Hezbollah demonstration protesting against the PLO-Israeli agreement.

There were immediate and positive results from the signing of the Declaration of Principles for both Israel and the PLO. On 14 September Rabin was received in Morocco by King Hassan, in the first official visit by an Israeli Prime Minister to any Arab country other than Egypt. On the same day in Washington, Israeli and Jordanian representatives signed an agreement on an agenda for forthcoming negotiations between the two states. A number of issues of concern to Jordan were covered, including the return of Jordanian territory (adjoining the Dead Sea) occupied by Israel since the late 1960s; the fate of Palestinian refugees in Jordan; water rights; and a number of security issues. Jordan also committed itself not to threaten Israel by force and to work towards the removal of weapons of mass destruction from the Middle East. Meanwhile, Arafat was being fêted by the media networks in the USA and enjoying the sort of rehabilitation in the eyes of the US public that would have been unthinkable only a few months previously. There was a developing awareness among all the parties who wished to see the peace process maintain its momentum that future progress depended on the ability of Arafat to demonstrate to his own constituency that the benefits of the deal outweighed its obvious shortcomings. Particularly important, PLO officials stressed, was the immediate commitment of the international community to the kind of substantial aid package that would be needed to revitalize the economy and to improve social conditions in the Occupied Territories. The Clinton Administration responded to these pleas by organizing a donors' conference in Washington that secured promises of US $2,300m. in emergency aid for the West Bank and Gaza over the following five years; the EU and the USA pledged $600m. and $500m. respectively.

PLO LEADERSHIP CRISIS

Securing promises of substantial financial aid was an important fillip for the PLO Chairman in managing the scepticism with which the Oslo Accords were still regarded within PLO circles. In mid-October 1993 the PLO's Central

Council met in Tunis to debate the Accords. The boycotting of the meeting by the Popular and Democratic Fronts (for the Liberation of Palestine) and the other opposition groups ensured that the ratification of the Accords was passed by a bigger majority (63 votes to eight, with 11 abstentions) than might have been expected. Yet, despite the margin of the victory, the Central Council session and subsequent meetings in Tunis were not the triumph that Arafat loyalists claimed. Delegates complained that there was little substantive discussion of the Accords and no attempt to map out a coherent negotiating strategy in the forthcoming talks with Israel over their implementation. Moreover, Arafat's autocratic handling of the meetings revived fears that the PLO Chairman lacked the requisite political skills to resist Israeli pressure to make further concessions, or, for that matter, to transform the Palestinian struggle from one of national liberation to one of nation-building. Abdel Shafei, the erstwhile chief Palestinian negotiator in the peace process, signalled his own lack of faith in the ability and motives of the PLO leadership by announcing his resignation from his post. The lack of confidence in the political leadership extended to the Damascus-based opposition, in particular to the PFLP and DFLP, which were widely criticized for boycotting the Tunis meetings and for their preference for sloganeering rather than establishing an alternative programme to the autonomy proposals. It also appeared increasingly obvious that the secular opposition was being outflanked and outmanoeuvred by Hamas. After the 'rejectionist' PLO factions had announced their intention to boycott a proposed Palestinian reconciliation conference in the Yemeni capital, San'a, Hamas informed Arafat that it would be attending. Behind the Islamist movement's contradictory pronouncements on its intended relationship with the new Palestinian authority (in contrast to the Popular and Democratic Fronts which insisted that they would have no dealings with the new autonomous Palestinian institutions) many observers claimed to detect a bid by Hamas to posit itself as the only credible opposition to the Arafat wing of the PLO.

FURTHER NEGOTIATIONS

Israeli-Palestinian negotiations on the implementation of the first stages of the Declaration of Principles began in Cairo and the Red Sea resort of Taba on 13 October 1993. It quickly emerged during the first round of talks that there were several potentially serious obstacles to be overcome. Firstly, the Israeli and Palestinian delegations had widely differing definitions of what constituted the geographical area referred to as Jericho. According to the chief Palestinian negotiator, Nabil Sha'ath, Jericho referred to the old British Mandate Administrative Area comprising some 390 sq km and currently encompassing a number of Israeli settlements, as well as Arab villages. According to his Israeli counterpart, Gen. Amnon Shahak, the area in question was Jericho limited to its present municipal boundaries of a mere 25 sq km. More emotively, the two sides failed to agree on a timetable for the release of the estimated 11,000 Palestinian political prisoners in Israeli prisons. For the Palestinian side a comprehensive release of Palestinian prisoners was crucial to the maintenance of any degree of popular support for the autonomy plan. However, its request that Israel should draw up a timetable for release bore little fruit. A total of 617 prisoners were released on 25 October as a confidence-building measure. However, the majority of these were Fatah loyalists, leading one of the Palestinian negotiators to remark that they were 'trying to make peace between Palestinians and Israelis, not between Israel and a faction of the PLO'. Israel responded by saying that it would wait until the Palestinian police force was in place before releasing the majority of the detainees. Shortly afterwards it bowed to right-wing pressure and ended nearly all releases. The moratorium provoked one prominent Palestinian, Ziad Abu Ziad, to tender his resignation from the negotiating team. The issue of border security proved just as intractable. From Israel's point of view, this was its most sensitive domestic concern and, as such, the one area of the autonomy negotiations where it was least likely to compromise. On 1 November the Israeli delegation submitted proposals on security and the withdrawal of troops from the self-governing enclaves of Gaza and Jericho. These envisaged not so much the withdrawal of troops from Gaza as their redeployment in buffer zones around the Gaza Strip's Jewish settlements. They also proposed the retention of 20 checkpoints along the 1967 border to ensure the security of soldiers and settlers, and Israeli control over crossing points into and out of the autonomous enclaves. The Israeli proposals were condemned as unacceptable by Sha'ath, who withdrew the Palestinian delegation from the negotiations; it only returned after the Israeli delegation agreed to revise its plans for the redeployment of the IDF in Gaza. Palestinian critics of the autonomy proposals commented that this early dispute over security went to the core of their dissatisfaction with the Declaration of Principles, namely its studied refusal to address the status of Jewish settlements. 'If Israelis and Palestinians can't agree that the settlements are illegal entities on our land,' commented one Gazan economist, 'then we are saying that in the Occupied Territories there are *de facto* two separate entities and that these are somehow equivalent. They are both legal or legitimate presences.' An inescapable corollary of this failure to define the status of the settlements was implicit acceptance of the long-held Israeli view that the West Bank and Gaza were not so much occupied territories as disputed ones.

VIOLENCE CONTINUES

Hopes that the signing of the Declaration of Principles would lead to a reduction in violent incidents in Gaza and the West Bank were also frustrated. In Gaza the impending transfer of power to a PLO authority gave rise to a secret feud within Fatah that claimed the lives of three top figures in the Organization, including that of As'ad Saftawi, a co-founder of the Fatah movement and its leading activist in Gaza. At the same time, the IDF maintained its policy of pursuing wanted activists, killing and arresting gunmen of all political factions, including those identified as Fatah loyalists. Protests from the Palestinian negotiators that the targeting of activists was a violation of the spirit of the newly signed Accords failed to end the operations of Israeli undercover units. The killing of Hamas's senior military leader in Gaza in November 1993 gave rise to a massive increase in confrontations which were reignited two weeks later when a leading Fatah 'hawk', Ahmad Abu Rish, was shot dead by an Israeli undercover unit in Khan Yunis. Only a few days before his killing Abu Rish had received a much publicized amnesty from the Israeli authorities for obeying an Arafat directive and surrendering his weapon. His colleagues subsequently announced that they would resume their military operations unless Israel stopped pursuing wanted activists. Hamas, which was the principal target of the IDF's operations in Gaza, had never shown any sign of de-escalating its attacks on Israeli targets. Despite the deaths and arrests of scores of its activists, it continued to demonstrate that it was by far the most effective Palestinian military force in the Occupied Territories. Seemingly impervious to penetration by the Israeli security services, it was able to inflict regular casualties on both soldiers and settlers. Indeed, the killing of Jewish settlers by Palestinian gunmen during the autumn of 1993 produced fierce right-wing reprisals that escalated with every passing incident. Arguably more opposed to their Government's agreement with the PLO than the Islamists of Hamas, the settlers' desire to avenge attacks on their own community became intertwined with a desire to derail the negotiation process. Such was the scale of the assaults on Palestinian targets that Israeli newspapers started to refer to a 'Jewish *intifada*'. Right-wing spokesmen hinted darkly that as long as the twin provocations of Palestinian violence and government talks with the PLO existed, there was every likelihood of the re-emergence of the kind of settler underground movement that had operated during the late 1970s and early 1980s. At a nationalist rally in Jerusalem, settlers were urged to 'rise up against this government of iniquity, against the evil ruling over us', and were told that 'these are not days of peace but of war'. The warnings proved to be prophetic. In mid-December, after two settlers were killed in an attack by Hamas fighters near Hebron, Israeli gunmen shot dead three young Palestinian workers in retaliation.

CRISIS WITHIN FATAH

The cycle of violence made the prospect of an agreement on withdrawal from Gaza and Jericho by the 13 December 1993 deadline (as set down in the Declaration of Principles) increasingly unlikely. The main obstacles remained security and the size of the Jericho enclave. At a joint press conference in Cairo on 12 December, the Israeli and Palestinian negotiators announced their failure to meet the deadline. Rabin complained that the PLO Chairman 'lacked the inner strength' to reach an agreement, while the Israeli Chief of Staff, Gen. Ehud Barak, stated that it was unlikely that the IDF would hand over Gaza to the Palestinians as long as the PLO seemed unable to halt the violence there. Unlike Rabin, who appeared unperturbed by the delay and made a point of stating that the timetable laid out in the Declaration of Principles was not a rigid one, Arafat was visibly upset. Failure to meet the deadline had further undermined dwindling support for the peace process—in the student council elections at Bir Zeit University, long regarded as a good indicator of Palestinian public opinion, Fatah had lost control of the student body to a coalition of 'rejectionist' groups—and was an undoubted reverse for the beleaguered Chairman. While he did receive grudging recognition for his refusal to accept Israel's proposals for the redeployment of the IDF to protect Jewish settlements in the Gaza Strip, this was small comfort when compared with the renewed chorus of criticism of the style and substance of his leadership. Calls for a clearer negotiating strategy and the democratization of the PLO were too loud to be ignored and compelled the PLO leader to accept demands for a dialogue with the nationalist opposition. Yet for some Fatah elements in Gaza patience with the PLO leadership had clearly expired. At the end of December three senior Fatah members resigned their posts in protest at the 'cronyism and favouritism' that had characterized political advancement in the Occupied Territories. They were articulating a concern of many Palestinians from within the Occupied Territories: that local cadres belonging to the *intifada* generation of activists were being marginalized by the imposition of political appointees from outside the Occupied Territories, and by 'salon spokesmen', with little experience of activism, from within. These were not new criticisms, but such a public airing of them at such a sensitive time pointed to an ever-deepening crisis within the Fatah movement.

PLO RELATIONS WITH JORDAN

Arafat also had to contend with a crisis in the PLO's relationship with Jordan. While the PLO and Israel had been struggling to overcome their differences on the autonomy accords, Israel and Jordan had been making swift progress in their own talks in Washington, DC. The claim, by an Israeli minister, that everything with Jordan 'is tied up and signed' hardly pleased the PLO leader. There was also irritation with Jordan for signing a memorandum with Israel that allowed the opening of branches of Jordanian banks in the Occupied Territories during the interim period. According to the PLO, Jordan should have waited to sign an agreement with the new Palestinian authority, and by not doing so it had undermined Palestinian attempts to secure practical acknowledgement of Palestinian sovereignty. As a result, Arafat refused to sign an agreement that would have allowed Jordan's Central Bank to regulate monetary policies in the Occupied Territories during the interim period. The difficulty was finally resolved in mid-January 1994 after a strong attack by the Jordanian monarch on the PLO's delaying tactics finally persuaded Arafat to dispatch Farouk Kaddoumi to Amman to sign an economic agreement. This allowed for the reopening of 20 branches of Jordanian banks closed in 1967 and confirmed the use of the Jordanian dinar in the Occupied Territories. The banks would be supervised by the Central Bank of Jordan until a Palestinian central bank was established.

SYRIAN REACTION

Syria, meanwhile, continued to smart at the perfidy of the Oslo Accords and at Jordan's apparently fruitful negotiations with Israel. King Hussein assured President Assad that Jordan would not sign a separate deal with Israel, despite pressure to do so from Rabin and President Clinton of the USA. Nevertheless, the feeling in Damascus remained one of perceived betrayal and injured pride, Syria regarding itself as the standard-bearer of Arab unity while all around the Arab world drifted into unprincipled accommodation with Israel. The USA's concern that Syrian isolation threatened to unbalance the peace process led to a summit meeting between the Syrian and US Presidents in Geneva, Switzerland, in January 1994. Assad stressed to Clinton that Syria could not consider a separate peace deal with Israel, and that he would not entertain a normalization of relations with Israel until Israel had committed itself to full withdrawal from the Golan Heights. President Assad did, however, confirm that peace with Israel was Syria's goal and intimated that, in return for an Israeli withdrawal from south Lebanon, the Syrian army would disarm Hezbollah. Fearing that the Assad-Clinton summit meeting was a dangerous step towards the rehabilitation of the Syrian President and a prelude to US pressure on Israel to make concessions over the Golan Heights, representatives of the Jewish settler movement delivered a letter of protest to the US embassy in Tel-Aviv stating that any US interference would be harmful to the peace process. Despite claims that 90% of Israelis were opposed to withdrawal from the Golan Heights, a radio opinion poll revealed that nearly one-half of the 12,000 Israeli settlers there had considered moving back to the pre-1967 borders of Israel. Several of the more 'dovish' members of the Israeli Cabinet, including the Deputy Minister of Foreign Affairs, Yosi Beilin, used the occasion of the Assad-Clinton meeting to concede that, given the proper security guarantees, Israel would be obliged to withdraw from the Golan Heights. Rabin distanced himself from such remarks, preferring to allude to withdrawal in the Golan Heights rather than from the Golan Heights. Interestingly, however, the Israeli Prime Minister hinted at greater Israeli flexibility with the assessment that the 'extent of the withdrawal will be as the extent of the peace'.

RENEWED DISCUSSIONS

Arafat and Peres met in Davos, Switzerland, in January 1994 for talks aimed at resolving the differences that were preventing the signing of an agreement on implementation of the Gaza-Jericho component of the Declaration of Principles. Sufficient progress was made for a resumption of talks in Cairo on 6 February. After three days of intense discussion it was announced that agreement had been reached on most of the issues that had been dividing the two sides. On the question of the control of border crossings between the autonomous zones and neighbouring states, it was agreed that Israel would maintain military control and have a veto over Palestinian visitors. The latter would be allowed to stay in Gaza and Jericho for a maximum period of four months only and would have to apply to the Israeli authorities for any extension of that time. The Palestinian presence at the borders was to be limited to flags, entry stamps, guards and immigration officials, although Israel acknowledged that the searching of Palestinian visitors would be largely a Palestinian responsibility. It was also agreed that the territory of Gaza would be divided into three zones: Israeli settlements and the Egyptian border area, which were to remain under Israeli control; a second area, encompassing the perimeter of the Israeli settlements and access roads, to be jointly patrolled; and the rest of the Gaza Strip, which was to be transferred to the new Palestinian authority. There was no resolution of the dispute over the precise size of the Jericho enclave, although Palestinian officials maintained that the 'size of Jericho will not be a problem in itself'.

PALESTINIAN REACTION

The agreement reached in Cairo was widely regarded as Palestinian capitulation to Israel's conception of what shape the interim autonomy period should take. In Damascus the 10 Palestinian rejectionist factions, grouped under the umbrella of the newly formed Alliance of Palestinian Forces (APF), condemned the new security arrangements and insisted that they would refuse to co-operate with the PLO or participate in elections scheduled for July 1994. The APF announced the formation of a new central council to rival that of the PLO and pledged an escalation of the *intifada*. The decision of the Palestinian rejection-ists, together with continued Fatah infighting, was further evidence of the painful process of disintegration and realignment that was steadily transforming the face of Palestinian politics. In Gaza, which continued to be affected by both inter-Palestinian violence and Israeli–Palestinian clashes, there were reports that huge numbers of arms were being stockpiled for the purpose of settling political differences once the Israeli forces withdrew. The visibility and availability of weapons led to allegations that the IDF was encouraging future disorder in Gaza by ignoring the organized gun-running to the Strip.

THE HEBRON MASSACRE

The peace process suffered a dramatic reverse on 25 February 1994 when Baruch Goldstein, an American-born adherent of the extremist Kach movement and resident of Kiryat Arba, carried out an armed attack on Palestinian worshippers in the Ibrahimi mosque in the centre of Hebron. Goldstein entered the mosque during early morning Ramadan prayers and fired his automatic weapon indis-criminately at the congregation. Twenty-nine people died before worshippers managed to overpower and kill their attacker. Palestinian fury at the massacre was heightened by reports that Israeli soldiers on duty at the mosque had contributed to the atrocity by failing to intercept Goldstein and by barring the doors of the mosque to fleeing worshippers. As news of the massacre spread, violent protests erupted throughout the Occupied Territories and among Arab communities inside Israel; a further 33 Palestinians were killed in the eight subsequent days, despite widespread curfews and massive troop deployment. The massacre and its bloody aftermath was roundly denounced in the Arab world. The Jordanian, Lebanese and Syrian Governments declared the suspen-sion of their participation in the peace process. The Rabin Government responded to the events in Hebron by announcing its intention to set up a commission of inquiry and ordering the detention of a small number of known settler extremists. A ban was also declared on Kach and the related organization, Kahane Lives. These measures failed to mollify Palestinians, who asserted that only the disarming of settlers and the dismantling of the settlements could guarantee Palestinian security in the Occupied Territories. PLO spokesmen demanded a revision of the Declaration of Principles to allow immediate discussion of the future of Israeli settlements and for the dispatch of an international protection force to the Occupied Territories, a suggestion that was endorsed by Arab states and the UN Secretary-General, but dismissed as 'neither particularly helpful or useful' by the USA. Several prominent PLO figures stated publicly that the removal of 400 or so militant settlers from the heart of Hebron was the *sine qua non* of the PLO's decision to resume talks with Israel. Both Hamas and Islamic Jihad vowed to take revenge for the Hebron massacre, a predictable response, but one that only added to the burden of pressure on the PLO leader. The massacre placed Arafat in a delicate position. Although it was believed that Hebron would allow the PLO Chairman to exact concessions from Israel in return for an early end to the Organization's suspen-sion of participation in the autonomy negotiations, it was unlikely that Rabin would entertain the PLO's demands for immediate action against core settler interests. The Labour Government had little ideological affinity with 'hardline' settlers; however, Rabin recognized that they were valuable 'bargaining chips' and that it would be a mistake to alienate them before the 'final status' negotiations. Moreover, it was clear to Arafat that the best hope to reinforce his own standing and to regain support for the peace process lay in demonstrating the benefits of the Oslo Accords by securing an early Israeli withdrawal from Gaza and Jericho. Any residual willingness of the PLO Chairman to delay in the hope of Israeli concessions was also undermined by Jordanian and Syrian assurances to the USA that their withdrawal from the peace talks with Israel was only temporary. The somewhat surprising stance of the Syrian Government was explained by its Minister of Foreign Affairs as a response to the PLO's 'isolationist' approach and its refusal to co-ordinate its position with the front-line Arab states. But it was also clear that the USA had lobbied hard in Damascus for a Syrian return to the negotiating table, primarily as a means of putting pressure on the PLO to end its boycott of the talks. The USA similarly promised that it would lift the naval blockade of the Jordanian port of Aqaba (in place since the Iraqi invasion of Kuwait) as a reward for Jordan's early resumption of talks with Israel. In the mean time, the USA maintained its pro-Israel diplomacy at the UN. Albright effectively delayed a vote on Resolution 904, which condemned the Hebron massacre and urged protection for Palestinians in the Occupied Territories, because the USA objected to the inclusion of paragraphs describing Jerusalem and the territories seized in 1967 as 'occupied Palestinian territory'. Resolution 904 was finally adopted by the Security Council on 10 March 1994, with the USA abstaining on two of its preambular paragraphs referring to occupied Palestinian territory. Albright justified the USA's abstentions on the grounds that it did not wish to prejudice the course of the 'final status' negotiations agreed upon in the Declaration of Principles. Nevertheless, Nasir el-Kidwa, the Palestinian observer at the UN, remarked that the USA's decision marked a disturbing departure from early US assurances that it regarded all of the 1967 territories as occupied. There was further Palestinian disappointment with Resolution 904's demand for their protection in the Occupied Territories. Instead of a UN armed force, as favoured by the PLO, the UN Security Council—again acting under US pressure—voted for a temporary observer force to be dispatched to Hebron. It was agreed that the force would not be under the control of the UN and that its mode of operations would be decided through negotiation between Israel and the PLO within the framework of the Declaration of Principles. Israel eventually agreed to the presence of 160 lightly armed observers, operating under ultimate Israeli control. The rather limited remit of the mainly Norwegian force was 'to monitor Palestinian safety' and to aid the return of Hebron to 'normal life'.

RETALIATION BY HAMAS

By the beginning of April 1994 the PLO had agreed to resume negotiations with Israel despite the failure to secure the reassurances on settlements that PLO leaders had initially demanded. Its decision was perceived negatively by many Palestinians in the Occupied Territories, where dwindling goodwill towards the Oslo process was undergoing further erosion as a result of IDF security operations. Several people were killed in Hebron and a number of houses were destroyed by rocket fire in an army attempt to flush out Hamas gunmen. At the end of March six members of a pro-Arafat Fatah security team were shot dead in an ambush in Gaza. The latter incident forced an apology by the IDF and underlined a belief shared by many in the Israeli political establishment that urgent action was required to reinforce Arafat's position and guarantee the viability of the peace process. The return of 47 Palestinian deportees, most of them senior PLO figures, was widely welcomed in the Occupied Territories. More importantly, the IDF began to redeploy its forces in response to news from Egypt that an agreement had been reached on the final issues dividing Israel and the PLO over the implementation of autonomy in the Gaza Strip and Jericho. However, even as the Oslo Accords were on the verge of being translated into reality, there came a deadly reminder of the fragility of that process. On 6 April a car bomb in the Israeli town of Afula killed seven Israelis and maimed scores of others, many of them schoolchildren. A week later five more people were killed in a similar attack in Hadera. Hamas claimed responsibility for both assaults, describing them as a response to the Hebron massacre. Some 300 Islamist militants were detained after the bombings and the Occupied Territories' boundaries were sealed. The Hamas spokesman in Amman stated that his organization would halt attacks on civilians in return for an end to the Israeli offensive. He also promised that Hamas would support a peace agreement with Israel in return for an Israeli withdrawal from all of the Palestinian territory occupied in 1967. The Hamas offer received no official reply from Israel except an appeal to Jordan to close Hamas's offices on its territory. Israel was also highly critical of an agreement reached in Gaza between Fatah and Hamas that had been precipitated by an outbreak of armed clashes between the two factions. Both sides agreed to a month-long moratorium on the killing of collaborators and 'an end to violence in Palestinian society'. Commenting on Israel's criticism of its talks with Hamas, a Fatah spokesman rejoined that the Organization's dealings with Hamas to secure order in the Gaza Strip would be on the PLO's terms and not Rabin's. He added: 'Our decision to co-operate with Hamas is an internal Palestinian issue and does not concern any other side. Fatah and Hamas are in the same boat and we will not allow anyone to sink it.'

AUTONOMY IN GAZA AND JERICHO

Against a background of weary anticipation and lawless confusion in Gaza, Israeli and Palestinian officials met in Cairo on 4 May 1994 for a signing ceremony to seal the successful conclusion of eight months of troubled talks on the implementation of an autonomy agreement for Gaza and Jericho. Yet, in ironic accordance with the problems that had bedevilled the negotiations from the start, the dignified proceedings turned to high farce when Arafat refused to sign one of the documents pertaining to the size of the Jericho enclave. A highly embarrassing moment for the assembled dignitaries and the Egyptian President was eventually resolved by a hasty adjournment and an agreement that Arafat would annotate the offending document with a comment to the effect that it was awaiting final agreement. On returning to Israel an outraged Rabin insinuated that the problems at the Cairo ceremony were symptomatic of the PLO Chairman's inability to provide leadership. Arafat was also reproached by members of the PLO Executive Committee for having failed to discuss the agreement about to be concluded with Israel at a meeting held just a few days before the Cairo signing. Many PLO executive members stayed away from Cairo in protest at Arafat's autocracy, while within the Occupied Territories deepening reservations over the style of Arafat's leadership and the substance of the agreement reached with Israel meant that the PLO Chairman experienced great difficulty in trying to persuade political figures to take seats on the 24-member Palestinian Autonomy Council, the body designed to oversee the implementation of the autonomy agreement. Nevertheless, the signing of the agreement in Cairo resulted in rapid change in Gaza and Jericho. The IDF hastened its withdrawal from centres of Palestinian population, and on 10 May the first contingent of the Palestinian police force arrived in Gaza. A further 400 arrived in Jericho a few days later. Israel had also announced the imminent release of 5,000 Palestinian detainees. On 13 May and 17 May, in Jericho and Gaza respectively, the IDF handed over its positions to the commanders of the Palestinian forces in simple ceremonies. The Chief of Palestinian Police Forces told crowds in Gaza that they were witnessing 'a historic day for the Palestinian people, the first step on the way to independence'. The following day, in the early hours of the morning, Israel evacuated its last position in Gaza City. Bitter memories of the occupation meant that even at this final hour there would be no dignity in the Israeli withdrawal. The departing troops left under a cloud of tear-gas and a shower of rocks and bottles, while tens of Palestinian gunmen joined members of the Palestinian police force in a deafening salute to the beginning of a somewhat different reality.

Finalization of the agreement on autonomy for Gaza and Jericho was met with scorn in Syria, where Arafat was widely perceived as having allowed the Palestinian national movement to be humiliated by Israel. Syria refused an invitation to attend the Cairo ceremony and the state-controlled media commented that, 'There can be no middle way. There can be no compromise over land and peace. Comprehensive peace in the Middle East depends on the return of all occupied land.' Syria's unwavering commitment to these principles was regarded by the USA as the principal obstacle to achieving a wider Middle East settlement. The US Secretary of State, Warren Christopher, was dispatched to the Middle East at the end of April 1994 and again in May in an attempt to reconcile the Syrian and Israeli positions. His mission proved largely fruitless. Rabin stated that he would entertain no greater compromise than a promise to dismantle some of the settlements on the Golan Heights and to make a phased withdrawal, over a number of years, from some areas of the Heights. This was unacceptable to President Assad, who insisted that a total Israeli withdrawal from occupied Syrian territory, accomplished within a one- to two-year period, must precede any peace agreement. Plans for a further visit by Christopher in June were abandoned after Rabin confirmed that negotiations with Syria were totally static and Syria reiterated that there was little purpose in further dialogue until Israel made a public pledge that its withdrawal from the Golan Heights would be total. Controversial Israeli military operations in Lebanon during May and June made it even less likely that Syria would soften its stance. On 22 May Mustafa ad-Dirani, a leader of the radical Iranian-supported Faithful Resistance Organization, was abducted by Israeli forces from the Beka'a valley. The raid, reminiscent of the abduction of Sheikh Obeid in 1989, was justified on the ground that ad-Dirani had information about the missing Israeli navigator, Ron Arad, who had been shot down over Lebanon in 1986. Ten days after ad-Dirani had been seized, Israeli aircraft were once again in action over Lebanon, attacking a Hezbollah training camp in the Beka'a valley and killing, according to Israeli sources, 36 Hezbollah fighters and wounding more than 100. The attack was of questionable political value and was regarded as an indication of a shift to the right in the governing Israeli Labour Party.

In Gaza and Jericho there was widespread jubilation at the departure of Israeli troops and an end to the curfews and restrictions that had been part of daily existence during the years of the *intifada*. Israel's own relief at being rid of the security problem of Gaza was marred, only two days after the withdrawal, when two Israeli soldiers were shot dead by Islamic Jihad gunmen near the Erez border crossing to Israel. Significantly, the IDF did not pursue the gunmen into Palestinian-controlled territory, and while the PLO assured Israel that it would try to curb such actions, it insisted that the disarming of Palestinian groups could only take place within the framework of broad factional agreement. Nevertheless, the agreed joint patrols by Israeli and Palestinian security forces along the demarcation lines of authority in Gaza and Jericho appeared to function in a spirit of comparative harmony.

ECONOMIC DIFFICULTIES

A far greater worry for Palestinians than security co-ordination with Israel, and one that was only briefly masked by the general euphoria, was the financial and administrative chaos in Gaza. The difficulty Arafat was experiencing in recruiting appointees to the new Palestinian Autonomy Council—to be composed of 15 personalities from inside the Occupied Territories and nine from the Palestinian diaspora—resulted in the 3,000-strong police force operating in a judicial and legal vacuum. This situation was aggravated by the absence of properly constituted structures to co-ordinate and implement administrative change. The extent of the financial crisis was epitomized by the fact that the new police force was having to subsist on munitions donated by the local population. Israel had placed a limit of 23,000 on the number of Gazan workers it was prepared to allow into Israel and had sealed its border completely in response to the killings at the Erez check-point; the consequent high unemployment exacerbated the situation. Under pressure from Israeli farmers, Rabin had also reneged on an earlier decision to allow the importation of Gazan agricultural produce into Israel. Further trouble loomed for the nascent Palestinian authority in Gaza with the prospect of having to pay the estimated 7,000 employees of the previous Israeli civilian administration. With little prospect of revenue from tax collection from a population for whom tax avoidance had been seen until now as a patriotic as well as a personal imperative, there were desperate pleas from the PLO for international aid. Palestinian economists had estimated that Palestinian self-rule would require an annual budget of US $240m., with a maximum of $127m. likely to be raised in tax revenues. First year start-up costs were likely to be in the region of $600m., leaving a huge budgetary deficit. Although $2,300m. had been promised to the Palestinians at the international donors' conference held in Washington, DC, in October 1993, the international community was reluctant to disburse funds until the Palestinians had established proper accounting procedures and clear project proposals. The PLO rejoined that without immediate funds to set up a basic administrative structure—which the donors were reluctant to subsidize—it would be impossible to meet the international requirements. Arafat expressed his personal fury at the implications of corruption and mismanagement and stated that he would not visit the autonomous regions to take charge of the transition until pledges of aid were forthcoming. The Israeli media appeared to take delight in the discomfort of the PLO leader and cited the financial wrangling as further evidence of his unredeemable political shortcomings. However, for once, Arafat's brinkmanship appeared to pay off. In a series of tense meetings in Paris, France, in June the donor countries agreed to the immediate release of $42m. in aid, with at least one-quarter of this sum going to fund the establishment of the Palestinian administration—without the *quid pro quo* of detailed accounting. They also agreed to take measures to cover the shortfall to meet the expected 1994 deficit. There were also positive developments in the West Bank and Gaza. By the end of June most of the 24 places on the Autonomy Council (which later became the Palestinian National Authority—PNA) had been filled, mostly by Arafat loyalists, but also by several quasi-independents and members of Fida, the faction of the DFLP led by Abd ar-Rabbuh. In Gaza the Palestinian police force had won an assurance from Hamas that the killing of collaborators would stop; and in Damascus the ageing leader of the PFLP, George Habash, marked a considerable softening of his organization's position on the new Palestinian authority by instructing his supporters 'not to take a negative stance towards the institutions that offer services during the interim phase'.

ARAFAT VISITS GAZA

The easing of the PLO's financial worries, coupled with criticism of Arafat's apparent hesitation in taking control of the Palestinian self-rule areas, was answered with a commitment by the PLO leader to make his long-awaited visit to the newly autonomous enclaves. On 1 July 1994, with little advance warning, Arafat crossed from Egypt into Gaza to set foot on Palestinian soil for the first time in 25 years. His reception was more muted than might have been expected for a returning leader who had for so many years been an international symbol of the Palestinian cause. Yet large crowds did gather both in Gaza City and in Jabalia refugee camp, birthplace of the *intifada*, to hear Arafat's address. There was little of note in either speech beyond the repeated pleas for Palestinian unity—directed principally at the Islamist opposition—and an acknowledgement that there was little popular enthusiasm for the Oslo Accords. Arafat reassured his audience that the Gaza and Jericho enclaves were the stepping-stones to an independent Palestinian state with Jerusalem as its capital. Similar sentiments were voiced two days later in Jericho. When the PLO Chairman ended his four-day visit to meet with Rabin and Peres in Paris, France, his aides announced that he would soon be returning 'for good' and that Gaza, rather than Jericho, would be the home of the new Palestinian administration. Arafat's visit had raised more questions than it had answered. Despite the affection extended to him, Arafat's performances failed to convince anybody that he possessed the requisite political skills to address the shortcomings of the autonomy accords or to build on their openings. The presence of the PLO

Chairman in Gaza and Jericho had as much symbolic resonance on the boulevards of Tel-Aviv as in the alley-ways of Gaza. The return of a personality who for more than two decades had been demonized by politicians and the media alike was seized on by the Israeli right wing as a focus to rally opposition to the Oslo Accords. A demonstration in Jerusalem organized by the nationalist right to protest at Arafat's visit ended as something of an 'own goal' for Likud when some 10,000 demonstrators left the main rally and rioted in East Jerusalem. Scenes of settlers and their supporters not only attacking Palestinians and their property, but also fighting with the Israeli security forces, were a severe embarrassment for the struggling Likud leader, Binyamin Netanyahu. Rabin lambasted the settlers as the Israeli equivalent of Hamas, while Likud quietly reflected that they had lost an opportunity to garner the moderate support needed to obstruct the PLO-Israeli agreement. Rabin's own fortunes were fortified in July with news that the orthodox Shas party would be rejoining the Labour coalition, as would Ye'ud, a splinter group from the right-wing Tzomet Party. There was no such comfort for Arafat. Shortly after returning to Gaza, the PLO leader became embroiled in the most serious incident of the Strip's two-month-old autonomy. In the early morning of 17 July a clash occurred at the Erez check-point between Palestinian labourers and units of the IDF attempting to check that they possessed the correct documentation for entry into Israel. Frustrations at the slowness of the process led to a full-scale riot, with the Palestinian workers burning down an Israeli bus depot and Israeli soldiers attempting to restore order with live ammunition. There then followed a prolonged gun battle between members of the Palestinian police force and soldiers of the IDF. Two Palestinians were killed in the clash and 75 were injured; 18 Israeli soldiers also suffered gun-shot wounds. The mutual recriminations that followed failed to obscure the underlying tensions that had given the incident an air of inevitability. Firstly, rather than easing the process by which Palestinian workers gained employment in Israel, the advent of autonomy had merely added to it a further tier of administrative bureaucracy. Secondly, the Erez violence confirmed the fears of Palestinians that the security arrangements agreed in Cairo had created a kind of Gaza *gulag*. Finally, the entire autonomy process appeared to be doomed to failure unless something could be done to address the perilous state of the Gazan economy. 'What happened in Gaza today,' the Palestinian Minister of Justice, Furaih Abu Middain, commented, 'was a battle for a loaf of bread.' The Israeli decision to seal off the Strip in response to the violence was condemned as incendiary by Palestinian sources and cast a further shadow over impending negotiations on the implementation of the next phase of the autonomy accords.

ISRAELI–JORDANIAN RELATIONS IMPROVE

The depressed mood that characterized Israeli–Palestinian relations was thrown into sharp relief by dramatic progress in Israel's bilateral talks with Jordan. On 9 July 1994 King Hussein announced to the Jordanian National Assembly that he was prepared to meet the Israeli Prime Minister, and on 18 July Jordanian and Israeli negotiators sat at a table straddling the countries' border to take part in the first bilateral talks to be held in the Middle East itself. The decision of the Jordanian monarch to make such a highly symbolic concession to Israel was widely interpreted as an exercise in pragmatic self-interest. Anxious to maintain the momentum for a comprehensive peace settlement in the Middle East, the USA had offered appealing incentives to King Hussein to move Israeli–Jordanian relations to the centre of the peace process. Not least among these was US President Clinton's promise that his Government would work towards the waiving of Jordan's $900m. debt to the USA, provide military assistance to Jordan and seek to persuade Saudi Arabia and the Gulf states to end their economic and political boycott of the Hashemite regime. An announcement by Peres in mid-July acknowledging the Golan Heights to be Syrian territory was seen as Israel's contribution to the wider US plan of muting Syrian criticism of Jordan's effective *coup de grâce* to the dying beast of Arab unity. That Jordan refrained from signing a full peace treaty with Israel did not disguise the fact that the normalization of Israeli–Jordanian relations was close. In Washington, DC, on 25 July King Hussein and Rabin formally ended the state of belligerency between their two nations in a ceremony that underlined not only the understanding that had been a feature of Israeli–Jordanian relations for many years, but also the personal warmth that existed between King Hussein and Rabin, a quality that was visibly absent from relations between the Israeli Prime Minister and the PLO Chairman. With the exception of the extreme right-wing fringe of Israeli politics, the country met the formal end of the state of war with Jordan with general acclaim, and a feeling that the key issues of contention with Jordan, the sharing of water resources and the return of a small area of Jordanian territory seized by Israel in the late 1960s, could be easily resolved. Jordan's citizens were less sanguine. Fundamentalist and left-wing groups were critical of the *rapprochement*, while the majority of the population saw the overtures to Israel as the inevitable price that had to be paid if Jordan was to solve the problem it had created for itself in the aftermath of Iraq's invasion of Kuwait in 1990. Palestinian reaction, in contrast, was sharply critical. There were strong suspicions that Israel, Jordan and the USA were engaged in a concerted effort to isolate the PLO and prepare for a reassertion of Hashemite control over the West Bank, leaving the PLO Chairman as 'mayor of Gaza'. There was particular concern at the inclusion in the document signed by King Hussein and Rabin in Washington of a paragraph acknowledging Jordan's 'special role' as guardian of the Muslim holy sites in Jerusalem. Assurances from King Hussein that there was no contradiction between Jordan reaching an understanding over guardianship of religious sites in East Jerusalem and Palestinian political sovereignty failed to convince the PLO leadership. On 20 July the PLO retaliated against Jordan's perceived treachery by banning the sale and distribution of the pro-Jordanian daily, *An-Nahar*, in the autonomous enclaves. Arafat reportedly justified the decision on the ground that he could not 'tolerate any undermining of Palestinian national interest in the name of press freedom'. The irony of a Palestinian authority restricting Palestinian freedom of speech was not lost on anyone, least of all Israel. The Arab world responded to both the Israeli-Jordanian agreement and the PLO's quarrel with Jordan with a large measure of indifference, damning evidence, if such was still needed, that the Arab world could not muster sufficient enthusiasm even to pay lip-service to the notion of Arab solidarity. Of the region's principal powers, only Syria condemned

Jordan's agreement with Israel, in a statement that was made much easier by an earlier refutation, by Rabin, of Peres' comment that Israel regarded the Golan Heights as Syrian territory.

ISRAELI-JORDANIAN PEACE TREATY

Israel's breakthrough in its relations with Jordan was succeeded by further diplomatic and political gains. On 1 September 1994 Morocco became only the second Arab nation to establish diplomatic ties with the Jewish state, while Tunisia announced that it would shortly be establishing its own links with Israel via the Belgian embassy in Tel-Aviv. At the end of the month the six GCC member states responded to US urgings and signalled the formal end of their long-standing economic boycott of companies trading with Israel. Meanwhile Israeli and Jordanian negotiators had reached agreement on outstanding disputes over territory and water. Israel acceded to the immediate diversion of 50m. cu m from the Sea of Galilee to meet Jordanian water needs and, in order to aid the construction of flood reservoirs on the Rivers Jordan and Yarmouk, agreed to supply a further 50m. cu m. The Israeli Government also recognized Jordanian sovereignty over contested border lands in return for a Jordanian commitment to lease back the territory to Israel. President Assad scorned this commitment as 'blasphemous', but despite his opposition and the resistance of Jordan's Islamist and leftist parties to the normalization of relations with their historic foe, King Hussein duly sealed the agreement with Israel on 26 October by signing a peace treaty with Rabin in the presence of US President Clinton. Israel and Jordan opened their respective embassies in Amman and Tel-Aviv less than two months later. Peace with Jordan was broadly welcomed in Israel and met with overwhelming approval in the Knesset; only the three deputies of the right-wing Moledet party voted against ratification of the peace treaty with Jordan, with a handful of Likud 'diehards' abstaining. Equally indicative of Israel's rapidly improving relations with the Arab world was the presence of a large Israeli delegation at a regional economic summit meeting in Casablanca, Morocco, at the end of October. The meeting attracted 2,000 business and political leaders from the Arab world and their main Western trading partners and was designed to further the peace process by encouraging economic co-operation. Although the summit concluded with few substantive proposals, Israel's high-profile presence was celebrated at home as both a political and economic victory.

FURTHER DEADLOCK ON DECLARATION OF PRINCIPLES

The Palestinian reaction to the Israeli-Jordanian peace treaty was, predictably, less welcoming. Arafat was not invited to the signing ceremony, and unallayed Palestinian suspicions regarding Hashemite designs on Jerusalem led to the burning of King Hussein's portrait in demonstrations on the West Bank. It was also feared that, having achieved peace with Jordan, the Israeli Government would feel under less pressure to pursue negotiations with Arafat's PNA on the implementation of the Declaration of Principles. Indeed, by late 1994 Israeli-Palestinian negotiations were effectively deadlocked. An early empowerment agreement had been reached between the Israeli Government and the PNA at the end of August for the transfer of control in the fields of education, tourism, taxation, health and social welfare from the Israeli civil administration to the PNA. However, this limited agreement was already several months behind the deadline stipulated in the Declaration of Principles and did nothing to resolve the serious differences preventing progress on the substantive issues of the interim phase negotiations. In Cairo, Egypt, Israeli negotiators emphasized that there could be no progress on IDF redeployment in the West Bank until they were satisfied that the Palestinian authorities had demonstrated an ability to curb the anti-Oslo violence of Islamist militants and PLO 'rejectionists'. There were further disputes over the function and composition of an elected Palestinian authority. Rabin reiterated a strong preference for a 24-member executive council whose legislative powers would be subject to an Israeli veto. Publicly, at least, PNA representatives argued for a 100-seat assembly with full executive and legislative authority. Without such a formula, Arafat realized that it would be increasingly difficult either to stem the tide of Palestinian disaffection with the course of the peace process or gain legitimacy for the PNA. There was already a growing conviction that the Palestinian negotiating team was being outmanoeuvred by its Israeli counterparts, and being drawn into a situation in which Israel's ostensible security concerns dominated the negotiating agenda. According to Palestinian sceptics, the 'security' issue served a dual purpose for Israel. First, it trapped the PNA in the role of Israeli gendarme and hence ensured continuing Palestinian divisions. Second, the failure to reach agreement on arrangements for the interim period allowed the Israeli Government to postpone a confrontation with Jewish settlers in the West Bank, while providing a breathing space to pursue the infrastructural development—road building and settlement expansion—on the West Bank and around Arab Jerusalem that would create the necessary 'facts' to prejudice the course and outcome of the 'final status' negotiations.

The fragility of the peace process and the character of the PNA's relationship with Israel were emphasized by a series of violent incidents towards the end of 1994. In mid-October an Israeli soldier, Nachshon Waxman, was abducted by Hamas militants demanding the release of 500 of their jailed comrades. Although there was no evidence that Waxman was being detained in the Gaza Strip, or, indeed, that his kidnappers came from there, Rabin stated publicly that he held Arafat and the PNA responsible for the soldier's safety. Under mounting Israeli pressure, Arafat ordered his security forces to detain several hundred known Hamas activists. However, it soon emerged that Waxman was in fact being held on the West Bank, where he and three of his captors died in a clumsily unsuccessful rescue operation by the IDF. Shortly after Waxman's killing Hamas struck again. Twenty-two Israelis were killed and tens were injured in the suicide bombing of a crowded Tel-Aviv bus. Rabin immediately ordered the sealing of the Gaza Strip and the West Bank, and, while he was more circumspect about blaming Arafat directly for the atrocity, he did urge the PNA to crush its Islamist opponents. He added that Israel reserved the right to intervene militarily in the Gaza Strip and on 2 November a leading member of Islamic Jihad in Gaza, Hani Abed, was killed by a car-bomb. The killing bore resemblance to previous Israeli covert operations and happened on the same day that Rabin stated that, while he was extending a hand of peace to Jordan, the other was 'pulling the trigger to hit the terrorists of

Hamas and Islamic Jihad'. The latter group took revenge 10 days later with a suicide attack on an IDF check-point in Gaza that left three Israeli soldiers dead and several injured. Some 200 Jihad sympathizers were arrested by the Palestinian police in the aftermath of the attack, while Rabin again harangued the PLO Chairman about his duty to 'dry out the swamp of terrorism in Gaza'. There was little doubt that this ugly cycle of violence severely undermined the PNA. The forces of militant Islam gained considerable sympathy from being perceived as victims of Arafat's heavy-handedness in the same way as the readiness with which Arafat was seen to be doing Rabin's bidding served to increase the alienation of those ordinary Palestinians already frustrated at the absence of a tangible 'peace dividend'. The presence of scores of Hamas and Islamic Jihad cadres in Palestinian prisons, together with the swelling ranks of the various Palestinian security forces, also marked the end of the delicate *modus vivendi* which the PNA had attempted to construct with the Islamist opposition.

SPECULATION OVER THE GOLAN HEIGHTS

At various times during the second half of 1994 prominent members of the Israeli Cabinet hinted that Israel was prepared to make more extensive concessions regarding the Golan Heights than had hitherto been entertained by the Labour-led coalition. However, the Prime Minister reiterated that any Israeli withdrawal from the Heights would be both gradual and modest. The apparent disunity within the Government on policy towards Syria was widely interpreted as a ploy to test domestic opinion on territorial compromise, and to entice Syria into making concessions. If true, there was little evidence to suggest that President Assad was about to soften his own position. Despite Warren Christopher's shuttle diplomacy and face-to-face meetings in Washington, DC, between the Israeli and Syrian ambassadors to the USA, it was conceded that 'wide differences' still existed between the two Governments and official bilateral talks remained suspended. Rumour did, however, spur the leaders of the 13,000 Israeli settlers on the Golan Heights into initiating a vigorous anti-withdrawal campaign. In TV advertisements and rallies throughout the country the settlers and their supporters denounced what they described as Rabin's treachery in reneging on his election promise to maintain an Israeli presence on the Golan Heights. Particularly disturbing for the Labour Prime Minister was the fact that the Golan settlers enjoyed the support of a significant section of the Labour establishment—seven Labour deputies tabled a bill that would have effectively ruled out withdrawal from the Golan Heights by making any change in the region's status subject to a 65% approval rating in a referendum. Opinion polls conducted in September also revealed that only 40% of the electorate would support a 'partial' withdrawal from the Golan Heights, while 35% opposed any withdrawal at all. This apparent lack of support in Israel for any compromise with Syria, together with a resurgence in the popularity of Likud, led well-placed Israeli sources to suggest that Rabin would be happy to place the Golan issue on hold until the 1996 elections. This view gained in currency after visits to Damascus by President Clinton and Christopher in October and December only resulted in an Israeli-Syrian agreement to restart talks on the understanding that they would be characterized as an 'exchange of ideas' rather than 'negotiations'.

INTER-PALESTINIAN CONFLICT

Arafat's relations with his Islamist opponents seriously deteriorated on 18 November 1994 when units of the Palestinian police fired on demonstrators as they left a Gaza City mosque. Twelve people died and 200 were injured, most of them Islamists, in the initial shootings and the gunfights which followed. Pro- and anti-Arafat rallies in the immediate aftermath of the killings, which were characterized by mutual threats and recriminations, maintained the high political tensions in the Gaza Strip. However, a realization that further confrontations could well tip Gaza into the abyss of civil war served eventually to cool tempers. The Palestinian police were prudently absent from the funeral marches of those killed on 18 November, while newspaper editors and political independents, most notably Abdel Shafei, gave support to hastily convened mediation committees. Their cause was aided in no small degree by the refusal of many Fatah cadres in Gaza to engage in the kind of provocation of Hamas in which the more ardent Arafat supporters in the West Bank had indulged. Arafat's own attempts to exploit the crisis beyond his Gaza headquarters proved only partially successful. By stressing the connection between civil unrest in Gaza and the dire economic situation there, he was able to persuade a conference of international donors in Brussels, Belgium, to promise an immediate aid package of US $125m. and a further $23m. for infrastructural projects. However, the PLO Chairman found it far more difficult to exploit the Gaza crisis to extract the concessions he and the PNA needed so urgently from Israel. Central to Arafat's and wider Palestinian unease were the continuing signals that Rabin, in contrast to the more conciliatory voices in the Cabinet, was intent on revising some of the fundamental articles of the Declaration of Principles. Speaking in mid-December, Rabin suggested that rather than completing its full withdrawal from Palestinian population centres in the West Bank prior to elections to the PNA, as stipulated in the Declaration of Principles, the IDF should redeploy only temporarily for the duration of the elections. The alternative, according to Rabin, was 'protracted negotiations' on the two issues. Arafat rejoined that the completion of the redeployment of the IDF by the eve of the elections was imperative, while one of the chief Palestinian negotiators stated that for Israel 'to come up with formulas and versions that contradict the Oslo Accords' would be 'the quickest way to destroy the peace process'. Events in the Gaza Strip and continued wrangling over the interpretation of the Declaration of Principles were thrown into sharp relief by the award of the Nobel Prize for Peace to Arafat, Rabin and Peres. As with many other awards, the decision of the Nobel committee had caused controversy when it was initially announced, but at the award ceremony in December it appeared particularly premature.

EXPANSION OF SETTLEMENTS

The sense of foreboding surrounding Israeli-Palestinian negotiations intensified at the beginning of 1995. On 2 January four Palestinian policemen were killed on the outskirts of Gaza City by Israeli soldiers who claimed that they had mistaken them for 'armed militants'. Yet this, the most serious breakdown to date in co-ordination between the Israeli and Palestinian security forces, was largely overshadowed by another furore over Israeli settlements. It was triggered by a decision of the settlement council of Efrat to expand its settlement on land adjoining the Palestinian village of Al-Khader and some 2 km away from the settlement itself. As Arab villagers and Israeli sympathizers confronted the bull-dozers, Palestinian leaders protested that the expansion violated the Declaration of Principles. The Israeli Cabinet eventually devised a compromise solution that 'froze' building on the initial site but allowed for the construction of new housing on lands next to Efrat. The compromise failed to assuage the anger of the PNA, but it was powerless to effect a reversal of this or other incidences of land confiscation and settlement building that had occurred on the West Bank since the signing of the Declaration of Principles. The USA made it clear that it would not intervene in a dispute which it regarded as a local matter, to be dealt with within the framework of the programme. Yet this provided little comfort for the opponents of Israel's settlement- and road-building programme. Under the Declaration, the issue of settlements had been assigned to the 'final status' negotiations and although a moratorium had been declared on the inauguration of new settlements, the expansion of existing ones had been implicitly accepted. Some 40,000 acres of Palestinian land had been confiscated since the signing of the Declaration of Principles, and construction had started on an additional 400 km of settlement roads. Their effect, in the words of Meron Benvenisti, a former deputy mayor of Jerusalem and a severe critic of the settlement programmes of successive Israeli governments, was to turn a 'huge expanse of the West Bank into a region in which it will be impossible to implement any final arrangement except by annexation to Israel'. Mahmud Abbas, Palestinian signatory of the Declaration of Principles in Washington, DC, added: 'If the confiscation of Palestinian land is not stopped we will not find anything to negotiate over in the future'. That the continued settlement activity in the West Bank violated the spirit if not the letter of the Declaration of Principles was tacitly acknowledged by sections of the Israeli Cabinet. However, spokesmen for the Israeli Prime Minister explained that Rabin was too weak politically—polls at the beginning of 1995 showed the Labour-led coalition badly trailing its Likud rivals—to implement the next stage of the Declaration of Principles or to tackle settler interests directly. Instead, Rabin insisted, with strong backing from the USA, that the course of the peace process would be determined by Israel's assessment of the impact of the autonomy experiment on its security concerns. It was a formula that the Palestinian opponents of the Declaration of Principles continued to exploit.

THE BEIT LID BOMBINGS

On 22 January 1995 two Islamic Jihad suicide bombers killed 22 Israelis, most of them soldiers, in a carefully planned attack at Beit Lid. Israel immediately sealed its borders with the Gaza Strip and the West Bank and arrested several hundred Islamist activists. Rabin also gave his backing to a proposal to build a 365-km (228-mile) long security fence in the West Bank that would 'physically segregate' Palestinians and Israelis. Arafat condemned the Beit Lid bombings and instructed his security forces to undertake a further and unpopular detention of Islamic Jihad cadres. The PNA leader attracted further criticism for his muted response to the security-fence plan. Many Palestinians feared that the separation calls were inspired by a desire unilaterally to seize Palestinian territory around Israel's border settlements and thus pre-empt negotiations on the 'final status' agreements. These concerns were aggravated on 25 January when the Israeli Cabinet committee for settlement voted in favour of the massive expansion of the Jewish satellite townships around Jerusalem. Attempts to limit the damage caused by the Beit Lid bombings produced few results. A beleaguered Arafat met Rabin in Gaza City on 9 February in an attempt to have the closure of the Gaza Strip and the West Bank lifted, and to obtain assurances on the redeployment of troops in the West Bank. He achieved neither of his aims, leading one Palestinian negotiator to describe the peace process as having 'reached a state beyond that of collapse'. A meeting of Egyptian, Israeli, Jordanian and Palestinian representatives in Washington, DC, three days later proved no more fruitful for Arafat, and Christopher gave his seal of approval to the crippling security closure of the Gaza Strip and the West Bank by commenting that free movement into and out of the territories could not be expected until the problem of terrorism had been addressed. Confirming Arab and Palestinian fears that the USA's agenda was broadly the same as Israel's, Christopher refused to address the problem of Palestinian detainees and did not criticize Israel for its refusal to adhere to the timetable set out in the Declaration of Principles.

INCREASING ARAB DISILLUSIONMENT

The Palestinians were not the only Arab party to despair at the deadlock in the peace process. By the beginning of 1995 President Mubarak of Egypt was clearly exasperated with Israeli policy. Having enthusiastically played the role of the key Arab Government in achieving a comprehensive regional peace, and having invested considerable political capital in the outcome of the peace process, Mubarak viewed Israel's obstructionism on fundamental issues as undermining his own regime. For Egypt to regain its place as leader of the Arab world, and for the Mubarak Government to erode support for Egypt's own violent Islamist opposition, Israel had to be seen to be dealing sensitively with Arab and Palestinian concerns. However, the Israeli Government's frequent humiliation of Arafat, its bellicose statements on Jerusalem and the ongoing concerns over the West Bank settlements strengthened Egypt's conviction that only by distancing itself from Israel could it avoid criticism that it was giving legitimacy to a process of which it was itself increasingly wary. Egypt signalled the rapid deterioration in its relations with Israel through clear and public support for Syria's terms for an Israeli-Syrian peace, and by announcing that it would not sign the renewal of the 1970 Nuclear Non-Proliferation Treaty (NPT) unless Israel, a non-signatory and the only known nuclear power in the region, also undertook to adhere to it. This stance won the backing of Arab states but was greeted with annoyance by Israel. Gentle persuasion by the USA led Israel to make a minor concession, to the effect that it would sign the NPT once a comprehensive Middle East peace had been achieved. Such a peace, however, would have to include peace treaties with such arch foes as Iran, Iraq and Libya. This concession failed to impress President Mubarak. Emboldened by Arab support and by charges of hypocrisy against the USA for its failure to pressurize Israel, the Egyptian President disregarded the USA's urgings to reconsider Egypt's position on the NPT. On 20 April Egypt reiterated that it would withhold its signature to the extension of the NPT because of Israel's refusal to ratify the Treaty. However, further persuasion by the USA and its threats to withhold aid led Egypt and the rest of the Arab states to agree to an extension of the NPT without Israel's signature. It was a victory for Israel, but one that emphasized its deteriorating relations with Egypt. An attempt by Israeli officials to blame the rift on the Egyptian Minister of Foreign Affairs, Amr Muhammad Moussa, failed to disguise the fact that Egypt's position was symptomatic of wider Arab disaffection with the lack of reciprocity in Arab–Israeli relations. The evidence of the previous six months gave credence to the Syrian belief that separate deals with Israel and an absence of inter-Arab co-ordination made Israel's neighbours vulnerable to manipulation. It was feared that Israel would achieve integration into the Arab world without having to make a commitment to withdraw from the territories it occupied. This somewhat belated assessment provided the impetus for Jordan to seek better relations with the PNA. King Hussein and Arafat signed a general co-operation agreement on 27 January covering trade, currency, banking, communications and administrative affairs. The Jordanian Prime Minister also promised that in future Jordanian policy towards Israel would be guided by the aim of achieving Palestinian sovereignty over East Jerusalem. The *rapprochement* with the Palestinians signalled a shift in Jordanian policy. Early in March the new Jordanian Minister of Foreign Affairs, Abdul Karim Kabariti, underlined Jordan's new priorities by warning Israel that the key to better Israeli-Jordanian relations lay in progress in negotiations with Syria and the Palestinians. In a meeting with Warren Christopher on 13 March King Hussein also admonished the US Administration for failing to honour pledges of increased economic and military assistance for Jordan. Without this promised assistance, the King argued, it would be difficult for him to persuade his subjects to see the value of peace with Israel. Moreover, Syria would be wary of any future US promises intended to encourage it to reach an agreement with Israel.

Israel gradually eased the restrictions it had imposed on Palestinians entering Israel following the Beit Lid bombings. Two months after the initial closure of its borders 20,000 workers were given permits to return to their jobs in Israel. This compared to 45,000 who had been working in Israel prior to the bombing and more than 100,000 who had worked in Israel before the Palestinian *intifada*. The presence in Israel of some 80,000 guest workers from Eastern Europe and Asia suggested that, despite the Gaza Strip's 50% unemployment rate, the Israeli Government had no plans to restore the number of Palestinians allowed to work in Israel to its pre-*intifada* level. The partial lifting of the blockade on Palestinian workers was agreed during talks between Arafat and Peres in Gaza on 9 March 1995. An optimistic Peres described their meeting as a 'breakthrough', but this was not an assessment shared by Palestinian negotiators. Although Peres promised to open up a road corridor between the Gaza Strip and Jericho, and to initiate discussion in the Israeli Cabinet on the release of some of the 7,000 Palestinians still held in Israeli prisons, there was still no agreement on the outstanding issues of IDF redeployment and Palestinian elections. Rabin had earlier suggested that Israel would agree to a town-by-town redeployment in the West Bank, with the proviso that Arafat would have to curb terror attacks.

PNA ANTI-TERRORISM ACTIVITIES

Peres confirmed in his meeting with Arafat on 9 March 1995 that negotiations on redeployment might be completed by July as long as 'specific actions were taken by the Palestinians against terror'. Such warnings hardly seemed necessary. With the tacit approval of Israel and the USA, Arafat had presided over the expansion of security forces in the Gaza Strip to some 17,000 personnel organized into six separate, competing branches. In the period since the Beit Lid bombings and an attack by DFLP fighters on an IDF patrol on 6 February they had detained scores of activists opposed to the Declaration of Principles. Additionally, the PNA had established special security courts administered by appointed security personnel. They were shortly to pass sentences of 25 years' imprisonment on members of the military wings of the Islamist opposition. Reports of the death in custody of Palestinian suspects and the routine torture of detainees provoked severe criticism from local and international human rights organizations. The harassment of journalists and the closure of opposition newspapers confirmed the increasingly authoritarian nature of the PNA regime. Arafat was also censured by former allies for his handling of negotiations with Israel, and in Gaza and the West Bank prominent independent activists had begun to seek support for a new political party committed to the democratization of the PNA. Especially troubling for the PLO leader was growing dissent from within his own Fatah ranks. At a stormy meeting of the Fatah central council in Tunis in late March Arafat came under strong pressure from erstwhile comrades-in-arms to suspend the peace process. Farouk Kaddoumi and Mahmud Abbas, founder members of Fatah, argued that it would be a grave error to pursue talks with Israel until a new and more accountable negotiating strategy had been devised. Breaking ranks even further, Kaddoumi publicly accused Arafat of embezzlement and of surrounding himself with corrupt opportunists. The meeting ended in uproar, but not before Arafat had won a narrow mandate to continue with the autonomy negotiations, with the proviso that a committee be set up to monitor the course of the negotiations and that dialogue be initiated with the opposition. (The sense that the largest faction of the PLO was moving towards violent division was given added weight by a series of feuds and turf wars in the West Bank that led to several deaths and scores of injuries.) No sooner had Arafat survived the Tunis meetings than the PNA became embroiled in further crisis. On 2 April a massive explosion in a residential apartment block in Gaza City killed four Palestinians and injured 30 others. Among the dead were key figures of Hamas' military wing, the *Izz ad-Din Qassam* Brigades. Hamas immediately accused the PNA authorities of collaborating with Israel in the bombing of the building. PNA representatives rejoined that the apartment had been blown up in an unsuccessful bomb-making operation. While Arafat's police produced a cache of arms and bomb-making equipment from the debris to support their claims, Hamas supporters demonstrated on the streets, vowing revenge for their slain comrades. On 9 April two suicide attacks on settlers and soldiers in Gaza left eight dead and more than 50 wounded. Hamas and Islamic Jihad claimed responsibility for the two operations. The Israeli Prime Minister ordered another closure of the West Bank and the Gaza Strip, a measure designed to deflect calls from right-wing political parties for an end to negotiations with the PNA over the extension of Palestinian autonomy in the West Bank. The closure did little to calm the rising passions in Gaza, however. Although Rabin confirmed that negotiations on the next phase of Palestinian self-rule would continue, there was little doubt that the events in Gaza had provided his Government with an opportunity to obtain both time and concessions from the embattled PNA. This was evidenced in Arafat's vetoing of a draft national-reconciliation treaty brokered between the various leftist and Islamist opposition groups in Gaza. Arafat's aides stated that he had opposed the agreement because it did not contain a condition that the opposition should respect his agreements with Israel.

NO PROGRESS ON SYRIAN TRACK

Negotiations between Israel and Syria remained stalled throughout early 1995. In the absence of progress, southern Lebanon once again became the arena for the pursuit of political objectives. A total of 80 attacks on IDF and SLA targets were reported during February, the highest monthly total for several years. Israel responded by subjecting the south Lebanese coast to a month-long blockade, an action that led to a loss of livelihood for some 1,800 Lebanese fishermen. On 31 March Israeli helicopter gunships attacked a car carrying a leading Hezbollah official, Rida Yasin. Both he and his companion died in an attack that was strongly reminiscent of the assassination of Hezbollah leader, Sheikh Abbas Moussawi, in 1992. Hezbollah fighters retaliated with rocket attacks on targets in northern Israel. A further escalation of hostilities was only averted by the intervention of the US State Department. In communications with the Israeli, Syrian and Lebanese leaders, Warren Christopher reminded the respondents of the agreements brokered in the wake of Israel's 'Operation Accountability' in 1993. Christopher's mediation reflected the high priority the Clinton Administration was giving to the Israeli-Syrian track of the peace process. The US President had stated that he hoped a peace agreement would be concluded between the two states prior to the 1996 elections in Israel and the USA. Mindful of the slow pace of negotiations, he announced in March that a representative from the State Department would participate in the ambassadorial talks taking place in Washington, DC. Conciliatory statements by Rabin to Syria prompted rumours that more progress was being made in the negotiations than the terse official summaries suggested. It emerged, nevertheless, that this optimism was largely misplaced. However, having failed to reduce differences on the crucial issue of Israel's withdrawal from the Golan Heights, Christopher urged the Israeli and Syrian delegations to postpone these discussions and concentrate on what security arrangements would be satisfactory to them in the wake of an Israeli evacuation of the Golan Heights. This change in emphasis appeared to bear fruit. Emboldened by Peres' further references to the Heights as Syrian territory, President Assad hinted that he would be prepared to share the Golan's water resources with Israel in the event of the latter's evacuation. In June Syria also conceded that the demilitarized zones on either side of the new border would not have to be of equal size; until this point Syria had insisted on 'symmetry' in all security arrangements. Despite these small shifts towards accommodation on security and water issues, there was little evidence of a breakthrough on the core issue of withdrawal. An opinion poll published in June indicated that 58% of the Israeli public remained opposed to a full withdrawal from the Golan in exchange for a comprehensive peace agreement with Syria. Disturbed by these findings, the Israeli Government repeated an earlier suggestion that an Israeli evacuation of land and settlements on the Golan Heights would have to be subject to a referendum. The idea was clearly irritating to the Syrian regime which saw it as evidence of Israel's unwillingness to give up the occupied land. Peres reassured Syria and the USA that, despite the pledge to hold a referendum, the Israeli Government was committed to its goal of peace with Syria. Supporters of Israel's continued presence on the Golan also found little comfort in the extent of opposition to withdrawal from the Heights. They were equally perturbed by Rabin's comment to the IDF's Golani Brigade that the Golan Heights was 'a tank land rather than a holy land'. In July three rebel Labour backbenchers sponsored legislation that sought to set a requirement of a majority of 70 in the 120-seat Knesset for any agreement to withdraw from the Golan. Rabin dismissed the proposed law as nonsense, adding that Israel had gone to war without such a mandate and could also make peace without one. The US Ambassador, Martin Indyk, lobbied vigorously prior to the vote, stating that if the law was approved it would effectively destroy the chances of a peace agreement with Syria. At the end of July the Knesset voted 59-59 on a first reading of the proposed legislation. The Speaker cast his vote against and declared the bill defeated.

NEW SETTLEMENT PLANS

At the end of April 1995 Rabin expressed his support for a plan of the Ministry of Housing to construct 7,000 new homes in East Jerusalem and announced plans to confiscate 130 acres of Arab land to facilitate the project. The scale of the proposed construction and its prejudicial impact on 'final status' negotiations on the future of Jerusalem caused an international furore. An irate Arafat authorized the tabling of a UN Security Council Resolution demanding that the decision be annulled. He did, however, resist a call from Haider Abdel Shafei to 'shock international opinion' by withdrawing from the peace talks, insisting that there was no alternative to a continuation of dialogue. Peres attempted to ease the pressure on the PLO leader with several minor concessions—increasing the number of Palestinians allowed to work in Israel to 31,000, simplifying bureaucratic procedures for the entry of goods into the Gaza Strip, promising to hasten the release of 250 Palestinians held in Israeli detention. But, in view of Palestinian outrage at the construction proposals, Peres' clumsy attempt to make them more acceptable only added insult to injury. The US reaction was similarly anodyne. Albright admitted that the new housing units 'pose problems as far as the peace process is concerned', but added that the Security Council was an inappropriate forum for the discussion of the issue. On 17 May the USA once again used its veto at the UN to defeat a resolution which insisted that Israel should rescind its construction plan. All of the other 14 voting countries supported the resolution. It was the 30th time since 1972 that the USA had used its veto to prevent the censure of Israel. If developments in the Security Council were wholly predictable owing to the strong pro-Israeli bias of the Clinton Administration, what followed was not. With the PNA reluctant to take the lead in mobilizing opposition to the construction proposals, it was left to a late intervention by the six deputies of the Arab Democratic Party and the Communist-led Hadash coalition to obstruct the Israeli plans. The two parties submitted a motion of 'no-confidence' in the Rabin Government, in spite of warnings from Arafat not to do anything that would cause the Israeli coalition to fall. When it emerged that Likud, despite their strong support for the confiscations, intended to seize the chance to defeat the Labour coalition and that vigorous attempts to encourage other parties to abstain on the vote had failed, Rabin was left with no option other than to suspend the plans to confiscate Arab land. The 'no-confidence' motion was withdrawn immediately.

NEGOTIATIONS ON IDF REDEPLOYMENT

During June 1995 Israeli and Palestinian representatives outlined their respective positions on the next, long-delayed phase of Palestinian autonomy: the redeployment of Israeli troops in the West Bank and the related issue of Palestinian elections. Arafat summarized the official PNA position on 18 June: there would be no elections until the IDF withdrew from all population centres in the West Bank. This was loyal to the text of the Declaration of Principles but at odds with Israel's own assessment of how stage two of the Declaration should be implemented. Advance warning of the rift was served by Rabin on 12 June when he commented that it would be impossible for Israel to reach agreement on redeployment by the target date of 1 July unless the PNA agreed to a partial redeployment of Israeli armed forces before the elections and further negotiations on full redeployment after them. The positions of the Israeli delegation involved in the redeployment talks were unveiled during June. A three-stage approach to the redeployment of the IDF was proposed. The first stage would involve the withdrawal of the IDF from towns and cities in the West Bank which were regarded as 'non-problematic'. These would include Jenin, Nablus, Tulkarm and Qalqilya. The IDF had stated that withdrawal from these towns could be completed by November 1995 as long as it only involved a retreat to the municipal boundaries—refugee camps and villages outside the boundaries would remain under Israeli control. The second stage of the Israeli delegation's approach referred to towns such as Ramallah and Bethlehem, which were contentious in Israeli eyes because they were adjoined by large Israeli settlements. For this reason there could be no withdrawal from these towns until the completion of 110 km of settler roads, a project that would not be completed until May 1996. The third stage of the Israeli approach to redeployment referred to settlements, Israeli-declared state lands and the city of Hebron with its central colony of 400 settlers. According to Israeli officials, there could be no withdrawal from these areas until the conclusion of the 'final status' agreement. There were hints that the PNA leadership might accept the idea of a phased Israeli withdrawal, but only as long as it was guaranteed that the second stage of the redeployment would take place within two months of Palestinian elections. For many Palestinians, already weary with the delays to the implementation of autonomy, the Israeli proposals were too radical a departure from the

Declaration of Principles to be entertained. As Israeli and Palestinian negotiators resumed their talks on the latest proposals it swiftly became obvious that no agreement would be reached before the target date of 1 July 1995. A later deadline of 25 July was set, but two days prior to this, in the midst of lengthy and secret negotiations, the PLO leader confirmed suspicions that the two sides were still some way from signing an agreement on the extension of Palestinian autonomy. On 25 July Hamas signalled its reaction to the impending agreement with the suicide bombing of a bus travelling through a Tel-Aviv suburb. Six Israelis were killed and dozens injured in the explosion. The prospect of an arrangement for withdrawal of the IDF from areas of the West Bank also led right-wing Israeli nationalists to stage land invasions and to occupy abandoned settlements throughout the occupied territory. Rabin ordered troops to break up the demonstrations leading to several days of clashes with settler groups and scores of arrests. On 21 August a suicide attack on a Jerusalem bus killed another five Israelis. Hamas's military wing immediately claimed that the female bomber responsible was one of its members and promised to carry out similar operations in the approach to the 1996 Israeli elections. The closure of the Gaza Strip and the West Bank followed; however, this was accompanied by statements from Rabin that suggested that the talks on the second phase of the Oslo Accords (Oslo II) would be delayed rather than cancelled.

NEGOTIATIONS OVER OSLO II

As Palestinian and Israeli negotiators engaged in round-the-clock talks in the Red Sea resort of Taba, reports from the negotiations appeared to confirm Israeli and Palestinian pessimism: that an agreement on Oslo II would not be signed by the new target month of September 1995. The status of Hebron was cited as the principal obstacle. However, the submission by Peres of a compromise proposal on the disputed city broke the impasse and facilitated a formal signing in Washington, DC, of an Israeli-Palestinian agreement on the interim stage of Oslo II (see Documents on Palestine, p. 388). Under the terms agreed by the two sides, Israel committed itself to the withdrawal of the IDF from six of the seven main towns and the 440 villages of the West Bank. Civil authority was to be transferred to the PNA in these areas of Palestinian population, although Israel reserved the right to intervene militarily in the villages. Israel also agreed to the establishment of an elected 82-member Palestinian Council with executive and legislative powers. While this represented a more flexible approach, the Israeli Prime Minister insisted that no amendments could be made to existing legislation without prior Israeli approval. On the issue of Hebron, the Palestinian negotiators acceded to Israel's demands that the IDF preserve full or partial authority over 25%–30% of the city's municipal area. This included the Ibrahimi mosque and five locations in the city centre where Jewish settlers and religious students were housed. There was no definitive resolution of the fate of Palestinians in Israeli prisons. Instead, Israel undertook to free up to 2,200 prisoners prior to elections to the Palestinian Legislative Council (PLC) and the remaining 3,000, somewhat cryptically, 'according to principles to be established separately'. However, Rabin remained adamant that there would be no freedom for those prisoners 'with Jewish blood on their hands'.

Palestinians were noticeably less enthusiastic in their response to the agreement reached at Taba than they had been two years previously, at the beginning of the Oslo process. This time there were no celebrations. A Hamas-inspired general strike shut down the city of Hebron on the day of the Washington signing and leaflets distributed by Islamists in the Gaza Strip and the West Bank castigated Arafat and declared the agreement null and void. In the refugee camps of Lebanon and Syria, Palestinians protested angrily at what they perceived as a further step towards marginalization. This rejection of the agreement was shared by their Arab hosts. Of Israel's neighbours, only Jordan was unconditional in its support for the Taba agreement. This contrasted sharply with King Hussein's initial hostility towards the first phase of the Oslo Accords (Oslo I) and appeared to confirm Jordan's increasing tendency to accommodate the USA's agenda for a Middle East peace. The Jordanian monarch's enthusiasm for the new agreement led to accusations in Arab circles that Jordan's improving relations with Israel and the USA had encouraged Israel to be less compromising in negotiations with the PNA.

The Israeli public's reaction to the Oslo II agreement, like that of the Palestinians, was characterized by indifference and resignation. Anti-Oslo II demonstrations organized by right-wing elements were unusually muted and poorly attended. The leader of the Likud party, Binyamin Netanyahu, initially refused to comment on a future Likud government's attitude towards Oslo II, but eventually conceded that his party would honour agreements between the Labour Party and the PNA. However, with obvious regard to his right-wing constituency, Netanyahu announced that he would renege on any clauses that might be considered harmful to Israel's security and added that the IDF would not refrain from pursuing 'terrorists' into areas of PNA control.

The Labour-led Government was also soon to prove that despite ongoing relations with Arafat's PNA, it had not adopted a more tolerant attitude towards more militant Palestinian factions. On 26 October 1995 the Islamic Jihad leader, Fathi Shqaqi, was assassinated in the streets of the Maltese capital, Valetta. Although the Israeli Government refused to confirm or deny that it was involved in Shqaqi's killing, it was widely acknowledged that the assassination showed signs of being a Mossad operation. Islamic Jihad cadres urged vengeance for the death of their leader and the news of the killing was followed by violent confrontations in towns of the West Bank. Elsewhere, however, the reaction to Shqaqi's death was decidedly low key. The Egyptian and Jordanian leaders declined to comment on the incident, while PNA spokesmen would go no further than to state that they would not be deflected from their commitment to the peace process. Hamas's reaction to the killing of an Islamist leader was also less strident than might have been expected. Unwilling to sour negotiations aimed at improving their relations with the PNA in the approach to elections to a PLC, Hamas's Gaza-based leaders confined their official reaction to a restrained leaflet.

PHASED IDF REDEPLOYMENT BEGINS

In accordance with the Taba agreements, the IDF began its phased redeployment on the West Bank in mid-October 1995. The village of Salfit was the first Palestinian locality to be evacuated by Israeli troops and this was swiftly followed by other villages. On 25 October Jenin became the first West Bank town to be relinquished by the IDF. However, Palestinian relief at seeing the Israeli occupation lifted for the first time in nearly 30 years was tempered by the limitations of the autonomy. In many instances Israeli troops withdrew not much further than municipal boundaries, confirming opponents of the Oslo Accords in their belief that the new agreements represented not so much an ending of the occupation as its reorganization. Meanwhile, Arab and Israeli leaders gathered in New York to celebrate the 50th anniversary of the founding of the UN. In a speech to the General Assembly, Arafat urged the UN to continue to support the Palestinian cause until the implementation of the Palestinians' 'inalienable rights' and insisted that the Palestinians wished to live side by side with the Israeli people in two independent states. The Saudi Arabian Minister of Defence, Prince Sultan bin Abd al-Aziz, stated that a comprehensive and just peace would have to be concluded before the Arab world could countenance the normalization of diplomatic or economic relations with Israel. For his part, Rabin thanked the international community for its support for the peace process and gave his undertaking that it would be pursued 'until we have brought peace to the region'.

ASSASSINATION OF RABIN

Rabin's ability to influence the course of the peace process was to be dramatically short-lived. On 4 November 1995 the Israeli Prime Minister was shot dead by a Jewish religious nationalist, Yigal Amir, as he was leaving a peace rally in Tel-Aviv. The assassination shocked Israeli society, not least because it had hitherto been unthinkable that a Jew would be responsible for the killing of the leader of the Jewish state. The Israeli internal security service, Shin Bet, came under severe criticism for its perceived complacency in not anticipating the threat of violence from the far right wing. This was particularly so given that Amir was well known on the extremist fringe of Israeli politics and his assassination plans were part of a wider conspiracy to attack Palestinian and pro-peace Israeli politicians, including Rabin's designated successor, Peres. While the manner and place of Rabin's death completed his metamorphosis from warrior to peace-maker and caused an outpouring of popular grief, it embarrassed the Israeli right wing. Likud leader Netanyahu was criticized for failing to distance himself from the increasingly rancorous verbal attacks on Rabin by the settler lobby and for thus contributing to the climate of opinion that made the assassination possible. Rabin's widow personally identified the Likud leader as morally responsible for her husband's death. An opinion poll conducted in the immediate aftermath of the assassination revealed only 20% support for Netanyahu compared with 54% for Peres.

There were widely different reactions in the Arab world to Rabin's death. Oman and Qatar sent high-ranking ministers to Jerusalem for Rabin's funeral, at which both King Hussein and Arafat paid effusive tribute to the memory of the Israeli premier. Neither Lebanon nor Syria offered any official comment on the killing, while in Lebanon Hezbollah and Palestinian fighters celebrated the death of an old foe with volleys of gunfire. Yet, despite the variety of responses to Rabin's killing, there existed a widespread belief, and not just in the region of conflict, that the peace process was at a challenging juncture. There could be no doubting Rabin's importance to the Oslo process and his credibility with those sections of Israeli society that had traditionally opposed compromise with their Arab neighbours.

PERES BECOMES PRIME MINISTER

Whether his immediate successor, Peres (regarded as more 'dovish' than his predecessor), possessed the political acumen to build a national consensus around the path taken by Rabin was the cause of much speculation. For Arafat's PNA there was comfort in the fact that the cornering of the Israeli right had created, albeit temporarily, a shift in the Israeli national consciousness and a mood that was far more hostile to settler interests in the West Bank and Gaza Strip. Syrian leaders noted that Peres' agenda was less strongly defined by security than Rabin's had been, and that the new Israeli Prime Minister was more amenable to their views on the Golan Heights. In talks with Western leaders, Syrian officials reportedly expressed enthusiasm for a resumption of their stalled negotiations with Israel, sentiments that clearly elicited excitement among Israeli and US officials. In early December 1995 Peres visited Cairo and Amman before making his first official trip as Israeli Prime Minister to Washington. At each venue Peres stressed that his administration would be prioritizing efforts to achieve a breakthrough with Syria. However, in spite of Peres' assertion that 'a new chapter' was about to open in Israeli-Syrian relations, the resumption of negotiations in Washington, DC, at the end of December failed to achieve significant progress. The main obstacle remained Syria's insistence that UN resolutions, and hence Israel's withdrawal from the Golan Heights, were the *sine qua non* of any agreement. Israeli demands for manned monitoring stations on the Golan Heights were rejected by Syria as a violation of its sovereignty and moves by Israel to tempt Damascus with joint economic and development initiatives proved no more successful. Hints from Washington that Syria's flexibility could lead to its removal from the US list of states which allegedly sponsored terrorism, and therefore open the way for US aid, also left President Assad unmoved.

PALESTINIAN ELECTIONS

The IDF's redeployment on the West Bank had been completed by the end of 1995 and without serious disagreement. The way was now open for elections to the PLC. There was considerable uncertainty in the approach to the January 1996 poll as to which political factions would participate. The PFLP and the DFLP were quick to urge Palestinians to boycott the elections, a stance that was apparently dictated by their Damascus-based leaderships, but was opposed by many of the parties' cadres in Gaza who argued that a boycott would deprive Palestinians of a secular left-wing voice in the Council. For many observers, the decision of the DFLP and the PFLP to boycott the elections without having developed a coherent alternative to the peace process was further evidence of their growing political irrelevance. Hamas' position on participation in the elections was initially more equivocal. Like all the other factions opposed to Arafat, it was highly critical of the first-past-the-post election system which seemed designed to guarantee the dominance of official Fatah candidates. However, a sizeable minority of pragmatists within Hamas was anxious to reach a *modus vivendi* with the PNA and called an early decision to boycott the elections 'unduly hasty and unwise'. The situation within Hamas was further complicated by the formation of a new Islamist party, the National Islamist Salvation Party (Khalas), instituted to contest the election and including several personalities closely identified with the moderate caucus in Hamas. By mid-December 1995 it appeared that the 'hardliners' had won the debate within Hamas. The movement reiterated its decision to boycott the elections and most of the figures associated with Hamas and connected to Khalas sought to distance themselves from the latter. This proved seriously damaging to Arafat's long-standing efforts to drive a wedge between Hamas' political and military wings. Nevertheless, talks between the two sides in Cairo at the end of the year did result in the issuing of a joint communiqué stressing the importance of national unity and the need for dialogue to resolve differences. Privately, Hamas also promised to refrain from attacking Israeli targets until after the elections, but it also stated that there could be no question of the movement renouncing 'the armed struggle'. That the resumption of suicide attacks against Israel would be sooner rather than later was signalled by the assassination, on 4 January 1996, of Yahya Ayyash. Known by the *nom de guerre* the 'Engineer', Ayyash was thought to have organized the spate of Hamas bus bombings in Israel and was therefore a prime target for Israeli agents. Killed in Gaza by a booby-trapped mobile telephone, Ayyash's funeral was attended by 100,000 Palestinians. The death of Ayyash, at a time when Hamas had for several months observed a *de facto* cease-fire, was regarded within the movement as vindicating the position of the 'hardliners'. Hamas and Islamic Jihad concurred that retaliation for Ayyash's death was an inevitability.

Some 676 candidates contested the 88 seats in the PLC. In a separate poll to elect the President of the PNA, Arafat was opposed by a single candidate, Samiha Khalil, a veteran women's activist and Fatah dissident. The result of the presidential vote was never seriously in doubt, even without Arafat's supporters' control of the nascent Palestinian radio and TV stations and of much of the print media. His capture of 88% of the votes cast for the position of PNA President was largely anticipated. The election of the Legislative Council was more interesting, not least because of the extremely high participation rate—90% of the electorate in Gaza and 68% on the West Bank voted (interestingly only in localities that were fully or partially under Israeli control, Hebron and East Jerusalem, was there low participation, of 35% and 40% respectively). As predicted, official Fatah candidates were successful, winning 50 of the Council seats. There was also a strong showing by independent candidates (many of them ex-Fatah cadres), who gained 35 seats. Haider Abdel Shafei won the poll in Gaza and in Jerusalem another independent activist, Ashrawi, came second to the incumbent Minister of Finance, Ahmed Quray. Overall, the results appeared to confirm the electorate's preference for candidates who had earned their political credentials through activism, as opposed to those who owed their position to Arafat's patronage. International observers declared the elections free and fair, an assessment that appeared to ignore not only Arafat's monopoly on media resources, but also widespread reports of electoral irregu-larities in the Hebron and Ramallah areas, and Israel's efforts to undermine Palestinian electioneering in Jerusalem. It led some commentators to conclude that the whole process had been 'rubber-stamped' under pressure from a US

Administration that was anxious to avoid further damage to the peace process. Yet, however flawed an exercise in democracy, the elections did represent a significant restructuring of Palestinian politics. They effectively signalled the end of Palestinian representation outside of the West Bank and the Gaza Strip, and with it a disintegration of the PLO institutions that had sustained the Palestinian struggle in the decades preceding the Oslo Accords. Exactly what the relationship would be between the Legislative Council and the PNC, theoretically the supreme decision-making body, was unclear. It seemed only a matter of time, nevertheless, before existing political forces realigned and transformed themselves into political parties.

RENEWED VIOLENCE AND SECURITY MEASURES

If the IDF's redeployment on the West Bank and the Palestinian elections were seen as proof of the workability of the peace process, what was shortly to occur provided that same process with its most serious test to date. On 25 February 1996, the second anniversary of the Ibrahimi mosque massacre, Palestinian suicide bombings in Jerusalem and Ashkelon claimed the lives of 25 Israelis and wounded some 55 others. On 3 and 4 March a second wave of bombings in Tel-Aviv and Jerusalem left a further 32 Israelis dead and scores more injured. Hamas' military wing (the *Izz ad-Din Qassam* Brigades) claimed responsibility for the bombings, although a series of contradictory communiqués issued in the aftermath of the attacks appeared to suggest a growing split between the more moderate Gaza-based leadership of Hamas and a dissident military faction that owed allegiance to political radicals stationed abroad. Speculation regarding the bombers' motives identified revenge for the killing of Yahya Ayyash and a desire to hinder the peace process by wrecking Peres' electoral chances. Either way, the response of the PNA and the Israeli Government was wholly predictable. Having so clearly tied his political future to that of the Israeli Labour Party, it came as no surprise that Arafat instructed the forces of the PNA to ameliorate the discomfort of the Israeli leader. The risk of bloody internecine conflict prevented Arafat from acting to dismantle Hamas' institutional base, as Israeli and US leaders would have liked, but he did earn grudging approval for a massive wave of arrests of Hamas and Islamic Jihad members in the areas under his control. On 3 March five Palestinian militias, including the *Izz ad-Din Qassam* Brigades, were officially outlawed by the PNA. On 6 March the PNA's Mahmud Abbas announced 'there is now no dialogue with either Hamas' political or military wings'. The Palestinian authorities' new, more severe, stance (as many as 12,000 Islamists were said to be in PNA custody by the end of March) was accompanied by Israel's announcement of an indefinite closure of the West Bank and Gaza Strip and restrictions on the movement of goods and people between autonomous areas on the West Bank. With the co-operation of the Palestinian security forces, the IDF also re-entered Palestinian villages to arrest suspects and several houses belonging to suspected Islamist militants were demolished in areas of Israeli control. However, despite Peres' and Arafat's co-ordinated attempts at damage limitation and the unequivocal condemnation of the bombings by a broad spectrum of Palestinian opinion, the suicide attacks heightened Israeli ambivalence towards the peace process. An opinion poll conducted shortly after the bombings revealed that the Likud leader had now overtaken his Labour rival, who had enjoyed a 30-point opinion-poll lead on becoming Prime Minister. Israeli observers suggested Netanyahu would have fared even better had Peres not been so uncompromising in his reaction to the spring's atrocities.

THE SHARM ESH-SHEIKH SUMMIT

In the wake of the suicide-bomb attacks the US Administration sought to bolster the peace process and its vulnerable participants by organizing what was described as an anti-terrorism conference and a 'Summit of the Peacemakers' in the Egyptian resort of Sharm esh-Sheikh on 13 March 1996. Twenty-seven nations were represented at the conference, including 12 Arab states, Israel and the nascent Palestinian entity. The conference concluded with a tame communiqué pledging the participants' support for the peace process and their commitment to combating terrorism. Iraq, Libya and Sudan were not invited to the conference. Lebanon and Syria declined their invitations, stating that the reconvening of the original Madrid peace conference would have been a more appropriate forum for discussion. Indeed, President Assad had already signalled his dissatisfaction with the state of the peace process by refusing to make public condemnation of the Hamas bombings in Israel.

'OPERATION GRAPES OF WRATH'

With progress in the Israeli-Syrian peace remaining elusive, the two states' proxy conflict in south Lebanon intensified. In a 16-day period in mid-March 1996 Hezbollah fighters killed six Israeli soldiers and wounded 27 others in and around Israel's self-declared security zone. At the end of the month Israeli tank fire killed two Lebanese civilians installing a water tank in the village of Yatar, prompting Hezbollah to fire rockets into northern Israel. On 8 April two Lebanese children were killed in an explosion on the edge of the security zone. Hezbollah blamed Israel for these attacks and fired more rockets into Galilee, wounding 13 people and driving hundreds more into air-raid shelters. Three days later Peres announced the beginning of 'Operation Grapes of Wrath', and, in an attempt to deliver a fatal blow to Hezbollah's military capabilities, launched combined air and artillery strikes against targets in south Lebanon, Beirut and the Beka'a valley. In a development reminiscent of Israel's bombardment of the Lebanese south in 1993, IDF commanders warned the populations of Tyre and surrounding villages to leave their homes, causing the displacement of an estimated 400,000 civilians northwards. During the following week Israeli forces expanded their area of attack. As well as firing several thousand shells at southern villages, Israel's navy bombarded the coast road south of Beirut and its air force struck against the Lebanese capital's power-stations and its international airport, killing several Lebanese and Syrian troops. With few, if any, fixed positions to defend, Hezbollah's highly mobile guerrillas appeared largely unscathed by the Israeli onslaught and were able to continue firing *Katyusha* rockets into Israel. These caused panic in the northern settlements but little damage and no loss of life. One week into 'Operation Grapes of Wrath' it had become evident that Israeli forces had been unable to achieve their military objective of silencing Hezbollah, and that they would not be able to do so without the commitment of ground troops, an option that Peres could not sanction in view of the casualties this would inevitably entail. Politically, Peres was also beginning to regret his decision to intensify the conflict on the northern borders. The indiscriminate nature of the attacks had, temporarily at least, healed the sectarian divisions in Lebanon and united the country behind Hezbollah. As hundreds of Shi'a youth volunteered to join the ranks of the Islamist militia, their Sunni and Christian countrymen hailed it as Lebanon's most potent symbol of national resistance. Moreover, with the exception of the USA, which once again blocked attempts by the UN formally to condemn the Israeli action, the international community was vocal in its opposition to what was widely interpreted as a cynical electioneering exercise by the Israeli Prime Minister.

THE QANA MASSACRE AND THE SUBSEQUENT CEASE-FIRE

Peres' discomfort was magnified on 18 April 1996 when Israeli shells landed on a UN base at the village of Qana, killing 105 civilian refugees who had been sheltering there and wounding scores of others, including Fijian soldiers serving with the UN. Israel's claim that the shelling of Qana had been the result of technical and procedural errors was rejected in a report commissioned by the UN Secretary-General. Whatever the truth about the tragedy at Qana, it did galvanize diplomatic efforts to bring about a cease-fire between the warring parties. Following the massacre at Qana, US President Clinton dispatched the US Secretary of State on a seven-day assignment, travelling between Jerusalem and Damascus. However, his six-point plan for securing a cease-fire—which included the disarming of Hezbollah and a Lebanese-Syrian guarantee of security for Israel's northern border—was regarded as too hopelessly pro-Israel to survive exploration (the Syrian President pointedly refused to receive Christopher in Damascus). Eventually Israel and the USA were obliged to submit to proposals which developed through the diplomatic efforts of the French Minister of Foreign Affairs, Hervé de Charette. What emerged was a new 'understanding' between the warring parties—essentially a return to the *status quo ante*. Written but unsigned, it stipulated the terms of engagement between the two sides to the conflict, principally that both parties would refrain from attacking civilians, that Hezbollah would not launch attacks from areas of civilian habitation and that Israel would not target civilian infrastructure. In addition, both parties agreed to retain the right of 'legitimate defence' within the understanding. The cease-fire was to be monitored by an Israel-Lebanon Monitoring Group (ILMG), consisting of Lebanon, Israel, France, Syria and the USA. Most observers saw the cease-fire terms as a victory for the Arab side, in that Hezbollah's standing had been enhanced through its ability to emerge from the conflict undefeated. The Lebanese Prime Minister, Rafik Hariri, insisted that the resistance would continue. Three days after the cease-fire of 27 April Hezbollah fighters were once again attacking the IDF and the SLA in the security zone.

US–ISRAELI RELATIONS

With its Middle East policy now so firmly linked to the victory of the Labour Party in the forthcoming Israeli elections, the USA was determined to boost the fortunes of its ally in the wake of the 'Grapes of Wrath' débâcle. At the end of

April 1996 the Israeli Prime Minister made an official visit to Washington, DC, where he was praised by and received the backing of President Clinton for his Lebanese adventure. He returned to Israel having obtained substantial US military and technological aid and promises to further develop mutual security, including the possible establishment of a formal defence treaty.

PALESTINIAN–ISRAELI RELATIONS

Arafat was also being urged to aid Peres' election campaign. On 24 April 1996 the PNC was convened in Gaza with the main intention of fulfilling Arafat's earlier promise to Rabin that the PNC would rescind those articles of the Palestinian National Charter which denied Israel's right to exist. This the PNC dutifully approved by an overwhelming majority of 504 to 62. Arafat's control of the debate was underlined by the heavy defeat of a motion tabled by his opponents that urged the Council to oppose any amendment if Israel did not acknowledge the Palestinians' right to self-determination. 'I am very happy to have fulfilled my commitments,' was the comment of the PLO leader. A delighted Peres described the PNC's decision—somewhat exaggeratedly—as 'the most significant ideological change in the Middle East in the last 100 years'. The *quid pro quo* for Arafat was the partial rehabilitation of the peace process in the aftermath of the suicide bombings and the crippling closure of the Palestinian territories. On 5 May Palestinian and Israeli negotiators met again in Taba to commence 'final status' talks on issues such as settlements, Jerusalem, refugees, borders and the status of a future Palestinian entity. As expected, the impending Israeli elections led to a ceremonial inauguration, brief procedural discussion and a formal adjournment of the talks until after the formation of a new Israeli government.

ISRAELI ELECTIONS

Israelis voted on 29 May 1996 to elect a new Knesset. For the first time ever there was also a separate vote to elect the Prime Minister directly. The campaign of suicide bombings earlier in the year had eroded the massive lead Peres had enjoyed over his Likud rival immediately following Rabin's assassination, and a close contest was predicted. The result of the election to the premiership was a win for Likud's Netanyahu by a margin of less than 1%, confirming the constancy of the left–right division of the Israeli electorate. Analysts attributed Netanyahu's victory partly to a dogged and opportunistic campaign that won the support of such diverse constituencies as the religious orthodox and the development town populations, and partly to a lacklustre performance by Peres. Following the legislative elections Likud's representation in the Knesset declined from 40 to 32 seats while the Labour Party lost 10 seats and its Meretz allies three. There was a particularly strong performance by the three religious parties, which captured 23 seats, and the Russian Immigrants' party, headed by the former Soviet dissident, Natan Scharansky, which won seven seats in the first election it had contested. Israel's Arab voters had voted overwhelmingly in favour of Peres to continue as Prime Minister, in spite of earlier threats to abstain because of the Israeli attack on Lebanon. In the Knesset Arab-dominated parties increased their representation from six to nine seats.

REACTION TO LIKUD VICTORY

The return to power of the Israeli right wing was viewed as little less than a disaster for the peace process. Netanyahu had long been associated with the nationalist 'hardliners' in Likud and his pre-election pronouncements had included a commitment to treble the settler population of the West Bank and the expression of his total opposition to Palestinian self-determination and to any change to the status of Jerusalem. Sensitive to the international disquiet that had accompanied his victory, Netanyahu's first major speech (to an adoring Likud crowd) was moderate and conciliatory as he paid generous tribute to his defeated predecessor and pledged to continue the peace process. Yet, even if Netanyahu was ultimately more of a pragmatic opportunist than a nationalist ideologue, as many commentators suspected, nothing could disguise the disappointment in Western and Arab capitals at Peres' loss of office. Arafat, struggling to manage a US $100m. budget deficit and the consequences of the 12-week closure of the PNA-ruled areas, was reported to be devastated by the Netanyahu victory, and not without good cause. For two years his policies had largely been predicated upon refraining from any course of action that would upset the electoral chances of Israel's Labour leaders. In the previous two months, and largely at Peres' bidding, Arafat had agreed to the delay of Israel's redeployment in Hebron, suppressed dissent in the PNA, imprisoned nearly 1,000 Palestinians and unilaterally changed the Palestinian National Charter. As his detractors now scornfully pointed out, the politics of acquiescence and accommodation had spectacularly backfired. Netanyahu, who refused to use the terms PNA or PLO, instructed a junior official at the Ministry of Foreign Affairs to inform Arafat's deputy, Mahmud Abbas, that a 'mechanism of contact' would be established in due course. The insult was deliberate. The Likud leader had already stated that he would not meet Arafat unless Israeli security deemed it necessary. As if this did not augur sufficiently badly for the future, Netanyahu went on to appoint the 'hardline' Ariel Sharon to head a ministry responsible for infrastructural development on the West Bank. The only comfort for Arafat and the PNA lay in Likud's ideological opposition to 'separation' and, hence, the prospect that there would be a gradual relaxation of the closure of the Occupied Territories. Sources close to Israel's internal security services also pointed out that Netanyahu would be foolish to jeopardize the established sharing of information by Israeli and Palestinian intelligence chiefs.

Egypt and Jordan were relatively sanguine in their official responses to the changes in Israel, with both of their Governments adopting a 'wait-and-see' attitude to the Likud leader. Lebanon and Syria displayed a degree of grim satisfaction, seeing in Netanyahu's victory a vindication of their refusal to join those Arab states who had moved to build relations with Israel. However, for neither Lebanon nor Syria was there any evidence that Netanyahu would advance bilateral relations. On the issue of Lebanon, the Likud leader differed little from his Labour predecessors. He had stated in his election campaign that Israel would maintain its security zone until the Lebanese army disarmed Hezbollah and assumed responsibility for security in the south. Netanyahu was notably more rigid in his views on the nature of Israeli–Syrian relations. There would be no withdrawal from the Golan Heights because it was vital to

Israel's security. Given Assad's insistence that an Israeli withdrawal from occupied lands was a prerequisite for any peace deal between the two countries, it was predicted that Israeli–Syrian relations were about to enter a potentially dangerous new era.

ARAB SUMMIT IN CAIRO

There was sufficient trepidation in the Arab world over the implications of the change in government in Israel for the Egyptian and Syrian Presidents to organize an Arab summit meeting in Cairo on 21–23 June 1996. The first of its kind since the Iraqi invasion of Kuwait in 1990, the meeting was attended by all of the Arab states with the exception of an uninvited Iraq. Syria had wanted the summit to produce a commitment by the Arab states to make any moves towards the normalization of relations with Israel dependent upon progress being made in the peace process. Fear of the USA's reaction prevented the Syrian proposal from being adopted, but the summit's final communiqué did reiterate that peace should be based on Israel's withdrawal from Arab lands, and that if Israel reneged on any of the agreements it had so far signed under the terms of the Oslo Accords, then the Arab states would have to reconsider the steps they had taken in the peace process. A series of important bilateral meetings took place in the context of the summit in the Egyptian capital, the most noteworthy being between the Syrian President and the Jordanian and Palestinian leaders. King Hussein, perhaps least threatened by the Netanyahu victory, promised to support Syrian demands for an Israeli withdrawal from the Golan Heights, and agreed with Assad that they would continue their dialogue as a means of improving their strained relations. Similar sentiments were expressed at the conclusion of Palestinian-Syrian discussions.

HOPES FOR PROGRESS RECEDE

Fears of a slide towards greater instability in the region were partially borne out in the two months following the Israeli election. In south Lebanon Hezbollah attacks claimed the lives of 11 Israeli soldiers, and on the West Bank five settlers and three soldiers were killed in attacks blamed on the PFLP and Abu Musa's faction of Fatah. Both Damascus-based groups had for a number of years allowed Islamist factions to take the leading role in armed activities in the West Bank and Gaza Strip. Meanwhile, the Netanyahu Government published plans to establish eight new settlements in the West Bank in line with election promises to increase the settler population to 500,000 by the end of the millennium. A decision was also taken by the new Minister of Defence, Itzhak Mordechai, to reintroduce IDF covert units to the West Bank and to expand their operations to include areas of PNA control. In mid-July 1996 one of these units was reported to be responsible for the killing of an Islamic Jihad activist in Ramallah, an area of the West Bank that, according to the terms of Oslo II, was supposed to be under exclusive Palestinian security control. The first contacts between the PNA and the Netanyahu Government also indicated that the future course of the peace process would not be smooth. Meeting Arafat on 19 July, David Levy, restored to the position of Minister of Foreign Affairs, informed the PLO leader that there could be no progress on resolving the outstanding issues of the interim phase—principally the stalled redeployment in Hebron—until certain

Israeli conditions were fulfilled. Levy detailed these as a halt to all PNA activity in Jerusalem, a moratorium on the release of Islamist suspects and the continued suppression of terrorist activities. He also refused to set a date for the resumption of 'final status' negotiations. The only concession that the Israeli Government was prepared to make was a verbal undertaking to increase by 10,000 to 35,000 the number of permits issued to Palestinians wanting to work in Israel.

During his first official visit to Washington, DC, as Israeli Prime Minister in mid-July 1996, Netanyahu did nothing to dispel Arab gloom or confirm Western hopes that he would reveal a more pragmatic bent. In a speech to the US Congress, Netanyahu dismissed the 'land-for-peace' formula and stated instead that the resolution of the Middle East conflict must be based on security, reciprocity and democracy. Equally uncompromising were his comments on the future of Jerusalem and the prospects of peace with his northern neighbours. On talks with Syria he told reporters: 'I can tell you that the first item on my agenda would be the cessation of all terrorist attacks from Syrian-controlled areas in Lebanon, via Hezbollah, or for that matter other terrorist attacks from groups based in Syria'.

At the end of July 1996 Arafat made his first visit to Damascus since 1993. Given the mistrust and personal enmities that had soured Syrian–Palestinian relations for more than a decade, it was perhaps inevitable that the discussions between the two sides concluded with little more than a commitment to work towards future co-ordination. However, the arrival of the Jordanian monarch in the Syrian capital only a few days after Arafat had departed seemed to suggest that the changes in Israel were producing tentative moves by its Arab neighbours to establish less unilateral strategies of dealing with the Jewish state.

CONTACTS ARE RE-ESTABLISHED

Amid increasing domestic unrest and cynicism with regard to the peace process, Arafat attempted to persuade the Israeli premier to meet for direct negotiations that would demonstrate that the Oslo process was again on track. Netanyahu remained aloof, judging correctly that delaying a resumption in the peace talks presented an opportunity to extract concessions from the PNA. By the end of July 1996 Palestinian negotiators were conceding that the agreements signed with the previous Labour Government on withdrawal from Hebron were open to revision. Equally controversially, Arafat bowed to Israeli demands that three Palestinian charitable institutions in Jerusalem, affiliated to the PNA, be closed. Both developments laid Arafat open to criticism from a broad spectrum of Palestinian opinion, particularly when Netanyahu signalled that his Government would not be guided by notions of reciprocity. Just days after the Jerusalem closures, Israeli troops demolished a Palestinian centre for the disabled in Jerusalem's Old City (supposedly on the pretext that it had been built without a licence) and announced that 900 new housing units would be built in a settlement near Ramallah. These were rebukes that the embattled Arafat could not afford to ignore. Declaring to the Legislative Council that 'Israel has declared war on us', he announced a four-hour general strike and warned that only a resumption of the *intifada* could end the current impasse with Israel. This latter announcement, together with a threat from President Mubarak to cancel November's Middle East and North Africa economic conference in Cairo unless

Israel began to meet its Oslo commitments, aroused sufficient concern in Washington, DC, and in European capitals for the Israeli leader to calculate that it was no longer in his interests to distance himself from the PNA, and from the peace process.

On 4 September 1996 Netanyahu met the PLO Chairman at the Erez checkpoint between Israel and the Gaza Strip to discuss a resumption of the Oslo talks. There was evident relief, not least in Washington, that the meeting had finally taken place. Christopher applauded the Israeli Prime Minister for having crossed 'a psychological threshold'. But US approval and declarations from the two negotiating sides that the meeting had produced positive results, failed to disguise the largely symbolic nature of the encounter. Israel did commit itself to resuming full contacts with the PNA, and to participation in a joint steering committee designed to direct implementation of the outstanding issues of Oslo's interim phase, yet when this committee first convened on 9 September in Jericho, there was an obvious divergence of opinion over the extent to which Israeli redeployment in Hebron could be renegotiated. In mid-September Arafat informed a meeting of Arab foreign ministers in Cairo that Israel was not committed to reaching consensus and that the peace process remained at a critical stage. On 23 September the Israeli Prime Minister announced that the Hasmonean tunnel, an ancient tunnel running beneath the Muslim quarter of Jerusalem's Old City, alongside the al-Aqsa mosque, was to be reopened. Given the already strained nature of Israeli–Palestinian relations and the acute Palestinian and Muslim sensitivities to the perceived threat to Jerusalem and its Islamic holy sites, the tunnel judgement was widely interpreted as provocative. Arafat denounced the rehabilitation of the tunnel as 'a crime against our holy places' and, to a chorus of popular indignation and support, advocated protests against the 'Judaization of Jerusalem', effectively endorsing a return to the politics of the *intifada*—the crucial difference at this stage being the existence of a legitimate armed Palestinian security force.

PNA POLICE CLASH WITH IDF

On 25 September 1996 several hundred Palestinian students, mobilized by the PNA and Fatah, confronted IDF positions on the outskirts of Ramallah. For a while the furious exchange of rocks and rubber bullets recalled the early days of the *intifada*, but after Israeli troops resorted to live ammunition and made incursions into areas under Palestinian control, Palestinian police observers of the protest became full participants in the battle. The following day the West Bank and Gaza witnessed the worst violence since the occupation of 1967 as Israeli and Palestinian troops engaged in lengthy exchanges of gunfire; in Ramallah and Gaza the Israeli army used helicopter gunships to fire on Palestinian positions, while in Nablus Palestinian security forces and armed militants overran the Israeli-held site of Joseph's Tomb, killing six soldiers in the process. After three days of bloody clashes, 55 Palestinians had been killed and around one hundred more had been wounded. Fourteen Israeli soldiers had also died in the violence and Israeli tanks had been moved into positions around the areas of PNA control amid speculation that Netanyahu was about to order the reoccupation of Palestinian population centres. The prospect of a full-scale conflagration prompted the US President to interrupt campaigning for November's presidential election and return to Washington. On 29 September President Clinton agreed to host a crisis summit between Arafat and Netanyahu and pledged his own participation in the talks. Invitations were also extended to the Egyptian and Jordanian leaders. In the West Bank and Gaza, meanwhile, Arafat ordered his forces to contain the demonstrations and to co-operate with the IDF which, in turn, imposed a closure of the major Palestinian population centres but refrained from further incursions. By the end of September only isolated incidents of violence were being reported from the West Bank and Gaza.

EUROPEAN REACTION

Internationally the crystallizing perception was that it was the Netanyahu Government's intransigence, rather than Arafat's manipulation, that was ultimately responsible for the latest débâcle. Amid reports that it intended to pursue a more pro-active role in the peace process, the EU emphasized its reservations concerning the policies of the Netanyahu Government by receiving the Palestinian leader in Luxembourg on the eve of the Washington, DC, summit. It was announced that negotiations would begin on a European-Palestinian trade agreement to accelerate the economic development of the West Bank and Gaza, and pledges of US $30m. in immediate aid were made. Shortly afterwards EU foreign ministers issued a statement on the recent escalation of violence on the West Bank and in Gaza, in which the IDF was accused of deploying disproportionate force in dealing with the Palestinians. The statement went on to comment: 'The EU recognizes that the recent incidents were precipitated by frustration and exasperation at the absence of any real progress in the peace process and . . . firmly believes that the absence of such progress is the root of the unrest'. The publication of the statement coincided with an announcement that the EU was for the first time to assign a special envoy to the Middle East. The eventual appointment of the Spanish diplomat, Miguel Moratinos, with a limited brief represented a defeat for a French-led attempt to have the post filled by a high-profile political personality with a wider-ranging mandate.

THE WASHINGTON SUMMIT

Realistic expectations of the Washington, DC, mini-summit did not exceed an easing of tensions. President Mubarak had declined an invitation to be present on the grounds that he doubted Israeli sincerity, while the looming US presidential election effectively precluded any significant political initiative from the Clinton Administration. Indeed, Netanyahu had prefaced his appearance in Washington by insisting that the controversial Jerusalem tunnel would remain open and was unequivocal in attributing responsibility for the renewed violence to the PNA. Yet despite the lack of progress in Washington—the two sides committed themselves to little more of substance than continued talks over Hebron—Arafat was not despondent as he left the US capital. Temporarily, at least, his standing had been strengthened by the crisis. Opinion polls published in October 1996 revealed overwhelming Palestinian support for the stance adopted by the PNA and for the actions of the security forces during the tunnel crisis. In addition to reaping the benefits of European frustration with Israel's new Government, Arafat had also drawn strength from a rapid deterioration in relations between Israel and Jordan. Jordan had been deeply angered by Israel's unilateral decision to open the tunnel (the Jordanian-Israeli treaty of 1994 recognized Jordan's special relationship with Islamic holy sites in Jerusalem) and King Hussein was reported privately to have expressed severe criticism of Netanyahu's policies. In a subsequent interview with the Saudi newspaper, *Asharq al-Awsat*, King Hussein warned that Israel's failure to meet its commitments as established by the Oslo Accords was raising the spectre of war in the region. In a clear gesture of support for the Palestinian leader, King Hussein made his first visit to the West Bank since the Israeli occupation of 1967. Speaking at a joint news conference with Arafat, in Jericho, he described an unprecedented improvement in Jordanian–Palestinian relations.

ARAB–ISRAELI ECONOMIC RELATIONS

Israeli–Egyptian relations remained less than cordial. In mid-October 1996 President Mubarak announced that he would not meet with Netanyahu until redeployment in Hebron was agreed, although his earlier threat to cancel the Middle East and North Africa economic conference was quietly abandoned in view of domestic economic interests and the US opposition to such a move. Nevertheless, for Israeli delegates the conference presented few opportunities. The Egyptian Chamber of Commerce had urged its members to boycott Israeli business stands while the Minister of Foreign Affairs, Amir Muhammad Musa, told reporters that Israel's isolation was the 'natural reaction from people in the region' and that 'inter-Arab co-operation should be the base of all regional co-operation'. A plan to build a natural gas pipeline from Egypt (through Gaza) to Israel, first proposed in 1993, was postponed indefinitely by its Italian contractor, and a joint Egyptian-Israeli-Jordanian project for tourist development along the shared coast of the Gulf of Aqaba became another victim of the soured atmosphere. (Earlier, on economic grounds, Israel had cancelled an agreement to buy natural gas exclusively from Qatar. The Qatari Government reacted by suspending moves towards normalization with Israel, thus isolating Oman as the only Gulf state continuing to develop trade links with Israel.)

DISCUSSIONS ON HEBRON

Whatever satisfaction Arafat derived from 'uniting the world against the Netanyahu Government' (his claim to the PLC), the formulation of a coherent strategy for future contacts with Israel had become increasingly problematic given Palestinian expectations that their negotiators would now be resolute in resisting Israeli pressure to alter agreements already signed under the terms of the Oslo Agreements. Discussions over the Hebron deployment were resumed and continued throughout the remainder of 1996 with the principal point of contention being Israel's insistence that its troops should have the right to intervene militarily in the 20% of the city that would remain in Israeli hands following the initial redeployment. Under the terms of Oslo's interim agreement, the IDF had preserved the right to enter Palestinian areas to 'bring an end to an act or incident' which threatened Israeli lives, but Netanyahu wanted this arrangement expanded to include, in the words of his chief media adviser, actions to 'pre-empt a terror attack as well as to pursue one'. There was little chance of Arafat agreeing to such a demand, given the support he had enjoyed internationally and locally in the wake of the September clashes. By the end of November the Israeli Prime Minister was accusing his Palestinian interlocutors of deliberately delaying any agreement on Hebron in an attempt to increase international pressure on Israel to make further concessions. Mutual distrust deepened following an announcement on 19 November that 1,200 new housing units were to be built in the West Bank settlement of Emmanuel. The PNA reacted to the announcement by urging 'popular confrontation' against Israeli settlement policy, and organized a brief blockade of the Netzarim settlement in Gaza. The prospects for agreement on Hebron appeared to recede even further during December. On 10 December the Jerusalem District Planning Authority approved the construction of 110 housing units in a Palestinian district of East Jerusalem. The following day a Jewish settler and her young son were shot dead by members of the PFLP near the Jewish settlement of Beit El on the West Bank. At the funeral of the two victims, attended by the Israeli Prime Minister, settler leaders demanded the immediate confiscation of land adjoining the settlement to make way for the building of 1,000 new homes. A belligerent Netanyahu seized on the mood of popular outrage and instructed his aides to draft a cabinet resolution approving the expansion sought by the settlers. This decision attracted opposition from unexpected quarters. In addition to the predictable fury emanating from Arab capitals and protests from the EU, US officials also expressed their dismay. However it was the opposition of Israel's security chiefs, who warned that implementation of the Beit El scheme might lead to a repeat of the September clashes, coupled with the misgivings of Levy and Mordechai, that persuaded the Israeli Premier to adopt a compromise on Beit El that involved a more modest expansion on land serving as an IDF base. Any goodwill that might have been engendered by this compromise was immediately eroded by an Israeli cabinet decision to reinstate subsidies and tax incentives to all settlements in the Occupied Territories by classifying them as 'national priority areas'. Clearly unimpressed by Netanyahu's assurances that the new ruling was largely symbolic and would not facilitate a new settlement initiative, the US State Department spokesman, Nicholas Burns, expressed the Clinton Administration's view that '. . settlement activity is unhelpful, and settlement activity clearly complicates the peace process'. His concern was shared by former high-ranking US officials who wrote to Netanyahu warning him 'not to take unilateral actions that would preclude a meaningful settlement and lasting peace'. The signatories of the letter included three former Secretaries of State (James Baker, Cyrus Vance and Lawrence Eagleburger) and three former national security advisers (Brent Scowcroft, Frank Carlucci and Zbigniew Brezsinski).

On 15 December 1996 the Palestinian and Israeli leaders resumed contact and committed themselves to renewed talks on Hebron redeployment. Two weeks later a Jewish settler and off-duty soldier made an indiscriminate machine-gun attack on shoppers in Hebron's crowded central market, wounding eight Palestinians before being overpowered and disarmed by Israeli troops. The realization that the incident could have claimed many lives lent new urgency to the negotiations. In a secret meeting in Gaza on 5 January 1997 the outstanding issues surrounding Israel's security redeployment in Hebron were effectively agreed between Arafat and Netanyahu. Nevertheless, continuing disagreement on future redeployments elsewhere forestalled the public announcement of a

Hebron deal. Instead the Israeli leader demanded that the deadline for Israel's final redeployment—from all West Bank territory except the settlements, municipal Jerusalem and certain military locations—should be postponed until April 1999, rather than September 1997 as stipulated under the Oslo timetable.

AGREEMENT ON HEBRON

Arafat's unwillingness and effective inability to agree to this proposal meant that agreement on Hebron appeared as elusive as ever. Attempts by the US special envoy, Dennis Ross, to persuade the Palestinians to accommodate Netanyahu's request earned a swift rebuttal, and it fell to King Hussein to broker a compromise. Travelling between Gaza and Tel-Aviv on 12 January 1997, the Jordanian monarch was able to secure Israeli and Palestinian acceptance of a proposal (originated by the Egyptian President) for Israel to complete its final West Bank redeployment by March 1998. The agreement was formalized by the signing of a protocol between Saeb Erekat and Dan Shomron, chief Palestinian and Israeli negotiators, on 15 January. Under the terms of the protocol, Israel agreed to withdraw from 80% of the city of Hebron, while retaining control over a central enclave housing 400 settlers and their 20,000 Palestinian neighbours for an interim period of at least two years. In addition, Israel agreed to begin immediate discussion of outstanding interim issues of Oslo II, most notably the questions of Palestinian detainees, Gaza's airport and a West Bank–Gaza corridor. There was no mention of the earlier insistence on the IDF's right of pre-emptive operations in the self-rule areas. For its part, the PNA reiterated its commitments to combating 'terror', finalizing the revision of the Palestinian National Charter and confiscating illegally held weapons in the areas under its control.

REACTION IN ISRAEL

A large majority of Knesset members supported the Hebron deal, as did the majority of Israel's population. The reaction of the nationalist right wing to the agreement also proved to be far more muted than their militant leaders had indicated. Attempts to disrupt the withdrawal through direct protest-action had been threatened but, in the event, failed to materialize. The Hebron agreement won the support of 11 of the 18 members of the Israeli Cabinet; of the seven dissenters only Binyamin Begin, the uncompromising Minister of Science, and son of the former Israeli Prime Minister, was prepared to express his opposition through resignation from the Government.

PALESTINIAN REACTION

The PNA leadership felt evident relief that the tortuous deliberations over Hebron had finally been concluded. There was satisfaction that the terms of the agreement were essentially in line with the Oslo Accords and that Arafat's strategy of internationalizing the negotiation process (and of discouraging Jordan from conducting a unilateral peace effort with Israel) had apparently been vindicated. The issue of Hebron had become for the Palestinians a crucial testing ground of relations with Likud. Palestinian concessions would have seriously undermined Arafat's position and made the Oslo process even more vulnerable to the revisionist intentions of the Israeli right wing. Nevertheless, while admitting that Palestinian negotiators had performed well in achieving the Hebron deal, sceptics of the Oslo process claimed that it was only mass participation in the September protests that had ultimately allowed Arafat to pursue such a course of inter-Arab co-operation and internationalization. Speaking to Arafat after he had addressed a large crowd in Hebron, Hamas leaders also adopted a conciliatory tone. Recognizing that the PLO Chairman was enjoying a rare moment of political success, they expressed disappointment with an agreement that left Israeli troops and settlers in control of the centre of Hebron, but promised that they would express their continued opposition to the Oslo Accords through 'democratic channels'.

DOMESTIC CRISIS FOR NETANYAHU

The optimism that had arisen from the January 1997 protocols proved to be short-lived. In Israel, at the end of January, it was alleged that Netanyahu had supported the appointment as Attorney-General of a little-known lawyer, Roni Bar-On, on the understanding that Bar-On would ensure lenient treatment of Aryeh Der'i, the leader of the orthodox Shas party, coalition ally of Likud, who was facing criminal proceedings on political and financial corruption charges. In return for leniency, it was reported, Shas party ministers were alleged to have pledged support for the Hebron withdrawal within the Cabinet. Bar-On resigned within 12 hours of his appointment; he was replaced by Elyaqim Rubenstein at the end of January. For a time, Netanyahu's impeachment seemed a distinct possibility, and this prospect exposed the growing rift between the nationalist 'hardliners' in Government and the pragmatic ideologues grouped around the Prime Minister. Mindful of Netanyahu's vulnerability, and still irate at the Hebron withdrawal, the nationalist wing of the coalition threatened to make Netanyahu's position untenable unless he agreed to a plan for the construction of a large new settlement on Palestinian-owned land to the south-east of Jerusalem. At the end of February the Ministerial Committee on Jerusalem approved the construction of a settlement (Har Homa) on the hilltop of Jabal Abu Ghunaim, just inside the municipal boundaries of Jerusalem. On completion, Har Homa would house some 32,000 settlers in 6,500 housing units, and complete the ring of settlements around Arab East Jerusalem. In a palliative move, Netanyahu simultaneously announced that his Government was granting 3,015 building permits to Palestinians in East Jerusalem.

HAR HOMA

The Har Homa issue aroused a predictable storm of protest. The EU described the decision as a 'major obstacle to peace', while President Clinton, who had recently been effusive in his praise of Netanyahu's accomplishment over Hebron, expressed the opinion that, 'The important thing is for these people on both sides to be building confidence and working together and so I would have preferred the decision not to have been made because I don't think it builds confidence, I think it builds distrust and I wish it had not been made'. Palestinian reaction to Har Homa was predictably fierce, with PNA spokesmen warning that it spelled the end of the peace process and would usher in a new era of confrontation. The rhetoric softened, however, after the USA cautioned against any repeat of the September 1996 armed clashes and Mordechai warned that contingency plans had been drafted for invasion of the autonomous areas if violence proceeded from the Har Homa decision. Nevertheless, a series of marches and protest strikes were urged by political and community organizations throughout the West Bank and Gaza. These reportedly failed to win the full support of Arafat, whose preferred response to the crisis was to attempt the diplomatic isolation of the Israeli Government. The PNA leader consulted EU leaders, King Hassan of Morocco and the Egyptian and Jordanian leaders in quick succession. Arafat's relatively restrained response to Har Homa led to speculation in the Israeli media that he had, at some time during negotiations with Israel, acquiesced to the construction of the settlement in return for swift progress on Israeli redeployments in the West Bank. Critics of Oslo repeated earlier assertions that what was happening at Har Homa was an inevitable consequence of the Accords' failure to curtail settlement activity during the interim period.

Following their success in helping to broker the Hebron agreement, the events surrounding Har Homa were received with alarm in Egypt and Jordan. On the day after the settlement was officially endorsed in Israel, King Hussein wrote to Netanyahu requesting his reappraisal of the decision and careful consideration of the consequences implicit in pursuing the project. To further demonstrate official Jordanian dissatisfaction, Crown Prince Hassan cancelled a scheduled visit to attend the inauguration of the Rabin Peace Centre at Tel-Aviv University. The Jordanian leader, however, stopped short of severing diplomatic links; Hussein had, after all, staked his regional policy on constructive engagement with Tel-Aviv. Yet the Jordanian monarch's perceived tolerance of Israeli provocation resulted in government policy that was severely at odds with a popular sentiment increasingly hostile to continued relations with Israel under Netanyahu. Public feeling in Egypt was similarly pitched against Israel. An ill-timed visit by Netanyahu to a Cairo trade fair in early March 1997 provoked overwhelming press hostility and the refusal of many prominent businessmen and intellectuals to accept invitations to be presented to the Israeli Prime Minister. On 7 March an EU-drafted UN resolution calling on Israel to refrain from settlement-building in East Jerusalem encountered the now customary US veto. Washington's newly appointed Ambassador to the UN, Bill Richardson, defended the use of the veto by stating that UN involvement in the current dispute could only serve to hinder progress.

Meanwhile, following lengthy cabinet discussion and considerable international pressure, Israel announced details of its first phase of West Bank troop redeployment, as required by the Oslo Accords and reaffirmed by the Hebron agreement. The Israeli proposal, which provided for the transfer of only 2% of 'new' West Bank territory to Palestinian control, was immediately rejected by the Palestinian negotiating team, which also challenged the level of total deployment quoted within the terms of the three-phase initiative. By 11 March 1997 negotiations had been suspended and all Palestinian officials had been instructed, by Arafat, to end all contacts with Israel. The deadline for the initiation of 'final status' talks, established by the Hebron agreement, was not observed by the Palestinians, who subsequently rejected an Israeli proposal to accelerate the timetable for the 'final status' negotiations, given that a satisfactory resolution of the outstanding provisions of Oslo II had yet to be achieved.

On 13 March 1997 seven Israeli schoolgirls visiting a border site in the Jordan Valley were killed when a Jordanian soldier discharged his automatic weapon on the school party. King Hussein condemned the massacre and curtailed an official visit in order to meet with the victims' families in Israel. His actions were widely applauded in Israel; less so in Jordan where his gesture was criticized as overly dramatic. On 19 March (the day after construction had begun at Har Homa) a Palestinian suicide bomber killed three women at a café in Tel-Aviv. Hamas' military wing in Jerusalem claimed responsibility for the attack, but the organization's political leaders in Gaza denied involvement. The Israeli Government immediately accused Arafat of having given tacit approval to his Islamist opposition to renew terror attacks and urged the PNA authorities to rectify the situation. One year previously the PNA had apprehended some 1,200 Islamist activists and sympathizers in the wake of a suicide-bombing campaign, but on this occasion Arafat felt little compulsion to respond so readily to Israeli demands. Arafat had made considerable efforts to build relations with Islamist organizations in the previous few months and was anxious not to antagonize this constituency with no prospect of reciprocity from Israel. Moreover, the issue of settlements had eroded residual support for the peace process in Palestinian communities and the prevalent mood was far less opposed to acts of violent resistance. Even Arafat's own Fatah faction was taking steps to distance itself from the policies of its nominal leader. On 23 March the Fatah Higher Committee in the West Bank called for an end to negotiations with Israel and an escalation of protests. There was an immediate response in the West Bank, particularly in Hebron, where there were prolonged clashes between Israeli soldiers and hundreds of demonstrators. Three Palestinian protesters were killed and more than 500 injured in the two weeks after the commencement of work at Har Homa.

ARAB FOREIGN MINISTERS' DECLARATION

Arab diplomatic protests were escalated in response to the commencement of construction on Jabal Abu Ghunaim. The GCC foreign ministers' meeting in the Saudi Arabian capital, Riyadh, the Islamic summit in Islamabad and the OIC Al-Quds (Jerusalem) Committee meeting in Rabat all produced statements denouncing Israel's settlement activity. More tangible opposition was expressed at an Arab foreign ministers' meeting in Cairo at the end of March when it was recommended that Arab League states should suspend involvement in multi-lateral negotiations with Israel, reassert the primary economic boycott and end moves towards normalization of relations, by closing the representative offices through which they were conducted. (Morocco, Mauritania, Oman, Qatar and Tunisia all had trade or representative offices in Tel-Aviv.) As these recommendations were non-binding and did not apply to Egypt, Jordan and the PNA, which had formal relations with Israel, it was unclear what practical impact they would have. (The Omani Government did prohibit Israeli participation at a Muscat trade fair in early April.) A group of states led by Syria had urged the imposition of more severe measures against Israel and the convening of a special Arab summit to authorize such action, but this proposal was vetoed by Egypt. There was little indication that the Netanyahu Government was unduly perturbed by the deterioration in relations with the Arab world;

although the previous Labour administration had regarded the development of closer relations with Arab states as a major dividend of the peace process, Israel's nationalist bloc had never been ideologically inclined to forge such links, given the cultural and political contempt in which it had long held the Arab world.

DIPLOMATIC INITIATIVES

With the peace process effectively stalled over Har Homa and the issue of redeployment on hold, attention turned to the USA, and Arab hopes that Clinton's successful re-election would allow him the political freedom to adopt a more uncompromising stance in his dealings with Israel. While Dennis Ross's assessment of the prevailing mood in the Middle East was sufficiently pessimistic for him to recommend that the newly appointed Secretary of State, Madeleine Albright, should cancel plans for a tour of the region, Arab and Israeli delegations made haste towards the White House. At the beginning of April 1997 the Jordanian monarch met President Clinton in Washington, DC, and expressed concerns that the precariousness of the current situation demanded that the USA play a more forthright role. However, Clinton replied that he was not willing to enforce an agreement. The end of King Hussein's visit coincided with the arrival in Washington of the Israeli Prime Minister. Netanyahu's visit was accompanied by an announcement that the USA was authorizing substantial new funds for Israel's anti-missile defence system, and no public expression of criticism of the Israeli leader was made by the US President. Their discussions, however, were described as 'frank', and privately Clinton aides revealed that the President had pressurized the Israeli leader to expedite a resumption of negotiations with the Palestinians by offering to suspend settlement in disputed areas, begin construction of Arab housing in Jerusalem and offer to negotiate on the next stage of redeployments. Netanyahu rejoined that under the terms of the Oslo Accords and the recent Hebron protocols Israel was under no obligation to move forward with the peace process while the Palestinians were failing to fulfil their 'security responsibilities'. This message was repeated to the PLO Chairman and the Palestinian delegation that held talks with US officials in Washington in mid-April. Arguing that the Palestinian side needed to undermine Israel's security argument, Clinton urged the Palestinians to renew security co-operation with Israel. Arafat duly complied, with an announcement that the PNA would 'temporarily' resume intelligence co-ordination.

INTER-PALESTINIAN PROBLEMS

Deaths and injuries were still occurring on much of the West Bank in continued demonstrations over Har Homa, and Arafat's decision on security was deeply unpopular, not least because Netanyahu pointedly refused to make concessions in return. Hamas, which was judged to be the main target of intelligence-sharing, registered its anger by boycotting a conference aimed at building better relations between the PNA and the Palestinian opposition. Arafat was beset by mounting difficulties throughout May and June, including the economic problems associated with a burgeoning budget deficit. In addition, Arafat's administration was severely undermined by allegations of widespread corruption and human rights abuses, and by a sustained strike by Palestinian teachers. Privately expressed hopes that domestic pressures would be relieved by the collapse of Netanyahu's Government were frustrated when investigation into the Der'i affair absolved the Israeli Prime Minister of any criminal wrongdoing. Instead Israeli–Palestinian relations further deteriorated into crisis after Israel accused the PNA of complicity in the murder of several Palestinians suspected of involvement in land sales to Israelis. PNA spokesmen denied the charge, although one week prior to the first killing the Authority's justice minister had stated that the selling of land to 'questionable land dealers' should become a capital offence.

ISRAELI RELATIONS WITH SYRIA AND LEBANON

Israel's relations with its northern neighbours had reverted to customary hostility following Syria's refusal to condemn Islamist attacks on Israeli civilian targets and the previous Israeli administration's subsequent decision to suspend bilateral negotiations. In August 1996 an attempt by the Netanyahu Government to entice Syria into a 'Lebanon first' agreement was rebuffed, while Israeli consideration of a plan to double the number of Jewish settlers on the Golan through the building of a new township seemed to cast doubt on the sincerity of Netanyahu's stated readiness to resume negotiations with Syria 'without preconditions'. Tension remained high between the two states in late 1996 when Syria deployed army units from the Lebanese coastal towns (as provided for by the Saudi-brokered Ta'if agreements between Lebanon and Syria) to the militarily sensitive area of the Beka'a valley. A substantial car-bomb attack in Damascus in late December that resulted in the deaths of a dozen people, and a machine-gun attack on a minibus transporting Syrian workers in Lebanon, were both attributed to Maronite elements working with Israel. Scores of Lebanese connected to the National Liberal Party, which had previously had close connections with Israeli intelligence services, were detained in the aftermath of the incidents. Netanyahu vehemently denied the charges of complicity in the attacks, while sections of the Israeli press carried ever more frequent stories of impending conflict with Syria, a proposition that was regarded as highly fanciful by most intelligence experts. Increasing security co-operation between Israel and Turkey, particularly the announcement in May 1997 of joint naval exercises with US warships in the Mediterranean, heightened Syrian concerns regarding territorial isolation and prompted renewed Syrian diplomatic efforts to persuade Arab states to block normalization with Israel. At the end of June Syria enlisted the support of Saudi Arabia in exerting pressure on Qatar to cancel the next post-Madrid economic summit due to take place in November with Israeli participation. The Saudi Crown Prince stated that the Kingdom would not be represented, a decision also taken by the United Arab Emirates. Syrian moves to establish more cordial relations with Iraq (the two states agreed to reopen border crossings and resume limited trade in June) and its attempts to broker improved relations between Iran and Iraq, on the one hand, and Iran and Saudi Arabia on the other, were all interpreted as a response to the perceived threat of an Israeli-Turkish axis. Meanwhile, the war of attrition in southern Lebanon continued at differing rates of intensity but with no sign of cessation. The deaths of 73 Israeli servicemen in February 1997, killed in a collision of helicopters while being transported to southern Lebanon, briefly provoked a debate on the future of Israel's presence in that country. Both left- and right-wing supporters in Israel argued that more was to be gained from abandoning the 'security zone' than maintaining it. However, this remained a minority opinion in the Knesset—a poll revealed that only 27 of the 120 deputies supported unilateral withdrawal—and was strongly opposed by Netanyahu and his defence minister. Reports also emerged that Israel had revised its counter-insurgency strategy with regard to Hezbollah and was relying more heavily on commando raids by élite parachute units. The IDF claimed this had been effective in disrupting Hezbollah's ability to engage in classic guerrilla warfare. However it did not prevent the Shi'a militia from continuing to inflict casualties on the IDF; 12 Israeli troops were killed in combat in southern Lebanon in the first half of 1997.

SPORADIC VIOLENCE CONTINUES

By the summer of 1997, and after months of stalled Israeli-Palestinian negotiations, many commentators were declaring the death of the Oslo process. Release from domestic scandal had fortified Netanyahu against US pressure to agree to the level of compromise on Har Homa that would facilitate the Palestinians' return to the negotiating table. However, evidence of increasing US frustration with Israeli policy emerged in May with the disclosure of a US intelligence report that claimed that many of the homes in Gaza's settlements and in the West Bank were lying empty. The report appeared seriously to undermine Netanyahu's principal public justification for continued settlement in the Occupied Territories, namely that land was needed to relieve Israel's chronic housing shortage. Netanyahu and settler leaders claimed the figures were groundless, but few doubted the accuracy of intelligence based on many years of field monitoring and satellite reconnaissance. Following the leak Israel agreed to two confidence-building measures suggested by the Clinton Administration: allowing the construction of more Arab housing in Jerusalem and suspending the policy of demolishing dwellings built without a licence. On the crucial issue of halting work on the Har Homa settlement, however, there was little sign of compromise, Cabinet 'hardliners' urging Netanyahu to ignore the pleas of the international community. The impasse ensured that the West Bank and Gaza remained in a state of high volatility. There were violent clashes in Gaza during May and June, provoked by settler attempts to encroach on neighbouring lands. Hebron also seemed to have descended into a state of permanent confrontation between stone-throwing youths and Israeli troops and armed settlers. The appearance in the city at the end of June of crudely offensive anti-Islamic posters prompted further large-scale unrest that provoked an Israeli ultimatum for the PNA to contain the protests or risk the reoccupation of the rest of the city. Some 200 unarmed Palestinian police were subsequently ordered onto the streets by Arafat to restore order. However, with the conflict in Hebron temporarily contained, another crisis arose when four Palestinian police-officers were arrested by Israeli troops outside Nablus on suspicion of planning attacks on Israeli targets. The discovery of a 'terror cell' was described by the Israeli defence minister as 'the gravest event since the Oslo Accords'. He also demanded the extradition of Jihad Masini, head of criminal investigations in Nablus, on suspicion of ordering an attack on a Jewish settler on 10 July. On 19 July Israel

Radio reported that Ghaza Jabali, Arafat's police chief, had authorized actions against West Bank settlers and that Netanyahu had ordered his removal. Masini and Jabali denied the Israeli allegations, but after receiving instructions from the USA to treat the Israeli charges with 'the highest degree of seriousness', a number of Palestinian police-officers, including Masini, were detained for investigation. Their arrest coincided with the discovery by the Palestinian police of what they termed a Hamas 'bomb factory' in the West Bank town of Beit Sahur. In the same week, the announcement that a permit had been granted for the building of a Jewish settlement in the densely-populated Palestinian district of Ras al-Amud aroused considerable international concern.

NEW INITIATIVE THWARTED

A sense of impending crisis in the Occupied Territories led to renewed US efforts to formulate an initiative that would save the Oslo process. In mid-July 1997 Clinton dispatched Thomas Pickering, the Under Secretary of State for Political Affairs, to meet with Israeli and Palestinian leaders. His presence in the region prompted speculation that the USA was close to securing the backing of both Israelis and Palestinians for a new proposal. Hopes were encouraged by a statement issued by Netanyahu expressing his opposition to the building of the settlement in Ras al-Amud and an interior ministry announcement that the permit for construction had been temporarily suspended. On 28 July Israel and the Palestinian negotiators announced that they would resume formal talks on the Oslo Accords within one week. The nature of the formula that had broken the deadlock remained unclear but was thought to have involved the possibility of suspension of works at Har Homa for between three and six months. It was also announced that Dennis Ross would be making an imminent visit to the region with a new series of proposals. A sense of relief that the peace process might yet be salvaged proved to be short-lived. On 30 July two suicide bombers attacked West Jerusalem's Mahane Yehuda market. Thirteen Israelis were killed and scores were wounded in the double explosion, responsibility for which was claimed initially by Islamic Jihad and subsequently by Hamas' military wing. There was little chance that the fledgling attempts to revive the peace process would survive the scenes of carnage in Jerusalem. The proposed resumption of formal negotiations was cancelled, as was Ross's visit to the region. Netanyahu charged Arafat with responsibility for the atrocity for his failure effectively to combat Islamist extremism. He pointedly refused to accept a message of condolence from the PNA Chairman and instead ordered the sealing of the Palestinian-controlled areas and the detention of suspected Islamist militants. Arafat aides described the measures as 'a declaration of war' on the Palestinian people. Despite the arrest of some Hamas and Islamic Jihad activists there was no immediate indication that the PNA was prepared to engage in the massive anti-activist campaign that Netanyahu declared to be the crucial prerequisite for both lifting of the siege and continuing the Oslo process.

The PLO Chairman's reluctance to accede to Israel's security demands was rooted in domestic vulnerability and ever-deepening mistrust of the Netanyahu Government. The day before the Jerusalem bombings, a report commissioned by the Legislative Council into the finances of the PNA had been presented and had concluded that corruption was endemic throughout the Authority. It recommended the dissolution of the existing executive and the prosecution of two Palestinian ministers. Following an announcement by Israel that, in addition to the closure of the West Bank and Gaza, further sanctions were to be applied including the withholding of tax revenues from the PNA, the 'freezing' of Authority assets in Israeli banks and the obstruction of broadcasts from Palestinian television and radio stations, there was little possibility that Arafat would risk further opprobrium and potential civil conflict by acquiescing in Israeli demands to dismantle the institutional base of his Islamist opposition. Instead, he attempted to counter Israeli belligerence by seeking to prevent further fracturing of his constituency. In mid-August 1997 he chaired a 'national unity' conference that was attended by representatives of both Hamas and Islamic Jihad. Although both organizations reiterated appeals for the PNA to abandon the Oslo process, their attendance at the conference was interpreted as a gesture of gratitude to Arafat for resisting Israeli demands for a more vigorous suppression of Islamist movements. The conference drew predictable criticism from the Netanyahu Government, which accused the PLO Chairman of 'colluding with terrorists'.

Having expended considerable diplomatic energy in attempting to reactivate Israeli-Palestinian negotiations, the aftermath of the Jerusalem bombings was viewed with particular dismay by the Clinton Administration. In mid-August 1997 the US Government announced that Madeleine Albright was to undertake her first tour of the region. Arab expectations of the visit were decidedly low. Albright's diplomatic career had established a firmly pro-Israeli profile in the Arab world, and her consistent response to the suicide attacks had been to echo Israeli demands for tighter security controls in the PNA-administered areas. However, greater encouragement was derived from the less partisan briefings of her spokesman, James Rubin, who, despite condemning Hamas and Islamic Jihad as 'enemies of peace', was careful not to criticize Arafat's recent meetings with them and also let it be known that the US Government opposed the economic sanctions that Israel had imposed on the Arab populations of the West Bank and Gaza. For their part, Palestinian officials warned that the Albright visit would provide the momentum for a resumption of the peace process only if Israel's security concerns were not the Secretary of State's principal focus. Such hopes were largely frustrated by a triple suicide bombing in Jerusalem the week before Albright's arrival. A further four Israelis were killed in the attack, which led to renewed demands from the Netanyahu Government for drastic action to be taken against Islamist militants. Albright repeatedly lent her voice to these calls in her first public statements in Jerusalem; however, she did go some way to addressing Arab concerns by criticizing Israel's withholding of Palestinian tax revenues and advising Israel against the 'unilateral actions' that were hindering the creation of a climate for peace. In Egypt Albright asserted that both the US and Egyptian Governments maintained that 'a permanent settlement must ensure real security for Israel and recognition of the legitimate rights of the Palestinian people'. Although such rhetorical flourishes won the Secretary of State guarded praise in some Arab quarters, Palestinian officials were less enthusiastic. They noted that there was 'a conspicuous dichotomy between our views and those of Albright on the concept of security and terrorism'. Even more worrying for Arafat and his loyalists, who had predicated their peace strategy on the expectation that the

US Government would act as a guarantor of Israeli adherence to the terms of the Oslo Accords, Albright had pointedly discounted the possibility of a more interventionist role for the USA. Continuing Palestinian despondency was a stark contrast to the satisfaction of the Israeli Government that the US Secretary of State's visit had committed Netanyahu to little more than the release of funds illegally withheld from the PNA and the resumption of negotiations with the Palestinians in the USA later in the month.

THE MESHAAL INCIDENT

Jordanian relations with Israel were plunged into renewed crisis at the end of September 1997 following a failed Mossad assassination attempt on Khalid Meshaal, a Jordanian citizen and head of the Hamas political bureau in Amman. Travelling with false Canadian passports, the two Israeli agents were over-powered on the streets of the Jordanian capital after they had injected Meshaal with a potentially lethal chemical agent. The Jordanian Government threatened to try the two Israeli operatives for murder and to sever diplomatic relations with Israel unless an antidote to the poison was supplied—it was immediately provided, probably saving Meshaal's life. Interviewed in the Arab press, King Hussein used the incident to initiate a bitter attack on Netanyahu and the role his Government had played in the search for a Middle East peace. Meanwhile, the Jordanian Government sought to undermine the gains made by its own Islamist opponents as a result of the Meshaal affair by exacting a high price for the return of the Israeli agents. The Government in Israel subsequently announced that it was to free from a lengthy prison sentence Sheikh Ahmad Yassin, the founder and spiritual leader of the Hamas movement. Although Israeli and Jordanian officials denied that an agreement had been negotiated, Yassin's release was followed by the deportation of the Israeli agents, and the further release of Jordanian and Palestinian prisoners. On returning to his native Gaza the ailing Yassin was fêted by thousands of well-wishers and given an official reception by the PNA leadership. The scenes in Gaza did little to diminish the Israeli embarrassment that had been generated by the assassination attempt and by the ensuing rupture in relations with Jordan. Given Netanyahu's repeated demands for the PNA to apprehend and contain Hamas cadres, the release of the movement's leader by Israel could scarcely have been more ill-timed.

ISRAELI CASUALTIES IN LEBANON

September 1997 witnessed the most serious resurgence of violence in the conflict in southern Lebanon since the Israeli bombardments of April 1996. A series of clashes involving the SLA and Hezbollah militias resulted in a number of Lebanese civilian casualties and the launch of rocket attacks against northern Israel. Israel responded with air raids on Hezbollah and Palestinian targets, and the bombing of a power station providing electricity to the port of Sidon. On 5 September a party of Israeli commandos was ambushed by a combined Hezbollah, Amal and Lebanese army force while mounting a raid on territory north of the 'security zone'. Twelve Israeli soldiers were killed and several were injured in the attack; two Lebanese soldiers and six Amal and Hezbollah militiamen also died during the IDF's evacuation of its wounded. The incident was significant not just for the number of Israeli casualties—the highest for more than a decade—but also because it illustrated a growing trend for regular Lebanese troops to engage the IDF and their SLA allies in battle. Further raids into Lebanon by Israeli forces on 12 and 13 September resulted in the deaths of six Lebanese soldiers and four Hezbollah fighters, and prompted Lebanese army commander Gen. Emile Lahoud to state that 'the Lebanese army will confront Israel until all our land is liberated'. Five more Israeli troops were killed in action in Lebanon during September, bringing the total number of IDF-SLA casualties during 1997 to 50 (compared to 48 Hezbollah deaths). Several reasons were advanced for the high number of casualties among Israeli and SLA forces. Defence commentators noted the deployment by Hezbollah of more sophisticated weaponry, particularly the *Sagar* missile, capable of penetrating the heavy armour of Israel's battle tanks. It was also suggested that Hezbollah had benefited from better intelligence; the activities of a 'double' agent were said to be behind the successful ambush of 5 September. Within Israel the mounting death toll in Lebanon provoked renewed public debate as to the wisdom of maintaining the occupation of the south. Yossi Beilin, a prominent member of the opposition Labour party, earned a rebuke from the new party leader, Ehud Barak, for campaigning for an immediate withdrawal from Lebanon. The mothers of serving troops also launched protests in Tel-Aviv, while opinion polls suggested that some 60% of the Israeli population was in favour of evacuation.

THE SETTLEMENT AND DEPLOYMENT ISSUES

The long hiatus in negotiations over implementation of the Oslo Accords ended in late September 1997 when the Israeli foreign minister met with his Palestinian counterpart in the US capital. This meeting prefaced more substantive negotiations in October. The key areas of concern for the Palestinian negotiators remained the question of settlements, the opening of the Gaza harbour and seaport, and the timing and extent of the long overdue Israeli redeployment on the West Bank. The former issue remained the most contentious. In pre-meeting declarations Arafat restated his intention to seek a halt to all construction of Jewish settlements. Netanyahu's interpretation of Albright's appeal for a suspension of 'unilateral steps' was predictably idiosyncratic. Speaking at a press conference in Jerusalem, Netanyahu elaborated his own understanding of Albright's rubric—Israel would temporarily undertake not to inaugurate new settlements, but would proceed with planned construction in existing settlements (including Har Homa) so as to 'accommodate natural population growth'. Given this divergence over such a core issue and continued friction over Israel's security demands, observers on both sides predicted that a breakthrough in the forthcoming negotiations was unlikely. Their pessimism appeared to be justified. By November Palestinian officials were accusing Israel of miring the talks in procedural issues so as to avoid broaching the subject of Israeli redeployment and settlements. For his part, Netanyahu stated that he 'would not hand over any more land to the Palestinians without knowing in advance how the features of the 'final status' settlement would look'. This remained unacceptable to the Palestinian side; indeed the only satisfaction that the Palestinian delegation derived from its presence in Washington, DC, was the sign of increasing impatience towards Israel from within the US Department of State. Press reports revealed that Albright had 'lambasted' the Israeli premier over his perceived lack of sincerity towards the Oslo process. The lack of progress in Washington also determined that the fourth Middle East and North Africa (MENA) economic conference in Qatar in mid-November would not substantially advance the development of trade links and development opportunities between Israel and the Arab world. The Syrian Government, which had distanced itself completely from the multilateral forums of the peace process, urged the cancellation of the conference. Morocco, Saudi Arabia and the United Arab Emirates, key US allies in the region, subsequently announced that they too would be boycotting the conference in response to Israeli policies. President Mubarak initially refused to commit Egypt to attendance or a boycott, his hesitation linked to the hope that the Israeli Government would smooth the way for Egyptian participation by announcing substantive movement in the peace process. With no such development, and with domestic opinion crystallized against Israel, Mubarak announced that Egypt would join the boycott of the MENA conference. Despite overt and covert US pressure, only five Arab states (Jordan, Kuwait, Mauritania, Oman and Yemen) sent delegations to Doha. The absence of Egypt and Saudi Arabia inevitably deprived the conference of much political and economic—not to mention symbolic—import. Nevertheless, the conference attracted 2,000 participants from 65 countries; this rivalled the attendance at the previous year's summit in Cairo. Qatari, Israeli and US officials expressed satisfaction with the gathering. Israel and Jordan announced commitments to a number of joint ventures, including the establishment of an industrial park in the Jordanian city of Irbid.

Far from reactivating the peace process, Israeli-Palestinian negotiations were soon marginalized as policy statements in Israel accentuated the chasm between the two sides. At the end of November 1997 the Israeli Cabinet issued a memorandum which underlined the Government's desire to radically rework the Oslo process. While agreeing in principle to a further redeployment of the IDF on the West Bank, the cabinet paper stated that this could only be accomplished in stages, and after the fulfilment of two conditions. The first of these would be the PNA's meeting certain Israeli demands: the revision of the Palestinian National Charter, and an end to 'terrorism' and political activity in East Jerusalem. The second would be an assessment by government agencies of those areas of the Occupied Territories to be retained indefinitely by Israel and not made subject to negotiation in the 'final status' talks. This was in direct contravention of the Oslo Agreement. Happily for Arafat, the Cabinet plan was rejected by Labour's Barak as 'totally irrelevant'. Of greater concern to the PNA was the response of the USA to Israel's posturing and the commitment of Albright to the provisions concerning redeployment as specified in the Oslo and Hebron interim agreements. As Palestinian officials indicated, according to these agreements, three redeployments were due to be completed by mid-1998. After this date the only areas of the Occupied Territories to remain under Israeli control would be borders, East Jerusalem, settlements and specified military locations. Ahmad Tibi, one of Arafat's advisers, estimated these areas to comprise no more than 11% of West Bank territory, considerably less than the 55% being claimed by some sections of the Israeli Government. In late December Albright flew to Europe to hold separate meetings with Netanyahu and Arafat in London and Paris, but neither these talks, nor a further trip to the

Middle East by Dennis Ross in January 1998 achieved an appreciable shift in positions. Ross's visit coincided with the announcement by Israel of a major expansion to two settlements in the Occupied Territories and the resignation of Israel's Deputy Prime Minister and Minister of Foreign Affairs, David Levy. Although Levy's resignation was forced primarily by disagreements over the Government's budget proposals, he was regarded as one of the more liberal voices in the Israeli Cabinet. His departure (not to mention the growing influence of Sharon) reinforced fears that there would be no relaxation in Israel's uncompromising approach to brokering an agreement with the PNA on IDF withdrawals. Two weeks after the failed Ross mission, Arafat and Netanyahu returned to Washington, DC, to hold separate talks with the US Administration. Prior to his appointment at the White House, the Israeli leader held a series of meetings with leading Republicans, including the Speaker of the House of Representatives, Newt Gingrich, and representatives of the evangelical Christian movement—both fiercely pro-Israel and anti-Clinton. If these high-profile engagements were intended as a warning to the Clinton Administration not to exert undue pressure on the Netanyahu Government, they proved to be barely necessary. With his presidency under threat from a rapidly escalating sex scandal, Clinton was keen to avoid a diplomatic confrontation with the Israeli leader. In seven hours of meetings, described as 'attritional', Clinton failed to persuade Netanyahu to accept a new US initiative. This was thought to involve a phased Israeli redeployment from 12%–15% of the West Bank territory in return for revision of the Palestinian National Charter and steps 'to fight terror and prevent violence' in the self-ruled areas. Netanyahu reportedly stated that his Cabinet would accept no more than a 9.5% withdrawal. Despite the fact that the US proposals represented far less than had been expected by the PNA only six months previously, Arafat was said to have reluctantly accepted the package. His decision was influenced, in part at least, by the possibility of Israeli rejection and Netanyahu's consequent diplomatic isolation. Netanyahu himself appeared unbowed by this eventuality. His supporters viewed the US trip as a diplomatic triumph—he had after all resisted the most modest of concessions. By contrast, Arafat's description of his meetings with Clinton as 'positive, fruitful and constructive' masked a deepening pessimism. For much of the wider Arab world also, the absence of real progress at meetings in the US capital signalled an end to hopes that the USA would be prepared to exert significant pressure on the Netanyahu Government.

ISRAELI INITIATIVE ON LEBANON

Since 1997 had been such a costly year for Israel in Lebanon, it was not surprising that the new year brought signs that the Netanyahu Government was prepared to respond to growing domestic unease with the human cost of the occupation. In an interview with a Lebanese daily newspaper, Mordechai stated that Israel would be prepared to consider a unilateral withdrawal from Lebanon in line with UN Security Council Resolution 425. He added that the withdrawal could only be undertaken if guarantees were forthcoming that the Lebanese army would be deployed to its southern border and would co-operate with the IDF in preventing 'terror and violence' against Israel. An Israeli foreign-ministry briefing also urged the incorporation of the SLA into the regular

Lebanese army in the same way that other militias had been absorbed at the end of the Lebanese civil war. Lebanon rejected the offer as unacceptable, a response that observers believed to be conditioned by Syria's long-held opposition to previous 'Lebanon first' proposals mooted by Israel. In mid-January 1998 the Israeli press carried reports that senior Lebanese officials had contacted Yossi Beilin, the guiding force behind the newly-constituted 'Movement for a Peaceful Departure from Lebanon', and assured him that in the event of an Israeli withdrawal the Lebanese army would establish full sovereignty over the evacuated areas. In March Netanyahu sought to secure international and regional backing for a more comprehensive version of the Mordechai proposals. Netanyahu reiterated Israel's desire for a withdrawal, but stated that any return to the international borders would occur in phases and be conditional on the negotiation of security guarantees from the Lebanese Government. The plan received the backing of the US Government but was rejected by Lebanon and Syria. On 3 April the Lebanese Prime Minister, Hariri, accused Israel of rewriting Resolution 425 and of attempting to drive a wedge between his country and Syria. He added that Lebanon would not support a 'security before peace' proposal and indicated that there was no prospect of an amnesty being awarded to the higher-ranking officers in the SLA. The Lebanese position received support from the French President, Jacques Chirac, who opined that Resolution 425 demanded a 'unilateral' and 'unconditional' withdrawal; this was also the majority opinion of the UN Security Council. After a closed meeting, the Council President, Hishashi Owada of Japan, reported that the body's consensus was that Security Council resolutions 'are mandatory and they should be implemented without preconditions'. Earlier the Iranian Minister of Foreign Affairs had stated that his Government believed Hezbollah should end its military campaign if Israel ended its occupation of southern Lebanon. He did, however, concur with the Syrian opinion that the Israeli proposal was 'a Zionist plot aimed at splitting the states in the region'. Later in the month the Lebanese President undertook a global tour to win international support for his country's refusal to accept the Israeli initiative.

INCREASED EUROPEAN INVOLVEMENT

In January 1998 the European Commission issued a detailed review of the EU's Middle East policies. The report argued that, as the region's largest aid donor, the EU should play a more active role in Middle Eastern affairs, particularly in relation to the faltering peace process. The report was careful to acknowledge the leading role played by the US Administration, but at the same time the author of the report, European Commissioner Manuel Marín, was unusually explicit in apportioning blame for the political and economic failures of the previous 12 months. Marín stated that Israeli policies, and in particular the restrictions imposed on trade and economic activity, had undermined EU aid initiatives and were responsible for a severe economic decline in the Palestinian territories. This was, Marín added, despite the injection of US $1,200m. of EU funds into the Palestinian economy during 1993–97. Within days of the presentation of the report, the European Commission President, Jacques Santer, embarked on a seven-day tour of the Middle East, his first official visit to the region. The visit was designed to raise the profile of the EU in the region and was punctuated by frequent expressions of the EU's irritation with the policies of the Netanyahu Government. Santer levelled specific criticism at Israel for blocking the opening of the European-financed airport in Gaza. Having held talks with both Palestinian and Israeli leaders, returned to Brussels accusing Netanyahu of generating 'contradictions' with regard to Israel's position: 'On the one hand, Prime Minister Netanyahu says he wants economic development in the Palestinian territories. On the other hand he won't allow the Palestinians to exploit their economic potential.' He also reiterated the European belief that Israel's security needs could best be assured by swift implementation of their obligations as laid down in the Oslo principles. Questioned as to what pressure the EU could bring to bear on Israel, Santer declared the Europeans 'powerless' to bring about a change in Israeli policies. He dismissed suggestions of sanctions being employed against Israel. European–Israeli relations deteriorated further in March, following a visit to the Middle East by the British Secretary of State for Foreign and Commonwealth Affairs, Robin Cook. Prior to the visit, Cook had gained EU support for a British initiative to 'unblock the peace process'. In essence, the six-point British plan called for the Palestinians and Israel to adhere to previously signed agreements. However, it also contained a specific appeal for Israel to implement substantial and credible redeployments on the West Bank and to 'freeze' all settlement activity. The proposals were dismissed by an Israeli Government spokesman as 'essentially Palestinian ideas' which only reinforced antipathy towards greater European involvement in the region. Cook's intended itinerary also raised Israeli ire. A proposed visit to the site of the Har Homa settlement in the company of Faisal Husseini, the PNA's Minister responsible for Jerusalem Affairs, was declared 'unacceptable' by Netanyahu. Cook eventually agreed to be escorted to Har Homa by Israel's Cabinet Secretary, David Naveh, a compromise that satisfied neither Israel nor the Palestinians. In the event, Cook's visit to Har Homa degenerated into an undignified spectacle as Israeli security personnel struggled to keep the British politician from being jostled by a crowd of right-wing settlers. Swiftly departing the scene, Cook travelled to East Jerusalem, where he met Husseini and laid a wreath to commemorate the Palestinian victims of the 1948 massacre at Deir Yassin. Netanyahu responded by cancelling an arranged dinner with Cook and truncating their scheduled meeting to a symbolic 15 minutes. The 15 EU foreign ministers issued a statement in support of Cook's visit, countering charges that it had irreparably damaged the chances of a more constructive EU role in the region. Netanyahu's refusal to pursue diplomatic channels in order to ease the strain on relations resulting from the visit suggested that the Israeli Prime Minister had seized on the incident as a means of forestalling the EU's political ambitions in the region.

RENEWED DEADLOCK

In early 1998, a renewed crisis in the USA's relations with Iraq, occasioned by Saddam Hussain's refusal to allow UN weapons-inspection teams free access to his presidential palaces, threw Arab dissatisfaction with the US Government's Middle East policy into sharp relief. The refusal of the Arab world to support US air strikes could be explained in part by the genuine desire to see an end to the hardships endured by ordinary Iraqis, but opposition to military action was also informed by a perception that the Clinton Administration was overly indulgent of Israel's reluctance to meet its responsibilities. There were few signs during the early months of 1998 to suggest that progress was about to be made. Further visits to the Middle East by Madeleine Albright in February and Dennis Ross in March failed to sway Netanyahu from his earlier insistence that Israel would only accept a redeployment of less than 10%. He deemed the US proposals 'an imposed solution that is neither desirable nor viable'. While Netanyahu's stance was reported to be causing exasperation in the US Administration, it did not lead to the public condemnation of Israel demanded by the Arab world. Arafat, meanwhile, was taking great risks with his own constituency in order to appease the US Government. Arrests of Hamas cadres had resumed in areas under PNA control, and during the Iraqi crisis pro-Iraqi demonstrations were dispersed by the security forces (it was also reported that, following Israeli allegations that the PNA was secretly releasing imprisoned Islamists, Arafat organized a tour of prisons for the US CIA to demonstrate that those arrested remained incarcerated). More importantly, Arafat had remained committed to the unpublished, but widely reported, US proposals to move the peace process forward. These proposals allegedly required Israel to redeploy from a further 13.1% of the West Bank's 'Area C' (under exclusive Israeli control) in three phases, and for 12% of this territory to be transferred to West Bank 'Area B' (under PNA civilian, but Israeli security control) rather than 'Area A' (under exclusive PNA civilian and security control). An additional 12% of 'Area B' territory would be converted to 'Area A', as a form of compensation. The US initiative fell far short of the 30%–40% redeployment originally anticipated by the Palestinians, yet PNA spokesmen believed that Arafat had no other option but to remain committed to the proposal. Egypt and Jordan had already given their reluctant support to the plan and had convinced Arafat that the US ideas represented the most realistic chance of success with Netanyahu. The PNA leader was also aware that rejection of the agreement would jeopardize US support for a more substantial third redeployment. The Israeli Government had already made it known that it wanted the third redeployment cancelled or at best merged into the 'final status' talks.

Relations between the Jordanian Government and the Israeli authorities remained frosty following the attempted assassination of Khalid Meshaal. Prospects of an improvement receded in mid-March 1998 when Ariel Sharon reportedly threatened to attempt another assassination of the Hamas chief. Jordan's foreign ministry summoned the Israeli Ambassador to demand an explanation of Sharon's comments; Sharon subsequently sent a letter to the Jordanian Government stating that his comments had been misunderstood and that Israel had no plans 'to attack Jordan or Jordanians'. In mid-April King Hussein and Netanyahu held an unscheduled meeting in Eilat to discuss the stalemate in the peace process. The details of the meeting were not revealed, although the Jordanian monarch later commented that 'not all the results of the meeting had been positive'. In a letter sent to Netanyahu on the day after the talks, King Hussein urged Israel to accept the US formula for withdrawal and warned that if he failed to do so he would bear responsibility for the collapse of the peace process.

During a visit to the Middle East at the end of April 1998 the British Prime Minister, Tony Blair, invited Israeli, Palestinian and US leaders to peace talks in

London to be conducted in May. All parties accepted the invitation which was presented, once again, as a final attempt to salvage what remained of the peace process. Following two days of bilateral talks in London on 4 and 5 May, there was little sign that the joint efforts of Blair and Albright had persuaded Israel to accept the US proposals. At the end of the talks Blair concluded, somewhat lamely, that there had been 'no breakthrough but no breakdown either'. Albright invited the Israeli and Palestinian leaders to meet President Clinton in Washington, DC, later in the month if Netanyahu could agree to the 13.1% redeployment. This was something that Netanyahu claimed his right-wing colleagues in the Cabinet were not prepared to countenance. He did, however, state that there were still issues to be explored with Albright, and in mid-May he flew to the USA. During his five-day trip to Washington and New York, Netanyahu once again displayed an adroit ability to manipulate the domestic US political scene. He argued his 'hardline' security agenda forcefully in the media, in the US Congress and to pro-Israeli lobby groups. He won both standing ovations and strong political backing from Republican legislators who were critical of the Clinton Administration's 'bullying' of Israel. The Republican Chair of the Committee for International Relations claimed that 'Congress will continue to stand shoulder-to-shoulder with Israel regardless of the obstacles that others may place before her'. Meetings with Albright and Ross concentrated on a formula to bridge the gap between the US redeployment proposals and Netanyahu's insistence that a withdrawal from more than 9.5% of West Bank territory would conflict with Israel's security needs. Before he flew back to Israel to take part in his nation's 50th anniversary celebrations, Netanyahu suggested that his policy differences with the US Administration were diminishing. He refused to elaborate on the reasons for his optimism but there was speculation that a bridging formula may have been agreed. Two potential scenarios were advanced unofficially. The first envisaged Israel implementing a 9.5% redeployment and agreeing to honour the remaining percentage only after the Palestinians had met certain security obligations. The second, more widely held view, involved the Israeli Government agreeing to the larger redeployment but demanding US support for a postponement of the all-important third deployment in compensation. If this was the case, it would be certain to cause a crisis within the PNA. Arafat had staked his negotiating strategy on the understanding, in accordance with the Oslo Accords, that he would be entering the 'final status' talks with at least 80% of the West Bank under his full or partial control. A postponement of the third redeployment would mean that these negotiations would begin with 60% of the West Bank under exclusive Israeli control. According to Hani al-Hassan of Fatah's central committee, this would inevitably lead to a 'final status' solution that involved the partitioning of the West Bank and the retention by Israel of 'around 45% of the territory'. This would be an arrangement, observed al-Hassan, 'that no Palestinian leader could endorse without falling'. The pessimism of Fatah was reflected in mounting frustration with regard to the peace process on the Palestinian streets. As Israelis were joyously marking the foundation of the Jewish State, Palestinians were marching through the streets of Gaza and the West Bank in officially sanctioned commemoration of the *Nabka*, the 'catastrophe' of 1948 that had led to their dispossession and dispersal. In a number of cities the thousands of demonstrators were joined by masked men carrying machine-guns and automatic rifles. Significantly, the majority of these were not the activists of Hamas and Islamic Jihad, but members of Arafat's increasingly estranged Fatah movement. In Nablus, the local leader of Hamas concluded a march by 15,000 people by firing a pistol into the air and calling for 'a new era of resistance'. Inevitably, several of the demonstrations erupted into violence as protesters vented their emotions on Israeli settlements and military positions. By the end of the day six Palestinians had been shot dead (five of them in Gaza) and scores had been wounded by live ammunition and rubber bullets.

STILL NO PROGRESS ON SYRIAN TRACK

The last week of May 1998 witnessed further fighting in southern Lebanon. Israeli naval vessels joined helicopter gunships in bombarding suspected Hezbollah targets around Sidon. On 26 May the Shi'a militia fired some 300 mortars at SLA positions, and on the following day two Israeli soldiers were killed on the edge of Israel's self-declared security zone. The deaths prompted Netanyahu to comment that an IDF withdrawal from Lebanon was 'more pressing than ever'. Tensions were heightened between Israel and its northern neighbours following reports that the Syrian authorities had been encouraging Hezbollah to intensify attacks on Israeli targets. In mid-June the Israeli daily newspaper *Ha'aretz* also reported that Syria had taken delivery of around 1,000 laser-guided anti-tank rockets, the first such shipment of advanced weaponry from Moscow since the demise of the USSR. A rare visit to Paris by President Assad in July suggested a developing strategic partnership between Syria and France. The visit also prompted speculation that renewed dialogue between Israel and Syria might be forthcoming. However, Netanyahu rejected a French proposal to resume talks on the basis of understandings already reached on the Israeli–Syrian track, owing to Syria's insistence that the previous Israeli Government had agreed, in principle, to an Israeli evacuation of the Golan Heights. Moreover, later in the month, the Israeli Knesset approved a bill, sponsored by the Third Way party, that would require any withdrawal from the Golan to be sanctioned by a national referendum. Syria deemed the vote 'a declaration of war against the peace process and a direct defiance of the international community'. In response, there was an immediate escalation of hostilities in Lebanon. Two Israeli soldiers and a civilian army employee were killed in Hezbollah attacks in the 'security zone' in mid-August, while the IDF shelled civilian areas in the south and, on 25 August, assassinated a prominent Amal leader. Hezbollah and its allied militias retaliated with *Katyusha* rocket attacks which wounded a number of civilians in northern Israel and forced residents of northern townships to seek the refuge of underground bunkers.

PALESTINIAN STATUS UPGRADED AT UN

The PNA secured a welcome diplomatic victory at the UN in early July 1998, when the General Assembly agreed by 124 votes to four to upgrade the observer status of the Palestinian representative. Henceforth the Palestinians would enjoy the same status as a full member state in all but voting and election rights. Israel and the USA were joined by the Marshall Islands and the Federated States of Micronesia in opposing the motion. An earlier draft resolution on the status of the Palestinian mission had been abandoned the previous December following

Arab failure to win the support of the EU for the proposal. That the EU was now prepared to put aside former misgivings and endorse such proposals underlined renewed European perceptions that Israel's obduracy was largely responsible for the parlous state of the peace process. For the Palestinian leader the vote could not have come at a better time. With the Israeli Government either unable or unwilling to address the latest US initiative on West Bank redeployment, Arafat had sought to stem the tide of domestic criticism of his handling of the peace process by stating his intention unilaterally to declare Palestinian statehood when the five-year interim period established by the Oslo Accords expired on 4 May 1999. Netanyahu, meanwhile, had warned that such a declaration would provoke the sternest of responses from Israel.

TALKS REVIVED

Israeli and Palestinian representatives resumed direct talks on the US initiative in Tel-Aviv in July 1998, but these ended in failure three days later, after the Palestinian side complained of Israel's 'obscure, sophistic formulations', a reference to an Israeli proposal that 3% of the designated 13.1% of territory slated for withdrawal should be classified as a 'nature reserve' in which neither Palestinian nor Israeli construction would be permitted. Pressure from the USA had compelled Arafat to instruct his negotiators to revive talks. The decision was not popular with many Palestinians, who argued that by returning to the negotiating table they were lending credibility to a process that had long been devoid of substance and only served to sustain the fiction that the Netanyahu Government was actively pursuing a peace settlement. Arafat's critics also complained that by resuming dialogue the Palestinians were implicitly accepting Israel's stance that the US initiative was still the subject of negotiation rather than implementation. Arafat was unwilling to accommodate dissent on this or other matters.

PNA RESHUFFLE

In June 1998 the PNA Cabinet resigned, apparently in order to obstruct an attempt by the PLC, which had published a highly critical report of widespread corruption in the PNA in July 1997, to pass a motion expressing 'no confidence' in it. Arafat accepted the resignation, but ministers were instructed to remain in office in a provisional capacity until new appointments were made. A new Cabinet appointed in August included several new ministers, but only one minister of the outgoing Cabinet was actually dismissed. On the day following the appointment of the new Cabinet, two prominent ministers resigned on the grounds that the Cabinet reshuffle had failed adequately to address the short-comings of the PNA. The new Cabinet was also criticized by officials of the principal international organizations granting funds to the PNA. In November, nevertheless, at a conference sponsored by the USA, donors agreed to grant the PNA more than US $3,000m., to be disbursed over the next five years.

DISENCHANTMENT IN THE OCCUPIED TERRITORIES

The mood of the region remained resolutely pessimistic during the summer of 1998, with local developments exacerbating the atmosphere of suspicion and mistrust. Unknown assailants killed three prominent Jewish West Bank settlers in August and Netanyahu responded by announcing the establishment of three permanent settlements in Nablus, Jerusalem and the centre of Hebron. This announcement, roundly condemned by the PNA, coincided with a report from the Washington-based Foundation for Middle East Peace which claimed that new homes were currently being constructed in the Occupied Territories at a rate of some 2,000 per year, compared to a rate of around 1,000 per year during 1996–97. The report also estimated the number of Jewish settlers living in the West Bank and Gaza to have increased by 12.4% in the 18 month-period to June 1998, bringing the total number of settlers in those areas to some 170,000. In September two prominent members of Hamas' military wing were killed in Hebron during a covert IDF operation. The killings brought thousands of Palestinians onto the streets of Gaza and the West Bank. Hamas leaders promised revenge attacks, raising the spectre of renewed suicide bombings. Spokesmen for the PNA condemned the assassinations as 'state-sponsored terrorism', but such sentiments failed to prevent charges of complicity being levelled against the PNA and its security apparatus. Despite the ongoing shuttle diplomacy of the US envoy, Dennis Ross, there was little evidence of progress on the redeployment proposals. Tellingly, the fifth anniversary of the signing of the Oslo Accords was marked by a low-key ceremony attended by Arafat and his older interlocutor, Peres. Netanyahu effectively snubbed the gathering, reporting instead to the Knesset that the PNA was failing in its 'pledge to combat terrorism' and therefore bore responsibility for any delay in reaching an agreement on second-phase redeployment.

LIMITED PROGRESS

Although the Netanyahu Government's prevarication with regard to the US peace proposals had been facilitated by President Clinton's embroilment in the sex scandal involving Monica Lewinsky, the Israeli Prime Minister recognized that it would not be possible to let the impasse continue indefinitely. The US Government was desperate for a foreign-policy success to distract attention from the President's personal embarrassment, and despite Israeli assertions of the PNA's failure to meet its security commitments, the international community was largely unanimous in its belief that Israel's intransigence was responsible for the lack of developments in the peace process. There were also domestic imperatives prompting Netanyahu to adopt a less uncompromising approach to a deal with the Palestinians. Israel's poor economic performance, an unpopular budget and simmering industrial unrest meant that the Israeli Prime Minister was almost as much in need of a diversion from internal difficulties as the US President. Signs of compromise emerged at a UN General Assembly debate in New York at the end of September 1998, when Netanyahu delivered a speech that was unusually conciliatory and affirmed Israel's commitment to achieving regional peace. For his part, Arafat elected not to jeopardize any new initiative by reiterating his plans for a unilateral declaration of statehood. Albright held talks with Arafat and Netanyahu in New York and secured their agreement to meet jointly with President Clinton on 28 September 1998—their first direct encounter since October 1997. The US President subsequently announced that he would host a bilateral summit at the Wye River Conference Centre in

Maryland in mid-October, with the express aim of reaching agreement on all outstanding provisions of the interim phase of the Oslo Accords. The portents in the weeks preceding the summit were not favourable. In late September a grenade attack on the IDF in Hebron resulted in injuries to 12 soldiers and a number of Palestinian civilians. A curfew was immediately imposed in the Israeli-controlled part of the city, but was frequently interrupted by clashes between soldiers and stone-throwing youths; scores of Palestinian injuries and at least one death were reported during the 13 days of the curfew. The violent intensity of the clashes was fuelled by a succession of developments regarding Israeli settlements in the West Bank. On 4 October the settlement of Ma'ate Hever, near Hebron, was expanded to include a further seven acres of confiscated Palestinian land. Three days later Netanyahu attended a ceremony to upgrade the status of Ariel, the West Bank's second-largest Jewish settlement, from that of a town to a city, while settlers in Hebron laid the cornerstone for a permanent settlement in the city centre. On 8 October it was announced that a further 150 housing units were to be built at a settlement near Ramallah. The Israeli Prime Minister also declared that Israel would annex all areas of the West Bank under Israeli control should Arafat proceed with his threatened declaration of statehood in May. Only days before the planned meeting at Wye Netanyahu assigned the vacant foreign-affairs portfolio to Ariel Sharon. While some observers interpreted the installation of such a prominent 'hawk' as a signal that a particularly uncompromising stance was to be taken at Wye, it was also suggested that Sharon's promotion was timed to mollify the nationalist right in the event of further territorial compromise.

THE WYE RIVER MEMORANDUM

The Wye summit was convened on 15 October 1998 and was scheduled to last four days, but continued for a further five. The Wye River Memorandum was signed on 23 October (see Documents on Palestine, p. 407). Moments of drama punctuated the steady procedures of the negotiating process. A visibly ailing King Hussein arrived mid-conference to help broker a deal, while the final agreement nearly collapsed at the last possible moment when Netanyahu attempted to trade his signature for the release of Jonathan Pollard, the US citizen convicted of spying for Israel and imprisoned in the USA in 1987. Netanyahu's attempt to link Pollard's release to the agreements reached at Wye mystified many observers as the consensus, internationally and in Israel, was that the terms of the agreement, broadly speaking, were more favourable to Israel than to the Palestinians. Although Wye did secure Israeli agreement to the 13.1% withdrawal proposed months earlier, Netanyahu had attached fairly stringent conditions: Israeli redeployment was to be undertaken in three phases, each being contingent on the PNA meeting 'concrete and verifiable' security measures. Should Israel be dissatisfied with Palestinian security compliance—to be overseen by the CIA—Netanyahu was empowered to suspend withdrawal. Oslo's putative third redeployment was to be discussed at sessions of a special committee but without commitments from Israel that it would ever be implemented. Negotiations on the 'final status' issues, *inter alia* refugees, settlements and Jerusalem, were to commence in November 1998 and continue until Oslo's timetabled expiry in May 1999. Netanyahu also won Arafat's commitment to convene a special session of the PNC to repeal formally those clauses of the Palestinian National Charter considered objectionable by Israel. For its part, Israel agreed to a schedule of release dates for gaoled Palestinians, and to facilitate the opening of Gaza airport and renew negotiations on a safe passage between Gaza and the West Bank.

VIOLENT REACTION TO THE MEMORANDUM

The announcement of territorial concessions was greeted with accusations of treason from Israeli nationalists, but the return to Israel of Sharon to assure supporters that 'this was the best agreement attainable', helped to marginalize the extreme right. Opinion polls published in Israel revealed 75% support for the Wye agreement. The Palestinian reaction to the Memorandum was far less favourable, despite the positive tone of declarations made by Arafat's spokesmen; there was a belief that too much had been conceded, and that the Wye Memorandum had strayed too far from the terms and the spirit of the original Oslo Agreements. Of particular concern was the realization that Israel would be entering the crucial 'final status' talks with control of security for 22% of the West Bank and absolute control of a further 60%. An additional cause of unease was the linkage of future redeployments to security compliance and the monitoring role given to the CIA. 'I'm afraid our entire security apparatus will become an extra-territorial department of the CIA', was the response of one PLC member. Decrees were issued curbing press freedoms, and the subsequent arrest of personalities critical of the Wye Memorandum convinced many observers that the erosion of civil liberties was a price that Arafat was prepared to pay for the peace process to be seen to be back on track. As the principal targets of any increase in security, the militant Islamists were unrestrained in their opposition to Wye. More than 60 Israelis had been wounded in a Hamas grenade attack in the city of Beersheba on 19 October 1998 and, at the end of the month, a suicide bomber attempted to drive his car into a bus carrying settler schoolchildren in Gaza. (He was intercepted by a military jeep, averting major bloodshed; one Israeli soldier and the bomber were killed in the incident.) Responsibility for the attack was promptly attributed to the *Izz ad-Din Qassam* Brigades. The Hamas political leadership attempted to distance itself from the operation, but an enraged Arafat ordered the detention of some 300 senior Hamas members and the immediate house arrest of its spiritual leader, Sheikh Ahmad Yassin. A Hamas military communiqué threatened to target PNA police officers in retaliation for the arrests, prompting both the PNA and the Hamas leadership to seek to prevent a further escalation in tensions. PNA spokesmen, therefore, sponsored the theory that the bombing had been orchestrated by an 'Iranian cell' within Hamas. Such conjecture was regarded as highly fanciful, but it did allow for the release of many of the political figures who had been arrested. Sheikh Yassin responded with a call for his movement to engage in dialogue with the PNA, while claiming that 'Palestinians must never turn their weapons against each other'. The relative moderation with which Arafat dealt with Hamas was conditioned, in part, by Fatah opposition to more extreme measures, the belief among Fatah activists being that if the PNA neutralized Hamas, then their own movement would become the principal target. In November further loss of life was also narrowly avoided, when explosives detonated prematurely while being transported by two Islamic Jihad bombers. Both men were killed and several Israelis were slightly injured by the explosion. In response, the PNA arrested scores of Islamic Jihad members and closed a kindergarten in Bethlehem closely identified with the organization.

RESPONSE IN ISRAEL

The attempted bomb attacks strengthened the opposition of the nationalist bloc in Israel to the Wye Memorandum and persuaded Netanyahu to postpone a cabinet vote on its provisions. The Knesset did signal effective support for the accord, although this was largely engineered by the right as a vote of confidence in the Government, and Netanyahu's ministers were more clearly undecided when the Cabinet eventually delivered its verdict on the first-stage withdrawal on 11 November 1998: eight votes were recorded in favour of the agreement, with four against, and five abstentions. On 17 November the Knesset ratified the Wye Memorandum by 75 votes to 19. While some of Wye's clauses were implemented without serious delay—most notably a redeployment (involving the transfer to complete Palestinian control of some 500 sq km) around the city of Jenin on 20 November and the opening of Gaza International Airport four days later—it soon became evident that the 'constructive ambiguity' that lay at the heart of the Wye Memorandum and, indeed, the whole Oslo process, would soon lead to serious disagreement. Before and after signing the memorandum the Palestinians had reluctantly accepted US assurances that Israeli settlement expansion 'would not take place beyond immediately contiguous areas'. However, Israel's chosen understanding of the settlement position was that the so-called 'contiguous areas' would only be realized once ongoing construction had been completed. This interpretation, coupled with the rightist imperative to assume and retain control of as much land on the West Bank as possible before the 'final status' talks, led to intensified settlement activity on the West Bank in the days and weeks after the Wye Conference. Much of this activity was officially sanctioned but there were also several instances of Jewish settlers seizing land in areas which were expected to be subject to negotiation in the 'final status' talks. The IDF did little to restrain the settlers and there was no attempt to conceal the Government's political and legal collusion with the encroachments. The issue of the release of prisoners was becoming equally contentious for the Palestinians. The PNA claimed that under the terms of the Wye Memorandum Israel was committed to release 750 Palestinians detained for politically motivated offences. However, the first batch of prisoners freed on 20 November was largely comprised of those detained for non-political crimes. When protests were made to the Israeli authorities, Netanyahu replied that he would not countenance the release of Islamists or those 'with Jewish blood on their hands'. Palestinian political prisoners staged a nine-day hunger strike in protest, and demonstrations on the West Bank resulted in several Palestinian deaths. In Nablus demonstrators supporting the prisoners also clashed with Palestinian security forces.

THE PROCESS FOUNDERS AGAIN

The steady erosion of trust between the PNA and the Israeli Government continued in the final weeks of 1998, as domestic pressures—on the streets of the West Bank, and inside the government offices in Israel—precluded the possibility of a dialogue of compromise. In mid-November Netanyahu claimed that the Wye Memorandum had made the PNA a more compliant interlocutor, ready to accept Israel's 'vital interests in Judaea and Samaria'. He also asserted that if a third-phase redeployment were to take place, it would involve an area no larger than 1% of the West Bank. Arafat responded by reaffirming his decision to declare Palestinian statehood on 4 May 1999 and to accept 'nothing short of an independent state with Jerusalem as its capital'. In a speech to the Fatah congress he assured his audience that 'we will brandish our guns ... to pray in Jerusalem'. Such rhetoric caused predictable disquiet in Israel. In early December Sharon informed Albright that the second Israeli withdrawal, scheduled for 18 December, would be suspended because of 'flagrant Palestinian violations of the accords, particularly incitement to renew the *intifada*'.

US RELATIONS WITH THE PNA

While relations with Israel once again teetered on the brink of collapse, the PNA's relations with the US Government exhibited a marked improvement. In December 1998 President Clinton visited the Gaza Strip for the formal inauguration of Gaza's airport, and also to address the assembled PNC at its reaffirmation of the abrogation of anti-Israel clauses in the Palestinian National Charter. Clinton's aides denied that the President's visit amounted to US recognition of Palestinian statehood. Nevertheless, Clinton's presence in PNA-administered territory had undoubted symbolic resonance, which was amplified by his address to the Council, during which he paid tribute to the Palestinian leadership and urged Israel to follow their example. He also referred to the Palestinians' 'history of dispossession and dispersal' and the need for Israel to develop an understanding of their plight. PNA officials hailed the President's visit as an important milestone on the road to statehood, but their enthusiasm was not universally shared. On the eve of Clinton's visit Palestinian opposition groups—including Hamas and Islamic Jihad—met in Damascus to recommend that Arafat be expelled from the PLO and that the amendments to the Palestinian National Charter be declared null and void. Twenty-eight members of the PNC also boycotted the Clinton visit in protest at the terms of the agreement concluded at Wye. Moreover, within days of his departure much of the goodwill expressed by ordinary Palestinians to the US President dissipated in angry protest at renewed US bombing of Iraq. The PNA security forces attempted to stifle the protests, and ordered the temporary closure of private television stations that were deemed excessively sympathetic to the anti-US demonstrations.

DOMESTIC DIFFICULTIES IN ISRAEL

The coalition difficulties troubling Netanyahu, meanwhile, were approaching their anticipated climax. Having repeatedly failed to secure Knesset approval for the 1999 budget, the Minister of Finance, Yaacov Ne'emen, resigned. Unable to appoint an obvious successor and under intense critical scrutiny from both pragmatic and nationalist wings of the Government over the progress of the peace process, Netanyahu made a final appeal to Labour to enter into talks on the formation of a government of national unity. Rebuffed by Labour leader Barak, Netanyahu bowed to the inevitable, and on 21 December 1998 voted in support of an opposition motion in the Knesset providing for early elections. Polls to elect a Prime Minister and a new legislature were subsequently scheduled for 17 May 1999. Both Israeli and Palestinian observers predicted that significant progress on the peace process would remain suspended until after the formation of a new Israeli government.

FIGHTING CONTINUES IN SOUTHERN LEBANON

In late November 1998 the IDF suffered several fatalities at the hands of Hezbollah. In December it was reported that 24 Israeli soldiers had been killed and more than 100 wounded in Lebanon during 1998. Around 40 SLA militiamen were killed and a further 45 were wounded during the same period. The end of the year witnessed another escalation in the conflict, beginning on 22 December when an attack by Israeli fighter aircraft in the Beka'a valley resulted in the deaths of one woman and six children. Hezbollah retaliated by firing salvos of *Katyusha* rockets into Galilee, wounding 17 inhabitants and causing substantial damage. Further Israeli air strikes in the Beka'a valley ensued, and the shelling of power lines and water pipelines in southern Lebanon prompted renewed speculation that Netanyahu was initiating a campaign to destroy the Lebanese communications infrastructure. Netanyahu was thought to have abandoned plans for a pre-election military adventure in Lebanon, but remained uncertain of his best response to the threat posed by Hezbollah and their Syrian supporters. At the end of 1998 Sharon introduced the possibility of staged withdrawal from Lebanese territory accompanied by the return to Syria of two Druze villages in the Golan Heights. This plan was promptly dismissed by Israel's northern neighbours. In February 1999 Israel took the controversial step of incorporating the semi-abandoned village of Arnoun into the Israeli-declared 'security zone', claiming it was being used by Hezbollah as a staging post for attacks on Israeli convoys. The Lebanese Prime Minister, Selim al-Hoss, was fiercely critical of the annexation. Hezbollah reacted with co-ordinated attacks on SLA and IDF positions, killing three Israeli officers and wounding a further five in a prolonged gun battle on 22 February. At the end of the month some 2,000 Lebanese students crossed a minefield and cut through fencing erected by the SLA to reclaim Arnoun. In early March rockets were again fired into Israel, and four Israeli soldiers (including Brig.-Gen. Erez Gerstein—the most senior member of the Israeli command to be killed in Lebanon since the 1982 occupation) were killed by a roadside bomb inside the 'security zone'. Israel retaliated with a series of air raids on Hezbollah targets, but resisted the demands of extremist elements inside the defence establishment to sanction tank incursions beyond the 'security zone'. The deaths of Israeli soldiers once again focused debate on the future of Israel's presence in Lebanon, with opinion polls demonstrating increased support for a unilateral withdrawal. The Labour candidate for the premiership, Barak, promised to effect an Israeli withdrawal from southern Lebanon within one year of being elected. Netanyahu baulked at such a time-bound commitment, but announced that he was hopeful of a withdrawal 'probably some time in the year 2000'. Later in March Netanyahu informed a Knesset defence and foreign affairs committee that he was preparing a redeployment of forces in southern Lebanon, exciting speculation that the SLA was about to abandon the Jezzine enclave and that the IDF would retreat to the southern bank of the Litani river. Policy statements from senior Hezbollah members suggested an increasingly uncompromising attitude towards Israel. Having previously stated that Israeli compliance with UN Resolution 425 would effectively end armed resistance, in March Hezbollah's chief spokesman, Ibrahim Mussawi, speculated that an Israeli withdrawal would not necessarily prompt Hezbollah to end its military campaign against the Jewish state. The reoccupation of Arnoun in April (following the killing of another Israeli soldier) provoked further clashes that resulted in several Israeli casualties and the death of the SLA's acting commander. Lebanon and Syria reacted vehemently to the Arnoun incursion, accusing Netanyahu of electioneering at the expense of the Lebanese people. Addressing a crowd of some 300,000 assembled celebrants at the Islamic festival of Ashoura, Hezbollah Secretary-General Hasan Nasrallah declared that his organization would 'never accept' an Israeli withdrawal in exchange for Lebanese security guarantees. Nasrallah also resurrected calls for his followers 'to eliminate Israel'.

DEATH OF KING HUSSEIN

King Hussein of Jordan died on 7 February 1999, after a long battle against cancer. His centrality to the peace process and his regional standing was emphasized in tributes from both Israel and the Arab world. Arafat effusively praised the man he had once dubbed a 'Zionist agent', while even leaders of Palestinian Islamist groups and the secular left were generous in their obituaries. In Israel, where respect for the Hashemite King had transformed in recent years into genuine public affection, flags flew at half-mast and the media carried numerous eulogies. It was widely acknowledged that King Hussein had neither trusted nor liked Netanyahu, whom he held responsible for the reversals of the Oslo process, and the Jordanian authorities made known their wish that Israel be represented at the King's funeral by its President, Ezer Weizman, rather than by its Prime Minister. However, calculating that his absence in Amman would be politically damaging, Netanyahu chose instead to risk upsetting reluctant hosts by his attendance. Syria was also represented by an impressive delegation, led by Hussein's long-term adversary, President Assad. King Hussein was succeeded by his eldest son, Abdullah. Popular with the armed forces but with little experience on the political stage, the new monarch was advised by fellow Arab leaders to strengthen ties with the Arab world and to attempt to co-ordinate policy on Israel. An early test of Israeli-Jordanian goodwill was presented by official Israeli warnings that agreed water quotas to Jordan would be reduced by up to 60% as a result of winter drought. Such a move struck at the core of Jordan's peace agreement with Israel and was condemned by the Jordanian parliament as 'a serious threat to the future peace, security and stability in the region'. It also lent impetus to a rapidly developing *rapprochement* with Syria. Following President Assad's unexpected attendance at King Hussein's funeral, at the end of April Assad's second son and heir apparent, Bashar, undertook a visit to Jordan. In mid-April King Abdullah made a high-profile trip to Damascus where agreement was made with the Syrian leader to put aside past differences and pursue future relations 'in a manner that will safeguard the interests of the Jordanian and Syrian people and the Arab nation'. Syria also pledged to provide water to Jordan during the summer months to compensate for any impending shortfall. In May Jordanian and Syrian officials met again to discuss ways of implementing the 1987 al-Wahdeh dam project for the Yarmouk river.

ARAFAT POSTPONES DECLARATION OF STATEHOOD

Preoccupation in Israel with the forthcoming elections precluded progress on implementing the provisions of the Wye Memorandum, and convinced Arafat to pursue a policy of isolation with regard to Netanyahu. However, there were certain risks attached to the PLO leader's approach. Having encouraged Palestinian expectation of a declaration of statehood on 4 May 1999, it was now evident that such a declaration would be likely to enhance Netanyahu's chances of re-election. Furthermore, in order to undermine Netanyahu's attempts to cite Palestinian non-compliance with Wye as an excuse for his own refusal to implement Israeli undertakings, Arafat had first to buttress his own administration's credibility with the USA by ensuring a degree of adherence to the deeply unpopular 'security commitments'. Inevitably this led to conflict with the Palestinian opposition. While Arafat berated the Israeli Government for its refusal to release Palestinian detainees, the PNA was itself under verbal attack from Islamist groups for its own refusal to free more than a handful of prisoners held in PNA custody. A hunger strike by Islamist detainees in early 1999 provoked a series of clashes between opposition supporters and the Palestinian security forces. However, Arafat's conflict with Hamas and Islamic Jihad was largely compensated by the US Administration's increasingly public disaffection with the Israeli Government. In February Martin Indyk, the US Assistant Secretary of State for the Near East, and a committed Zionist, explicitly rejected Netanyahu's claims that the PNA was not fulfilling its security obligations under the terms of the Wye Memorandum, and instead accused Israel of reneging on its commitments to the Palestinians. Of particular concern was the frenzied pace of settlement activity. In mid-April it was revealed that the Likud Government had during 1998 built nearly 4,000 housing units in the territories occupied in 1967 (compared to 1,680 in 1996 and 1,900 in 1997), and that 17 new 'hilltop' settlements had been established on the West Bank since the Wye summit. On 14 April US presidential spokesman James Rubin appeared to accuse the Israeli leader of duplicity when he commented that 'Netanyahu has told us at all levels and on many occasions that as a matter of policy, there would be no new settlements and no expansion of settlements beyond their contiguous periphery ... Contrary to what we were told, we see an accelerated pattern of Israeli actions that involve both construction of new settlements, as well as an expansion of settlements beyond their contiguous periphery'. He added that 'these Israeli activities ... make it very difficult to pursue peace'. While Arafat welcomed the US Administration's transparent support for the Labour Party in Israel's election campaign, the US State Department's avowed opposition to a declaration of Palestinian statehood posed a problem, especially since opinion polls revealed considerable support among the Palestinians of Gaza and the West Bank for such a declaration on 4 May. However, any residual commitment that Arafat might have felt to a statehood declaration was dispelled during world-wide 'consultations with friendly states' in the spring of 1999. A rapid tour of more than 50 nations achieved an upgrading of the PLO's representative status in six countries and recognition from the EU and Japan of the Palestinians' 'unqualified' right to self-determination (including the option of statehood), but Arafat was counselled against taking a step for which there had been inadequate preparation and which threatened to enhance the electoral fortunes of the Likud Prime Minister. The US Government tempered its own opposition to the statehood declaration with a letter of assurances which reportedly reaffirmed President Clinton's December 1998 support for the rights of Palestinians to 'determine their future as a free people on their land' and restated Washington's opposition to 'unilateral acts'. Clinton also suggested a one-year extension to Oslo's interim phase during which accelerated talks on a 'final status' agreement would be conducted. Arafat described the assurances as 'more than positive' and a vindication of the political energies expended in courting US support. For many Palestinians, however, Arafat's appraisal of the US position was excessively optimistic. It was argued that President Clinton's letter did not represent a shift in US policy, in that it neither recognized the right to Palestinian self-determination nor committed the USA to actively opposing Israeli settlement activity. Nevertheless, when the 180 members of the PLO Central Council met in Gaza at the end of April to make a 'final decision' on the declaration of statehood, a change of strategy had become inevitable. The Central Council agreed to postpone a decision on statehood, while lamely expressing 'grave concern' that Oslo's interim period had expired 'without implementing the requirements of this phase, such as the withdrawal of Israel's occupation of Palestinian lands'.

ELECTION OF BARAK

Netanyahu's bid for a second term as Prime Minister had much with which to contend, including the gradual disintegration of his coalition and the transfer of allegiance of a number of former allies. Mordechai was dismissed from his position as Minister of Defence in January 1999, accused of maintaining unauthorized contacts with the emerging Centre Party, a grouping that had already attracted the support of former senior Likud members, including Roni Milo and Dan Meridor. Moshe Arens was recruited to replace Mordechai, who went on to represent the Centre Party in the contest for the premiership. Meanwhile, Levy, Netanyahu's former foreign minister, announced his intention to ally himself with Labour leader Barak, while Binyamin Begin left the Likud right to resurrect the revisionist (New) Herut party. Attempting to reprise his successful vilification of Peres prior to the 1996 elections, Netanyahu chose to conduct an increasingly personal campaign against his principal adversaries. Netanyahu notably portrayed Barak as a serious danger to state security. Given Barak's distinguished military career and his image as a soldier-politician in the mould of Rabin, Netanyahu's charges failed to engage the electorate. Any hope on the part of the Likud campaign of the anti-Netanyahu vote being split between politically indistinguishable rivals, thus affording their candidate a theoretical chance of victory in a head-to-head contest with Barak, were frustrated in the days preceding the ballot, when Mordechai and two other candidates withdrew from the premiership contest. Victory for Barak over Netanyahu was now widely predicted, but the margin of victory on 17 May—56% to 44% of votes cast—surprised even the most optimistic Labour supporters. The 1999 campaign was particularly notable for the fact that it was the first election contest in over 20 years in which the issue of Arab–Israeli relations had not been the principal focus of public debate. Indeed, commentators considered Barak's victory to be less of a comment on the state of the peace process than a reflection of Netanyahu's poor handling of the economy. Disenchantment with Netanyahu's style of leadership and a perceived duplicity in his actions had also persuaded many former supporters to shift their support to Barak; this was particularly true of the Russian immigrant population. At the legislative elections neither the Labour Party (restyled the One Israel alliance), nor Likud fared particularly well. The greatest gains were made by the ultra-orthodox Shas party, which nearly doubled its share of the 1996 poll, to take 17 seats. Netanyahu resigned as Likud leader as soon as the scale of his defeat became known; Ariel Sharon was appointed as interim leader. Netanyahu, meanwhile, in accordance with electoral law, remained in office for a 45-day period during which Barak sought to build a coalition and form a government.

SYRIAN PEACE AND PALESTINIAN ISOLATION?

Netanyahu's defeat provoked barely concealed delight in the USA and Europe. However, the PNA's extension of a cautious welcome to the new leadership in Israel was tempered by the knowledge that Barak's most recent statements on the future of peace with the Palestinians had been distinctly uncompromising. He was a committed supporter of Israel's 'eternal' sovereignty over Jerusalem, was opposed to withdrawal to pre-1967 borders, considered that most West Bank settlements would remain *in situ* and under Israeli rule and rejected the idea of 'foreign armies' west of the Jordan river. It was also noted that Barak had been the only member of the former Peres Cabinet to abstain during a vote organized in support of the Oslo Accords. Palestinian fears were exacerbated by the suspicion that Barak's principal foreign-policy objective was the achievement of a peace treaty with Syria, and that if such a deal were struck, the Palestinians would be dangerously isolated. Privately, Palestinian officials admitted that having broken Arab ranks to pursue a separate peace with Israel, they were now in no position to demand co-ordination and a unified front from a disaffected President Assad. Barak remained resolutely non-committal on relations with his Palestinian neighbours as he sought to form a coalition. When Barak did finally break his silence in a lengthy interview with the Israeli daily newspaper, *Ha'aretz*, he said little to dispel Palestinian anxieties. Although he expressed a desire for a 'comprehensive' resolution of the conflict with the Arab world, Barak appeared to suggest that it was Syria, with its formidable military arsenal, rather than the Palestinians, 'the weakest of all our adversaries', who would be the focus of his attentions. Reports that President Assad was also ready to embark on serious negotiations with Israel appeared to confirm speculation that formal bilateral contacts would be resumed shortly.

SLA WITHDRAWS FROM JEZZINE

At the beginning of June 1999 the SLA began to withdraw from the Jezzine enclave adjoining Israel's 'security zone'. Although the withdrawal had been predicted for some months and was thought, in part, to reflect the IDF's increasing lack of faith in their Lebanese surrogates (the strength of the SLA was reported to have dwindled to just 400 armed operatives who were thought to have been heavily infiltrated by Hezbollah informers), there was a sense both in Israel and Lebanon that the Jezzine evacuation was a practice exercise for a more substantial future withdrawal. Hezbollah attacks increased following the Jezzine withdrawal, resulting in a number of Israeli casualties in the first week of June. Hezbollah's militiamen also claimed responsibility for the downing of an IDF helicopter, as engagements continued throughout the month. Later in June Israeli artillery wounded a Lebanese woman in the village of Qabrika, and Hezbollah responded with a rocket attack against the northern Israeli town of Kiryat Shemona. Two Israelis were killed in the attack—the first such casualties since 1995—and substantial damage was inflicted on buildings in the town. Israel retaliated immediately with air attacks against power plants, bridges and communications centres in Beirut and in southern Lebanon. Eight people were killed and some 70 were wounded in the raids. The cost of the bomb damage incurred was estimated at US $52m. The intensity of the air raids was thought to have been prompted by frustration in the Israeli defence establishment with Hezbollah's military successes and by Netanyahu's desire to undermine the peace efforts of his successor. Netanyahu confirmed that Barak had been informed but not consulted about the attacks, a version of events that was welcomed by the Syrian authorities. In a rare break with the official Syrian stance, Lebanese officials held both Barak and Netanyahu responsible for the bombardment. The Lebanese press also gave voice to the widespread belief that the escalation of hostilities between Israel and Hezbollah had been provoked by the political manoeuvring of Syria and Israel in the preamble to future peace talks.

BARAK ASSUMES OFFICE

Barak swore in a new Cabinet on 6 July 1999, having secured the support of an estimated 77 of the 120 Knesset deputies. The new Cabinet, which contained familiar political figures, including Levy (as Deputy Prime Minister and Minister of Foreign Affairs), Mordechai (Deputy Prime Minister and Minister of Transport) and Peres (Minister of Regional Co-operation), was considered well balanced between ministers with a 'dovish' outlook on the peace process and those of a more pragmatic persuasion. In his inaugural address to the Knesset, Barak announced his intention to achieve peace with all of Israel's neighbours. He stated that peace with Egypt, Jordan, Syria and the Palestinians was of equal importance since, 'if we don't place peace on all four pillars, peace will be unstable'. He added, 'I know not only the pain of my own people, but recognize the pain of the Palestinian people'. Anxious to demonstrate the sincerity of his commitment to the peace process, Barak announced that he would be making immediate visits to President Mubarak, Arafat and King Abdullah, before holding extensive talks with President Clinton in Washington, DC. At a joint press conference with Mubarak in Alexandria on 9 July, Barak vowed 'to turn every stone in order to find a way to go forward without risking our security or vital interests'.

HOPES RENEWED OVER WYE TWO

During August 1999 Israeli and Palestinian representatives met in Jerusalem to discuss the feasibility of reactivating the stalled Wye River Memorandum. Negotiations were encouraged by visiting delegations from Norway and the Netherlands (presiding over the EU at that time) and by an official visit to the region undertaken by Madeleine Albright in early September. Negotiations continued in Egypt, and on 4 September Barak and Arafat signed the Sharm esh-Sheikh Memorandum on the Implementation Timeline of Outstanding Commitments of Agreements Signed and the Resumption of Permanent Status Negotiations, also known as Wye Two (see Documents on Palestine, p. 412), which detailed a revised timetable for the outstanding provisions of the Wye River Memorandum of October 1998, including: the conclusion of permanent status negotiations within one year of the resumption of talks on this issue (to be commenced not later than 13 September 1999), with an agreed framework for these negotiations to be concluded by 13 February 2000; Israeli redeployments from a further 10% of the West Bank to be undertaken on 5 September 1999 (7%), 15 November 1999 (2%) and 20 January 2000 (1%); 200 Palestinian prisoners to be released on 5 September 1999, and a further 150 to be released on 8 October 1999; a southern safe passage to become operational from 1 October 1999, the location of a northern safe passage to be agreed by 5 October 1999; construction of Gaza sea port to begin on 1 October 1999; increased, immediate and effective security co-operation to be undertaken. The Israeli Cabinet approved the new Memorandum on the following day, and on 8 September the Knesset endorsed the first Israeli redeployment under the terms of the new agreement, scheduled for 13 September. Some 200 Palestinian 'security prisoners' were released by the Israeli authorities on 9 September. (Although the document stipulated that the first troop withdrawal and release of prisoners should take place on 5 September, the Israeli authorities invoked a clause which allowed one week for 'technical preparations'.) Transfer of control of the initial 400 sq km of West Bank territory (7%) was initiated on 10 September with the signing of relevant maps; control of police operations and postal and public services was to be completed within three days. On 13 September Israeli and Palestinian delegations inaugurated the 'final status' negotiations at a ceremony at the Erez check-point.

REACTIONS TO WYE TWO

Evidence that progress in the Israeli-Palestinian peace process had resumed was greeted with relief in Western and regional capitals. Many Palestinians, however, remained sanguine at the latest developments. Although Arafat aides described the Wye Two agreements as an improvement on the original Wye Memorandum, both Israeli and Palestinian commentators viewed the Framework Agreement on Permanent Status (FAPS) as a political 'coup' for Barak. Effectively, it would allow his Government to test PNA amenability on settlements, Jerusalem and refugees before agreeing to the scope and timetable for the all-important third redeployment. Levy heightened the pressure at the 'final status' 'relaunch' on 13 September 1999 by indicating that a failure to achieve the FAPS by the mid-February 2000 deadline would mean that there would be no agreement on 'final status' by September 2000. The fear in the West Bank and Gaza was that in an effort to expedite the Wye Two timetable and secure Israeli acceptance of a Palestinian 'state', Arafat might sign up to a vaguely worded framework agreement that would allow for 'interpretation' at a later stage. Observers also advanced the theory that the PNA's negotiators would be pressured into deferring agreements indefinitely on the most contentious 'final status' issues. In an interview with Israeli state radio on 11 September 1999, Barak had already opined that the 'final status' talks might well result in a series of 'long-term interim arrangements', rather than a permanent settlement. There was also concern among Palestinians that the Sharm esh-Sheikh summit had not led to a better deal on settlements or prisoners. On the latter issue, Israel agreed that prisoner releases should be targeted at those detained for politically-related offences, but had stipulated that the number of prisoners to be released should be reduced to 350 (the PNA had asked for 750). Barak also widened the criteria of those ineligible for release (hitherto Islamists and those convicted of serious attacks on Israelis) to include those Palestinians arrested after the Oslo signing or those resident in East Jerusalem.

IMPLEMENTATION AND ACTION AGAINST HAMAS

The southern safe passage between Gaza and Tarqimiya on the West Bank was opened on 5 October 1999. The delay was occasioned by initial PNA resistance to Israeli demands for a security veto over which Palestinians could use the passage. Arafat eventually agreed to a protocol that necessitated Israeli approval of applicants to use the passage. However, Palestinian negotiator Jamil at-Tarifi claimed he had received a 'gentleman's agreement' from his Israeli counterpart not to exercise powers of arrest on the new highway. Israel's apparent magnanimity reportedly stemmed from an acceptance, in the words of a PNA security official, that 'the same people Israel wants are wanted by us as well'. Indeed, despite profound unease regarding so many issues in the peace process, there appeared to be a firm consensus between Israel, the PNA and Jordan on the need to contain the threat posed by Islamist opponents of the peace process. In an apparently co-ordinated operation PNA and Israeli security forces detained scores of Hamas activists in areas of respective control during the summer of 1999. On 30 August Jordanian police closed down Hamas offices in the capital, arrested 12 of its leading figures and issued warrants for the detention of politburo members who were visiting Iran. These included its spokesman, Ibrahim Ghosheh, and Meshaal, bureau chief and victim of Mossad's 1997 assassination attempt. Hamas had hitherto been allowed to operate with relative freedom in Jordan. The Jordanian Prime Minister defended the actions on the grounds that Hamas was 'an illegal organization in violation of Jordanian laws'. Nevertheless, the abrupt shift in policy drew sharp criticism from some pro-Government parties as well as opposition groups. The latter decried the arrests as politically motivated and designed to ingratiate the Government with the USA, Israel and the PNA. On their return to Jordan three of the senior Hamas figures, all Jordanian citizens, were arrested and later exiled to Qatar. In a statement issued after the deportations the Jordanian Government upheld Hamas's right to organize in the West Bank and Gaza, but stated that it would 'firmly confront any attempt to use

Jordan illegally'. Observers believed that the assault on Hamas reflected King Abdullah's desire to divorce political activity in Jordan from the issue of Palestine and to facilitate the 'Jordanianization' of political life in the Kingdom.

BARAK AND THE SETTLEMENT ISSUE

There had been hopes that Barak's election would result in settlement becoming less of an obstacle to moves to improve relations between Israel and the Arab world. While the new Israeli Government proved to be far more circumspect in its promises to the settler lobby than the Netanyahu administration, it quickly became clear that Barak had neither the political will nor the inclination to revise policy towards settlement in the West Bank and Gaza. Commitment to the concept of the 'natural growth' of existing settlements was forcibly underlined. In the first three months of the Barak administration the Ministry of Construction and Housing issued tenders for the construction of 2,600 housing units in the settlements; this compared to an annual average of 3,000 under Netanyahu. The new Government also gave notice that it was to construct a further five bypass roads in the West Bank. The IDF's confiscation of 25,000 dunums of mainly arable and pasture land during September and October 1999 lent further weight to the Palestinian contention that Israel was 'creating the facts' that would predetermine the territorial aspect of a 'final status' agreement. Under fire from the peace lobby for the aggressive nature of his land and settlement policies, Barak confirmed that on this issue his political sympathies were closer to those of the fiercely pro-settler National Religious Party than the left-wing Meretz party (both factions were coalition partners). In mid-October the ministerial commit-tee on settlement, newly formed to mediate policy between the pro- and anti-settlement factions in the Government, met to decide on the fate of the 42 outpost settlements established in the final months of the Netanyahu administration. Although it was initially agreed that 15 of these settlements were 'illegal' and would have to be removed, Barak revised this number to 10—only five of which were inhabited—after government talks with the leaders of the settler council. The settler movement later leaked details of a government promise to incorpo-rate three of the five populated settlements scheduled for evacuation into officially sanctioned settler blocs and allow for the 'orderly and legal' return of settlers at a future date. The PNA's chief negotiator, Yasser Abd ar-Rabbuh, condemned Barak's settlement initiatives as 'unprecedented colonialist aggres-sion', while Arafat claimed that the retention of the outpost settlements violated an undertaking given by the Israeli leader at the Wye Two meetings.

OBSTACLES TO PROGRESS

Israeli-Palestinian talks on the framework of a 'final status' agreement finally began in the West Bank town of Ramallah on 8 November 1999. A week earlier Arafat and Barak had met with President Clinton in Oslo during ceremonies to mark the anniversary of the assassination of Rabin. Clinton characterized their summit talks as having 'revitalized' the peace process. He stressed the impor-tance of the two sides' meeting the February 2000 deadline for the Framework Agreement, and pledged regular visits to the region by his special envoy, Dennis Ross, to ensure that focus was maintained. But despite the positive sentiments from the US President, the gulf in expectations appeared as unbridgeable as ever.

While Palestinian negotiators prefaced their attendance at the Ramallah talks with insistence on the applicability of UN resolutions, the right of refugees to repatriation and compensation, and the illegality of Israeli settlement, Israel's leadership reiterated its adherence to the 'national consensus' stance of no return to the June 1967 borders, no evacuation of the main settlement blocs, and a united Jerusalem under Israeli sovereignty. Barak also stated in a cabinet meeting on the eve of the Ramallah talks that UN Resolution 242 did not apply to the West Bank and Gaza because it pertained to sovereign states and not organizations. Palestinian anger at this new interpretation was exacerbated by developments in parallel talks on outstanding issues from Oslo's interim phase—foremost among these being the transfer of 5% of the West Bank still outstanding from the Wye Two agreement. PNA negotiators refused to sign the maps detailing the lands to be handed over (3% to PNA civilian control and 2% to full control) on the grounds that the territories were either sparsely populated or too far removed from the main areas of PNA control. Barak rejoined that the maps had Cabinet approval and would not be altered. His aides accused Arafat of 'stonewalling' in an attempt to force sympathetic intervention from the USA (which, in any event, failed to materialize). Commentators on both sides interpreted the dispute over redeployment as evidence of their leaders' desire to surrender as little as possible while the Framework Agreement talks continued to promise little in the way of substantive progress. A mediation mission to the region by Ross failed to win Arafat's approval for the Israeli redeployment proposals, and on 6 December 1999 Abd ar-Rabbuh stated that he was suspending Palestinian involvement in the 'final status' talks because of continuing settlement activity.

RAPPROCHEMENT WITH SYRIA?

Barak's election commitment to effect an Israeli withdrawal from Lebanon and his declared intention to achieve a peace treaty with Syria had prompted speculation that there would be a swift resumption of the bilateral talks suspended in 1996. Initial developments seemed to suggest otherwise. Speaking in August 1999 the Syrian Minister of Foreign Affairs, Farouk ash-Shara', conceded that Syria would be prepared to accommodate Israel's security fears by accepting an international force in the Golan Heights. But despite this apparent softening of the Syrian position, ash-Shara' informed US intermediaries that Damascus would only contemplate a resumption of talks if it received assurances that Barak would negotiate on the basis of the understandings purportedly reached with the Rabin Government (i.e. that Israel was committed to a withdrawal from the occupied Golan). In September Albright held talks in Damascus with President Assad. Reportedly she brought an Israeli proposal to resume negotiations on the Golan Heights in return for an end to Hezbollah attacks in southern Lebanon. Inevitably this was rejected by Syria, who complained to Albright of Israeli time-wasting and requested that the USA become more involved in brokering a deal between the two sides. Syrian impatience stemmed in part from the fear that the following year's US presidential election would irrevocably delay the securing of a deal on the Golan. There was also a suspicion that the US Administration's perceived reluctance to pressurize Israel flowed from a desire to defer a breakthrough on the Syria-Israel track until a time convenient to the election campaign of the Democratic presidential hopeful (and incumbent Vice-President), Al Gore. By October commentaries in the official Syrian press were more vociferous in their criticism of the USA for its role in missing 'an exceptional chance to achieve peace'. Under pressure from a strongly anti-withdrawal campaign led by the newly elected Likud leader, Ariel Sharon, Barak's policy messages on his administration's approach to relations with Syria appeared inconsistent. In an interview with the London-based *Jewish Chronicle*, the Israeli leader spoke of his admiration for the leadership qualities of President Assad and of his belief that a formula would soon be achieved that would allow negotiations to resume. Privately, however, the Israeli leader remained irritated by Syrian preconditions for a resumption of their dialogue. In October he announced that there would be no moratorium on the ongoing construction of 700 housing units on the Golan Heights. The Israeli Government also conferred 'national priority' status on the region, enabling residents to benefit from extra government aid and tax advantages. Syria reacted angrily to the announcements, and accused Israel of trying to sabotage the peace process. Israeli observers interpreted the concessions to the settlers as a means of forcing a response from Damascus. The liberal Israeli daily newspaper, *Ha'aretz*, commented that the Golan decision was 'apparently designed to signal to the Syrian president that the window of opportunity will not wait indefinitely, and that ultimate delay could generate a mass of concrete and mortar, and above all, of inhabitants that would populate the area to an extent that will not allow the settlements to be dismantled'. The failure of Assad and Barak to translate initial goodwill into public progress continued to find expression in the hills and villages of southern Lebanon. After a lull in fighting in the aftermath of Israel's June bombing raids, there was a steady increase in the number of attacks carried out by Hezbollah and its militia allies. Intent on reducing the level of IDF casualties, Barak ordered a change of tactics in the war over Israel's northern border. Troop-deployment levels were reduced and aggressive counter-insurgency operations by ground forces largely abandoned in favour of air strikes. Meanwhile, the Israeli Prime Minister continued to assert his commitment to his election promise of a withdrawal of all forces from southern Lebanon by July 2000. At the beginning of December 1999 Albright undertook another visit to the Middle East, meeting both Israeli and Syrian leaders. Department of State aides downplayed expectations that her diplomacy might revive the Israeli-Syrian track of the peace process. However, after Albright's talks with President Assad and then Barak, President Clinton announced that Barak and ash-Shara' would be meeting in Washington, DC, on 15 December in order formally to resume negotiations 'from the point where they left off' in February 1996. There was no attempt by either side to elaborate on the 'point' at which the negotiations would be resumed, although consensual opinion had it that President Assad would not have agreed for his Minister of Foreign Affairs to journey to the USA without having received assurances that Israel was prepared to retreat to its June 1967 borders with Syria. At the Washington ceremony to mark the relaunch of their negotiations, Albright spoke of her optimism that Israel and Syria would find a peaceful resolution to their disputes, while President Clinton stressed US willingness to meet a substantial proportion of the cost of a future peace deal. He added that, 'For the first time in history, there is a chance of a comprehensive peace between Israel and Syria and, indeed, all its neighbours'.

PALESTINIAN REACTION

The prospect of a peace treaty between Israel and Syria was greeted with alarm by Arafat. It was accepted as an article of faith within the PNA that while Israel was embroiled in the intricate processes of peace-making with Syria, the Israeli-Palestinian track would be put on hold—not just by Israel but also by the USA. Furthermore, with Israeli settlements and attendant infrastructural development gradually eroding the Palestinian patrimony, the scenarios attached to further extensions of the Oslo process looked bleak indeed. Although the Palestinians might gain theoretical protection from a more co-ordinated Arab approach to relations with Israel, this remained a distant prospect as long as President Assad nurtured such a deep antipathy for the PLO leader. Within the Occupied Territories the mild optimism with which many Palestinians had greeted the election of Barak had been replaced by rising discontent, much of it directed against Arafat. Opinion polls conducted at the end of 1999 revealed the latter's personal popularity rating to be at an all-time low. In November demonstrators took to the streets of Gaza to protest against the economic policies of the PNA and Arafat's deeply unpopular economic 'adviser', Khalid Salem. Later in the same month several prominent Palestinian personalities were arrested after signing a petition castigating the PNA and its leadership for the failure of Oslo and for the perceived endemic corruption of the regime. Arafat's isolation was heightened by Albright's December visit: ignoring the entreaties of the PNA leader, she refused to become involved in the argument over the stalled second-phase redeployment. On 22 December Arafat met with Barak and abandoned his earlier opposition to Israel's proposed redeployment. His aides mitigated the reverse with suggestions that Barak had promised to revise the third phase of the second redeployment (whereby 6.1% of the West Bank would come under exclusive Palestinian control by 20 January 2000) to take into account Palestinian requests for the transfer of villages around Jerusalem. The overdue second redeployment was duly implemented on 6–7 January 2000. However, on 14 January Barak announced a unilateral delay of the third-phase redeployment for a period of three weeks. When Barak and Arafat met on 17 January, the Israeli Prime Minister stated that Israel had the right under the terms of Wye Two to delay deployments. He also demanded that the Palestinians accept a degree of flexibility over the 13 February deadline for reaching the FAPS issues. Arafat responded that he would prefer negotiations to be intensified in order to expedite the agreed timetable. The Palestinian leader put this preference to President Clinton in Washington, DC, on 20 January, but discovered that the US position on the substance and timetabling of the Framework Agreement was largely in line with the latest Israeli interpretations. According to the Department of State's spokesman, James Rubin, the mid-February date for the draft of a Framework Agreement was a 'target' rather than a 'deadline'. US officials also communicated their belief that the Framework Agreement should be a broad declaration of principles rather than the detailed draft peace treaty favoured by Arafat. His dismay at US support for Israeli revisions was only slightly tempered by the promise of US $900m. in aid for infrastructural projects in areas of PNA control and the prospect that the third-phase redeployment would deliver the PNA a foothold near Jerusalem and other 'quality' lands. With this expectation Arafat received Barak in Gaza on

3 February to discuss the details of the postponed redeployment. On the previous day the Israeli press had confidently speculated that Arafat would be rewarded for delays on the Framework Agreement and the third redeployment by taking control of 'two villages north-east of Jerusalem'. Yet, when the maps for the redeployment were published on 3 February, they were found to be identical to those drawn up before the mid-January deferral. Moreover, Barak proposed that the timetables for achieving the Framework and 'final status' agreements be shifted to mid-August 2000 and mid-June 2001 respectively. He also suggested that the crucial third redeployment should be collapsed into the 'final status' negotiations. As PNA officials pointed out, this was an identical position to that of his Likud predecessor. According to PNA sources, Arafat left the meeting 'beside himself with rage', having rejected the redeployment proposals and the revised timetables. He immediately implored the USA to intervene in the peace process to guarantee the integrity of the Wye agreements. After meetings with Palestinian negotiators on 5 February, Ross rejoined that the US role was to support and facilitate the peace process, not to act as a guarantor. Echoing Barak's own view on US intervention, he commented that the US Government would not take 'fateful decisions' that 'must be owned by the parties themselves'. The PLO Central Council responded to the latest development by granting Arafat the authority to declare a Palestinian state in September 2000. Support for this was forthcoming from Egypt and Jordan. Having agreed in Moscow on 31 January to revive the long-dormant multilateral negotiations, the Egyptian Minister of Foreign Affairs, Amr Muhammad Moussa, declared on 5 February that if Israel was not prepared to honour the timetable on a 'final status' agreement, then its Arab neighbours would not be bound by the schedules agreed in Moscow. Following a visit by Barak to Jordan the following day, Jordanian officials also intimated that a proposed first visit to Israel by King Abdullah would not take place as long as Israel was obstructing progress in its peace process with the Palestinians.

THE SHEPHERDSTOWN TALKS

Israeli and Syrian delegations led by Barak and ash-Shara' met in Shepherdstown, West Virginia, USA, on 3 January 2000. It was hoped that this would be the culmination of the process begun at the Madrid conference in 1991 and would lead, by late spring, to the drafting of a full peace treaty between Israel and Syria. Four committees were set up to address the key areas of concern: borders, water, security and diplomatic relations. Albright remained closely involved in the negotiations, but after eight days the meetings broke up without obvious agreement. Albright commended the two delegations on the seriousness of their endeavours, and arranged a further round of talks for 19 January. All parties to the negotiations pointedly refused to comment on the substance and progress of the negotiations. Although his regime faced little in the way of organized domestic opposition, President Assad had prefaced his foreign affairs minister's trip to Shepherdstown with the arrest of scores of suspected Islamist sympathizers and members of radical Palestinian factions. Barak had a far stiffer test of his resolve in pursuing peace with Damascus. An opinion poll published during the Shepherdstown talks revealed that 53% of

Israelis opposed a comprehensive withdrawal from the Golan Heights in return for a 'full peace' with Syria. More problematic for Barak was the opposition of two of his coalition partners—the National Religious Party and Natan Sharansky's Israel B'Aliyah—to an Israeli evacuation of the Golan. On the eve of the second round of talks President Assad signalled that Syria would not be returning to Shepherdstown. His decision was made in protest at Israel's disclosure of the details of a US framework document presented during the Shepherdstown talks. This document revealed that while Israel and Syria had minimized differences on water, security and diplomatic relations, there had been no undertaking by Israel to meet the Syrian demand of a retreat to the borders of 4 June 1967. For the Syrian President, who had repeatedly stated that Israeli agreement to such a withdrawal was the *sine qua non* of any negotiations, the revelation was a major embarrassment: even more so given the vilification that had been heaped on Arafat for his perceived weakness and lack of principle in his dealings with Israel. Ash-Shara' spelled out the Syrian position on latest developments in an interview with the Lebanese daily newspaper, *As-Safir*: 'we have put up with Ehud Barak's manoeuvring for a long time, as well as his false promises ... without a commitment to the line of June 4th our return to the negotiating table would be absurd'. Despite these uncompromising words, it was believed that talks would not be in abeyance for long. On 18 January the Lebanese Prime Minister, Selim al-Hoss, reversed his Government's position of refusing to give Israel any guarantees on post-withdrawal security arrangements along the common border by stating that he would be prepared to maintain security as part of a full peace treaty. Hezbollah's Secretary-General, Nasrallah, also made some conciliatory gestures, confirming later in January that his movement was working hard to locate the whereabouts of Ron Arad, an Israeli military pilot missing since 1986. However, he also commented that his movement was fully opposed to any normalization of relations with Israel in the event of the latter's withdrawal from Arab lands, and that the military campaign against Israel would be pursued without respite—as long as the occupation of the south continued. With Israeli–Syrian relations once again soured by mistrust, the fighting in South Lebanon entered another phase of intensification. Five Israeli soldiers and an SLA engineer were killed in a series of raids by Hezbollah units on Israel's self-designated 'security zone' in late January, and on 30 January the SLA's second-in-command, Col Aql Hashem, was assassinated by a Hezbollah unit in the occupation zone. These were the first Israeli deaths in Lebanon since August of the previous year, and the scale of the losses attracted a severe response. On 4 February a helicopter gunship succeeded in wounding a senior Hezbollah official as he travelled in a car near Tyre. Three nights later Israeli military aircraft carried out heavy bombing raids against Lebanese power stations in the northern port of Tripoli, Ba'albek and near Beirut. The damage was reported to be even more extensive than that incurred in the air raids of June 1999, and the assaults provoked condemnation throughout the Arab world. On 19 February President Mubarak made the first ever visit by an Egyptian leader to Lebanon. Speaking in Beirut, he vented Arab anger over the bombing raids, and with Israeli and US procrastination with regard to the Palestinian track of the peace process, by endorsing the resistance activities of Hezbollah. Mubarak was followed to Beirut by the Kuwaiti, PNA and Jordanian ministers responsible for foreign affairs. In a rare show of Arab unity, the Arab League also voted to move the venue of its foreign ministers' summit, scheduled for mid-March, from Cairo to Beirut. Two further Israeli soldiers were killed in early February, and on 11 February Israeli delegates walked out of the five nation ILMG, established to monitor the April 1996 'understanding' regarding the avoidance of civilian targets in the Lebanese–Israeli conflict, protesting that Hezbollah was launching attacks from populated areas, in violation of the 'understanding'. The Lebanese Prime Minister rejected the accusation, as did Israel's foremost military commentator, Ze'ev Schiff. Hezbollah maintained its offensive into March, inflicting several casualties on the increasingly demoralized SLA. Crown Prince Abdullah of Saudi Arabia visited Lebanon in early March and endorsed Hezbollah. Asserting that the Arab side had 'already compromised all it can', he urged Israel to 'relaunch the peace process and renounce the language of arms'. More radical sentiments were expressed in an 18-point communiqué issued after the Arab League foreign ministers' summit on 11 March: this called *inter alia* for Arab states to reassess their relations with Israel, for Palestinian refugees in Lebanon to be repatriated, and for an international tribunal to be established to try Israel for war crimes in Lebanon. Meanwhile, Israel's Minister of Foreign Affairs, Levy, made an uncharacteristically 'hawkish' speech in the Knesset in which he promised 'blood for blood and child for child' in the war with Hezbollah and its allies. At the beginning of March, furthermore, the Knesset gave majority assent to Likud-sponsored legislation that sought to change the terms of a future referendum on a withdrawal from the Golan Heights by demanding a 'yes' vote of 50% of all registered voters, rather than 50% of voter turn-out. The bill was supported by three of the government coalition parties, including the Shas party. Given the escalation of the 'proxy war' in Lebanon, the Syrian response to the Knesset vote was noticeably muted. Restraint from Damascus suggested that channels of communication between Israel and Syria had remained open and active. Observers were not therefore unduly surprised when it was announced that Presidents Clinton and Assad had arranged to meet in Geneva on 26 March. It seemed unlikely that the ailing Assad, a reluctant traveller at the best of times, would have been persuaded to make the trip to Switzerland without the expectation that Clinton would be conveying Barak's assurances on an Israeli withdrawal from the Golan. In the event, however, the talks ended without agreement. While President Clinton claimed he had brought with him a proposal from Barak that was 'serious, detailed and comprehensive', ash-Shara' rejoined, 'We had no illusions, but we were surprised that the US President did not bring anything new from Israel. Instead, he came asking Syria to help Ehud Barak get out of his difficulties over the Golan. We think he put himself in that position'. Syrian anger was apparently provoked by Barak's insistence that Israel should maintain sovereignty over the shores of Lake Tiberias and the waters of the Jordan river following any withdrawal from the Golan Heights. This option had already been rejected by President Assad, although the British writer on Middle Eastern affairs, Patrick Seale, who had served as an intermediary between the Israeli and Syrian leaders, had suggested that Assad would be willing to accept some form of overlapping jurisdiction along parts of the Tiberias shoreline. The failure of the summit prompted widespread accusations that the Geneva talks had never been intended by Barak or Clinton to serve as a forum for the clinching of a peace deal. Rather, they had allowed Barak to blame Syria for the failure to reach agreement and thus to avoid the territorial concessions that might precipitate the collapse of his fragile coalition and the fall of his Government. The Arab world rounded on Israel and the USA for their perceived duplicity in Geneva, while the official Syrian press warned that Barak 'bears responsibility for absence of opportunity for achieving peace and for the opening of the region to danger'. Both Jordan and Oman postponed negotiations with Israel on economic initiatives, in response to the breakdown on the Israeli-Syrian track.

ARAFAT UNDER PRESSURE

On 9 March 2000 President Mubarak hosted Barak and Arafat at the resort of Sharm esh-Sheikh. Overcoming February's acrimony, the two leaders were able to agree a formula for a resumption of talks. In exchange for Israel's abandoning its suggestion of extending deadlines on the Framework and 'final status' agreements (these now set for mid-May and mid-September 2000), the Palestinian leader accepted Israel's proposed map for the final phase of the second-stage redeployment. This was scheduled to commence on 21 March, and would transfer to Arafat's civilian control some 60% of the Palestinian population of the West Bank. Meanwhile, at the beginning of March, and acting on intelligence from PNA security sources, the IDF uncovered a Hamas cell in the Israeli Arab town of Taibe. Four of the group were killed and a fifth was captured, while substantial amounts of bomb-making equipment were seized. Shortly afterwards, and presumably acting on information received from the arrested Hamas member, PNA forces uncovered explosives in Gaza and a 'bomb factory' in Tulkarm, and arrested two Hamas fugitives in Nablus. While these reverses for the main Islamist organization were reported to have set back any plans to re-embark on a suicide-bombing campaign, disaffection with Arafat's governance ensured that public support for radical Islamist politics remained high in the West Bank and Gaza. The April elections for the student council of Bir Zeit University saw Hamas defeat their Fatah rivals for the second successive year. The secular opposition also voiced fears over Arafat's stewardship of the peace process in an open letter to the Israeli public. The 135 signatories warned that the kind of settlement being discussed between Barak and Arafat would not guarantee a future peace. The letter argued that an imposed solution based on the security and territorial ambitions of the stronger party, rather than the principles of justice and equality, would sow the seeds for future conflict. The Palestinian leader received much-needed but purely symbolic support during the first papal visit to Israel and the PNA-administered areas on 22–26 March. Speaking in Bethlehem, Pope John Paul II expressed the Vatican's support for the right of the Palestinian people to a homeland 'on the basis of international law and the relevant UN resolutions and declarations'. However, the volatility of the area was once more underlined when, after a visit by the Pope to the Dheisheh refugee camp on the West Bank, dispersing crowds began stoning PNA police-officers. A full-scale riot ensued, engulfing the camp for several hours and resulting in many injuries. Tensions in the West Bank and Gaza remained high as the Israeli press reported extensively on Barak's vision of a 'final status' agreement. According to these reports, Israel's Prime Minister would be prepared to recognize Palestinian statehood and transfer some 60% of the territory to Palestinian control. In return, however, he would demand the formal annexation of the main settlement blocs, amounting to 10% of the West Bank, and the deferral of any agreement on the remaining 30%. Resolution of the refugee and Jerusalem issues would also be deferred. The Palestinian negotiators responded to the reports by reiterating their commitment to the achievement of a state encompassing all the West Bank and Gaza with Jerusalem as its capital. Fearful of being 'steamrollered' by Israel, Arafat sought and obtained from President Clinton the promise of more active US participation in the Framework Agreement talks. Ongoing negotiations, punctuated by regular crises, continued to make little apparent progress. At the start of the third round of talks, in Eilat on 30 April, Palestinian negotiators walked out in protest at Israeli proposals to expand the settlement of Ma'aleh Edomin. This apparently violated an earlier undertaking that no new tenders for settlement construction would be issued while the Framework Agreement talks were in session. Barak persuaded the Palestinians to return to the negotiating table, insisting that he had not authorized the tenders and would investigate the issue. By the time Dennis Ross made his promised visit on Eilat on 3 May, it was obvious that the mid-May deadline for the Framework Agreement, like so many other deadlines in the Oslo process, would not be fulfilled. On the following day the Palestinian team walked out of the talks once again, after an Israeli map of a future Palestinian entity was unveiled. It depicted a territorial arrangement on the West Bank whereby 66% of the land would be under Palestinian control, 20% annexed to Israel and the remainder of indeterminate status and subject to further negotiation. Ross tried to assuage Palestinian ire by claiming that the map was not a firm proposal or a 'final offer'. He held a crisis meeting with Barak and Arafat on 7 May in Ramallah and was able to secure their agreement to continue talking until he returned to the Middle East at the end of the month. It was also reported that Barak offered Arafat the immediate transfer of three villages bordering Jerusalem—Abu Dis, Azariya and Sawahara—to full PNA control in exchange for the postponement of the third redeployment, scheduled for June 2000. Frustration with the tardiness and opacity of the negotiation process was finding increasingly violent expression on the streets of the West Bank and Gaza. Demonstrations in support of hunger-striking Palestinian prisoners in Israeli gaols had begun in a noisy but largely peaceful fashion on 10 May, but the protests quickly escalated in scale and militancy and on 15 May, the 52nd anniversary of the 1948 declaration of the State of Israel, confrontations between youths and Israeli troops erupted throughout the West Bank and Gaza. In several locations Palestinian security forces were drawn into gun battles with Israeli soldiers, in scenes reminiscent of the violence that had followed the reopening of the Hasmonean tunnel in 1996. By the end of 17 May six Palestinians had been shot dead and more than 800 injured; several Israeli soldiers also suffered serious injury in the clashes. The confrontations had subsided by the following day. Israel's intelligence services had been warning for some weeks that Arafat would respond to slow progress in the peace process by orchestrating violent protests in the West Bank and Gaza. The role played by Fatah cadres in leading the prisoners' hunger strikes and in marshalling the street protests appeared to lend weight to Israeli charges that the violence had been encouraged at the highest levels of the PNA. A senior Arafat aide predictably rejected the Israeli allegations and accused Israel of 'pushing' the Palestinian people 'to the brink'.

ISRAELI DEPARTURE FROM SOUTHERN LEBANON

With progress in the peace process between Syria and Israel apparently stalled, attention once again focused on Israel's proposed withdrawal from southern Lebanon. The Israeli Cabinet ratified an early July departure date in a vote on 6 March 2000, but the Prime Minister and the Ministry of Defence continued to promote ambiguity over the withdrawal arrangements with a series of often contradictory disclosures concerning such issues as the fate of the SLA and whether Barak intended to maintain fortified border enclaves on Lebanese territory. Meanwhile, the conflict continued to claim victims. Following the deaths of two women in an SLA artillery attack at the beginning of May, Hezbollah fighters fired *Katyusha* rockets into northern Israel for the first time in 11 months; a soldier was killed in the barrage. Israel responded with air raids on power plants in Beirut and Tripoli and the bombing of a suspected Hezbollah arms dump. In mid-May, when the IDF began redeploying its forces prior to the final evacuation, it rapidly became clear that the days of the occupation were numbered. Fortified positions handed over to the SLA were almost immediately abandoned as the 'client' militia began to dissolve: SLA members deserted in large numbers, and Hezbollah and its civilian supporters overran villages and military outposts in the occupation zone. The IDF command thus realized that an orderly retreat was impossible, and by 24 May the last Israeli soldier had left Lebanon—leaving behind a considerable amount of equipment and ordnance. Israeli predictions of a bloody anarchy descending on the evacuated areas were not fulfilled. Plans drawn up between UNIFIL, the Lebanese Government and the various militia groups saw a largely disciplined take-over of the south by the Lebanese police and armed irregulars. To minimize the potential for revenge attacks and a return to the 'confessional' conflicts of the 1970s and 1980s, responsibility for the security of Christian villages was handed to secular leftist militias, while Druze militias maintained a presence in Druze villages. Hezbollah and Amal units were afforded a triumphal welcome in the predominantly Shi'ite areas. Some 6,000 SLA militiamen and their families were given refuge in Israel, and a further 1,500 surrendered to Hezbollah and the Lebanese police. Thousands of Lebanese and Palestinian civilians flocked to the south in the immediate aftermath of the SLA's collapse and the IDF's departure; 25 May was declared a 'National Liberation Day' by the Lebanese Government, and on the following day Hezbollah held a victory rally close to the Israeli border. Addressing a crowd of 30,000, Nasrallah warned that the conflict would continue until Israel withdrew from 'every inch' of Lebanese territory, ceased violations of its airspace and territorial waters, and released the 19 Lebanese still being held in Israeli gaols. However, he also urged restraint in dealing with those who had collaborated with the occupation. Confusion surrounded conflicting Israeli and Lebanese claims as to whether the former had indeed evacuated all Lebanese territory. The initial assessment of UN cartographers supported the Israeli assertion that the withdrawal was complete. This was challenged by President Lahoud, who alleged that Israel still controlled three parcels of land belonging to Lebanon, including the 25-sq km enclave of the Shebaa farms (most experts agreed that this was Syrian rather than Lebanese territory). The inability of the UN and the Government of Lebanon to agree on the delineation of the international frontier delayed the proposed deployment of the Lebanese army in the border region. Lebanese jubilation at the recovery of occupied territory was shared throughout the Arab world. It was evident none the less that President Assad's satisfaction at seeing Israel expelled from Lebanon was diluted by the knowledge that, with an ending of the conflict in southern Lebanon, Syria had lost important leverage in its dealings with Israel. Furthermore, Israeli withdrawal would increase pressure for the withdrawal of Syria's own troops from Lebanon. For the Palestinians of the Occupied Territories, inevitable comparisons were drawn between the successes of the Hezbollah-led resistance in forcing an Israeli withdrawal and their own achievements via the path of negotiation. 'The way to recover our usurped rights,' commented one Gaza-based Palestinian newspaper, 'is not through secret talks or security co-ordination with the usurpers, but through determined resistance, strong faith and patience.' Arafat responded defensively to the implicit criticism of his own leadership by controversially downplaying the role of Hezbollah in securing Israel's withdrawal from Lebanon. Nasrallah replied that Arafat was 'embarrassed by the resistance's victory', and that he should be confronting Israel rather than 'locking up Palestinian freedom fighters to please Israel'. Within Israel, unease at the manner of the withdrawal was outweighed by relief that the IDF would no longer be mired in the 'mini-Viet Nam' represented by its involvement in southern Lebanon. Barak and Levy continued to warn that any incidences of cross-border violence would be met with massive Israeli retaliation.

DEATH OF PRESIDENT ASSAD

The death of President Hafiz al-Assad of Syria was announced on 10 June 2000. As had been widely anticipated, Assad's eldest surviving son, Bashar, was nominated as President by the ruling Baath party. Arafat made his first trip to Damascus in six years to visit the new Syrian ruler, amid hopes of an improvement in PLO-Syrian relations. In contrast to the respectful eulogies that appeared in the Arab world, Israeli commentators responded to the death of their country's most intractable foe with scarcely concealed satisfaction. They shared the speculation in Europe and the USA that Bashar al-Assad, who was formally confirmed as President following a national referendum held on 10 July, would liberalize the governing regime and open up to the West.

SECRET CONTACTS IN STOCKHOLM, CAMP DAVID
TALKS ANNOUNCED

Meanwhile, in mid-May 2000 it emerged that the PNA and the Israeli Government had been engaging in secret talks in Stockholm, Sweden. Negotiations had been broken off by Barak in protest at the recent upsurge in violence in the West Bank and Gaza, but had resumed after Arafat responded to US overtures to calm the disturbances. The chief Palestinian negotiator to the 'official' team at the 'final status' talks, ar-Rabbuh, resigned on hearing of the Stockholm meetings, warning of the readiness of figures in the PNA leadership to make unacceptable concessions to Israel. Conflicting messages emerged from these meetings and from the 'shuttle diplomacy' of Albright. While Albright and the Israeli leader were positive about the progress that had been made in Stockholm and reconvened talks in Israel, Arafat complained that he would not be corralled by Israel into achieving a draft Framework Agreement as long as critical interim issues—the final redeployment, the fate of Palestinian detainees and a 'freeze' on settlements—remained unresolved. Following a meeting between Arafat and President Clinton in Washington, DC, on 15 June, and a further visit to the region by Albright at the end of the month, it became evident that the US leadership was determined to find a solution to the impasse. The sense of urgency in the USA was heightened by the decision of the PLO's Central Council on 3 July to empower Arafat to declare a Palestinian state at the conclusion of the interim period on 13 September. Barak responded with a warning that a unilateral declaration of statehood would be answered by Israeli annexation of settlement blocs on the West Bank and a security blockade along the Jordan valley. Spurred by this escalation in political tensions, on 5 July President Clinton issued a formal invitation to Barak and Arafat to attend an open-ended summit at Camp David. Although it was acknowledged that there must have been progress in the recent rounds of talks for the US President to choose such a symbolic venue, there was little to suggest that positions on core issues had narrowed sufficiently for the crucial Framework Agreement to be easily brokered. Pessimism over the outcome of the intended summit was fuelled by the coalition difficulties of the Israeli leader. In June the three ministers belonging to the secular Meretz grouping had resigned from the Cabinet in protest at Barak's bowing to demands from the ultra-orthodox Shas party for extra state funding for religious schools. Worse was to follow for Barak in the days preceding his departure for Camp David on 10 July. Complaining that they had not been consulted over the extent of the concessions that Barak would be prepared to make in the USA, the leaders of Barak's nationalist allies—Israel B'Aliyah, the National Religious Party and Shas—withdrew support for the Government in quick succession. Responding to accusations from settlers and other right-wingers that he was preparing for treasonable concessions to the Palestinians, Barak claimed that he had an electoral mandate to pursue a policy of peace. He gave an undertaking that any agreements reached at Camp David would be put before the nation in a national referendum. Narrowly surviving an opposition-tabled motion of 'no confidence', Barak warned in the Knesset that the summit was 'a moment of truth for Israel'. He stressed that he was not going alone to the USA but with 'two million voters, citizens who want to give change a chance, who hope for a different Israel at peace with its neighbours'. Opinion polls published on the eve of his departure for the summit suggested that 52% of Israelis supported his mission. Arafat, aware that he would be facing enormous pressures to depart from the minimum demands of the Palestinian consensus, took a large and unusually broadly-based team to Camp David. This included representatives of the left-wing DFLP and People's Party. Hamas and the PFLP were reportedly invited to send representatives to the talks but declined to do so. It was also announced that any agreements reached on permanent status would be subject to a national referendum.

THE CAMP DAVID SUMMIT

A news embargo prevailed for most of the 15 days that the Camp David talks were in session. With the exception of a brief absence to attend the summit of the Group of Eight industrialized nations (G-8) in Okinawa, Japan, the US

President was present throughout. In their regular briefings presidential spokes-men characterized the negotiations as hard and serious, and at various stages in the proceedings both Israeli and Palestinian delegations reportedly threatened to walk out in protest at the intransigence of the other side. While there had been a long tradition of such actions over the years of Arab–Israeli negotiations, unofficial dispatches from the conference rooms suggested that despite some progress, there would be no draft agreement on the permanent status issues. Although there were conflicting reports on the depth of the understandings reached on borders, refugees and settlements—with the Palestinian side claim-ing less progress than the Israeli—by the end of the first week it was evident that the future status of Jerusalem was the principal stumbling-block. It was reported that the Israeli side had agreed to a form of enhanced Palestinian autonomy over the east of the city, with a shared sovereignty over this part of the city; in return, Israel claimed the right formally to annex those settlements abutting the existing municipal boundaries. This was rejected by the Palestinian side. According to Palestinian Minister of State Ziad abu Ziad, Arafat had proposed Palestinian sovereignty over all of East Jerusalem, including the Old City, but with individual religions having control over their holy places. With no prospect of bridging the divide over Jerusalem, the summit ended in acrimony on 25 July, each side accusing the other of responsibility for the failure. Barak claimed that the Palestinians had been unprepared to make 'the necessary concessions' to secure a peace deal. He also stated that he was withdrawing concessions made on the 'final status' issues. In his post-summit press con-ference the US President signalled his belief that Israel had been the more flexible at Camp David. He commended Barak for showing 'particular vision and courage', while faintly praising Arafat for being 'committed to the path of peace'. In a scarcely veiled reference to Arafat's intended declaration of Palestinian statehood, Clinton warned against the dangers of 'unilateral' actions. Initially at least, Israeli reaction to the failure of the summit was divided along the right–left fault line, with the liberal establishment expressing disappointment and a belief that, despite the formal failure of the summit, Camp David had created a new set of understandings that augured well for the future. To little surprise, the nationalists were jubilant at the collapse of the negotiations. Commenting on the failure at Camp David, an erstwhile ally of Barak's from the National Religious Party declared his party to be 'fully satisfied' with the outcome. For the Palestinians, and much of the Arab world, there were fewer recriminations. Pride and relief that Arafat had not succumbed to a 'dishonourable peace' appeared to outweigh any other consideration. 'He can show how he did not buckle under the pressure. That he did stand up to the US and the Israelis. He will be seen as a hero,' commented one Arab diplomat. Sensitive to Barak's political vulnerability after Camp David, and to the disappointment of the international community, officials of the US Department of State emphasized that permanent status negotiations had been adjourned rather than ended.

AFTER CAMP DAVID

In subsequent weeks the USA revived as a 'bargaining chip' the issue of the location of its embassy in Israel: by hinting that he would consider relocating the mission from Tel-Aviv to Jerusalem, President Clinton apparently sought to force Arafat to refrain from a unilateral declaration of Palestinian statehood on 13 September 2000. None the less, despite an assertion, ahead of separate meetings with Barak and Arafat at the UN millennium summit in New York on 6 September, that chances for peace in the Middle East were 'fleeting and about to pass', Clinton remained determined that the final months of his presidency should witness, if not a final agreement on permanent status, then at least a further major breakthrough in the peace process. US influence was evident when, following a two-day meeting in Gaza, on 10 September the Palestinian Central Council endorsed a recommendation made by Arafat to delay the declaration of a Palestinian state, pending a further round of peace talks. On 19 September, however, Israel cancelled a scheduled round of talks with Palestinian negotiators in Jerusalem, citing the Palestinians' failure to devise proposals to break the deadlock in the peace process following the Camp David summit. The Palestinians responded that Israel had rejected out of hand their proposal to place the site of Temple Mount, or Haram ash-Sharif, under the administration of the Al-Quds (Jerusalem) Committee of the OIC. Barak and Arafat did meet at the Israeli premier's home on 25 September, for their first talks since the failure of the Camp David summit. As negotiators from both sides were reportedly preparing for further talks in the USA, Israel's acting Minister of Foreign Affairs, Shlomo Ben-Ami, was said to be seeking support for a compromise whereby sovereignty over Temple Mount/Haram ash-Sharif would be accorded to the five permanent members of the UN Security Council.

THE AL-AQSA UPRISING

Throughout the latter part of September 2000 there were conflicting signals from the Israeli Prime Minister as to his intentions regarding the resumption of negotiations with the PNA. On 23 September Barak publicly questioned the usefulness of resuming contacts with Arafat, but the two did meet at the Israeli premier's home on 25 September and it was announced that they would meet again on 29 September. With both sides' positions apparently more deeply entrenched since the collapse of the Camp David summit, few observers predicted an easy or an early end to the stalemate in the peace process. The proposed meeting never materialized. On 28 September the controversial leader of the Likud opposition, Ariel Sharon, toured the al-Aqsa compound at Temple Mount/Haram ash-Sharif in Jerusalem's Old City. Regarded by many Palestinians as a provocative attempt to demonstrate Israeli sovereignty over one of Islam's holiest sites, the visit provoked scuffles and stone-throwing. The next day Palestinians in the al-Aqsa compound demonstrated at the conclusion of Friday's midday prayers. Israeli security forces responded with rubber bullets and live ammunition, leaving seven Palestinians dead and more than 200 wounded. Palestinians reacted to the deaths by taking to the streets in huge numbers to throw rocks and petrol bombs at Israeli soldiers. In a number of localities in Gaza and the West Bank Palestinian security forces engaged Israeli troops in prolonged gun battles. Mutual recriminations characterized proximity talks and direct encounters between Arafat and Barak hosted by Albright in Paris, France, on 4 October, and the Israeli premier did not proceed with

Albright and Arafat to Sharm esh-Sheikh for further talks led by President Mubarak. Meanwhile, Palestinian casualties mounted, with each death fanning the flames of a revolt that was soon being referred to as the al-Aqsa *intifada*. By 9 October 90 Palestinians, 18 of them children, had been shot dead in clashes with Israeli security forces, and more than 2,500 wounded; 13 of those killed were Arab citizens of Israel, as protests in support of Palestinians in the Occupied Territories were quelled with unprecedented force. Although mass street protests reminiscent of the early months of the previous *intifada* remained an important characteristic of this new rebellion, the uprising swiftly came under the leadership and direction of the Tanzim militias affiliated to Arafat's Fatah movement. The Tanzim concentrated firepower on Israel's more exposed military and civilian settlements in the West Bank and Gaza, notably forcing the evacuation of Israeli soldiers from the outpost at Joseph's Tomb in Nablus. Elsewhere, but primarily at the Netzarim crossroads in Gaza and around the settler enclave in Hebron, the IDF responded to Palestinian attacks with fire from tanks and helicopter gunships.

Barak did not delay in attributing responsibility for the dramatic upsurge in violence to the Palestinian leader. US-mediated efforts to broker a cease-fire were unsuccessful, despite a series of meetings between Israeli and Palestinian military commanders. Arafat asserted that Israel's refusal to withdraw its forces from around Palestinian population centres was at the heart of the failure to agree a cessation of hostilities. He also called for an international commission of inquiry to examine the cause of the violence, a proposal that was rejected by Israel. Alarmed by the scale of the violence, President Clinton invited Barak, Arafat and representatives from Egypt and Jordan to attend a crisis summit to be held at Sharm esh-Sheikh. Popular support within the Arab states for the plight of the Palestinians led to mass demonstrations—a reported 700,000 Moroccans marched in Rabat to show their solidarity with the *intifada*—and calls for Arab governments to take action. The uprising brought early pledges of support from the leadership of Lebanon's Hezbollah, which had long exhorted Palestinians to abandon the path of negotiation with Israel in favour of armed resistance. Both Israeli and Arab commentators cited the perceived successes of the Hezbollah guerrilla campaign against the Israeli occupation of southern Lebanon as having inspired the Palestinian revolt. In a potentially dangerous escalation of the regional crisis, Hezbollah fighters ambushed and abducted three Israeli soldiers from the disputed Shebaa Farms on 7 October 2000. Hezbollah leaders claimed that the abductions had been carried out to facilitate the release of Arab prisoners held in Israel and also out of support for the *intifada*. Israel threatened reprisals against Lebanon and Syria for the Shebaa Farms incident—leading the Syrian Government to inform the USA that it wanted no escalation, and Egypt to warn Israel that it would not tolerate any aggression against Syria. Popular anger at the bloodshed in the West Bank and Gaza persuaded Arab heads of state to bring forward the date of their scheduled summit from January 2001 to 21 October. Meanwhile, on 7 October the UN Security Council adopted Resolution 1322, which condemned the 'provocation carried out' at the al-Aqsa compound on 28 September and the 'excessive use of force' against Palestinians that had followed it. The US Ambassador to the UN abstained in the vote on the resolution, which was carried by 14 votes to none.

CRISIS TALKS AT SHARM ESH-SHEIKH

Following the mob killing on 12 October 2000 of two Israeli soldiers being held in a police station in Ramallah, Israel launched air and naval attacks on PNA buildings and installations in the major cities of Gaza and the West Bank. Although there were no deaths in the bombardments, there were many casualties and heavy damage was inflicted. Polarization widened with these events and their aftermath, confirming convictions that neither the Israeli nor the Palestinian leader was in a mood to make a success of the Sharm esh-Sheikh summit—which both had agreed to attend following intense diplomacy by the UN Secretary-General, Kofi Annan—when it convened on 16 October. After a day of rancorous exchanges the predictions of failure appeared to be confirmed. Barak refused to revoke the military sieges in the West Bank and Gaza (which had been sealed since 6 October), and only reluctantly agreed to an international investigation—by an inquiry panel to be appointed by the US President—into the causes of the violence. It was also clear that in advance of the Arab League summit there was little incentive for the PLO Chairman to act to calm the violence. The meeting ended on 17 October with an unsigned statement committing the two parties to take steps to return to the situation that had existed before 28 September. This 'compromise' was immediately rejected by militia leaders in the Occupied Territories for not meeting the 'minimal expectations' of the Palestinian people. Israelis were also angered that 60 Islamist prisoners held in PNA prisons in Gaza and Nablus had been freed during the bombardments of 12 October. There were growing signs of military co-operation and co-ordination between the Fatah militias and those owing allegiance to Hamas and Islamic Jihad. There was also a shift in strategy; by the end of the third week of the uprising there had been a steady rise in the number of 'hit-and-run' attacks on peripheral settlements and on settler traffic on the roads of the West Bank and Gaza. The aim, according to one Tanzim leader, was 'to persuade the settlers that they would be safer within the Green Line than beyond it', and to convince the international community of the impossibility of peace as long as Israeli settlements remained in the Occupied Territories.

THE ARAB LEAGUE SUMMIT

Arab heads of state met for their emergency summit in Cairo on 21–22 October. Given that their meeting had been brought forward specifically to address the situation created by the new *intifada*, Palestinians hoped that the Arab leaders would adopt measures that would both deter Israel from military escalation and also raise the international profile of the conflict. To reinforce their demand for concerted Arab action, Fatah leaders ensured that the summit took place against a background of intensified protest in Gaza and the West Bank; 20 Palestinians were killed during 20–22 October. However, the outcome of the summit proved to be largely disappointing for Arafat and the Palestinians. Although Libya's Col al-Qaddafi and the more radical Arab leaders had urged the severing of all ties with Israel and the use of the petroleum 'weapon' to counterbalance US support for Israel, the final communiqué of the summit reflected the determination of most Arab governments not to antagonize the US Administration. This was particularly true of the Egyptian host, President Mubarak, who had earlier emphasized the need for Arab leaders to be 'reasonable and practical' and to avoid 'emotive' decisions. As expected, the summit document professed strong support for the Palestinians, but little in the way of tangible action. Avoiding calls for the closure of diplomatic missions, Arab leaders asked instead for a halt to the establishment of new ties with Israel. (Oman and Tunisia had closed their trade offices in Tel-Aviv prior to the Cairo meeting, and Morocco followed suit the day after the Arab declaration. In mid-November Qatar also formally succumbed to pressure to shut an Israeli mission in Doha.) Other measures adopted in Cairo—the halt to the already moribund multilateral negotiations with Israel on regional issues, and calls for the UN Security Council to form a tribunal on Israeli war crimes—were dismissed by Palestinians as mere token-ism. A Saudi Arabian proposal to set up two funds—one of US $800m. to preserve the Arab identity of Jerusalem, and the other of—$200m. to support the families of those killed in the uprising, was warmly welcomed by the PNA.

VIOLENCE CONTINUES

Several Israeli soldiers were killed in Palestinian attacks at the beginning of November 2000, with reprisal assaults on suspected militia targets claiming a further six Palestinian lives. Arafat had met with Peres on 1 November, briefly raising hopes that a mechanism had been agreed to contain the violence, but the optimism proved short-lived. On 2 November a car bombing by Islamic Jihad killed two Israelis in West Jerusalem. The PNA leadership condemned the attack, and issued a statement urging Palestinians to 'ensure that the *intifada* maintains its popular and peaceful course'. Such comments were seen as largely disingenuous. Most analysts shared the view that while Arafat was not in control of every action in the rebellion, he remained in charge of its strategic direction. Having so forcefully demonstrated the Palestinian rejection of the humiliations of the Oslo process, the PLO leader was not going to ease the pressure on Israel nor spare the discomfort of the USA by abandoning the revolt. After a brief lull in the fighting in mid-November the cycle of violence was once again renewed on 20 November when a mortar attack on a settler bus transporting pupils to a school in a Gaza settlement killed two people and seriously wounded several others, including a number of children. Arafat promised to 'investigate' the incident, but although his spokesman reiterated the PNA's opposition to 'all kinds of violence in principle', retaliation appeared inevitable. That evening Israeli navy gunboats, tanks and helicopters sustained a three-hour-long assault on a variety of military and civilian targets in Gaza, leaving 120 injured and a Palestinian policeman dead. Many buildings belonging to the PNA and its security forces were reduced to rubble in the bombardment. The Israeli action was condemned as 'state terror' by the PNA, and was viewed with sufficient concern in Cairo for the Egyptian Ambassador to Israel to be recalled for only the second time in 21 years (the first had been in response to the Sabra and Chatila massacres in Lebanon). Egypt's action was welcomed by Arafat. However, the Palestinian leader's attempt to capitalize on international con-demnation of the Israeli attack by renewing calls for an international protection force to be sent to the West Bank and Gaza failed to dissuade either the UN Secretary-General or President Clinton that the dispatch of an international force to the region would require the approval of the Israeli Government. With Israel historically determined to resist any Arab or Palestinian attempt to internationalize the Middle East conflict, Barak reiterated his Government's opposition to such a force.

At the end of November 2000 the Israeli Prime Minister abandoned his battle to keep together a governing coalition that commanded only minority support in the Knesset. Confronted by an opposition-sponsored bill for dissolution and elections, Barak signalled his willingness to go to the polls early. The popularity he had enjoyed in the initial months of his premiership had been eroded by a series of broken promises: the perception was that his Government had failed to deliver on peace with the Palestinians or with Syria, and at home the country was suffering rising unemployment and an underfunded social-welfare system. Although Israel's Arab citizens (some 20% of the electorate) had voted over-whelmingly for Barak in 1999, attracted by his twin pledges of regional peace and greater government funding for Arab municipalities, they had been alienated by the lethal response to their protests in solidarity with the Palestinian uprising and the rising toll of deaths and injuries in the Occupied Territories. Opinion polls conducted in November showed Barak trailing far behind Ariel Sharon. These same polls revealed that Barak's election prospects would be revived if he were able to use his remaining time in office to achieve a peace deal with the Palestinians. There seemed little hope of such a development. Nevertheless, two days after the election announcement Barak made public a proposal that Israel recognize Palestinian statehood and redeploy from a further 10% of the Occupied Territories in return for the annexation of some settlement blocs and the deferral of agreement on issues such as Jerusalem, settlements, refugees and borders. Barak himself conceded that these proposals rated 'not more than a 10%' chance of success. Given that Arafat had rejected a more generous offer at Camp David, it came as little surprise that the proposal was dismissed by a Palestinian leadership apparently disinclined to boost the electoral fortunes of Israel's Prime Minister. Speaking on 2 December, Marwan Barghouti, a leader of the Fatah movement on the West Bank, pledged that the uprising and 'armed resistance' against soldiers and settlers would continue. Arafat was no more conciliatory the following day, when he in turn affirmed that 'our people' would continue their revolt against the Israeli presence in Gaza and the West Bank.

THE CLINTON PLAN

Palestinian and Israeli officials met in Washington, DC, on 19 December 2000 at the invitation of the outgoing US President. PNA negotiators admitted that their attendance at the talks had been motivated by a desire not to be accused of intransigence, rather than by faith in the continuation of the Oslo process. The head of the Palestinian delegation, Erekat, commented that without an Israeli commitment to return to the borders of 4 June 1967 and to accept the principle of a return of refugees, 'there would be no point in conducting further negotiations'. Details of Clinton's proposals appeared in the Israeli and Arab media in late December. Unlikely not to have been given prior approval by the Israeli premier, the Clinton plan envisaged a non-militarized Palestinian state in all of Gaza and 95% of the West Bank. Israel would annex 5% of the West Bank to incorporate the three settlement blocs of Ma'aleh Edomin, Ariel and Gush Etzion. The Palestinians would be compensated by the acquisition of 3% of land from within Israel's 1967 borders. In East Jerusalem the Palestinians would be given sovereignty over Arab districts, but Israel would extend its sovereignty over the Jewish settlements built within the city's annexed and enlarged municipal boundaries. Israel would annex the Jewish quarter of the Old City and the Western Wall, and would have 'shared functional sovereignty' under the al-Aqsa compound, and 'behind' the Western Wall. On the issue of the 3.7m. Palestinian refugees, Clinton proposed a right to return to their homeland in a West Bank-Gaza state but not to their original lands in what was now Israel. Those unwilling to accept this option would be entitled to compensation and resettlement. Although Arafat was wary of rejecting the proposal outright, his negotiating team submitted a detailed rebuttal of the Clinton plan on 1 January 2001. They argued that the provisions for Israeli annexation of settlement blocs on the West Bank and Jerusalem would 'cantonize' the Palestinian state and jeopardize its viability. Moreover, the Palestinians rejected the notion that refugees should forswear their right of return: 'There is no historical precedent for a people abandoning their fundamental right to return to their homes, whether they were forced to leave or fled in fear', explained the document; 'We will not be the first people to do so.' The publication of this text made anything other than a diplomatic rejection of the Clinton proposals very difficult for the PNA President. Under pressure from Egypt and the EU not to dismiss the plan, Arafat met with the US President in Washington, DC, on 3 January to express reservations and ask for clarifications. Clinton rejoined that these proposals would only be on offer until he left office on 20 January. The Oslo experience had made Palestinians acutely aware of the dangers of endorsing vague agreements that lacked implementation guarantees and which Israel, as the stronger party, could reinterpret and renege upon without sanction. But despite Arafat's decision not to embrace the Clinton plan, he was equally mindful of Israel's impending prime ministerial election, scheduled for 6 February, and the importance of avoiding actions that would bolster Ariel Sharon's campaign. On 10 January Palestinian and Israeli negotiators agreed in Cairo to a CIA-devised plan to reduce the violence in the Occupied Territories. This produced a significant, albeit temporary, drop in shooting incidents. The two sides also agreed to a resumption of direct negotiations in the Egyptian resort of Taba on 21 January. Arafat's sanctioning of these developments was reputedly motivated not only through fear of an election victory for Sharon, but also by the Occupied Territories' parlous economic state. According to the PNA's Minister of Finance, the Palestinian economy had lost US $2,900m. since Israel's sealing of the West Bank and Gaza in October 2000. With unemployment and poverty indices at unprecedentedly high levels, and the PNA on the edge of bankruptcy, Arafat was clearly desperate for some respite for his beleaguered administration.

ARIEL SHARON WINS THE ISRAELI PREMIERSHIP

A slight lessening of tension in the Occupied Territories was never likely to overturn the Likud leader's commanding lead in the opinion polls. Sharon's pledge to deal firmly with the Palestinian uprising—one of his campaign mottoes was 'Let the IDF Win'—struck a chord with the large number of electors who had lost all faith in the idea of Arafat as a peace partner. Until recently Sharon had been regarded as the unacceptable face of the nationalist right wing in Israel, but his 'rebranding' as a tough but benignly paternal politician had been sufficiently skilful for the Likud leader to appeal to Israel's notoriously fickle political centre ground. Aided by an unconvincing Barak campaign and a widely observed boycott of the polls by Israel's Arab voters, Sharon secured an overwhelming victory over his Labour rival in the prime-ministerial election. In the prelude to the ballot Sharon had made no secret of his preference for a government of national unity, and was quick to invite Labour politicians to join his coalition. After some prevarication Barak declined the invitation, but Peres accepted the post of Deputy Prime Minister and Minister of Foreign Affairs in a Cabinet that also included representatives of the extreme right of Israeli politics. Peres was criticized by many of his Labour colleagues for lending a veneer of respectability to a Government headed by an uncompromising right-winger with a reputation for military adventurism. Binyamin Ben-Eliezer, a notably 'hawkish' Labour figure, also joined the Sharon Cabinet as Minister of Defence.

GEORGE W. BUSH ASSUMES THE US PRESIDENCY

The international community greeted Sharon's election victory with a mixture of stoicism and dismay. Given the new Prime Minister's pledge to increase Israeli settlement on the West Bank and to maintain undiluted sovereignty over all areas of Jerusalem, it was difficult to see how there could be a retreat from the bloodshed in Israel and the Occupied Territories and a revival of the peace process. In the Arab world and in Europe there was a general consensus that the policies of the new US Administration of George W. Bush (the son of George Bush, Sr, President in 1989–93) would be critical in determining the parameters of the crisis in the Middle East. During his election campaign Bush had promised a less partisan approach to the Arab–Israeli conflict, but had also indicated that he did not advocate direct US involvement in negotiations between the Arabs and Israel and would not be appointing a special Middle East Co-ordinator to replace Dennis Ross (who had been closely involved in the Oslo process under both the Administrations of Bush, Sr and Clinton). The appointment as Secretary of State of Gen. Colin Powell (who had been Chairman of the US Joint Chiefs of Staff at the time of the Gulf conflict) appeared to confirm commentators' belief that the containment of Saddam Hussain's regime in Iraq would henceforth be the principal objective of US Middle East policy. In late February 2001, during his first tour of the Middle East as Secretary of State, Powell met both Barak and Sharon and reiterated pledges of US support for Israel; he also joined in their calls for an 'end to violence'. Keen perhaps to demonstrate the USA's new even-handedness, Powell then travelled to Ramallah to meet with Arafat. There he endorsed the PNA President's demand for Israel to release millions of dollars of tax revenue withheld from the Authority. This appeal coincided with the publication of a report by the US Department of State that was strongly critical of Israel's policy of assassinating Palestinian political figures and of the ongoing closure of the West Bank and Gaza.

HOSTILITIES CONTINUE

On 4 March 2001 a Hamas suicide bomber killed three Israelis and injured scores of others in an attack on the Israeli coastal town of Netanya. The previous day Hamas's military wing had warned that it had 10 volunteers ready to carry out suicide attacks against Israeli targets in retaliation for the continued killings of

Palestinian civilians in the Occupied Territories. In a rare address to the PLC a week later, Arafat acknowledged that peace remained the 'strategic option' of the Palestinians but cautioned the new Israeli Prime Minister that he demanded a settlement based on 'international legitimacy'. In an interview with a Saudi newspaper the following day the PNA President asserted that the '*intifada* would continue', and that future negotiations must resume from the point at which they had left off under the Barak Government. Sharon reiterated that he would not entertain negotiations while violence persisted in the Occupied Territories, and scorned the notion that his administration would be bound by any promises made by his Labour predecessor. Instead, the Likud leader revealed a new tactic to quell the rebellion—ordering the IDF to ring Palestinian population centres with a series of deep trenches and earth barricades. These measures added to the economic hardship in the territories, and briefly revitalized large-scale civilian protests, but had little obvious impact on the ability of the Palestinian militias to wage their guerrilla campaign. 'Drive-by' shootings of soldiers and settlers on the West Bank, and mortar attacks on Israeli settlements in the Gaza Strip, had become almost daily occurrences. These attacks were often perpetrated by the Popular Resistance Committees (PRCs), which claimed cross-factional support. Inevitably such assaults on settlers brought their own response from a section of Israeli society that had been emboldened by Sharon's election victory and which was enjoying unprecedented sympathy from a hitherto antipathetic Israeli public. Human-rights organizations estimated that in the first six months of the *intifada* settlers were responsible for an estimated 40 Palestinian deaths, in addition to widespread destruction of agricultural land and property.

The killing of a 10-month-old Jewish girl in a Palestinian gun attack on the settler enclave in Hebron on 26 March 2001 ensured that the cycle of violence was sustained. While armed settlers set fire to Palestinian houses in the PNA-controlled parts of the city, Israeli tank fire targeted districts linked to the Palestinian militants. A number of Palestinians were seriously injured in the bombardments. Over the next two days militants from Hamas and Islamic Jihad used the indiscriminate weapon of the suicide bomb in three attacks on Israeli civilians. Two young students were killed and many injured in the explosions, which the bombers claimed were in reprisal for the assault on Hebron. At an emergency cabinet meeting convened to consider a response to the bombings, Sharon held Arafat responsible for the deaths and pledged 'no restraint in the war against terror'. On the night of 29 March Israeli helicopters attacked barracks of Arafat's Force 17 presidential guard in Gaza and Ramallah, killing three and wounding 64. The following day seven Palestinians were shot dead on the outskirts of Nablus and Ramallah during traditional Land Day protests. Battles between Palestinian militiamen and the IDF in Hebron and Beit Jala in the West Bank were reported to have lasted for many hours. Arafat was visibly shaken while touring the wreckage of the Force 17 bases in Gaza. While publicly invoking experience of the 1982 siege of Beirut to warn Sharon of Palestinian 'steadfastness', he was reported privately to have offered a cease-fire in return for an Israeli military pull-back from Palestinian population centres and a renewal of negotiations on 'final status' issues. The Israeli premier rejected the offer as a ploy to coerce Israel into negotiating 'under fire', something he had vowed he would not do. In a move destined to ensure no lessening in the political temperature, Israel's media reported that the Ministry of Construction and

Housing was preparing to commence work on 6,000 new homes in the area between Bethlehem and Hebron.

The absence of tangible political support from the Arab world was a major contributory factor to Arafat's political vacillation. Arab League heads of state met in Amman on 27–28 March 2001, but as in Cairo the previous October, the rhetorical expressions of support for the *intifada* were not translated into the actions hoped for by the Palestinians. Some measures were welcomed by the PNA. These included the reinstatement of the secondary economic boycott of Israel; the commitment to sever relations with any country transferring its embassy from Tel-Aviv to Jerusalem; and the disbursement of emergency funds to Arafat's destitute administration.

EGYPTIAN-JORDANIAN PEACE PROPOSALS

Israel continued its policy of assassinations of Palestinian activists and political leaders in early April 2001 targeting both Islamists and Fatah members with some success. In response, PRC fighters intensified mortar attacks on Israeli settlements within Gaza, and also fired on the Israeli town of Sederot, just north of the Gaza Strip. This proved a provocation too far for the Sharon Government. On the night of 17 April Israeli gunboats and helicopters once again undertook rocket attacks on Palestinian installations in Gaza, while Israeli tanks and bulldozers crossed into PNA-controlled areas in the north-east of the Gaza Strip, occupying the town of Beit Hanoun. The IDF announced that its occupation would last as long as was needed to deter Palestinian mortar fire. However, following a stern rebuke from the US Administration at what constituted Israel's most serious violation of PNA territory, Sharon ordered the immediate withdrawal of Israeli forces—although he denied that he had acted in response to US pressure. The daily litany of violent incidents in the Occupied Territories overshadowed efforts by the Governments in Egypt and Jordan to prevent the seemingly inexorable descent into full-scale military conflict. The Egyptian-Jordanian plan was essentially a modification of the proposals agreed, but never implemented, at the Sharm esh-Sheikh summit in October 2000. It urged the withdrawal of Israeli forces from Palestinian civilian areas; an end to the siege of the West Bank and Gaza; and the transfer by Israel of US $430m. in tax revenues to the PNA. For its part, the PNA would rein in the gunmen operating from areas under its control and resume security co-operation with Israel. After a six-week 'cooling-off' period, Israel and the PNA would resume negotiations on 'final status' issues for a period lasting no more than 12 months. The USA and members of the EU were reported to have given strong backing to the plan. Arafat had also moved from a position of scepticism to one of support. To underline his stated commitment to the proposals, and in the wake of another suicide bombing that left one Israeli killed, Arafat ordered an end to attacks on Israelis from Palestinian civilian areas and authorized renewed contacts with Israeli security personnel. The PNA President's redis-covered enthusiasm for the concepts outlined at Sharm esh-Sheikh was inter-preted in Palestinian circles more as a ploy to isolate the Israeli premier than as an expression of belief in their viability. Sharon had initially rejected the Egyptian-Jordanian plan in a meeting with the Jordanian Minister of Foreign Affairs, Abd al-Ilah al-Khatib, on 16 April, but—apparently realizing the dangers of being exposed as the sole detractor—he revised his position on 25 April, characterizing the new initiative as 'important' but 'in need of some changes and improvements'. The Likud leader once again emphasized that negotiations could only take place once there had been a total cessation of violence. This remained an unlikely prospect. Despite Arafat's clear message that he believed it expedient, for the time being at least, to scale down the use of arms, the dynamic of the conflict dictated otherwise. On 26 April four Fatah activists, including the leader of the southern Gaza PRC, were killed near the Egyptian border. The circumstances surrounding their deaths remained mysterious, but Gaza's chief of police insisted that the men had been 'assassinated' by an explosive device. Fatah militiamen retaliated with renewed mortar fire against the Israeli settlements of Gush Qatif and Kfar Darom on 28–29 April; among those injured in the attacks were five children. Clearly embarrassed, Arafat ordered an end to such 'security breaches' and the disbanding of the PRCs. Both calls were quietly ignored, and Arafat refrained from attempting to impose his will through force of arms.

TENSIONS IN LEBANON

Meanwhile, Hezbollah guerrillas maintained their sporadic attacks against the disputed Shebaa Farms region. On 16 February 2001 an attack on an Israeli patrol in the area resulted in a number of Israeli casualties. Two months later another Israeli soldier was killed in a Hezbollah rocket attack against an Israeli tank. Israel responded with the bombing of a Syrian radar station at Dahr al-Baydar, east of Beirut, killing and wounding an undisclosed number of Syrian military personnel. The attack was roundly condemned in Beirut and Damascus, with the Syrian Minister of Foreign Affairs promising a response 'at an appropriate time'. Israel denied that the attack represented an escalation of the situation, but a spokesman warned that the new Government would not follow the 'policy of restraint' exercised by Barak's administration. The attack on Dahr al-Baydar was justified by Israeli officials on the grounds that Syria allegedly remained the conduit for the flow of Iranian arms to Hezbollah, and that Syria should pay the price for facilitating aggression against Israel. The resurgence of tension along the Israeli–Lebanese border prompted further calls from the USA, the UN and EU members for the Lebanese army to deploy as far as the Israeli border and thus take control of the border region from Hezbollah. Despite this pressure, President Emile Lahoud insisted that the Lebanese state would not provide security for Israel until peace agreements were reached with both Lebanon and Syria. Lebanon's Prime Minister, Rafik Hariri, was less tolerant of the activities of the Hezbollah militias, having publicly decried the adverse impact of their paramilitary activities on foreign investment. Nevertheless, in a meeting with President Bush in late April, he reportedly endorsed the presidential (and Syrian) stance on Lebanese army deployment. UN officials meanwhile announced plans for the phased reduction of UNIFIL forces stationed in Lebanon.

THE MITCHELL REPORT

On 5 May 2001 the international fact-finding commission established by the previous October's Sharm esh-Sheikh summit to investigate the causes of the al-Aqsa *intifada* presented its initial findings. Chaired by former US Senator George Mitchell, the committee produced a report (the full text of which was published on 20 May) that trod a finely balanced line between Israeli and Palestinian narratives of the conflict (see Documents on Palestine, p. 416). The report absolved Ariel Sharon of direct responsibility for precipitating the uprising, but criticized his September tour of the al-Aqsa compound as 'provocative'. The report also concluded that Israel had used excessive lethal force against Palestinian demonstrators, but rejected the PNA's demands for an international protection force because the Israeli Government was so vehemently opposed to such a force. There was harsh condemnation of Palestinian 'terrorism' and criticism of Palestinian gunmen for firing at Israeli soldiers and settlers from PNA-controlled areas. While these comments made uncomfortable reading for the PNA leadership, there was considerable satisfaction in the commission's conclusion that Israel's settlements were obstacles to a search for a regional peace and that 'a cessation of Palestinian–Israeli violence will be particularly hard to sustain unless the Government of Israel freezes all settlement construction activity', and that Israel should 'freeze all settlement activity, including the "natural growth" of existing settlements'. The PNA leadership endorsed the Mitchell recommendations, secure in the knowledge that the report had the backing of the USA, Russia, the EU, Jordan and Egypt, but had caused consternation in Israeli government circles. Sharon and Peres categorically rejected the link between a 'freeze' on settlement and an end to violence as a 'reward' for 'terrorism'. In the two weeks following the release of the draft Mitchell report, Israel initiated an unusually high number of attacks on Palestinian targets, killing at least 17 and wounding hundreds more. The victims included a four-month-old baby killed during the shelling of a market at the Khan Yunis refugee camp in Gaza, and five Palestinian policemen killed when an IDF unit inexplicably raked their check-point with automatic gunfire. There were also an estimated 24 incursions into PNA-controlled territory, in what some observers interpreted as a clear attempt to heighten tension and provoke a response from the Palestinians at a time when international focus was on Israel's settlement policy. Two Israeli teenagers were beaten to death in mid-May, and 15 mortars were fired at Israeli settlements on 11–13 May. A subsequent bombardment along Gaza's coastline destroyed several PNA and Fatah positions.

On 19 May 2001 another Hamas suicide bomber penetrated the security cordons around the West Bank, killing five Israelis in the coastal town of Netanya. Shortly afterwards F-16 fighter jets of Israel's air force fired missiles at the PNA's intelligence service headquarters in Ramallah and at its prison in Nablus, demolishing both buildings and killing 13 policemen in the process. While the PNA leadership denounced Israel's first use of jet fighters against the West Bank since the June war of 1967, the US Administration did not selectively condemn the air strikes—despite the high toll of Palestinian casualties. Instead, the US Vice-President, Dick Cheney, asked both sides to reflect on the dangers that flowed from taking the road of escalation. On the specific issue of Israel's use of F-16s against the Palestinian police, Cheney would only comment that it was a 'delicate situation'. Even more reassuring for Israel's Prime Minister was the apparent revision by Powell of the international (and Palestinian) community's interpretation of the Mitchell Report's cease-fire recommendations.

Speaking on 21 May, the US Secretary of State opined that there was no link between the Mitchell Report's demand for an immediate cessation of violence and the need for subsequent confidence-building measures which might well include a moratorium on settlement construction. Having earlier expressed his 'reservations' over this key element of Mitchell's findings, Sharon now declared his readiness to accept 'in principle' all the report's recommendations. In a bid to pressure Arafat and answer the critics of the air strikes of 19 May, Sharon also declared on 22 May that the IDF would refrain from 'all initiated pre-emptive operations against Palestinians except in cases of extreme danger'. He urged the PNA to reciprocate and to desist from further violence. His appeal was disregarded by Arafat, who embarked on a tour of Europe and the Far East to muster support for the Palestinian contention that a settlement 'freeze' was integral to a cessation of violence in the West Bank and Gaza. On 27 May, during talks with William Burns, US Ambassador to Jordan and designated Assistant Secretary of State for Near Eastern Affairs, Arafat outlined the preconditions for a Palestinian cease-fire. These consisted not only of a settlement 'freeze' but also of an end to the blockades of population centres, the implementation of Oslo's third redeployment and a resumption of 'final status' negotiations from the point they had reached under Barak's premiership. There was little likelihood that the Sharon Government would accede to any of these demands. What was more important from Arafat's point of view was that the US Administration recognize that calm in the Occupied Territories could only be brought about by means of substantive Palestinian political gains.

This assertion was rudely undermined on the night of 1 June 2001 with another Hamas suicide bombing outside a Tel-Aviv night-club, as a result of which 20 young Israelis—most of them immigrants from the former USSR— were killed and more than 100 injured. It was widely predicted that the deadliest such outrage of the *intifada* would be answered with massive Israeli retaliation against Palestinian targets in the West Bank and Gaza. This did not materialize for two principal reasons. Firstly, the Sharon Government was persuaded not to take action that would detract from the international sympathy accorded Israel in the wake of the bombing. Secondly, the PNA came under intense pressure from the EU states and the USA to call an immediate cease-fire. Powell reportedly warned Arafat that without such a declaration the USA would sever relations with the PLO and do nothing to moderate Israeli reprisals. On 2 June Arafat duly abandoned his earlier conditions for a cessation of violence and announced that the PNA would 'do all that is necessary to achieve an immediate, unconditional, real and effective cease-fire'. This would not, however, include the arrests of Islamist militants demanded by Israel and the USA. To have done so would not only have shattered national unity, cited by many Palestinians as the major achievement of the uprising, but it would also have raised the spectre of civil war. Instead, he appealed to factional leaders to recognize his predicament and endorse the calls for a cease-fire. Such entreaties from a leader renowned for his often autocratic approach to dissent were evidence of the extent to which the *intifada* had shifted the balance of power within the Palestinian national movement. It was equally telling that although Fatah agreed to an end to actions from within the PNA-administered areas and inside Israel, the Islamist factions and the PFLP reserved the right to carry out 'resistance' activities anywhere.

TENET'S 'CEASE-FIRE'

The enforced cease-fire was a major political reverse for Arafat and his attempt to mobilize international opinion around the Mitchell Report's recommendations for a moratorium on settlements. President Bush moved swiftly to consolidate the cease-fire declaration by sending the Director of the CIA, George Tenet, to the Middle East to mediate its terms. Following meetings with Israeli and Palestinian leaders on 9–10 June 2001, Tenet presented his proposals on 12 June. In essence, these confirmed the Israeli position that there would need to be a cessation of violence for a significant period (six weeks according to the Israelis) before other confidence-building measures could be considered: these included a return to negotiations or a 'freeze' on settlement construction. In order to facilitate an end to the violence, the PNA would be required to 'arrest, question and incarcerate terrorists in the West Bank and Gaza'. Israel would also be allowed to maintain the 'buffer' zones it had created in the Palestinian territories during the course of the previous nine months. Arafat accepted the cease-fire conditions, albeit with grave reservations. It was evident to observers that he would not pursue its implementation with the energy or the focus demanded by the US Administration. Several Palestinians were arrested for continuing mortar assaults on settlements in Gaza, but the large-scale detentions of Islamists that had been ordered after the suicide bombings of the mid-1990s did not materialize. The PNA leadership might have felt under greater pressure to abide by 'Tenet's truce' if the Israeli side had itself exercised more restraint. Three sleeping Palestinian women were killed in Gaza by Israeli tank fire on 10 June, while three Islamic Jihad members were reportedly the subjects of Israeli targeted killings in the West Bank in subsequent days. These deaths brought the inevitable Palestinian retaliation and a swift return to the dialogue of assassination and ambush. By the third week in June, and despite the professed commitment of both Israel and the PNA to a reduction in violence, the cease-fire existed in name only. Three Israeli settlers were shot dead on 20–21 June in road ambushes in the West Bank; the following day a Hamas suicide bomber killed two soldiers in the Gaza Strip. On 23 June Israeli forces entered PNA territory in southern Gaza and demolished a number of houses; on 24 June a Fatah activist was assassinated in Nablus.

POWELL RETURNS

The fiction of the cease-fire was maintained during Powell's second visit to the region on 27–28 June 2001. Acknowledging that there had been no significant reduction in the levels of violence in the Occupied Territories, the US Secretary of State proposed that there should be a seven-day period of 'quiet' before the 'cooling-off period' itself began. His suggestion that the period of quiet should begin as soon as he had left the region had no impact in reality: five Palestinian activists from Hamas and Islamic Jihad were killed in targeted assassinations on 1 July. Two car bombs were detonated in Tel-Aviv, and three Israelis were killed in the West Bank in the first week of July, leading right-wing members of the Israeli Cabinet to demand an end to Sharon's policy of 'restraint'. Such calls intensified on 6 July, following the deaths of two Israeli soldiers in a suicide bombing in Tel-Aviv (the first attack of its kind since the night-club bombing at the beginning of June). The deaths were followed by the shelling of the

Palestinian towns of Jenin and Tulkarm and an assault by helicopter gunship on a farm in Bethlehem that left a Hamas activist and three others dead. On 12 July two settlers were killed outside the Kiryat Arba settlement near Jerusalem, and a week later an extremist settler organization claimed responsibility for an attack on a Palestinian vehicle near Hebron that killed three members of one family and wounded four others; among the dead was a 10-week-old baby, the youngest victim of the *intifada* to date. The following day missiles were fired at Fatah offices in PNA-controlled Hebron, killing one and injuring 10. With the Palestinian factions pronouncing the 'cease-fire' to be dead and the violence threatening to escalate into an ever more serious conflict, the leaders of the G-8, meeting in Genoa, Italy, announced that 'third party monitoring, accepted by both sides' would be the most effective way of implementing the Mitchell Report and the Tenet cease-fire. Opposed in principle to the presence of any kind of international force in the Occupied Territories, but discomforted by the settler attack near Hebron, Sharon reluctantly noted that he might be willing to see more CIA personnel involved in the dormant Israeli-Palestinian security committees. This was far removed from the ideas of the PNA leader, who in recent weeks had devoted more and more of his political energies into securing the backing of the international community for an independent monitoring force to be dispatched to the West Bank and Gaza. Such a development would represent a significant milestone in the PNA's determination to internationalize the conflict. It was also believed that Arafat would require a political gain of this magnitude if he was to be able to reassert his authority over the militia groups that were increasingly determining the course of the *intifada*. It was not just Arafat's ruling élite in the PNA leadership that was watching the ascendancy of the armed militants with unease. Many Palestinians viewed the militarization of the uprising as not only detracting from attempts to develop its character as a popular revolt but also as an obstacle to the democratization of the Palestinian national movement.

ARAB REACTION

President Mubarak expressed his own fears with regard to the deterioration of the situation in the Palestinian territories in an unprecedented verbal attack on the Israeli premier in an interview carried by Egypt's official news agency on 19 July 2001. Describing Sharon as 'a man who knows only murder, violence and war', he despaired of any progress being made in the peace process under the incumbent Israeli leadership. Equally fearful of the possibility of the situation in the Occupied Territories developing into a wider conflict, the Saudi Arabian Government meanwhile attempted to pressure the Bush Administration into restraining its Israeli ally. At a meeting with Powell in Paris, France, at the end of June, Crown Prince Abdullah voiced Riyadh's unhappiness with the USA's perceived pro-Israeli bias. In mid-July it was reported in the *New York Times* that the Saudi authorities had restricted the kind of ordnance that US forces were allowed to bring into the Prince Sultan military base (from where US aircraft patrolled Iraq's southern air-exclusion zone). The newspaper also carried reports of increasing friction between US and Saudi military personnel at the Prince Sultan base. On 18 July, at a meeting in Cairo of the Arab League's committee to support the decisions of the October 2000 Arab summit on the

Palestinian uprising, the USA was formally urged 'to live up to its responsibility as a sponsor of the Middle East peace process by halting Israeli practices which threaten the chances of peace in the region'.

FURTHER ESCALATION: THE 'PIZZA RESTAURANT' BOMBING

On 30 July 2001 six Fatah members were killed in an explosion at the Fara'a refugee camp in the West Bank. Palestinians accused Israel of responsibility for the bombing as part of its policy of assassination, a charge denied by Israel. On the same day in the Gaza Strip a PNA policeman and an Islamic Jihad member were killed by IDF snipers at the Munzar crossing into Israel. The following day Israeli helicopters fired missiles into Hamas offices in Nablus, killing eight people—among them two leading Hamas activists, a visiting journalist and two children. While a Fatah official described the two days of attrition as marking 'a point of no return' in the 10-month conflict, a Hamas spokesman warned of 'resistance against Israel by all means and in all places'. During the first week in August several settlers were injured and one killed in ambushes by Palestinian militias. On 5 August a lone gunman launched a machine-gun attack on the Ministry of Defence in Tel-Aviv, wounding nine soldiers and two civilians before being shot dead. Two attempts by Palestinians to detonate explosive devices on Israeli buses were also thwarted, heightening the vigilance of the Israeli public in the face of Islamist threats to avenge the deaths of those killed in Nablus. The expected retaliation came with brutal force on 9 August, when 15 Israelis were killed and many injured in the suicide bombing of a busy restaurant in the centre of West Jerusalem. Hamas claimed responsibility for the bombing, which it described as just retribution for 'terrorist Zionist attacks'. Although the PNA leadership condemned the targeting of Israeli civilians, Arafat's spokesman blamed the policies of the Sharon Government for provocations that led Palestinians to commit such desperate acts. The US Administration, although not directly blaming the PNA for the bombing, urged Arafat to 'act now to arrest those responsible and take immediate, sustained action to prevent future terrorist attacks'. There was little chance that Arafat would order his security forces—themselves frequent victims of Israeli missile and bomb attacks—to arrest those being lauded by many Palestinians as 'heroes of the resistance'. Israel's Prime Minister was once again caught between the conflicting pressures of international appeals for restraint and the urgings of cabinet ministers and a large section of the Israeli public to unleash a massive assault on Arafat's PNA. In the event, Sharon's response was swift but not on the scale initially feared. On the night of 9 August Israeli fighter jets demolished a Palestinian police station in Ramallah. The station had been evacuated in anticipation of just such an attack, and few casualties were reported. More controversially, Sharon ordered his police to seize Orient House, the PLO's unofficial headquarters in East Jerusalem and for many years the most visible bricks-and-mortar symbol of the Palestinians' political claim to East Jerusalem. Orient House had long been regarded as a provocation by the nationalist right wing in Israel. Attempts by the previous Likud Prime Minister, Netanyahu, to close the building had been abandoned after strong warnings from the international community. The Jerusalem bombing had, however, provided the Sharon Government with a context in which to fly the Israeli flag over a compound described by an official spokesman as 'a virtual hub and nerve centre of terrorists'. Despite the strong expressions of revulsion in Washington, DC, and in Europe at the carnage visited by Hamas on the streets of Jerusalem, the seizure of Orient House was criticized by Western governments as unnecessary and as representing a political escalation of the conflict. Israeli peace groups also stated their opposition to the take-over; their protest vigils outside the newly occupied building were violently dispersed by Israeli police. Three days after the Jerusalem blast a suicide bombing carried out in the name of Islamic Jihad wounded 20 young Israelis outside a café in the northern city of Haifa. Israel responded to the attack by sending tanks and bulldozers into the heart of the Palestinian-controlled city of Jenin in the early hours of 14 August. There they demolished the main police station and several other PNA offices. Israel justified the attack on the grounds that this northern West Bank city was the principal staging-post for suicide attacks on Israeli targets. Palestinian leaders denounced the violation of their sovereignty, accusing Israel of engaging in a concerted campaign to destroy the institutions of the PNA and to create chaos in the Occupied Territories. This interpretation of Sharon's policy was shared by influential Israeli defence analysts. 'This is a rolling war,' commented one security commentator, 'We are rolling towards an all-out war with the Palestinians. What happened in the last few days was that we were not making war against terrorist individuals but against the Palestinians.' On 27 August the leader of the PFLP, Abu Ali Moustafa, was assassinated by Israeli troops in the West Bank. The assassination was roundly condemned in the Arab world. Although he had led an organization that had maintained uncompromising opposition to the Oslo process, unlike most recent victims of Israel's assassination policy, 'Abu Ali' was widely seen as a political personality with little involvement in his movement's military activities. The PFLP vowed 'qualitative revenge' for the killing. On the same night Palestinian gunmen in Beit Jala opened fire on the settlement of Gilo, prompting a temporary reoccupation by Israeli tanks of a town dubbed 'a sniper's nest' by an Israeli government spokesman. Similar incursions by the IDF into 'Area A' locations of the West Bank and Gaza during the first week of September left 11 Palestinians dead and several homes demolished. Hamas and Islamic Jihad responded in predictably bloody fashion on 9 September, killing five Israeli civilians and wounding many more in a series of co-ordinated bomb and gun attacks in Israel and the Jordan Valley. Sharon dismissed the PNA's condemnation of the attacks and ordered retaliatory strikes against PNA and Fatah infrastructure targets across the West Bank and Gaza. In the early hours of 11 September Israeli tanks and bulldozers were again dispatched to Jenin where they were met with uncommonly fierce resistance from numerically and technologically inferior Palestinian forces. There followed the most sustained Israeli ground assault on PNA territory in the year-old *intifada*. Six Palestinians were killed and every PNA barracks and police station in Jenin was destroyed during a seven-day campaign. The offensive was barely registered by the international media as attention focused on the terrorist attacks on the USA which occurred on 11 September and on related events in subsequent days.

GLOBAL INSECURITY

The events of 11 September 2001 and the USA's subsequent decision to prosecute a 'war against international terrorism', presented President Bush with a foreign-policy challenge not dissimilar to that which had arisen during his father's presidency 11 years earlier. In its attempt to build regional support for military action against Iraq following that country's invasion of Kuwait in 1990, the USA had needed to appreciate the conflicting demands and sensitivities of Israel and the Arab states on the question of Palestine. In order to gain legitimacy for a military campaign to depose the Taliban regime in Afghanistan and dismantle the al-Qa'ida (Base) organization held responsible for the attacks on the USA, it was again required to manage the differing agendas of the Arabs and Israel. With the exception of Saddam Hussain, Arab leaders were swift to denounce the attacks in New York and Washington, DC. But while it was evident that the Arab states did not wish to incur President Bush's wrath by opposing his initiative on global terrorism, there were two issues on which they sought assurances: the scale and legal framework of any military action and the nature of future US engagement with the Arab–Israeli conflict, which, hitherto, the Arab nations had perceived as insufficient and favourable to Israel. Prior to 11 September there had been growing disquiet in the Arab world regarding the US role in the region. Speaking in Alexandria in August, President Mubarak had condemned 'the complete and utter American bias in Israel's favour' and in early September the foreign ministers of the GCC released a statement accusing the USA of threatening regional security by condoning what he described as Israel's 'racist' policy of aggression towards the Palestinians. It was also reported that Saudi Crown Prince Abdullah had refused to accept an invitation to visit the USA because of US detachment from the crisis in the Occupied Territories.

For Arafat the new political realities offered an exit strategy from the *intifada*, a rebellion which daily grew more threatening to the PNA and its leader. Arafat believed that the US need to garner Arab support for an anti-terrorist front would exacerbate tensions in Israel's ruling coalition and lead to the elections that would return a premier less fundamentally opposed to Palestinian aspirations than was Sharon. In the days following the attacks the PNA made every effort to demonstrate Palestinian readiness to accommodate American sensitivities. Greatly disturbed by television footage of small groups of Palestinians celebrating the suicide attacks on the World Trade Center, Arafat invited journalists to witness his donation of blood to the American victims. On 17 September, and before an audience of foreign dignitaries, Arafat also declared that he had 'issued strong and clear instructions for a full commitment to a cease-fire'. Predictions that US-Israeli relations would be strained by the countries' competing priorities following the changes occasioned by the attacks appeared to be supported by both Governments' actions. Sharon's public expression of his belief in the equivalence of Arafat and the al-Qa'ida leader, Osama bin Laden, and his demand that the nascent 'coalition against terror' should target the 'terrorist organization led by Arafat' annoyed and embarrassed the US Administration. Israel's escalating assaults on the West Bank and Gaza further discomfited President Bush. During the week following the attacks 28 Palestinians were killed in 18 separate incursions into the West Bank and Gaza. With the belief that Sharon was, on balance, detrimental to US planning gaining currency in the US State Department, Powell urged Israel to constrain its military operations against the PNA and to respond positively to Arafat's cease-fire proposal. The Israeli premier reluctantly announced a halt to 'offensive actions', although initially, at least, he refused US and EU requests that the cease-fire be consolidated through a meeting between the PLO leader and Peres. Although Sharon was to concede that the period of calm needed before such a meeting could be sanctioned would be reduced from seven to two days, he vetoed the prospect of Arafat-Peres talks five times in the two weeks following 11 September. This was despite Israeli intelligence assessments that there had been a significant decrease in Palestinian armed activity following Arafat's cease-fire instruction on 17 September. Peres responded with vehemence to the obstacles being placed in the way of talks with Arafat, commenting that Sharon's insistence that a cessation of violence must precede negotiations on a cease-fire had made Israel a 'laughing stock in the eyes of the world'.

SITUATION DETERIORATES FURTHER

Peres finally met with Arafat on 26 September 2001. The cease-fire agreed between the two men lasted only a few hours. Later that day Palestinian guerrillas wounded three Israeli soldiers in an attack on an army base on Gaza's border with Egypt. Shortly afterwards Israeli tanks and bulldozers carried out a raid on the town of Rafah, killing four, wounding 30 and destroying a number of houses. Sources within the Labour Party alleged that certain IDF commanders had colluded with Sharon to undermine the cease-fire. Even if this were the case many observers believed it was unlikely that the tensions of a violent September could have been contained with the uprising's first anniversary approaching. A further 12 Palestinians died in violent incidents on 28–29 September; this number included four militants killed in a land-mine explosion near Rafah. Rumours that the PNA were sending policemen to quell anti-Israeli protests in Gaza following this incident led to angry crowds sacking three police stations. Further challenges to Arafat's authority occurred at the beginning of October when suicide bombers and gunmen aligned to both Islamist groups and Fatah committed attacks on a variety of civilian and military targets inside Israel and the Occupied Territories, killing six people. In Hebron Israeli forces killed nine as they staged a three-day occupation of a Palestinian district in response to the wounding of two Israeli women in the settler enclave. A further six Palestinians were killed in the north of Gaza after Palestinian gunmen killed two Israelis in a settlement straddling Gaza's northern border. Questioned over whether he believed Arafat was capable of preventing such attacks, Sharon ventured that he had no trust in the PLO leader and that he did not consider him 'a partner for anything'. Although the US and European assessment of Arafat was more generous, there was clear impatience with the PNA's reluctance or inability to take action against the factions that targeted civilians inside Israel. The Palestinian leader once again faced the choice of alienating the USA or risking internecine conflict. Over the past year the PNA had sought to preserve the notion of Palestinian unity and there had been few arrests of Islamist opponents. However, with Sharon's confident disregard of US pleas for reduced tension in the West Bank and Gaza souring US-Israeli relations and the imperatives for an expanded US role in the region appearing more urgent than they had for many months, Arafat's closest advisers calculated that they could not jeopardize the strategic objective of US involvement by refusing to act. Arafat ordered the arrest of three senior Hamas and Islamic Jihad activists, including the Hamas leader in Tulkarm. This was arguably the minimum he could to do to mollify the Bush Administration, but the arrests were unpopular with a domestic constituency that was increasingly scornful of Arafat's trust in the USA. While the PNA leadership had welcomed the announcement by President Bush that his Government supported the creation of a 'viable Palestinian state', much of Palestinian opinion had interpreted the US Administration's renewed interest in the Middle East conflict as a cynical attempt to win support in the Arab and Islamic world for a military campaign in Afghanistan. On 8 October, the day after the initiation of such military action, students from the Islamic University in Gaza took to the streets to protest against what they perceived as 'the war against Islam'. PNA policeman opened fire on the demonstrators, killing three and wounding several dozen. In the ensuing riots police stations were attacked and the PNA airline's office ransacked. The use of live ammunition on unarmed protesters was widely denounced. Demands for an investigation into the shootings were accompanied by the urgings of the Fatah movement for all factions to observe the 'unity of Palestinian blood'. Arafat reportedly ordered his security personnel to seize all footage of the incident.

Wary of the ambiguities and future direction of the US campaign against terrorism (the scope of which was not necessarily limited to Afghanistan, according to US sources), the Arab states had been reluctant to translate their avowed political support into military assistance. Despite intensive diplomacy by the US Secretary of Defense, Donald Rumsfeld, and by Powell, the USA's key allies in the region maintained a cautious distance from the military preparations. Both Oman and Saudi Arabia stated they would not be pre-pared for the USA to use their military bases for offensive actions. US-Israeli relations also remained strained in the prelude to military action against Afghanistan. Although the Sharon Government could have expected that the USA would decline its offer of direct military assistance, the latter's overtures to Iran and Syria had engendered resentment, which grew following the perceived insult of Rumsfeld's electing not to visit Israel during his tour of the USA's regional allies in late September. More irritating for the Israeli premier was the USA's expectation that the IDF should exercise restraint in its operations against Palestinian 'terrorism' in order that US forces might enjoy a favourable political climate for their own actions. Sharon's anger was expressed in characteristic fashion at a press conference in early October. Likening Israel's situation to that faced by Czechoslovakia in 1938, he urged the USA not to 'appease the Arab states at Israel's expense'. He added that 'Israel won't be another Czechoslovakia. Israel will fight terrorism.' US officials were surprised by the vehemence of Sharon's statement and com-mented that his allegations were 'unacceptable.' Appreciating that his populist remarks risked alienating US government opinion, Sharon subsequently issued a statement stressing the depth and closeness of Israel's alliance with the USA.

THE ASSASSINATION OF ZE'EVI

On 17 October 2001 Palestinian gunmen of the PFLP assassinated Israel's Minister of Tourism, Rehavam Ze'evi, in a Jerusalem hotel. Ze'evi led a party on the extreme right of the Israeli political spectrum, which advocated the expulsion of the Arab populations of Israel and the Occupied Territories. Ze'evi's killing, claimed as retribution for the death of Abu Ali Mustafa, came hours before he was due to withdraw from the Government in protest at Sharon's earlier admission that Palestinian sovereignty over parts of the West Bank was an inevitability. In a strongly worded condemnation of the assassi-nation, and a further equivalence between Palestinian attacks and those on the USA in September, Sharon stated that the killing of Ze'evi was 'Israel's own Twin Towers'. He demanded that the PNA either surrender those responsible for the assassination, including the new leader of the PFLP, or risk being defined as 'an entity that supports terror'. There was no possibility of the PNA extraditing wanted Palestinians to Israel, nor was it likely that the PNA's condemnation of Ze'evi's killing or its detention of numerous PFLP activists and the outlawing of its military wing would deflect Israel from the military reprisals indicated by Sharon's rhetoric. On 18 October Israeli tanks and bulldozers encircled Jenin and entered deep into Ramallah in an operation that many analysts regarded as pre-planned and for which the Ze'evi killing had provided the necessary pretext. Following further Palestinian fire against Gilo, Israeli forces took control of Beit Jala and entered Bethlehem. On 20 October tanks also entered Qalqilya and Tulkarm. The fighting provoked by the Israeli advances proved fiercest in Bethlehem, where 14 Palestinians were killed over a five-day period. Arafat responded to this, the most serious assault on the PNA, with statements urging his people 'to resist the invaders' and pleas to the USA and the international community to force restraint on Israel. On 22 October a US State Department spokesman urged Sharon to halt the IDF's offensive and withdraw forces from Palestinian areas. It was not a message that Sharon initially appeared ready to heed. He insisted that the IDF would remain in its zones of control until 'terrorism, violence and incitement' had ended. Expressions of unease with the escalation in violence were made during regional visits by the German Minister of Foreign Affairs, Joschka Fischer, and the British Prime Minister, Tony Blair. There was particular disapproval of the daily battles around the Christian landmarks of Bethlehem, many of which were televised. On 28 October Sharon announced a withdrawal of troops from Bethlehem and Beit Jala. Elsewhere in the West Bank and Gaza the incursions, assassinations and mass arrests of suspected militants from all Palestinian factions continued. Palestinian groups also demonstrated their ability to penetrate Israeli security control and exact indiscriminate revenge against Israeli civilians. Four women were killed by Islamic Jihad in the town of Hadera on 28 October; a week later two youths were killed when their bus was fired upon in a Jewish settlement of East Jerusalem. On 4 November, three weeks after an offensive that had left 79 Palestinians dead, scores detained and several hundred more injured, Israel's defence minister announced that the incursions had achieved their military objectives. He authorized a phased withdrawal from 'Area A', 'subject to security assessments in each location'. The following day Sharon acknowledged that the USA was seeking a rapid

Israeli retreat from the areas reoccupied but denied that he was under any pressure to effect this from the Bush Administration. He did, however, cancel a visit to Washington, DC, scheduled for 4 November, thus avoiding the possibility of confrontation with the US President. EU mediation led to the arrangement of an informal meeting between Arafat and Peres in Belgium on 5 November. That Sharon was willing to tolerate his Minister of Foreign Affairs meeting with the man now routinely referred to as a 'terrorist' reflected renewed confidence in Israel's position. Only a few months previously the IDF's first incursion into an area of full PNA control had ended abruptly after stern warnings from the Bush Administration that it was opposed to such operations. Now Israel had concluded a lengthy campaign against the PNA which had provoked only relatively mild rebuke in the West, and the IDF remained in control of strategic areas at the heart of PNA territory. Furthermore, although both Blair and Fischer had conveyed their belief that an enduring cease-fire was not sustainable without Israel ending its policy of assassination, lifting its siege of Palestinian areas and returning to the negotiating table, the EU had joined the USA in echoing more forcefully Israel's demand that the neutralization of the factions that continued to commit acts of violence in Israel was the *sine qua non* of the revival of the peace process.

The West had ignored Sharon's attempts to characterize Arafat as the 'Palestinian bin Laden'. However, any comfort the PLO leader may have derived from the perceived European and US belief that he remained their only interlocutor was offset by the knowledge that he could not rely indefinitely on the promise of US re-engagement to guarantee the Mitchell principles and provide support for the PNA. The incursions of October 2001 had consolidated the cantonization of the West Bank and appeared to confirm the assessment of both Israeli and Palestinian analysts that Sharon's notion of a Palestinian state encompassed little more than the arrangements offered to the African 'homelands' under apartheid rule in South Africa. The Israeli Government's insistence that withdrawal from the recently reoccupied areas would be dependent upon the conclusion of local security arrangements appeared to prefigure such a settlement. As it was, the steady attrition against the PNA's infrastructure had meant that in some areas, most notably in Jenin on the West Bank and around Rafah and Khan Yunis in the Gaza Strip, Arafat's PNA exercised little control over the local populations. There, as elsewhere, groups of gunmen determined the course of the *intifada*. Opinion polls revealed that support for Hamas continued to grow at Arafat's expense and there was mounting evidence of fighters owing nominal allegiance to Arafat's Fatah organization co-operating militarily with Islamist militias. Arafat's failure to exert control over the uprising, articulate his strategic vision or respond to calls for greater democracy and accountability within the PNA was also alienating political leaders who had hitherto been supportive of his stewardship. One of Arafat's principal lieutenants in Gaza, the territory's Security Chief, Muhammad Dahlan, tendered his resignation in mid-November over the executive's refusal to suspend the police chief responsible for the shooting of students on 8 October and in protest at the ongoing arrests of PFLP activists. He was subsequently persuaded to withdraw his resignation and reaffirm loyalty to Arafat.

US POLICY DEVELOPMENTS

In early November 2001 President Bush outlined US policy on the Middle East in a speech to the UN General Assembly in New York. Prior to the speech he had declined to meet or even shake the hand of the Palestinian President. Despite this, there was much in the speech to raise the spirits of the beleaguered Arafat. Citing the applicability of UN Security Council Resolutions 242 and 338 to any settlement, Bush also proclaimed that he was 'working towards a day when two states, Israel and Palestine, live peacefully within secure and recognized borders'. This was followed by a joint statement with the Russian President, Vladimir Putin, advocating the immediate resumption of talks between Israelis and Palestinians. In his own speech to the General Assembly Arafat offered his 'deepest appreciation' for the commitment of the US President. On 19 November Powell expanded upon his President's words with a long-anticipated policy speech. He confirmed the Administration's commitment to a 'just and lasting peace between Israel and its Arab neighbours' based on relevant Security Council Resolutions. Although stating that Israel's occupation of the West Bank, Gaza and East Jerusalem 'must end', he made it clear to listeners that the first stage in achieving this goal would necessarily be an end to violence in Israel and the Occupied Territories. He announced the appointment of Gen. (retd) Anthony Zinni as a new US envoy to the region. Zinni's 'immediate mission' would be the achievement of a cease-fire between Israel and the Palestinians. Primary responsibility for the success or failure of the Zinni mission, Powell confirmed, lay with Arafat's PNA. He described the *intifada* as being 'mired in the quicksand of self-defeating violence and terror directed against Israel'. The Palestinian leadership, he contended, 'must make a 100% effort to end violence and to end terror. There must be real results, not just words and declarations. The Palestinian leadership must arrest, prosecute and punish perpetrators of acts of terror'. Developments in the West Bank and Gaza continued to remind Arafat of the difficulties of the problem assigned to him by the USA. In mid-November the arrest by the PNA's security police in Jenin of an Islamic Jihad activist wanted on suspicion of planning a suicide-bombing operation in Israel led to a crowd of 2,000 besieging offices of the Preventative Security Force. Another Jihad activist was freed from PNA custody by an armed crowd in Gaza and a committee to defend political prisoners won cross-factional support. The Palestinian High Court had also ordered the release of some of the arrested PFLP members on the grounds that their arrests had been unlawful. Meanwhile, in elections to the student council at al-Najah University in Nablus, the first to be held since the beginning of the uprising, Islamist groups won 48 of the 81 seats, Fatah supporters winning only 28. This steady shift of the Islamist movements from the margins to the mainstream of Palestinian political life was perhaps the main factor militating against the success of any cease-fire initiative. Powell had unambiguously established the position for future progress in the peace process: the PNA would be obliged to resume its commitment to an alliance with the IDF and the CIA against its Islamist opposition. Having recently been included by the US State Department in a list of organizations which would be subject to financial sanctions in the campaign against terrorism, it was evident that both Hamas and Islamic Jihad had a vested interest in subverting the formation of such an axis. Popularity on the Palestinian street, significantly greater than it had been during the bombing campaign of the mid-1990s, would be a major weapon in their defiance.

ISRAELI STRATEGIC RESPONSE

The US Administration's strong reaffirmation of its commitment to UN Resolutions 242 and 338 may have irritated Sharon, but it was unlikely to have surprised him. Nor was Zinni's mission to the region regarded as especially troubling to Sharon. Immediate responsibility for ensuring the success of the cease-fire lay with the embattled PLO leader's ability to impose authority over his fractured domain. There was no certainty that such an outcome could be achieved. To the annoyance of the USA and the EU, Sharon also announced that 'seven days of peace and quiet' would be necessary before the commencement of formalised talks on a cease-fire. In effect, commentators observed, this would bestow the power of veto upon any Palestinian wielding a gun. Sharon's optimistic mood originated in part from developments outside the region. The sudden collapse of the Taliban regime in Afghanistan had rendered the US need for public Arab support less urgent. President Bush had also commented that the war against terrorism 'could not wait for a Palestinian state.' While the USA had been cautious in being seen to give validation to the Israeli-drawn parallels between the battles waged by the USA against al-Qa'ida and their own fight against the second *intifada*, Israeli officials expressed satisfaction that several Palestinian factions, as well as Lebanese Hezbollah, had been formally listed as 'terrorist' organizations by the US State Department. Hezbollah received the support of the Lebanese and Syrian Governments in rejecting the designation. Speaking on 6 November 2001 the Lebanese finance minister echoed views expressed in Damascus during the recent visit of the British Prime Minister. He declared that he would not sequester the movement's assets, in accordance with US wishes, because the Lebanese Government 'views the group as a resistance movement and not a terrorist organization'. The US National Security Adviser, Condoleezza Rice, acknowledged that Hezbollah 'has a side which conducts social and political activities', but insisted that the movement also possessed a 'terrorist branch which is responsible for many problems in the Middle East'. The US Ambassador in Beirut accused Hezbollah of having a global terrorist reach and of fuelling the violence in Israel and the Occupied Territories through its assistance to Palestinian Islamist organizations. Following visits to Damascus and Beirut in mid-December, the US envoy, William Burns, gave no sign that the USA would drop its demand that the Lebanese Government take action against Hezbollah. He did add, however, that the USA would pursue its goals through 'a practical and quiet dialogue'. The omission of Hezbollah's military wing from the EU's list of terrorist organizations was warmly welcomed in Beirut and Damascus.

SUICIDE BOMBINGS AND ISRAEL'S MILITARY RESPONSE

A period of comparative calm in the Occupied Territories came to an end on 22 November 2001 with the deaths of 5 Palestinian minors in Khan Yunis, apparently after they activated a booby-trapped device intended for fighters operating in the area. The following day, the first Friday in the Muslim holy month, Ramadan, an Israeli missile attack on the West Bank resulted in the death of Mahmud Abu Hanud, a senior Hamas military leader, and two of his bodyguards. Hamas announced publicly that it would seek to avenge the assassination. Elsewhere in the Occupied Territories four other Palestinians were killed in violent incidents. Hamas fulfilled its threat of retribution for the death of 'Abu Hanud' with two devastating suicide bombings in West Jerusalem and Haifa on 1 and 2 December, respectively. A total of 25 Israelis were killed and scores injured in the attacks. Hamas' spiritual leader, Sheikh Ahmed Yassin, defended the bombings as just retaliation for the cycle of violence initiated by Israel on 22 November. He denied that they were intended to forestall Zinni's impending visit to the region. Sharon truncated a visit to the USA in response to the bombings, but not before receiving US approval to take stern action against the PNA. On 3 December Sharon delivered a nationwide address in which he accused the PNA and Arafat of sole responsibility for 'this war of terror forced upon us'. The widely anticipated retaliatory actions against the PNA were initiated the same day. F-16 fighters and helicopter gunships struck against numerous PNA targets throughout the West Bank and Gaza. Arafat's helicopter fleet in Gaza was disabled in the operation and a number of fuel dumps were destroyed. During the night Israeli bulldozers tore up the runway at Gaza International Airport. For once, the customary US pleas for restraint were not forthcoming. Speaking after the first round of attacks, the spokesman for the US presidency, Ari Fleischer, said that Israel 'had a right to defend itself'. Arafat had moved to Ramallah in anticipation of Israeli attacks against his headquarters in Gaza. On 4 December as Israeli tanks encircled Palestinian towns and cities, Arafat's compound in the town was fired upon by helicopter gunships. An IDF spokesman denied that it was intended to physically harm the Palestinian leader, but confirmed that they would not allow him to move from Ramallah until he had complied with their requests to arrest a list of named militants wanted for planning attacks on Israel. To demonstrate the extent of the Palestinian leader's humiliation, an Israeli tank was positioned less than 200 m from Arafat's residence. The PNA leadership had reiterated its opposition to the targeting of Israeli civilians in the immediate aftermath of the first suicide bombing in Jerusalem and had ordered all hostile operations against Israel to cease. More than 100 prominent Islamists were also arrested across the West Bank and Gaza in the week following the bombings. This proved insufficient not only for Israel and the USA but also for EU leaders. On 10 December they urged Arafat to bring an end to the *intifada* and to 'dismantle the terrorist networks' of Hamas and Islamic Jihad. The following day Palestinian gunmen ambushed a settler convoy on the West Bank, killing 10 people. In the previous few days Sharon had ordered restraint on the IDF, apparently unwilling to expose Israel to accusations of excessive military force or redirect international attention from the discomfort he had imposed on Arafat. However, these latest killings, in which Arafat's Fatah had been implicated, prompted a resumption of aggressive incursions. Scores of activists were arrested in sweeps across the Occupied Territories and many killed in the unequal struggle against Israeli armour. Sharon also escalated his rhetoric against Arafat, declaring him to be 'irrelevant' to the political process. This, in turn, prompted EU leaders meeting for an end-of-year summit to issue a statement reminding the Israeli Prime Minister that Arafat was the partner Israel needed 'in order to eradicate terrorism and to work towards peace'. Sharon's words and deeds led to inevitable speculation over his strategic intentions. If Arafat was no longer relevant to the search for a settlement to the conflict, which Palestinian figures did the Israeli Government view as viable—or even likely—alternatives? Analysts also pondered on the logic of demanding Arafat tackle the Islamist opponents of accommodation with Israel while at the same time targeting the physical and human resources needed to achieve such a goal. Egypt's President Mubarak attempted to ameliorate Arafat's isolation by sending the Egyptian Minister of Foreign Affairs, Ahmed Maher, to Israel on 6 December. Maher failed to win any undertaking to lessen the pressure on the PNA or its leader. A week later the USA vetoed a draft resolution at the UN Security Council, co-sponsored by Egypt, which condemned 'all acts of violence and terror resulting in deaths and injuries among Palestinian and Israeli civilians'. The draft also proposed condemnation of breaches of the Geneva Conventions, which the US Ambassador to the UN, John Negroponte, determined was intended to 'isolate' Israel. On 6 December the Conference of the 114 High Contracting Parties to the Fourth Geneva Convention had met in Geneva, Switzerland, and decided unanimously that the Conventions did apply to the Occupied Territories and that Israel was in serious violation of many of the articles. The Conference was boycotted by both Israel and the USA.

On 16 December 2001 Arafat acceded to international opinion and, in a televised address, reiterated his demand 'for a complete cessation of military activities, especially suicide attacks, which we have always condemned'. He said that the PNA would locate and punish 'planners', 'executors' and 'violators' of the cease-fire. He also ordered the closure of 30 institutions affiliated to the Islamist movement. Hamas spokesmen attacked Arafat, stating that his announcement and the measures taken against their institutional bases were tantamount to 'legitimizing the occupation'. Similar sentiments were expressed by Islamic Jihad and the PFLP. Nevertheless, recognizing the precariousness of Arafat's position, the two main Islamist organizations were reported to have given an undertaking to suspend military operations inside Israel. The low-level warfare in the West Bank and Gaza continued, albeit with a lesser intensity. Israeli forces assassinated a Hamas activist in Gaza on 17 December and killed a policeman in Nablus on the same day. Palestinian guerrillas responded with mortar fire against settlements in Gaza and attacks on settlers on the West Bank. Arafat, meanwhile, remained confined to his Ramallah compound. President Mubarak reported that Arafat had been informed that his request to attend the meeting of the OIC in Doha, Qatar, on 10 December would only be granted if he did not return. Sharon also refused to allow Arafat to attend the Christmas celebrations in Bethlehem, including Midnight Mass. On 30 December Israeli forces killed six Palestinians, three of them children, during an incursion in the north of the Gaza Strip.

The year 2001 thus proved to be the bloodiest in Israel and the Occupied Territories since 1967. More than 1,000 Palestinians and nearly 200 Israelis had now lost their lives in the 15 months of the second *intifada*. The prospect of Arafat regaining his previous status seemed remote, and the apparent absence of an alternative leader with the will and ability to command a broad base of Palestinian support indicated that the deterioration in relations in the early 2000s was unlikely to be attenuated in the immediate future.

On 3 January 2002 Israeli naval commandos seized the freighter *Karine A* in international waters of the Red Sea. The ship was carrying some 50 metric tons of weapons, including rockets and missiles, which Israel claimed were *en route* from Iran to the PA in Gaza. Both Iran and the Palestinian leadership denied knowledge of the *Karine A* or its cargo, although the vessel was commanded by a lieutenant-colonel in the PA naval police. Israeli officials held up the seizure of the arms as evidence of Arafat's commitment to a war of terror against Israel. This message was forcibly relayed to Anthony Zinni on his return visit to the region later on the same day. The US special envoy did not, however, comment publicly on Israeli claims of PA complicity in the *Karine A* affair, reflecting the reported uncertainty within the US State Department regarding the stewardship of the project.

The gun-running charges were an embarrassment for the PA. However Arafat's standing in the USA had been improved by the Palestinian factions' continued observance of his appeal for a cease-fire in the previous month; this was despite the deaths of some 20 Palestinians in Israeli military operations in the three weeks following the declaration. On 6 January 2002 Zinni met with Israeli and Palestinian security officials to outline the confidence-building measures to be taken prior to the implementation of the Mitchell and Tenet recommendations for ending the violence and restarting the peace process: the PA was required to arrest and prosecute the 33 Palestinians named on an Israeli list of 'terrorist' suspects, while Israel would reciprocate by ending its sieges of Palestinian population centres. Additionally, Zinni made it clear in his discussions with Arafat that the Bush Administration expected the 'terrorist infrastructure' in Gaza and the West Bank to be dismantled. The formula was an old one, and no more palatable to a PA leadership reliant on the goodwill of Islamist and dissident PLO militias to maintain the calm in the Occupied Territories that Arafat believed necessary to expose the Israeli leader's lack of commitment to the implementation of the Mitchell principles. Nevertheless, Arafat instructed his security forces to target militant groups; six Islamic Jihad members, including one named on Israel's list, were detained in a large-scale PA security sweep in Jenin in early January. A week later Abu Ali Moustafa's successor as leader of the PFLP, Ahmad Saadat, who was sought in connection with the killing of Rehavam Ze'evi in October 2001, was arrested in Ramallah, prompting the PFLP to make threats against the lives of PA security chiefs. A brief lull in the violence in the West Bank and Gaza came to an abrupt end on 9 January with a Hamas assault on an IDF base near Rafah. Four soldiers and two assailants were killed in the operation, which a Hamas spokesman claimed as retaliation for Israel's killing of three Palestinian children in the north of Gaza at the end of December. The following day Israeli troops launched a major incursion into the Rafah refugee camp, bulldozing 60 houses. Attacks were also launched against PA police and naval bases on Gaza's southern coast and against Gaza international airport. On 14 January 2002 the leader of Fatah's al-Aqsa Martyrs Brigades in Tulkarm was assassinated while nominally under the protective custody of the PA. The Brigades immediately joined the other militant factions in declaring 'the hoax of the cease-fire cancelled'. Three days later a gunman from the organization attacked a Bar Mitzvah celebration in the Israeli town of Hadera, killing six people and wounding 30 others. Israel responded with ground and air assaults on PA targets throughout the West Bank. Tanks were once again positioned outside Arafat's compound in Ramallah, and the broadcasting facilities of the PA's television station in the city were blown up.

The Israeli Prime Minister was subjected to unusually sharp media criticism for his perceived part in reigniting the *intifada*. An editorial in the conservative daily newspaper, *Ma'ariv*, charged Sharon with not being 'really interested in peace and quiet, only in gradually breaking the Palestinian Authority and its leader'. Editors also questioned the value of pursuing a policy of assassination when these actions invited such bloody retaliation as had occurred in Hadera. Yet although there was little evidence that the Israeli public believed that Sharon possessed a viable vision for his nation's future relations with the Palestinians, his coalition Government remained solid. An attempt by the Labour 'dove' Yossi Beilin to force his party's withdrawal from the Likud-led coalition was roundly defeated at a meeting of its Central Committee in mid-January 2002, not least because Labour politicians appeared unwilling to give up on power, or Sharon, as long as the Prime Minister's military escalations against the PA did not destabilize relations with the USA. A rift appeared a distant prospect. George Bush's State of the Union address at the end of the month (*inter alia* characterizing Iraq, Iran and North Korea as forming an 'axis of evil') demonstrated that in the aftermath of the 11 September 2001 attacks, his avowed commitment to wage war on terrorism and its sponsors was undiminished. The US Administration's rhetoric also sat increasingly uneasily with the Arab world's hopes of a less partisan approach to the Middle East conflict. Concerns that the US position was moving ever closer to the formulations of the Likud leader grew stronger with the hardening of criticisms directed at the PA and its leader. At the end of January the US President stated, 'I am disappointed in Yasser Arafat. He must make a fuller effort to root out terror in the Middle East'. Assurances that the USA would maintain pressure on the PA leader were given to Sharon during his visit to Washington, DC, in the first week of February. Although these fell short of a US commitment to cease dealing with the Palestinian leader, Israel's Minister of Defence, Ben Eliezer, none the less confided that US Vice-President Dick Cheney's attitudes towards Arafat were 'more extreme' than his own.

European leaders shared Arab fears that the USA's willingness and ability to deal with the complexities of the continuing crisis in the Middle East had been dangerously compromised by the simplistic frameworks generated by the suicide attacks of September 2001. EU foreign ministers met in Brussels in mid-February 2002 to discuss ideas for de-escalating the conflict and revitalizing the search for a political solution. Proposals reportedly included an early declaration of Palestinian statehood and the convening of an international conference. Neither Israel nor the USA was prepared to extend its backing to the European plans, on the grounds that the security imperatives outlined by Mitchell and Tenet must have priority over restarting a political process. Lack of unanimity or clarity among EU nations, and in particular German and British opposition to undermining US policy, effectively scuppered the initiative, to the evident satisfaction of the Israeli Government. Sharon did meet with three of Arafat's deputies at the end of January. These sought the lifting of the siege of Palestinian towns, the ending of targeted killings and freedom of movement for the PA leader (who was still confined to his Ramallah compound). According to Israeli press reports, Sharon replied that none of the requests could be granted until Arafat and the PA put an end to 'terrorism' and 'incitement' and carried out the arrest of named individuals.

With all the Palestinian factions having abandoned a cease-fire which Israeli forces had never observed, there was a steady escalation in violent incidents in the West Bank and Gaza and within Israel. On 22 January 2002 the IDF killed four wanted Hamas members in a raid on Nablus. Within a week several armed attacks had been carried out on Israeli civilians in Tel-Aviv and Jerusalem. On 27 January a Palestinian woman blew herself up in West Jerusalem. Her death represented another bloody milestone of the *intifada*, not only because she was the first female suicide bomber, but also because it marked a commitment by the nationalists of the al-Aqsa Martyrs Brigades to emulate the Islamist organizations in employing this most feared and indiscriminate of weapons. (The avowed secularists and nominal Marxists of the PFLP would also soon be dispatching 'martyrs' against Israeli targets.) In mid-February Hamas deployed a new weapon in the conflict, firing two home-made rockets from Gaza into Israel. Dubbed the *Qassam 2*, the weapons were crude in design, modest in performance and had little conventional military value: both fell harmlessly in fields. Nevertheless, their use was seized on by Sharon 'as an act of war'. Israeli military aircraft were sent to bomb PA buildings in Gaza City and suspected mortar factories in the Jabalia refugee camp. The IDF also launched a major ground assault in the central area of the Gaza Strip, taking over PA security bases and dividing the Strip into two northern and two southern enclaves. Several PA security police and militiamen were killed in the attacks. In an ambush reminiscent of the Hezbollah guerrilla war in southern Lebanon, an Israeli tank was blown up and three of its occupants killed in a landmine explosion during the incursion. In the West Bank attacks on military and settler targets were reported daily. The intensification of the conflict and the growing number of casualties on both sides had a polarizing effect on the political debate within Israel. In late January more than 50 IDF reservists signed a declaration announcing their intention of refusing to do military service in the West Bank and Gaza. They stated they would 'no longer fight in the war for the welfare of the settlements in the Territories. We will not continue to fight beyond the Green Line for the purpose of dominating, expelling, starving and humiliating an entire people'. The declaration served to revitalize the Israeli peace movement; rallies in Tel-Aviv brought together activists from Peace Now, Meretz and the 'dovish' wing of the Labour Party into a new 'Peace Coalition'. While there was a reluctance on the part of these representatives of the political mainstream to endorse the call of the 'refuseniks', opinion polls released in the weeks following the publication of the declaration revealed that the reservists had the support of 15%–25% of the Israeli public. At the other end of the political spectrum, advocates of the expulsion or 'transfer' of the Palestinian populations were reported in an opinion poll published in the daily newspaper *Ma'ariv* to have the backing of 35% of Israeli Jews.

THE SAUDI ARABIAN INITIATIVE

In mid-February 2002 substance was given to rumours of a new Middle East peace plan with the announcement by Saudi Arabia's Crown Prince Abdullah of an initiative for a comprehensive resolution of the Arab–Israeli conflict. The central idea of the Saudi proposals was for the Arab states collectively to normalize relations with Israel within its pre-June 1967 borders in return for the establishment of a Palestinian state in the West Bank and Gaza with East Jerusalem as its capital. According to US and Arab media reports, the basic tenets of the Saudi plan had been formulated in Washington, DC, the previous November, but had not been promoted by George W. Bush because he had felt that US credibility in the Arab world could not risk further harm through failure of an official peace initiative. Saudi Arabia had its own reasons for now accepting authorship of the proposals. It would help repair the rift in relations with the USA after revelations that many of those involved in the September 2001 attacks had come from the Kingdom. Moreover, Saudi Arabia perceived sponsorship of a US-originated peace plan as strengthening its bid to rival Cairo as the West's favoured interlocutor in the Arab world. Fittingly, Crown Prince Abdullah stated that the plan would be officially launched at the summit meeting of Arab League heads of state to be held in Beirut at the end of March. EU ministers of foreign affairs praised the Saudi proposals as making a 'significant contribution' to the search for a regional peace. With the exception of Syria and Libya, Arab responses were also largely positive. Seeing Crown Prince Abdullah's plan as a chance to isolate Sharon internationally and exacerbate tensions within the Likud-led coalition, PA officials expressed full support for the Saudi formula; full acceptance, however, would be conditional on Israel's lifting of the siege of Yasser Arafat's Ramallah compound and allowing him to attend the Arab summit in Beirut. This stance was endorsed by GCC foreign ministers meeting with their EU counterparts in Granada, Spain, at the end of February. Oman's Minister of Foreign Affairs commented that if Arafat was not freed to attend, 'we shall all consider that Israel does not take the initiative seriously'. Indeed, that appeared to be the official attitude of the Sharon Government.

Encouraged by the lukewarm reception extended to the Saudi plan in Washington, and in particular the emphasis placed by spokesmen for the Bush Administration on the need for a cessation of violence to precede political dialogue, the Israeli Government appeared unwilling to engage with the Saudi offer. Nor was it predisposed to ease regional tensions. In a televised address on 22 February 2002 Sharon signalled the IDF's readiness to take the war against Palestinian militants to the 'terrorist nests' of the refugee camps. Six days later major assaults were launched against the Balata and Jenin refugee camps on the West Bank, killing 30 Palestinians, injuring more than 200, and causing widespread destruction. Balata was the West Bank stronghold of the al-Aqsa Martyrs Brigades, and the organization was quick to vow and exact retaliation. On 2 March responsibility was claimed for a suicide bombing in an ultra-orthodox Jewish district of Jerusalem in which nine Israelis, including four young children, were killed. The following day a lone Palestinian sniper shot dead seven soldiers and three settlers at an army check-point on the West Bank. Charging that the Palestinians would need to be 'hit hard—so that they understand that terrorism will achieve nothing', Sharon ordered gunboat, fighter aircraft and helicopter strikes against a variety of PA targets in the West Bank and Gaza and tank-led incursions against refugee camps in both areas. The PA called on Palestinians to 'confront the invaders', but despite fierce resistance from Palestinian policemen and assorted militia groups, the overwhelmingly superior forces of the IDF were able to reoccupy Ramallah and carry out arrests and weapons seizures throughout the Occupied Territories. By the end of the third week in March some 200 Palestinians, many of them civilians, had been killed in the Israeli assaults. Palestinian gun and bomb attacks inside Israel contributed to a rising toll of civilian deaths and a growing sense of vulnerability in the towns and cities that would marshal popular support behind the uncompromising military responses of the Israel Prime Minister.

RESOLUTION 1397

The ferocity of Israel's attacks on the Palestinian territories caused alarm in the USA, not least because of the Bush Administration's renewed focus on achieving 'regime change' in Iraq. With US Vice-President Dick Cheney already scheduled to tour Middle Eastern capitals to garner Arab acquiescence in, if not support for, military action against Iraq, the US President announced that he would also be sending Anthony Zinni back to the region in an attempt to broker another cease-fire. Annoyed that Sharon's adventurism was apparently undermining his principal foreign policy objective, Bush was moved to direct rare criticism at his ally, declaring that, while he understood the need to defend against terrorism, Israel's 'recent actions aren't helpful'. Elsewhere, stronger words were directed against Israeli policies. The EU condemned Israel's excessive use of force, and warned that there was 'no military solution to the conflict'. The UN Secretary-General, Kofi Annan, was unusually forthright in attributing responsibility for the deepening of the conflict. He stated that the indiscriminate killing of civilians by Palestinian suicide bombings was 'morally repugnant' and politically counter-productive. He asserted that Israel had 'the right to live in peace and security within internationally recognized borders, but called on Israel to end 'illegal occupation'. 'More urgently,' he continued, Israel 'must stop the bombing of civilian areas, the assassinations, the unnecessary use of lethal force, the house demolitions, and the daily humiliations of ordinary Palestinians. Such actions gravely erode Israel's standing in the international community, and further fuel the fires of hatred, despair and extremism among Palestinians.' On 12 March 2002 the UN Security Council adopted Resolution 1397 (See Documents on Palestine, p. 437). This was the first UN Resolution to affirm the 'vision' of a Palestinian state. It was also noteworthy for being the first resolution on the Middle East to be sponsored by the USA for 25 years. Syria abstained in the vote. The Arab grouping at the UN had attempted to formulate a resolution calling for protection under the Fourth Geneva Convention (pertaining to protection for civilians in time of war) for the Palestinians of the Occupied Territories. This would have been unacceptable to the USA. However, rather than being seen to exercise yet another veto in Israel's favour at a time when the USA was canvassing Arab support for its policies against Iraq, the US Ambassador drafted a compromise which would be adopted as Resolution 1397. The resolution also welcomed the recent Saudi peace initiative, demanded 'immediate cessation of all acts of violence', and called on Israel and the Palestinians to co-operate in implementing the Tenet and Mitchell proposals with a view to resuming negotiations on a political settlement. Although the mention of a Palestinian state was welcomed by the PA and the Arab world, the enshrining of the security-based Tenet and Mitchell proposals in a UN plan of action was viewed by some Palestinian analysts as unwelcome.

THE BEIRUT DECLARATION

Sharon ordered a pull-back of his forces from Palestinian population centres on the eve of Zinni's arrival on 15 March 2002. However, IDF tanks remained on the outskirts of Ramallah and other 'Area A' territories, while the IDF Chief of Staff, Shaul Mofaz, warned that he was prepared to call up reservists and occupy all PA territories if required to do so. Meanwhile, US Vice-President Cheney's tour of Arab states failed to elicit support for military action against Iraq. The USA's key allies in the region, Egypt, Jordan and Saudi Arabia, all voiced strong opposition to a US strike on Iraq. King Abdullah of Jordan asserted that such a development would represent 'a catastrophe for Iraq and the region in general', while Saudi Arabia's Minister of Foreign Affairs stated that the Kingdom would not sanction the use of its airbases for an assault. Even Kuwaiti leaders were reported to have informed Cheney that they preferred political dialogue to military action in dealing with the problem of their northern neighbour. Just as disconcerting for the US Vice-President was Arab unanimity in insisting that it was the issue of Palestine, not Iraq, that was the major cause of instability in the region. These priorities were forcibly underlined at the 14th Arab League summit in Beirut on 27–28 March. Responding to Crown Prince Abdullah's keynote speech in which he reiterated the principles of his peace plan, Arab leaders assented to a text calling for Israel's full withdrawal from lands occupied in 1967, and what were termed 'territories still occupied in southern Lebanon', the creation of a Palestinian state in the West Bank and Gaza Strip with East Jerusalem as its capital, and a 'just solution' to the refugee issue, based on the principles of repatriation or compensation in accordance with UN General Assembly Resolution 194 (See Documents on Palestine, p. 331). In return, the Arab world would 'consider the Arab–Israeli conflict at an end and enter into a peace agreement with Israel'. A snub was also delivered to the USA with the public reconciliation of Kuwaiti and Saudi delegation leaders with the Vice-President of the Iraqi Revolutionary Command Council, Izzat Ibrahim. The summit declaration welcomed Iraq's assurances that it would respect the 'independence, sovereignty and security' of the state of Kuwait, and emphasized its rejection of 'threats of aggression against some Arab states, particularly Iraq'. Yasser Arafat did not attend the summit, having failed to secure Israeli guarantees that he would be able to return. Egypt's President Mubarak and Jordan's King Abdullah also stayed away, and were represented in Beirut by their respective prime ministers. Solidarity with the PA leader was cited as the official reason for their absence; however, most commentators explained their decision not to attend the summit as a response to concerns that their continued diplomatic links with Sharon's Israel would come under an unwelcome spotlight.

'OPERATION DEFENSIVE SHIELD'

Undoubtedly mindful of the impending summit in Beirut, militant Islamist and nationalist organizations sought to heighten tension in the region with a series of deadly suicide attacks against Israelis, designed in the words of one Fatah leader 'to destroy Sharon' and 'create mayhem from Cairo to the Galilee'. On 20 March 2002 seven Israelis, including four soldiers, were killed by a suicide bomber acting for Islamic Jihad. Over the next week attacks in Jerusalem, Tel-Aviv and

Haifa resulted in 16 civilian fatalities and many scores of injuries. Responsibility was claimed by Hamas and the al-Aqsa Martyrs Brigades, and the frequency of the attacks deepened the sense of panic and outrage among the Israeli population. On 27 March a Hamas bomber blew himself up in a restaurant in Netanya, causing the deaths of 29 mainly elderly Israelis gathered for a Passover celebration and injuring more than 100 others. This was the deadliest Palestinian attack of the 18 months of the *intifada*, and was destined to elicit a formidable response. At a crisis meeting of the Cabinet following the bombing Sharon authorized a major assault on PA-controlled areas of the West Bank. In the early morning of 29 March tanks and troops entered Ramallah and forced their way through the perimeter walls of Arafat's compound. With the exception of a few rooms in which the PA leader was allowed refuge with assorted advisers, security personnel and journalists, the compound was soon under tight Israeli control. After several hours of street fighting, and at a cost of some 30 Palestinian lives, the rest of the city was also placed under a tight curfew while Israeli troops carried out searches and arrested more than 700 people. Sharon subsequently appeared on Israeli television to announce that the country was at war and that the IDF were embarking on 'Operation Defensive Shield', a rolling campaign designed to 'vanquish the Palestinian terror infrastructure'. The PLO leader was declared an enemy who was to be 'isolated'—an apparent climbdown for the Israeli leader, who had only been deterred from his preferred option of arresting and expelling Arafat after stern warnings from the US Administration. In subsequent days, and with overwhelming domestic support, the IDF overran Qalqilya, Tulkarm and Bethlehem, causing widespread destruction and loss of life. More than 100 Palestinian police and militiamen sought refuge with clerics and other non-combatants inside Bethlehem's Church of the Nativity. With the central areas of the West Bank reconquered, Israel turned its attention to the militant strongholds of Nablus and Jenin. After four days of stiff resistance to combined air and ground assaults, the militias of Nablus and its refugee camps surrendered to the IDF; 74 people, fighters and civilians alike, were killed in the offensive. Here, as in other parts of the West Bank, Palestinians reported that the IDF systematically destroyed educational, media and research facilities belonging to the PA and independent Palestinian organizations. However, it was in the northern town of Jenin and its adjacent refugee camp where the IDF met the most sustained and fierce resistance. It took a week of house-to-house fighting and the loss of 28 of its soldiers before Israel's security forces were able to exert control over the refugee camp adjoining the town. Much of the central area of the Jenin camp was destroyed in the Israeli assault. Palestinian sources claimed a massacre had taken place, allegations that were strenuously denied by Israel, which continued to deny independent access to the area.

Having endorsed what they considered to be a comprehensive and historic peace offer to Israel at the Beirut summit, Arab states responded angrily to Israel's offensive on the West Bank. Demonstrations took place across the Arab world. In Cairo and Alexandria at least one person was killed and many were injured as students clashed with riot police deployed to protect US multinational companies. Responding to the mood of popular outrage, President Mubarak announced that Egypt would suspend all ties with Israel except those links that might 'help the Palestinian cause'. This was deemed insufficient by opposition groups, which demanded that Cairo sever its peace treaty with Israel and supply weapons to the Palestinians. Similar calls were made in Jordan, where protesters took to the streets to demand a firm Arab response to the unfolding crisis on the West Bank. Jordan's Minister of Foreign Affairs, Marwan al-Muasher, summoned the Israeli Ambassador to Jordan on 31 March 2002 and warned that action would be taken against Israel unless the IDF withdrew from the Palestinian areas it had recently occupied and the siege on Arafat's compound was lifted. Jordanian officials informed reporters that measures under consideration included the severing of diplomatic ties and the closure of Israel's embassy in Amman and the Jordanian embassy in Tel-Aviv. Lebanon also witnessed joint Palestinian-Lebanese demonstrations organized by student, Islamist and professional groups. Significantly, Lebanon's Christian clerics and politicians, not normally known for their pro-Palestinian sentiments, also added their voices to the chorus of condemnation of Israeli aggression. On 7 April an officially sanctioned rally in support of the Palestinians in the Moroccan capital, Rabat, drew a crowd of some 500,000–800,000. Images conveyed via Arab satellite television stations of the destruction and bloodshed in the West Bank were regarded as having contributed to the scale and size of the anti-Israeli and anti-US protests. On Israel's northern border Hezbollah stepped up its attacks on the disputed Shebaa Farms enclave in an attempt to divert Israeli military attention from the Palestinian territories.

That the Bush Administration accorded a low-key reception to adoption by the Beirut summit of Crown Prince Abdullah's initiative was interpreted as reflecting anger at the rebuff delivered to Vice-President Cheney on his recent Middle East tour and the subsequent Arab reconciliation with Iraq in Beirut. Initial reaction to Israel's 'Operation Defensive Shield' was also muted, and contrasted sharply to the animated responses in European as well as Arab capitals. The carnage inflicted by Palestinian suicide bombers inside Israeli cities had a powerful resonance with a US public well versed in its leadership's policy and rhetoric on terrorism. The early comments from US officials appeared to confirm that the Israeli Prime Minister had received a degree of advance support from the USA for its assault on the West Bank. Speaking on consecutive days at the beginning of the attack, both Secretary of State Powell and President Bush placed the responsibility for initiating and also for easing the crisis on the beleaguered Arafat and his willingness to act against those Palestinians responsible for orchestrating the violence against Israelis. Israel's role, in Bush's assessment, was to 'keep in mind there must be an avenue towards a peaceful settlement'. On 30 March 2002 the USA voted in favour of UN Security Council Resolution 1402, which expressed grave concern at the further deterioration of the situation, including the suicide bombings in Israel and the military attack against the headquarters of the PA President, and called *inter alia* for both Israel and the Palestinians to move immediately towards a 'meaningful' cease-fire and for Israel to withdraw troops from Ramallah and other Palestinian cities. There was some surprise that the USA was prepared to vote for a resolution nominally critical of Israel. However, analysts pointed out that the absence of detail on a timetable or enforcement rendered the resolution less problematic for Israel. Israel's ambassador to the UN, Yehuda Lancry, subsequently told Israel Army Radio that 'US officials' concurred with the Israeli view that his country did not have to act immediately.

With anti-US sentiment rising in the Arab world as the human and material costs of Israel's offensive spiralled, the Bush Administration signalled a volte-face in its support for Sharon's West Bank campaign. Addressing world media from the White House on 4 April 2002, the US President urged Israeli forces to withdraw from Palestinian areas 'without delay'. Although once again castigating Yasser Arafat for lack of leadership and for betraying 'the hopes of his people', he also called for Israeli settlement activity to cease and for an end to the Israeli occupation in accordance with UN Resolutions 242 and 338. Recognizing, moreover, EU and Arab appeals for the USA to 're-engage' with the Middle East conflict, Bush announced that he would be dispatching the US Secretary of State to the region with a brief to secure a cease-fire and restart the political process. His speech won immediate support from the EU, and deflected calls from some member states for an independent European initiative on the Arab–Israeli conflict—including the imposition of trade sanctions against Israel. The French Minister of Foreign Affairs, Hubert Védrine, considered to be a critic of the USA's Middle East policy, confirmed European backing for the Powell's peace mission as 'the best way of moving forward, the most intelligent thing we can do'. The Israeli Government appeared unconcerned by the implicit ultimatum from Washington, and responded to Bush's speech by reiterating that it would not halt its offensive on the West Bank until the objectives of 'Operation Defensive Shield' had been achieved. Although reportedly angry at Sharon's obduracy, the US President avoided a confrontation. It was announced that Powell's departure from the USA would not take place for several days; nor would he fly direct to the conflict zone, with stop-over visits to Morocco, Egypt, Jordan and Spain before arriving in Israel and the West Bank. The delay to the Powell mission and its circuitous itinerary were interpreted in the Arab world as further evidence of US collusion with Israel's military goals on the West Bank. In talks with Arab leaders in Morocco, Egypt and Jordan, the US Secretary of State was urged to apply pressure to Israel to end its offensive against the Palestinians and allow the free movement of the PA President. It was also reported that Jordan's King Abdullah emphasized to Powell that the stability of pro-Western Arab governments was threatened by the violence in the Occupied Territories.

By the time Powell arrived in Israel on 11 April 2002 the IDF had withdrawn from several areas of the West Bank, although troops continued to besiege Arafat's Ramallah compound and the Church of the Nativity in Bethlehem. Smaller-scale operations against other towns and villages in the West Bank continued, and Israeli forces remained in tight control of Jenin. Shortly before Powell's visit the rationale for 'Operation Defensive Shield' was violently reinforced with a suicide attack on a bus near Haifa in which eight people died. Several people were killed in a further bombing in Jerusalem on 12 April, perpetrated within the hearing of the visiting US Secretary of State. Powell's scheduled meeting with the PA leader was delayed in response to the latter attack, but after Arafat issued an explicit condemnation of the suicide bombings the US mission travelled on to Arafat's bunker in Ramallah. The talks were said to be cordial, but there was little common ground. Arafat refused to countenance a cease-fire as long as Israeli forces remained in occupation of 'Area A' Palestinian territories. In response to Powell's insistence that the PA suppress Palestinian militants, the PA's chief negotiator, Saeb Erakat, informed his guest that 'The Palestinian Authority has ceased to exist'. In his four-hour meeting with the Israeli Prime Minister, Powell also failed to dissuade Sharon from his insistence that a cessation of military activity would only be secured through the destruction of the Palestinian militias and the PA's handing over of terrorist suspects, including those responsible for the assassination of Rehavam Ze'evi. After the failure of the Powell-Arafat talks on 14 April, Sharon proposed the convening of an international peace conference to be chaired by the USA and to include Palestinians and front-line Arab states, but not Yasser Arafat. In order for the conference to go ahead, there would need to be a cessation of violence in Israel and the Occupied Territories. PA officials dismissed these ideas as unacceptable. On 15 April Israeli forces arrested the West Bank's Fatah leader, Marwan Barghouthi, a veteran of the resistance to Israeli occupation frequently mentioned as a likely successor to Yasser Arafat.

After concentrating its military operation in the central and northern areas of the West Bank, in mid-April 2002 Israeli troops turned their attentions to the south, occupying the towns of Dura, Dhahiriya, Yatta and Sammu. The pattern of these operations mirrored those that had taken place in other areas of the West Bank, with large numbers of Palestinian casualties reported as well as mass arrests and the deliberate targeting of the infrastructural symbols of self-rule. On 29 April the PA-controlled areas of Hebron witnessed an invasion by 100 tanks and armoured personnel carriers. Nine Palestinians were reported to have been killed in the initial attack, and some 20 people on Israel's 'wanted' list were arrested. However, the details of the IDF's incursions into Palestinian population centres in the south of the West Bank were overshadowed by the continued controversy surrounding Israel's 13-day assault on the Jenin refugee camp. On 16 April the first independent observers entered the camp to witness the massive scale of the destruction. Claim and counter-claim by Palestinians and Israel over allegations of a massacre in Jenin dominated subsequent news reports. Preliminary investigations by outside agencies, including the International Committee of the Red Cross and the human rights organization Amnesty International, did not support Palestinian claims of a massacre, but did suggest that serious violations of human rights had been committed by Israeli forces. On 19 April the UN Security Council adopted Resolution 1405, which expressed concern at the 'dire humanitarian situation of the Palestinian population, in particular reports from the Jenin refugee camp of an unknown number of deaths and destruction', and welcomed an initiative by the Secretary-General for a fact-finding team to be sent to Jenin to report on recent events in the camp. Although Israel initially agreed to co-operate with an independent mission, having conceived the idea with the USA in the first place, the Sharon Government swiftly adopted a less accommodating stance. There were a number of objections. First, Sharon considered that the proposed team, to be led by former Finnish President Martti Ahtisaari, had too much of a 'humanitarian' composition and too little military expertise objectively to evaluate the Jenin events. Second, there was strong Israeli opposition to the idea that the UN team would be allowed to make observations on what happened in Jenin in addition to reporting the strict facts. Finally, Israel was opposed to allowing team members free access to serving military personnel, and demanded a prior guarantee of immunity from prosecution by a third party. After a week of fitful negotiations and last minute delays to the dispatch of the team, the Israeli Government announced on 28 April that it would not co-operate with the mission and would deny its members entry. Relaying this decision to the media, Minister of Communications Reuven Rivlin explained, 'This awful United Nations committee is out to get us and is likely to smear Israel and to force us to do things which Israel is not prepared even to hear about, such as interrogating soldiers and officers who took part in the fighting. No country in the world would agree to such a thing'. Under US pressure, the Security Council chose not to try to send the team to Jenin without the co-operation of Israel. Instead, it was decided that the fact-finding mission on the Jenin events would be downgraded to a report compiled by UN staff commissioned by the Secretary-General.

The Bush Administration apparently lent its support to Israel's blocking of the UN investigation into Jenin in return for an Israeli promise of flexibility in resolving Yasser Arafat's continued incarceration in Ramallah and an end to the siege of the Church of the Nativity in Bethlehem. At the end of April 2002 Sharon agreed to lift the siege of the PA leader in return for guarantees that Palestinians who were sheltering in the compound and who had been convicted under PA jurisdiction for the assassination of Rehavam Ze'evi would serve their gaol terms under the supervision of US and British prison warders. A compromise deal between the PA and the Israeli Government on the fate of the wanted Palestinians in the Church of the Nativity was also brokered by US and European diplomats. The siege finally came to an end on 10 May with the transfer of 26 of the gunmen to the Gaza Strip and the transportation to Cyprus, under international guard, of the 13 higher-level cadres described by Israel as 'senior terrorists'. The latter were to be dispersed to permanent exile in various EU member states (one remained in Cyprus), while it was unclear whether trial by a Palestinian court of those deported to the Gaza Strip, as envisaged under the agreement, would actually take place.

PRESSURE FOR REFORM OF THE PA

For most of the five weeks during which he was confined to a tiny enclave within his Ramallah headquarters, Yasser Arafat enjoyed his highest popularity ratings among the Palestinians of the West Bank and Gaza for many years. However, the tumultuous applause that he received when he emerged onto the streets of Ramallah at the beginning of May 2002 failed to conceal the dissatisfaction among political and civic leaders with the PA's leadership in the period leading up to Israel's rolling reoccupation of the self-rule areas. At an angry meeting of the Palestinian leadership on 3 May Fatah representatives lambasted the PA for its weakness in the face of the Israeli incursions and demanded elections to determine a new cabinet. Arafat walked out of the meeting, only to return to announce the appointment of committees to oversee political reform and national reconstruction. These were to be headed by two of Arafat's closest associates, Muhammad Rashid and Nabil Shaath. Both men had been tainted by charges of corruption, and neither had broad political support. Arafat's popularity declined further with the disclosure of the deal to end the siege of the Church of the Nativity. The PA President's approval of a formula that resulted in the exile of Palestinian militants was seen as breaching a central tenet of Palestinian nationalism and was widely condemned. A scheduled visit by Arafat to view the destruction in Jenin in mid-May was cancelled by his officials, fearing that Arafat would face too hostile a reception. Calls for the reform of the PA were also being made in the USA and in Israel. Speaking on 8 May after meeting with the visiting Israeli Prime Minister, George W. Bush echoed his guest's assertions that progress towards meaningful dialogue between Israel and the Palestinians could only be made if the PA's political, security and financial institutions were restructured to make them more democratic and accountable. Signalling that the attitude of his Administration had moved yet further towards Sharon's characterization of Arafat as an enemy, rather than an ally, in the search for peace, Bush declared, 'What is an accurate reflection of my opinion is that Mr Arafat has let the Palestinian people down. He hasn't led. And as a result, the Palestinian people suffer'. Sharon was more strident, warning in an address to the Knesset on 14 May that there could be no peace with a 'corrupt, terror regime' and that 'everything must be overhauled' within the PA before political negotiations could resume. Palestinians regarded US and Israeli championing of democratization of the PA with heavy cynicism. Supporters of internal reform were quick to point out that successive US and Israeli governments had ignored the autocratic nature of Arafat's rule and the PA's human rights abuses as long as violence against Israelis was being contained. Nevertheless, caught between internal and external pressures for structural change within the PA, Arafat reluctantly proceeded with a reform programme. He approved the adoption of legislation intended to separate judicial and executive functions in the PA, and it was announced that municipal elections would be held by the end of 2002. It was also widely reported that the 13 different branches of the PA's security and police forces were to be streamlined and placed under the control of the Ministry of the Interior.

Meanwhile, on 7 May 2002 15 Israelis were killed in a Hamas suicide bombing in the town of Rishon Le Zion. The blast exposed the limitations of 'Operation Defensive Shield' and Sharon's exclusively security-based response to the Palestinian *intifada*. Cutting short his visit to Washington, DC, and brushing aside Yasser Arafat's strong denunciation of the attack, Sharon convened an emergency cabinet meeting at Tel-Aviv's airport. The session was followed by an emergency call-up of IDF reservists and a movement of Israeli armour southwards. The Gaza Strip had thus far been spared the large-scale incursions visited on Palestinian population centres of the West Bank, but now military assault appeared to have been signposted. That it failed to materialize was explained by Israel's Minister of Defence as a response to 'too much public discussion of the scheduled operation, including details of targets'. However, it was felt to be more likely that the expected invasion had been deferred by the realization that any assault on the densely populated cities and camps of Gaza would result in unacceptably high casualties among the IDF and Palestinian civilians and would have uncertain political and military outcomes. Meanwhile, and despite consistently high levels of domestic support for his premiership, Sharon suffered a political defeat at the hands of his party rival, ex-Prime Minister Binyamin Netanyahu, at Likud's Central Committee Meeting. In a debate charged with personal acrimony the former Likud leader secured majority backing on a vote committing the party to oppose the creation of a Palestinian state, even the fragmented and vague entity envisaged by Sharon. The Israeli Prime Minister also had to face the problem of Israel's economic downturn. Foreign investment in Israel had declined in response to the continuing violence, and the transfer of capital out of the country had contributed to the national currency's loss of 20% of its value in the first five months of 2002. Likud's coalition partners in the Shas party were expelled from of the Cabinet in May for opposing government proposals for budget cuts.

Israeli incursions and suicide attacks continued through the late spring of 2002. Qalqilya, Bethlehem, Tulkarm and Jenin were all reoccupied by Israeli forces in the last week of May 2002. The assaults had been preceded by a spate of suicide bombings which had killed 10 Israeli civilians. On 5 June an Islamic Jihad suicide bomber targeted a bus at the Megiddo junction in northern Israel, killing 17 Israelis—14 of them soldiers. The following day a Hamas attack on a West Bank settlement left three settlers dead. Israel responded by sending tanks once again onto the streets of Ramallah, where they carried out scores of arrests while the town's 120,000 inhabitants were confined to their houses under a tight curfew. This latest upsurge in the violence came amid renewed US diplomatic efforts to manage the crisis. On 4 June CIA Director George Tenet met with the Palestinian leader in Ramallah in an attempt to adopt US suggestions for the overhaul of Palestinian security forces. Tenet urged Arafat to amalgamate his security forces into one body, reporting to a national security council to be advised by US, European and Egyptian officials. The proposals were rejected by the PA President. On 8–9 June Egypt's President Mubarak attended talks with the US President at Camp David. At their post-summit media briefing Bush made it clear that although he shared the vision of a Palestinian state, internal reform of the PA and the fight against Palestinian 'terror' remained his Administration's principal focus. Mubarak's assertion that a timetable was needed for the creation of a Palestinian state went unacknowledged by his US host. Questioned directly on the possibility of Israel's expelling the Palestinian leader, Bush did not express US opposition to Arafat's removal but declared that he did not think Arafat was 'the issue'. After discussions with Israel's Prime Minister on 10 June, the US President echoed Sharon's assessment that there was no obvious partner for peace on the Palestinian side. Referring to the PA President's recent unveiling of a new Cabinet (which saw most ministries allocated to Fatah members or independents loyal to Arafat) Bush declared, 'No one has confidence in the emerging Palestinian government'.

'OPERATION DETERMINED PATH'

The limitations of Israel's spring offensive in the West Bank to deliver security to its citizens was once again underlined in mid-June 2002 with two devastating suicide attacks in Jerusalem. On 18 June at least 19 people were killed in a bus bombing in Gilo; seven were killed the following day at a bus stop in another Jewish area of East Jerusalem. The attacks were claimed by Hamas and Fatah. On 20 June a gunman from the PFLP infiltrated a settlement near Nablus and shot dead five Israelis. These were provocations too far for the Israeli leader. After another crisis meeting of his Cabinet it was announced that the IDF was initiating 'Operation Determined Path', the indefinite reoccupation of any PA territory Israel deemed necessary to meet its security needs. Within days Israeli troops and armour had taken control of most of the major towns and cities of the West Bank without encountering significant Palestinian resistance. Curfews were imposed on the newly occupied population centres, and the Ministry of Defence declared that the families of suicide bombers would be deported from the West Bank to the Gaza Strip. In a separate but related development, the

Government confirmed that it had completed the first stage in the construction of a 'security wall' that was intended to follow the entire length of the West Bank and prevent would-be suicide bombers from penetrating Israeli cities.

Palestinian bombings prompted George W. Bush to delay a policy statement on the Middle East. The US Administration under his presidency had been repeatedly criticized for lack of coherence in its policy towards the Arab–Israeli conflict, and it was hoped that his speech would signal renewed US commitment to pursuit of a regional peace settlement. However, the vision elucidated outside the White House on 24 June 2002 was judged by most commentators to be too partisan to offer a workable way forward. Bush stated that he would offer US support for a 'provisional' Palestinian state once 'Palestinians embrace democracy, confront corruption and firmly reject terror'. It was made clear that this could not be achieved under Arafat's stewardship. Bush opined, 'I call on the Palestinian people to elect new leaders, leaders not compromised by terror'. Only after the Palestinians had effected progress on security issues would Israel be required to stop its settlement activity and begin working towards a 'final status' agreement. At the end of this process Israel's occupation would be 'ended through a settlement negotiated between the parties, based on UN Resolutions 242 and 338, with Israeli withdrawal to secure and recognized borders'. The address was not well received in the Arab world. There was disappointment that Bush had not referred to the Arab initiative elaborated in Beirut in March, and that the Palestinians had not been given a timetable for independence, but rather the prospect of open-ended negotiations on the establishment of an entity with powers and borders that were undefined. That these negotiations would only commence once the Palestinians had ended resistance and installed a leadership acceptable to the USA was seen as particularly discouraging. By contrast, there was little in the Bush speech to concern Sharon, and much to cause satisfaction. Two key demands of the Israeli premier—for Palestinian resistance to end before negotiations could begin and for Yasser Arafat's removal as a political player—had now been adopted as US policy. Reference to Israeli withdrawal to 'secure borders', rather than to the lines of 4 June 1967, was also regarded as a concession to Sharon's interpretation of Resolution 242 as calling for a withdrawal within, but not from, the territories occupied in the June war. Indeed, such was the perceived bias in the Bush speech that Israeli commentators suggested that it could easily have been penned by Sharon himself. Surprisingly, the Palestinian leader responded positively to Bush's statement, choosing to praise the vision of a Palestinian state and to interpret the call for a new leadership as an endorsement of the reform process currently under way within the PA—and not as a demand for him to step down. Arafat's welcome caught his Arab neighbours off guard. While Bush's stance was being vilified in the press and among the Arab people, Jordan's King Abdullah praised its positive elements and stated that it represented 'the beginning of the end of the conflict between Arabs and Israelis'. In interviews with Arab newspapers on 29 June the Jordanian monarch was, however, more critical, rejecting the idea of a 'provisional' state and charging that it was up to the Palestinian people 'to determine the fate of Yasser Arafat'. President Mubarak of Egypt made similar assessments in his reaction to the Washington statement. Privately, EU leaders were reported to be dismayed by Bush's proposals. Gathered at the G-8 summit in Kananaskis, Canada, at the end of June, French President Jacques Chirac and

British Prime Minister Tony Blair made public their differences with the Bush Administration. Although in broad agreement on the need for reform of the PA, both distanced themselves from the US demand for 'regime change'. 'We have a simple position: it is for the Palestinians to designate their representatives,' stated Chirac, continuing, 'We cannot ask them to vote and then tell them who to elect'. EU officials insisted that the Union would remain in close contact with Arafat.

Meanwhile, there was a heightening of tension along Israel's northern border. On several occasions in mid-June 2002 Hezbollah militants fired anti-aircraft batteries at Israeli military aircraft overflying the country. Several shells fell in the waters of Lake Tiberias, leading a senior IDF commander to comment that an escalation in the simmering conflict with Hezbollah fighters and their Syrian sponsors was unavoidable. Israeli intelligence reports claimed, moreover, that Hezbollah had taken delivery of long-range *Fajr* rockets which it had stockpiled in caves in southern Lebanon. A US State Department official delivered warnings to Beirut, Damascus and Tehran in response to Israel's allegations regarding the new weaponry and further claims that al-Qa'ida operatives were based in the country's Palestinian refugee camps. These allegations were categorically denied by the Lebanese Minister of Foreign Affairs in a meeting with representatives of the five permanent members of the UN Security Council, and the US delegate declared himself satisfied with the assurances. Syria, for its part, continued to reject US demands that it should condemn Palestinian attacks on Israeli civilians and suppress Hezbollah and Palestinian military organizations operating from Syria.

Arafat's domestic position was generally regarded as having been strengthened by the US Administration's apparent attempts to sideline him. Earlier speculation that the PA leader would face a serious challenge in forthcoming elections was now ended with all potential candidates, including those personalities favoured by the USA, declaring that they would not be seen to be doing the Bush Administration's bidding by standing against the PLO veteran. Arafat continued the tentative reform process within his administration, dismissing his head of security in the West Bank and Gaza's unpopular police chief. In mid-July 2002 Israeli and Palestinian ministers held their first meetings in three months to discuss ways of easing the humanitarian crisis caused by the curfews and travel bans on the West Bank. Shimon Peres agreed to increase access to besieged PA areas, to facilitate the withdrawal of troops from some of the towns currently under occupation, and also to release a proportion of the US $600m. in tax revenues owed to the PA. Saudi Arabia, Jordan, Egypt and the EU were reported to be mediating discussions between the different Palestinian factions, with the aim of reaching agreement on a cease-fire within Israel and the Occupied Territories. There were, however, few signs of Hamas, Islamic Jihad or the al-Aqsa Martyrs Brigades eschewing military attacks in the West Bank and Gaza: a Hamas gunman killed 10 Israelis in an ambush on a settler bus outside Nablus on 16 July, although Hamas leaders did state that they would call a halt to attacks on civilians inside Israel in return for the IDF's withdrawal from Palestinian cities, the release of prisoners and an end to the assassination policy. Doubts that the Israeli Prime Minister would respond to such an offer were confirmed in the early hours of 23 July, when an F-16 fighter of the Israeli air force fired a rocket into an apartment block in Gaza City, reducing it to rubble.

The intended target of the attack, Hamas military leader Salah Shihada, was killed outright, as were 14 other Palestinians, nine of them children. Sharon lauded as a 'great success' an operation that drew international condemnation. UN Secretary-General Kofi Annan stated that Israel 'has the legal and moral responsibility to take all measures to avoid the loss of civilian life; it clearly failed to do so in using a missile against an apartment building'. Javier Solana, the EU's High Representative for foreign and security policy, implicitly questioned Israeli motivation for carrying out such a provocative action at a time 'when both Israelis and Palestinians were working very seriously to curb violence'. For the White House, spokesman Ari Fleischer commented that the US President regretted the loss of innocent lives and believed that 'this heavy-handed action does not contribute to peace'. Arab reaction was far less circumspect. Both Yasser Arafat and Egypt's Minister of Foreign Affairs, Ahmad Maher, termed the Gaza killings a 'war crime'. Tens of thousands blocked the streets of Gaza for the funeral of the victims of the attack. Predictably, Hamas vowed to exact a terrible revenge, with a spokesman decaring that 'Hamas will not accept any conditions for halting resistance operations to avenge the Palestinian martyrs'. In the days after the Shihada assassination several settlers were killed in the West Bank, despite the massive IDF presence in the territory and a strict regime of curfews and closures. On 31 July a bomb was detonated in a cafeteria of the Hebrew University in Jerusalem, killing at least seven students—five of them US citizens. The PA leader added his voice to those condemning the bombing, but stated that the Israeli Prime Minister bore partial responsibility because of Israel's policy of 'destruction, killing and collective punishment'. On 4 August nine people were killed in a Hamas suicide bombing on a bus in northern Israel. Three people were killed in a gun battle outside the Old City of Jerusalem on the same day and two settlers were shot dead in an ambush on their car in the West Bank. Israel responded with a major incursion into the Old City of Nablus and the declaration of a total ban on Palestinians travelling in the northern sector of the West Bank. The IDF also continued its policy of destroying the homes of suicide bombers, and Israel's Minister of Defence confirmed that he would pursue the policy of deporting to Gaza relatives of Palestinians held responsible for attacks on Israelis. This was despite a legal challenge in the Israeli courts, as well as warnings from the EU and the USA that such measures were both illegal and counter-productive.

On 1 August 2002 the UN released its long awaited report into Israel's spring invasion of the West Bank, and in particular events in the Jenin camp. The report concluded that there was no evidence to support Palestinian claims of a massacre. It stated that 52 Palestinians had died during the days of the Israeli assault, the same number that had been reported by Israeli officials. In the period 1 March–7 May a recorded 497 Palestinians had been killed during Israeli incursions into the West Bank, over 1,400 had been wounded and more than 17,000 made homeless. More than 100 Israelis had died in Palestinian attacks within Israel during the same period. Israeli forces were criticized for the widespread destruction of Palestinian property, and both they and Palestinian militias were considered to have disregarded the safety of civilians. Although it had refused to co-operate with the reporting team and denied access to Jenin, the Israeli Government welcomed the findings as exposing Palestinian 'fabrication' and 'false propaganda'. The UN Secretary-General stated that he believed the report to be a 'fair representation of a complex situation', but added that Palestinians were still suffering severe 'humanitarian consequences' as a result of Israeli policies in the West Bank and Gaza.

In the second week of August 2002 the political leadership of the different Palestinian factions met once again in Gaza to try to arrive at a common position on the tactical and strategic direction of the *intifada*. Top of the agenda were proposals for a united leadership and an agreement to cease attacks on civilian targets inside Israel. Although initial reports suggested that the three main groupings, Fatah, Hamas and Islamic Jihad, had resolved their differences, final agreement proved elusive. Hamas's military cadres joined forces with leaders outside the Occupied Territories in declaring opposition to any dilution of their operational autonomy. Moreover, after the IDF's killing of a senior al-Aqsa Martyrs Brigade member near Jenin on 12 August, the militia declared that it would continue suicide operations inside Israel proper until Israel ordered an end to the assassination of Palestinian militants and the release of all prisoners. For their part, Israeli leaders also appeared unwilling to create conditions to support cease-fire proposals. On 18 August Israel's Minister of Defence, Binyamin Ben Eliezer, met with his Palestinian counterpart and agreed to ease the military restrictions on Bethlehem and Gaza. However, although the PA opined that the agreement demonstrated the efficacy of non-military approaches to the conflict, the Israeli Prime Minister was quick to dampen expectations of wider under-standings with the Palestinians. Following anger from right-wing coalition partners at talk of a 'Gaza-Bethlehem first' deal, Sharon stressed that 'the removal of a few jeeps from the streets of Bethlehem' was not the precursor to a softening of Israel's grip on Palestinian population centres. Events on the ground supported the Prime Minister's reassurances. The last two weeks of August saw several large-scale sweeps by the IDF through towns and villages on the West Bank and Gaza, leading to the detention of scores more Palestinians and further house demolitions. The raids also contributed to a rising toll in Palestinian casualties. According to the liberal Israeli daily newspaper, *Ha'aretz*, 39 Palestinian civilians were killed from 1 August to 1 September.

The PLC met in Yasser Arafat's Ramallah compound on 9 September 2002. The PA leader used his address to condemn not only Israeli policies in the West Bank and Gaza, but also suicide attacks against civilians in Israel. The latter tactic, he admonished, had given the Sharon Government the pretext to reoccupy Palestinian territories and maintain its stranglehold over civil and economic affairs. For many of the assembled deputies and particularly those representing the younger generation of Fatah leaders, culpability for their current plight also lay with the leadership failures of Arafat and his loyalist coterie in the PA. His opponents had two key demands. Firstly, the dismissal of eight ministers accused of corruption; and second, the appointment of a prime minister. A partial victory was gained by the reformers on the first issue, with Arafat's Cabinet resigning *en masse* rather than subjecting itself to a vote of 'no confidence'. Yet the PLO Chairman refused to commit himself on the creation of the post of prime minister, claiming privately that such a development was part of an Israeli-US plot to remove him as Palestinian leader. His main concession to the voices of reform within the PLC and beyond was a renewed commitment to the principle of holding elections in January 2003. Nevertheless, Arafat added the caveat that elections could not take place while Israeli tanks surrounded Palestinian cities.

Arafat's woes were heightened following two suicide bombings in Tel-Aviv on 18 and 19 September 2002. Claimed by Hamas and Islamic Jihad, respectively, the attacks ended six weeks of relative calm within Israel and left seven people dead and more than 60 injured. The Israeli Cabinet immediately authorized an assault on Arafat's Muqatta compound in Ramallah, code-named 'Operation Matter of Time'. By nightfall on 19 September IDF bulldozers and tanks had forced their way into the centre of the compound, leading the PLO Chairman to seek refuge with 250 others in an inner sanctum. The Israeli Government demanded the surrender of 50 'fugitives' sheltering with Arafat as the price for lifting the siege. This was rejected by the PA leadership. Their resolve was strengthened by the thousands of Palestinians who defied the curfews in West Bank cities to demonstrate support for Arafat, and was further boosted by mounting international criticism of Israel. On 24 September, the day after an Israeli raid on Gaza had claimed the lives of nine Palestinians, the UN Security Council passed Resolution 1435 which demanded that Israel 'immediately cease measures in and around Ramallah' and expedite a swift withdrawal from Palestinian cities. The USA abstained on the resolution. However, in a meeting with a senior Sharon aide in Washington, DC, the US National Security Adviser, Condoleezza Rice, voiced the Bush Administration's firm opposition to the Israeli operation against Arafat's headquarters. Shortly afterwards Israeli troops withdrew from the Muqatta. Arafat emerged to berate the Israelis for perpetrating a 'fraud' on the UN for not withdrawing completely from Ramallah. His domestic standing was undoubtedly enhanced, albeit temporarily, by his latest ordeal at the hands of Sharon. Acknowledging that this was not the time for displays of national disunity, the previously rebellious opposition in the PLC granted Arafat a further month to form a new cabinet. On 2 October the Central Council of Arafat's Fatah movement also agreed not to raise the issue of a Palestinian prime minister.

US pressure on Israel over the Ramallah siege was not predicated upon any residual belief in Arafat's political leadership. Indeed, in recent months the most senior figures in the US Administration had been only marginally less restrained in their expressions of antipathy towards the Palestinian leader than their Israeli counterparts. However, as the USA escalated its war of words against Saddam Hussein's regime in Iraq during the late summer of 2002, it was evident that attempts to win Arab acquiescence in a US-led military campaign in Iraq were being jeopardized by the scenes of destruction from the occupied Palestinian territories and rumours that the Israeli Cabinet had drawn up plans for Arafat's deportation. As it was, animosity towards the USA in the Arab world was running at its highest level for many years. Just as the Bush Administration evoked the imagery of 11 September 2001 as a context for policy towards Iraq, so the Arab street viewed the USA's aggressive denunciations of Iraq's violation of UN resolutions through the prism of perceived US indulgence of Israel's own contraventions of international law. Writing in the *New York Times* in August, the former Secretary of State during the presidency of George Bush, Sr, James Baker, had commented that 'accomplishing regime change in Iraq is made more difficult by the way our policy on the Arab–Israeli dispute is perceived around the world'. This was a view widely accepted to have been shared by Secretary of State Colin Powell. Yet, although the US President wished to avoid an eruption in the Israeli–Palestinian dispute and was anxious to restrain Sharon from committing his Government to some of the more extreme anti-Palestinian measures demanded by cabinet hardliners, he still appeared unprepared to commit his Administration to the resurrection of the peace process. For his part, the Israeli Prime Minister was determined not to be shackled to US policy imperatives. This was despite heading a Government outspoken in favour of deposing Saddam Hussain. The USA had requested and received assurances from Itzhak Shamir, Sharon's Likud predecessor during the Gulf War of 1991, that Israel would not retaliate in the event of an Iraqi attack. The Israeli Prime Minister was adamant that he would give no such undertaking in the event of a new conflict with Iraq. Moreover, while bending to belated US pressure over the IDF's siege of Arafat in Ramallah, there was no sign of an easing of military operations elsewhere. Some 17 Palestinians were killed and up to 80 wounded during an Israeli raid on Khan Yunis in the Gaza Strip on 7 October. The attack, during which a hospital came under fire, earned a mild rebuke from US officials and the advice from a National Security Council spokesman that Israel 'should take every measure to prevent the loss of innocent life in fighting terror'. Prior to a mid-October visit to Washington, DC, by Ariel Sharon, the US Ambassador to Israel, Dan Kurtzer, met with the Israeli Prime Minister to press for an amelioration of the conditions faced by Palestinians in the West Bank and Gaza. According to Israeli press reports, these included the release of US $400m. of illegally withheld tax revenues to the PA, an easing of the restrictions on Palestinian movement within the West Bank and an early withdrawal from some West Bank cities. Sharon responded that there would be a partial with-drawal of the IDF from PA areas of Hebron and that Israel would transfer some of the revenues due to the PA. He added that further remittances would be dependent on assurances that the monies would 'be kept away from terror groups and not used to strengthen Yasser Arafat's regime'. These gestures ensured that the Israeli Prime Minister received a warm welcome when he met with George Bush on 16 October in Washington, DC. Sharon reciprocated effusively, proclaiming that Israel had 'never had such a co-operation in every-thing as we have with the current Administration'.

There was little enthusiasm in European capitals for the US Administration's push for confrontation with Iraq. In the absence of a Middle East peace process, and with Israeli forces firmly entrenched in the Occupied Territories, the European consensus held that Western credibility in the Arab world and the wider campaign against global terrorism would be seriously undermined by precipitate military action in Iraq. However, notwithstanding US pressure on Israel not to escalate regional tensions, the Bush Administration remained at odds with Europe in pointedly resisting the linkage of 'regime change' in Iraq with progress towards an Israeli-Palestinian settlement. The US President's key European ally, British Prime Minister Tony Blair, won overwhelming support at the governing Labour Party's annual conference in October 2002 for his insis-tence that a revived and credible search for a resolution of the core Middle East conflict was a necessary corollary of the international community's addressing of the Iraqi regime's alleged weapons programmes. Predictably, Blair's speech was accorded a cool reception in the USA and an even frostier one in Israel. Relations between Israel and the EU continued to deteriorate during late 2002. At a meeting of the Israel-EU Co-operation Council in Luxembourg in October, EU ministers issued a strongly worded statement demanding that Israel bring an 'immediate end to activities that are inconsistent with international humanitarian law and human rights'. Officials also emphasized to Israel's delegation, led by the Minister of Foreign Affairs, Shimon Peres, the urgency of reaching an agreement on the long-standing dispute over Israel's export to Europe of goods produced in Israeli enterprises established in occupied Arab territories. Under EU customs legislation, products originating in Israeli settlements were not entitled to the same special tariffs eligible for goods originating in Israel proper. By not declaring the origin of these exports, the EU estimated that customs duties amounting to approximately €7m. were going unpaid each year. Although Peres pointed out that these products represented only 1% of the value of Israel's total exports to the EU, neither side failed to appreciate the political and diplomatic importance of the dispute. In future, EU officials insisted, goods originating in Israeli settlements would be liable to customs duties. EU ministers also made it clear that they expected full Israeli co-operation with the as yet unpublished 'roadmap' for an Israeli-Palestinian peace, recently drawn up by the Quartet group (comprising the EU, the USA, Russia and the UN). Other Israeli ministers visiting Europe also complained of having decidedly unsympathetic encounters with their hosts; such reports only served to confirm the belief that prejudice and hostility towards Israel was too firmly rooted in European perceptions of the Middle East conflict for the EU to play anything other than a marginal role in determining the course of any future peace process.

On 21 October 2002 militants from Islamic Jihad were able to evade Israel's security cordon around the West Bank and ram a car laden with explosives into an Israeli bus. Fourteen were killed in the attack near Hadera and more than 40 were injured. Most of the dead were soldiers on their way to rejoin their units. A spokesman for Islamic Jihad claimed the bombing as retaliation for Israeli 'massacres' in southern Gaza (eight Palestinian civilians had been killed in Rafah on 17 October in addition to the 17 killed in Khan Yunis on 7 October). The Israeli Government immediately ordered the suspension of the planned redeployment from parts of Hebron. Six days later Israeli forces killed four Palestinian militants in the West Bank, including a senior Islamic Jihad activist from Jenin. On 30 October a gunman affiliated to Arafat's Fatah movement infiltrated a settlement in the north of the West Bank, killing three Israelis (two of them children). The cycle of violence continued a few days later with the killing of seven Palestinians in separate attacks in Gaza and Nablus and the deaths of two Israelis in a further suicide bombing near Tel-Aviv.

The international community's pessimism at this latest round of violence was deepened by political events in Israel. At the end of October 2002 the acting Labour leader, Minister of Defence Binyamin Ben Eliezer, announced that he was withdrawing the Labour Party from the ruling coalition. His decision followed an ultimatum to Prime Minister Sharon to divert US $150m. from the settlement budget to increase benefits for socially disadvantaged groups. Although the sum amounted to less than 0.25% of the total budget, internal political considerations suggested that it was in neither Sharon's nor Ben Eliezer's interest to reach a compromise. Both men were facing leadership contests, with the principal threats coming from their right and left wings, respectively. Adopting the mantle of 'champion of the underprivileged' was regarded as a shrewd political move by Ben Eliezer's supporters, even though Israeli analysts viewed his showdown with the Israeli Prime Minister as an exercise in cynical self-preservation. Similarly, Sharon's support of settler interests was calculated as boosting his standing with nationalist hardliners leaning towards Sharon's old rival, Binyamin Netanyahu. The Likud leader proved unable to put together a viable new coalition and called general elections for early 2003. In the mean time, the post of Minister of Defence was awarded to Shaul Mofaz, the hardline former IDF Chief of Staff. The foreign affairs portfolio was offered to Netanyahu who, after some deliberation, accepted the position.

Meanwhile, the Palestinian leader was having to face rebellious elements within his own legislature. Buoyed by his latest experiences under Israeli siege in Ramallah, and declaring that any challenge to his authority would serve US and Israeli plans to remove his from power, Arafat was able to cajole and bully Fatah deputies in the PLC into approving a Cabinet that was largely the same as the discredited old one. In a further victory for the PLO leader, the Fatah Central Council confirmed that the new post of prime minister would only be created once a Palestinian state had been established. Few outside Arafat's web of patronage welcomed these developments. The continued presence in the Cabinet of personalities routinely tainted with corruption was viewed with distaste, not only by the vast majority of ordinary Palestinians, but also by many in Arafat's own Fatah movement. Few believed that the new administration possessed the qualities to provide leadership at a time of continued political crisis and many blamed outside pressure to sideline Arafat as proving a major obstacle to internal Palestinian reform. With the new draft roadmap calling for the creation of an 'empowered prime minister', it had become easier for Arafat and his supporters to accuse advocates of internal reform of engaging in externally inspired 'plots'. According to some analysts, the survival of Arafat as political leader was increasingly equated with the Palestinian national interest.

The unrest in Israel and the Palestinian territories continued to worsen during November 2002, whenviolent incidents were recorded on an almost daily basis. Islamic Jihad's military chief in the northern West Bank, Iyad Sawalha, was successfully targeted by the IDF in Jenin. A few days later a lone Fatah gunman shot dead five people (three of them children) in a kibbutz near the 1967 border with Israel. The attack was condemned by both the PA and the Fatah leadership. The IDF, nevertheless, stepped up operations in both the West Bank and Gaza, targeting buildings they claimed were being used to manufacture arms and launching attacks against Palestinians accused of belonging to armed factions. At least 10 Palestinians were killed in the raids; according to Palestinian sources, most of the dead were non-combatants and at least three were children. On 15 November the Israeli military suffered one of its worst days of the two-year-old *intifada* when Islamic Jihad gunmen ambushed an army unit close to the Kiryat Arba settlement near Hebron. Nine soldiers and three paramilitary guards were killed in the gun battle which also claimed the lives of three of the attackers. Among the Israeli dead was the IDF's commander in Hebron. The Israeli Government responded to the reverse by demolishing six Palestinian houses in the area where the ambush had taken place and uprooting vineyards and orchards near Kiryat Arba. Scores were also arrested during a tightly imposed curfew on the 150,000 Palestinian inhabitants. Touring the city on 17 November, the Israeli Prime Minister declared that his Government would no longer abide by the 1997 Hebron Protocol and promised that 'the Jewish presence in Hebron' would be 'expanded and strengthened'. The day after his visit it was reported that a new settlement outpost had been established on the site of bulldozed Palestinian fields outside Kiryat Arba. On 21 November a Hamas suicide bomber detonated a bomb on a bus in Jerusalem, killing 11 Israelis and injuring tens more.

On 8 November 2002 the UN Security Council passed Resolution 1441, which afforded the Iraqi regime of Saddam Hussain a final opportunity to comply with its disarmament obligations. Syria, the only Arab state on the Security Council, had been widely expected to abstain from the final vote. Although relations between Syria and Iraq had been acrimonious for many years, their two Governments had achieved a *rapprochement* in 1998. Relations had since been cemented by trade and economic agreements worth some US $4,000m. Syria's self-declared role as guardian of authentic Arab nationalism also made its vote in favour of Resolution 1441 somewhat surprising. Syria explained its positive vote at the UN by claiming that it had received assurances from the USA that the resolution did not provide an automatic pretext for war. However, it was widely acknowledged that the Syrian decision had been brought about by heavy-handed US diplomacy. On the eve of the UN vote, the US Secretary of State, Colin Powell, was alleged to have threatened, in a phone conversation with President Bashar al-Assad, that if Syria did not support 1441, Washington would demand *inter alia* that the offices of militant Palestinian factions in Damascus be shut down and their leaders handed over. Although the al-Assad regime had co-operated with the USA's 'war on terror' by cracking down on individuals suspected of involvement with the al-Qaida network, Syria was vocal in its defence of both the militant Palestinian groups and Lebanese Hezbollah, which it continued to characterize as legitimate resistance movements. Syria withstood calls from the USA to close down Islamic Jihad's offices in Syria following the group's claim of responsibility for the Hebron ambush.

Arab anxiety at the impending war with Iraq was mirrored by barely concealed satisfaction in Israel. The nationalist right was particularly enthused by the growing influence of the 'neo-conservative' agenda in the US Administration's policy-making, and the prospect that 'regime change' in Iraq would be the first stage in realizing the strategic vision of a reshaped political landscape in the Middle East—one that was far less hostile to Israel. The conflict with Iraq also provided an immediate opportunity for increased economic assistance from the USA. At a meeting with Condoleezza Rice on 25 November 2002, Israeli officials gained a sympathetic hearing for their requests for an extra US $4,000m. in military aid and $10,000m. in loan guarantees. Speaking on National Public Radio two days later, US Secretary of State Powell conceded that the aid would offset the costs of the IDF's military operations in the West Bank and Gaza. He also claimed that 'none of this aid will be underwriting settlement activity'. However, as observers pointed out, the dollars granted in aid to the Israeli Government would simply release money to fund settlement activity in the Occupied Territories.

Amram Mitzna, a career soldier and Mayor of Haifa, defeated Ben-Eliezer for the leadership of the Labour Party. Regarded as 'dovish' in his approach to the Palestinian issue, Mitzna campaigned on a platform of total Israeli withdrawal from Gaza and the immediate resumption of political negotiations with the

Palestinians. In the contest for the Likud leadership, Sharon won an expected victory over Binyamin Netanyahu. The voting was marred by an attack by two al-Aqsa Martyrs Brigade gunmen on a Likud party polling station in the town of Beit Shean. Six Israelis were killed in the attack, most of them party members waiting to cast their votes. The PA issued an unusually strong denunciation of the killings. 'These attacks', read their communiqué, 'do not serve the just cause of the Palestinian people but cause us great damage on every level and strengthen the warmongers and settlements of Israel'. The PA also emphasized that the al-Aqsa Brigades were a separate entity to the mainstream Fatah movement. A week prior to the Beit Shean attack, the PLO General Secretary, Mahmud Abbas (Abu Mazen), had delivered his own withering critique of the *intifada*, condemning its slide into militarism and accusing the gunmen of distorting the initial popular character of the uprising. By relying on armed struggle, Abu Mazen opined, the *intifada* had played to Israel's strongest suit and had brought about 'the total destruction of all we have built and all that had been built before that'. He argued that the way forward lay in ending armed actions and exposing Sharon's intransigence through a return to the negotiating table. He also called for the reconstitution of the PA and the initiation of a national dialogue to bring about factional consensus on the future direction of the *intifada*. The new mood had been forged in part by a recognition that the only chance of boosting the electoral fortunes of the Labour Party lay in an end to the violence.

EU governments echoed Abu Mazen's belief in the futility of Palestinian armed attacks. In a statement issued during a summit in Copenhagen, Denmark, in mid-December 2002, the EU singled out suicide bombings as 'causing irreparable damage to the Palestinian cause'. Israeli policies in the Occupied Territories also received a fierce rebuke. Following on from comments by the Danish Minister of Foreign Affairs that settlement activity had made the Palestinian territories look like a 'Swiss cheese', the EU statement warned that the continued expansion of Israeli settlements 'violates international law, inflames an already volatile situation and reinforces the fear of Palestinians that Israel is not genuinely committed to ending the occupation'. EU leaders also continued to push strongly for the formal launch of the roadmap for an Israeli-Palestinian peace. The US Administration showed considerably less enthusiasm for its early adoption, with President Bush informing French President Jacques Chirac on 11 December that the USA 'was not quite ready to adopt' the new peace proposals. US reticence was shared by the Israeli Prime Minister, who insisted that he would not engage with new peace proposals until after the Israeli general election scheduled for 28 January 2003.

The urgency of the revival of the peace process was underlined by the rising toll of death and destruction in the Occupied Territories. According to Palestinian sources, 75 Palestinians were killed by Israeli forces in December 2002 and more than 650 were injured. During the same period eight Israelis died in Palestinian attacks (compared to 44 in November), all of these taking place in the West Bank and Gaza. The scale of the Palestinian casualties and the continued demolition of homes and property in IDF operations strained Egyptian-mediated talks in Cairo between the different Palestinian factions, aimed at forging a common approach to the *intifada* and an agreement on terms for a cease-fire. The scepticism expressed by Egyptian officials over the pro-spects of a breakthrough in the negotiations was reinforced by a double suicide

295

bombing in Tel-Aviv on 5 January 2003. Twenty-three people were killed in the explosions and more that 100 were wounded; many of the dead and injured were reported to be migrant workers. Authorship of the atrocity was claimed by the al-Aqsa Martyrs Brigade, although the subsequent confirmations and denials in militia statements emanating from different cities of the West Bank and Gaza lent weight to speculation that the Brigade had fractured into semi-autonomous groupings. The Tel-Aviv bombing was the deadliest attack of its kind since Hamas' Netanya bombing of March 2002, which had led to the IDF's recon-quest of the West Bank. This time Sharon's response was limited to further aerial assaults on suspected arms factories and to imposing a ban on Palestinian delegates attending a conference on PA reform hosted by the UK Prime Minister in London. The tempered nature of the Israeli reaction was seen largely as a product of Israel's promise not to aggravate the situation in the Middle East while the crisis with Iraq was unfolding. Israel was also mindful not to prejudice final agreement on its request for increased US aid and US \$10,000m. in loan guarantees. The USA had earlier vetoed a Syrian-drafted UN Security Council Resolution condemning Israel's destruction of a World Food Programme ware-house in the Gaza Strip and the killing of a British UN worker in Jenin. In the previous week, Syria had been the sole member of the Council to vote against condemnation of November's suspected al-Qaida attacks on an Israeli hotel and airline in Kenya.

The London Conference on Palestinian Reform was held on 14 January 2003. Palestinians from the Occupied Territories, barred from leaving by Israel, participated through a live video link. The Israeli Prime Minister declared himself opposed to the whole notion of a conference that would afford legitimacy to Arafat's governance of the PA. Aware of the importance of being seen to be proactive in the pursuit of an Israeli-Palestinian peace after being widely criticized for unprincipled subservience to President Bush over the Iraq crisis, the UK Prime Minister, Tony Blair, was not unduly troubled by Sharon's pique. Although all the participants in the conference welcomed an international spotlight on their collaborative efforts to move peace-making forward, it was also understood that its primary function was a public relations exercise. The most noteworthy development was the presentation by Egypt's intelligence chief of a framework document for the realization of a Palestinian cease-fire. This offered an immediate end to military operations inside Israel, in return for a commitment from Israel to end its 'assassination' policy, and the prospect of a cessation of all armed attacks once Israel had withdrawn to its pre-*intifada* positions. More controversially, the document enshrined Yasser Arafat and his PA as 'the sole authority mandated to negotiate with Israel for the purpose of reaching an agreement'. It was reported that the draft had the approval of Arafat's Fatah faction, but it remained to be seen whether the principal Islamist group, Hamas, would accept the limitations on its military arena, and recognize Arafat's sole authority. The Egyptian Government extended invitations to all the Palestinian factions to take part in further talks. However, the chances of cross-factional agreement being achieved in Cairo receded with an IDF incur-sion into the heart of Gaza City on the night of 25 January. Fourteen people were killed, over 60 injured and scores of buildings were destroyed before the tanks and troops withdrew. Against the background of such an assault, militia leaders warned that the calls for revenge attacks were now far louder than those calling for restraint. The destruction visited on Gaza did nothing to dent the electoral fortunes of Israel's Likud party and its leader, Ariel Sharon. At the Israeli elections on 28 January, Likud emerged as a clear victor, winning nearly 30% of the vote and doubling its parliamentary representation to 40 seats. On a far lower-than-average turn-out, right-wing parties fared particularly well, but the anti-clerical centrists of the Shinui party achieved the most spectacular success, winning 15 seats. Labour's representation in the new Knesset fell from 26 to 19 seats, and the liberal left Meretz party's from 10 to 6. Many commentators believed that it was the traditional Labour and left-wing voters who had stayed away from the polls. Sharon's victory was seen as all the more impressive given Israel's failing economy. However, his uncompromising attitude towards Arafat and the PA resonated well with a public that distrusted Palestinian protestations of commitment to reaching a peace settlement. The Likud leader indicated that he would not rush to establish a new coalition, but his preferred option of a renewal of the national unity government appeared unlikely. Following the election results, Labour's Mitzna reiterated his pledge that his party would not enter into a coalition with Likud.

The PA leader extended his congratulations to Sharon on his election victory and offered to resume negotiations immediately. The Israeli Prime Minister's office rejoined that Arafat 'is not and will not be a negotiating partner'. The PLO leader's fortunes dipped even further after heavy lobbying from the Quartet group forced Arafat to backtrack on his earlier opposition to the creation of the prime ministerial post. On 14 February 2003 he gave his assent 'in principle' to the appointment of a Palestinian prime minister. The Quartet also called for the amalgamation of the PA and the PLO into a body that would take responsibility for managing the reform process and for negotiating with Israel. The ongoing talks in Cairo between the Palestinian factions, meanwhile, failed to deliver agreement on the terms for a cease-fire. Hamas leaders declared that the organization would be opposed to any moratorium on attacks on civilians inside Israel unless it had assurances that the IDF would halt the targeting of its military cadres. These were conditions that Israel rejected in both word and deed. Israeli security forces killed seven leading Hamas members in Gaza within a 48-hour period in mid February. This followed a Hamas ambush of an Israeli tank in the Gaza Strip which claimed the lives of four soldiers. On 19 February the IDF made its second large incursion into Gaza, leaving 11 people dead. A further six were killed on 25 February during an incursion into the town of Beit Hanoun straddling the Israeli border. By the end of February 41 Palestinians had been killed in Gaza alone. March began in a similarly bloody fashion. Hamas fighters continued to direct home-made rockets from Gaza into Israel and on 5 March claimed responsibility for the bombing of a bus in Haifa that left 18 Israelis dead and many more injured. Over the following two days Israeli raids on Gaza claimed 17 lives in Gaza, including that of a senior Hamas military commander. Twelve more people were killed in the Strip on 16 and 17 March, including a young US peace activist.

Sharon's attempts to form a ruling coalition had borne fruit by the end of March 2003. He was successful in wooing the 15 Shinui party Knesset members (MKs) into a Government that would also be buttressed by the 13 MKs of the far right Haichud-Haleumi and the National Religious Party. Binyamin Netanyahu accepted the challenging post of Minister of Finance, with the position's previous incumbent, Silvan Shalom, moving to the foreign ministry. Shaul Mofaz retained the defence portfolio. In the estimation of many observers of the Israeli political scene, the new Sharon-led Government was the most right-wing in Israel's history. The possibility that such a Government would accept the 'painful concessions' for peace with the Palestinians alluded to previously by Sharon appeared remote. However, with a US-led military campaign against the Iraqi regime now accepted as inevitable, the new Government would as yet not to have to face the requirements of the much touted but still unpublished blueprint for a future settlement.

Squeezed between internal demands for reform and the Quartet group's insistence that the creation of the post of Palestinian prime minister was the *sine qua non* for the viability of the roadmap, the PLO's Central Council approved the appointment of Arafat nominee, Mahmud Abbas, to the new position. Under the new division of powers ratified by the PLC on 10 March 2003, Arafat would retain control over foreign policy (including negotiations with Israel) and the PLO's so-called 'national security' forces. Abbas would be responsible for internal government and policing in the self-rule areas. As one of the founder members of Fatah, Abbas had been a long-term deputy to Arafat. He lacked an independent power base among Palestinians in the Occupied Territories, but was regarded by the USA and Israel as an acceptable candidate.

The invasion of Iraq by US and British forces in mid-March 2003 and the subsequent collapse of Saddam Hussain's regime shifted the international spotlight onto the Israeli–Palestinian conflict and the long awaited roadmap. The US President had been criticized by the French President for the delays to its launch, and at the summit in the Azores, Portugal, prior to the Iraq war and again in Belfast, Northern Ireland, on 7 April the British Prime Minister lobbied hard for a US commitment to reviving the Middle East peace process. Anxious to demonstrate to the Arab world that the British Government at least was sensitive to their concerns over Western policy in their region, the British Foreign Secretary Jack Straw acknowledged 'double standards' in relation to the implementation of UN resolutions pertaining to Iraq and Israel and the Palestinian territories. He also alluded to the 'profound sense of injustice felt by the Palestinians'. Such comments were irksome to the Sharon Government, which was now anxious to play down expectations of a significant break-through in the search for a regional settlement. Speaking to the Israeli daily newspaper *Ha'aretz* in April, the Israeli Prime Minister stated that he had '14 or 15' reservations on the draft version of the roadmap. He also insisted that, although he foresaw a Palestinian state at some point in the future, this could not come about until Palestinian terrorism had been defeated. Similarly, any Israeli moves towards a 'freeze' on settlement would be conditional upon a prolonged cease-fire by Palestinian groups. In the mean time, Sharon under-lined that there would be no softening of security measures in the West Bank and Gaza. IDF incursions into the Strip continued with the same levels of intensity, creating further casualties among combatants and civilians alike. The Likud leader courted further international controversy by announcing that the West Bank 'security fence' would be diverted to incorporate Jewish settlements deep inside northern areas of the territory. Earlier, in March, he had also signalled that the fence should be extended to the east, effectively creating an internal barrier between the West Bank highlands and the Jordan valley.

Mahmud Abbas's early tenure as Prime Minister proved to be a troubled one. His attempts to entice opposition factions—Hamas, Islamic Jihad and the PFLP—into the new administration were rebuffed on the grounds that new elections were required to legitimize its mandate. His urgings on the importance of reaching a cease-fire were being undermined by Israel's daily military operations, and elicited an equally negative response. The Palestinian Prime Minister also faced a battle of political wills with Yasser Arafat over the composition of the new Cabinet. Abbas' initial ministerial choices reflected his desire to limit the influence of Arafat loyalists within the PA Cabinet, and in particular to deny the critical post of Minister of the Interior to the President's loyal supporter, Hani al-Hassan. Arafat succeeded in getting most of his supporters reinstated, but after coming under direct pressure from Tony Blair and US Secretary of State Colin Powell, he agreed a compromise. Arafat loyalists would hold the majority of the ministries in return for Abbas being confirmed as Minister of the Interior as well as Prime Minister. The newly created position of Minister of State for Security would go to Muhammad Dahlan, the USA's first and only choice. US influence in ensuring that key portfolios were held by personalities deemed sympathetic to the Bush Administration's agenda, namely the disarming of the militias, inevitably led to charges of collaboration and collusion being levelled at Abbas and Dahlan. However, despite their public quarrel over the new Cabinet, there was not perceived to be significant policy disagreement between the PA President and Prime Minister. Both men sought the end of the armed *intifada*. Abbas believed that this should happen unconditionally, while Arafat was convinced that this was an unrealistic prospect without an easing of Israeli military pressure on the West Bank and Gaza. The two men staged a public reconciliation on 23 April 2003.

THE ROADMAP

The much-vaunted roadmap (See Documents on Palestine, p. 437) was formally presented to the Israeli and Palestinian Prime Ministers on 30 April 2003, the day before President Bush declared an end to hostilities in Iraq. Supposedly drafted and revised by the Quartet group over the previous nine months, the main provisions of the new peace plan had already been leaked to the media. They set out three main stages for the achievement of a 'final and comprehensive settlement'. The first phase, initially scheduled to be completed by the end of May, would see 'restructured and reformed' Palestinian security forces ending 'violence, terrorism and incitement' emanating from the PA areas. This would be coupled with political and constitutional reform to prepare the way for statehood and 'free, fair and open elections'. For its part, the Israeli Government would 'withdraw from Palestinian areas occupied from September 28th 2000' and 'freeze all settlement activity, consistent with the Mitchell Report'. Settlement outposts constructed since March 2001, would have to be dismantled. Israel would also be expected to issue an 'unequivocal statement affirming its commitment to the two-state vision of an independent, viable, sovereign, Palestinian state living in peace and security alongside Israel'. During the second phase, from June–December 2003, 'efforts are focused on the option of creating an independent Palestinian state with provisional borders and attributes of sovereignty'. The Palestinian leadership would have to continue to demonstrate its willingness and ability to act 'decisively against terror' and to 'build a practising democracy'. Phase three would see the beginning of Israeli-Palestinian negotiations on permanent status agreements—borders, refugees, Jerusalem and settlements. Negotiations would commence with the convening of an international conference, which would also 'support progress towards a comprehensive Middle East settlement between Israel and Lebanon and Israel and Syria'. This final phase was due to be completed by the end of 2005. Following the release of the roadmap, US Secretary of State Powell visited the Middle East to garner support from regional leaders and to secure Palestinian and Israeli agreement to the plan. Privately, the Palestinian leadership entertained grave reservations over the new peace proposal. Objections centred on the vagueness of the language and the emphasis on conditionality rather than reciprocity. Palestinians feared that the Israeli Government would once again be able to exploit the inherent ambiguities in the text to ensure that negotiations would be subject to obfuscation and delay. In the mean time, Israel would continue to create the 'facts on the ground' which would prejudice final outcomes. Nevertheless, despite these concerns, the Palestinians judged that in the prevailing geopolitical climate they had no option other than to accept the roadmap. On 11 May 2003 in Jericho the Palestinian Prime Minister told Colin Powell that the PA accepted the roadmap 'as it is'. The same day in Jerusalem the Israeli Prime Minister declared that his Government could not accept the roadmap as it currently stood. In a statement issued by the Israeli Ministry of Foreign Affairs, Sharon outlined his Government's position on the roadmap. Paradoxically, the absence of guarantees on conditionality were chief among the Israeli objections. Without the PA disarming and uprooting the Palestinian militias, the Israeli Government would not be prepared to engage with the process, including the demands for a settlement 'freeze'. The ministry statement also confirmed that Israel would not extend recognition of a Palestinian state until Palestinians had renounced their right of return. Sharon was invited to address these reservations with President Bush in Washington, DC.

Powell's tour of the Middle East also involved brief stop-overs in Damascus and Beirut. The Syrian regime had been severely criticized by the US Administration during the war with Iraq for allegedly supplying military equipment to the Iraqi army and for allowing its territory to be used as a staging post for foreign fighters seeking to confront US forces in Iraq. In the latter stages of the conflict the US Secretary of Defense, Donald Rumsfeld, also accused Syria of sheltering wanted Iraqi officials. The USA's vigorous sabre-rattling prompted Syria to undertake a series of measures designed to mollify the Bush Administration. In addition to sealing its border with Iraq and introducing visa requirements for Iraqi citizens, Syria also instructed Palestinian factions based in the country to close some of their offices and to maintain a low media profile. The US President acknowledged that Syria was 'getting the message', but Powell maintained the pressure in his talks with the Syrian leader, Bashar al-Assad. He stated that he expected Syria to give its full backing to the roadmap, withdraw troops from Lebanon and end its support for Lebanese Hezbollah and militant Palestinian groups. Commenting on his meeting with the Syrian President, Powell stated later, 'There are no illusions in his mind as to what we are looking for from Syria'. An equally stern warning was delivered to Lebanese leaders regarding the USA's expectation that Hezbollah be 'dismantled' and that the Lebanese army be deployed to the country's border with Israel. The Lebanese Government expressed no enthusiasm for either request, while Hezbollah considered that Lebanese support for 'the resistance' was too strong for opinions to be swayed by US belligerency. The radical Shi'a group also received tacit support from UNIFIL spokesman, Timor Goksel. Interviewed in the English language *Lebanese Daily Star*, Goksel noted that there had only been three Hezbollah attacks on the disputed Shebas Farms enclave in the previous year, and that the organization had played no small part in thwarting infiltration into Israel by Palestinian groups.

On 18 May 2003 Mahmud Abbas met with the Israeli Prime Minister for the first time in an attempt to win his public backing for the roadmap. This was not forthcoming. However, on 23 May the US Administration stated that it would 'fully and seriously' address the Israeli Government's reservations over the roadmap. The Israeli Cabinet subsequently voted narrowly (by 12 votes to seven, with four abstentions) to accept the new peace initiative. Opinion polls suggested that 56% of the Israeli public supported the government decision, while the depressed Tel-Aviv stock market rose by 7% following news of the Cabinet's decision. For the Arab world, the US assurances to Sharon fed the old belief that the USA was an unsuitable guardian of the peace process, being either unable or unwilling to apply the levels of pressure on Israel that would make the roadmap viable.

The US President chose to formally celebrate Israeli and Palestinian acceptance of the roadmap with back-to-back summits in Egypt and Jordan at the beginning of June 2003. The first, hosted by the Egyptian President at the Red Sea resort of Sharm esh-Sheikh, brought together several US Arab allies to endorse both the roadmap and to renew commitment to the 'war against terror'. Alongside George W. Bush and Mahmud Abbas were the leaders of Egypt, Saudi Arabia, Jordan and Bahrain. Tellingly, neither Syria nor the Secretary-General of the Arab League were invited, while other Arab allies, including the Moroccan monarch and leaders of the Gulf States, pleaded illness or prior commitments to excuse their absence. Having achieved a public display of regional support for the roadmap, George Bush journeyed the short distance to the Jordanian port of Aqaba, to preside over declarations of commitment to the new peace initiative by the Israeli Prime Minister and his Palestinian counterpart. In an address that appeared to have been scripted in part at least by the USA, Mahmud Abbas declared that he would bring about the end of the armed *intifada* while denouncing 'terrorism against Israelis wherever they might be'. Although this formulation won the Palestinian Prime Minister plaudits from the international community, the implicit characterization of all Palestinian military operations, including those directed against soldiers and armed settlers, as 'terrorism' caused a tide of anger in the West Bank and Gaza, where such actions were universally accepted as the legitimate response of an occupied population to the agents of occupation. Palestinian listeners to the speech were similarly alarmed by Abbas's assertion that the destination of the roadmap was an ending to 'the occupation and suffering of Palestinians and Israelis' rather than to secure, in accordance with UN resolutions, a full Israeli withdrawal from the territories it occupied in 1967 (including East Jerusalem), and a just resolution to the issue of Palestinian refugees. In his own speech, Ariel Sharon declared that he understood 'the importance of territorial contiguity in the West Bank for a viable Palestinian state', promised to resume 'direct negotiations according to the steps in the roadmap' and to dismantle 'unauthorized' settler outposts. He did not mention any commitment to the settlement 'freeze' demanded under the terms of the roadmap. Nevertheless, even a commitment to remove a few flags and caravans from the bleak hillsides of the West Bank was deemed sufficient a betrayal of settler interests to provoke a 40,000-strong demonstration in Jerusalem on 6 June. This display of far right anger was of minimal annoyance to Ariel Sharon compared to the political storm encountered by the Palestinian Prime Minister on his return to Gaza. On 7 June Islamist and PLO factions issued a statement harshly criticizing 'the results of Aqaba and Sharm esh-Sheikh' and reaffirming their commitment to 'national unity, the *intifada* and resistance'. In a withering attack on what its leaders were calling 'a security arrangement' rather than a peace plan, Hamas concluded with the announcement that it was ending its cease-fire negotiations with the PA. Visibly shaken by the depth of negative feeling generated by his Aqaba address, the Palestinian Prime Minister accepted at a press conference in Ramallah on 9 June that he may have been 'misunderstood'. He stated that his goal remained the creation of a Palestinian state on all of the territories occupied in 1967, with Jerusalem as its capital. He also insisted that he was committed to the removal of Israeli settlements and the right of return for Palestinian refugees. However, even prior to Abu Mazen's reaffirmation of the nationalist consensus, Palestinian militants had underlined their rejection of Aqaba with separate ambushes in Gaza and Hebron on 8 June 2003, which left five Israeli soldiers dead. Two days later, Hamas' senior political leader in Gaza, Abd al-Aziz ar-Rantisi was wounded in an attempted assassination strike by Israeli helicopter gunships. The following day a Hamas suicide bomber carried out the inevitable retaliation, killing 16 people in a devastating attack on a bus in West Jerusalem. Over the following week a series of retaliatory attacks left more than a score of people dead (the overwhelming majority Palestinian) and threatened to leave the new peace process stillborn. It took the dispatch of US Secretary of State Powell to the region on 19 June to reduce the violence. Powell urged Sharon to scale down his offensives against the Palestinian groups in order to give the Palestinian Prime Minister political breathing space and a chance to reconstitute the Palestinian security forces. Despite early comments from the US President stating that he was 'troubled' by the assassination attempt on ar-Rantisi, the US Secretary of State maintained an uncompromising hostility towards Hamas in his public statements, calling the organization 'an enemy of peace'. The Israeli Prime Minister, meanwhile, chose Powell's visit to demonstrate his Government's compliance with the stipulations of the roadmap on the removal of 'unauthorized' settler outposts on the West Bank. On 19 June Israeli police forces overcame the resistance of several hundred settlers and their supporters to remove a few empty caravans from sites on the West Bank. Although the televised tussles with the extremist fringes of the settler movement would allow Sharon to claim Israel was living up to its commitments, many analysts dismissed the police actions as mere political theatre. This view hardened following reports a few days later that Sharon had exhorted settler leaders to continue expanding their settlements but 'without talking about it'.

At the end of June 2003 Hamas, Islamic Jihad and the Fatah dissidents of the al-Aqsa Martyrs Brigades announced a three-month cease-fire. During this period they declared that they would suspend all attacks on Israeli targets within Israel, and in the Occupied Territories. They demanded in return a halt to 'acts of aggression against the Palestinian people' and the freeing of Palestinians held in Israeli prisons. The cease-fire declaration followed months of Egyptian-mediated negotiations between the Palestinian factions and the PA, and was seen as an important boost to the Palestinian Prime Minister in his struggle to garner domestic and international credibility. Although the roadmap was explicit in its stipulation that the PA should disarm and dismantle the Palestinian militias, Abbas remained reluctant to employ his security forces to pursue such an end. As welcome as the cease-fire was to a Palestinian populace exhausted by the three years of the al-Aqsa *intifada*, there was no appetite for the civil war that would follow the PA's confrontation with Hamas and Islamic Jihad. Behind their uncompromising rhetoric, the Islamist organizations also understood that much was to be gained in calling a halt to their military campaign, and not just because such a declaration would be greeted with relief by ordinary Palestinians. The post-Iraq climate in the USA was uniformly opposed to any kind of accommodation with groups such as Hamas and, as Egyptian officials were quick to point out to the leadership of the Islamist factions, the US Administration would not restrain the Sharon Government if it opted for an all-out war against them. Israeli leaders reacted with cynicism to the cease-fire declaration, complaining that it would allow the Palestinian factions to rearm and reorganize after the reversals of the previous months. Nevertheless, the USA persuaded Israel not to undermine the cease-fire and with it the ability of Abu Mazen to develop the authority to bring about disarmament. Although pledging to refrain from targeted assassinations and to ease restrictions on Palestinian movement in the West Bank and Gaza, Israeli government officials expressed doubts over the willingness of the PA to dismantle the 'terror networks'.

Despite these misgivings, the Israeli Prime Minister authorized the IDF's withdrawal from Bethlehem and from the northern parts of the Gaza Strip. Check-points were also removed from the main highway running through the Strip. On 1 July 2003 the Israeli and Palestinian Prime Ministers met to discuss the way forward for the roadmap. Public warmth between the two men reportedly masked serious private disagreements. Sharon continued to press for a commitment from Abbas to begin disarming the Palestinian militias. Abbas responded that he would prefer to achieve this through negotiation rather than confrontation and called upon the Israeli leader to abide by a promise made at Aqaba to release a substantial number of the 7,000 or more Palestinian prisoners held in Israeli gaols. The Israeli Cabinet balked at the release of any more than a small number of detainees, but eventually agreed to free some 400 as a 'goodwill' gesture. Members of Islamist organizations as well as prisoners 'with blood on their hands' would not be included. According to Sharon, any future releases would be 'carried out in small numbers and will be conditioned on proof that the Palestinians are living up to their security commitments'. The extent of the proposed releases and Sharon's warning not to expect swift implementation came as a bitter blow to a Palestinian premier in no doubt that his political fortunes were intimately tied to his ability to demonstrate concrete outcomes for his embrace of the roadmap and the achievement of a cease-fire. Warning of the fragility of the process came on 7 July with the death of an Israeli woman in a suicide attack in northern Israel.

The killing was nominally claimed by Islamic Jihad as a response to Israel's refusal to include its cadres in the proposed prisoner releases. However, spokesmen from the organization distanced Islamic Jihad from the attack. They claimed that it had not been authorized by the leadership and asserted their continued observance of the cease-fire.

July 2003 witnessed a dramatic fall in the number of violent incidents in Israel and the Occupied Territories, yet relations between Israel and the Palestinians became increasingly acrimonious. A meeting between Abbas and Sharon on 20 July in Jerusalem reportedly involved heated exchanges between the two men over Israel's continued settlement activity on the West Bank and Sharon's deferral of a decision on prisoner releases. Abbas's request that the siege of Yasser Arafat's Ramallah headquarters be lifted was also met with a negative response. At the end of July both men made separate trips to Washington, DC, to report on progress made towards implementation of the roadmap. While in Washington, the Palestinian Prime Minister received promises of further US aid and a sympathetic hearing for his complaints about Israel's 'hesitant implementation' of its obligations under the roadmap, but no indication that the US President shared his sense of concern over the sluggish pace of the peace process. Ariel Sharon followed Abbas to Washington to deliver his own cautious and unexpectedly hardline assessment of the progress of the roadmap. 'I wish to move forward with a political process with our Palestinian neighbours', commented the Israeli Prime Minister, 'and the right way to do that is only after a complete cessation of terror, violence and incitement, full dismantlement of terror organizations, and completion of the reform process of the Palestinian Authority'. He added that he expected the 'welcome quiet' of the cease-fire would not last because of the PA's failure to tackle Palestinian militant groups. This was despite intelligence reports suggesting that both Hamas and Islamic Jihad were generally keeping a tight rein on their activists. US President Bush concurred with Sharon's view that 'terrorist groups' posed the greatest threat to the peace process. However, the US Administration also indicated that it regarded Israeli settlement activity and its security fence as a major hindrance to progress. Having recently seen Congress approve US $9,000m. in loan guarantees to Israel, the Bush Administration warned in early August that it would consider reducing the guarantee in direct proportion to the sums spent on the security wall.

Prior to his visit to Washington, DC, the Israeli Prime Minister had secured cabinet approval for increasing the number of prospective prisoner releases to 542 and to include Hamas and Islamic Jihad members among those being freed. Following a gun attack on an Israeli car near Bethlehem on 3 August 2003, in which a woman and her child were injured, Israel said it would only be releasing 342 security detainees and 97 common criminals. Israel's Minister of Defence also announced that the IDF would suspend further redeployments from Palestinian territory. Abbas declared that Sharon had reneged on his earlier pledge on prisoner releases and cancelled a scheduled meeting with the Israeli leader. The subsequent release of 335 prisoners on 6 August did little to assuage the PA's anger. Many of those released were coming to the end of their sentences while others had been held without charge or trial. The atmosphere soured further on 8 August with Israel's assassination of two leading Hamas activists in Nablus. An Israeli defence spokesman claimed that the two men were planning an attack on an Israeli target. Hamas declared the killings a breach of the cease-fire understanding and promised to exact revenge. On 12 August two suicide bombings, one next to the West Bank settlement of Ariel, and the other in the Israeli town of Rosh Ha'ayin, left the two bombers and two Israelis dead. Hamas claimed the Ariel attack as a response to the deaths in Nablus, while a branch of the increasingly fractured al-Aqsa Martyrs Brigade claimed that their movement was responsible for the bombing in Israel. Faith in the sustainability of the cease-fire ebbed further over the following days with Israel's killing of Mohammed Sidr, Hebron commander of Islamic Jihad, and the assassination in the same city of a high-ranking Hamas activist, Abdullah Kawasme. Meanwhile, in the north of Israel a teenage boy was killed when anti-aircraft shells fired by Hezbollah fell on the town of Shlomi. The militia claimed that they had targeted Israeli warplanes violating Lebanese airspace, but this charge was rejected by Israeli defence officials. On 10 August Israeli helicopters struck at suspected Hezbollah positions in the south of the country.

Amid fears that Israeli–Palestinian relations were on the brink of descent into a further spiral of violence, the Bush Administration urged both sides to intensify efforts to bolster the six-week-old cease-fire agreement. After several days of negotiations between Israeli and Palestinian security officials, it was reported that an agreement had been reached on the staged withdrawal of Israeli troops from four West Bank cities: Qalqilya, Jericho, Tulkarm and Ramallah. Israel had also agreed to a Palestinian proposal that 400 militants responsible for attacks on Israelis be confined to PA-supervised towns rather than face impri-sonment, as had originally been demanded by the Israeli Government. Hopes that the new agreements would rescue the cease-fire proved to be short-lived. While the Palestinian Prime Minister was meeting with Islamist leaders in Gaza on 19 August 2003 to persuade them to refrain from further attacks on Israeli targets, news broke of another suicide bombing in Jerusalem. Twenty people were killed, six of them children, and more than 100 were injured in an explosion on a bus in the centre of the city. Although a claim of responsibility came from Hamas, the group's leaders in the West Bank and Gaza claimed not to have authorized the attack and insisted that they were still observing the truce. Israel responded to the bus bombing by 'freezing' all negotiations with the PA and calling off plans to withdraw its forces from the West Bank cities. The PA swiftly condemned the attack and also broke off contact with Hamas and Islamic Jihad. The EU added their voice to US calls for the Palestinian leadership to take decisive action to prevent further attacks. Israel exacted its own revenge on 21 August with the assassination in Gaza of Ismail Abu Shanab and two of his bodyguards. As one of Hamas' more pragmatic and moderate leaders, the Israeli decision to target Abu Shanab was viewed as puzzling by some observers. Despite pleas from the Egyptian Government for the PA to be given time to deal with the Islamist forces, Israeli officials warned that they would strike hard against Hamas and Islamic Jihad if the Palestinian leadership failed to control the organizations. Predictably, both Hamas and Islamic Jihad responded to the killing of Abu Shanab by declaring their cease-fire at an end.

Amid the IDF's sustained targeting of suspected Hamas militants, the Israeli Cabinet announced on 1 September 2003 that it was suspending all contacts with PA officials. The Israeli move sealed the fate of the PA Prime Minister. Abbas had staked his political credibility on his ability to deliver and sustain a

Palestinian cease-fire and it was difficult to see how his uncertain authority would survive the collapse of the 40-day truce he had brokered. On 6 September he resigned as Prime Minister. His closest political ally, Security Minister Muhammad Dahlan, followed suit the next day. Abbas claimed to the Legislative Assembly in Ramallah that it was the impasse created by Israel's refusal to implement the roadmap and the USA's reluctance to exert pressure, that 'fundamentally' lay behind his decision to quit. However, his additional references to the problem of 'domestic incitement', hinted more accurately at the reasons for his departure. During his brief tenure as Prime Minister, Abbas had been locked in an often bitter struggle with the PA President. Control of the Authority's myriad security services provided the focus of their dispute, with Abbas's attempts to reform and unify the services, in line with the roadmap requirements, being consistently resisted by Arafat. US and, to a lesser extent, Israeli, backing for Abbas had also undermined his domestic standing and tainted his political reform programme. At a time of stagnation in the peace process, economic hardship in the West Bank and Gaza and the demonization of Arafat, it had become easy for the President's supporters to accuse Abu Mazen of collusion with the USA and to deflect the wider demands for reform. Abbas was visibly upset after being abused and jostled by Arafat supporters on 4 September.

For the USA and Israel, Abbas's resignation was further evidence of Arafat's role in undermining the peace process. In response, senior figures in the Israeli Government called for the PA President to be deported, while members of far right parties and settler organizations called for his 'liquidation'. Although Sharon was not yet prepared to sanction Arafat's exile, there would be no respite in the pursuit of Hamas members. In the three weeks after the Jerusalem bus bombing, 12 Hamas leaders were killed in Gaza alone. Just hours after the resignation of Abbas, the Israeli air force struck an apartment block in Gaza City in a failed attempt to assassinate Sheikh Ahmad Yassin, Hamas's founder and spiritual leader. Meanwhile, at a meeting of EU foreign ministers in Italy on 5–6 September 2003 it was agreed that Hamas should be placed on the EU's list of terrorist organizations, a move committing member states to freeze the Islamist group's assets and to block the channelling of further funds to it. Egypt's foreign minister voiced his concern that the European decision would encourage an intensification of Israeli incursions in the Occupied Territories.

Hamas suicide bombers struck in Tel-Aviv and Jerusalem on 9 September 2003. Eight soldiers and seven civilians were killed in the attacks, which the organization's spokesmen claimed as revenge for the deaths of their operatives in Gaza and for the attempted killing of Sheikh Yassin. As before, the Israeli Government accused Arafat of ultimate responsibility for the carnage. At an emergency cabinet meeting the decision was taken 'in principle' to 'remove' the PA President. There was widespread consternation outside Israel at the most explicit threat to date to exile or assassinate the elected leader of the Palestinians. In the UN Security Council on 16 September, the US Ambassador vetoed a draft resolution condemning the Israeli threat. When the resolution was put to the vote in the General Assembly three days later, it was passed by 133 votes to 4, with 15 abstentions (the USA and Israel were joined by Micronesia and the Marshall Islands in voting against the resolution). Despite siding with the

Sharon Government against an 'unbalanced' resolution, and sharing its distaste for the Palestinian leader, the USA warned the Israeli Prime Minister against overthrowing Arafat. It was feared that such a move would not only bring about anarchy in the Occupied Territories, but would also create a shockwave in the Arab world of significant magnitude to jeopardize the US project in Iraq. Nevertheless, there were no senior voices in the Administration signalling dissent from the policy of continued isolation of Yasser Arafat. It was also evident that the hope of fostering a more compliant leadership alternative to the PA President had diminished—in the short term at least—with the departure of Mahmud Abbas. The extent to which the USA acknowledged Swedish foreign minister Lindh's assertion that US-Israeli exclusion of Arafat had been 'very dangerous' for Abbas, remained unknown.

Abbas's nominated successor as prime minister was Ahmed Quray (Abu Ala), identified with the Fatah mainstream and considered more of an Arafat loyalist than his predecessor. His early statements suggested that his preference would be to demonstrate independence from the USA rather than from Arafat. On the core issues of a cease-fire and the roadmap, Quray stuck to formulations that had the imprimatur of the Palestinian President. A Palestinian cease-fire and implementation of the PA's responsibilities under the roadmap could only be brought about through US and international pressure on Israel to cease assassinations, ease the blockade of Palestinian areas and commit to end settlement activity. He also stated that the Israeli boycott of Arafat would have to end 'because I cannot work without his support'. Both the USA and Israel reacted coolly to Abu Ala's nomination, observing that he would be judged on his willingness to challenge the PA President's monopoly on power and disarm the Palestinian armed groups. Quray had to face an early test of his attitudes towards the radical organizations. On 4 October 2003 a female suicide bomber belonging to Islamic Jihad detonated explosives in a café in the Israeli city of Haifa. Nineteen people were killed and tens injured in the outrage, many of them from the city's minority Arab community. Quray joined Arafat in strong condemnation of the bombing. 'This is an unjustified attack on innocent civilians', opined the prime minister-designate, 'the Palestinian Authority condemns this act of terror and offers condolences to the bereaved families.' Quray's words were dismissed by the Israeli Government, which repeated its demand that the PA act decisively against the Islamists. This was not a course of action that Quray was willing to take. He insisted that he would not risk a Palestinian civil war and that he preferred the path of dialogue. Israeli officials rejoined that there could be no meeting with a new Palestinian government as long as it refused to tackle the extremists.

Israeli retaliation for the Haifa bombing was anticipated, but the target chosen was not. In the early hours of 5 October 2003 Israeli jets bombed a military training facility north of the Syrian capital, Damascus, causing widespread damage but no fatalities. Israeli spokesmen justified the raid on the grounds that the facility, purportedly run by the pro-Syrian PFLP-General Command organization, was being used by members of Islamic Jihad. The authenticity of Syrian denials of the Israeli claim was difficult to verify, although independent reports from Damascus did suggest that the radical Palestinian organizations were far less visible in Syria following the USA's earlier insistence that President al-Assad should close their offices and withdraw other facilities. Given that the destruction of a training facility in Syria would have negligible impact upon the ability of Islamic Jihad to wage a campaign of terror inside Israel, Sharon's motivation in ordering the attack was not transparent. US hostility towards Syria during and after the Iraqi conflict had certainly removed some of the political sensitivities attached to such action. President Bush's refusal to condemn the attack on Syria—he commented that Israel should avoid escalation of tensions but 'must not feel constrained, in terms of defending the homeland'—added some weight to speculation that Israel and the USA were working together to maintain pressure on the Syrian regime. The USA's UN Ambassador, John Negroponte, acceded to a request to debate aggression claimed by Syria to be a serious violation of the UN Charter. Negroponte subsequently used the discussion to accuse Syria of being 'on the wrong side' in the war against terrorism and to implicitly condone the Israeli raid. On 16 October the US House of Representatives passed the Syria Accountability and Lebanese Sovereignty Restoration Act. The Act mandated President Bush to impose economic and diplomatic sanctions on Syria until it could be certified that the country had removed its troops from Lebanon, ceased supporting terrorist groups and abandoned its non-conventional weapons programme. The Act was approved by the Senate four weeks later.

Israel continued to court international controversy during the autumn of 2003 with the ongoing construction of its separation fence. In early October John Dugard, special *rapporteur* for the UN Commission on Human Rights to the Occupied Territories, published a report that was sharply critical of the new barrier. Dugard estimated that the wall had brought about *de facto* Israeli annexation of large parts of the West Bank and would incorporate one-half of the combined settler population of the West Bank and East Jerusalem. While acknowledging the legitimacy of Israeli security fears, he commented that 'the time has come to condemn the wall as an unlawful act of annexation'. The Israeli Government, which had refused to meet with Dugard, denounced the report as 'biased and one-sided'. EU leaders meeting in Brussels on 17 October 2003 also charged that the new barrier was adding to the humanitarian hardships of Palestinian communities. Moreover, they voiced fears that Israel's proposed route for the wall could 'make the two-state solution physically impossible to implement'. The first draft of this detailed statement from Brussels had contained language that was far harsher in its criticism of Israel, but the text had reportedly been amended in response to appeals from the USA. The USA had also shielded Israel in the UN Security Council on 15 October, vetoing a draft resolution which condemned the wall as illegal and called for it to be dismantled. The US Ambassador once again explained the use of the veto on the grounds of imbalance. He said the resolution had 'failed to address terrorism and the security problems that Israel has faced for years'. Despite the use of its veto, US policy was officially anti-wall in so far as the new structure deviated from the 'Green Line' separating Israel from the West Bank. The USA had already warned Israel that it might register its disapproval by withholding a proportion of the US $9,000m. in loan guarantees granted by the Bush Administration.

The security situation in the Occupied Territories continued to deteriorate during October 2003. This was especially the case in Gaza. In the second week of the month Israeli forces staged a series of raids into the southern city of Rafah.

At least 15 people were killed (including children and other non-combatants) and more than 100 homes destroyed in a rolling operation claimed by the IDF as designed to destroy tunnels used for smuggling weapons from Egypt. On 15 October Palestinian militants appeared to signal their preparedness dramatically to escalate the three-year-old *intifada*. A road-side bomb in the north of the Gaza Strip targeted vehicles belonging to a US diplomatic mission on its way to interview Palestinians academics applying for study scholarships. The convoy was being escorted by PA police. Three US security personnel were killed in the explosion. All the known military groups active in Gaza denied involvement, although this type of ambush bore the hallmark of the cross-factional PRCs. Anger at the US veto of the UN Resolution condemning the Israeli security wall was cited by many Palestinians as the possible motive. Arafat and Quray both denounced the attack and the latter promised a joint Palestinian-US investigation. Several suspects associated with the PRC were arrested in the immediate aftermath of the bombing. Al-Aqsa Martyrs Brigade gunmen, meanwhile, killed three Israeli soldiers in an ambush on the West Bank, and on 19 October Hamas fighters fired eight rockets into Israel from Gaza. Israel retaliated with a further round of air strikes on alleged Hamas targets. Fourteen people were killed in the assaults, including seven in a single incident at the Nusseirat refugee camp.

Ahmed Quray struggled to maintain a semblance of political independence from Arafat. Quray's task had been made more difficult by the surge in popularity for the PA President following Israel's call for his removal. The new Prime Minister also had to contend with Arafat's exploitation of his new-found standing to reassert presidential authority over powers nominally devolved to the post of prime minister. Political manoeuvring by the veteran leader saw control of the PA's Security Forces placed before a reincorporated National Security Council headed by Arafat. (This was the issue which had ultimately forced Abbas's exit.) Quray had wanted the crucial interior ministry position to be assigned to a supporter, Nasr Yusuf, who had occupied the post in the emergency government installed after the Haifa bombing. The appointment of Quray's nominee was opposed by Arafat, who mounted a smear campaign against Yusuf, accusing him of working in accordance with an Israeli and US agenda. Quray tendered his resignation, but was persuaded by Arafat to withdraw it. The new PA Government was finally unveiled on 12 November 2003. A large majority of the 24-member Cabinet was identified as loyal to Arafat, confirming that despite the combined efforts of the US and Israeli Governments, the PLO leader had reasserted control over the levers of power. For the foreseeable future, the authority of the Prime Minister would be subordinate to that of the president. When questioned on this apparent contravention of the provisions of the roadmap, Quray closed ranks with Arafat, declaring that the roadmap was 'not the Bible'. He reiterated, however, his Government's commitment to bringing about a Palestinian cease-fire, but once again stated that he would expect reciprocity from Israel. The prospect of the PA authority disarming the militias remained remote: the new secretary of the National Security Council had already commented that 'while Israel occupies our land, we cannot treat Hamas and Islamic Jihad as terrorist groups'. For their part, the Islamist opposition had stated to Egyptian mediators that they were prepared to observe a cease-fire in return for a public commitment by Israel to do likewise. As it was, Hamas was already hinting that it might suspend attacks on civilians inside

Israel in favour of stepping up its campaign against military and settler targets inside the Occupied Territories. Hamas and Islamic Jihad had mounted a joint raid on the Netzarim settlement in Gaza on 24 October, killing three Israeli soldiers. Prior to the attack, spokesmen for the two groups had announced that they were attempting to co-ordinate their armed operations. Meanwhile, the extensive social and charitable works sponsored by the Islamist groups, programmes widely regarded as untainted by the corruption and inefficiency associated with official PA agencies, contributed to an impressive bedrock of popular support.

GENEVA ACCORDS

In mid-November 2003 the Israeli Prime Minister indicated that he would be prepared to meet with Ahmed Quray. Israeli officials also gave cautious encouragement to the PA Prime Minister's attempts to bring about a Palestinian cease-fire. Having so recently predicated any Israeli re-engagement with the peace process on the marginalization of Arafat and the disarming of Palestinian militants, Sharon's volte-face surprised some observers. The retreat from apparently entrenched positions stemmed from growing domestic unrest with an approach to the conflict with the Palestinians that was being derided as dangerously mono-dimensional. Although Sharon had learned to live with Labour Party and left-wing criticism that his management of the conflict relied on nothing more creative than the application of superior military force, the disenchantment of powerful figures associated with the nationalist centre had discomfited the Israeli leader. At the beginning of the month the IDF's Chief of Staff, Moshe Ya'alon, a noted hardliner, warned that the hardship being inflicted on the Palestinian population was 'strengthening terrorist organizations rather than weakening them'. He also conceded that the military policies carried out in the West Bank and Gaza had served to undermine Abu Mazen and buttress Yasser Arafat. Several days later Ya'alon's concerns were amplified in interviews given by four former chiefs of Israel's internal intelligence service, Shin Bet. This group (which included a well-known pacifist, Ami Ayalon) argued that the Prime Minister was 'leading Israel to catastrophe by failing to pursue peace with the Palestinians'. This indictment from senior members of the security establishment was thrown into sharper relief by developing international support for an extra-governmental Israeli-Palestinian peace initiative. Authored on the Israeli side by Yossi Beillin, chief architect of the Oslo Accords, and on the Palestinian side by former information minister Yasser Abed Rabbo, the self-styled Geneva Accords presented a development of the solutions proposed at Camp David in the summer of 2000 and at Taba several months later. Their more noteworthy provisions included the enshrining of an Israeli veto over the Palestinian Right of Return, shared sovereignty in East Jerusalem and the evacuation of most of the West Bank settlements and their settlers. The Palestinians were to be given territorial compensation for the settlement blocs around Jerusalem that would be formally annexed to Israel. The achievement of a 'virtual' Israeli Palestinian peace was celebrated in the glare of the world's media on 1 December 2003, but was dismissed by the Israeli Government. However, Sharon's dismissive bluster over the event in Geneva only served to highlight the absence of alternatives emanating from the Prime Minister's office.

Significantly, it was only a matter of days before Israel's Minister of Trade and Industry, Ehud Olmert, substantiated the Prime Minister's earlier warnings that he was prepared for 'painful concessions' in the Occupied Territories. Interviewed in the popular daily newspaper, *Yedioth Aharonoth*, Olmert cited the demographic time bomb of a rapidly increasing Palestinian population to warn of a scenario where 'more and more Palestinians will say "We don't need a Palestinian state. All we want is voting rights".' According to the Likud minister, this would spell the end to Israel's viability as a Jewish state. His recommended alternative, and presumably Sharon's, was separation from the Palestinians and the surrender of most of the Occupied Territories. Olmert drew predictable fire from the nationalist right and the settler lobby for suggesting an abandonment of the Greater Israel project.

The enthusiastic reception of the Geneva initiative by EU member states (in contrast to a far more measured response from the USA) came at a time of strained relations between the EU and the Israeli Government. An opinion poll conducted across EU member states during October 2003 showed that a majority of those questioned (59%) singled out Israel as the country posing the greatest threat to world peace (Iran, North Korea and the USA tied for second place). There was predictable outrage in Israel at the findings of the poll, which were blamed on the prejudicial and distorted image of the country as portrayed in the European media and disseminated by its politicians. Italy's foreign minister, Franco Frattini, attempted to defuse Israeli anger, declaring that the poll results were at variance with the policy positions of member governments. There were still reminders that more substantive issues divided Israel and the EU. In mid-November the Israeli Minster of Foreign Affairs, Silvan Shalom, was involved in a public quarrel with senior EU figures (including the EU High Representative, Javier Solana, and the Commissioner responsible for External Relations, Chris Patten) over Israel's boycott of EU representatives who met with the 'terrorist' Yasser Arafat. The EU figures warned that a continuation of the ban would have a negative impact on future relations. They reiterated strong opposition to the construction of the security fence and to recent plans to expand settlements on the West Bank. Shalom had already warned the Europeans that a failure to establish greater balance in their approach to Arab–Israeli relations would mean that they would have no part to play in the search for a regional peace settlement. Following the adoption on 19 November of UN Security Council Resolution 1515, which confirmed support for the roadmap and the central role to be played by the Quartet group in its implementation, Israel insisted that it held the USA to be the peace plan's sole arbiter. At their meeting in mid-December, EU leaders rejoined that they intended to play a more prominent role in the Middle East with the resolution of the Arab–Israeli conflict deemed 'a strategic priority'.

Opinion polls conducted in the Occupied Territories suggested that more than one-half of Palestinians backed the terms of the Geneva Accords. This result was at odds with the judgements of the political parties, all of which, with differing degrees of vehemence, stated their opposition to the initiative. Insistence by the supporters of the Accords that the proposals were a tactical initiative designed to isolate the Sharon Government internationally failed to mollify the militant organizations. The proposed Palestinian relinquishment of the right to return aroused the fiercest passions and resulted in accusations of treason being levelled at those personalities attending the ceremony in Geneva; shots were fired at the Ramallah home of Yasser Abed Rabbo on 29 November. Yasser Arafat remained aloof from the proposals, refraining from either endorsement or condemnation. He did, however, grant security force protection to Palestinian personalities making the journey to Geneva.

A lull in Palestinian-Israeli violence during November 2003 increased speculation that Ahmed Quray would be able to win commitment for a Palestinian cease-fire during talks mediated by Egypt in Cairo on 4 December 2003. Twelve factions were present in the Egyptian capital, but the talks broke up after four days without agreement. It was reported that Fatah and several other groups wanted an unconditional end to attacks on civilians inside the 1967 borders as a first step towards the negotiation of a total cessation of military activities. Israel would be expected, in return, to lift its blockade of Palestinian communities and halt construction of the West Bank barrier. The principal Islamist organizations rejected any moratorium on the use of weapons until Israel issued assurances that it was also prepared to observe a truce. They were unmoved by the moderates' old argument that the declaration of a Palestinian truce would isolate and weaken the Israeli premier.

The failure of the talks to bring about a cease-fire was a blow to Quray, who was now left to rely on the mediatory efforts of his Egyptian hosts to try to secure the guarantees from Israel which might yet deliver an Islamist truce. There were few signs that the Israeli Prime Minister would be receptive to such an approach. The IDF's restraint failed to last into December 2003, despite the absence of attacks inside Israel and a reduction in armed actions in the West Bank and Gaza. Israel mounted several raids into Palestinian towns during the month, including large-scale incursions into Rafah and Nablus. On 25 December an Israeli helicopter attack on a car in Gaza killed two Islamic Jihad cadres and three other Palestinians. This was the first assassination of Palestinian activists carried out by Israel for nearly two months. Shortly afterwards, a suicide attack killed three Israelis at a Tel-Aviv bus stop. Responsibility for the bombing was claimed by the PFLP.

The Israeli Prime Minister delivered a major policy speech in Herziliya on 18 December 2003. He warned that the PA's failure to fulfil its obligations under the terms of the roadmap would result in a 'unilateral step of disengagement from the Palestinians'. According to Sharon, the PA had 'a few months' to demonstrate its compliance before Israel imposed its own solution to the conflict.

Documents on Palestine

DECLARATION OF FIRST WORLD ZIONIST CONGRESS

The Congress, convened in Basle by Dr Theodor Herzl in August 1897, adopted the following programme.*

The aim of Zionism is to create for the Jewish people a home in Palestine secured by public law.

The Congress contemplates the following means to the attainment of this end:

1. The promotion on suitable lines, of the settlement of Palestine by Jewish agriculturists, artisans and tradesmen.

2. The organization and binding together of the whole of Jewry by means of appropriate institutions, local and general, in accordance with the laws of each country.

3. The strengthening of Jewish sentiment and national consciousness.

4. Preparatory steps towards obtaining government consent as are necessary, for the attainment of the aim of Zionism.

McMAHON CORRESPONDENCE†

Ten letters passed between Sir Henry McMahon, British High Commissioner in Cairo, and Sherif Husain of Mecca from July 1915 to March 1916. Husain offered Arab help in the war against the Turks if Britain would support the principle of an independent Arab state. The most important letter is that of 24 October 1915, from McMahon to Husain:

... I regret that you should have received from my last letter the impression that I regarded the question of limits and boundaries with coldness and hesitation; such was not the case, but it appeared to me that the time had not yet come when that question could be discussed in a conclusive manner.

I have realized, however, from your last letter that you regard this question as one of vital and urgent importance. I have, therefore, lost no time in informing the Government of Great Britain of the contents of your letter, and it is with great pleasure that I communicate to you on their behalf the following statement, which I am confident you will receive with satisfaction:

The two districts of Mersina and Alexandretta and portions of Syria lying to the west of the districts of Damascus, Homs, Hama and Aleppo cannot be said to be purely Arab, and should be excluded from the limits demanded.

With the above modification, and without prejudice to our existing treaties with Arab chiefs, we accept those limits.

As for those regions lying within those frontiers wherein Great Britain is free to act without detriment to the interest of her ally, France, I am empowered in the name of the Government of Great Britain to give the following assurances and make the following reply to your letter:

* Text supplied by courtesy of Josef Fraenkel.
† British White Paper, Cmd. 5957, 1939.

(1) Subject to the above modifications, Great Britain is prepared to recognize and support the independence of the Arabs in all the regions within the limits demanded by the Sherif of Mecca.

(2) Great Britain will guarantee the Holy Places against all external aggression and will recognize their inviolability.

(3) When the situation admits, Great Britain will give to the Arabs her advice and will assist them to establish what may appear to be the most suitable forms of government in those various territories.

(4) On the other hand, it is understood that the Arabs have decided to seek the advice and guidance of Great Britain only, and that such European advisers and officials as may be required for the formation of a sound form of administration will be British.

(5) With regard to the *vilayets* of Baghdad and Basra, the Arabs will recognize that the established position and interests of Great Britain necessitate special administrative arrangements in order to secure these territories from foreign aggression, to promote the welfare of the local populations and to safeguard our mutual economic interests.

I am convinced that this declaration will assure you beyond all possible doubt of the sympathy of Great Britain towards the aspirations of her friends the Arabs and will result in a firm and lasting alliance, the immediate results of which will be the expulsion of the Turks from the Arab countries and the freeing of the Arab peoples from the Turkish yoke, which for so many years has pressed heavily upon them. ....

ANGLO-FRANCO-RUSSIAN AGREEMENT (SYKES—PICOT AGREEMENT)
April-May 1916

The allocation of portions of the Ottoman empire by the three powers was decided between them in an exchange of diplomatic notes. The Anglo-French agreement* dealing with Arab territories became known to Sherif Husain only after publication by the new Bolshevik Government of Russia in 1917:

1. That France and Great Britain are prepared to recognize and protect an independent Arab State or a Confederation of Arab States in the areas (A) and (B) marked on the annexed map (*not reproduced here—Ed.*), under suzerainty of an Arab Chief. That in area (A) France, and in area (B) Great Britain shall have priority of right of enterprises and local loans. France in area (A) and Great Britain in area (B) shall alone supply foreign advisers or officials on the request of the Arab State or the Confederation of Arab States.

2. France in the Blue area and Great Britain in the Red area shall be at liberty to establish direct or indirect administration or control as they may desire or as they may deem fit to establish after agreement with the Arab State or Confederation of Arab States.

3. In the Brown area there shall be established an international administration of which the form will be decided upon after consultation with Russia, and

---

* E. L. Woodward and Rohan Butler (Eds.). *Documents on British Foreign Policy 1919–1939*. First Series, Vol. IV, 1919. London, HMSO, 1952.

after subsequent agreement with the other Allies and the representatives of the Sherif of Mecca.

4. That Great Britain be accorded

(*a*) The ports of Haifa and Acre;

(*b*) Guarantee of a given supply of water from the Tigris and the Euphrates in area (A) for area (B).

His Majesty's Government, on their part, undertake that they will at no time enter into negotiations for the cession of Cyprus to any third Power without the previous consent of the French Government.

5. Alexandretta shall be a free port as regards the trade of the British Empire and there shall be no discrimination in treatment with regard to port dues or the extension of special privileges affecting British shipping and commerce; there shall be freedom of transit for British goods through Alexandretta and over railways through the Blue area, whether such goods are going to or coming from the Red area, area (A) or area (B); and there shall be no differentiation in treatment, direct or indirect, at the expense of British goods on any railway or of British goods and shipping in any port serving the areas in question.

Haifa shall be a free port as regards the trade of France, her colonies and protectorates, and there shall be no differentiation in treatment or privilege with regard to port dues against French shipping and commerce. There shall be freedom of transit through Haifa and over British railways through the Brown area, whether such goods are coming from or going to the Blue area, area (A) or area (B), and there shall be no differentiation in treatment, direct or indirect, at the expense of French goods on any railway or of French goods and shipping in any port serving the areas in question.

6. In area (A), the Baghdad Railway shall not be extended southwards beyond Mosul, and in area (B), it shall not be extended northwards beyond Samarra, until a railway connecting Baghdad with Aleppo along the basin of the Euphrates will have been completed, and then only with the concurrence of the two Governments.

7. Great Britain shall have the right to build, administer and be the sole owner of the railway connecting Haifa with area (B). She shall have, in addition, the right in perpetuity and at all times of carrying troops on that line. It is understood by both Governments that this railway is intended to facilitate communication between Baghdad and Haifa, and it is further understood that, in the event of technical difficulties and expenditure incurred in the maintenance of this line in the Brown area rendering the execution of the project impracticable, the French Government will be prepared to consider plans for enabling the line in question to traverse the polygon formed by Banias-Umm Qais-Salkhad-Tall 'Osda-Mismieh before reaching area (B).

Clause 8 referred to customs tariffs.

9. It is understood that the French Government will at no time initiate any negotiations for the cession of their rights and will not cede their prospective rights in the Blue area to any third Power other than the Arab State or Confederation of Arab States, without the previous consent of His Majesty's Government who, on their part, give the French Government a similar undertaking in respect of the Red area.

10. The British and French Governments shall agree to abstain from acquiring and to withhold their consent to a third Power acquiring territorial possessions in the Arabian Peninsula; nor shall they consent to the construction by a third Power of a naval base in the islands on the eastern seaboard of the Red Sea. This, however, will not prevent such rectification of the Aden boundary as might be found necessary in view of the recent Turkish attack.

11. The negotiations with the Arabs concerning the frontiers of the Arab State or Confederation of Arab States shall be pursued through the same channel as heretofore in the name of the two Powers.

12. It is understood, moreover, that measures for controlling the importation of arms into the Arab territory will be considered by the two Governments.

BALFOUR DECLARATION

2 November 1917

Balfour was British Foreign Secretary, Rothschild the British Zionist leader.

Dear Lord Rothschild,

I have much pleasure in conveying to you on behalf of His Majesty's Government the following declaration of sympathy with Jewish Zionist aspirations, which has been submitted to and approved by the Cabinet.

'His Majesty's Government view with favour the establishment in Palestine of a national home for the Jewish people, and will use their best endeavours to facilitate the achievement of this object, it being clearly understood that nothing shall be done which may prejudice the civil and religious rights of existing non-Jewish communities in Palestine, or the rights and political status enjoyed by Jews in any other country.'

I should be grateful if you would bring this declaration to the knowledge of the Zionist Federation.

Yours sincerely,

Arthur James Balfour.

HOGARTH MESSAGE*

4 January 1918

The following is the text of a message which Commander D. G. Hogarth, CMG, RNVR, of the Arab Bureau in Cairo, was instructed on 4 January 1918 to deliver to King Husain of the Hijaz at Jeddah:

1. The *Entente* Powers are determined that the Arab race shall be given full opportunity of once again forming a nation in the world. This can only be achieved by the Arabs themselves uniting, and Great Britain and her Allies will pursue a policy with this ultimate unity in view.

2. So far as Palestine is concerned, we are determined that no people shall be subject to another, but—

---

* British White Paper, Cmd. 5964, 1939.

(*a*) In view of the fact that there are in Palestine shrines, Wakfs and Holy places, sacred in some cases to Moslems alone, to Jews alone, to Christians alone, and in others to two or all three, and inasmuch as these places are of interest to vast masses of people outside Palestine and Arabia, there must be a special régime to deal with these places approved of by the world.

(*b*) As regards the Mosque of Omar, it shall be considered as a Moslem concern alone, and shall not be subjected directly or indirectly to any non-Moslem authority.

3. Since the Jewish opinion of the world is in favour of a return of Jews to Palestine, and inasmuch as this opinion must remain a constant factor, and, further, as His Majesty's Government view with favour the realization of this aspiration, His Majesty's Government are determined that in so far as is compatible with the freedom of the existing population, both economic and political, no obstacle should be put in the way of the realization of this ideal.

In this connection the friendship of world Jewry to the Arab cause is equivalent to support in all States where Jews have political influence. The leaders of the movement are determined to bring about the success of Zionism by friendship and co-operation with the Arabs, and such an offer is not one to be lightly thrown aside.

ANGLO-FRENCH DECLARATION*

7 November 1918

The object aimed at by France and Great Britain in prosecuting in the East the war let loose by the ambition of Germany is the complete and definite emancipation of the peoples so long oppressed by the Turks and the establishment of national Governments and Administrations deriving their authority from the initiative and free choice of the indigenous populations.

In order to carry out these intentions France and Great Britain are at one in encouraging and assisting the establishments of indigenous Governments and Administrations in Syria and Mesopotamia, now liberated by the Allies, and in the territories the liberation of which they are engaged in securing and recognizing these as soon as they are actually established.

Far from wishing to impose on the populations of these regions any particular institutions they are only concerned to ensure by their support and by adequate assistance the regular working of Governments and Administrations freely chosen by the populations themselves. To secure impartial and equal justice for all, to facilitate the economic development of the country by inspiring and encouraging local initiative, to favour the diffusion of education, to put an end to dissensions that have too long been taken advantage of by Turkish policy which the two Allied Governments uphold in the liberated territories.

---

* Report of a Committee set up to consider Certain Correspondence between Sir Henry McMahon and the Sherif of Mecca in 1915 and 1916, 16 March 1939 (British White Paper, Cmd. 5974).

RECOMMENDATIONS OF THE KING—CRANE COMMISSION*

28 August 1919

The Commission was set up by President Wilson of the USA to determine which power should receive the Mandate for Palestine. The following are extracts from their recommendations on Syria:

1. We recommend, as most important of all, and in strict harmony with our Instructions, that whatever foreign administration (whether of one or more Powers) is brought into Syria, should come in, not at all as a colonising Power in the old sense of that term, but as a Mandatory under the League of Nations with the clear consciousness that 'the well-being and development' of the Syrian people form for it a 'sacred trust'.

2. We recommend, in the second place, that the unity of Syria be preserved, in accordance with the earnest petition of the great majority of the people of Syria.

3. We recommend, in the third place, that Syria be placed under one mandatory Power, as the natural way to secure real and efficient unity.

4. We recommend, in the fourth place, that Amir Faisal be made the head of the new united Syrian State.

5. We recommend, in the fifth place, serious modification of the extreme Zionist program for Palestine of unlimited immigration of Jews, looking finally to making Palestine distinctly a Jewish State.

(1) The Commissioners began their study of Zionism with minds predisposed in its favor, but the actual facts in Palestine, coupled with the force of the general principles proclaimed by the Allies and accepted by the Syrians have driven them to the recommendation here made.

(2) The Commission was abundantly supplied with literature on the Zionist program by the Zionist Commission to Palestine; heard in conferences much concerning the Zionist colonies and their claims; and personally saw something of what had been accomplished. They found much to approve in the aspirations and plans of the Zionists, and had warm appreciation for the devotion of many of the colonists, and for their success, by modern methods in overcoming great, natural obstacles.

(3) The Commission recognised also that definite encouragement had been given to the Zionists by the Allies in Mr Balfour's often-quoted statement, in its approval by other representatives of the Allies. If, however, the strict terms of the Balfour Statement are adhered to—favoring 'the establishment in Palestine of a national home for the Jewish people', 'it being clearly understood that nothing shall be done which may prejudice the civil and religious rights of existing non-Jewish communities in Palestine'—it can hardly be doubted that the extreme Zionist program must be greatly modified. For 'a national home for the Jewish people' is not equivalent to making Palestine into a Jewish State; nor can the erection of such a Jewish State be accomplished without the gravest trespass upon the 'civil and religious rights of existing non-Jewish communities in Palestine'. The fact came out repeatedly in the Commission's conference with Jewish representatives, that the Zionists looked forward to a practically

---

* US Department of State. *Papers Relating to the Foreign Relations of the United States. The Paris Peace Conference 1919.* Vol. XII. Washington, 1947.

complete dispossession of the present non-Jewish inhabitants of Palestine, by various forms of purchase.

In his address of 4 July 1918, President Wilson laid down the following principle as one of the four great 'ends for which the associated peoples of the world were fighting': 'The settlement of every question, whether of territory, of sovereignty, of economic arrangement, or of political relationship upon the basis of the free acceptance of that settlement by the people immediately concerned, and not upon the basis of the material interest or advantage of any other nation or people which may desire a different settlement for the sake of its own exterior influence or mastery.' If that principle is to rule, and so the wishes of Palestine's population are to be decisive as to what is to be done with Palestine, then it is to be remembered that the non-Jewish population of Palestine—nearly nine-tenths of the whole—are emphatically against the entire Zionist program. The tables show that there was no one thing upon which the population of Palestine were more agreed than upon this. To subject a people so minded to unlimited Jewish immigration, and to steady financial and social pressure to surrender the land, would be a gross violation of the principle just quoted, and of the people's rights, though it kept within the forms of law.

It is to be noted also that the feeling against the Zionist program is not confined to Palestine, but shared very generally by the people throughout Syria, as our conferences clearly showed. More then 72%—1,350 in all—of all the petitions in the whole of Syria were directed against the Zionist program. Only two requests—those for a united Syria and for independence—had a larger support. This general feeling was duly voiced by the General Syrian Congress in the seventh, eighth and tenth resolutions of their statement.

The Peace Conference should not shut its eyes to the fact that the anti-Zionist feeling in Palestine and Syria is intense and not lightly to be flouted. No British officer, consulted by the Commissioners, believed that the Zionist program could be carried out except by force of arms. The officers generally thought that a force of not less than 50,000 soldiers would be required even to initiate the program. That of itself is evidence of a strong sense of the injustice of the Zionist program, on the part of the non-Jewish populations of Palestine and Syria. Decisions requiring armies to carry out are sometimes necessary, but they are surely not gratuitously to be taken in the interests of serious injustice. For the initial claim, often submitted by Zionist representatives, that they have a 'right' to Palestine, based on an occupation of 2,000 years ago, can hardly be seriously considered.

There is a further consideration that cannot justly be ignored, if the world is to look forward to Palestine becoming a definitely Jewish State, however gradually that may take place. That consideration grows out of the fact that Palestine is the Holy Land for Jews, Christians, and Moslems alike. Millions of Christians and Moslems all over the world are quite as much concerned as the Jews with conditions in Palestine, especially with those conditions which touch upon religious feelings and rights. The relations in these matters in Palestine are most delicate and difficult. With the best possible intentions, it may be doubted whether the Jews could possibly seem to either Christians or Moslems proper guardians of the holy places, or custodians of the Holy Land as a whole.

The reason is this: The places which are most sacred to Christians—those having to do with Jesus—and which are also sacred to Moslems, are not only not sacred to Jews, but abhorrent to them. It is simply impossible, under those circumstances, for Moslems and Christians to feel satisfied to have these places in Jewish hands, or under the custody of Jews. There are still other places about which Moslems must have the same feeling. In fact, from this point of view, the Moslems, just because the sacred places of all three religions are sacred to them, have made very naturally much more satisfactory custodians of the holy places than the Jews could be. It must be believed that the precise meaning in this respect of the complete Jewish occupation of Palestine has not been fully sensed by those who urge the extreme Zionist program. For it would intensify, with a certainty like fate, the anti-Jewish feeling both in Palestine and in all other portions of the world which look to Palestine as the Holy Land.

In view of all these considerations, and with a deep sense of sympathy for the Jewish cause, the Commissioners feel bound to recommend that only a greatly reduced Zionist program be attempted by the Peace Conference, and even that, only very gradually initiated. This would have to mean that Jewish immigration should be definitely limited, and that the project for making Palestine distinctly a Jewish commonwealth should be given up.

There would then be no reason why Palestine could not be included in a united Syrian State, just as other portions of the country, the holy places being cared for by an international and inter-religious commission, somewhat as at present, under the oversight and approval of the Mandatory and of the League of Nations. The Jews, of course, would have representation upon this commission.

ARTICLE 22 OF THE COVENANT OF THE LEAGUE OF NATIONS

1. To those colonies and territories which as a consequence of the late War have ceased to be under the sovereignty of the States which formerly governed them and which are inhabited by peoples not yet able to stand by themselves under the strenuous conditions of the modern world, there should be applied the principle that the well-being and development of such peoples form a sacred trust of civilization and that securities for the performance of this trust should be embodied in this Covenant.

2. The best method of giving practical effect to this principle is that the tutelage of such peoples should be entrusted to advanced nations who by reason of their resources, their experience or their geographical position can best undertake this responsibility, and who are willing to accept it, and that this tutelage should be exercised by them as Mandatories on behalf of the League.

3. The character of the Mandate must differ according to the stage of the development of the people, the geographical situation of the territory, its economic conditions and other similar circumstances.

4. Certain communities formerly belonging to the Turkish Empire have reached a stage of development where their existence as independent nations can be provisionally recognized subject to the rendering of administrative advice and assistance by a Mandatory until such time as they are able to stand alone.

The wishes of these communities must be a principal consideration in the selection of the Mandatory.

Articles 5 and 6 refer chiefly to issues affecting Mandated Territories other than Palestine.

7. In every case of Mandate, the Mandatory shall render to the Council an annual report in reference to the territory committed to its charge.

8. The degree of authority, control, or administration to be exercised by the Mandatory shall, if not previously agreed upon by the Members of the League, be explicitly defined in each case by the Council.

9. A permanent Commission shall be constituted to receive and examine the annual reports of the Mandatories and to advise the Council on all matters relating to the observance of the Mandates.

MANDATE FOR PALESTINE*

24 July 1922

The Council of the League of Nations:

Whereas the Principal Allied Powers have agreed, for the purpose of giving effect to the provisions of Article 22 of the Covenant of the League of Nations to entrust to a Mandatory selected by the said Powers the administration of the territory of Palestine, which formerly belonged to the Turkish Empire, within such boundaries as may be fixed by them; and

Whereas the Principal Allied Powers have also agreed that the Mandatory should be responsible for putting into effect the declaration originally made on 2 November 1917 by the Government of His Britannic Majesty, and adopted by the said Powers, in favour of the establishment in Palestine of a National Home for the Jewish people, it being clearly understood that nothing should be done which might prejudice the civil and religious rights of existing non-Jewish communities in Palestine, or the rights and political status enjoyed by Jews in any other country; and

Whereas recognition has thereby been given to the historical connection of the Jewish people with Palestine and to the grounds for reconstituting their National Home in that country; and

Whereas the Principal Allied Powers have selected His Britannic Majesty as the Mandatory for Palestine; and

Whereas the Mandate in respect of Palestine has been formulated in the following terms and submitted to the Council of the League for approval; and

Whereas His Britannic Majesty has accepted the Mandate in respect of Palestine and undertaken to exercise it on behalf of the League of Nations in conformity with the following provisions; and

Whereas by the aforementioned Article 22 (paragraph 8), it is provided that the degree of authority, control or administration to be exercised by the Mandatory, not having been previously agreed upon by the Members of the League, shall be explicitly defined by the Council of the League of Nations;

Confirming the said Mandate, defines its terms as follows:

---

* British White Paper, Cmd. 1785.

ARTICLE 1. The Mandatory shall have full powers of legislation and of administration, save as they may be limited by the terms of this Mandate.

ARTICLE 2. The Mandatory shall be responsible for placing the country under such political, administrative and economic conditions as will secure the establishment of the Jewish National Home, as laid down in the preamble, and the development of self-governing institutions, and also for safeguarding the civil and religious rights of all the inhabitants of Palestine, irrespective of race and religion.

ARTICLE 3. The Mandatory shall, so far as circumstances permit, encourage local autonomy.

ARTICLE 4. An appropriate Jewish Agency shall be recognized as a public body for the purpose of advising and co-operating with the Administration of Palestine in such economic, social and other matters as may affect the establishment of the Jewish National Home and the interests of the Jewish population in Palestine, and, subject always to the control of the Administration, to assist and take part in the development of the country.
The Zionist organization, so long as its organization and constitution are in the opinion of the Mandatory appropriate, shall be recognized as such agency. It shall take steps in consultation with His Britannic Majesty's Government to secure the co-operation of all Jews who are willing to assist in the establishment of the Jewish National Home.

ARTICLE 5. The Mandatory shall be responsible for seeing that no Palestine territory shall be ceded or leased to, or in any way placed under the control of, the Government of any foreign Power.

ARTICLE 6. The Administration of Palestine, while ensuring that the rights and position of other sections of the population are not prejudiced, shall facilitate Jewish immigration under suitable conditions and shall encourage, in co-operation with the Jewish Agency referred to in Article 4, close settlement by Jews on the land, including State lands and waste lands not required for public purposes.

ARTICLE 7. The Administration of Palestine shall be responsible for enacting a nationality law. There shall be included in this law provisions framed so as to facilitate the acquisition of Palestinian citizenship by Jews who take up their permanent residence in Palestine.

ARTICLE 13. All responsibility in connection with the Holy Places and religious buildings or sites in Palestine, including that of preserving existing rights and of securing free access to the Holy Places, religious buildings and sites and the free exercise of worship, while ensuring the requirements of public order and decorum, is assumed by the Mandatory, who shall be responsible solely to the League of Nations in all matters connected herewith, provided that nothing in this Article shall prevent the Mandatory from entering into such arrangements as he may deem reasonable with the Administration for the purpose of carrying the provisions of this Article into effect; and provided also that nothing in this Mandate shall be construed as conferring upon the Mandatory authority to interfere with the fabric of the management of purely Moslem sacred shrines, the immunities of which are guaranteed.

ARTICLE 14. A special Commission shall be appointed by the Mandatory to study, define and determine the rights and claims in connection with the Holy Places and the rights and claims relating to the different religious communities in Palestine. The method of nomination, the composition and the functions of this Commission shall be submitted to the Council of the League for its approval, and the Commission shall not be appointed or enter upon its functions without the approval of the Council.

ARTICLE 28. In the event of the termination of the Mandate hereby conferred upon the Mandatory, the Council of the League of Nations shall make such arrangements as may be deemed necessary for safe-guarding in perpetuity, under guarantee of the League, the rights secured by Articles 13 and 14, and shall use its influence for securing, under the guarantee of the League, that the Government of Palestine will fully honour the financial obligations legitimately incurred by the Administration of Palestine during the period of the Mandate, including the rights of public servants to pensions or gratuities.

CHURCHILL MEMORANDUM*

3 June 1922

The Secretary of State for the Colonies has given renewed consideration to the existing political situation in Palestine, with a very earnest desire to arrive at a settlement of the outstanding questions which have given rise to uncertainty and unrest among certain sections of the population. After consultation with the High Commissioner for Palestine the following statement has been drawn up. It summarizes the essential parts of the correspondence that has already taken place between the Secretary of State and a Delegation from the Moslem Christian Society of Palestine, which has been for some time in England, and it states the further conclusions which have since been reached.

The tension which has prevailed from time to time in Palestine is mainly due to apprehensions, which are entertained both by sections of the Arab and by sections of the Jewish population. These apprehensions, so far as the Arabs are concerned, are partly based upon exaggerated interpretations of the meaning of the Declaration favouring the establishment of a Jewish National Home in Palestine, made on behalf of His Majesty's Government on 2 November 1917. Unauthorized statements have been made to the effect that the purpose in view is to create a wholly Jewish Palestine. Phrases have been used such as that Palestine is to become 'as Jewish as England is English.' His Majesty's Government regard any such expectation as impracticable and have no such aim in view. Nor have they at any time contemplated, as appears to be feared by the Arab Delegation, the disappearance or the subordination of the Arabic population, language or culture in Palestine. They would draw attention to the fact that the terms of the Declaration referred to do not contemplate that Palestine as a whole should be converted into a Jewish National Home, but that such a Home should be founded *in Palestine*. In this connection it has been observed with satisfaction that at the meeting of the Zionist Congress, the supreme governing body of the Zionist Organization, held at Carlsbad in September 1921, a resolution was

---

* Palestine, Correspondence with the Palestine Arab Delegation and the Zionist Organization (British White Paper, Cmd. 1700), pp. 17–21.

passed expressing as the official statement of Zionist aims 'the determination of the Jewish people to live with the Arab people on terms of unity and mutual respect, and together with them to make the common home into a flourishing community, the upbuilding of which may assure to each of its peoples an undisturbed national development.'

It is also necessary to point out that the Zionist Commission in Palestine, now termed the Palestine Zionist Executive, has not desired to possess, and does not possess, any share in the general administration of the country. Nor does the special position assigned to the Zionist Organization in Article IV of the Draft Mandate for Palestine imply any such functions. That special position relates to the measures to be taken in Palestine affecting the Jewish population, and contemplates that the Organization may assist in the general development of the country, but does not entitle it to share in any degree in its Government.

Further, it is contemplated that the status of all citizens of Palestine in the eyes of the law shall be Palestinian, and it has never been intended that they, or any section of them, should possess any other juridical status.

So far as the Jewish population of Palestine are concerned, it appears that some among them are apprehensive that His Majesty's Government may depart from the policy embodied in the Declaration of 1917. It is necessary, therefore, once more to affirm that these fears are unfounded, and that the Declaration, re-affirmed by the Conference of the Principal Allied Powers at San Remo and again in the Treaty of Sèvres, is not susceptible of change.

During the last two or three generations the Jews have recreated in Palestine a community, now numbering 80,000, of whom about one-fourth are farmers or workers upon the land. This community has its own political organs; an elected assembly for the direction of its domestic concerns; elected councils in the towns; and an organization for the control of its schools. It has its elected Chief Rabbinate and Rabbinical Council for the direction of its religious affairs. Its business is conducted in Hebrew as a vernacular language, and a Hebrew Press serves its needs. It has its distinctive intellectual life and displays considerable economic activity. This community, then, with its town and country population, its political, religious and social organizations, its own language, its own customs, its own life, has in fact 'national' characteristics. When it is asked what is meant by the development of the Jewish National Home in Palestine, it may be answered that it is not the imposition of a Jewish nationality upon the inhabitants of Palestine as a whole, but the further development of the existing Jewish community, with the assistance of Jews in other parts of the world, in order that it may become a centre in which the Jewish people as a whole may take, on grounds of religion and race, an interest and a pride. But in order that this community should have the best prospect of free development and provide a full opportunity for the Jewish people to display its capacities, it is essential that it should know that it is in Palestine as of right and not on sufferance. That is the reason why it is necessary that the existence of a Jewish National Home in Palestine should be internationally guaranteed, and that it should be formally recognized to rest upon ancient historic connection.

This, then, is the interpretation which His Majesty's Government place upon Declaration of 1917, and, so understood, the Secretary of State is of opinion that it does not contain or imply anything which need cause either alarm to the Arab population of Palestine or disappointment to the Jews.

For the fulfilment of this policy it is necessary that the Jewish community in Palestine should be able to increase its numbers by immigration. This immigration cannot be so great in volume as to exceed whatever may be the economic capacity of the country at the time to absorb new arrivals. It is essential to ensure that the immigrants should not be a burden upon the people of Palestine as a whole, and that they should not deprive any section of the present population of their employment. Hitherto the immigration has fulfilled these conditions. The number of immigrants since the British occupation has been about 25,000. ...

REPORT OF PALESTINE ROYAL COMMISSION (PEEL COMMISSION)*

July 1937

The Commission under Lord Peel was appointed in 1936. The following are extracts from recommendations made in Ch. XXII:

Having reached the conclusion that there is no possibility of solving the Palestine problem under the existing Mandate (or even under a scheme of cantonization), the Commission recommend the termination of the present Mandate on the basis of Partition and put forward a definite scheme which they consider to be practicable, honourable and just. The scheme is as follows:

The Mandate for Palestine should terminate and be replaced by a Treaty System in accordance with the precedent set in Iraq and Syria.

Under Treaties to be negotiated by the Mandatory with the Government of Transjordan and representatives of the Arabs of Palestine on the one hand, and with the Zionist Organization on the other, it would be declared that two sovereign independent States would shortly be established—(1) an Arab State consisting of Transjordan united with that part of Palestine allotted to the Arabs, (2) a Jewish State consisting of that part of Palestine allotted to the Jews. The Mandatory would undertake to support any requests for admission to the League of Nations made by the Governments of the Arab and Jewish States. The Treaties would include strict guarantees for the protection of minorities. Military Conventions would be attached to the Treaties.

A new Mandate should be instituted to execute the trust of maintaining the sanctity of Jerusalem and Bethlehem and ensuring free and safe access to them for all the world. An enclave should be demarcated to which this Mandate should apply, extending from a point north of Jerusalem to a point south of Bethlehem, and access to the sea should be provided by a corridor extending from Jerusalem to Jaffa. The policy of the Balfour Declaration would not apply to the Mandated Area.

The Jewish State should pay a subvention to the Arab State. A Finance Commission should be appointed to advise as to its amount and as to the division of the public debt of Palestine and other financial questions.

In view of the backwardness of Transjordan, Parliament should be asked to make a grant of £2,000,000 to the Arab State.

* *Palestine Royal Commission: Report,* 1937 (British Blue Book, Cmd. 5479).

WHITE PAPER*

May 1939

The main recommendations are extracted below:

10. ... His Majesty's Government make the following declaration of their intentions regarding the future government of Palestine:

(i) The objective of His Majesty's Government is the establishment within ten years of an independent Palestine State in such treaty relations with the United Kingdom as will provide satisfactorily for the commercial and strategic requirements of both countries in the future. This proposal for the establishment of the independent State would involve consultation with the Council of the League of Nations with a view to the termination of the Mandate.

(ii) The independent State should be one in which Arabs and Jews share in government in such a way as to ensure that the essential interests of each community are safeguarded.

(iii) The establishment of the independent State will be preceded by a transitional period throughout which His Majesty's Government will retain responsibility for the government of the country. During the transitional period the people of Palestine will be given an increasing part in the government of their country. Both sections of the population will have an opportunity to participate in the machinery of government, and the process will be carried on whether or not they both avail themselves of it.

(iv) As soon as peace and order have been sufficiently restored in Palestine steps will be taken to carry out this policy of giving the people of Palestine an increasing part in the government of their country, the objective being to place Palestinians in charge of all the Departments of Government, with the assistance of British advisers and subject to the control of the High Commissioner. With this object in view His Majesty's Government will be prepared immediately to arrange that Palestinians shall be placed in charge of certain Departments, with British advisers. The Palestinian heads of Departments will sit on the Executive Council, which advises the High Commissioner. Arab and Jewish representatives will be invited to serve as heads of Departments approximately in proportion to their respective populations. The number of Palestinians in charge of Departments will be increased as circumstances permit until all heads of Departments are Palestinians, exercising the administrative and advisory functions which are at present performed by British officials. When that stage is reached consideration will be given to the question of converting the Executive Council into a Council of Ministers with a consequential change in the status and functions of the Palestinian heads of Departments.

(v) His Majesty's Government make no proposals at this stage regarding the establishment of an elective legislature. Nevertheless they would regard this as an appropriate constitutional development, and, should public opinion in Palestine hereafter show itself in favour of such a

---

* British White Paper, Cmd. 6019.

development, they will be prepared, provided that local conditions permit, to establish the necessary machinery.

(vi) At the end of five years from the restoration of peace and order, an appropriate body representative of the people of Palestine and of His Majesty's Government will be set up to review the working of the constitutional arrangements during the transitional period and to consider and make recommendations regarding the Constitution of the independent Palestine State.

(vii) His Majesty's Government will require to be satisfied that in the treaty contemplated by sub-paragraph (i) or in the Constitution contemplated by sub-paragraph (vi) adequate provision has been made for:

(*a*) the security of, and freedom of access to, the Holy Places, and the protection of the interests and property of the various religious bodies;

(*b*) the protection of the different communities in Palestine in accordance with the obligations of His Majesty's Government to both Arabs and Jews and for the special position in Palestine of the Jewish National Home;

(*c*) such requirements to meet the strategic situation as may be regarded as necessary by His Majesty's Government in the light of the circumstances then existing.

His Majesty's Government will also require to be satisfied that the interests of certain foreign countries in Palestine, for the preservation of which they are presently responsible, are adequately safeguarded.

(viii) His Majesty's Government will do everything in their power to create conditions which will enable the independent Palestine State to come into being within ten years. If, at the end of ten years, it appears to His Majesty's Government that, contrary to their hope, circumstances require the postponement of the establishment of the independent State, they will consult with representatives of the people of Palestine, the Council of the League of Nations and the neighbouring Arab States before deciding on such a postponement. If His Majesty's Government come to the conclusion that postponement is unavoidable, they will invite the co-operation of these parties in framing plans for the future with a view to achieving the desired objective at the earliest possible date.

14. they believe that they will be acting consistently with their Mandatory obligations to both Arabs and Jews, and in the manner best calculated to serve the interests of the whole people of Palestine by adopting the following proposals regarding immigration:

(i) Jewish immigration during the next five years will be at a rate which, if economic absorptive capacity permits, will bring the Jewish population up to approximately one-third of the total population of the country. Taking into account the expected natural increase of the Arab and Jewish populations, and the number of illegal Jewish immigrants now in the country, this would allow for the admission, as from the beginning of April this year, of some 75,000 immigrants over the next five years. These immigrants would, subject to the criterion of economic absorptive capacity, be admitted as follows:

(*a*) For each of the next five years a quota of 10,000 Jewish immigrants will be allowed, on the understanding that a shortage in any one year may be added to the quotas for subsequent years, within the five-year period, if economic absorptive capacity permits.

(*b*) In addition, as a contribution towards the solution of the Jewish refugee problem, 25,000 refugees will be admitted as soon as the High Commissioner is satisfied that adequate provision for their maintenance is ensured, special consideration being given to refugee children and dependants.

(ii) The existing machinery for ascertaining economic absorptive capacity will be retained, and the High Commissioner will have the ultimate responsibility for deciding the limits of economic capacity. Before each periodic decision is taken, Jewish and Arab representatives will be consulted.

(iii) After the period of five years no further Jewish immigration will be permitted unless the Arabs of Palestine are prepared to acquiesce in it.

(iv) His Majesty's Government are determined to check illegal immigration, and further preventive measures are being adopted. The numbers of any Jewish illegal immigrants who, despite these measures, may succeed in coming into the country and cannot be deported will be deducted from the yearly quotas.

15. His Majesty's Government are satisfied that, when the immigration over five years which is now contemplated has taken place they will not be justified in facilitating, nor will they be under any obligation to facilitate, the further development of the Jewish National Home by immigration regardless of the wishes of the Arab population.

16. The Administration of Palestine is required, under Article 6 of the Mandate, 'while ensuring that the rights and position of other sections of the population are not prejudiced,' to encourage 'close settlement by Jews on the land,' and no restriction has been imposed hitherto on the transfer of land from Arabs to Jews. The Reports of several expert Commissions have indicated that, owing to the natural growth of the Arab population and the steady sale in recent years of Arab land to Jews, there is now in certain areas no room for further transfers of Arab land, whilst in some other areas such transfers of land must be restricted if Arab cultivators are to maintain their existing standard of life and a considerable landless Arab population is not soon to be created. In these circumstances, the High Commissioner will be given general powers to prohibit and regulate transfers of land. These powers will date from the publication of this statement of Policy and the High Commissioner will retain them throughout the transitional period.

17. The policy of the Government will be directed towards the development of the land and the improvement, where possible, of methods of cultivation. In the light of such development it will be open to the High Commissioner, should he be satisfied that the 'rights and position' of the Arab population will be duly

preserved, to review and modify any orders passed relating to the prohibition or restriction of the transfer of land.

BILTMORE PROGRAMME*

11 May 1942

The following programme was approved by a Zionist Conference held in the Biltmore Hotel, New York City:

1. American Zionists assembled in this Extraordinary Conference reaffirm their unequivocal devotion to the cause of democratic freedom and international justice to which the people of the United States, allied with the other United Nations, have dedicated themselves, and give expression to their faith in the ultimate victory of humanity and justice over lawlessness and brute force.

2. This Conference offers a message of hope and encouragement to their fellow Jews in the Ghettos and concentration camps of Hitler-dominated Europe and prays that their hour of liberation may not be far distant.

3. The Conference sends its warmest greetings to the Jewish Agency Executive in Jerusalem, to the Va'ad Leumi, and to the whole Yishuv in Palestine, and expresses its profound admiration for their steadfastness and achievements in the face of peril and great difficulties. ...

4. In our generation, and in particular in the course of the past twenty years, the Jewish people have awakened and transformed their ancient homeland; from 50,000 at the end of the last war their numbers have increased to more than 500,000. They have made the waste places to bear fruit and the desert to blossom. Their pioneering achievements in agriculture and in industry, embodying new patterns of co-operative endeavour, have written a notable page in the history of colonization.

5. In the new values thus created, their Arab neighbours in Palestine have shared. The Jewish people in its own work of national redemption welcomes the economic, agricultural and national development of the Arab peoples and states. The Conference reaffirms the stand previously adopted at Congresses of the World Zionist Organization, expressing the readiness and the desire of the Jewish people for full co-operation with their Arab neighbours.

6. The Conference calls for the fulfilment of the original purpose of the Balfour Declaration and the Mandate which '*recognizing the historical connexion of the Jewish people with Palestine*' was to afford them the opportunity, as stated by President Wilson, to found there a Jewish Commonwealth.

The Conference affirms its unalterable rejection of the White Paper of May 1939 and denies its moral or legal validity. The White Paper seeks to limit, and in fact to nullify Jewish rights to immigration and settlement in Palestine, and, as stated by Mr Winston Churchill in the House of Commons in May 1939, constitutes 'a breach and repudiation of the Balfour Declaration'. The policy of the White Paper is cruel and indefensible in its denial of sanctuary to Jews fleeing from Nazi persecution; and at a time when Palestine has become a focal

---

* Text supplied by courtesy of Josef Fraenkel.

point in the war front of the United Nations, and Palestine Jewry must provide all available manpower for farm and factory and camp, it is in direct conflict with the interests of the allied war effort.

7. In the struggle against the forces of aggression and tyranny, of which Jews were the earliest victims, and which now menace the Jewish National Home, recognition must be given to the right of the Jews of Palestine to play their full part in the war effort and in the defence of their country, through a Jewish military force fighting under its own flag and under the high command of the United Nations.

8. The Conference declares that the new world order that will follow victory cannot be established on foundations of peace, justice and equality, unless the problem of Jewish homelessness is finally solved.

The Conference urges that the gates of Palestine be opened; that the Jewish Agency be vested with control of immigration into Palestine and with the necessary authority for upbuilding the country, including the development of its unoccupied and uncultivated lands; and that Palestine be established as a Jewish Commonwealth integrated in the structure of the new democratic world.

Then and only then will the age old wrong to the Jewish people be righted.

UN GENERAL ASSEMBLY RESOLUTION ON THE FUTURE GOVERNMENT OF PALESTINE (PARTITION RESOLUTION)

29 November 1947

The General Assembly,

Having met in special session at the request of the mandatory Power to constitute and instruct a special committee to prepare for the consideration of the question of the future government of Palestine at the second regular session;

Having constituted a Special Committee and instructed it to investigate all questions and issues relevant to the problem of Palestine, and to prepare proposals for the solution of the problem, and

Having received and examined the report of the Special Committee (document A/364) including a number of unanimous recommendations and a plan of partition with economic union approved by the majority of the Special Committee,

Considers that the present situation in Palestine is one which is likely to impair the general welfare and friendly relations among nations;

Takes note of the declaration by the mandatory Power that it plans to complete its evacuation of Palestine by 1 August 1948;

Recommends to the United Kingdom, as the mandatory Power for Palestine, and to all other Members of the United Nations the adoption and implementation, with regard to the future government of Palestine, of the Plan of Partition with Economic Union set out below;

Requests that

(a) The Security Council take the necessary measures as provided for in the plan for its implementation;

(*b*) The Security Council consider, if circumstances during the transitional period require such consideration, whether the situation in Palestine constitutes a threat to the peace. If it decides that such a threat exists, and in order to maintain international peace and security, the Security Council should supplement the authorization of the General Assembly by taking measures, under Articles 39 and 41 of the Charter, to empower the United Nations Commission, as provided in this resolution, to exercise in Palestine the functions which are assigned to it by this resolution;

(*c*) The Security Council determine as a threat to the peace, breach of the peace or act of aggression, in accordance with Article 39 of the Charter, any attempt to alter by force the settlement envisaged by this resolution;

(*d*) The Trusteeship Council be informed of the responsibilities envisaged for it in this plan;

Calls upon the inhabitants of Palestine to take such steps as may be necessary on their part to put this plan into effect;

Appeals to all Governments and all peoples to refrain from taking any action which might hamper or delay the carrying out of these recommendations. . .

Official Records of the second session of the General Assembly, Resolutions, p. 131.

UN GENERAL ASSEMBLY RESOLUTION 194 (III)
11 December 1948

The Resolution's terms have been reaffirmed every year since 1948.

11. ... the refugees wishing to return to their homes and live at peace with their neighbours should be permitted to do so at the earliest practicable date, and that compensation should be paid for the property of those choosing not to return and for the loss of or damage to property which, under principles of international law or in equity, should be made good by the Governments or authorities responsible;

Official Records of the third session of the General Assembly, Part I, Resolutions, p. 21.

UN GENERAL ASSEMBLY RESOLUTION ON THE INTERNATIONALIZATION OF JERUSALEM
9 December 1949

The General Assembly,

Having regard to its resolution 181 (II) of 29 November 1947 and 194 (III) of 11 December 1948,

Having studied the reports of the United Nations Conciliation Commission for Palestine set up under the latter resolution,

I. Decides

In relation to Jerusalem,

Believing that the principles underlying its previous resolutions concerning this matter, and in particular its resolution of 29 November 1947, represent a just and equitable settlement of the question,

1. To restate, therefore, its intention that Jerusalem should be placed under a permanent international regime, which should envisage appropriate guarantees for the protection of the Holy Places, both within and outside Jerusalem, and to confirm specifically the following provisions of General Assembly resolution 181 (II): (1) The City of Jerusalem shall be established as a *corpus separatum* under a special international regime and shall be administered by the United Nations; (2) The Trusteeship Council shall be designated to discharge the responsibilities of the Administering Authority...; and (3) The City of Jerusalem shall include the present municipality of Jerusalem plus the surrounding villages and towns, the most eastern of which shall be Abu Dis; the most southern, Bethlehem; the most western, Ein Karim (including also the built-up area of Motsa); and the most northern, Shu'fat, as indicated on the attached sketchmap; ... [*map not reproduced: Ed.*]

Official Records of the fourth session of the General Assembly, Resolutions, p. 25.

TEXT OF UN SECURITY COUNCIL RESOLUTION 242

22 November 1967

The Security Council,

Expressing its continued concern with the grave situation in the Middle East,

Emphasizing the inadmissibility of the acquisition of territory by war and the need to work for a just and lasting peace in which every state in the area can live in security,

Emphasizing further that all Member States in their acceptance of the Charter of the United Nations have undertaken a commitment to act in accordance with Article 2 of the Charter

1. *Affirms* that the fulfilment of Charter principles requires the establishment of a just and lasting peace in the Middle East which should include the application of both the following principles:

    (i) Withdrawal of Israel armed forces from territories occupied in the recent conflict;

    (ii) Termination of all claims or states of belligerency and respect for the acknowledgement of the sovereignty, territorial integrity and political independence of every State in the area and their right to live in peace within secure and recognized boundaries free from threats or acts of force.

2. *Affirms further* the necessity

    (*a*) For guaranteeing freedom of navigation through international waterways in the area;

    (*b*) For achieving a just settlement of the refugee problem;

    (*c*) For guaranteeing the territorial inviolability and political independence of every State in the area, through measures including the establishment of demilitarized zones;

3. *Requests* the Secretary-General to designate a Special Representative to proceed to the Middle East to establish and maintain contacts with the States concerned in order to promote agreement and assist efforts to achieve a peaceful

and accepted settlement in accordance with the provisions and principles in this resolution;

4. *Requests* the Secretary-General to report to the Security Council on the progress of the efforts of the Special Representative as soon as possible.

Source: UN Document S/RES/242 (1967).

PALESTINIAN NATIONAL CHARTER (PLO COVENANT)

Resolutions of the Palestine National Council, July 1–17, 1968

In September 1993 Yasser Arafat declared those articles of the PLO Covenant which deny Israel's right to exist or are inconsistent with the PLO's commitments to Israel under the terms of subsequent accords to be invalid. Revision of those articles, presented here in italics, was to be undertaken as part of the ongoing peace process.

The following is the complete and unabridged text of the Palestinian National Covenant, as published officially in English by the PLO.

Article I:

Palestine is the homeland of the Arab Palestinian people; it is an indivisible part of the Arab homeland, and the Palestinian people are an integral part of the Arab nation.

Article II:

Palestine, with the boundaries it had during the British Mandate, is an indivisible territorial unit.

Article III:

The Palestinian Arab people possess the legal right to their homeland and have the right to determine their destiny after achieving the liberation of their country in accordance with their wishes and entirely of their own accord and will.

Article IV:

The Palestinian identity is a genuine, essential, and inherent characteristic; it is transmitted from parents to children. The Zionist occupation and the dispersal of the Palestinian Arab people, through the disasters which befell them, do not make them lose their Palestinian identity and their membership in the Palestinian community, nor do they negate them.

Article V:

The Palestinians are those Arab nationals who, until 1947, normally resided in Palestine regardless of whether they were evicted from it or have stayed there. Anyone born, after that date, of a Palestinian father—whether inside Palestine or outside it—is also a Palestinian.

Article VI:

The Jews who had normally resided in Palestine until the beginning of the Zionist invasion will be considered Palestinians.

Article VII:

That there is a Palestinian community and that it has material, spiritual, and historical connection with Palestine are indisputable facts. It is a national duty to bring up individual Palestinians in an Arab revolutionary manner. All means of information and education must be adopted in order to acquaint the Palestinian with his country in the most profound manner, both spiritual and material, that is possible. He must be prepared for the armed struggle and ready to sacrifice his wealth and his life in order to win back his homeland and bring about its liberation.

Article VIII:

The phase in their history, through which the Palestinian people are now living, is that of national (watani) struggle for the liberation of Palestine. Thus the conflicts among the Palestinian national forces are secondary, and should be ended for the sake of the basic conflict that exists between the forces of Zionism and of imperialism on the one hand, and the Palestinian Arab people on the other. On this basis the Palestinian masses, regardless of whether they are residing in the national homeland or in diaspora (mahajir) constitute—both their organizations and the individuals—one national front working for the retrieval of Palestine and its liberation through armed struggle.

Article IX:

Armed struggle is the only way to liberate Palestine. This is the overall strategy, not merely a tactical phase. The Palestinian Arab people assert their absolute determination and firm resolution to continue their armed struggle and to work for an armed popular revolution for the liberation of their country and their return to it. They also assert their right to normal life in Palestine and to exercise their right to self-determination and sovereignty over it.

Article X:

Commando action constitutes the nucleus of the Palestinian popular liberation war. This requires its escalation, comprehensiveness, and the mobilization of all the Palestinian popular and educational efforts and their organization and involvement in the armed Palestinian revolution. It also requires the achieving of unity for the national (watani) struggle among the different groupings of the Palestinian people, and between the Palestinian people and the Arab masses, so as to secure the continuation of the revolution, its escalation, and victory.

Article XI:

The Palestinians will have three mottoes: national (wataniyya) unity, national (qawmiyya) mobilization, and liberation.

Article XII:

The Palestinian people believe in Arab unity. In order to contribute their share toward the attainment of that objective, however, they must, at the present stage of their struggle, safeguard their Palestinian identity and develop their consciousness of that identity, and oppose any plan that may dissolve or impair it.

Article XIII:

Arab unity and the liberation of Palestine are two complementary objectives, the attainment of either of which facilitates the attainment of the other. Thus, Arab unity leads to the liberation of Palestine, the liberation of Palestine leads to Arab unity; and work towards the realization of one objective proceeds side by side with work towards the realization of the other.

Article XIV:

The destiny of the Arab nation, and indeed Arab existence itself, depend upon the destiny of the Palestine cause. From this interdependence springs the Arab nation's pursuit of, and striving for, the liberation of Palestine. The people of Palestine play the role of the vanguard in the realization of this sacred (qawmi) goal.

Article XV:

The liberation of Palestine, from an Arab viewpoint, is a national (qawmi) duty and it attempts to repel the Zionist and imperialist aggression against the Arab homeland, and aims at the elimination of Zionism in Palestine. Absolute responsibility for this falls upon the Arab nation—peoples and governments—with the Arab people of Palestine in the vanguard. Accordingly, the Arab nation must mobilize all its military, human, moral, and spiritual capabilities to participate actively with the Palestinian people in the liberation of Palestine. It must, particularly in the phase of the armed Palestinian revolution, offer and furnish the Palestinian people with all possible help, and material and human support, and make available to them the means and opportunities that will enable them to continue to carry out their leading role in the armed revolution, until they liberate their homeland.

Article XVI:

The liberation of Palestine, from a spiritual point of view, will provide the Holy Land with an atmosphere of safety and tranquility, which in turn will safeguard the country's religious sanctuaries and guarantee freedom of worship and of visit to all, without discrimination of race, color, language, or religion. Accordingly, the people of Palestine look to all spiritual forces in the world for support.

Article XVII:

The liberation of Palestine, from a human point of view, will restore to the Palestinian individual his dignity, pride, and freedom. Accordingly the Palestinian Arab people look forward to the support of all those who believe in the dignity of man and his freedom in the world.

Article XVIII:

The liberation of Palestine, from an international point of view, is a defensive action necessitated by the demands of self-defense. Accordingly the Palestinian people, desirous as they are of the friendship of all people, look to freedom-loving, and peace-loving states for support in order to restore their legitimate rights in Palestine, to re-establish peace and security in the country, and to enable its people to exercise national sovereignty and freedom.

Article XIX:

The partition of Palestine in 1947 and the establishment of the state of Israel are entirely illegal, regardless of the passage of time, because they were contrary to the will of the Palestinian people and to their natural right in their homeland, and inconsistent with the principles embodied in the Charter of the United Nations, particularly the right to self-determination.

Article XX:

The Balfour Declaration, the Mandate for Palestine, and everything that has been based upon them, are deemed null and void. Claims of historical or religious ties of

Jews with Palestine are incompatible with the facts of history and the true conception of what constitutes statehood. Judaism, being a religion, is not an independent nationality. Nor do Jews constitute a single nation with an identity of its own; they are citizens of the states to which they belong.

Article XXI:

The Arab Palestinian people, expressing themselves by the armed Palestinian revolution, reject all solutions which are substitutes for the total liberation of Palestine and reject all proposals aiming at the liquidation of the Palestinian problem, or its internationalization.

Article XXII:

Zionism is a political movement organically associated with international imperialism and antagonistic to all action for liberation and to progressive movements in the world. It is racist and fanatic in its nature, aggressive, expansionist, and colonial in its aims, and fascist in its methods. Israel is the instrument of Zionist movement, and geographical base for world imperialism placed strategically in the midst of the Arab homeland to combat the hopes of the Arab nation for liberation, unity, and progress. Israel is a constant source of threat vis-à-vis peace in the Middle East and the whole world. Since the liberation of Palestine will destroy the Zionist and imperialist presence and will contribute to the establishment of peace in the Middle East, the Palestinian people look for the support of all the progressive and peaceful forces and urge them all, irrespective of their affiliations and beliefs, to offer the Palestinian people all aid and support in their just struggle for the liberation of their homeland.

Article XXIII:

The demand of security and peace, as well as the demand of right and justice, require all states to consider Zionism an illegitimate movement, to outlaw its existence, and to ban its operations, in order that friendly relations among peoples may be preserved, and the loyalty of citizens to their respective homelands safeguarded.

Article XXIV:

The Palestinian people believe in the principles of justice, freedom, sovereignty, self-determination, human dignity, and in the right of all peoples to exercise them.

Article XXV:

For the realization of the goals of this Charter and its principles, the Palestine Liberation Organization will perform its role in the liberation of Palestine in accordance with the Constitution of this Organization.

Article XXVI:

The Palestine Liberation Organization, representative of the Palestinian revolutionary forces, is responsible for the Palestinian Arab people's movement in its struggle—to retrieve its homeland, liberate and return to it and exercise the right to self-determination in it—in all military, political, and financial fields and also for whatever may be required by the Palestine case on the inter-Arab and international levels.

Article XXVII:

The Palestine Liberation Organization shall co-operate with all Arab states, each according to its potentialities; and will adopt a neutral policy among them in the light of the requirements of the war of liberation; and on this basis it shall not interfere in the internal affairs of any Arab state.

Article XXVIII:

The Palestinian Arab people assert the genuineness and independence of their national (wataniyya) revolution and reject all forms of intervention, trusteeship, and subordination.

Article XXIV:

The Palestinian people possess the fundamental and genuine legal right to liberate and retrieve their homeland. The Palestinian people determine their attitude toward all states and forces on the basis of the stands they adopt vis-à-vis to the Palestinian revolution to fulfil the aims of the Palestinian people.

Article XXX:

Fighters and carriers of arms in the war of liberation are the nucleus of the popular army which will be the protective force for the gains of the Palestinian Arab people.

Article XXXI:

The Organization shall have a flag, an oath of allegiance, and an anthem. All this shall be decided upon in accordance with a special regulation.

Article XXXII:

Regulations, which shall be known as the Constitution of the Palestinian (sic) Liberation Organization, shall be annexed to this Charter. It will lay down the manner in which the Organization, and its organs and institutions, shall be constituted; the respective competence of each; and the requirements of its obligation under the Charter.

Article XXXIII:

This Charter shall not be amended save by [vote of] a majority of two-thirds of the total membership of the National Congress of the Palestine Liberation Organization [taken] at a special session convened for that purpose.

English rendition as published in Basic Political Documents of the Armed Palestinian Resistance Movement; Leila S. Kadi (Ed.), Palestine Research Centre, Beirut, December 1969, pp. 137–141.

UN SECURITY COUNCIL RESOLUTION ON JERUSALEM

25 September 1971

The resolution, No. 298 (1971), was passed nem. con., *with the abstention of Syria.*

The Security Council,

Recalling its Resolutions 252 (1968) of 21 May 1968, and 267 (1969) of 3 July 1969, and the earlier General Assembly resolution 2253 (ES-V) and 2254 (ES-V) of 4 and 14 July 1967, concerning measures and actions by Israel designed to change the status of the Israeli-occupied section of Jerusalem,

Having considered the letter of the Permanent Representative of Jordan on this situation in Jerusalem and the reports of the Secretary-General, and having heard the statements of the parties concerned in the question,

Recalling the principle that acquisition of territory by military conquest is inadmissible,

Noting with concern the non-compliance by Israel with the above-mentioned resolutions,

Noting with concern also that since the adoption of the above-mentioned resolutions Israel has taken further measures designed to change the status and character of the occupied section of Jerusalem.

1. *Reaffirms* its resolutions 252 (1968) and 267 (1969);

2. *Deplores* the failure of Israel to respect the previous resolutions adopted by the United Nations concerning measures and actions by Israel purporting to affect the status of the City of Jerusalem;

3. *Confirms* in the clearest possible terms that all legislative and administrative actions taken by Israel to change the status of the City of Jerusalem, including expropriation of land and properties, transfer of populations and legislation aimed at the incorporation of the occupied section, are totally invalid and cannot change that status;

4. *Urgently calls upon* Israel to rescind all previous measures and actions and to take no further steps in the occupied section of Jerusalem which may purport to change the status of the City, or which would prejudice the rights of the inhabitants and the interests of the international community, or a just and lasting peace;

5. *Requests* the Secretary-General, in consultation with the President of the Security Council and using such instrumentalities as he may choose, including a representative or a mission, to report to the Council as appropriate and in any event within 60 days on the implementation of the present resolution.

Source: UN Document S/RES/298 (1971).

UN SECURITY COUNCIL RESOLUTION 338

22 October 1973

UN Resolutions between 1967 and October 1973 reaffirmed Security Council Resolution 242 (see above). In an attempt to end the fourth Middle East war, which had broken out between the Arabs and Israel on 6 October 1973, the UN Security Council passed the following Resolution:

The Security Council,

1. *Calls upon* all parties to the present fighting to cease all firing and terminate all military activity immediately, not later than 12 hours after the moment of the adoption of the decision, in the positions they now occupy;

2. *Calls upon* the parties concerned to start immediately after the ceasefire the implementation of Security Council Resolution 242 (1967) in all of its parts;

3. *Decides that,* immediately and concurrently with the ceasefire negotiations start between the parties concerned under appropriate auspices aimed at establishing a just and durable peace in the Middle East.

Source: UN Document PR/73/29 (1973).

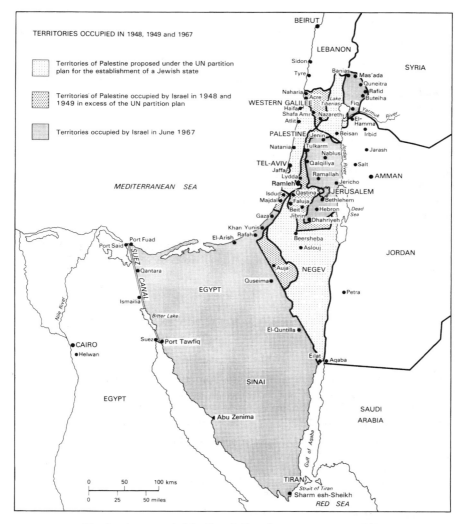

TERRITORIES OCCUPIED IN 1948, 1949 and 1967

Territories of Palestine proposed under the UN partition plan for the establishment of a Jewish state

Territories of Palestine occupied by Israel in 1948 and 1949 in excess of the UN partition plan

Territories occupied by Israel in June 1967

Territories occupied by Israel. See also maps on page 341.

UN SECURITY COUNCIL RESOLUTION 340

25 October 1973

The Security Council,

Recalling its Resolutions 338 (1973) of 22 October 1973 and 339 (1973) of 23 October 1973,

Noting with regret the reported repeated violations of the ceasefire in non-compliance with Resolutions 338 (1973) and 339 (1973),

Noting with concern from the Secretary-General's report that the UN military observers have not yet been enabled to place themselves on both sides of the ceasefire line,

1. *Demands* that an immediate and complete ceasefire be observed and that the parties withdraw to the positions occupied by them at 16.50 hours GMT on 22 October 1973;

2. *Requests* the Secretary-General as an immediate step to increase the number of UN military observers on both sides;

3. *Decides* to set up immediately under its authority a UN emergency force to be composed of personnel drawn from member states of the UN, except the permanent members of the Security Council, and requests the Secretary-General to report within 24 hours on the steps taken to this effect.

4. *Requests* the Secretary-General to report to the Council on an urgent and continuing basis on the state of implementation of this Resolution, as well as Resolutions 338 (1973) and 339 (1973);

5. *Requests* all member states to extend their full co-operation to the UN in the implementation of this Resolution, as well as Resolutions 338 (1973) and 339 (1973).

Source: UN Document PR/73/31 (1973).

DECLARATION OF EEC FOREIGN MINISTERS ON THE MIDDLE EAST SITUATION

6 November 1973

The Nine Governments of the European Community have exchanged views on the situation in the Middle East. While emphasizing that the views set out below are only a first contribution on their part to the search for a comprehensive solution to the problem, they have agreed on the following:

1. They strongly urge that the forces of both sides in the Middle East conflict should return immediately to the positions they occupied on 22 October in accordance with Resolutions 339 and 340 of the Security Council. They believe that a return to these positions will facilitate a solution to other pressing problems concerning prisoners of war and the Egyptian Third Army.

2. They have the firm hope that, following the adoption by the Security Council of Resolution 338 of 22 October, negotiations will at last begin for the restoration in the Middle East of a just and lasting peace through the application of Security Council Resolution 242 in all of its parts. They declare themselves ready to do all in their power to contribute to that peace. They believe that those negotiations must take place in the framework of the United Nations. They recall that the Charter has entrusted to the Security Council the principal responsibility for international peace and security. The Council and the Secretary-General have a special role to play in the making and keeping of peace through the application of Council Resolutions 242 and 338.

3. They consider that a peace agreement should be based particularly on the following points:

(i) the inadmissibility of the acquisition of territory by force;

(ii) the need for Israel to end the territorial occupation which it has maintained since the conflict of 1967;

(iii) respect for the sovereignty, territorial integrity and independence of every state in the area and their right to live in peace within secure and recognized boundaries;

(iv) recognition that in the establishment of a just and lasting peace account must be taken of the legitimate rights of the Palestinians.

Article 4 calls for the dispatch of peace-keeping forces to the demilitarized zones.

Source: *Bulletin of the European Communities Commission,* No. 10, 1973, p. 106.

EGYPTIAN-ISRAELI AGREEMENT ON DISENGAGEMENT OF FORCES IN PURSUANCE OF THE GENEVA PEACE CONFERENCE

(signed by the Egyptian and Israeli Chiefs of Staff, 18 January 1974)

This agreement was superseded by the second Egyptian-Israeli Disengagement Agreement signed in September 1975 (see p. 344 below) and then by the Peace Treaty between Egypt and Israel signed on 26 March 1979 (see p. 349 below). A map showing the boundaries of the first agreement is reproduced herewith.

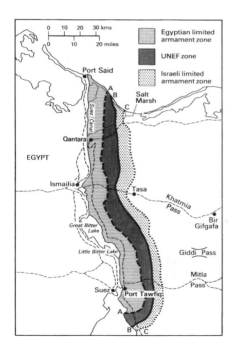

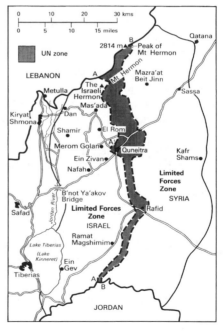

Disengagement Agreement of 18 January 1974 between Israel and Egypt.

Disengagement Agreement of 31 May 1974 between Israel and Syria.

341

DISENGAGEMENT AGREEMENT BETWEEN SYRIAN AND ISRAELI FORCES AND PROTOCOL TO AGREEMENT ON UNITED NATIONS DISENGAGEMENT OBSERVER FORCE (UNDOF)

(signed in Geneva, 31 May 1974)

(Annex A)

A.　Israel and Syria will scrupulously observe the cease-fire on land, sea and air and will refrain from all military actions against each other, from the time of signing this document in implementation of the United Nations Security Council Resolution 338 dated 22 October 1973.

B.　The military forces of Israel and Syria will be separated in accordance with the following principles:

1. All Israeli military forces will be west of a line designated line A on the map attached hereto (*reproduced below*), except in Quneitra (Kuneitra) area, where they will be west of a line A-1.

2. All territory east of line A will be under Syrian administration and Syrian civilians will return to this territory.

3. The area between line A and the line designated as line B on the attached map will be an area of separation. In this area will be stationed UNDOF established in accordance with the accompanying Protocol.

4. All Syrian military forces will be east of a line designated as line B on the attached map.

5. There will be two equal areas of limitation in armament and forces, one west of line A and one east of line B as agreed upon.

C.　In the area between line A and line A-1 on the attached map there shall be no military forces.

D.　*Paragraph D deals with practical details of signing and implementation.*

E.　Provisions of paragraphs A, B and C shall be inspected by personnel of the United Nations comprising UNDOF under the Agreement.

F.　*Paragraphs F and G deal with repatriation of prisoners and return of bodies of dead soldiers.*

H.　This Agreement is not a peace agreement. It is a step towards a just and durable peace on the basis of the Security Council Resolution 338 dated 22 October 1973.

A Protocol to the Disengagement Agreement outlined the functions of the United Nations Disengagement Observer Force (UNDOF).

RESOLUTION OF CONFERENCE OF ARAB HEADS OF STATE

Rabat, 28 October 1974

The Conference of the Arab Heads of State:

1. *Affirms* the right of the Palestinian people to return to their homeland and to self-determination.

2. *Affirms* the right of the Palestinian people to establish an independent national authority, under the leadership of the PLO in its capacity as the sole legitimate representative of the Palestine people, over all liberated territory. The

Arab States are pledged to uphold this authority, when it is established, in all spheres and at all levels.

3. *Supports* the PLO in the exercise of its national and international responsibilities, within the context of the principle of Arab solidarity.

4. *Invites* the kingdom of Jordan, Syria and Egypt to formalize their relations in the light of these decisions and in order that they be implemented.

5. *Affirms* the obligation of all Arab States to preserve Palestinian unity and not to interfere in Palestinian internal affairs.

Sources: *Le Monde: Problèmes Politiques et Sociaux*, 7 March 1975; *Arab Report and Record*.

UN GENERAL ASSEMBLY RESOLUTION 3236 (XXIX)

22 November 1974

The General Assembly,

Having considered the question of Palestine,

Having heard the statement of the Palestine Liberation Organization, the representative of the Palestinian people,

Having also heard other statements made during the debate,

Deeply concerned that no just solution to the problem of Palestine has yet been achieved and recognizing that the problem of Palestine continues to endanger international peace and security,

Recognizing that the Palestinian people is entitled to self-determination in accordance with the Charter of the United Nations,

Expressing its grave concern that the Palestinian people has been prevented from enjoying its inalienable rights, in particular its right to self-determination,

Guided by the purposes and principles of the Charter,

Recalling its relevant resolutions which affirm the right of the Palestinian people to self-determination,

1. *Reaffirms* the inalienable rights of Palestinian people in Palestine, including:

(*a*) The right to self-determination without external interference;

(*b*) The right to national independence and sovereignty;

2. *Reaffirms also* the inalienable right of the Palestinians to return to their homes and property from which they have been displaced and uprooted, and calls for their return;

3. *Emphasizes* that full respect for and the realization of these inalienable rights of the Palestinian people are indispensable for the solution of the question of Palestine;

4. *Recognizes* that the Palestinian people is a principal party in the establishment of a just and durable peace in the Middle East;

5. *Further Recognizes* the right of the Palestinian people to regain its rights by all means in accordance with the purposes and principles of the Charter of the United Nations;

6. *Appeals* to all States and international organizations to extend their support to the Palestinian people in its struggle to restore its rights, in accordance with the Charter;

7. *Requests* the Secretary-General to establish contacts with the Palestinian Liberation Organization on all matters concerning the question of Palestine;

8. *Requests* the Secretary-General to report to the General Assembly at its thirtieth session on the implementation of the present resolution;

9. *Decides* to include the item 'Question of Palestine' in the provisional agenda of its thirtieth session.

Source: UN Document BR/74/55 (1974).

SECOND INTERIM PEACE AGREEMENT BETWEEN EGYPT AND ISRAEL

(signed 4 September 1975)

This agreement was superseded by the Peace Treaty between Egypt and Israel signed on 26 March 1979 (see p. 349 below).

DEVELOPMENTS 1975–78

At the 30th Meeting of the UN General Assembly in November 1975, General Assembly Resolution 3236 (XXIX) was reaffirmed and a 20-nation Committee (the Committee on Palestine Rights) was set up to report on the 'Exercise of the Inalienable Right of the Palestine People' by 1 June 1976.

At the UN Security Council a draft resolution which would have affirmed the rights of the Palestinian people to self-determination, including the right to establish an independent state, was vetoed by the USA on 26 January 1976. A Security Council draft resolution criticizing Israeli policies in East Jerusalem and on the West Bank of the Jordan was also vetoed by the USA on 25 March 1976.

The Committee on Palestine Rights presented its report in June 1976 and recommended that Israel should withdraw from all occupied territories by June 1977. A resolution in the Security Council, stemming from the report, affirmed the 'inalienable rights of the Palestinians' and called for the creation of a 'Palestine entity' in the West Bank and Gaza. This resolution was vetoed by the USA on 29 June 1976. The Committee on Palestine Rights then submitted its report to the UN General Assembly in November 1976 in the form of a resolution. The Resolution (No. 20, of 24 November 1976) was adopted by a vote of 90 to 16 (30 members abstained; 10 were absent). The USA and 10 other Western countries (including the UK) opposed the Resolution.

Other General Assembly resolutions in December 1976 called for the reconvening of the Geneva Middle East peace conference by March 1977 and the participation in the negotiations of the PLO. Neither of these resolutions was implemented.

After a meeting in London of the nine EC heads of government at the end of June 1977, a statement was issued reaffirming earlier statements and stating that 'The Nine have affirmed their belief that a solution to the conflict in the Middle East will be possible only if the legitimate rights of the Palestinian people to give effective expression to its national identity is translated into fact, which would take into account the need for a homeland for the Palestinian people. .... In the context of an overall settlement Israel must be ready to recognize the legitimate rights of the Palestinian people; equally, the Arab side must be ready to recognize the right of Israel to live in peace within secure and recognized boundaries'.

A UN General Assembly Resolution of 25 November 1977 (32/30) 'called anew' for the early convening of the Geneva Middle East peace conference.

A further UN General Assembly Resolution (33/29 of 7 December 1978) repeated the call for the convening of the Geneva Middle East peace conference. The main focus of attention, however, had now moved away from the UN. President Sadat of Egypt visited Jerusalem in November 1977, and after protracted negotiations, President Sadat and Menachem Begin first of all signed two agreements at Camp David in the USA under the auspices of the US President, Jimmy Carter, and subsequently signed a Peace Treaty in Washington on 26 March 1979. The Arab League Council, angry at Egypt's unilateral action, met in Baghdad on 27 March and passed a series of resolutions aimed at isolating Egypt from the Arab world.

CAMP DAVID: THE FRAMEWORK FOR PEACE IN THE MIDDLE EAST

Muhammad Anwar as-Sadat, President of the Arab Republic of Egypt, and Menachem Begin, Prime Minister of Israel, met with President Carter of the USA at Camp David from 5 September to 17 September 1978, and agreed on the following framework for peace in the Middle East. They invited other parties to the Arab–Israeli conflict to adhere to it.

Preamble:

The search for peace in the Middle East must be guided by the following:

The agreed basis for a peaceful settlement of the conflict between Israel and its neighbours is UN Security Council Resolution 242 in all its parts.

The historic initiative by President Sadat in visiting Jerusalem and the reception accorded to him by the Parliament, Government and people of Israel, and the reciprocal visit of Prime Minister Begin to Ismailia, the peace proposals made by both leaders, as well as the warm reception of these missions by the peoples of both countries, have created an unprecedented opportunity for peace which must not be lost if this generation and future generations are to be spared the tragedies of war.

The provisions of the Charter of the UN and the other accepted norms of international law and legitimacy now provide accepted standards for the conduct of relations between all states.

To achieve a relationship of peace, in the spirit of article 2 of the UN Charter, future negotiations between Israel and any neighbour prepared to negotiate peace and security with it, are necessary for the purpose of carrying out all the provisions and principles of Resolutions 242 and 338.

Peace requires respect for the sovereignty, territorial integrity and political independence of every state in the area and their right to live in peace within secure and recognized boundaries free from threats or acts of force. Progress toward that goal can accelerate movement towards a new era of reconciliation in the Middle East marked by co-operation in promoting economic development, in maintaining stability and in assuring security. . . .

Framework

Taking these factors into account, the parties are determined to reach a just, comprehensive and durable settlement of the Middle East conflict through the conclusion of peace treaties based on Security Council Resolutions 242 and 338 in all their parts. Their purpose is to achieve peace and good neighbourly relations. They recognize that, for peace to endure, it must involve all those who have been most deeply affected by the conflict. They therefore agree that this framework as appropriate is intended by them to constitute a basis for peace not only between Egypt and Israel but also between Israel and each of its other neighbours which is prepared to negotiate peace with Israel on this basis. With that objective in mind, they have agreed to proceed as follows:

A. West Bank and Gaza

1. Egypt, Israel, Jordan and the representatives of the Palestinian people should participate in negotiations on the resolution of the Palestinian problem in all its aspects to achieve that objective, negotiations relating to the West Bank and Gaza should proceed in three stages.

(A) Egypt and Israel agree that, in order to ensure a peaceful and orderly transfer of authority, and taking into account the security concerns of all the parties, there should be transitional arrangements for the West Bank and Gaza for a period not exceeding five years. In order to provide full autonomy to the inhabitants, under these arrangements the Israeli military government and its civilian administration will be withdrawn as soon as a self-governing authority has been freely elected by the inhabitants of these areas to replace the existing military government.

To negotiate the details of transitional arrangement, the Government of Jordan will be invited to join the negotiations on the basis of this framework. These new arrangements should give due consideration to both the principle of self-government by the inhabitants of these territories and to the legitimate security concerns of the parties involved.

(B) Egypt, Israel and Jordan will agree on the modalities for establishing the elected self-governing authority in the West Bank and Gaza. The delegations of Egypt and Jordan may include Palestinians from the West Bank and Gaza or other Palestinians as mutually agreed. The parties will negotiate an agreement which will define the powers and responsibilities of the self-governing authority to be exercised in the West Bank and Gaza. A withdrawal of Israeli armed forces will take place and there will be a redeployment of the remaining Israeli forces into specified security locations.

The negotiations shall be based on all the provisions and principles of UN Security Council Resolution 242. The negotiations will resolve, among other matters, the location of the boundaries and the nature of the security arrangements. The solution from the negotiations must also recognize the legitimate rights of the Palestinian people and their just requirements. In this way, the Palestinians will participate in the determination of their own future through:

(i) The negotiations among Egypt, Israel, Jordan and the representatives of the inhabitants of the West Bank and Gaza to agree on the final status of the West Bank and Gaza and other outstanding issues by the end of the transitional period.

(ii) Submitting their agreement to a vote by the elected representatives of the inhabitants of the West Bank and Gaza.

(iii) Providing for the elected representatives of the inhabitants of the West Bank and Gaza to decide how they shall govern themselves consistent with the provisions of their agreement.

(iv) Participating as stated above in the work of the committee negotiating the peace treaty between Israel and Jordan.

The agreement will also include arrangements for assuring internal and external security and public order. A strong local police force will be established, which may include Jordanian citizens. In addition, Israeli and Jordanian forces will participate in joint patrols and in the manning of control posts to assure the security of the borders.

(C) When the self-governing authority (administrative council) in the West Bank and Gaza is established and inaugurated, the transitional period of five years will begin. As soon as possible, but not later than the third year after the beginning of the transitional period, negotiations will take place to determine the final status of the West Bank and Gaza and its relationship with its neighbours, and to conclude a peace treaty between Israel and Jordan by the end of the transitional period. These negotiations will be conducted among Egypt, Israel, Jordan and the elected representatives of the inhabitants of the West Bank and Gaza.

Two separate but related committees will be convened; one committee, consisting of representatives of the four parties which will negotiate and agree on the final status of the West Bank and Gaza, and its relationship with its neighbours, and the second committee, consisting of representatives of Israel and representatives of Jordan to be joined by the elected representatives of the inhabitants of the West Bank and Gaza, to negotiate the peace treaty between Israel and Jordan, taking into account the agreement reached on the final status of the West Bank and Gaza.

2. All necessary measures will be taken and provisions made to assure the security of Israel and its neighbours during the transitional period and beyond. To assist in providing such security, a strong local police force will be constituted by the self-governing authority. It will be composed of inhabitants of the West Bank and Gaza. The police will maintain continuing liaison on internal security matters with the designated Israeli, Jordanian and Egyptian officers.

3. During the transitional period, the representatives of Egypt, Israel, Jordan and the self-governing authority will constitute a continuing committee to decide by agreement on the modalities of admission of persons displaced from the West Bank and Gaza in 1967, together with necessary measures to prevent disruption and disorder. Other matters of common concern may also be dealt with by this committee.

4. Egypt and Israel will work with each other and with other interested parties to establish agreed procedures for a prompt, just and permanent implementation of the resolution of the refugee problem.

B. Egypt-Israel

1. Egypt and Israel undertake not to resort to the threat or the use of force to settle disputes. Any disputes shall be settled by peaceful means in accordance with the provisions of article 33 of the Charter of the UN.

2. In order to achieve peace between them, the parties agree to negotiate in good faith with a goal of concluding within three months from the signing of this framework a peace treaty between them, while inviting the other parties to the conflict to proceed simultaneously to negotiate and conclude similar peace treaties with a view to achieving a comprehensive peace in the area. The framework for the conclusion of a peace treaty between Egypt and Israel will govern the peace negotiations between them. The parties will agree on the modalities and the timetable for the implementation of their obligations under the treaty.

Associated principles

1. Egypt and Israel state that the principles and provisions described below should apply to peace treaties between Israel and each of its neighbours—Egypt, Jordan, Syria and Lebanon.

2. Signatories shall establish among themselves relationships normal to states at peace with one another. To this end, they should undertake to abide by all the provisions of the Charter of the UN. Steps to be taken in this respect include:

   (a) Full recognition.

   (b) Abolishing economic boycotts.

   (c) Guaranteeing that under their jurisdiction the citizens of the other parties shall enjoy the protection of the due process of law.

3. Signatories should explore possibilities for economic development in the context of final peace treaties, with the objective of contributing to the atmosphere of peace, co-operation, and friendship which is their common goal.

4. Claims commissions may be established for the mutual settlement of all financial claims.

5. The United States shall be invited to participate in the talks on matters related to the modalities of the implementation of the agreements and working out the time-table for the carrying out of the obligation of the parties.

6. The UN Security Council shall be requested to endorse the peace treaties and ensure that their provisions shall not be violated. The permanent members of the Security Council shall be requested to underwrite the peace treaties and ensure respect for their provisions. They shall also be requested to conform their policies and actions with the undertakings contained in this framework.

The second agreement signed at Camp David was a framework for the conclusion of a peace treaty between Egypt and Israel. The actual Treaty was signed on 26 March 1979, and is reproduced below.

THE PEACE TREATY BETWEEN EGYPT AND ISRAEL SIGNED IN WASHINGTON ON 26 MARCH 1979

The Government of the Arab Republic of Egypt and the Government of the State of Israel:

Preamble

Convinced of the urgent necessity of the establishment of a just, comprehensive and lasting peace in the Middle East in accordance with Security Council Resolutions 242 and 338:

Reaffirming their adherence to the 'Framework for Peace in the Middle East agreed at Camp David', dated 17 September 1978:

Noting that the aforementioned framework as appropriate is intended to constitute a basis for peace not only between Egypt and Israel but also between Israel and each of the other Arab neighbours which is prepared to negotiate peace with it on this basis:

Desiring to bring to an end the state of war between them and to establish a peace in which every state in the area can live in security:

Convinced that the conclusion of a treaty of peace between Egypt and Israel is an important step in the search for comprehensive peace in the area and for the attainment of the settlement of the Arab–Israeli conflict in all its aspects:

Inviting the other Arab parties to this dispute to join the peace process with Israel guided by and based on the principles of the aforementioned framework:

Desiring as well to develop friendly relations and co-operation between themselves in accordance with the UN Charter and the principles of international law governing international relations in times of peace:

Agree to the following provisions in the free exercise of their sovereignty, in order to implement the 'framework for the conclusion of a peace treaty between Egypt and Israel'.

Article I

1. The state of war between the parties will be terminated and peace will be established between them upon the exchange of instruments of ratification of this treaty.

2. Israel will withdraw all its armed forces and civilians from the Sinai behind the international boundary between Egypt and Mandated Palestine, as provided in the annexed protocol (annexed), and Egypt will resume the exercise of its full sovereignty over the Sinai.

3. Upon completion of the interim withdrawal provided for in Annex 1, the parties will establish normal and friendly relations, in accordance with Article II (3).

Article II

The permanent boundary between Egypt and Israel is the recognized international boundary between Egypt and the former Mandated Territory of Palestine, as shown on the map at Annex 2 (*not reproduced here—Ed.*), without prejudice to the issue of the status of the Gaza Strip. The parties recognize this boundary as inviolable. Each will respect the territorial integrity of the other, including their territorial waters and airspace.

Article III

1. The parties will apply between them the provisions of the Charter of the UN and the principles of international law governing relations among states in times of peace.

In particular:

A. They recognize and will respect each other's sovereignty, territorial integrity and political independence.

B. They recognize and will respect each other's right to live in peace within their secure and recognized boundaries.

C. They will refrain from the threat of use of force, directly or indirectly, against each other and will settle all disputes between them by peaceful means.

2. Each party undertakes to ensure that acts or threats of belligerency, hostility, or violence do not originate from and are not committed from within its territory, or by any forces subject to its control or by any other forces stationed on its territory, against the population, citizens or property of the other party. Each party also undertakes to refrain from organizing, instigating, inciting, assisting or participating in acts or threats of belligerency, hostility, subversion or violence against the other party, anywhere, and undertakes to ensure that perpetrators of such acts are brought to justice.

3. The parties agree that the normal relationship established between them will include full recognition, diplomatic, economic and cultural relations, termination of economic boycotts and discriminatory barriers to the free movement of people and goods, and will guarantee the mutual enjoyment by citizens of the due process of law. The process by which they undertake to achieve such a relationship parallel to the implementation of other provisions of this treaty is set out in the annexed protocol (Annex 3).

Article IV

1. In order to provide maximum security for both parties on the basis of reciprocity, agreed security arrangements will be established including limited force zones in Egyptian and Israeli territory, and UN forces and observers, described in detail as to nature and timing in Annex 1, and other security arrangements the parties may agree upon.

2. The parties agree to the stationing of UN personnel in areas described in Annex 1, the parties agree not to request withdrawal of the UN personnel and that these personnel will not be removed unless such removal is approved by the Security Council of the UN, with the affirmative vote of the five members, unless the parties otherwise agree.

3. A joint commission will be established to facilitate the implementation of the treaty, as provided for in Annex 1.

4. The security arrangements provided for in paragraphs 1 and 2 of this article may at the request of either party be reviewed and amended by mutual agreement of the parties.

Article V

Article V deals with rights of passage of shipping through the Suez Canal, the Strait of Tiran and the Gulf of Aqaba.

Article VI

1. This treaty does not affect and shall not be interpreted as affecting in any way the rights and obligations of the parties under the Charter of the UN.

2. The parties undertake to fulfil in good faith their obligations under this treaty, without regard to action or inaction of any other party and independently of any instrument external to this treaty.

3. They further undertake to take all the necessary measures for the application in their relations of the provisions of the multilateral conventions to which they are parties. Including the submission of appropriate notification to the Secretary-General of the UN and other depositories of such conventions.

4. The parties undertake not to enter into any obligation in conflict with this treaty.

5. Subject to Article 103 of the UN Charter, in the event of a conflict between the obligations of the parties under the present treaty and any of their other obligations, the obligations under this treaty will be binding and implemented.

Article VII

1. Disputes arising out of the application or interpretation of this treaty shall be resolved by negotiations.

2. Any such disputes which cannot be settled by negotiations shall be resolved by conciliation or submitted to arbitration.

Article VIII

The parties agree to establish a claims commission for the mutual settlement of all financial claims.

Article IX

1. This treaty shall enter into force upon exchange of instruments of ratification.

2. This treaty supersedes the agreement between Egypt and Israel of September 1975.

3. All protocols, annexes, and maps attached to this treaty shall be regarded as an integral part hereof.

4. The treaty shall be communicated to the Secretary-General of the UN for registration in accordance with the provisions of Article 102 of the Charter of the UN.

Annex 1—military and withdrawal arrangements:

Israel will complete withdrawal of all its armed forces and civilians from Sinai within three years of the date of exchange of instruments of ratification of the treaty. The withdrawal will be accomplished in two phases, the first, within nine months, to a line east of Al Arish and Ras Muhammad; the second to behind the international boundary. During the three-year period, Egypt and Israel will maintain a specified military presence in four delineated security zones (see map—*not reproduced here—Ed.*), and the UN will continue its observation and supervisory functions. Egypt will exercise full sovereignty over evacuated territories in Sinai upon Israeli withdrawal. A joint commission will supervise the withdrawal, and security arrangements can be reviewed when either side asks but any change must be by mutual agreement.

Annex 2—maps (*not reproduced here*).

Annex 3—normalization of relations:

Ambassadors will be exchanged upon completion of the interim withdrawal. All discriminatory barriers and economic boycotts will be lifted and, not later than six months after the completion of the interim withdrawal, negotiations for a trade and commerce agreement will begin. Free movement of each other's nationals and transport will be allowed and both sides agree to promote 'good neighbourly relations'. Egypt will use the airfields left by Israel near Al Arish, Rafah, Ras an-Naqb and Sharm ash-Shaikh, only for civilian aircraft. Road, rail, postal, telephone, wireless and other forms of communications will be opened between the two countries on completion of interim withdrawal.

Exchange of letters

Negotiations on the West Bank and Gaza—Negotiations on autonomy for the West Bank and Gaza will begin within one month of the exchange of the instruments of ratification. Jordan will be invited to participate and the Egyptian and Jordanian delegations may include Palestinians from the West Bank and Gaza, or other Palestinians as mutually agreed. If Jordan decides not to take part, the negotiations will be held by Egypt and Israel. The objective of the negotiations is the establishment of a self-governing authority in the West Bank and Gaza 'in order to provide full autonomy to the inhabitants'.

Egypt and Israel hope to complete negotiations within one year so that elections can be held as soon as possible. The self-governing authority elected will be inaugurated within one month of the elections at which point the five year transitional period will begin. The Israeli military Government and its civilian administration will be withdrawn, Israeli armed forces withdrawn and the remaining forces redeployed 'into specified security locations'.

MAIN POINTS OF THE RESOLUTIONS PASSED BY THE ARAB LEAGUE COUNCIL IN BAGHDAD ON 27 MARCH 1979

—To withdraw the ambassadors of the Arab states from Egypt immediately.

—To recommend the severance of political and diplomatic relations with the Egyptian Government. The Arab governments will adopt the necessary measures to apply this recommendation within a maximum period of one month from the date of the issue of this decision, in accordance with the constitutional measures in force in each country.

—To consider the suspension of the Egyptian Government's membership in the Arab League as operative from the date of the Egyptian Government's signing of the peace treaty with the Zionist enemy. This means depriving it of all rights resulting from that membership.

—To make the city of Tunis, capital of the Tunisian Republic, the temporary headquarters of the Arab League, its general secretariat, the competent ministerial councils and the permanent technical committees, as of the date of signing of the treaty between the Egyptian Government and the Zionist enemy. This shall be communicated to all international and regional organizations and bodies. They will also be informed that dealings with the Arab League will be conducted with its secretariat in its new temporary headquarters.

—To condemn the policy that the United States is practising regarding its role in concluding the Camp David agreements and the Egyptian-Israeli treaty.

The Arab League Council, at the level of Arab Foreign and Economy Ministers, has also decided the following:

—To halt all bank loans, deposits, guarantees or facilities, as well as all financial or technical contributions and aid by Arab Governments or their establishments to the Egyptian Government and its establishments as of the treaty-signing date.

—To ban the extension of economic aid by the Arab funds, banks and financial establishments within the framework of the Arab League and the joint Arab co-operation to the Egyptian Government and its establishments.

—The Arab governments and institutions shall refrain from purchasing the bonds, shares, postal orders and public credit loans that are issued by the Egyptian Government and its financial foundations.

—Following the suspension of the Egyptian Government's membership in the Arab League, its membership will also be suspended from the institutions, funds and organisations deriving from the Arab League.

—In view of the fact that the ill-omened Egyptian-Israeli treaty and its appendices have demonstrated Egypt's commitment to sell oil to Israel, the Arab states shall refrain from providing Egypt with oil and its derivatives.

—Trade exchanges with the Egyptian state and with private establishments that deal with the Zionist enemy shall be prohibited.

Source: *MEED Arab Report,* 11 April 1979, p. 9.

UN SECURITY COUNCIL RESOLUTION ON ISRAELI SETTLEMENTS

1 March 1980

The resolution, No. 465, was adopted unanimously by the 15 members of the Council. The USA repudiated its vote in favour of the resolution on 3 March 1980 (see below).

The Security Council, taking note of the reports of the Commission of the Security Council established under resolution 446 (1979) to examine the situation relating to the settlements in the Arab territories occupied since 1967, including Jerusalem, contained in documents S/13450 and S/13679,

—Taking note also of letters from the permanent representative of Jordan (S/13801) and the permanent representative of Morocco, Chairman of the Islamic Group (S/13802),

—Strongly deploring the refusal by Israel to co-operate with the Commission and regretting its formal rejection of resolutions 446 (1979) and 452 (1979),

—Affirming once more that the fourth Geneva Convention relative to the protection of civilian persons in time of war of 12 August 1949 is applicable to the Arab territories occupied by Israel since 1967, including Jerusalem,

—Deploring the decision of the Government of Israel to officially support Israeli settlement in the Palestinian and other Arab territories occupied since 1967,

—Deeply concerned over the practices of the Israeli authorities in implementing that settlement policy in the occupied Arab territories, including Jerusalem, and its consequences for the local Arab and Palestinian population,

—Taking into account the need to consider measures for the impartial protection of private and public land and property, and water resources,

—Bearing in mind the specific status of Jerusalem and, in particular, the need for protection and preservation of the unique spiritual and religious dimension of the holy places in the city,

—Drawing attention to the grave consequences which the settlement policy is bound to have on any attempt to reach a comprehensive, just and lasting peace in the Middle East,

—Recalling pertinent Security Council resolutions, specifically resolutions 237 (1967) of 14 June 1967, 252 (1968) of 21 May 1968, 267 (1969) of 3 July 1969, 271 (1969) of 15 September 1969 and 298 (1971) of 25 September 1971, as well as the consensus statement made by the President of the Security Council on 11 November 1976,

—Having invited Mr Fahd Qawasmah, Mayor of Al-Khalil (Hebron), in the occupied territories, to supply it with information pursuant to rule 39 of provisional rules of procedure,

1. Commends the work done by the Commission in preparing the report contained in document S/13679,

2. Accepts the conclusions and recommendations contained in the above-mentioned report of the Commission,

3. Calls upon all parties, particularly the Government of Israel, to co-operate with the Commission,

4. Strongly deplores the decision of Israel to prohibit the free travel of Mayor Fahd Qawasmah in order to appear before the Security Council, and requests Israel to permit his free travel to the United Nations headquarters for that purpose,

5. Determines that all measures taken by Israel to change the physical character, demographic composition, institutional structure or status of the Palestinian and other Arab territories occupied since 1967, including Jerusalem, or any part thereof, have no legal validity and that Israel's policy and practices of settling parts of its population and new immigrants in those territories constitute a flagrant violation of the Fourth Geneva Convention relative to the protection of civilian persons in time of war and also constitute a serious obstruction to achieving a comprehensive, just and lasting peace in the Middle East,

6. Strongly deplores the continuation and persistence of Israel in pursuing those policies and practices and calls upon the Government and people of Israel to rescind those measures, to dismantle the existing settlements and in particular to cease, on an urgent basis, the establishment, construction and planning of settlements in the Arab territories occupied since 1967, including Jerusalem,

7. Calls upon all states not to provide Israel with any assistance to be used specifically in connection with settlements in the occupied territories,

8. Requests the Commission to continue to examine the situation relating to settlements in the Arab territories occupied since 1967 including Jerusalem, to investigate the reported serious depletion of natural resources, particularly the water resources, with a view of ensuring the protection of those important natural resources of the territories under occupation, and to keep under close scrutiny the implementation of the present resolution,

9. Requests the Commission to report to the Security Council before 1 September 1980, and decides to convene at the earliest possible date thereafter in order to consider the report and the full implementation of the present resolution.

PRESIDENT CARTER'S STATEMENT REPUDIATING US VOTE IN SUPPORT OF UN SECURITY COUNCIL RESOLUTION 465
3 March 1980

I want to make it clear that the vote of the US in the Security Council of the UN does not represent a change in our position regarding the Israeli settlements in the occupied areas nor regarding the status of Jerusalem.

While our opposition to the establishment of the Israeli settlements is long-standing and well-known, we made strenuous efforts to eliminate the language with reference to the dismantling of settlements in the resolution. This call for dismantling was neither proper nor practical. We believe that the future disposition of the existing settlements must be determined during the current autonomy negotiations.

As to Jerusalem, we strongly believe that Jerusalem should be undivided with free access to the holy places for all faiths, and that its status should be determined in the negotiations for a comprehensive peace settlement.

The US vote in the UN was approved with the understanding that all references to Jerusalem would be deleted. The failure to communicate this clearly resulted in a vote in favour of the resolution rather than abstention.

EEC STATEMENT ON THE MIDDLE EAST
Issued in Venice, 13 June 1980

1. The heads of state and government and the ministers of foreign affairs held a comprehensive exchange of views on all aspects of the present situation in the Middle East, including the state of negotiations resulting from the agreements signed between Egypt and Israel in March 1979. They agreed that growing tensions affecting this region constitute a serious danger and render a comprehensive solution to the Israeli–Arab conflict more necessary and pressing than ever.

2. The nine member-states of the European Community consider that the traditional ties and common interests which link Europe to the Middle East oblige them to play a special role and now require them to work in a more concrete way towards peace.

3. In this regard, the nine countries of the Community base themselves on Security Council Resolutions 242 and 338 and the positions which they have expressed on several occasions, notably in their declarations of 29 June 1977, 19 September 1978, 26 March and 18 June 1979, as well as the speech made on their

behalf on 25 September 1979, by the Irish Minister of Foreign Affairs at the thirty-fourth United Nations General Assembly.

4. On the bases thus set out, the time has come to promote the recognition and implementation of the two principles universally accepted by the international community: the right to existence and to security of all the states in the region, including Israel, and justice for all the peoples which implies the recognition of the legitimate rights of the Palestinian people.

5. All of the countries in the area are entitled to live in peace within secure, recognized and guaranteed borders. The necessary guarantees for a peace settlement should be provided by the United Nations by a decision of the Security Council and, if necessary, on the basis of other mutually agreed procedures. The Nine declared that they are prepared to participate within the framework of a comprehensive settlement in a system of concrete and binding international guarantees, including (guarantees) on the ground.

6. A just solution must finally be found to the Palestinian problem, which is not simply one of refugees. The Palestinian people, which is conscious of existing as such, must be placed in a position, by an appropriate process defined within the framework of the comprehensive peace settlement, to exercise fully its right to self-determination.

7. The achievement of these objectives requires the involvement and support of all the parties concerned in the peace settlement which the Nine are endeavouring to promote in keeping with the principles formulated in the declaration referred to above. These principles apply to all the parties concerned, and thus the Palestinian people, and to the PLO, which will have to be associated with the negotiations.

8. The Nine recognize the special importance of the role played by the question of Jerusalem for all the parties concerned. The Nine stress that they will not accept any unilateral initiative designed to change the status of Jerusalem and that any agreement on the city's status should guarantee freedom of access for everyone to the holy places.

9. The Nine stress the need for Israel to put an end to the territorial occupation which it has maintained since the conflict of 1967, as it has done for part of Sinai. They are deeply convinced that the Israeli settlements constitute a serious obstacle to the peace process in the Middle East. The Nine consider that these settlements, as well as modifications in population and property in the occupied Arab territories, are illegal under international law.

10. Concerned as they are to put an end to violence, the Nine consider that only the renunciation of force or the threatened use of force by all the parties can create a climate of confidence in the area, and constitute a basic element for a comprehensive settlement of the conflict in the Middle East.

11. The Nine have decided to make the necessary contacts with all the parties concerned. The objective of these contacts would be to ascertain the position of the various parties with respect to the principles set out in this declaration and in the light of the result of this consultation process to determine the form which such an initiative on their part could take.

Subsequent UN Resolutions (General Assembly Resolutions ES-7/2, 29 July 1980; Security Council Resolution 478, 20 August 1980; General Assembly Resolutions

35-169 and 35-207 of 15 and 16 December 1980, etc.) have reaffirmed earlier resolutions and condemned the Israeli 'Jerusalem Bill' of July 1980, which stated explicitly that Jerusalem should be for ever the undivided Israeli capital and seat of government, parliament and judiciary. A UN General Assembly Resolution of 6 February 1982, condemned Israel's annexation of the Golan Heights. UN Resolutions in June 1982 condemned the Israeli invasion of Lebanon, and called for the withdrawal of Israeli forces.

THE FAHD PLAN

In August 1981 Crown Prince Fahd of Saudi Arabia launched an 8-point peace plan for the Middle East. During the remainder of 1981 some Arab states showed their support, but failure to agree on the 'Fahd Plan' caused the break-up of the Fez Arab Summit in November only a few hours after it had opened. The plan is as follows:

1. Israel to withdraw from all Arab territory occupied in 1967, including Arab Jerusalem.

2. Israeli settlements built on Arab land after 1967 to be dismantled.

3. A guarantee of freedom of worship for all religions in holy places.

4. An affirmation of the right of the Palestinian Arab people to return to their homes, and compensation for those who do not wish to return.

5. The West Bank and Gaza Strip to have a transitional period under the auspices of the United Nations for a period not exceeding several months.

6. An independent Palestinian state should be set up with Jerusalem as its capital.

7. All states in the region should be able to live in peace.

8. The UN or member-states of the UN to guarantee carrying-out of these principles.

THE REAGAN PLAN

After the Israeli invasion of Lebanon in June 1982, and the consequent evacuation of the PLO from Beirut, the US Government made strenuous efforts to continue the Camp David peace process and find a permanent solution that would ensure peace in the Middle East. On 1 September 1982 President Reagan outlined the following proposals in a broadcast to the nation from Burbank, California:

'... First, as outlined in the Camp David accords, there must be a period of time during which the Palestinian inhabitants of the West Bank and Gaza will have full autonomy over their own affairs. Due consideration must be given to the principle of self-government by the inhabitants of the territories and to the legitimate security concerns of the parties involved.

The purpose of the 5-year period of transition, which would begin after free elections for a self-governing Palestinian authority, is to prove to the Palestinians that they can run their own affairs and that such Palestinian autonomy poses no threat to Israel's security.

The United States will not support the use of any additional land for the purpose of settlements during the transition period. Indeed, the immediate adoption of a settlement freeze by Israel, more than any other action, could create the confidence needed for wider participation in these talks. Further settlement activity is in no way necessary for the security of Israel and only diminishes the confidence of the Arabs that a final outcome can be freely and fairly negotiated.

I want to make the American position well understood: The purpose of this transition period is the peaceful and orderly transfer of authority from Israel to the Palestinian inhabitants of the West Bank and Gaza. At the same time, such a transfer must not interfere with Israel's security requirements.

Beyond the transition period, as we look to the future of the West Bank and Gaza, it is clear to me that peace cannot be achieved by the formation of an independent Palestinian state in those territories. Nor is it achievable on the basis of Israeli sovereignty or permanent control over the West Bank and Gaza.

So the United States will not support the establishment of an independent Palestinian state in the West Bank and Gaza, and we will not support annexation or permanent control by Israel.

There is, however, another way to peace. The final status of these lands must, of course, be reached through the give-and-take of negotiations. But it is the firm view of the United States that self-government by the Palestinians of the West Bank and Gaza in association with Jordan offers the best chance for a durable, just and lasting peace.

We base our approach squarely on the principle that the Arab-Israeli conflict should be resolved through negotiations involving an exchange of territory for peace. This exchange is enshrined in UN Security Council Resolution 242, which is, in turn, incorporated in all its parts in the Camp David agreements. UN Resolution 242 remains wholly valid as the foundation stone of America's Middle East peace effort.

It is the United States' position that—in return for peace—the withdrawal provision of Resolution 242 applies to all fronts, including the West Bank and Gaza.

When the border is negotiated between Jordan and Israel, our view on the extent to which Israel should be asked to give up territory will be heavily affected by the extent of true peace and normalization and the security arrangements offered in return.

Finally, we remain convinced that Jerusalem must remain undivided, but its final status should be decided through negotiations.

In the course of the negotiations to come, the United States will support positions that seem to us fair and reasonable compromises and likely to promote a sound agreement. We will also put forward our own detailed proposals when we believe they can be helpful. And, make no mistake, the United States will oppose any proposal—from any party and at any point in the negotiating process—that threatens the security of Israel. America's commitment to the security of Israel is ironclad. And, I might add, so is mine.'

FEZ SUMMIT PEACE PROPOSAL

A further Fez Arab Summit was held in September 1982, and produced a set of peace proposals. The following excerpts are from the official English-language text of the final declaration on 9 September 1982, and are reproduced from American Arab Affairs, No 2:

I. The Israeli-Arab conflict:

The summit adopted the following principles:

1. The withdrawal of Israel from all Arab territories occupied in 1967 including Arab Al Qods (East Jerusalem).

2. The dismantling of settlements established by Israel on the Arab territories after 1967.

3. The guarantee of freedom of worship and practice of religious rites for all religions in the holy shrine.

4. The reaffirmation of the Palestinian people's right to self-determination and the exercise of its imprescriptible and inalienable national rights under the leadership of the Palestine Liberation Organization (PLO), its sole and legitimate representative, and the indemnification of all those who do not desire to return.

5. Placing the West Bank and Gaza Strip under the control of the United Nations for a transitory period not exceeding a few months.

6. The establishment of an independent Palestinian state with Al Qods as its capital.

7. The Security Council guarantees peace among all states of the region including the independent Palestinian state.

8. The Security Council guarantees the respect of these principles.

II. The Israeli aggression against Lebanon:

The summit was informed of the Lebanese Government's decision to put an end to the mission of the Arab deterrent forces in Lebanon. To this effect, the Lebanese and Syrian governments will start negotiations on measures to be taken in the light of the Israeli withdrawal from Lebanon.

JOINT JORDAN–PLO PEACE PROPOSALS

After a series of negotiations which began in January 1984, establishing a platform for joint action, King Hussein of Jordan and Yasser Arafat, Chairman of the PLO, announced their proposals for a Middle East peace settlement in Amman, on 23 February 1985. The failure of these proposals to further the peace process was acknowledged by King Hussein on 19 February 1986, when he abandoned Jordan's political collaboration with the PLO. The PLO did not formally abrogate the Amman agreement until the 18th session of the PNC in Algiers in April 1987. The following is the entire text of the joint agreement in an English-language version distributed by the Jordanian Government.

A PLAN OF JOINT ACTION

Proceeding from the spirit of the Fez summit resolutions approved by the Arab states and from UN resolutions on the Palestinian question, in accordance with international legitimacy, and proceeding from a common understanding on the building of a special relationship between the Jordanian and Palestinian peoples, the Government of the Hashemite Kingdom of Jordan and the Palestine Liberation Organization have agreed to work together with a view to a just and peaceful settlement of the Middle East crisis and to the termination of the occupation by Israel of the occupied Arab territories, including Jerusalem, on the basis of the following principles:

1. The return of all territories occupied in 1967 in exchange for a comprehensive peace, as stipulated in the resolutions of the United Nations and its Security Council.

2. The right of the Palestinian people to self-determination: in this respect the Palestinians will exercise their inalienable right to self-determination within the context of the formation of the proposed confederated states of Jordan and Palestine.

3. The solution of the Palestinian refugee problem in accordance with United Nations resolutions.

4. The solution of all aspects of the Palestinian question.

5. On this basis, negotiations should be undertaken under the auspices of an international conference to be attended by the five permanent members of the United Nations Security Council and all parties to the conflict, including the Palestine Liberation Organization, which is the sole legitimate representative of the Palestinian people, in the form of a joint delegation (a joint Jordanian–Palestinian delegation).

THE SHULTZ PLAN

At the beginning of February 1988 the Government of the USA announced a new plan for the resolution of the Palestine issue, which came to be known as the 'Shultz Plan', after the US Secretary of State, George Shultz. The presentation of the plan followed more than a year of diplomatic activity during which the idea of an international peace conference under the auspices of the UN, which had been agreed in principle by Shimon Peres, the Israeli Minister of Foreign Affairs, and King Hussein of Jordan, had won increasing support. The main provisions of the plan, as they were subsequently clarified, were for a six-month period of negotiations between Israel and a joint Jordanian/Palestinian delegation, to determine the details of a transitional autonomy arrangement for the West Bank and the Gaza Strip, which would last for three years; during the transitional period a permanent settlement would be negotiated by the Israeli and Jordanian/Palestinian delegations; both sets of negotiations would run concurrently with and, if necessary, with reference to, an international peace conference, involving the five permanent members of the UN Security Council and all the interested parties (including the Palestinians in a joint Jordanian/Palestinian delegation), which, like the separate Israeli-Jordanian/Palestinian negotiations, would be conducted on the basis of all the participants' acceptance of UN Security Council Resolutions 242 and 338, but would have no power to impose a settlement.

On 6 March 1988, the Israeli newspaper, Yedioth Aharonoth, *published a photocopy of a letter from George Shultz to the Israeli Prime Minister, Itzhak Shamir, containing details of his peace proposals. The contents of the letter, identical versions of which were believed to have been delivered to the governments of Egypt, Jordan and Syria, were as follows:*

Dear Mr. Prime Minister,

I set forth below the statement of understandings which I am convinced is necessary to achieve the prompt opening of negotiations on a comprehensive peace. This statement of understandings emerges from discussions held with you and other regional leaders. I look forward to the letter of reply of the government of Israel in confirmation of this statement.

The agreed objective is a comprehensive peace providing for the security of all the States in the region and for the legitimate rights of the Palestinian people.

Negotiations will start on an early date certain between Israel and each of its neighbors which is willing to do so. Those negotiations could begin by May 1, 1988. Each of these negotiations will be based on United Nations Security Council Resolutions 242 and 338, in all their parts. The parties to each bilateral negotiation will determine the procedure and agenda of their negotiation. All participants in the negotiations must state their willingness to negotiate with one another.

As concerns negotiations between the Israeli delegation and Jordanian-Palestinian delegation, negotiations will begin on arrangements for a transitional period, with the objective of completing them within six months. Seven months after transitional negotiations begin, final status negotiations will begin, with the objective of completing them within one year. These negotiations will be based on all the provisions and principles of the United Nations Security Council Resolution 242. Final status talks will start before the transitional period begins. The transitional period will begin three months after the conclusion of the transitional agreement and will last for three years. The United States will participate in both negotiations and will promote their rapid conclusion. In particular, the United States will submit a draft agreement for the parties' consideration at the outset of the negotiations on transitional arrangements.

Two weeks before the opening of negotiations, an international conference will be held. The Secretary-General of the United Nations will be asked to issue invitations to the parties involved in the Arab-Israeli conflict and the five permanent members of the United Nations Security Council. All participants in the conference must accept United Nations Security Council Resolutions 242 and 338, and renounce violence and terrorism. The parties to each bilateral negotiations may refer reports on the status of their negotiations to the conference, in a manner to be agreed. The conference will not be able to impose solutions or veto agreements reached.

Palestinian representation will be within the Jordanian-Palestinian delegation. The Palestinian issue will be addressed in the negotiations between the Jordanian-Palestinian and Israeli delegations. Negotiations between the Israeli delegation and the Jordanian-Palestinian delegation will proceed independently of any other negotiations.

This statement of understandings is an integral whole. The United States understands that your acceptance is dependent on the implementation of each element in good faith.

Sincerely yours,

George P. Shultz.

DECLARATION OF PALESTINIAN INDEPENDENCE

In November 1988, the 19th session of the Palestine National Council (PNC) culminated in the declaration 'in the name of God and the Palestinian Arab people' of the independent State of Palestine, with the Holy City of Jerusalem as its capital. The opportunity for the PLO to assert sovereignty over a specific area arose through the decision of King Hussein of Jordan, in July 1988, to sever Jordan's 'administrative and legal links' with the West Bank. The Declaration of Independence cited United Nations General Assembly Resolution 181 of 1947, which partitioned Palestine into two states, one Arab and one Jewish, as providing the legal basis for the right of the Palestinian Arab people to national sovereignty and independence. At the end of the session, the PNC issued a political statement. Details of the Declaration of Independence, and of the political statement, set out below, are taken from an unofficial English-language translation of the proceedings, distributed by the PLO.

'The National Council proclaims, in the name of God and the Palestinian Arab people, the establishment of the State of Palestine on our Palestinian land, with the Holy City of Jerusalem as its capital.

The State of Palestine is the state of Palestinians wherever they may be. In it they shall develop their national and cultural identity and enjoy full equality in rights. Their religious and political beliefs and their human dignity shall be safeguarded under a democratic parliamentary system of government built on the freedom of opinion; and on the freedom to form parties; and on the protection of the rights of the minority by the majority and respect of the decisions of the majority by the minority; and on social justice and equal rights, free of ethnic, religious, racial or sexual discrimination; and on a constitution that guarantees the rule of law and the independence of the judiciary; and on the basis of total allegiance to the centuries-old spiritual and civilizational Palestinian heritage of religious tolerance and coexistence.

The State of Palestine is an Arab state, an integral part of the Arab nation and of that nation's heritage, its civilization and its aspiration to attain its goals of liberation, development, democracy and unity. Affirming its commitment to the Charter of the League of Arab states and its insistence on the reinforcement of joint Arab action, the State of Palestine calls on the people of its nation to assist in the completion of its birth by mobilizing their resources and augmenting their efforts to end the Israeli occupation.

The State of Palestine declares its commitment to the principles and objectives of the United Nations, and to the Universal Declaration of Human Rights, and to the principles and policy of non-alignment.

The State of Palestine, declaring itself a peace-loving state committed to the principles of peaceful coexistence, shall strive with all states and peoples to attain a permanent peace built on justice and respect of rights, in which humanity's constructive talents can prosper, and creative competition can flourish, and fear of tomorrow can be abolished, for tomorrow brings nothing but security for the just and those who regain their sense of justice.

As it struggles to establish peace in the land of love and peace, the State of Palestine exhorts the United Nations to take upon itself a special responsibility for the Palestinian Arab people and their homeland; and exhorts the peace-loving, freedom-cherishing peoples and states of the world to help it attain its objectives and put an end to the tragedy its people are suffering by providing them with security and endeavouring to end the Israeli occupation of the Palestinian territories.

The State of Palestine declares its belief in the settlement of international and regional disputes by peaceful means in accordance with the Charter and resolutions of the United Nations; and its rejection of threats of force or violence or terrorism and the use of these against its territorial integrity and political independence or the territorial integrity of any other state, without prejudice to its natural right to defend its territory and independence.

The Palestine National Council resolves:

First: On the escalation and continuity of the intifada

A. To provide all the means and capabilities needed to escalate our people's *intifada* in various ways and on various levels to guarantee its continuation and intensification.

B. To support the popular institutions and organizations in the occupied Palestinian territories.

C. To bolster and develop the Popular Committees and other specialized popular and trade union bodies, including the attack group and the popular army, with a view to expanding their role and increasing their effectiveness.

D. To consolidate the national unity that emerged and developed during the *intifada*.

E. To intensify efforts on the international level for the release of the detainees, the repatriation of the deportees, and the termination of the organized, official acts of repression and terrorism against our children, our women, our men, and our institutions.

F. To call on the United Nations to place the occupied Palestinian land under international supervision for the protection of our people and the termination of the Israeli occupation.

G. To call on the Palestinian people outside our homeland to intensify and increase their support, and to expand the family-assistance program.

H. To call on the Arab nation, its people, forces, institutions and governments, to increase their political, material and informational support of the *intifada*.

I. To call on all free and honorable people worldwide to stand by our people, our revolution, our *intifada* against the Israeli occupation, the repression, and the organized, fascist official terrorism to which the occupation forces and the armed fanatic settlers are subjecting our people, our universities, our institutions, our national economy, and our Islamic and Christian holy places.

Second: In the political field

Proceeding from the above, the Palestine National Council, being responsible to the Palestinian people, their national rights and their desire for peace as expressed in the Declaration of Independence issued on November 15, 1988; and in response to the humanitarian quest for international entente, nuclear disarmament and the settlement of regional conflicts by peaceful means, affirms the determination of the Palestine Liberation Organization to arrive at a political settlement of the Arab–Israeli conflict and its core, the Palestinian issue, in the framework of the UN Charter, the principles and rules of international legitimacy, the edicts of international law, the resolutions of the United Nations, the latest of which are Security Council Resolutions 605, 607 and 608, and the resolutions of the Arab summits, in a manner that assures the Palestinian Arab people's right to repatriation, self-determination and the establishment of their independent state on their national soil, and that institutes arrangements for the security and peace of all states in the region.

Towards the achievement of this, the Palestine National Council affirms:

1. The necessity of convening an international conference on the issue of the Middle East and its core, the Palestinian issue, under the auspices of the United Nations and with the participation of the permanent members of the Security Council and all parties to the conflict in the region, including, on an equal footing, the Palestine Liberation Organization, the sole legitimate representative of the Palestinian people; on the understanding that the international conference will be held on the basis of Security Council Resolutions 242 and 338 and the safeguarding of the legitimate national rights of the Palestinian people, foremost among which is the right to self-determination, in accordance with the principles and provisions of the UN Charter as they pertain to the right of peoples to self-determination, and the inadmissibility of the acquisition of others' territory by force or military conquest, and in accordance with the UN resolutions relating to the Palestinian issue.

2. The withdrawal of Israel from all the Palestinian and Arab territories it occupied in 1967, including Arab Jerusalem.

3. The annulment of all expropriation and annexation measures and the removal of the settlements established by Israel in the Palestinian and Arab territories since 1967.

4. Endeavouring to place the occupied Palestinian territories, including Arab Jerusalem, under the supervision of the United Nations for a limited period, to protect our people, to create an atmosphere conducive to the success of the proceedings of the international conference toward the attainment of a comprehensive political settlement and the achievement of peace and security for all on the basis of mutual consent, and to enable the Palestinian state to exercise its effective authority in these territories.

5. The settlement of the issue of the Palestinian refugees in accordance with the pertinent United Nations resolutions.

6. Guaranteeing the freedom of worship and the right to engage in religious rites for all faiths in the holy place in Palestine.

7. The Security Council shall draw up and guarantee arrangements for the security of all states concerned and for peace between them, including the Palestinian state.

The Palestine National Council confirms its past resolutions that the relationship between the fraternal Jordanian and Palestinian peoples is a privileged one and that the future relationship between the states of Jordan and Palestine will be built on confederal foundations, on the basis of the two fraternal peoples' free and voluntary choice, in consolidation of the historic ties that bind them and the vital interests they hold in common.

The National Council also renews its commitment to the United Nations resolutions that affirm the right of peoples to resist foreign occupation, imperialism and racial discrimination, and their right to fight for their independence; and it once more announces its rejection of terrorism in all its forms, including state terrorism, emphasizing its commitment to the resolutions it adopted in the past on this subject, and to the resolutions of the Arab summit in Algiers in 1988, and to UN Resolutions 42/159 of 1967 and 61/40 of 1985, and to what was stated in this regard in the Cairo Declaration of 7/11/85.

Third: In the Arab and international fields

The Palestine National Council emphasizes the importance of the unity of Lebanon in its territory, its people and its institutions, and stands firmly against the attempts to partition the land and disintegrate the fraternal people of Lebanon. It further emphasizes the importance of the joint Arab effort to participate in a settlement of the Lebanese crisis that helps crystallize and implement solutions that preserve Lebanese unity. The Council also stresses the importance of consecrating the right of the Palestinians in Lebanon to engage in political and informational activity and to enjoy security and protection; and of working against all the forms of conspiracy and aggression that target them and their right to work and live; and of the need to secure the conditions that assure them the ability to defend themselves and provide them with security and protection.

The Palestine National Council affirms its solidarity with the Lebanese nationalist Islamic forces in their struggle against the Israeli occupation and its agents in the Lebanese South; expresses its pride in the allied struggle of the Lebanese and Palestinian peoples against the aggression and toward the termination of the Israeli occupation of parts of the South; and underscores the importance of bolstering this kinship between our people and the fraternal, combative people of Lebanon.

And on this occasion, the Council addresses a reverent salute to the long-suffering people of our camps in Lebanon and its South, who are enduring the aggression, massacres, murder, starvation, air raids, bombardments and sieges perpetrated against the Palestinian camps and Lebanese villages by the Israeli army, air force and navy, aided and abetted by hireling forces in the region; and it rejects the resettlement conspiracy, for the Palestinians' homeland is Palestine.

The Council emphasizes the importance of the Iraq–Iran cease-fire resolution toward the establishment of a permanent peace settlement between the two countries and in the Gulf Region; and calls for an intensification of the efforts being exerted to ensure the success of the negotiations toward the establishment of peace on stable and firm foundations; affirming, on this occasion, the price of the Palestinian Arab people and the Arab nation as a whole in the steadfastness and triumphs of fraternal Iraq as it defended the eastern gate of the Arab nation.

The National Council also expresses its deep pride in the stand taken by the peoples of our Arab nation in support of our Palestinian Arab people and of the Palestine Liberation Organization and of our people's *intifada* in the occupied homeland; and emphasizes the importance of fortifying the bonds of combat among the forces, parties and organizations of the Arab national liberation movement, in defense of the right of the Arab nation and its peoples to liberation, progress, democracy and unity. The Council calls for the adoption of all measures needed to reinforce the unity of struggle among all members of the Arab national liberation movement.

The Palestine National Council, as it hails the Arab states and thanks them for their support of our people's struggle, calls on them to honour the commitments they approved at the summit conference in Algiers in support of the Palestinian people and their blessed *intifada*. The Council, in issuing this appeal, expresses its great confidence that the leaders of the Arab nation will remain, as we have known them, a bulwark of support for Palestine and its people.

The Palestine National Council reiterates the desire of the Palestine Liberation Organization for Arab solidarity as the framework within which the Arab nation and its states can organize themselves to confront Israel's aggression and American support of that aggression, and within which Arab prestige can be enhanced and the Arab role strengthened to the point of influencing international policies to the benefit of Arab rights and causes.

The Palestine National Council expresses its deep gratitude to all the states and international forces and organizations that support the national rights of the Palestinians; affirms its desire to strengthen the bonds of friendship and co-operation with the Soviet Union, the People's (Republic of) China, the other socialist countries, the non-aligned states, the Islamic states, the African states, the Latin American states and the other friendly states; and notes with satisfaction the signs of positive evolution in the positions of some West European states and Japan in the direction of support for the rights of the Palestinian people, applauds this development, and urges intensified efforts to increase it.

The National Council affirms the fraternal solidarity of the Palestinian people and the Palestine Liberation Organization with the struggle of the peoples of Asia, Africa and Latin America for their liberation and the reinforcement of their independence; and condemns all American attempts to threaten the independence of the states of Central America and interfere in their affairs.

The Palestine National Council expresses the support of the Palestine Liberation Organization for the national liberation movements in South Africa and Namibia. . . .

The Council notes with considerable concern the growth of the Israeli forces of fascism and extremism and the escalation of their open calls for the implementation of the policy of annihilation and individual and collective expulsion of our people from their homeland, and calls for intensified efforts in all areas to confront this fascist peril. The Council at the same time expresses its appreciation of the role and courage of the Israeli peace forces as they resist and expose the forces of fascism, racism and aggression, support our people's struggle and their valiant *intifada* and back our people's right to self-determination and the establishment of an independent state. The Council confirms its past resolutions regarding the reinforcement and development of relations with these democratic forces.

The Palestine National Council also addresses itself to the American people, calling on them all to strive to put an end to the American policy that denies the Palestinian people's national rights, including their sacred right to self-determination, and urging them to work toward the adoption of policies that conform to the Declaration of Human Rights and the international conventions and resolutions and serve the quest for peace in the Middle East and security for all its peoples, including the Palestinian people.

The Council charges the Executive Committee with the task of completing the formation of the Committee for the Perpetuation of the Memory of the Martyr-Symbol Abu Jihad, which shall initiate its work immediately upon the adjournment of the Council.

The Council sends its greetings to the United Nations Committee on the Exercise of the Inalienable Rights of the Palestinian People, and to the fraternal

and friendly international and non-governmental institutions and organizations, and to the journalists and media that have stood and still stand by our
people's struggle and *intifada*.

The National Council expresses deep pain at the continued detention of
hundreds of combatants from among our people in a number of Arab countries,
strongly condemns their continued detention, and calls upon those countries to
put an end to these abnormal conditions and release those fighters to play their
role in the struggle.

In conclusion, the Palestine National Council affirms its complete confidence
that the justice of the Palestinian cause and of the demands for which the
Palestinian people are struggling will continue to draw increasing support from
honorable and free people around the world; and also affirms its complete
confidence in victory on the road to Jerusalem, the capital of our independent
Palestinian state.'

THE ISRAELI PEACE INITIATIVE

*In May 1989 the Government of Israel approved a four-point peace initiative for a
resolution of the Middle East conflict, the details of which had first been announced
during a meeting between US President George Bush and Israeli Prime Minister,
Itzhak Shamir, in Washington on 6 April. Based largely on peace proposals made
by Israeli Defence Minister, Itzhak Rabin, in January 1989, the new plan followed
increased international diplomatic pressure on Israel to respond to the uprising in
the Occupied Territories with constructive action to end the conflict. The main
proposals of the Israeli initiative were that elections should be held in the West
Bank and Gaza Strip in order to facilitate the formation of a delegation of
appropriate interlocutors (i.e. non-PLO representatives) to take part in negotiations on a transitional settlement, when a self-ruling authority might be established.
The transitional period would serve as a test of co-operation and coexistence and
would be followed by negotiations on a final agreement in which Israel would be
prepared to discuss any option presented; that Israel, Egypt and the USA should
reconfirm their commitment to the Camp David Agreements of 1979; that the USA
and Egypt should seek to persuade Arab countries to desist from hostility towards
Israel; and that an international effort should be made to solve the 'humanitarian
issue' of the inhabitants of refugee camps in Judaea, Samaria and the Gaza Strip.
In July 1989 four amendments to the Israeli peace initiative were approved by the
central committee of the Likud. These stipulated that residents of East Jerusalem
would not be allowed to take part in the proposed elections in the West Bank and
Gaza; that violent attacks by Palestinians must cease before elections could be held
in the Occupied Territories; that Jewish settlement should continue in the
Territories and that foreign sovereignty should not be conceded in any part of
Israel; and that the establishment of a Palestinian state west of the River Jordan
was out of the question, as were negotiations with the PLO. At the end of July,
however, the Israeli Cabinet once again endorsed the peace initiative in its original
form.*

*In September 1989 President Mubarak of Egypt sought ten assurances from the
Israeli Government with regard to its peace initiative: (i) a commitment to accept
the results of the elections proposed by the peace initiative; (ii) the vigilance of
international observers at the elections; (iii) the granting of immunity to all elected*

representatives; (iv) the withdrawal of the Israel Defence Force from the balloting area; (v) a commitment by the Israeli Government to begin talks on the final status of the Occupied Territories on a specific date within three to five years; (vi) an end to Jewish settlement activities in the Occupied Territories; (vii) a ban on election propaganda; (viii) a ban on the entry of Israelis into the Occupied Territories on the day of the proposed elections; (ix) permission for residents of East Jerusalem to participate in the elections; (x) a commitment by the Israeli Government to the principle of exchanging land for peace. Mubarak also offered to host talks between Palestinian and Israeli delegations prior to the holding of the elections, but a proposal by the Labour component of the Israeli Government to accept his invitation was rejected by Israel's 'inner' Cabinet in October 1989. In the same month the US Secretary of State, James Baker, put forward a series of unofficial proposals which aimed to give new impetus to the Israeli peace initiative and the subsequent clarification proposed by President Mubarak. On the basis of its understanding that a dialogue between Israeli and Palestinian delegations would take place, the USA, through the 'Baker plan', sought assurances that Egypt could not and would not substitute itself for the Palestinians in any future negotiations, and that both Israel and the Palestinians would take part in any future dialogue on the basis of the 'Shamir plan'.

THE 1991 MIDDLE EAST PEACE CONFERENCE

On 30 October 1991 the first, symbolic session of a Middle East peace conference, sponsored by the USA and the USSR and attended by Israeli, Syrian, Egyptian, Lebanese and Palestinian/Jordanian delegations, commenced in Madrid, Spain. The text of the invitation sent to the participants by the US and Soviet Presidents is reproduced from Al-Hayat, London

After extensive consultations with Arab states, Israel and the Palestinians, the US and the Soviet Union believe that an historic opportunity exists to advance the prospects for genuine peace throughout the region. The US and the Soviet Union are prepared to assist the parties to achieve a just, lasting and comprehensive peace settlement, through direct negotiations along two tracks, between Israel and the Palestinians, based on UN Security Council resolutions 242 and 338. The objective of this process is real peace.

Towards that end, the president of the US and the president of the USSR invite you to a peace conference, which their countries will co-sponsor, followed immediately by direct negotiations. The conference will be convened in Madrid on 30 October 1991.

President Bush and President Gorbachev request your acceptance of this invitation no later than 6.00pm Washington time, 23 October 1991, in order to ensure proper organisation and preparation of the conference.

Direct bilateral negotiations will begin four days after the opening of the conference. Those parties who wish to attend multilateral negotiations will convene two weeks after the opening of the conference to organise those negotiations. The co-sponsors believe that those negotiations should focus on regionwide issues such as arms control and regional security, water, refugee issues, environment, economic development, and other subjects of mutual interest.

The co-sponsors will chair the conference which will be held at ministerial level. Governments to be invited include Israel, Syria, Lebanon and Jordan. Palestinians will be invited and attend as part of a joint Jordanian-Palestinian delegation. Egypt will be invited to the conference as a participant. The EC will be a participant in the conference alongside the US and Soviet Union and will be represented by its presidency. The GCC will be invited to send its secretary-general to the conference as an observer, and GCC member states will be invited to participate in organising the negotiations on multilateral issues. The UN will be invited to send an observer, representing the secretary-general.

DECLARATION OF PRINCIPLES ON PALESTINIAN SELF-RULE

13 September 1993

The Government of the State of Israel and the Palestinian team (in the Jordanian-Palestinian delegation to the Middle East Peace Conference) (the 'Palestinian Delegation') representing the Palestinian people, agree that it is time to put an end to decades of confrontation and conflict, recognize their mutual legitimate and political rights, and strive to live in peaceful coexistence and mutual dignity and security and achieve a just, lasting and comprehensive peace settlement and historic reconciliation through the agreed political process.

Accordingly, the two sides agree to the following principles:

Article I

Aim of the negotiations

The aim of the Israeli-Palestinian negotiations within the current Middle East peace process is, among other things, to establish a Palestinian Interim Self-Government Authority, the elected Council, (the 'Council') for the Palestinian people in the West Bank and the Gaza Strip, for a transitional period not exceeding five years, leading to a permanent settlement based on Security Council Resolutions 242 and 338.

It is understood that the interim arrangements are an integral part of the overall peace process and that final status negotiations will lead to the implementation of Security Council Resolutions 242 and 338.

Article II

Framework for the interim period

The agreed framework for the interim period is set forth in the Declaration of Principles.

Article III

Elections

1. In order that the Palestinian people in the West Bank and Gaza Strip may govern themselves according to democratic principles, direct, free and general political elections will be held for the Council under agreed supervision and international observation, while the Palestinian police will ensure public order.

2. An agreement will be concluded on the exact mode and conditions of the elections in accordance with the protocol attached as Annex I, with the goal of holding the elections not later than nine months after the entry into force of this Declaration of Principles.

369

3. These elections will constitute a significant interim preparatory step toward the realization of the legitimate rights of the Palestinian people and their just requirements.

Article IV

Jurisdiction of the Council will cover West Bank and Gaza Strip territory, except for issues that will be negotiated in the permanent status negotiations. The two sides view the West Bank and the Gaza Strip as a single territorial unit, whose integrity will be preserved during the interim period.

Article V

Transitional period and permanent status negotiations

1. The five-year transitional period will begin upon the withdrawal from the Gaza Strip and Jericho area.

2. Permanent status negotiations will commence as soon as possible, but not later than the beginning of the third year of the interim period, between the Government of Israel and the Palestinian people representatives.

3. It is understood that these negotiations shall cover remaining issues, including Jerusalem, refugees, settlements, security arrangements, borders, relations and co-operation with other neighbours, and other issues of common interest.

4. The two parties agree that the outcome of the permanent status negotiations should not be prejudiced or pre-empted by agreements reached for the interim period.

Article VI

Preparatory transfer of powers and responsibilities

1. Upon the entry into force of this Declaration of Principles and the withdrawal from the Gaza Strip and Jericho area, a transfer of authority from the Israeli military government and its Civil Administration to the authorized Palestinians for this task, as detailed herein, will commence. This transfer of authority will be of preparatory nature until the inauguration of the Council.

2. Immediately after the entry into force of this Declaration of Principles and the withdrawal from the Gaza Strip and Jericho area, with the view to promoting economic development in the West Bank and Gaza Strip, authority will be transferred to the Palestinians in the following spheres: education and culture, health, social welfare, direct taxation, and tourism. The Palestinian side will commence in building the Palestinian police force, as agreed upon. Pending the inauguration of the Council, the two parties may negotiate the transfer of additional powers and responsibilities as agreed upon.

Article VII

Interim agreement

1. The Israeli and Palestinian delegations will negotiate an agreement on the interim period (the 'Interim Agreement').

2. The Interim Agreement shall specify, among other things, the structure of the Council, the number of its members, and the transfer of powers and responsibilities from the Israeli military government and its Civil Administration to the Council. The Interim Agreement shall also specify the

Council's executive authority, legislative authority in accordance with Article IX below, and the independent Palestinian judicial organs.

3. The Interim Agreement shall include arrangements, to be implemented upon the inauguration of the Council, for the assumption by the Council of all of the powers and responsibilities transferred previously in accordance with Article VI above.

4. In order to enable the Council to promote economic growth, upon its inauguration, the Council will establish, among other things, a Palestinian Electricity Authority, a Gaza Sea Port Authority, a Palestinian Development Bank, a Palestinian Export Promotion Board, a Palestinian Environmental Authority, a Palestinian Land Authority and a Palestinian Water Administration Authority, and any other authorities agreed upon, in accordance with the Interim Agreement that will specify their powers and responsibilities.

5. After the inauguration of the Council, the Civil Administration will be dissolved, and the Israeli military government will be withdrawn.

Article VIII
Public order and security
In order to guarantee public order and internal security for the Palestinians of the West Bank and the Gaza Strip, the Council will establish a strong police force, while Israel will continue to carry the responsibility for defending against external threats, as well as the responsibility for overall security of the Israelis to protect their internal security and public order.

Article IX
Laws and military orders
1. The Council will be empowered to legislate, in accordance with the Interim Agreement, within all authorities transferred to it.

2. Both parties will review jointly laws and military orders presently in force in remaining spheres.

Article X
Joint Israeli-Palestinian liaison committee
In order to provide for a smooth implementation of this Declaration of Principles and any subsequent agreements pertaining to the interim period, upon the entry into force of this Declaration of Principles, a Joint Israeli-Palestinian Liaison Committee will be established in order to deal with issues requiring co-ordination, other issues of common interest, and disputes.

Article XI
Israeli-Palestinian co-operation in economic fields
Recognizing the mutual benefit of co-operation in promoting the development of the West Bank, the Gaza Strip and Israel, upon the entry into force of this Declaration of Principles, an Israeli-Palestinian Economic Co-operation Committee will be established in order to develop and implement in a co-operative manner the programmes identified in the protocols attached as Annex III and Annex IV.

Article XII

Liaison and co-operation with Jordan and Egypt

The two parties will invite the Governments of Jordan and Egypt to participate in establishing further liaison and co-operation arrangements between the Government of Israel and the Palestinian representatives, on one hand, and the Governments of Jordan and Egypt, on the other hand, to promote co-operation between them. These arrangements will include the constitution of a Continuing Committee that will decide by agreement on the modalities of the admission of persons displaced from the West Bank and Gaza Strip in 1967, together with necessary measures to prevent disruption and disorder. Other matters of common concern will be dealt with by this Committee.

Article XIII

Redeployment of Israeli forces

1. After the entry into force of this Declaration of Principles, and not later than the eve of elections for the Council, a redeployment of Israeli military forces in the West Bank and the Gaza Strip will take place, in addition to withdrawal of Israeli forces carried out in accordance with Article XIV.

2. In redeploying its military forces, Israel will be guided by the principle that its military forces should be redeployed outside the populated areas.

3. Further redeployments to specified locations will be gradually implemented commensurate with the assumption of responsibility for public order and internal security by the Palestinian police force pursuant to Article VIII above.

Article XIV

Israeli withdrawal from the Gaza Strip and Jericho area

Israel will withdraw from the Gaza Strip and Jericho area, as detailed in the protocol attached as Annex II.

Article XV

Resolution of disputes

1. Disputes arising out of the application or interpretation of this Declaration of Principles, or any subsequent agreements pertaining to the interim period, shall be resolved by negotiations through the Joint Liaison Committee to be established pursuant to Article X above.

2. Disputes which cannot be settled by negotiations may be resolved by a mechanism of conciliation to be agreed upon by the parties.

3. The parties may agree to submit to arbitration disputes relating to the interim period, which cannot be settled through conciliation. To this end, upon the agreement of both parties, the parties will establish an Arbitration Committee.

Article XVI

Israel-Palestinian co-operation concerning regional programs

Both parties view the multilateral working groups as an appropriate instrument for promoting a 'Marshall Plan,' the regional programs and other programs, including special programs for the West Bank and Gaza Strip, as indicated in the protocol atttached as Annex IV.

Article XVII

Miscellaneous provisions

1. This Declaration of Principles will enter into force one month after its signing.

2. All protocols annexed to this Declaration of Principles and Agreed Minutes pertaining thereto shall be regarded as an integral part hereof.

Annex 1—protocol on the mode and conditions of elections

1. Palestinians of Jerusalem who live there will have the right to participate in the election process, according to an agreement between the two sides.

2. In addition, the election agreement should cover, among other things, the following issues:

   a. the system of elections,

   b. the mode of the agreed supervision and international observation and their personal composition, and

   c. rules and regulations regarding election campaign, including agreed arrangements for the organizing of mass media, and the possibility of licensing a broadcasting and TV station.

3. The future status of displaced Palestinians who were registered on 4th June 1967 will not be prejudiced because they are unable to participate in the election process due to practical reasons.

Annex 2—protocol on withdrawal of Israeli forces from the Gaza Strip and Jericho Area

1. The two sides will conclude and sign within two months from the date of entry into force of this Declaration of Principles, an agreement on the withdrawal of Israeli military forces from the Gaza Strip and Jericho area. This agreement will include comprehensive arrangements to apply in the Gaza Strip and the Jericho area subsequent to the Israeli withdrawal.

2. Israel will implement an accelerated and scheduled withdrawal of Israeli military forces from the Gaza Strip and Jericho area, beginning immediately with the signing of the agreement on the Gaza Strip and Jericho area and to be completed within a period not exceeding four months after the signing of this agreement.

3. The above agreement will include, among other things:

   a. Arrangements for a smooth and peaceful transfer of authority from the Israeli military government and its Civil Administration to the Palestinian representatives.

   b. structure, powers and responsibilities of the Palestinian authority in these areas, except, external security, settlements, Israelis, foreign relations, and other subjects mutually agreed upon.

   c. Arrangements for assumption of internal security and public order by the Palestinian police force consisting of police officers recruited locally and from abroad (holding Jordanian passports and Palestinian documents issued by Egypt). Those who will participate in the Palestinian police force coming from abroad should be trained as police and police officers.

d. A temporary international or foreign presence, as agreed upon.

e. Establishment of a joint Palestinian-Israeli co-ordination and co-operation committee for mutual security purposes.

f. An economic development and stablization program, including the establishment of an Emergency Fund, to encourage foreign investment, and financial and economic support. Both sides will co-ordinate and co-operate jointly and unilaterally with regional and international parties to support these aims.

g. Arrangements for a safe passage for persons and transportation between the Gaza Strip and Jericho area.

4. The above agreement will include arrangements for co-ordination between both parties regarding passages:

a. Gaza – Egypt; and

b. Jericho – Jordan.

5. The offices responsible for carrying out the powers and responsibilities of the Palestinian authority under this Annex II and Article VI of the Declaration of Principles will be located in the Gaza Strip and in the Jericho area pending the inauguration of the Council.

6. Other than these agreed arrangements, the status of the Gaza Strip and Jericho area will continue to be an integral part of the West Bank and Gaza Strip, and will not be changed in the interim period.

PROTOCOL ON ISRAELI-PALESTINIAN CO-OPERATION IN ECONOMIC AND DEVELOPMENT PROGRAMS

The two sides agree to establish an Israeli-Palestinian Continuing Committee for Economic Co-operation, focusing, among other things, on the following:

1. Co-operation in the field of water, including a Water Development Program prepared by experts from both sides, which will also specify the mode of co-operation in the management of water resources in the West Bank and Gaza Strip, and will include proposals for studies and plans on water rights of each party, as well as on the equitable utilization of joint water resources for implementation in and beyond the interim period.

2. Co-operation in the field of electricity, including an Electricity Development Program, which will also specify the mode of co-operation for the production, maintenance, purchase and sale of electricity resources.

3. Co-operation in the field of energy, including an Energy Development Program, which will provide for the exploitation of oil and gas for industrial purposes, particularly in the Gaza Strip and in the Negev, and will encourage further joint exploitation of other energy resources. This Program may also provide for the construction of a Petrochemical industrial complex in the Gaza Strip and the construction of oil and gas pipelines.

4. Co-operation in the field of finance, including a Financial Development and Action Program for the encouragement of international investment in the West Bank and the Gaza Strip, and in Israel, as well as the establishment of a Palestinian Development Bank.

5. Co-operation in the fields of transport and communications, including a Program, which will define guidelines for the establishment of a Gaza Sea Port Area, and will provide for the establishing of transport and communications lines to and from the West Bank and the Gaza Strip to Israel and to other countries. In addition, this Program will provide for carrying out the necessary construction of roads, railways, communications lines, etc.

6. Co-operation in the field of trade, including studies, and Trade Promotion Programs, which will encourage local, regional and inter-regional trade, as well as a feasibility study of creating free trade zones in the Gaza Strip and in Israel, mutual access to these zones, and co-operation in other areas related to trade and commerce.

7. Co-operation in the field of industry, including industrial Development Programs, which will provide for the establishment of joint Israeli-Palestinian Research and Development Centers, will promote Palestinian-Israeli joint ventures, and provide guidelines for co-operation in the textile, food, pharmaceutical, electronics, diamonds, computer and science-based industries.

8. A program for co-operation in, and regulation of, labour relations and co-operation in social welfare issues.

9. A Human Resources Development and Co-operation Plan, providing for joint Israeli-Palestinian workshops and seminars, and for the establishment of joint vocational training centres, research institutes and data banks.

10. An Environmental Protection Plan, providing for joint and/or co-ordinated measures in this sphere.

11. A program for developing co-ordination and co-operation in the field of communication and media.

12. Any other programs of mutual interest.

PROTOCOL ON ISRAELI-PALESTINIAN CO-OPERATION CONCERNING REGIONAL DEVELOPMENT PROGRAMS

1. The two sides will co-operate in the context of the multilateral peace efforts in promoting a Development Program for the region, including the West Bank and the Gaza Strip, to be initiated by the G-7. The parties will request the G-7 to seek the participation in this program of other interested states, such as members of the Organization for Economic Co-operation and Development, regional Arab states and institutions, as well as members of the private sector.

2. The Development Program will consist of two elements:

   a) an Economic Development Program for the West Bank and the Gaza Strip;

   b) a Regional Economic Development Program

A. The Economic Development Program for the West Bank and the Gaza Strip will consist of the following elements:

   (1) A Social Rehabilitation Program, including a Housing and Construction Program.

   (2) A Small and Medium Business Development Plan.

(3) An Infrastructure Development Program (water, electricity, transportation and communications, etc.)

(4) A Human Resources Plan.

(5) Other programs.

B. *The Regional Economic Development Program* may consist of the following elements:

(1) The establishment of a Middle East Development Fund, as a first step, and a Middle East Development Bank, as a second step.

(2) The development of a joint Israeli-Palestinian-Jordanian Plan for co-ordinated exploitation of the Dead Sea area.

(3) The Mediterranean Sea (Gaza)—Dead Sea Canal.

(4) Regional Desalinization and other water development projects.

(5) A regional plan for agricultural development, including a co-ordinated regional effort for the prevention of desertification.

(6) Interconnection of electricity grids.

(7) Regional co-operation for the transfer, distribution and industrial exploitation of gas, oil and other energy resources.

(8) A regional Tourism, Transportation and Telecommunications Development Plan.

(9) Regional co-operation in other spheres.

3. The two sides will encourage the multilateral working groups, and will co-ordinate towards its success. The two parties will encourage international activities, as well as pre-feasibility and feasibility studies, within the various multilateral working groups.

AGREED MINUTES TO THE DECLARATION OF PRINCIPLES ON INTERIM SELF-GOVERNMENT ARRANGEMENTS

A. General Understandings and Agreements

Any powers and responsibilites transferred to the Palestinians pursuant to the Declaration of Principles prior to the inauguration of the Council will be subject to the same principles pertaining to Article IV, as set out in these Agreed Minutes below.

B. Specific Understandings and Agreements

Article IV

It is understood that:

1. Jurisdiction of the Council will cover West Bank and Gaza Strip territory, except for issues that will be negotiated in the permanent status negotiations: Jerusalem, settlements, military locations and Israelis.

2. The Council's jurisdiction will apply with regard to the agreed powers, responsibilities, spheres and authorities transferred to it.

Article VI (2)

It is agreed that the transfer of authority will be as follows:

(1) The Palestinian side will inform the Israeli side of the names of the authorized Palestinians who will assume the powers, authorities and responsibilities that will be transferred to the Palestinians according to the Declaration of Principles in the following fields: education and culture, health, social welfare, direct taxation, tourism, and any other authorities agreed upon.

(2) It is understood that the rights and obligations of these offices will not be affected.

(3) Each of the spheres described above will continue to enjoy existing budgetary allocations in accordance with arrangements to be mutually agreed upon. These arrangements also will provide for the necessary adjustments required in order to take into account the taxes collected by the direct taxation office.

(4) Upon the execution of the Declaration of Principles, the Israeli and Palestinian delegations will immediately commence negotiations on a detailed plan for the transfer of authority on the above offices in accordance with the above understandings.

Article VII (2)

The Interim Agreement will also include arrangements for co-ordination and co-operation.

Article VII (5)

The withdrawal of the military government will not prevent Israel from exercising the powers and responsibilities not transferred to the Council.

Article VIII

It is understood that the Interim Agreement will include arrangements for co-operation and co-ordination between the two parties in this regard. It is also agreed that the transfer of powers and responsibilities to the Palestinian police will be accomplished in a phased manner, as agreed in the Interim Agreement.

Article X

It is agreed that, upon the entry into force of the Declaration of Principles, the Israeli and Palestinian delegations will exchange the names of the individuals designated by them as members of the Joint Israeli-Palestinian Liaison Committee.

It is further agreed that each side will have an equal number of members in the Joint Committee. The Joint Committee will reach decisions by agreement. The Joint Committee may add other technicians and experts, as necessary. The Joint Committee will decide on the frequency and place or places of its meetings.

Annex II

It is understood that, subsequent to the Israeli withdrawal, Israel will continue to be responsible for external security, and for internal security and public order of settlements and Israelis. Israeli military forces and civilians may continue to use roads freely within the Gaza Strip and the Jericho area.

Article XVI

Israeli-Palestinian Co-operation Concerning Regional Programs

Both parties view the multilateral working groups as an appropriate instrument for promoting a 'Marshall Plan,' the regional programs and other programs, including special programs for the West Bank and Gaza Strip, as indicated in the protocol attached as Annex IV.

Article XVII

Miscellaneous Provisions

1. This Declaration of Principles will enter into force one month after its signing.

2. All protocols annexed to this Declaration of Principles and Agreed Minutes pertaining thereto shall be regarded as an integral part hereof.

THE CAIRO AGREEMENT ON THE GAZA STRIP AND JERICHO
4 May 1994

The Government of the State of Israel and the Palestine Liberation Organization (hereinafter 'the PLO'), the representative of the Palestinian people;

Preamble

Within the framework of the Middle East peace process initiated at Madrid in October 1991;

Reaffirming their determination to live in peaceful co-existence, mutual dignity and security, while recognizing their mutual legitimate and political rights;

Reaffirming their desire to achieve a just, lasting and comprehensive peace settlement through the agreed political process;

Reaffirming their adherence to the mutual recognition and commitments expressed in the letters dated September 9, 1993, signed by and exchanged between the Prime Minister of Israel and the Chairman of the PLO;

Reaffirming their understanding that the interim self-government arrangements, including the arrangements to apply in the Gaza Strip and the Jericho Area contained in this Agreement, are an integral part of the whole peace process and that the negotiations on the permanent status will lead to the implementation of Security Council Resolutions 242 and 338;

Desirous of putting into effect the Declaration of Principles on Interim Self-Government Arrangements signed at Washington, D.C. on September 13, 1993, and the agreed minutes thereto (hereinafter 'The Declaration of Principles'), and in particular the protocol on withdrawal of Israeli forces from the Gaza Strip and the Jericho Area:

Hereby agree to the following arrangements regarding the Gaza Strip and the Jericho Area:

Article I

Definitions

For the purpose of this Agreement:

  a. The Gaza Strip and the Jericho Area are delineated on Map Nos. 1 and 2 attached to this Agreement (*Maps not reproduced—Ed.*);

b. 'The settlements' means the Gush Katif and Erez settlement areas, as well as the other settlements in the Gaza Strip, as shown on attached Map No. 1;

c. 'The military installation area' means the Israeli military installation area along the Egyptian border in the Gaza Strip, as shown on Map No. 1; and

d. The term 'Israelis' shall also include Israeli statutory agencies and corporations registered in Israel.

Article II

Scheduled withdrawal of Israeli military forces

1. Israel shall implement an accelerated and scheduled withdrawal of Israeli military forces from the Gaza Strip and from the Jericho Area to begin immediately with the signing of this Agreement. Israel shall complete such withdrawal within three weeks from this date.

2. Subject to the arrangements included in the Protocol concerning withdrawal of Israeli military forces and security arrangements attached as Annex I, the Israeli withdrawal shall include evacuating all military bases and other fixed installations to be handed over to the Palestinian Police, to be established pursuant to Article IX below (hereinafter 'the Palestinian Police').

3. In order to carry out Israel's responsibility for external security and for internal security and public order of settlements and Israelis, Israel shall, concurrently with the withdrawal, redeploy its remaining military forces to the settlements and the military installation area, in accordance with the provisions of this Agreement. Subject to the provisions of this Agreement, this redeployment shall constitute full implementation of Article XIII of the Declaration of Principles with regard to the Gaza Strip and the Jericho Area only.

4. For the purposes of this Agreement, 'Israeli military forces' may include Israeli police and other Israeli security forces.

5. Israelis, including Israeli military forces, may continue to use roads freely within the Gaza Strip and the Jericho Area. Palestinians may use public roads crossing the settlements freely, as provided for in Annex I.

6. The Palestinian Police shall be deployed and shall assume responsibility for public order and internal security of Palestinians in accordance with this Agreement and Annex I.

Article III

Transfer of authority

1. Israel shall transfer authority as specified in this Agreement from the Israeli military government and its Civil Administration to the Palestinian Authority, hereby established, in accordance with Article V of this Agreement, except for the authority that Israel shall continue to excercise as specified in this Agreement.

2. As regards the transfer and assumption of authority in civil spheres, powers and responsibilities shall be transferred and assumed as set out in the Protocol concerning civil affairs attached as Annex II.

3. Arrangements for a smooth and peaceful transfer of the agreed powers and responsibilities are set out in Annex II.

4. Upon the completion of the Israeli withdrawal and the transfer of powers and responsibilities as detailed in Paragraphs 1 and 2 above and in Annex II, the Civil Administration in the Gaza Strip and the Jericho Area will be dissolved and the Israeli military government will be withdrawn. The withdrawal of the military government shall not prevent it from continuing to excercise the powers and responsibilities specified in this Agreement.

5. A joint Civil Affairs Co-ordination and Co-operation Committee (hereinafter 'the CAC') and two joint regional civil affairs subcommittees for the Gaza Strip and the Jericho Area respectively shall be established in order to provide for co-ordination and co-operation in civil affairs between the Palestinian Authority and Israel, as detailed in Annex II.

6. The offices of the Palestinian Authority shall be located in the Gaza Strip and the Jericho Area pending the inauguration of the council to be elected pursuant to the Declaration of Principles.

Article IV

Structure and composition of the Palestinian Authority

1. The Palestinian Authority will consist of one body of 24 members which shall carry out and be responsible for all the legislative and executive powers and responsibilities transferred to it under this Agreement, in accordance with this article, and shall be responsible for the excercise of judicial functions in accordance with Article VI, subparagraph 1.b of this Agreement.

2. The Palestinian Authority shall administer the departments transferred to it and may establish, within its jurisdiction, other departments and subordinate administrative units as necessary for the fulfilment of its responsibilities. It shall determine its own internal procedures.

3. The PLO shall inform the Government of Israel of the names of the members of the Palestinian Authority and any change of members. Changes in the membership of the Palestinian Authority will take effect upon an exchange of letters between the PLO and the Government of Israel.

4. Each member of the Palestinian Authority shall enter into office upon undertaking to act in accordance with this Agreement.

Article V

Jurisdiction

1. The authority of the Palestinian Authority encompasses all matters that fall within its territorial, functional and personal jurisdiction, as follows:

    a. The territorial jurisdiction covers the Gaza Strip and the Jericho Area territory, as defined in Article I, except for settlements and the military installation area.
    Territorial jurisdiction shall include land, subsoil and territorial waters, in accordance with the provisions of this Agreement.

    b. The functional jurisdiction encompasses all powers and responsibilities as specified in this Agreement. This jurisdiction does not include foreign relations, internal security and public order of settlements and the military installation area and Israelis, and external security.

c. The personal jurisdiction extends to all persons within the territorial jurisdiction referred to above, except for Israelis, unless otherwise provided in this Agreement.

2. The Palestinian Authority has, within its authority, legislative, executive and judicial powers and responsibilities, as provided for in this Agreement.

3. a. Israel has authority over the settlements, the military installation area, Israelis, external security, internal security and public order of settlements, the military installation area and Israelis, and those agreed powers and responsibilities specified in this Agreement.

b. Israel shall exercise its authority through its military government, which for that end, shall continue to have the necessary legislative, judicial and executive powers and responsibilities, in accordance with international law. This provision shall not derogate from Israel's applicable legislation over Israelis in personam.

4. The exercise of authority with regard to the electromagnetic sphere and airspace shall be in accordance with the provisions of this Agreement.

5. The provisions of this article are subject to the specific legal arrangements detailed in the Protocol concerning legal matters attached as Annex III. Israel and the Palestinian Authority may negotiate further legal arrangements.

6. Israel and the Palestinian Authority shall co-operate on matters of legal assistance in criminal and civil matters through the legal subcommittee of the CAC.

Article VI

Powers and responsibilities of the Palestinian Authority

1. Subject to the provisions of this Agreement, the Palestinian Authority, within its jurisdiction:

a. has legislative powers as set out in Article VII of this Agreement, as well as executive powers;

b. will administer justice through an independent judiciary:

c. will have, inter alia, power to formulate policies, supervise their implementation, employ staff, establish departments, authorities and institutions, sue and be sued and conclude contracts; and

d. will have, inter alia, the power to keep and administer registers and records of the population, and issue certificates, licenses and documents.

2. a. In accordance with the Declaration of Principles, the Palestinian Authority will not have powers and responsibilities in the sphere of foreign relations, which sphere includes the establishment abroad of embassies, consulates or other types of foreign missions and posts or permitting their establishment in the Gaza Strip or the Jericho Area, the appointment of or admission of diplomatic and consular staff, and the exercise of diplomatic functions.

b. Notwithstanding the provisions of this paragraph, the PLO may conduct negotiations and sign agreements with states or international organizations for the benefit of the Palestinian Authority in the following cases only:

(1) Economic agreements, as specifically provided in Annex IV of this Agreement;

(2) Agreements with donor countries for the purpose of implementing arrangements for the provision of assistance to the Palestinian Authority;

(3) Agreements for the purpose of implementing the regional development plans detailed in Annex IV of the Declaration of Principles or in agreements entered into in the framework of the multilateral negotiations; and

(4) Cultural, scientific and education agreements.

   c. Dealings between the Palestinian Authority and representatives of foreign states and international organizations, as well as the establishment in the Gaza Strip and the Jericho Area of representative offices other than those described in subparagraph 2.a, above, for the purpose of implementing the agreements referred to in subparagraph 2.b above, shall not be considered foreign relations.

Article VII

Legislative powers of the Palestinian Authority

1. The Palestinian Authority will have the power, within its jurisdiction, to promulgate legislation, including basic laws, laws, regulations and other legislative acts.

2. Legislation promulgated by the Palestinian Authority shall be consistent with the provisions of this Agreement.

3. Legislation promulgated by the Palestinian Authority shall be communicated to a legislation subcommittee to be established by the CAC (hereinafter 'the Legislation Subcommittee'). During a period of 30 days from the communication of the legislation, Israel may request that the Legislation Subcommittee decide whether such legislation exceeds the jurisdiction of the Palestinian Authority or is otherwise inconsistent with the provisions of this Agreement.

4. Upon receipt of the Israeli request, the Legislation Subcommittee shall decide, as an initial matter, on the entry into force of the legislation pending its decision on the merits of the matter.

5. If the Legislation Subcommittee is unable to reach a decision with regard to the entry into force of the legislation within 15 days, this issue will be referred to a Board of Review. This Board of Review shall be comprised of two judges, retired judges or senior jurists (hereinafter 'Judges'), one from each side, to be appointed from a compiled list of three judges proposed by each.

6. Legislation referred to the Board of Review shall enter into force only if the Board of Review decides that it does not deal with a security issue which falls under Israel's responsibility, that it does not seriously threaten other significant Israeli interests protected by this Agreement and that the entry into force of the legislation could not cause irreparable damage or harm.

7. The Legislation Subcommitte shall attempt to reach a decision on the merits of the matter within 30 days from the date of the Israeli request. If this subcommittee is unable to reach such a decision within this period of 30 days, the matter shall be referred to the joint Israeli-Palestinian Liaison Committee referred to in Article XV below (hereinafter 'the Liaison Committee'). This

Liaison Committee will deal with the matter immediately and will attempt to settle it within 30 days.

8. Where the legislation has not entered into force pursuant to paragraphs 5 or 7 above, this situation shall be maintained pending the decision of the Liaison Committee on the merits of the matter, unless it has decided otherwise.

9. Laws and military orders in effect in the Gaza Strip or the Jericho Area prior to the signing of this Agreement shall remain in force, unless amended or abrogated in accordance with this Agreement.

Article VIII
Arrangements for security and public order

1. In order to guarantee public order and internal security for the Palestinians of the Gaza Strip and the Jericho Area, the Palestinian Authority shall establish a strong police force, as set out in Article IX below. Israel shall continue to carry the responsibility for defence against external threats, including the responsibility for protecting the Egyptian border and the Jordanian line, and for defence against external threats from the sea and from the air, as well as the responsibility for overall security of Israelis and settlements, for the purpose of safeguarding their internal security and public order, and will have all the powers to take the steps necessary to meet this responsibility.

2. Agreed security arrangements and co-ordination mechanisms are specified in Annex I.

3. A Joint Co-ordination and Co-operation committee for mutual security purposes (hereinafter 'the JSC'), as well as three joint district co-ordination and co-operation offices for the Gaza District, the Khan Younis District and the Jericho District respectively (hereinafter 'the DCOS') are hereby established as provided for in Annex I.

4. The security arrangements provided for in this Agreement and in Annex I may be reviewed at the requests of either party and may be amended by mutual agreement of the parties. Specific review arrangements are included in Annex I.

Article IX
The Palestinian Directorate of Police Force

1. The Palestinian Authority shall establish a strong police force, the Palestinian Directorate of Police Force (hereinafter 'the Palestinian Police'). The duties, functions, structure, deployment and composition of the Palestinian Police, together with provisions regarding its equipment and operation, are set out in Annex I, Article III. Rules of conduct governing the activities of the Palestinian Police are set out in Annex I, Article VIII.

2. Except for the Palestinian Police referred to in this article and the Israeli military forces, no other armed forces shall be established or operate in the Gaza Strip or the Jericho Area.

3. Except for the arms, ammunition and equipment of the Palestinian Police described in Annex I, Article III, and those of the Israeli military forces, no organization or individual in the Gaza Strip and the Jericho Area shall manufacture, sell, acquire, possess, import or otherwise introduce into the Gaza Strip or the Jericho Area any firearms, ammunition, weapons, explosives, gunpowder or any related equipment, unless otherwise provided for in Annex I.

Article X

Passages

Arrangements for co-ordination between Israel and the Palestinian Authority regarding the Gaza–Egypt and Jericho–Jordan passages, as well as any other agreed international crossings, are set out in Annex 1.

Article XI

Safe passage between the Gaza Strip and the Jericho Area

Arrangements for safe passage of persons and transportation between the Gaza Strip and the Jericho Area are set out in Annex I, Article IX.

Article XII

Relations between Israel and the Palestinian Authority

1. Israel and the Palestinian Authority shall seek to foster mutual understanding and tolerance and shall accordingly abstain from incitement, including hostile propaganda, against each other and, without derogating from the principle of freedom of expression, shall take legal measures to prevent such incitement by any organizations, groups or individuals within their jurisdiction.

2. Without derogating from the other provisions of this agreement, Israel and the Palestinian Authority shall co-operate in combating criminal activity which may affect both sides, including offences related to trafficking in illegal drugs and psychotropic substances, smuggling, and offences against property, including offences related to vehicles.

Article XIII

Economic relations

The economic relations between the two sides are set out in the Protocol on Economic Relations signed in Paris on April 29, 1994 and the appendixes thereto, certified copies of which are attached as Annex IV, and will be governed by the relevant provisions of this agreement and its annexes.

Article XIV

Human rights and the rule of law

Israel and the Palestinian Authority shall exercise their powers and responsibilities pursuant to this Agreement with due regard to internationally-accepted norms and principles of human rights and the rule of law.

Article XV

The Joint Israeli-Palestinian Liaison Committee

1. The Liaison Committee established pursuant to Article X of the Declaration of Principles shall ensure the smooth implementation of this Agreement. It shall deal with issues requiring co-ordination, other issues of common interest and disputes.

2. The Liaison Committee shall be composed of an equal number of members from each party. It may add other technicians and experts as necessary.

3. The Liaison Committee shall adopt its rules of procedure, including the frequency and place or places of its meetings.

4. The Liaison Committee shall reach its decision by agreement.

Article XVI

Liaison and Co-operation with Jordan and Egypt

1. Pursuant to Article XII of the Declaration of Principles, the two parties shall invite the governments of Jordan and Egypt to participate in establishing further Liaison and Co-operation Arrangements between the Government of Israel and the Palestinian Representatives on the one hand, and the governments of Jordan and Egypt on the other hand, to promote co-operation between them. These arrangements shall include the constitution of a Continuing Committee.

2. The Continuing Committee shall decide by agreement on the modalities of admission of persons displaced from the West Bank and the Gaza Strip in 1967, together with necessary measures to prevent disruption and disorder.

3. The Continuing Committee shall deal with other matters of common concern.

Article XVII

Settlement of differences and disputes

Any difference relating to the application of this agreement shall be referred to the appropriate co-ordination and co-operation mechanism established under this agreement. The provisions of Article XV of the Declaration of Principles shall apply to any such difference which is not settled through the appropriate co-ordination and co-operation mechanism, namely:

1. Disputes arising out of the application or interpretation of this agreement or any subsequent agreements pertaining to the interim period shall be settled by negotiations through the Liaison Committee.

2. Disputes which cannot be settled by negotiations may be settled by a mechanism of conciliation to be agreed between the parties.

3. The parties may agree to submit to arbitration disputes relating to the interim period, which cannot be settled through conciliation. To this end, upon the agreement of both parties, the parties will establish an arbitration committee.

Article XVIII

Prevention of hostile acts

Both sides shall take all measures necessary in order to prevent acts of terrorism, crime and hostilities directed against each other, against individuals falling under the other's authority and against their property, and shall take legal measures against offenders. In addition, the Palestinian side shall take all measures necessary to prevent such hostile acts directed against the settlements, the infrastructure serving them and the military installation area, and the Israeli side shall take all measures necessary to prevent such hostile acts emanating from the settlements and directed against Palestinians.

Article XIX

Missing persons

The Palestinian Authority shall co-operate with Israel by providing all necessary assistance in the conduct of searches by Israel within the Gaza Strip and the Jericho Area for missing Israelis, as well as by providing information about missing Israelis. Israel shall co-operate with the Palestinian Authority in searching for, and providing necessary information about, missing Palestinians.

Article XX

Confidence-building measures

With a view to creating a positive and supportive public atmosphere to accompany the implementation of this agreement, and to establish a solid basis of mutual trust and good faith, both parties agree to carry out confidence-building measures as detailed herewith:

1. Upon the signing of this agreement, Israel will release, or turn over, to the Palestinian Authority within a period of 5 weeks, about 5,000 Palestinian detainees and prisoners, residents of the West Bank and the Gaza Strip. Those released will be free to return to their homes anywhere in the West Bank or the Gaza Strip. Prisoners turned over to the Palestinian Authority shall be obliged to remain in the Gaza Strip or the Jericho Area for the remainder of their sentence.

2. After the signing of this Agreement, the two parties shall continue to negotiate the release of additional Palestinian prisoners and detainees, building on agreed principles.

3. The implementation of the above measures will be subject to the fulfilment of the procedures determined by Israeli law for the release and transfer of detainees and prisoners.

4. With the assumption of Palestinian Authority, the Palestinian side commits itself to solving the problem of those Palestinians who were in contact with the Israeli authorities. Until an agreed solution is found, the Palestinian side undertakes not to prosecute these Palestinians or to harm them in any way.

5. Palestinians from abroad whose entry into the Gaza Strip and the Jericho Area is approved pursuant to this agreement, and to whom the provisions of this article are applicable, will not be prosecuted for offences committed prior to September 13, 1993.

Article XXI

Temporary international presence

1. The parties agree to a temporary international or foreign presence in the Gaza Strip and the Jericho Area (hereinafter 'the TIP'), in accordance with the provisions of this article.

2. The TIP shall consist of 400 qualified personnel, including observers, instructors and other experts, from 5 or 6 of the donor countries.

3. The two parties shall request the donor countries to establish a special fund to provide finance for the TIP.

4. The TIP will function for a period of 6 months. The TIP may extend this period, or change the scope of its operation, with the agreement of the two parties.

5. The TIP shall be stationed and operative within the following cities and villages: Gaza, Khan Younis, Rafah, Deir al-Balah, Jabalya, Absan, Beit Hanun and Jericho.

6. Israel and the Palestinian Authority shall agree on a special protocol to implement this article, with the goal of concluding negotiations with the donor countries contributing personnel within two months.

Article XXII

Rights, liabilities and obligations

1. a. The transfer of all powers and responsibilities to the Palestinian Authority, as detailed in Annex II, includes all related rights, liabilities and obligations arising with regard to acts or omissions which occurred prior to the transfer. Israel will cease to bear any financial responsibility regarding such acts or omissions and the Palestinian Authority will bear all financial responsibility for these and for its own functioning.

   b. Any financial claim made in this regard against Israel will be referred to the Palestinian Authority.

   c. Israel shall provide the Palestinian Authority with the information it has regarding pending and anticipated claims brought before any court or tribunal against Israel in this regard.

   d. Where legal proceedings are brought in respect of such a claim, Israel will notify the Palestinian Authority and enable it to participate in defending the claim and raise any arguments on its behalf.

   e. In the event that an award is made against Israel by any court or tribunal in respect of such a claim, the Palestinian Authority shall reimburse Israel the full amount of the award.

   f. Without prejudice to the above, where a court or tribunal hearing such a claim finds that liability rests solely with an employee or agent who acted beyond the scope of the powers assigned to him or her, unlawfully or with willful malfeasance, the Palestinian Authority shall not bear financial responsibility.

2. The transfer of authority in itself shall not affect rights, liabilities and obligations of any person or legal entity, in existence at the date of signing of this Agreement.

Article XXIII

Final clauses

1. This Agreement shall enter into force on the date of its signing.

2. The arrangements established by this Agreement shall remain in force until and to the extent superseded by the Interim Agreement referred to in the Declaration of Principles or any other Agreement between the parties.

3. The five-year Interim Period referred to in the Declaration of Principles commences on the date of the signing of this Agreement.

4. The parties agree that, as long as this Agreement is in force, the security fence erected by Israel around the Gaza Strip shall remain in place and that the line demarcated by the fence, as shown on attached Map No. 1, shall be authoritative only for the purpose of this Agreement.

5. Nothing in this Agreement shall prejudice or pre-empt the outcome of the negotiations on the Interim Agreement or on the Permanent Status to be conducted pursuant to the Declaration of Principles. Neither party shall be

deemed, by virtue of having entered into this Agreement, to have renounced or waived any of its existing rights, claims or positions.

6. The two parties view the West Bank and the Gaza Strip as a single territorial unit, the integrity of which will be preserved during the Interim Period.

7. The Gaza Strip and the Jericho Area shall continue to be an integral part of the West Bank and the Gaza Strip, and their status shall not be changed for the period of this Agreement. Nothing in this Agreement shall be considered to change this status.

8. The preamble to this Agreement, and all Annexes, Appendices and Maps attached hereto, shall constitute an integral part hereof.

ISRAELI-PALESTINIAN INTERIM AGREEMENT ON THE WEST BANK AND THE GAZA STRIP
28 September 1995

The Interim Agreement was signed by the Chairman of the PLO, Yasser Arafat, and the Israeli Minister of Foreign Affairs, Shimon Peres, in Washington, DC, USA. The Agreement was witnessed by representatives of the USA, Russia, Egypt, Jordan, Norway and the European Union (EU). Considerable additional detail was contained in seven annexes (not reproduced here) to the Agreement (the most expansive of which—Annex I—concerned redeployment and security arrangements) and a map (not reproduced here, although an overview is provided by the map on p. 403) in which the boundaries of first-phase redeployment areas 'A' and 'B' were defined.

The Government of the State of Israel and the Palestine Liberation Organization (hereinafter the 'PLO'), the representative of the Palestinian people;

Preamble

WITHIN the framework of the Middle East peace process initiated at Madrid in October 1991;

REAFFIRMING their determination to put an end to decades of confrontation and to live in peaceful coexistence, mutual dignity and security, while recognizing their mutual legitimate and political rights;

REAFFIRMING their desire to achieve a just, lasting and comprehensive peace settlement and historic reconciliation through the agreed political process;

RECOGNIZING that the peace process and the new era that it has created, as well as the new relationship established between the two Parties as described above, are irreversible, and the determination of the two Parties to maintain, sustain and continue the peace process;

RECOGNIZING that the aim of the Israeli-Palestinian negotiations within the current Middle East peace process is, among other things, to establish a Palestinian Interim Self-Government Authority, i.e. the elected Council (hereinafter 'the Council' or 'the Palestinian Council'), and the elected Ra'ees of the Executive Authority, for the Palestinian people in the West Bank and the Gaza Strip, for a transitional period not exceeding five years from the date of signing the Agreement on the Gaza Strip and the Jericho Area (hereinafter 'the

Gaza-Jericho Agreement') on May 4, 1994, leading to a permanent settlement based on Security Council Resolutions 242 and 338;

REAFFIRMING their understanding that the interim self-government arrangements contained in this Agreement are an integral part of the whole peace process, that the negotiations on the permanent status, that will start as soon as possible but not later than May 4, 1996, will lead to the implementation of Security Council Resolutions 242 and 338, and that the Interim Agreement shall settle all the issues of the interim period and that no such issues will be deferred to the agenda of the permanent status negotiations;

REAFFIRMING their adherence to the mutual recognition and commitments expressed in the letters dated September 9, 1993, signed by and exchanged between the Prime Minister of Israel and the Chairman of the PLO;

DESIROUS of putting into effect the Declaration of Principles on Interim Self-Government Arrangements signed at Washington, DC on September 13, 1993, and the Agreed Minutes thereto (hereinafter 'the DOP') and in particular Article III and Annex I concerning the holding of direct, free and general political elections for the Council and the Ra'ees of the Executive Authority in order that the Palestinian people in the West Bank, Jerusalem and the Gaza Strip may democratically elect accountable representatives;

RECOGNIZING that these elections will constitute a significant interim preparatory step toward the realization of the legitimate rights of the Palestinian people and their just requirements and will provide a democratic basis for the establishment of Palestinian institutions;

REAFFIRMING their mutual commitment to act, in accordance with this Agreement, immediately, efficiently and effectively against acts or threats of terrorism, violence or incitement, whether committed by Palestinians or Israelis;

FOLLOWING the Gaza-Jericho Agreement; the Agreement on Preparatory Transfer of Powers and Responsibilities signed at Erez on August 29, 1994 (hereinafter 'the Preparatory Transfer Agreement'); and the Protocol on Further Transfer of Powers and Responsibilities signed at Cairo on August 27, 1995 (hereinafter 'the Further Transfer Protocol'); which three agreements will be superseded by this Agreement;

HEREBY AGREE as follows:

CHAPTER 1—THE COUNCIL

ARTICLE I
Transfer of Authority

1. Israel shall transfer powers and responsibilities as specified in this Agreement from the Israeli military government and its Civil Administration to the Council in accordance with this Agreement. Israel shall continue to exercise powers and responsibilities not so transferred.

2. Pending the inauguration of the Council, the powers and responsibilities tranferred to the Council shall be exercised by the Palestinian Authority established in accordance with the Gaza-Jericho Agreement, which shall also have all the rights, liabilities and obligations to be assumed by the Council in this regard. Accordingly, the term 'Council' throughout this Agreement shall,

pending the inauguration of the Council, be construed as meaning the Palestinian Authority.

3. The transfer of powers and responsibilities to the police force established by the Palestinian Council in accordance with Article XIV below (hereinafter 'the Palestinian Police') shall be accomplished in a phased manner, as detailed in this Agreement and in the Protocol concerning Redeployment and Security Arrangements attached as Annex I to this Agreement (hereinafter 'Annex I').

4. As regards the transfer and assumption of authority in civil spheres, powers and responsibilities shall be transferred and assumed as set out in the Protocol Concerning Civil Affairs attached as Annex III to this Agreement (hereinafter 'Annex III').

5. After the inauguration of the Council, the Civil Administration in the West Bank will be dissolved, and the Israeli military government shall be withdrawn. The withdrawal of the military government shall not prevent it from exercising the powers and responsibilities not transferred to the Council.

6. A Joint Civil Affairs Co-ordination and Co-operation Committee (hereinafter 'the CAC'), Joint Regional Civil Affairs Subcommittees, one for the Gaza Strip and the other for the West Bank, and District Civil Liaison Offices in the West Bank shall be established in order to provide for co-ordination and co-operation in civil affairs between the Council and Israel, as detailed in Annex III.

7. The offices of the Council, and the offices of its Ra'ees and its Executive Authority and other committees, shall be located in areas under Palestinian territorial jurisdiction in the West Bank and the Gaza Strip.

ARTICLE II

Elections

1. In order that the Palestinian people of the West Bank and the Gaza Strip may govern themselves according to democratic principles, direct, free and general political elections will be held for the Council and the Ra'ees of the Executive Authority of the Council in accordance with the provisions set out in the Protocol concerning Elections attached as Annex II to this Agreement (hereinafter 'Annex II').

2. These elections will constitute a significant interim preparatory step towards the realization of the legitimate rights of the Palestinian people and their just requirements and will provide a democratic basis for the establishment of Palestinian institutions.

3. Palestinians of Jerusalem who live there may participate in the election process in accordance with the provisions contained in this Article and in Article VI of Annex II (Election Arrangements concerning Jerusalem).

4. The elections shall be called by the Chairman of the Palestinian Authority immediately following the signing of this Agreement to take place at the earliest practicable date following the redeployment of Israeli forces in accordance with Annex I, and consistent with the requirements of the election timetable as provided in Annex II, the Election Law and the Election Regulations, as defined in Article I of Annex II.

ARTICLE III

Structure of the Palestinian Council

1. The Palestinian Council and the Ra'ees of the Executive Authority of the Council constitute the Palestinian Interim Self-Government Authority, which will be elected by the Palestinian people of the West Bank, Jerusalem and the Gaza Strip for the transitional period agreed in Article I of the DOP.

2. The Council shall possess both legislative power and executive power, in accordance with Articles VII and IX of the DOP. The Council shall carry out and be responsible for all the legislative and executive powers and responsibilities transferred to it under this Agreement. The exercise of legislative powers shall be in accordance with Article XVIII of this Agreement (Legislative Powers of the Council).

3. The Council and the Ra'ees of the Executive Authority of the Council shall be directly and simultaneously elected by the Palestinian people of the West Bank, Jerusalem and the Gaza Strip, in accordance with the provisions of this Agreement and the Election Law and Regulations, which shall not be contrary to the provisions of this Agreement.

4. The Council and the Ra'ees of the Executive Authority of the Council shall be elected for a transitional period not exceeding five years from the signing of the Gaza-Jericho Agreement on May 4, 1994.

5. Immediately upon its inauguration, the Council will elect from among its members a Speaker. The Speaker will preside over the meetings of the Council, administer the Council and its committees, decide on the agenda of each meeting, and lay before the Council proposals for voting and declare their results.

6. The jurisdiction of the Council shall be as determined in Article XVII of this Agreement (Jurisdiction).

7. The organization, structure and functioning of the Council shall be in accordance with this Agreement and the Basic Law for the Palestinian Interim Self-Government Authority, which Law shall be adopted by the Council. The Basic Law and any regulations made under it shall not be contrary to the provisions of this Agreement.

8. The Council shall be responsible under its executive powers for the offices, services and departments transferred to it and may establish, within its jurisdiction, ministries and subordinate bodies, as necessary for the fulfillment of its responsibilities.

9. The Speaker will present for the Council's approval proposed internal procedures that will regulate, among other things, the decision-making processes of the Council.

ARTICLE IV

Size of the Council

The Palestinian Council shall be composed of 82 representatives and the Ra'ees of the Executive Authority, who will be directly and simultaneously elected by the Palestinian people of the West Bank, Jerusalem and the Gaza Strip.

ARTICLE V

The Executive Authority of the Council

1. The Council will have a committee that will exercise the executive authority of the Council, formed in accordance with paragraph 4 below (hereinafter 'the Executive Authority').

2. The Executive Authority shall be bestowed with the executive authority of the Council and will exercise it on behalf of the Council. It shall determine its own internal procedures and decision making processes.

3. The Council will publish the names of the members of the Executive Authority immediately upon their initial appointment and subsequent to any changes.

4. a. The Ra'ees of the Executive Authority shall be an ex officio member of the Executive Authority.

   b. All of the other members of the Executive Authority, except as provided in subparagraph c. below, shall be members of the Council, chosen and proposed to the Council by the Ra'ees of the Executive Authority and approved by the Council.

   c. The Ra'ees of the Executive Authority shall have the right to appoint some persons, in number not exceeding twenty percent of the total membership of the Executive Authority, who are not members of the Council, to exercise executive authority and participate in government tasks. Such appointed members may not vote in meetings of the Council.

   d. Non-elected members of the Executive Authority must have a valid address in an area under the jurisdiction of the Council.

ARTICLE VI

Other Committees of the Council

1. The Council may form small committees to simplify the proceedings of the Council and to assist in controlling the activity of its Executive Authority.

2. Each committee shall establish its own decision-making processes within the general framework of the organization and structure of the Council.

ARTICLE VII

Open Government

1. All meetings of the Council and of its committees, other than the Executive Authority, shall be open to the public, except upon a resolution of the Council or the relevant committee on the grounds of security, or commercial or personal confidentiality.

2. Participation in the deliberations of the Council, its committees and the Executive Authority shall be limited to their respective members only. Experts may be invited to such meetings to address specific issues on an ad hoc basis.

ARTICLE VIII

Judicial Review

Any person or organization affected by any act or decision of the Ra'ees of the Executive Authority of the Council or of any member of the Executive Authority, who believes that such act or decision exceeds the authority of the

Ra'ees or of such member, or is otherwise incorrect in law or procedure, may apply to the relevant Palestinian Court of Justice for a review of such activity or decision.

ARTICLE IX

Powers and Responsibilities of the Council

1. Subject to the provisions of this Agreement, the Council will, within its jurisdiction, have legislative powers as set out in Article XVIII of this Agreement, as well as executive powers.

2. The executive power of the Palestinian Council shall extend to all matters within its jurisdiction under this Agreement or any future agreement that may be reached between the two Parties during the interim period. It shall include the power to formulate and conduct Palestinian policies and to supervise their implementation, to issue any rule or regulation under powers given in approved legislation and administrative decisions necessary for the realization of Palestinian self-government, the power to employ staff, sue and be sued and conclude contracts, and the power to keep and administer registers and records of the population, and issue certificates, licenses and documents.

3. The Palestinian Council's executive decisions and acts shall be consistent with the provisions of this Agreement.

4. The Palestinian Council may adopt all necessary measures in order to enforce the law and any of its decisions, and bring proceedings before the Palestinian courts and tribunals.

5. a. In accordance with the DOP, the Council will not have powers and responsibilities in the sphere of foreign relations, which sphere includes the establishment abroad of embassies, consulates or other types of foreign missions and posts or permitting their establishment in the West Bank or the Gaza Strip, the appointment of or admission of diplomatic and consular staff, and the exercise of diplomatic functions.

   b. Notwithstanding the provisions of this paragraph, the PLO may conduct negotiations and sign agreements with states or international organizations for the benefit of the Council in the following cases only:

   (1) Economic agreements, as specifically provided in Annex V of this Agreement;

   (2) Agreements with donor countries for the purpose of implementing arrangements for the provision of assistance to the Council;

   (3) Agreements for the purpose of implementing the regional development plans detailed in Annex IV of the DOP or in agreements entered into in the framework of the multilateral negotiations; and

   (4) Cultural, scientific and educational agreements.

   c. Dealings between the Council and representatives of foreign states and international organizations, as well as the establishment in the West Bank and the Gaza Strip of representative offices other than those described in subparagrah 5.a above, for the purpose of implementing the agreements referred to in subparagraph 5.b above, shall not be considered foreign relations.

6. Subject to the provisions of this Agreement, the Council shall, within its jurisdiction, have an independent judicial system composed of independent Palestinian courts and tribunals.

CHAPTER 2—REDEPLOYMENT AND SECURITY ARRANGEMENTS

ARTICLE X
Redeployment of Israeli Military Forces

1. The first phase of the Israeli military forces redeployment will cover populated areas in the West Bank—cities, towns, villages, refugee camps and hamlets—as set out in Annex I, and will be completed prior to the eve of the Palestinian elections, i.e., 22 days before the day of the elections.

2. Further redeployments of Israeli military forces to specified military locations will commence after the inauguration of the Council and will be gradually implemented commensurate with the assumption of responsibility for public order and internal security by the Palestinian Police, to be completed within 18 months from the date of the inauguration of the Council as detailed in Articles XI (Land) and XIII (Security), below and in Annex I.

3. The Palestinian Police shall be deployed and shall assume responsibility for public order and internal security for Palestinians in a phased manner in accordance with Article XIII (Security) below and Annex I.

4. Israel shall continue to carry the responsibility for external security, as well as the responsibility for overall security of Israelis for the purpose of safe-guarding their internal security and public order.

5. For the purpose of this Agreement, 'Israeli military forces' includes Israeli Police and other Israeli security forces.

ARTICLE XI
Land

1. The two sides view the West Bank and the Gaza Strip as a single territorial unit, the integrity and status of which will be preserved during the interim period.

2. The two sides agree that West Bank and Gaza Strip territory, except for issues that will be negotiated in the permanent status negotiations, will come under the jurisdiction of the Palestinian Council in a phased manner, to be completed within 18 months from the date of the inauguration of the Council, as specified below:

   a. Land in populated areas (Areas A and B), including government and Al Waqf land, will come under the jurisdiction of the Council during the first phase of redeployment.

   b. All civil powers and responsibilities, including planning and zoning, in Areas A and B, set out in Annex III, will be transferred to and assumed by the Council during the first phase of redeployment.

   c. In Area C, during the first phase of redeployment Israel will transfer to the Council civil powers and responsibilities not relating to territory, as set out in Annex III.

d. The further redeployments of Israeli military forces to specified military locations will be gradually implemented in accordance with the DOP in three phases, each to take place after an interval of six months, after the inauguration of the Council, to be completed within 18 months from the date of the inauguration of the Council.

e. During the further redeployment phases to be completed within 18 months from the date of the inauguration of the Council, powers and responsibilities relating to territory will be transferred gradually to Palestinian jurisdiction that will cover West Bank and Gaza Strip territory, except for the issues that will be negotiated in the permanent status negotiations.

f. The specified military locations referred to in Article X, paragraph 2 above will be determined in the further redeployment phases, within the specified time-frame ending not later than 18 months from the date of the inauguration of the Council, and will be negotiated in the permanent status negotiations.

3. For the purpose of this Agreement and until the completion of the first phase of the further redeployments:

a. 'Area A' means the populated areas delineated by a red line and shaded in brown on attached map No. 1 (*not reproduced here—Ed.*);

b. 'Area B' means the populated areas delineated by a red line and shaded in yellow on attached map No. 1, and the built-up area of the hamlets listed in Appendix 6 to Annex I; and

c. 'Area C' means areas of the West Bank outside Areas A and B, which, except for the issues that will be negotiated in the permanent status negotiations, will be gradually transferred to Palestinian jurisdiction in accordance with this Agreement.

ARTICLE XII

Arrangements for Security and Public Order

1. In order to guarantee public order and internal security for the Palestinians of the West Bank and the Gaza Strip, the Council shall establish a strong police force as set out in Article XIV below. Israel shall continue to carry the responsibility for defence against external threats, including the responsibility for protecting the Egyptian and Jordanian borders, and for defence against external threats from the sea and from the air, as well as the responsibility for overall security of Israelis and Settlements, for the purpose of safeguarding their internal security and public order, and will have all the powers to take the steps necessary to meet this responsibility.

2. Agreed security arrangements and co-ordination mechanisms are specified in Annex I.

3. A Joint Co-ordination and Co-operation Committee for Mutual Security Purposes (hereinafter 'the JSC'), as well as Joint Regional Security Committees (hereinafter 'RSCs') and Joint District Co-ordination Offices (hereinafter 'DCOs'), are hereby established as provided for in Annex I.

4. The security arrangements provided for in this Agreement and in Annex I may be reviewed at the request of either Party and may be amended by mutual agreement of the Parties. Specific review arrangements are included in Annex I.

5. For the purpose of this Agreement, 'the Settlements' means, in the West Bank—the settlements in Area C; and in the Gaza Strip—the Gush Katif and Erez settlement areas, as well as the other settlements in the Gaza Strip, as shown on attached map No. 2 (*not reproduced—Ed.*).

ARTICLE XIII
Security

1. The Council will, upon completion of the redeployment of Israeli military forces in each district, as set out in Appendix 1 to Annex I, assume the powers and responsibilities for internal security and public order in Area A in that district.

2. a. There will be a complete redeployment of Israeli military forces from Area B. Israel will transfer to the Council and the Council will assume responsibility for public order for Palestinians. Israel shall have the overriding responsibility for security for the purpose of protecting Israelis and confronting the threat of terrorism.

   b. In Area B the Palestinian Police shall assume the responsibility for public order for Palestinians and shall be deployed in order to accommodate the Palestinian needs and requirements in the following manner:

      (1) The Palestinian Police shall establish 25 police stations and posts in towns, villages, and other places listed in Appendix 2 to Annex I and as delineated on map No. 3 (*not reproduced—Ed.*). The West Bank RSC may agree on the establishment of additional police stations and posts, if required.

      (2) The Palestinian Police shall be responsible for handling public order incidents in which only Palestinians are involved.

      (3) The Palestinian Police shall operate freely in populated places where police stations and posts are located, as set out in paragraph b(1) above.

      (4) While the movement of uniformed Palestinian policemen in Area B outside places where there is a Palestinian police station or post will be carried out after co-ordination and confirmation through the relevant DCO, three months after the completion of redeployment from Area B, the DCOs may decide that movement of Palestinian policemen from the police stations in Area B to Palestinian towns and villages in Area B on roads that are used only by Palestinian traffic will take place after notifying the DCO.

      (5) The co-ordination of such planned movement prior to confirmation through the relevant DCO shall include a scheduled plan, including the number of policemen, as well as the type and number of weapons and vehicles intended to take part. It shall also include details of arrangements for ensuring continued co-ordination through appropriate communication links, the exact schedule of

movement to the area of the planned operation, including the destination and routes thereto, its proposed duration and the schedule for returning to the police station or post.

The Israeli side of the DCO will provide the Palestinian side with its response, following a request for movement of policemen in accordance with this paragraph, in normal or routine cases within one day and in emergency cases no later than 2 hours.

(6) The Palestinian Police and the Israeli military forces will conduct joint security activities on the main roads as set out in Annex 1.

(7) The Palestinian Police will notify the West Bank RSC of the names of the policemen, number plates of police vehicles and serial numbers of weapons, with respect to each police station and post in Area B.

(8) Further redeployments from Area C and transfer of internal security responsibility to the Palestinian Police in Areas B and C will be carried out in three phases, each to take place after an interval of six months, to be completed 18 months after the inauguration of the Council, except for the issues of permanent status negotiations and of Israel's overall responsibility for Israelis and borders.

(9) The procedures detailed in this paragraph will be reviewed within six months of the completion of the first phase of redeployment.

ARTICLE XIV

The Palestinian Police

1. The Council shall establish a strong police force. The duties, functions, structure, deployment and composition of the Palestinian Police, together with provisions regarding its equipment and operation, as well as rules of conduct, are set out in Annex I.

2. The Palestinian police force established under the Gaza-Jericho Agreement will be fully integrated into the Palestinian Police and will be subject to the provisions of this Agreement.

3. Except for the Palestinian Police and the Israeli military forces, no other armed forces shall be established or operate in the West Bank and the Gaza Strip.

4. Except for the arms, ammunition and equipment of the Palestinian Police described in Annex I, and those of the Israeli military forces, no organization, group or individual in the West Bank and the Gaza Strip shall manufacture, sell, acquire, possess, import or otherwise introduce into the West Bank or the Gaza Strip any firearms, ammunition, weapons, explosives, gunpowder or any related equipment, unless otherwise provided for in Annex I.

ARTICLE XV

Prevention of Hostile Acts

1. Both sides shall take all measures necessary in order to prevent acts of terrorism, crime and hostilities directed against each other, against individuals

falling under the other's authority and against their property, and shall take legal measures against offenders.

2. Specific provisions for the implementation of this Article are set out in Annex I.

ARTICLE XVI
Confidence Building Measures

With a view to fostering a positive and supportive public atmosphere to accompany the implementation of this Agreement, to establish a solid basis of mutual trust and good faith, and in order to facilitate the anticipated co-operation and new relations between the two peoples, both Parties agree to carry out confidence building measures as detailed herewith:

1. Israel will release or turn over to the Palestinian side, Palestinian detainees and prisoners, residents of the West Bank and the Gaza Strip. The first stage of release of these prisoners and detainees will take place on the signing of this Agreement and the second stage will take place prior to the date of the elections. There will be a third stage of release of detainees and prisoners. Detainees and prisoners will be released from among categories detailed in Annex VII (Release of Palestinian Prisoners and Detainees). Those released will be free to return to their homes in the West Bank and the Gaza Strip.

2. Palestinians who have maintained contact with the Israeli authorities will not be subjected to acts of harassment, violence, retribution or prosecution. Appropriate ongoing measures will be taken, in co-ordination with Israel, in order to ensure their protection.

3. Palestinians from abroad whose entry into the West Bank and the Gaza Strip is approved pursuant to this Agreement, and to whom the provisions of this Article are applicable, will not be prosecuted for offences committed prior to September 13, 1993.

CHAPTER 3—LEGAL AFFAIRS

ARTICLE XVII
Jurisdiction

1. In accordance with the DOP, the jurisdiction of the Council will cover West Bank and Gaza Strip territory as a single territorial unit, except for:

    a. Issues that will be negotiated in the permanent status negotiations: Jerusalem, settlements, specified military locations, Palestinian refugees, borders, foreign relations and Israelis; and

    b. Powers and responsibilities not transferred to the Council.

2. Accordingly, the authority of the Council encompasses all matters that fall within its territorial, functional and personal jurisdiction, as follows:

    a. The territorial jurisdiction of the Council shall encompass Gaza Strip territory, except for the Settlements and the Military Installation Area shown on map No. 2, and West Bank territory, except for Area C which, except for the issues that will be negotiated in the permanent status negotiations, will be gradually transferred to Palestinian jurisdiction in three phases, each to take place after an interval of six months, to be completed 18 months after the inauguration of the Council. At this time, the jurisdiction of the Council will cover West Bank and Gaza Strip territory, except for the issues that will be negotiated in the permanent status negotiations.

Territorial jurisdiction includes land, subsoil and territorial waters, in accordance with the provisions of this Agreement.

b. The functional jurisdiction of the Council extends to all powers and responsibilities transferred to the Council, as specified in this Agreement or in any future agreements that may be reached between the Parties during the interim period.

c. The territorial and functional jurisdiction of the Council will apply to all persons, except for Israelis, unless otherwise provided in this Agreement.

d. Notwithstanding subparagraph a. above, the Council shall have functional jurisdiction in Area C, as detailed in Article IV of Annex III.

3. The Council has, within its authority, legislative, executive and judicial powers and responsibilities, as provided for in this Agreement.

4. a. Israel, through its military government, has the authority over areas that are not under the territorial jurisdiction of the Council, powers and responsibilities not transferred to the Council and Israelis.

b. To this end, the Israeli military government shall retain the necessary legislative, judicial and executive powers and responsibilities, in accordance with international law. This provision shall not derogate from Israel's applicable legislation over Israelis in personam.

5. The exercise of authority with regard to the electromagnetic sphere and air space shall be in accordance with the provisions of this Agreement.

6. Without derogating from the provisions of this Article, legal arrangements detailed in the Protocol Concerning Legal Matters attached as Annex IV to this Agreement (hereinafter 'Annex IV') shall be observed. Israel and the Council may negotiate further legal arrangements.

7. Israel and the Council shall co-operate on matters of legal assistance in criminal and civil matters through a legal committee (hereinafter 'the Legal Commmittee'), hereby established.

8. The Council's jurisdiction will extend gradually to cover West Bank and Gaza Strip territory, except for the issues to be negotiated in the permanent status negotiations, through a series of redeployments of the Israeli military forces. The first phase of the redeployment of Israeli military forces will cover populated areas in the West Bank—cities, towns, refugee camps and hamlets, as set out in Annex I—and will be completed prior to the eve of the Palestinian elections, i.e. 22 days before the day of the elections. Further redeployments of Israeli military forces to specified military locations will commence immediately upon the inauguration of the Council and will be effected in three phases, each to take place after an interval of six months, to be concluded no later than eighteen months from the date of the inauguration of the Council.

ARTICLE XVIII

Legislative Powers of the Council

1. For the purposes of this Article, legislation shall mean any primary and secondary legislation, including basic laws, laws, regulations and other legislative acts.

2. The Council has the power, within its jurisdiction as defined in Article XVII of this Agreement, to adopt legislation.

3. While the primary legislative power shall lie in the hands of the Council as a whole, the Ra'ees of the Executive Authority of the Council shall have the following legislative powers:

    a. The power to initiate legislation or to present proposed legislation to the Council;

    b. The power to promulgate legislation adopted by the Council; and

    c. The power to issue secondary legislation, including regulations, relating to any matters specified and within the scope laid down in any primary legislation adopted by the Council.

4. a. Legislation, including legislation which amends or abrogates existing laws or military orders, which exceeds the jurisdiction of the Council or which is otherwise inconsistent with the provisions of the DOP, this Agreement, or of any other agreement that may be reached between the two sides during the interim period, shall have no effect and shall be void ab initio.

    b. The Ra'ees of the Executive Authority of the Council shall not promulgate legislation adopted by the Council if such legislation falls under the provisions of this paragraph.

5. All legislation shall be communicated to the Israeli side of the Legal Committee.

6. Without derogating from the provisions of paragraph 4 above, the Israeli side of the Legal Committee may refer for the attention of the Committee any legislation regarding which Israel considers the provisions of paragraph 4 apply, in order to discuss issues arising from such legislation. The Legal Committee will consider the legislation referred to it at the earliest opportunity.

ARTICLE XIX

Human Rights and the Rule of Law

Israel and the Council shall exercise their powers and responsibilities pursuant to this Agreement with due regard to internationally-accepted norms and principles of human rights and the rule of law.

ARTICLE XX

Rights, Liabilities and Obligations

1. a. Transfer of powers and responsibilities from the Israeli military government and its civil administration to the Council, as detailed in Annex III, includes all related rights, liabilities and obligations arising with regard to acts or omissions which occurred prior to such transfer. Israel will cease to bear any financial responsibility regarding such acts or

omissions and the Council will bear all financial responsibility for these and for its own functioning.

b. Any financial claim made in this regard against Israel will be referred to the Council.

c. Israel shall provide the Council with the information it has regarding pending and anticipated claims brought before any court or tribunal against Israel in this regard.

d. Where legal proceedings are brought in respect of such a claim, Israel will notify the Council and enable it to participate in defending the claim and raise any arguments on its behalf.

e. In the event that an award is made against Israel by any court or tribunal in respect of such a claim, the Council shall immediately reimburse Israel the full amount of the award.

f. Without prejudice to the above, where a court or tribunal hearing such a claim finds that liability rests solely with an employee or agent who acted beyond the scope of the powers assigned to him or her, unlawfully or with willful malfeasance, the Council shall not bear financial responsibility.

2. a. Notwithstanding the provisions of paragraphs 1.d through 1.f above, each side may take the necessary measures, including promulgation of legislation, in order to ensure that such claims by Palestinians, including pending claims in which the hearing of evidence has not yet begun, are brought only before Palestinian courts or tribunals in the West Bank and the Gaza Strip, and are not brought before or heard by Israeli courts or tribunals.

b. Where a new claim has been brought before a Palestinian court or tribunal subsequent to the dismissal of the claim pursuant to subparagraph a. above, the Council shall defend it and, in accordance with subparagraph 1.a above, in the event that an award is made for the plaintiff, shall pay the amount of the award.

c. The Legal Committee shall agree on arrangements for the transfer of all materials and information needed to enable the Palestinian courts or tribunals to hear such claims as referred to in sub-paragraph b. above, and, when necessary, for the provision of legal assistance by Israel to the Council in defending such claims.

3. The transfer of authority in itself shall not affect rights, liabilities and obligations of any person or legal entity, in existence at the date of signing of this Agreement.

4. The Council, upon its inauguration, will assume all the rights, liabilities and obligations of the Palestinian Authority.

5. For the purpose of this Agreement, 'Israelis' also includes Israeli statutory agencies and corporations registered in Israel.

ARTICLE XXI

Settlement of Differences and Disputes

Any difference relating to the application of this Agreement shall be referred to the appropriate co-ordination and co-operation mechanism established under this Agreement. The provisions of Article XV of the DOP shall apply to any such difference which is not settled through the appropriate co-ordination and co-operation mechanism, namely:

1. Disputes arising out of the application or interpretation of this Agreement or any related agreements pertaining to the interim period shall be settled through the Liaison Committee.

2. Disputes which cannot be settled by negotiations may be settled by a mechanism of conciliation to be agreed between the Parties.

3. The Parties may agree to submit to arbitration disputes relating to the interim period, which cannot be settled through conciliation. To this end, upon the agreement of both Parties, the Parties will establish an Arbitration Committee.

CHAPTER 4—CO-OPERATION

ARTICLE XXII
Relations between Israel and the Council

1. Israel and the Council shall seek to foster mutual understanding and tolerance and shall accordingly abstain from incitement, including hostile propaganda, against each other and, without derogating from the principle of freedom of expression, shall take legal measures to prevent such incitement by any organizations, groups or individuals within their jurisdiction.

2. Israel and the Council will ensure that their respective educational systems contribute to the peace between the Israeli and Palestinian peoples and to peace in the entire region, and will refrain from the introduction of any motifs that could adversely affect the process of reconciliation.

3. Without derogating from the other provisions of this Agreement, Israel and the Council shall co-operate in combating criminal activity which may affect both sides, including offenses related to trafficking in illegal drugs and psycho-tropic substances, smuggling, and offenses against property, including offenses related to vehicles.

ARTICLE XXIII
Co-operation with Regard to Transfer of Powers and Responsibilities

In order to ensure a smooth, peaceful and orderly transfer of powers and responsibilities, the two sides will co-operate with regard to the transfer of security powers and responsibilities in accordance with the provisions of Annex I, and the transfer of civil powers and responsibilities in accordance with the provisions of Annex III.

ARTICLE XXIV
Economic Relations

The economic relations between the two sides are set out in the Protocol on Economic Relations, signed in Paris on April 29, 1994, and the Appendices thereto, and the Supplement to the Protocol on Economic Relations, all attached as Annex V, and will be governed by the relevant provisions of this Agreement and its Annexes.

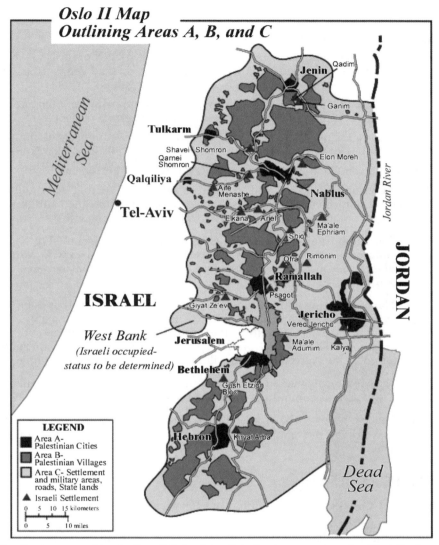

Oslo II Map
Outlining Areas A, B, and C

LEGEND

- ■ Area A- Palestinian Cities
- ▨ Area B- Palestinian Villages
- ▢ Area C- Settlement and military areas, roads, State lands
- ▲ Israeli Settlement

0   5   10 15 kilometers

0   5   10 miles

Territories covered by the Israeli-Palestinian Interim Agreement on the West Bank and the Gaza Strip ('Oslo II').

ARTICLE XXV

Co-operation Programmes

1. The Parties agree to establish a mechanism to develop programmes of co-operation between them. Details of such co-operation are set out in Annex VI.

2. A Standing Co-operation Committee to deal with issues arising in the context of this co-operation is hereby established as provided for in Annex VI.

ARTICLE XXVI

The Joint Israeli-Palestinian Liaison Committee

1. The Liaison Committee established pursuant to Article X of the DOP shall ensure the smooth implementation of this Agreement. It shall deal with issues requiring co-ordination, other issues of common interest and disputes.

2. The Liaison Committee shall be composed of an equal number of members from each Party. It may add other technicians and experts as necessary.

3. The Liaison Committee shall adopt its rules of procedures, including the frequency and place or places of its meetings.

4. The Liaison Committee shall reach its decisions by agreement.

5. The Liaison Committee shall establish a subcommittee that will monitor and steer the implementation of this Agreement (hereinafter 'the Monitoring and Steering Committee'). It will function as follows:

   a. The Monitoring and Steering Committee will, on an ongoing basis, monitor the implementation of this Agreement, with a view to enhancing the co-operation and fostering the peaceful relations between the two sides.

   b. The Monitoring and Steering Committee will steer the activities of the various joint committees established in this Agreement (the JSC, the CAC, the Legal Committee, the Joint Economic Committee and the Standing Co-operation Committee) concerning the ongoing implementation of the Agreement, and will report to the Liaison Committee.

   c. The Monitoring and Steering Committee will be composed of the heads of the various committees mentioned above.

   d. The two heads of the Monitoring and Steering Committee will establish its rules of procedures, including the frequency and places of its meetings.

ARTICLE XXVII

Liaison and Co-operation with Jordan and Egypt

1. Pursuant to Article XII of the DOP, the two Parties have invited the Governments of Jordan and Egypt to participate in establishing further liaison and co-operation arrangements between the Government of Israel and the Palestinian representatives on the one hand, and the Governments of Jordan and Egypt on the other hand, to promote co-operation between them. As part of these arrangements a Continuing Committee has been constituted and has commenced its deliberations.

2. The Continuing Committee shall decide by agreement on the modalities of admission of persons displaced from the West Bank and the Gaza Strip in 1967, together with necessary measures to prevent disruption and disorder.

3. The Continuing Committee shall also deal with other matters of common concern.

ARTICLE XXVIII

Missing Persons

1. Israel and the Council shall co-operate by providing each other with all necessary assistance in the conduct of searches for missing persons and bodies of persons which have not been recovered, as well as by providing information about missing persons.

2. The PLO undertakes to co-operate with Israel and to assist it in its efforts to locate and to return to Israel Israeli soldiers who are missing in action and the bodies of soldiers which have not been recovered.

CHAPTER 5—MISCELLANEOUS PROVISIONS

ARTICLE XXIX

Safe Passage between the West Bank and the Gaza Strip

Arrangements for safe passage of persons and transportation between the West Bank and the Gaza Strip are set out in Annex 1.

ARTICLE XXX

Passages

Arrangements for co-ordination between Israel and the Council regarding passage to and from Egypt and Jordan, as well as any other agreed international crossings, are set out in Annex I.

ARTICLE XXXI

Final Clauses

1. This Agreement shall enter into force on the date of its signing.

2. The Gaza-Jericho Agreement, the Preparatory Transfer Agreement and the Further Transfer Protocol will be superseded by this Agreement.

3. The Council, upon its inauguration, shall replace the Palestinian Authority and shall assume all the undertakings and obligations of the Palestinian Authority under the Gaza-Jericho Agreement, the Preparatory Transfer Agreement, and the Further Transfer Protocol.

4. The two sides shall pass all necessary legislation to implement this Agreement.

5. Permanent status negotiations will commence as soon as possible, but not later than May 4, 1996, between the Parties. It is understood that these negotiations shall cover remaining issues, including: Jerusalem, refugees, settlements, security arrangements, borders, relations and co-operation with other neighbours, and other issues of common interest.

6. Nothing in this Agreement shall prejudice or preempt the outcome of the negotiations on the permanent status to be conducted pursuant to the DOP. Neither Party shall be deemed, by virtue of having entered into this Agreement, to have renounced or waived any of its existing rights, claims or positions.

7. Neither side shall initiate or take any step that will change the status of the West Bank and the Gaza Strip pending the outcome of the permanent status negotiations.

8. The two Parties view the West Bank and the Gaza Strip as a single territorial unit, the integrity and status of which will be preserved during the interim period.

9. The PLO undertakes that, within two months of the date of the inauguration of the Council, the Palestinian National Council will convene and formally approve the necessary changes in regard to the Palestinian Covenant, as undertaken in the letters signed by the Chairman of the PLO and addressed to the Prime Minister of Israel, dated September 9, 1993 and May 4, 1994.

10. Pursuant to Annex I, Article IX of this Agreement, Israel confirms that the permanent checkpoints on the roads leading to and from the Jericho Area (except those related to the access road leading from Mousa Alami to the Allenby Bridge) will be removed upon the completion of the first phase of redeployment.

11. Prisoners who, pursuant to the Gaza-Jericho Agreement, were turned over to the Palestinian Authority on the condition that they remain in the Jericho Area for the remainder of their sentence, will be free to return to their homes in the West Bank and the Gaza Strip upon the completion of the first phase of redeployment.

12. As regards relations between Israel and the PLO, and without derogating from the commitments contained in the letters signed by and exchanged between the Prime Minister of Israel and the Chairman of the PLO, dated September 9, 1993 and May 4, 1994, the two sides will apply between them the provisions contained in Article XXII, paragraph 1, with the necessary changes.

13. a. The Preamble to this Agreement, and all Annexes, Appendices and maps attached hereto (*not reproduced—Ed.*), shall constitute an integral part hereof.

   b. The Parties agree that the maps (*not reproduced—Ed.*) attached to the Gaza-Jericho Agreement as:

   c. map No. 1 (The Gaza Strip), an exact copy of which is attached to this Agreement as map No. 2 (in this Agreement 'map No. 2');

   d. map No. 4 (Deployment of Palestinian Police in the Gaza Strip), an exact copy of which is attached to this Agreement as map No. 5 (in this Agreement 'map No. 5'); and

   e. map No. 6 (Maritime Activity Zones), an exact copy of which is attached to this Agreement as map No. 8 (in this Agreement 'map No. 8');

are an integral part hereof and will remain in effect for the duration of this Agreement.

14. While the Jeftlik area will come under the functional and personal jurisdiction of the Council in the first phase of redeployment, the area's transfer to the territorial jurisdiction of the Council will be considered by the Israeli side in the first phase of the further redeployment phases.

THE WYE RIVER MEMORANDUM

The Wye River Memorandum was signed by Israeli Prime Minister Binyamin Netanyahu and PNA President Yasser Arafat, and witnessed by US President Bill Clinton, on 23 October 1998 at the Wye Plantation, Maryland, USA. The Memorandum was to enter into force 10 days after this date. An attachment to the Memorandum detailed a 'time line' for the implementation of the terms of the Interim Agreement and the Memorandum.

The following are steps to facilitate implementation of the Interim Agreement on the West Bank and Gaza Strip of September 28, 1995 (the 'Interim Agreement') and other related agreements including the Note for the Record of January 17, 1997 (hereinafter referred to as 'the prior agreements') so that the Israeli and Palestinian sides can more effectively carry out their reciprocal responsibilities, including those relating to further redeployments and security respectively. These steps are to be carried out in a parallel phased approach in accordance with this Memorandum and the attached time line. They are subject to the relevant terms and conditions of the prior agreements and do not supersede their other agreements.

I. FURTHER REDEPLOYMENTS

A. Phase One and Two Further Redeployments

1. Pursuant to the Interim Agreement and subsequent agreements, the Israeli side's implementation of the first and second F.R.D. will consist of the transfer to the Palestinian side of 13% from Area C as follows:

1% to Area (A)
12% to Area (B)

The Palestinian side has informed that it will allocate an area/areas amounting to 3% from the above Area (B) to be designated as Green Areas and/or Nature Reserves. The Palestinian side has further informed that they will act according to the established scientific standards, and that therefore there will be no changes in the status of these areas, without prejudice to the rights of the existing inhabitants in these areas including Bedouins; while these standards do not allow new construction in these areas, existing roads and buildings may be maintained.

The Israeli side will retain in these Green Areas/Nature Reserves the overriding security responsibility for the purpose of protecting Israelis and confronting the threat of terrorism. Activities and movements of the Palestinian Police forces may be carried out after co-ordination and confirmation; the Israeli side will respond to such requests expeditiously.

2. As part of the foregoing implementation of the first and second F.R.D., 14.2% from Area (B) will become Area (A).

B. Third Phase of Further Redeployments

With regard to the terms of the Interim Agreement and of Secretary Christopher's letters to the two sides of January 17, 1997 relating to the further redeployment process, there will be a committee to address this question. The United States will be briefed regularly.

II. SECURITY

In the provisions on security arrangements of the Interim Agreement, the Palestinian side agreed to take all measures necessary in order to prevent acts of terrorism, crime and hostilities directed against the Israeli side, against individuals falling under the Israeli side's authority and against their property, just as the Israeli side agreed to take all measures necessary in order to prevent acts of terrorism, crime and hostilities directed against the Palestinian side, against individuals falling under the Palestinian side's authority and against their property. The two sides also agreed to take legal measures against offenders within their jurisdiction and to prevent incitement against each other by any organizations, groups or individuals within their jurisdiction.

Both sides recognize that it is in their vital interests to combat terrorism and fight violence in accordance with Annex I of the Interim Agreement and the Note for the Record. They also recognize that the struggle against terror and violence must be comprehensive in that it deals with terrorists, the terror support structure, and the environment conducive to the support of terror. It must be continuous and constant over a long-term, in that there can be no pauses in the work against terrorists and their structure. It must be co-operative in that no effort can be fully effective without Israeli-Palestinian co-operation and the continuous exchange of information, concepts, and actions.

Pursuant to the prior agreements, the Palestinian side's implementation of its responsibilities for security, security co-operation, and other issues will be as detailed below during the time periods specified in the attached time line:

A. Security Actions

1. *Outlawing and Combating Terrorist Organizations*

    a. The Palestinian side will make known its policy of zero tolerance for terror and violence against both sides.

    b. A work plan developed by the Palestinian side will be shared with the U.S. and thereafter implementation will begin immediately to ensure the systematic and effective combat of terrorist organizations and their infrastructure.

    c. In addition to the bilateral Israeli-Palestinian security co-operation, a U.S.-Palestinian committee will meet biweekly to review the steps being taken to eliminate terrorist cells and the support structure that plans, finances, supplies and abets terror. In these meetings, the Palestinian side will inform the U.S. fully of the actions it has taken to outlaw all organizations (or wings of organizations, as appropriate) of a military, terrorist or violent character and their support structure and to prevent them from operating in areas under its jurisdiction.

    d. The Palestinian side will apprehend the specific individuals suspected of perpetrating acts of violence and terror for the purpose of further investigation, and prosecution and punishment of all persons involved in acts of violence and terror.

    e. A U.S.-Palestinian committee will meet to review and evaluate information pertinent to the decisions on prosecution, punishment or other legal measures which affect the status of individuals suspected of abetting or perpetrating acts of violence and terror.

2. *Prohibiting Illegal Weapons*

   a. The Palestinian side will ensure an effective legal framework is in place to criminalize, in conformity with the prior agreements, any importation, manufacturing or unlicensed sale, acquisition or possession of firearms, ammunition or weapons in areas under Palestinian jurisdiction.

   b. In addition, the Palestinian side will establish and vigorously and continuously implement a systematic programme for the collection and appropriate handling of all such illegal items in accordance with the prior agreements. The U.S. has agreed to assist in carrying out this programme.

   c. A U.S.-Palestinian-Israeli committee will be established to assist and enhance co-operation in preventing the smuggling or other unauthorized introduction of weapons or explosive materials into areas under Palestinian jurisdiction.

3. *Preventing Incitement*

   a. Drawing on relevant international practice and pursuant to Article XXII (1) of the Interim Agreement and the Note for the Record, the Palestinian side will issue a decree prohibiting all forms of incitement to violence or terror, and establishing mechanisms for acting systematically against all expressions or threats of violence or terror. This decree will be comparable to the existing Israeli legislation which deals with the same subject.

   b. A U.S.-Palestinian-Israeli committee will meet on a regular basis to monitor cases of possible incitement to violence or terror and to make recommendations and reports on how to prevent such incitement. The Israeli, Palestinian and U.S. sides will each appoint a media specialist, a law enforcement representative, an educational specialist and a current or former elected official to the committee.

B. Security Co-operation

The two sides agree that their security co-operation will be based on a spirit of partnership and will include, among other things, the following steps:

1. *Bilateral Co-operation*

There will be full bilateral security co-operation between the two sides which will be continuous, intensive and comprehensive.

2. *Forensic Co-operation*

There will be an exchange of forensic expertise, training, and other assistance.

3. *Trilateral Committee*

In addition to the bilateral Israeli-Palestinian security co-operation, a high-ranking U.S.-Palestinian-Israeli committee will meet as required and not less than biweekly to assess current threats, deal with any impediments to effective security co-operation and co-ordination and address the steps being taken to combat terror and terrorist organizations. The committee will also serve as a forum to address the issue of external support for terror. In these meetings, the Palestinian side will fully inform the members of the committee of the results of its investigations concerning terrorist suspects already in custody and the participants will exchange additional relevant information. The committee will report regularly to the leaders of the two sides on the status of co-operation, the results of the meetings and its recommendations.

C. Other Issues

1. Palestinian Police Force

    a. The Palestinian side will provide a list of its policemen to the Israeli side in conformity with the prior agreements.

    b. Should the Palestinian side request technical assistance, the U.S. has indicated its willingness to help meet their needs in co-operation with other donors.

    c. The Monitoring and Steering Committee will, as part of its functions, monitor the implementation of this provision and brief the U.S.

2. PLO Charter

The Executive Committee of the Palestine Liberation Organization and the Palestinian Central Council will reaffirm the letter of 22 January 1998 from PLO Chairman Yasser Arafat to President Clinton concerning the nullification of the Palestinian National Charter provisions that are inconsistent with the letters exchanged between the PLO and the Government of Israel on 9–10 September 1993. PLO Chairman Arafat, the Speaker of the Palestine National Council, and the Speaker of the Palestinian Council will invite the members of the PNC, as well as the members of the Central Council, the Council, and the Palestinian Heads of Ministries to a meeting to be addressed by President Clinton to reaffirm their support for the peace process and the aforementioned decisions of the Executive Committee and the Central Council.

3. Legal Assistance in Criminal Matters

Among other forms of legal assistance in criminal matters, the requests for arrest and transfer of suspects and defendants pursuant to Article II (7) of Annex IV of the Interim Agreement will be submitted (or resubmitted) through the mechanism of the Joint Israeli-Palestinian Legal Committee and will be responded to in conformity with Article II (7) (f) of Annex IV of the Interim Agreement within the twelve week period. Requests submitted after the eighth week will be responded to in conformity with Article II (7) (f) within four weeks of their submission. The U.S. has been requested by the sides to report on a regular basis on the steps being taken to respond to the above requests.

4. Human Rights and the Rule of Law

Pursuant to Article XI (1) of Annex I of the Interim Agreement, and without derogating from the above, the Palestinian Police will exercise powers and responsibilities to implement this Memorandum with due regard to internationally accepted norms of human rights and the rule of law, and will be guided by the need to protect the public, respect human dignity, and avoid harassment.

III. INTERIM COMMITTEES AND ECONOMIC ISSUES

1. The Israeli and Palestinian sides reaffirm their commitment to enhancing their relationship and agree on the need actively to promote economic development in the West Bank and Gaza. In this regard, the parties agree to continue or to reactivate all standing committees established by the Interim Agreement, including the Monitoring and Steering Committee, the Joint Economic Committee (JEC), the Civil Affairs Committee (CAC), the Legal Committee, and the Standing Co-operation Committee.

2. The Israeli and Palestinian sides have agreed on arrangements which will permit the timely opening of the Gaza Industrial Estate. They also have concluded a 'Protocol Regarding the Establishment and Operation of the International Airport in the Gaza Strip During the Interim Period'.

3. Both sides will renew negotiations on Safe Passage immediately. As regards the southern route, the sides will make best efforts to conclude the agreement within a week of the entry into force of this Memorandum. Operation of the southern route will start as soon as possible thereafter. As regards the northern route, negotiations will continue with the goal of reaching agreement as soon as possible. Implementation will take place expeditiously thereafter.

4. The Israeli and Palestinian sides acknowledge the great importance of the Port of Gaza for the development of the Palestinian economy, and the expansion of Palestinian trade. They commit themselves to proceeding without delay to conclude an agreement to allow the construction and operation of the port in accordance with the prior agreements. The Israeli-Palestinian Committee will reactivate its work immediately with a goal of concluding the protocol within sixty days, which will allow commencement of the construction of the port.

5. The two sides recognize that unresolved legal issues adversely affect the relationship between the two peoples. They therefore will accelerate efforts through the Legal Committee to address outstanding legal issues and to implement solutions to these issues in the shortest possible period. The Palestinian side will provide to the Israeli side copies of all of its laws in effect.

6. The Israeli and Palestinian sides will launch a strategic economic dialogue to enhance their economic relationship. They will establish within the framework of the JEC an Ad Hoc Committee for this purpose. The committee will review the following four issues: (1) Israeli purchase tax; (2) co-operation in combating vehicle theft; (3) dealing with unpaid Palestinian debts; and (4) the impact of Israeli standards as barriers to trade and the expansion of the A1 and A2 lists. The committee will submit an interim report within three weeks of the entry into force of this Memorandum, and within six weeks will submit its conclusions and recommendations to be implemented.

7. The two sides agree on the importance of continued international donor assistance to facilitate implementation by both sides of agreements reached. They also recognize the need for enhanced donor support for economic development in the West Bank and Gaza. They agree jointly to approach the donor community to organize a Ministerial Conference before the end of 1998 to seek pledges for enhanced levels of assistance.

IV. PERMANENT STATUS NEGOTIATIONS

The two sides will immediately resume permanent status negotiations on an accelerated basis and will make a determined effort to achieve the mutual goal of reaching an agreement by May 4, 1999. The negotiations will be continuous and without interruption. The U.S. has expressed its willingness to facilitate these negotiations.

V. UNILATERAL ACTIONS

Recognizing the necessity to create a positive environment for the negotiations, neither side shall initiate or take any step that will change the status of the West Bank and the Gaza Strip in accordance with the Interim Agreement.

SHARM ESH-SHEIKH MEMORANDUM ON THE IMPLEMENTATION TIMELINE OF OUTSTANDING COMMITMENTS OF AGREEMENTS SIGNED AND THE RESUMPTION OF PERMANENT STATUS NEGOTIATIONS (WYE TWO)

The implementation of the Wye River Memorandum having stalled under the Netanyahu administration in Israel, in September 1999 the new Israeli Prime Minister, Ehud Barak, and the PNA President, Yasser Arafat, met in the Egyptian resort of Sharm esh-Sheikh to discuss the possible reactivation of the Memorandum. On 4 September the two leaders signed the Sharm esh-Sheikh Memorandum (also known as Wye Two), which detailed a revised timetable for the outstanding provisions of the October 1998 Memorandum. The Memorandum was witnessed by President Hosni Mubarak for Egypt, Secretary of State Madeleine Albright for the USA, and King Abdullah of Jordan.

The Government of the State of Israel and the Palestine Liberation Organization (PLO) commit themselves to full and mutual implementation of the Interim Agreement and all other agreements concluded beween them since September 1993 (hereinafter 'the prior agreements'), and all outstanding commitments emanating from the prior agreements. Without derogating from the other requirements of the prior agreements, the two sides have agreed as follows:

1. Permanent Status Negotiations

    a. In the context of the implementation of the prior agreements, the two sides will resume the Permanent Status negotiations in an accelerated manner and will make a determined effort to achieve their mutual agenda, i.e. the specific issues reserved for Permanent Status negotiators and other issues of common interest;

    b. The two sides reaffirm their understanding that the negotiations on the Permanent Status will lead to the implementation of Security Council Resolutions 242 and 338;

    c. The two sides will make a determined effort to conclude a Framework Agreement on all Permanent Status issues in five months from the resumption of the Permanent Status negotiations;

d. The two sides will conclude a comprehensive agreement on all Permanent Status issues within one year from the resumption of the Permanent Status negotiations;

e. Permanent Status negotiations will resume after the implementation of the first stage of release of prisoners and the second stage of the First and Second Further Redeployments and not later than September 13, 1999. In the Wye River Memorandum, the United States has expressed its willingness to facilitate these negotiations.

2. Phase One and Phase Two of the Further Redeployments

The Israeli side undertakes the following with regard to Phase One and Phase Two of the Further Redeployments:

a. On September 5, 1999, to transfer 7% from Area C to Area B;

b. On November 15, 1999, to transfer 2% from Area B to Area A and 3% from Area C to Area B;

c. On January 20, 2000, to transfer 1% from Area C to Area A, and 5.1% from Area B to Area A.

3. Release of Prisoners

a. The two sides shall establish a joint committee that shall follow up on matters related to the release of Palestinian prisoners;

a. The Government of Israel shall release Palestinian and other prisoners who committed their offences prior to September 13, 1993, and were arrested prior to May 4, 1994. The Joint Committee shall agree on the names of those who will be released in the first two stages. Those lists shall be recommended to the relevant Authorities through the Monitoring and Steering Committee;

b. The first stage of release of prisoners shall be carried out on September 5, 1999 and shall consist of 200 prisoners. The second stage of release of prisoners shall be carried out on October 8, 1999 and shall consist of 150 prisoners;

c. The joint committee shall recommend further lists of names to be released to the relevant Authorities through the Monitoring and Steering Committee;

d. The Israeli side will aim to release Palestinian prisoners before next Ramadan.

4. Committees

a. The Third Further Redeployment Committee shall commence its activities not later than September 13, 1999;

b. The Monitoring and Steering Committee, all Interim Committees (i.e. Civil Affairs Committee, Joint Economic Committee, Joint Standing Committee, legal committee, people to people), as well as Wye River Memorandum committees shall resume and/or continue their activity, as the case may be, not later than September 13, 1999. The Monitoring and Steering Committee will have on its agenda, inter alia, the Year 2000, Donor/PA projects in Area C, and the issue of industrial estates;

c. The Continuing Committee on displaced persons shall resume its activity on October 1, 1999 (Article XXVII, Interim Agreement);

d. Not later than October 30, 1999, the two sides will implement the recommendations of the Ad-hoc Economic Committee (article 111-6, Wye River Memorandum).

5. Safe Passage

a. The operation of the Southern Route of the Safe Passage for the movement of persons, vehicles, and goods will start on October 1, 1999 (Annex I, Article X, Interim Agreement) in accordance with the details of operation, which will be provided for in the Safe Passage Protocol that will be concluded by the two sides not later than September 30, 1999;

b. The two sides will agree on the specific location of the crossing point of the Northern Route of the Safe Passage as specified in Annex I, Article X, provision c-4, in the Interim Agreement not later than October 5, 1999;

c. The Safe Passage Protocol applied to the Southern Route of the Safe Passage shall apply to the Northern Route of the Safe Passage with relevant agreed modifications;

d. Upon the agreement on the location of the crossing point of the Northern Route of the Safe Passage, construction of the needed facilities and related procedures shall commence and shall be ongoing. At the same time, temporary facilities will be established for the operation of the Northern Route not later than four months from the agreement on the specific location of the crossing-point;

e. In between the operation of the Southern crossing point of the Safe Passage and the Northern crossing point of the Safe Passage, Israel will facilitate arrangements for the movement between the West Bank and the Gaza Strip, using non-Safe Passage routes other than the Southern Route of the Safe Passage;

f. The location of the crossing points shall be without prejudice to the Permanent Status negotiations (Annex I, Article X, provision e, Interim Agreement).

6. Gaza Sea Port

The two sides have agreed on the following principles to facilitate and enable the construction works of the Gaza Sea Port. The principles shall not prejudice or pre-empt the outcome of negotiations on the Permanent Status:

a. The Israeli side agrees that the Palestinian side shall commence construction works in and related to the Gaza Sea Port on October 1, 1999;

b. The two sides agree that the Gaza Sea Port will not be operated in any way before reaching a joint Sea Port protocol on all aspects of operating the Port, including security;

c. The Gaza Sea Port is a special case, like the Gaza Airport, being situated in an area under the responsibility of the Palestinian side and serving as an international passage. Therefore, with the conclusion of a joint Sea Port Protocol, all activities and arrangements relating to the construction of the Port shall be in accordance with the provisions of the Interim Agreement, especially those relating to international passages, as adapted in the Gaza Airport Protocol;

d. The construction shall ensure adequate provision for effective security and customs inspection of people and goods, as well as the establishment of a designated checking area in the Port;

e. In this context, the Israeli side will facilitate on an ongoing basis the works related to the construction of the Gaza Sea Port, including the movement in and out of the Port of vessels, equipment, resources, and material required for the construction of the Port;

f. The two sides will co-ordinate such works, including the designs and movement, through a joint mechanism.

7. Hebron Issues

a. The Shuhada Road in Hebron shall be opened for the movement of Palestinian vehicles in two phases. The first phase has been carried out, and the second shall be carried out not later than October 30, 1999;

b. The wholesale market Hasbahe will be opened not later than November 1, 1999, in accordance with arrangements which will be agreed upon by the two sides;

c. A high-level Joint Liaison Committee will convene not later than September 13, 1999 to review the situation in the Tomb of the Patriarchs/Al Haram Al Ibrahimi (Annex I, Article VII, Interim Agreement and as per the January 15, 1998 US Minute of Discussion).

8. Security

a. The two sides will, in accordance with the prior agreements, act to ensure the immediate, efficient and effective handling of any incident involving a threat or act of terrorism, violence or incitement, whether committed by Palestinians or Israelis. To this end, they will co-operate in the exchange of information and co-ordinate policies and activities. Each side shall immediately and effectively respond to the occurrence of an act of terrorism, violence or incitement and shall take all necessary measures to prevent such an occurrence;

b. Pursuant to the prior agreements, the Palestinian side undertakes to implement its responsibilities for security, security co-operation, ongoing obligations and other issues emanating from the prior agreements, including, in particular, the following obligations emanating from the Wye River Memorandum:

   1. continuation of the programme for the collection of the illegal weapons, including reports;

   2. apprehension of suspects, including reports;

   3. forwarding of the list of Palestinian policemen to the Israeli side not later than September 13, 1999;

   4. beginning of the review of the list by the Monitoring and Steering Committee not later than October 15, 1999.

9. The two sides call upon the international donor community to enhance its commitment and financial support to the Palestinian economic development and the Israeli-Palestinian peace process.

10. Recognizing the necessity to create a positive environment for the negotiations, neither side shall initiate or take any step that will change the status of the West Bank and the Gaza Strip in accordance with the Interim Agreement.

11. Obligations pertaining to dates which occur on holidays or Saturdays shall be carried out on the first subsequent working day.

This memorandum will enter into force one week from the date of its signature.

It is understood that, for technical reasons, implementation of Article 2a and the first stage mentioned in Article 3c will be carried out within a week from the signing of this Memorandum.

REPORT OF THE SHARM ESH-SHEIKH FACT-FINDING COMMITTEE (THE MITCHELL REPORT)

Violence between Israeli forces and Palestinians broke out in late September 2000, following a visit by the leader of Israel's Likud party, Ariel Sharon, to the site of the Temple Mount/Haram ash-Sharif, in East Jerusalem. A period of intense international diplomatic activity ensued, in an attempt to bring about an end to the violent confrontations which had swiftly spread throughout the West Bank and Gaza Strip. On 14 October UN Secretary-General Kofi Annan secured the agreement of the Israeli Prime Minister, Ehud Barak, and the PNA President, Yasser Arafat, to lead delegations to a summit meeting in Sharm esh-Sheikh, Egypt, with mediation by US President Bill Clinton. The summit duly proceeded on 16 October, concluding the following day with what Clinton termed agreement on 'immediate concrete measures' to end the violence. (Subsequent truce agreements, based on understandings brokered by Clinton at Sharm esh-Sheikh, failed to hold, and violence continued throughout mid-2001.) Agreement was reached at the summit on the formation of a US-appointed international fact-finding commission to investigate the clashes. The committee—chaired by former US Senator George Mitchell and comprising also former President Süleyman Demirel of Turkey, Norwegian Minister of Foreign Affairs Thorbjørn Jagland, former US Senator Warren Rudman, and the High Representative for the Common Foreign and Security Policy of the European Union, Javier Solana—was appointed by Clinton in early November. Reproduced is the full text of the committee's report, published on 20 May 2001. [Footnotes to the report—principally references to statements and submissions of the Government of Israel and the PLO, which made submissions to the committee on behalf of the Palestinians—have been omitted].

SUMMARY OF RECOMMENDATIONS

The Government of Israel and the Palestinian [*National*] Authority (PA) must act swiftly and decisively to halt the violence. Their immediate objectives then should be to rebuild confidence and resume negotiations.

During this mission our aim has been to fulfil the mandate agreed at Sharm esh-Sheikh. We value the support given our work by the participants at the summit, and we commend the parties for their co-operation. Our principal recommendation is that they recommit themselves to the Sharm esh-Sheikh spirit and that they implement the decisions made there in 1999 and 2000. We believe that the summit participants will support bold action by the parties to achieve these objectives.

The restoration of trust is essential, and the parties should take affirmative steps to this end. Given the high level of hostility and mistrust, the timing and sequence of these steps are obviously crucial. This can be decided only by the parties. We urge them to begin the process of decision immediately.

Accordingly, we recommend that steps be taken to:

END THE VIOLENCE

The Government of Israel and the PA should reaffirm their commitment to existing agreements and undertakings and should immediately implement an unconditional cessation of violence.

The Government of Israel and PA should immediately resume security co-operation.

REBUILD CONFIDENCE

The PA and Government of Israel should work together to establish a meaningful 'cooling-off period' and implement additional confidence-building measures, some of which were detailed in the October 2000 Sharm esh-Sheikh Statement and some of which were offered by the US on January 7, 2001 in Cairo [see Recommendations section for further description].

The PA and Government of Israel should resume their efforts to identify, condemn and discourage incitement in all its forms.

The PA should make clear through concrete action to Palestinians and Israelis alike that terrorism is reprehensible and unacceptable, and that the PA will make a 100 percent effort to prevent terrorist operations and to punish perpetrators. This effort should include immediate steps to apprehend and incarcerate terrorists operating within the PA's jurisdiction.

The Government of Israel should freeze all settlement activity, including the 'natural growth' of existing settlements.

The Government of Israel should ensure that the IDF [*Israeli Defence Forces*] adopt and enforce policies and procedures encouraging non-lethal responses to unarmed demonstrators, with a view to minimizing casualties and friction between the two communities.

The PA should prevent gunmen from using Palestinian populated areas to fire upon Israeli populated areas and IDF positions. This tactic places civilians on both sides at unnecessary risk.

The Government of Israel should lift closures, transfer to the PA all tax revenues owed, and permit Palestinians who had been employed in Israel to return to their jobs; and should ensure that security forces and settlers refrain from the destruction of homes and roads, as well as trees and other agricultural property in Palestinian areas. We acknowledge the Government of Israel's position that actions of this nature have been taken for security reasons. Nevertheless, the economic effects will persist for years.

The PA should renew co-operation with Israeli security agencies to ensure, to the maximum extent possible, that Palestinian workers employed within Israel are fully vetted and free of connections to organizations and individuals engaged in terrorism.

The PA and Government of Israel should consider a joint undertaking to preserve and protect holy places sacred to the traditions of Jews, Muslims, and Christians.

The Government of Israel and PA should jointly endorse and support the work of Palestinian and Israeli non-governmental organizations involved in cross-community initiatives linking the two peoples.

RESUME NEGOTIATIONS

In the spirit of the Sharm esh-Sheikh agreements and understandings of 1999 and 2000, we recommend that the parties meet to reaffirm their commitment to signed agreements and mutual understandings, and take corresponding action.This should be the basis for resuming full and meaningful negotiations.

INTRODUCTION

On October 17, 2000, at the conclusion of the Middle East Peace Summit at Sharm esh-Sheikh, Egypt, the President of the United States spoke on behalf of the participants (the Government of Israel, the Palestinian Authority, the Governments of Egypt, Jordan, and the United States, the United Nations, and the European Union). Among other things, the President stated that:

The United States will develop with the Israelis and Palestinians, as well as in consultation with the United Nations Secretary-General, a committee of fact-finding on the events of the past several weeks and how to prevent their recurrence. The committee's report will be shared by the US President with the UN Secretary-General and the parties prior to publication. A final report shall be submitted under the auspices of the US President for publication.

On November 7, 2000, following consultations with the other participants, the President asked us to serve on what has come to be known as the Sharm esh-Sheikh Fact-Finding Committee. In a letter to us on December 6, 2000, the President stated that:

The purpose of the Summit, and of the agreement that ensued, was to end the violence, to prevent its recurrence, and to find a path back to the peace process. In its actions and mode of operation, therefore, the Committee should be guided by these overriding goals ... [T]he Committee should strive to steer clear of any step that will intensify mutual blame and finger-pointing between the parties. As I noted in my previous letter, 'the Committee should not become a divisive force or a focal point for blame and recrimination but rather should serve to forestall violence and confrontation and provide lessons for the future.' This should not be a tribunal whose purpose is to determine the guilt or innocence of individuals or of the parties; rather, it should be a fact-finding committee whose purpose is to determine what happened and how to avoid it recurring in the future.

After our first meeting, held before we visited the region, we urged an end to all violence. Our meetings and our observations during our subsequent visits to the region have intensified our convictions in this regard. Whatever the source, violence will not solve the problems of the region. It will only make them worse. Death and destruction will not bring peace, but will deepen the hatred and harden the resolve on both sides. There is only one way to peace, justice, and security in the Middle East, and that is through negotiation.

Despite their long history and close proximity, some Israelis and Palestinians seem not to fully appreciate each other's problems and concerns. Some Israelis appear not to comprehend the humiliation and frustration that Palestinians must endure every day as a result of living with the continuing effects of occupation, sustained by the presence of Israeli military forces and settlements in their midst, or the determination of the Palestinians to achieve independence and genuine self-determination. Some Palestinians appear not to comprehend the extent to which terrorism creates fear among the Israeli people and undermines their belief in the possibility or co-existence, or the determination of the Government of Israel to do whatever is necessary to protect its people.

Fear, hate, anger, and frustration have risen on both sides. The greatest danger of all is that the culture of peace, nurtured over the previous decade, is being shattered. In its place there is a growing sense of futility and despair, and a growing resort to violence.

Political leaders on both sides must act and speak decisively to reverse these dangerous trends; they must rekindle the desire and the drive for peace. That will be difficult. But it can be done and it must be done, for the alternative is unacceptable and should be unthinkable.

Two proud peoples share a land and a destiny. Their competing claims and religious differences have led to a grinding, demoralizing, dehumanizing conflict. They can continue in conflict or they can negotiate to find a way to live side-by-side in peace.

There is a record of achievement. In 1991 the first peace conference with Israelis and Palestinians took place in Madrid to achieve peace based on UN Security Council Resolutions 242 and 338. In 1993, the Palestine Liberation Organization (PLO) and Israel met in Oslo for the first face-to-face negotiations; they led to mutual recognition and the Declaration of Principles (signed by the parties in Washington, D.C. on September 13, 1993), which provided a road map to reach the destination agreed in Madrid. Since then, important steps have been taken in Cairo, in Washington, and elsewhere. Last year the parties came very close to a permanent settlement.

So much has been achieved. So much is at risk. If the parties are to succeed in completing their journey to their common destination, agreed commitments must be implemented, international law respected, and human rights protected. We encourage them to return to negotiations, however difficult. It is the only path to peace, justice and security.

DISCUSSION

It is clear from their statements that the participants in the summit of last October hoped and intended that the outbreak of violence, then less than a month old, would soon end. The US President's letters to us, asking that we make recommendations on how to prevent a recurrence of violence, reflect that intention.

Yet the violence has not ended. It has worsened. Thus the overriding concern of those in the region with whom we spoke is to end the violence and to return to the process of shaping a sustainable peace. That is what we were told, and were asked to address, by Israelis and Palestinians alike. It was the message conveyed to us as well by President Mubarak of Egypt, King Abdullah of Jordan, and UN Secretary-General Annan.

Their concern must be ours. If our report is to have effect, it must deal with the situation that exists, which is different from that envisaged by the summit participants. In this report, we will try to answer the questions assigned to us by the Sharm esh-Sheikh summit: What happened? Why did it happen?

In light of the current situation, however, we must elaborate on the third part of our mandate: How can the recurrence of violence be prevented? The relevance and impact of our work, in the end, will be measured by the recommendations we make concerning the following:

Ending the Violence.
Rebuilding Confidence.
Resuming Negotiations.

WHAT HAPPENED?

We are not a tribunal. We complied with the request that we do not determine the guilt or innocence of individuals or of the parties. We did not have the power to compel the testimony of witnesses or the production of documents. Most of the information we received came from the parties and, understandably, it largely tended to support their arguments.

In this part of our report, we do not attempt to chronicle all of the events from late September 2000 onward. Rather, we discuss only those that shed light on the underlying causes of violence.

In late September 2000, Israeli, Palestinian, and other officials received reports that Member of the Knesset (now Prime Minister) Ariel Sharon was planning a visit to the Haram ash-Sharif/Temple Mount in Jerusalem. Palestinian and US officials urged then Prime Minister Ehud Barak to prohibit the visit. Mr Barak told us that he believed the visit was intended to be an internal political act directed against him by a political opponent, and he declined to prohibit it.

Mr Sharon made the visit on September 28 accompanied by over 1,000 Israeli police officers. Although Israelis viewed the visit in an internal political context, Palestinians saw it as highly provocative to them. On the following day, in the same place, a large number of unarmed Palestinian demonstrators and a large Israeli police contingent confronted each other. According to the US Department of State, 'Palestinians held large demonstrations and threw stones at police in the vicinity of the Western Wall. Police used rubber-coated metal bullets and live ammunition to disperse the demonstrators, killing 4 persons and injuring about 200.' According to the Government of Israel, 14 Israeli policemen were injured.

Similar demonstrations took place over the following several days. Thus began what has become known as the 'Al-Aqsa Intifada' (Al-Aqsa being a mosque at the Haram ash-Sharif/Temple Mount).

The Government of Israel asserts that the immediate catalyst for the violence was the breakdown of the Camp David negotiations on July 25, 2000 and the 'widespread appreciation in the international community of Palestinian responsibility for the impasse'. In this view, Palestinian violence was planned by the PA leadership, and was aimed at 'provoking and incurring Palestinian casualties as a means of regaining the diplomatic initiative.'

The Palestine Liberation Organization (PLO) denies the allegation that the intifada was planned. It claims, however, that 'Camp David represented nothing less than an attempt by Israel to extend the force it exercises on the ground to negotiations,' and that 'the failure of the summit, and the attempts to allocate blame on the Palestinian side only added to the tension on the ground ...'

From the perspective of the PLO, Israel responded to the disturbances with excessive and illegal use of deadly force against demonstrators; behavior which, in the PLO's view, reflected Israel's contempt for the lives and safety of Palestinians. For Palestinians, the widely seen images of the killing of 12-year-old Muhammad ad-Durra in Gaza on September 20, shot as he huddled behind his father, reinforced that perception.

From the perspective of the Government of Israel, the demonstrations were organized and directed by the Palestinian leadership to create sympathy for their cause around the world by provoking Israeli security forces to fire upon demonstrators, especially young people. For Israelis, the lynching of two military reservists, First Sergeant Vadim Novesche and First Corporal Yosef Avrahami, in Ramallah on October 12, reflected a deep-seated Palestinian hatred of Israel and Jews.

What began as a series of confrontations between Palestinian demonstrators and Israeli security forces, which resulted in the Government of Israel's initial restrictions on the movement of people and goods in the West Bank amd Gaza Strip (closures), has since evolved into a wider array of violent actions and responses. There have been exchanges of fire between built-up areas, sniping incidents and clashes between Israeli settlers and Palestinians. There have also been terrorist acts and Israeli reactions thereto (characterized by the Government of Israel as counter-terrorism), including killings, further destruction of property and economic measures. Most recently, there have been mortar attacks on Israeli locations and IDF ground incursions into Palestinian areas.

From the Palestinian perspective, the decision of Israel to characterize the current crisis as 'an armed conflict short of war' is simply a means 'to justify its assassination policy, its collective punishment policy, and its use of lethal force.' From the Israeli perspective, 'The Palestinian leadership have instigated, orchestrated and directed the violence. It has used, and continues to use, terror and attrition as strategic tools.'

In their submissions, the parties traded allegations about the motivation and degree of control exercised by the other. However, we were provided with no persuasive evidence that the Sharon visit was anything other than an internal political act; neither were we provided with persuasive evidence that the PA planned the uprising.

Accordingly, we have no basis on which to conclude that there was a deliberate plan by the PA to initiate a campaign of violence at the first opportunity; or to conclude that there was a deliberate plan by the Government of Israel to respond with lethal force.

However, there is also no evidence on which to conclude that the PA made a consistent effort to contain the demonstrations and control the violence once it began; or that the Government of Israel made a consistent effort to use non-lethal means to control demonstrations of unarmed Palestinians. Amid rising anger, fear, and mistrust, each side assumed the worst about the other and acted accordingly.

The Sharon visit did not cause the 'Al-Aqsa Intifada'. But it was poorly timed and the provocative effect should have been foreseen; indeed it was foreseen by those who urged that the visit be prohibited. More significant were the events that followed: the decision of the Israeli police on September 29 to use lethal means against the Palestinian demonstrators; and the subsequent failure, as noted above, of either party to exercise restraint.

WHY DID IT HAPPEN?

The roots of the current violence extend much deeper than an inconclusive summit conference. Both sides have made clear a profound disillusionment with the behavior of the other in failing to meet the expectations arising from the peace process launched in Madrid in 1991 and then in Oslo in 1993. Each side has accused the other of violating undertakings and undermining the spirit of their commitment to resolving their political differences peacefully.

Divergent Expectations:
We are struck by the divergent expectations expressed by the parties relating to the implementation of the Oslo process. Results achieved from this process were unthinkable less than 10 years ago. During the latest round of negotiations, the parties were closer to a permanent settlement than ever before.

None the less, Palestinians and Israelis alike told us that the promise on which the Oslo process is based—that tackling the hard 'permanent status' issues be deferred to the end of the process—has gradually come under serious pressure. The step-by-step process agreed to by the parties was based on the assumption that each step in the negotiating process would lead to enhanced trust and confidence. To achieve this, each party would have to implement agreed-upon commitments and abstain from actions that would be seen by the other as attempts to abuse the process in order to predetermine the shape of the final outcome. If this requirement is not met, the Oslo road map cannot successfully lead to its agreed destination. Today, each side blames the other for having ignored this fundamental aspect, resulting in a crisis in confidence. This problem became even more pressing with the opening of permanent status talks.

The Government of Israel has placed primacy on moving toward a Permanent Status Agreement in a non-violent atmosphere, consistent with commitments contained in the agreements between the parties. 'Even if slower than was initially envisaged, there has, since the start of the peace process in Madrid in 1991, been steady progress towards the goal of a Permanent Status Agreement without the resort to violence on a scale that has characterized recent weeks.' The 'goal' is the Permanent Status Agreement, the terms of which must be negotiated by the parties.

The PLO view is that delays in the process have been the result of an Israeli attempt to prolong and solidify the occupation. Palestinians 'believed that the

Oslo process would yield an end to Israeli occupation in five years,' the time frame for the transitional period specified in the Declaration of Principles. Instead there have been, in the PLO's view, repeated Israeli delays culminating in the Camp David summit, where, 'Israel proposed to annex about 11.2% of the West Bank (excluding Jerusalem)...' and offered unacceptable proposals concerning Jerusalem, security and refugees. 'In sum, Israel's proposals at Camp David provided for Israel's annexation of the best Palestinian lands, the perpetuation of Israeli control over East Jerusalem, a continued Israeli military presence on Palestinian territory, Israeli control over Palestinian natural resources, airspace and borders, and the return of fewer than 1% of refugees to their homes.'

Both sides see the lack of full compliance with agreements reached since the opening of the peace process as evidence of a lack of good faith. This conclusion led to an erosion of trust even before the permanent status negotiations began.

Divergent Perspectives:
During the last seven months, these views have hardened into divergent realities. Each side views the other as having acted in bad faith; as having turned the optimism of Oslo into the suffering and grief of victims and their loved ones. In their statements and actions, each side demonstrates a perspective that fails to recognize any truth in the perspective of the other.

The Palestinian Perspective:
For the Palestinian side, 'Madrid' and 'Oslo' heralded the prospect of a State, and guaranteed an end to the occupation and a resolution of outstanding matters within an agreed time frame. Palestinians are genuinely angry at the continued growth of settlements and at their daily experiences of humiliation and disruption as a result fo Israel's presence in the Palestinian territories. Palestinians see settlers and settlements in their midst not only as violating the spirit of the Oslo process, but also as an application of force in the form of Israel's overwhelming military superiority, which sustains and protects the settlements.

> The Interim Agreement provides that 'the two parties view the West Bank and Gaza as a single territorial unit, the integrity and status of which will be preserved during the interim period.' Coupled with this, the Interim Agreement's prohibition on taking steps which may prejudice permanent status negotiations denies Israel the right to continue its illegal expansionist settlement policy. In addition to the Interim Agreement, customary international law, including the Fourth Geneva Convention, prohibits Israel (as an occupying power) from establishing settlements in occupied territory pending an end to the conflict.

The PLO alleges that Israeli political leaders 'have made no secret of the fact that the Israeli interpretation of Oslo was designed to segregate the Palestinians in non-contiguous enclaves, surrounded by Israeli military-controlled borders, with settlements and settlement roads violating the territories' integrity.' According to the PLO, 'In the seven years since the [Declaration of Principles], the settler population in the West Bank, excluding East Jerusalem and the Gaza Strip, has doubled to 200,000, and the settler population in East Jerusalem has risen to 170,000. Israel has constructed approximately 30 new settlements, and expanded a number of existing ones to house these new settlers.'

The PLO also claims that the Government of Israel has failed to comply with other commitments such as the further withdrawal from the West Bank and the release of Palestinian prisoners. In addition, Palestinians expressed frustration with the impasse over refugees and the deteriorating economic circumstances in the West Bank and Gaza Strip.

The Israeli Perspective:
From the Government of Israel perspective, the expansion of settlement activity and the taking of measures to facilitate the convenience and safety of settlers do not prejudice the outcome of permanent status negotiations.

> *Israel understands that the Palestinian side objects to the settlements in the West Bank and Gaza Strip. Without prejudice to the formal status of the settlements, Israel accepts that the settlements are an outstanding issue on which there will have to be agreement as part of any permanent status resolution between the sides. This point was acknowledged and agreed upon in the Declaration of Principles of 13 September 1993 as well as other agreements between the two sides. There has in fact been a good deal of discussion on the question of settlements between the two sides in the various negotiations toward a permanent status agreement.*

Indeed, Israelis point out that at the Camp David summit and during subsequent talks the Government of Israel offered to make significant concessions with respect to settlements in the context of an overall agreement.

Security, however, is the key Government of Israel concern. The Government of Israel maintains that the PLO has breached its solemn commitments by continuing the use of violence in the pursuit of political objectives. 'Israel's principal concern in the peace process has been security. This issue is of overriding importance ... [S]ecurity is not something on which Israel will bargain or compromise. The failure of the Palestinian side to comply with both the letter and spirit of the security provisions in the various agreements has long been a source of disturbance in Israel.'

According to the Government of Israel, the Palestinian failure takes several forms: institutionalized anti-Israel, anti-Jewish incitement; the release from detention of terrorists; the failure to control illegal weapons; and the actual conduct of violent operations, ranging from the insertion of riflemen into demonstrations to terrorist attacks on Israeli civilians. The Government of Israel maintains that the PLO has explicitly violated its renunciation of terrorism and other acts of violence, thereby significantly eroding trust between the parties. The Government of Israel perceives 'a thread, implied but nonetheless clear, that runs throughout the Palestinian submissions. It is that Palestinian violence against Israel and Israelis is somehow explicable, understandable, legitimate.'

END THE VIOLENCE

For Israelis and Palestinians alike the experience of the past several months has been intensely *personal*. Through relationships of kinship, friendship, religion, community and profession, virtually everyone in both societies has a link to someone who has been killed or seriously injured in the recent violence. We were touched by their stories. During our last visit to the region, we met with the families of Palestinian and Israeli victims. These individual accounts of grief were heart-rending and indescribably sad. Israeli and Palestinian families used virtually the same words to describe their grief.

When the widow of a murdered Israeli physician—a man of peace whose practice included the treatment of Arab patients—tells us that it seems that Palestinians are interested in killing Jews for the sake of killing Jews, Palestinians should take notice. When the parents of a Palestinian child killed while in his bed by an errant .50 calibre bullet draw similar conclusions about the respect accorded by Israelis to Palestinian lives, Israelis need to listen. When we see the shattered bodies of children we know it is time for adults to stop the violence.

With widespread violence, both sides have resorted to portrayals of the other in hostile stereotypes. This cycle cannot be easily broken. Without considerable determination and readiness to compromise, the rebuilding of trust will be impossible.

Cessation of Violence:

Since 1991, the parties have consistently committed themselves, in all their agreements, to the path of non-violence. They did so most recently in the two Sharm esh-Sheikh summits of September 1999 and October 2000. To stop the violence now, the PA and Government of Israel need not 'reinvent the wheel'. Rather, they should take immediate steps to end the violence, reaffirm their mutual commitments, and resume negotiations.

Resumption of Security Co-operation:

Palestinian security officials told us that it would take some time—perhaps several weeks—for the PA to reassert full control over armed elements nominally under its command and to exert decisive influence over other armed elements operating in Palestinian areas. Israeli security officials have not disputed these assertions. What is important is that the PA make an all-out effort to enforce a complete cessation of violence and that it be clearly seen by the Government of Israel as doing so. The Government of Israel must likewise exercise a 100 percent effort to ensure that potential friction points, where Palestinians come into contact with armed Israelis, do not become stages for renewed hostilities.

The collapse of security co-operation in early October reflected the belief by each party that the other had committed itself to a violent course of action. If the parties wish to attain the standard of 100 percent effort to prevent violence, the immediate resumption of security co-operation is mandatory.

We acknowledge the reluctance of the PA to be seen as facilitating the work of Israeli security services absent an explicit political context (i.e., meaningful negotiations) and under the threat of Israeli settlement expansion. Indeed, security co-operation cannot be sustained without such negotiations and with ongoing actions seen as prejudicing the outcome of negotiations. However, violence is much more likely to continue without security co-operation. Moreover, without effective security co-operation, the parties will continue to regard all acts of violence as officially sanctioned.

In order to overcome the current deadlock, the parties should consider how best to revitalize security co-operation. We commend current efforts to that end. Effective co-operation depends on recreating and sustaining an atmosphere of confidence and good personal relations.

It is for the parties themselves to undertake the main burden of day-to-day co-operation, but they should remain open to engaging the assistance of others in facilitating that work. Such outside assistance should be by mutual consent, should not threaten good bilateral working arrangements, and should not act as a tribunal or interpose between the parties. There was good security co-operation until last year that benefited from the good offices of the US (acknowledged by both sides as useful), and was also supported indirectly by security projects and assistance from the European Union. The role of outside assistance should be that of creating the appropriate framework, sustaining goodwill on both sides, and removing friction where possible. That framework must be seen to be contributing to the safety and welfare of both communities if there is to be acceptance by those communities of these efforts.

REBUILD CONFIDENCE

The historic handshake between Chairman Arafat and the late Prime Minister Rabin at the White House in September 1993 symbolized the expectation of both parties that the door to the peaceful resolution of differences had been opened. Despite the current violence and mutual loss of trust, both communities have repeatedly expressed a desire for peace. Channelling this desire into substantive progress has proved difficult. The restoration of trust is essential, and the parties should take affirmative steps to this end. Given the high level of hostility and mistrust, the timing and sequence of these steps are obviously crucial. This can be decided only by the parties. We urge them to begin the process of decision immediately.

Terrorism:

In the September 1999 Sharm esh-Sheikh Memorandum, the parties pledged to take action against 'any threat or act of terrorism, violence or incitement.' Although all three categories of hostilities are reprehensible, it was no accident that 'terrorism' was placed at the top of the list.

Terrorism involves the deliberate killing and injuring of randomly selected non-combatants for political ends. It seeks to promote a political outcome by spreading terror and demoralization throughout a population. It is immoral and ultimately self defeating. We condemn it and we urge that the parties co-ordinate their security efforts to eliminate it.

In its official submissions and briefings, the Government of Israel has accused the PA of supporting terrorism by releasing incarcerated terrorists, by allowing PA security personnel to abet, and in some cases to conduct, terrorist operations, and by terminating security co-operation with the Government of Israel. The PA vigorously denies the accusations. But Israelis hold the view that the PA's leadership has made no real effort over the past seven months to prevent anti-Israeli terrorism. The belief is, in and of itself, a major obstacle to the rebuilding of confidence.

We believe that the PA has a responsibility to help rebuild confidence by making clear to both communities that terrorism is reprehensible and unacceptable, and by taking all measures to prevent terrorist operations and to punish perpetrators. This effort should include immediate steps to apprehend and incarcerate terrorists operating within the PA's jurisdiction.

Settlements:

The Government of Israel also has a responsibility to help rebuild confidence. A cessation of Palestinian–Israeli violence will be particularly hard to sustain unless the Government of Israel freezes all settlement construction activity. The Government of Israel should also give careful consideration to whether settlements that are focal points for substantial friction are valuable bargaining chips for future negotiations or provocations likely to preclude the onset of productive talks.

The issue is, of course, controversial. Many Israelis will regard our recommendation as a statement of the obvious, and will support it. Many will oppose it. But settlement activities must not be allowed to undermine the restoration of calm and the resumption of negotiations.

During the half-century of its existence, Israel has had the strong support of the United States. In international forums, the US has at times cast the only vote on Israel's behalf. Yet, even in such a close relationship there are some differences. Prominent among those differences is the US Government's longstanding opposition to the Government of Israel's policies and practices regarding settlements. As the then Secretary of State, James A. Baker, III, commented on May 22, 1991:

Every time I have gone to Israel in connection with the peace process, on each of my four trips, I have been met with the announcement of new settlement activity. This does violate United States policy. It's the first thing that Arabs—Arab Governments, the first thing that the Palestinians in the territories—whose situation is really quite desperate—the first thing they raise when we talk to them. I don't think there is any bigger obstacle to peace than the settlement activity that continues not only unabated but at an enhanced pace.

The policy desribed by Secretary Baker, on behalf of the Administration of President George H.W. Bush, has been, in essence, the policy of every American administration over the past quarter century.

Most other countries, including Turkey, Norway, and those of the European Union, have also been critical of Israeli settlement activity, in accordance with their views that such settlements are illegal under international law and not in compliance with previous agreements.

On each of our two visits to the region there were Israeli announcements regarding expansion of settlements, and it was almost always the first issue raised by Palestinians with whom we met. During our last visit, we observed the impact of 6,400 settlers on 140,000 Palestinians in Hebron and 6,500 settlers on over 1,100,000 Palestinians in the Gaza Strip. The Government of Israel describes its policy as prohibiting new settlements but permitting expansion of existing settlements to accommodate 'natural growth'. Palestinians contend that there is no distinction between 'new' and 'expanded' settlements; and that, except for a brief freeze during the tenure of Prime Minister Itzhak Rabin, there has been a continuing, aggressive effort by Israel to increase the number and size of settlements.

The subject has been widely discussed within Israel. The *Ha'aretz* English Language Edition editorial of April 10, 2001 stated:

> *A government which seeks to argue that its goal is to reach a solution to the conflict with the Palestinians through peaceful means, and is trying at this stage to bring an end to the violence and terrorism, must announce an end to construction in the settlements.*

The circumstances in the region are much changed from those which existed nearly 20 years ago. Yet, President Reagan's words remain relevant: 'The immediate adoption of a settlement freeze by Israel, more than any other action, could create the confidence needed [...]'

Beyond the obvious confidence-building qualities of a settlement freeze, we note that many of the confrontations during this conflict have occurred at points where Palestinians, settlers, and security forces protecting the settlers, meet. Keeping both the peace and these friction points will be very difficult.

Reducing Tension:

We were told by both Palestinians and Israelis that emotions generated by the many recent deaths and funerals have fuelled additional confrontations, and, in effect, maintained the cycle of violence. We cannot urge one side or the other to refrain from demonstrations. But both sides must make clear that violent demonstrations will not be tolerated. We can and do urge that both sides exhibit a greater respect for human life when demonstrators confront security personnel. In addition, a renewed effort to stop the violence might feature, for a limited time, a 'cooling off' period during which public demonstrations at or near friction points will be discouraged in order to break the cycle of violence. To the extent that demonstrations continue, we urge that demonstrators and security personnel keep their distance from one another to reduce the potential for lethal confrontation.

Actions and Responses:

Members of the Committee staff witnessed an incident involving stone throwing in Ramallah from the perspectives, on the ground, of both sides. The people confronting one another were mostly young men. The absence of senior leadership on the IDF side was striking. Likewise, the absence of responsible security and other officials counselling restraint on the Palestinian side was obvious.

Concerning such confrontations, the Government of Israel takes the position that 'Israel is engaged in an armed conflict short of war. This is not a civilian disturbance or a demonstration or a riot. It is characterized by live-fire attacks on a *significant scale* [emphasis added]...[T]he attacks are carried out by a well-armed and organized militia...' Yet, the Government of Israel acknowledges that of some 9,000 'attacks' by Palestinians against Israelis, 'some 2,700 [about 30 percent] involved the use of automatic weapons, rifles, hand guns, grenades, [and] explosives of other kinds.'

Thus, for the first three months of the current uprising, most incidents *did not* involve Palestinian use of firearms and explosives. B'Tselem *[the Israeli*

Information Centre for Human Rights in the Occupied Territories] reported that, 'according to IDF figures, 73 percent of the incidents [from September 29 to December 2, 2000] did not include Palestinian gunfire. Despite this, it was in these incidents that most of the Palestinians [were] killed and wounded...' Altogether, nearly 500 people were killed and over 10,000 injured over the past seven months; the overwhelming majority in both categories were Palestinian. Many of these deaths were avoidable, as were many Israeli deaths.

Israel's characterization of the conflict, as noted above, is overly broad, for it does not adequately describe the variety of incidents reported since late September 2000. Moreover, by thus defining the conflict, the IDF has suspended its policy of mandating investigations by the Department of Military Police Investigations whenever a Palestinian in the territories dies at the hands of an IDF soldier in an incident not involving terrorism. In the words of the Government of Israel, 'Where Israel considers that there is reason to investigate particular incidents, it does so, although, given the circumstances of armed conflict, it does not do so routinely.' We believe, however, that by abandoning the blanket 'armed conflict short of war' characterization and by re-instituting mandatory military police investigations, the Government of Israel could help mitigate deadly violence and help rebuild mutual confidence. Notwithstanding the danger posed by stone-throwers, an effort should be made to differentiate between terrorism and protests.

Controversy has arisen between the parties over what Israel calls the 'targeting of individual enemy combatants.' The PLO describes these actions as 'extra-judicial executions', and claims that Israel has engaged in an 'assassination policy' that is 'in clear violation of Article 32 of the Fourth Geneva Convention...' The Government of Israel states that, 'whatever action Israel has taken has been taken firmly within the bounds of the relevant and accepted principles relating to the conduct of hostilities.'

With respect to demonstrations, the Government of Israel has acknowledged 'that individual instances of excessive response may have occurred. To a soldier or a unit coming under Palestinian attack, the equation is not that of the Israeli army versus some stone throwing Palestinian protesters. It is a personal equation.'

We understand this concern, particularly since rocks can maim or even kill. It is no easy matter for a few young soldiers, confronted by large numbers of hostile demonstrators, to make fine legal distinctions on the spot. Still, this 'personal equation' must fit within an organizational ethic; in this case, *The Ethical Code of the Israel Defence Forces.* which states, in part:

> *The sanctity of human life in the eyes of the IDF servicemen will find expression in all of their actions, in deliberate and meticulous planning, in safe and intelligent training and in proper execution of their mission. In evaluating the risk to self and others, they will use the appropriate standards and will exercise constant care to limit injury to life to the extent required to accomplish the mission.*

Those required to respect the IDF ethical code are largely draftees, as the IDF is a conscript force. Active duty enlisted personnel, non-commissioned officers and junior officers—the categories most likely to be present at friction points—are young, often teenagers. Unless more senior career personnel or reservists are stationed at friction points, no IDF personnel present in these sensitive areas have experience to draw upon from previous violent Israeli–Palestinian confrontations. We think it is essential, especially in the context of restoring confidence by minimizing deadly confrontations, that the IDF deploy more senior, experienced soldiers to these sensitive points.

There were incidents where IDF soldiers have used lethal force, including live ammunition and modified metal-cored rubber rounds, against unarmed demonstrators throwing stones. The IDF should adopt crowd-control tactics that minimize the potential for deaths and casualties, withdrawing metal-cored rubber rounds from general use and using instead rubber baton rounds without metal cores.

We are deeply concerned about the public safety implications of exchanges of fire between populated areas, in particular between Israeli settlements and neighbouring Palestinian villages. Palestinian gunmen have directed small arms fire at Israeli settlements and at nearby IDF positions from within or adjacent to civilian dwellings in Palestinian areas, thus endangering innocent Israeli and Palestinian civilians alike. We condemn the positioning of gunmen within or near civilian dwellings. The IDF often responds to such gunfire with heavy calibre weapons, sometimes resulting in deaths and injuries to innocent Palestinians. An IDF officer told us at the Ministry of Defence on March 23, 2001 that, 'When shooting comes from a building we respond, and sometimes there are innocent people in the building.' Obviously, innocent people are injured and killed during exchanges of this nature. We urge that such provocations cease and that the IDF exercise maximum restraint in its responses if they do occur. Inappropriate or excessive uses of force often lead to escalation.

We are aware of IDF sensitivities about these subjects. More than once we were asked: 'What about Palestinian rules of engagement? What about a Palestinian code of ethics for their military personnel?' These are valid questions.

On the Palestinian side there are disturbing ambiguities in the basic areas of responsibility and accountability. The lack of control exercised by the PA over its own security personnel and armed elements affiliated with the PA leadership is very troubling. We urge the PA to take all necessary steps to establish a clear and unchallenged chain of command for armed personnel operating under its authority. We recommend that the PA institute and enforce effective standards of conduct and accountability, both within the uniformed ranks and between the police and the civilian political leadership to which it reports.

Incitement:

In their submissions and briefings to the Committee, both sides expressed concerns about hateful language and images emanating from the other, citing numerous examples of hostile sectarian and ethnic rhetoric in the Palestinian and Israeli media, in school curricula and in statements by religious leaders, politicians and others.

We call on the parties to renew their formal commitments to foster mutual understanding and tolerance and to abstain from incitement and hostile propaganda. We condemn hate language and incitement in all its forms. We suggest that the parties be particularly cautious about using words in a manner that suggests collective responsibility.

Economic and Social Impact of Violence:

Further restrictions on the movement of people and goods have been imposed by Israel on the West Bank and the Gaza Strip. These closures take three forms: those which restrict movement between the Palestinian areas and Israel; those (including curfews) which restrict movement within the Palestinian areas; and those which restrict movement from the Palestinian areas to foreign countries. These measures have disrupted the lives of hundreds of thousands of Palestinians; they have increased Palestinian unemployment to an estimated 40 percent, in part by preventing some 140,000 Palestinians from working in Israel; and have stripped away about one-third of the Palestinian gross domestic product. Moreover, the transfer of tax and customs duty revenues owed to the PA by Israel has been suspended, leading to a serious fiscal crisis in the PA.

Of particular concern to the PA has been the destruction by Israeli security forces and settlers of tens of thousands of olive and fruit trees and other agricultural property. The closures have had other adverse effects, such as preventing civilians from access to urgent medical treatment and preventing students from attending school.

The Government of Israel maintains that these measures were taken in order to protect Israeli citizens from terrorism. Palestinians characterize these measures as 'collective punishment'. The Government of Israel denies the allegations:

> Israel has not taken measures that have had an economic impact simply for the sake of taking such measures or for reasons of harming the Palestinian economy. The measures have been taken for reasons of security. Thus, for example, the closure of the Palestinian territories was taken in order to prevent, or at least minimize the risks of, terrorist attacks... The Palestinian leadership has made no attempt to control this activity and bring it to an end.

Moreover, the Government of Israel points out that violence in the last quarter of 2000 cost the Israeli economy $1.2 billion [US $1,200m.], and that the loss continues at a rate of approximately $150 million per month.

We acknowledge Israel's security concerns. We believe, however, that the Government of Israel should lift closures, transfer to the PA all revenues owed, and permit Palestinians who have been employed in Israel to return to their jobs. Closure policies play into the hands of extremists seeking to expand their constituencies and thereby contribute to escalation. The PA should resume co-operation with Israeli security agencies to ensure that Palestinian workers employed within Israel are fully vetted and free of connections to terrorists and terrorist organizations.

International development assistance has from the start been an integral part of the peace process, with an aim to strengthen the socio-economic foundations for peace. This assistance today is more important than ever. We urge the international community to sustain the development agenda of the peace process.

Holy Places:

It is particularly regrettable that places such as the Temple Mount/Haram ash-Sharif in Jerusalem, Joseph's Tomb in Nablus, and Rachel's Tomb in Bethlehem have been the scenes of violence, death and injury. These are places of peace, prayer and reflection which must be accessible to all believers.

Places deemed holy by Muslims, Jews, and Christians merit respect, protection and preservation. Agreements previously reached by the parties regarding holy places must be upheld. The Government of Israel and the PA should create a joint initiative to defuse the sectarian aspect of their political dispute by preserving and protecting such places. Efforts to develop inter-faith dialogue should be encouraged.

International Force:

One of the most controversial subjects raised during our inquiry was the issue of deploying an international force to the Palestinian areas. The PA is strongly in favour of having such a force to protect Palestinian civilians and their property from the IDF and from settlers. The Government of Israel is just as adamantly opposed to an 'international protection force', believing that it would prove unresponsive to Israeli security concerns and interfere with bilateral negotiations to settle the conflict.

We believe that to be effective such a force would need the support of both parties. We note that international forces deployed in this region have been or are in a position to fulfil their mandates and make a positive contribution only when they were deployed with the consent of all of the parties involved.

During our visit to Hebron we were briefed by personnel of the Temporary International Presence in Hebron (TIPH), a presence to which both parties have agreed. The TIPH is charged with observing an explosive situation and writing reports on their observations. If the parties agree, as a confidence-building measure, to draw upon TIPH personnel to help them manage other friction points, we hope that TIPH contributors could accommodate such a request.

Cross-Community Initiatives:

Many described to us the near absolute loss of trust. It was all the more inspiring, therefore, to find groups (such as the Parent's Circle and the Economic Co-operation Foundation) dedicated to cross-community understanding in spite of all that has happened. We commend them and their important work.

Regrettably, most of the work of this nature has stopped during the current conflict. To help rebuild confidence, the Government of Israel and PA should jointly endorse and support the work of Israeli and Palestinian non-governmental organizations (NGOs) already involved in confidence-building through initiatives linking both sides. It is important that the PA and Government of Israel support cross-community organizations and initiatives, including the provision of humanitarian assistance to Palestinian villages by Israeli NGOs. Providing travel permits for participants is essential. Co-operation between the humanitarian organizations and the military/security services of the parties should be encouraged and institutionalized.

Such programmes can help build, albeit slowly, constituencies for peace among Palestinians and Israelis and can provide safety nets during times of turbulence. Organizations involved in this work are vital for translating good intentions into positive actions.

RESUME NEGOTIATIONS

Israeli leaders do not wish to be perceived as 'rewarding violence'. Palestinian leaders do not wish to be perceived as 'rewarding occupation'. We appreciate the political constraints on leaders of both sides. Nevertheless, if the cycle of violence is to be broken and the search for peace resumed, there needs to be a new bilateral relationship incorporating both security co-operation and negotiations.

We cannot prescribe to the parties how best to pursue their political objectives. Yet the construction of a new bilateral relationship solidifying and transcending an agreed cessation of violence requires intelligent risk-taking. It requires, in the first instance, that each party again be willing to regard the other as a *partner*. Partnership, in turn, requires at this juncture something more than was agreed in the Declaration of Principles and in subsequent agreements. Instead of declaring the peace process to be 'dead', the parties should determine how they will conclude their common journey along their agreed 'road map' a journey which began in Madrid and continued in spite of problems—until very recently.

To define a starting point is for the parties to decide. Both parties have stated that they remain committed to their mutual agreements and undertakings. It is time to explore further implementation. The parties should declare their intention to meet on this basis, in order to resume full and meaningful negotiations, in the spirit of their undertakings at Sharm esh-Sheikh in 1999 and 2000.

Neither side will be able to achieve its principal objectives unilaterally or without political risk. We know how hard it is for leaders to act—especially if the action can be characterized by political opponents as a concession—without getting something in return. The PA must—as it has at previous critical junctures—take steps to reassure Israel on security matters. The Government of Israel must—as it has in the past—take steps to reassure the PA on political matters. Israelis and Palestinians should avoid, in their own actions and attitudes, giving extremists, common criminals and revenge seekers the final say in defining their joint future. This will not be easy if deadly incidents occur in spite of effective co-operation. Notwithstanding the daunting difficulties, the very foundation of the trust required to re-establish a functioning partnership consists of each side making such strategic reassurances to the other.

RECOMMENDATIONS

The Government of Israel and the PA must act swiftly and decisively to halt the violence. Their immediate objectives then should be to rebuild confidence and resume negotiations. What we are asking is not easy. Palestinians and Israelis—not just their leaders, but two publics at large—have lost confidence in one another. We are asking political leaders to do, for the sake of their people, the politically difficult: to lead without knowing how many will follow.

During this mission our aim has been to fulfil the mandate agreed at Sharm esh-Sheikh. We value the support given our work by the participants at the summit, and we commend the parties for their co-operation. Our principal recommendation is that they recommit themselves to the Sharm esh-Sheikh spirit, and that they implement the decisions made there in 1999 and 2000. We believe that the summit participants will support bold action by the parties to achieve these objectives.

END THE VIOLENCE

The Government of Israel and the PA should reaffirm their commitment to existing agreements and undertakings and should immediately implement an unconditional cessation of violence.

Anything less than a complete effort by both parties to end the violence will render the effort itself ineffective, and will likely be interpreted by the other side as evidence of hostile intent.

The Government of Israel and PA should immediately resume security co-operation.

Effective bilateral co-operation aimed at preventing violence will encourage the resumption of negotiations. We are particularly concerned that, absent effective, transparent security co-operation, terrorism and other acts of violence will continue and may be seen as officially sanctioned whether they are or not. The parties should consider widening the scope of security co-operation to reflect the priorities of both communities and to seek acceptance for these efforts from those communities.

We acknowledge the PA's position that security co-operation presents a political difficulty absent a suitable political context, i.e., the relaxation of stringent Israeli security measures combined with ongoing, fruitful negotiations. We also acknowledge the PA's fear that, with security co-operation in hand, the Government of Israel may not be disposed to deal forthrightly with Palestinian political concerns. We believe that security co-operation cannot long be sustained if meaningful negotiations are unreasonably deferred, if security measures 'on the ground' are seen as hostile, or if steps are taken that are perceived as provocative or as prejudicing the outcome of negotiations.

REBUILD CONFIDENCE

The PA and Government of Israel should work together to establish a meaningful 'cooling-off period' and implement additional confidence-building measures, some of which were proposed in the October 2000 Sharm esh-Sheikh Statement and some of which were offered by the US on January 7, 2001 in Cairo.

The PA and Government of Israel should resume their efforts to identify, condemn and discourage incitement in all its forms.

The PA should make clear through concrete action to Palestinians and Israelis alike that terrorism is reprehensible and unacceptable, and that the PA will make a 100 percent effort to prevent terrorist operations and to punish perpetrators. This effort should include immediate steps to apprehend and incarcerate terrorists operating within the PA's jurisdiction.

The Government of Israel should freeze all settlement activity, including the 'natural growth' of existing settlements.

The kind of security co-operation desired by the Government of Israel cannot for long co-exist with settlement activity described very recently by the European Union as causing 'great concern' and by the US as 'provocative'.

The Government of Israel should give careful consideration to whether set-tlements which are focal points for substantial friction are valuable bargaining chips for future negotiations, or provocations likely to preclude the onset of productive talks.

The Government of Israel may wish to make it clear to the PA that a future peace would pose no threat to the territorial contiguity of a Palestinian State to be established in the West Bank and the Gaza Strip.

The IDF should consider withdrawing to positions held before September 28, 2000 which will reduce the number of friction points and the potential for violent confrontations.

The Government of Israel should ensure that the IDF adopt and enforce policies and procedures encouraging non-lethal responses to unarmed demon-strators, with a view to minimizing casualties and friction between the two communities. The IDF should:

Re-institute, as a matter of course, military police investigations into Palestinian deaths resulting from IDF actions in the Palestinian territories in incidents not involving terrorism. The IDF should abandon the blanket characterization of the current uprising as 'an armed conflict short of war', which fails to discriminate between terrorism and protest.

Adopt tactics of crowd-control that minimize the potential for deaths and casualties, including the withdrawal of metal-cored rubber rounds from gen-eral use.

Ensure that experienced, seasoned personnel are present for duty at all times at known friction points.

Ensure that the stated values and standard operating procedures of the IDF effectively instil the duty of caring for Palestinians in the West Bank and Gaza Strip as well as Israelis living there, consistent with The Ethical Code of the IDF.

The Government of Israel should lift closures, transfer to the PA all tax revenues owed, and permit Palestinians who had been employed in Israel to return to their jobs; and should ensure that security forces and settlers refrain from the destruction of homes and roads, as well as trees and other agricul-tural property in Palestinian areas. We acknowledge the Government of Israel's position that actions of this nature have been taken for security reasons. Nevertheless, their economic effects will persist for years.

The PA should renew co-operation with Israeli security agencies to ensure, to the maximum extent possible, that Palestinian workers employed within Israel are fully vetted and free of connections to organizations and individuals engaged in terrorism.

The PA should prevent gunmen from using Palestinian populated areas to fire upon Israeli populated areas and IDF positions. This tactic places civilians on both sides at unnecessary risk.

The Government of Israel and IDF should adopt and enforce policies and procedures designed to ensure that the response to any gunfire emanating from Palestinian populated areas minimizes the danger to the lives and property of Palestinian civilians, bearing in mind that it is probably the objective of gunmen to elicit an excessive IDF response.

435

The Government of Israel should take all necessary steps to prevent acts of violence by settlers.

The parties should abide by the provisions of the Wye River Agreement prohibiting illegal weapons.

The PA should take all necessary steps to establish a clear and unchallenged chain of command for armed personnel operating under its authority.

The PA should institute and enforce effective standards of conduct and accountability, both within the uniformed ranks and between the police and the civilian political leadership to which it reports.

The PA and Government of Israel should consider a joint undertaking to preserve and protect holy places sacred to the traditions of Muslims, Jews, and Christians. An initiative of this nature might help to reverse a disturbing trend: the increasing use of religious themes to encourage and justify violence.

The Government of Israel and PA should jointly endorse and support the work of Palestinian and Israeli non-governmental organizations (NGOs) involved in cross-community initiatives linking the two peoples. It is important that these activities, including the provision of humanitarian aid to Palestinian villages by Israeli NGOs, receive the full backing of both parties.

RESUME NEGOTIATIONS

We reiterate our belief that a 100 percent effort to stop the violence, an immediate resumption of security co-operation and an exchange of confidence-building measures are all important for the resumption of negotiations. Yet none of these steps will long be sustained absent a return to serious negotiations.

It is not within our mandate to prescribe the venue, the basis or the agenda of negotiations. However, in order to provide an effective political context for practical co-operation between the parties, negotiations must not be unreasonably deferred and they must, in our view, manifest a spirit of compromise, reconciliation and partnership, notwithstanding the events of the past seven months.

In the spirit of the Sharm esh-Sheikh agreements and understandings of 1999 and 2000, we recommend that the parties meet to reaffirm their commitment to signed agreements and mutual understandings, and take corresponding action. This should be the basis for resuming full and meaningful negotiations.

The parties are at a crossroads. If they do not return to the negotiating table, they face the prospect of fighting it out for years on end, with many of their citizens leaving for distant shores to live their lives and raise their children. We pray they make the right choice. That means stopping the violence now. Israelis and Palestinians have to live, work, and prosper together. History and geography have destined them to be neighbours. That cannot be changed. Only when their actions are guided by this awareness will they be able to develop the vision and reality of peace and shared prosperity.

UN SECURITY COUNCIL RESOLUTION 1397

March 2002

Resolution 1397 affirmed for the first time the UN Security Council's 'vision' of both Israeli and Palestinian states. It was the first US-sponsored resolution on the Middle East for some 25 years, and was adopted by 14 votes to none; Syria abstained in the vote.

The Security Council

Recalling all its previous relevant resolutions, in particular resolutions 242 (1967) and 338 (1973),

Affirming a vision of a region where two States, Israel and Palestine, live side by side within secure and recognized borders,

Expressing its grave concern at the continuation of the tragic and violent events that have taken place since September 2000, especially the recent attacks and the increased number of casualties,

Stressing the need for all concerned to ensure the safety of civilians,

Stressing also the need to respect the universally accepted norms of international humanitarian law.

Welcoming and encouraging the diplomatic efforts of special envoys from the United States of America, the Russian Federation, the European Union and the United Nations Special Coordinator and others, to bring about a comprehensive, just and lasting peace in the Middle East,

Welcoming the contribution of Saudi Crown Price Abdullah,

1. *Demands* immediate cessation of all acts of violence, including all acts of terror, provocation, incitement and destruction;

2. *Calls upon* the Israeli and Palestinian sides and their leaders to cooperate in the implementation of the Tenet work plan and Mitchell Report recommendations with the aim of resuming negotiations on a political settlement;

3. *Expresses* support for the efforts of the Secretary- General and others to assist the parties to halt the violence and to resume the peace process;

4. *Decides* to remain seized of the matter. UN Document S/Res/1397 (2002).

A PERFORMANCE-BASED ROADMAP TO A PERMANENT TWO-STATE SOLUTION TO THE ISRAELI-PALESTINIAN CONFLICT

30 April 2003

The 'roadmap' was presented to both Israeli and Palestinian leaders on 30 April 2003, having been drafted in late 2002 by the Quartet group, comprising the USA, the UN, the European Union (EU) and Russia. Publication of the roadmap, which was intended to lead to an immediate resumption of Israeli-Palestinian negotiations, followed the naming of a new Palestinian Cabinet by the recently appointed Palestinian Prime Minister, Mahmud Abbas (Abu Mazen).

The following is a performance-based and goal-driven roadmap, with clear phases, timelines, target dates, and benchmarks aiming at progress through reciprocal steps by the two parties in the political, security, economic, humanitarian, and institution-building fields, under the auspices of the Quartet [the United States, European Union, United Nations, and Russia]. The destination is a final and comprehensive settlement of the Israel-Palestinian conflict by 2005, as presented in President Bush's speech of 24 June, and welcomed by the EU, Russia and the UN in the 16 July and 17 September Quartet Ministerial statements.

A two-state solution to the Israeli-Palestinian conflict will only be achieved through an end to violence and terrorism, when the Palestinian people have a leadership acting decisively against terror and willing and able to build a practising democracy based on tolerance and liberty, and through Israel's readiness to do what is necessary for a democratic Palestinian state to be established, and a clear, unambiguous acceptance by both parties of the goal of a negotiated settlement as described below. The Quartet will assist and facilitate implementation of the plan, starting in Phase I, including direct discussions between the parties as required. The plan establishes a realistic timeline for implementation. However, as a performance-based plan, progress will require and depend upon the good faith efforts of the parties, and their compliance with each of the obligations outlined below. Should the parties perform their obligations rapidly, progress within and through the phases may come sooner than indicated in the plan. Non-compliance with obligations will impede progress.

A settlement, negotiated between the parties, will result in the emergence of an independent, democratic, and viable Palestinian state living side by side in peace and security with Israel and its other neighbors. The settlement will resolve the Israel-Palestinian conflict, and end the occupation that began in 1967, based on the foundations of the Madrid Conference, the principle of land for peace, UNSCRs 242, 338 and 1397, agreements previously reached by the parties, and the initiative of Saudi Crown Prince Abdullah—endorsed by the Beirut Arab League Summit—calling for acceptance of Israel as a neighbor living in peace and security, in the context of a comprehensive settlement. This initiative is a vital element of international efforts to promote a comprehensive peace on all tracks, including the Syrian-Israeli and Lebanese-Israeli tracks.

The Quartet will meet regularly at senior levels to evaluate the parties' performance on implementation of the plan. In each phase, the parties are expected to perform their obligations in parallel, unless otherwise indicated.

Phase I: Ending Terror And Violence, Normalizing Palestinian Life, and Building Palestinian Institutions—Present to May 2003

In Phase I, the Palestinians immediately undertake an unconditional cessation of violence according to the steps outlined below; such action should be accompanied by supportive measures undertaken by Israel. Palestinians and Israelis resume security co-operation based on the Tenet work plan to end violence, terrorism, and incitement through restructured and effective Palestinian security services. Palestinians undertake comprehensive political reform in preparation for statehood, including drafting a Palestinian constitution, and free, fair and open elections upon the basis of those measures. Israel takes all necessary steps to help normalize Palestinian life. Israel withdraws from Palestinian areas occupied from September 28, 2000 and the two sides restore the status quo that existed at that time, as security performance and co-operation progress. Israel also freezes all settlement activity, consistent with the Mitchell report.

At the outset of Phase I:

- Palestinian leadership issues unequivocal statement reiterating Israel's right to exist in peace and security and calling for an immediate and unconditional ceasefire to end armed activity and all acts of violence against Israelis anywhere. All official Palestinian institutions end incitement against Israel.
- Israeli leadership issues unequivocal statement affirming its commitment to the two-state vision of an independent, viable, sovereign Palestinian state living in peace and security alongside Israel, as expressed by President Bush, and calling for an immediate end to violence against Palestinians everywhere. All official Israeli institutions end incitement against Palestinians.

Security

- Palestinians declare an unequivocal end to violence and terrorism and undertake visible efforts on the ground to arrest, disrupt, and restrain individuals and groups conducting and planning violent attacks on Israelis anywhere.
- Rebuilt and refocused Palestinian Authority security apparatus begins sustained, targeted, and effective operations aimed at confronting all those engaged in terror and dismantlement of terrorist capabilities and infrastructure. This includes commencing confiscation of illegal weapons and consolidation of security authority, free of association with terror and corruption.
- GOI takes no actions undermining trust, including deportations, attacks on civilians; confiscation and/or demolition of Palestinian homes and property, as a punitive measure or to facilitate Israeli construction; destruction of Palestinian institutions and infrastructure; and other measures specified in the Tenet work plan.
- Relying on existing mechanisms and on-the-ground resources, Quartet representatives begin informal monitoring and consult with the parties on establishment of a formal monitoring mechanism and its implementation.
- Implementation, as previously agreed, of US rebuilding, training and resumed security co-operation plan in collaboration with outside oversight board (US-Egypt-Jordan). Quartet support for efforts to achieve a lasting, comprehensive cease-fire.
  - All Palestinian security organizations are consolidated into three services reporting to an empowered Interior Minister.
  - Restructured/retrained Palestinian security forces and IDF counterparts progressively resume security co-operation and other undertakings in implementation of the Tenet work plan, including regular senior-level meetings, with the participation of US security officials.
- Arab states cut off public and private funding and all other forms of support for groups supporting and engaging in violence and terror.
- All donors providing budgetary support for the Palestinians channel these funds through the Palestinian Ministry of Finance's Single Treasury Account.
- As comprehensive security performance moves forward, IDF withdraws progressively from areas occupied since September 28, 2000 and the two sides restore the status quo that existed prior to September 28, 2000. Palestinian security forces redeploy to areas vacated by IDF.

Palestinian Institution-Building

- Immediate action on credible process to produce draft constitution for Palestinian statehood. As rapidly as possible, constitutional committee circulates draft Palestinian constitution, based on strong parliamentary democracy and cabinet with empowered prime minister, for public comment/debate. Constitutional committee proposes draft document for submission after elections for approval by appropriate Palestinian institutions.
- Appointment of interim prime minister or cabinet with empowered executive authority/decision-making body.
- GOI fully facilitates travel of Palestinian officials for PLC and Cabinet sessions, internationally supervised security retraining, electoral and other reform activity, and other supportive measures related to the reform efforts.
- Continued appointment of Palestinian ministers empowered to undertake fundamental reform. Completion of further steps to achieve genuine separation of powers, including any necessary Palestinian legal reforms for this purpose.
- Establishment of independent Palestinian election commission. PLC reviews and revises election law.
- Palestinian performance on judicial, administrative, and economic benchmarks, as established by the International Task Force on Palestinian Reform.
- As early as possible, and based upon the above measures and in the context of open debate and transparent candidate selection/electoral campaign based on a free, multi-party process, Palestinians hold free, open, and fair elections.
- GOI facilitates Task Force election assistance, registration of voters, movement of candidates and voting officials. Support for NGOs involved in the election process.
- GOI reopens Palestinian Chamber of Commerce and other closed Palestinian institutions in East Jerusalem based on a commitment that these institutions operate strictly in accordance with prior agreements between the parties.

Humanitarian Response

- Israel takes measures to improve the humanitarian situation. Israel and Palestinians implement in full all recommendations of the Bertini report to improve humanitarian conditions, lifting curfews and easing restrictions on movement of persons and goods, and allowing full, safe, and unfettered access of international and humanitarian personnel.
- AHLC reviews the humanitarian situation and prospects for economic development in the West Bank and Gaza and launches a major donor assistance effort, including to the reform effort.
- GOI and PA continue revenue clearance process and transfer of funds, including arrears, in accordance with agreed, transparent monitoring mechanism.

Civil Society

- Continued donor support, including increased funding through PVOs/NGOs, for people to people programs, private sector development and civil society initiatives.

Settlements

- GOI immediately dismantles settlement outposts erected since March 2001.

- Consistent with the Mitchell Report, GOI freezes all settlement activity (including natural growth of settlements).

Phase II: Transition—June 2003–December 2003

In the second phase, efforts are focused on the option of creating an independent Palestinian state with provisional borders and attributes of sovereignty, based on the new constitution, as a way station to a permanent status settlement. As has been noted, this goal can be achieved when the Palestinian people have a leadership acting decisively against terror, willing and able to build a practicing democracy based on tolerance and liberty. With such a leadership, reformed civil institutions and security structures, the Palestinians will have the active support of the Quartet and the broader international community in establishing an independent, viable, state.

Progress into Phase II will be based upon the consensus judgment of the Quartet of whether conditions are appropriate to proceed, taking into account performance of both parties. Furthering and sustaining efforts to normalize Palestinian lives and build Palestinian institutions, Phase II starts after Palestinian elections and ends with possible creation of an independent Palestinian state with provisional borders in 2003. Its primary goals are continued comprehensive security performance and effective security co-operation, continued normalization of Palestinian life and institution-building, further building on and sustaining of the goals outlined in Phase I, ratification of a democratic Palestinian constitution, formal establishment of office of prime minister, consolidation of political reform, and the creation of a Palestinian state with provisional borders.

- **International Conference:** Convened by the Quartet, in consultation with the parties, immediately after the successful conclusion of Palestinian elections, to support Palestinian economic recovery and launch a process, leading to establishment of an independent Palestinian state with provisional borders.
  - Such a meeting would be inclusive, based on the goal of a comprehensive Middle East peace (including between Israel and Syria, and Israel and Lebanon), and based on the principles described in the preamble to this document.
  - Arab states restore pre-*intifada* links to Israel (trade offices, etc.).
  - Revival of multilateral engagement on issues including regional water resources, environment, economic development, refugees, and arms control issues.
- New constitution for democratic, independent Palestinian state is finalized and approved by appropriate Palestinian institutions. Further elections, if required, should follow approval of the new constitution.
- Empowered reform cabinet with office of prime minister formally established, consistent with draft constitution.
- Continued comprehensive security performance, including effective security co-operation on the bases laid out in Phase I.
- Creation of an independent Palestinian state with provisional borders through a process of Israeli-Palestinian engagement, launched by the international conference. As part of this process, implementation of prior agreements, to enhance maximum territorial contiguity, including further

action on settlements in conjunction with establishment of a Palestinian state with provisional borders.

- Enhanced international role in monitoring transition, with the active, sustained, and operational support of the Quartet.
- Quartet members promote international recognition of Palestinian state, including possible UN membership.

Phase III: Permanent Status Agreement and End of the Israeli–Palestinian Conflict—2004–2005

Progress into Phase III, based on consensus judgment of Quartet, and taking into account actions of both parties and Quartet monitoring. Phase III objectives are consolidation of reform and stabilization of Palestinian institutions, sustained, effective Palestinian security performance, and Israeli-Palestinian negotiations aimed at a permanent status agreement in 2005.

- **Second International Conference:** Convened by Quartet, in consultation with the parties, at beginning of 2004 to endorse agreement reached on an independent Palestinian state with provisional borders and formally to launch a process with the active, sustained, and operational support of the Quartet, leading to a final, permanent status resolution in 2005, including on borders, Jerusalem, refugees, settlements; and, to support progress toward a comprehensive Middle East settlement between Israel and Lebanon and Israel and Syria, to be achieved as soon as possible.
- Continued comprehensive, effective progress on the reform agenda laid out by the Task Force in preparation for final status agreement.
- Continued sustained and effective security performance, and sustained, effective security co-operation on the bases laid out in Phase I.
- International efforts to facilitate reform and stabilize Palestinian institutions and the Palestinian economy, in preparation for final status agreement.
- Parties reach final and comprehensive permanent status agreement that ends the Israel-Palestinian conflict in 2005, through a settlement negotiated between the parties based on UNSCR 242, 338, and 1397, that ends the occupation that began in 1967, and includes an agreed, just, fair, and realistic solution to the refugee issue, and a negotiated resolution on the status of Jerusalem that takes into account the political and religious concerns of both sides, and protects the religious interests of Jews, Christians, and Muslims worldwide, and fulfils the vision of two states, Israel and sovereign, independent, democratic and viable Palestine, living side-by-side in peace and security.
- Arab state acceptance of full normal relations with Israel and security for all the states of the region in the context of a comprehensive Arab-Israeli peace.

Political Profiles of Prominent Figures in Arab–Israeli Relations

ABBAS, Mahmud ('Abu Mazen'): Prime Minister of the Palestinian Authority, March–October 2003; b. 26 March 1935, in Safed, British Palestine Mandate. *Education:* he studied law in Cairo and obtained a doctorate in Moscow. *Career:* his doctoral thesis, which examined the secret links between Zionism and Nazism, identified him as a controversial figure from a relatively early stage. He was forced into exile following the publication of the book based on his thesis, which provoked allegations of holocaust denial. While in exile in Qatar he met a number of figures who would become influential in the Palestinian opposition to Israel, including Yasser Arafat (q.v.) and, in 1957, was a founder member of Fatah. He travelled with what became the leadership of the PLO as its base moved around the Arab world. Allegations by a former ally that he was involved in the funding of the terrorist attacks on Israeli athletes during the Olympic Games in Munich, Germany, in 1972 have never been corroborated. It is clear that he became a senior political figure in the PLO, and led its delegations in various negotiations. This process culminated in his participation in the negotiations leading to the Oslo Accords in 1993. He remained a senior figure in the PLO, as Secretary-General, while Arafat became the face of the emerging Palestinian political entity. When it became clear in the early 2000s that Israel and, later, the USA had abandoned hope of being able to negotiate successfully with Arafat, pressure grew for reform of the Palestinian Authority (PA) and the appointment of an executive Prime Minister. As a senior PLO figure with generally a more moderate position than Arafat, Abbas was an obvious choice for Palestinians, and he was considered an acceptable candidate by Israel and the international community. Following protracted negotiations on the necessary reforms of the PA, he became Prime Minister in March 2003. His tenure was marked from its beginning by disputes with Arafat, chiefly over security policy and the delineations of the executive powers of the presidency and the premiership. Despite the re-emergence of accusations of holocaust denial regarding his book, he maintained relatively good relations with Israel, and led the Palestinian delegations in the early negotiations on the 'roadmap' peace proposals. However, his moderate, pragmatic position brought him into conflict with the Palestinian paramilitary groups, and as his relationship with Arafat continued to deteriorate, his position soon became untenable. He resigned in September 2003, claiming that he enjoyed the support of neither Arafat, nor the paramilitaries, nor Israel. He remained in office until the formation of a new government by his successor, Ahmed Quray (q.v.) in October. *Address:* c/o Palestinian Authority, Ramallah, West Bank.

ARAFAT, Yasser (Muhammad Abd ar-Raouf Arafat as Qudwa al-Husseini): Chairman of the PLO 1968–, Palestinian Executive President 1996–; b. 24 August 1929, in Cairo, Egypt; m. Sulia Tawil in 1991, one d. *Education:* he studied civil engineering at King Fuad University, Cairo. *Career:* While at university, Arafat joined the League of Palestinian Students, becoming its President in 1952. Following the completion of his studies, and after fighting with the Egyptian army in the conflict with Israel in 1956, he established an engineering business in Kuwait. He remained politically active, however, and in 1957 he formed, together with 'Abu Jihad' (Khalil al-Wazir, q.v.), the clandestine Palestinian movement, Fatah. Arafat took the group into the PLO in 1968, becoming its Chairman. Following the Arab League's recognition of the PLO as the sole legitimate representative of the Palestinian people in 1974, Arafat addressed the UN General Assembly, warning of violence if proposals for a Palestinian state were not considered. The conflict which ensued throughout the 1970s and 1980s and the problems it caused for Israel's neighbours forced Arafat to move the Organization's headquarters from Jordan to Lebanon in 1970 and from there to Tunisia following the invasion of Israeli troops and subsequent siege of Beirut in 1982. Discontent at Arafat's personal style of politics caused two prominent members, 'Abu Musa' and 'Abu Saleh', to dispute his leadership the following year, although the discord was eventually resolved by the intervention of Saudi Arabian diplomats. Throughout his period as PLO leader Arafat was the target of assassination attempts and suffered from ill health. However, he was able to maintain power, sometimes precariously, whenever threatened. In November 1988 he declared that the PLO would renounce armed insurgency and recognize the state of Israel. While this improved the Organization's relations with the West, Arafat's subsequent decision to support the Iraqi invasion of Kuwait in 1990 not only caused relations with the USA and its allies in the ensuing conflict to deteriorate but also deprived the PLO of crucial funding from the Arab petroleum-producing nations. Following the conclusion of the war, Arafat entered into a series of secret negotiations with the Israeli Government in Norway, following which he concluded a 'Declaration of the Principles of Self-Rule in the Occupied Territories' (known as the Oslo Accords) in November 1993. For his efforts he received the Nobel Prize for Peace, jointly with the Israeli Prime Minister, Itzhak Rabin (q.v.), and Minister of Foreign Affairs, Shimon Peres (q.v.), the following October. Although he had been successful in securing a certain amount of self-rule in the Occupied Territories, delegates at a subsequent PLO conference regarding the Oslo Accords criticized his handling of the discussions as being autocratic and one of his aides who had attended the negotiations, Haider Abdel Shafei, resigned. At the signing of documents providing for elections in the Gaza Strip and Jericho in May 1994, his refusal to sign an agreement with Israel relating to the size of the Jericho enclave caused a further crisis of confidence in his leadership and prompted several members to boycott a conference in Cairo. Nevertheless, in January 1996, he was elected President of the Palestinian National Authority, gaining 87.1% of votes cast. During his first years as President he again encountered criticism for his autocratic style of leadership, particularly for his delay of 10 months in accepting the resignation of leading members of the Cabinet accused of corruption in 1998. In 1998 he concluded the Wye River Memorandum with the Israeli Prime minister, Binyamin Netanyahu (q.v.).

Amid the deterioration in Israeli–Palestinian relations resulting from the Al-Aqsa *intifada* in 2000–01, the Israeli Government was increasingly critical of Arafat, claiming that he was not making sufficient effort to detain members of Islamist groups responsible for attacks on Israel. However, the increasing popularity of these groups among Palestinians following Israel's military responses made Arafat's position as the leader of the Palestinians, hitherto seemingly impregnable, appear vulnerable to challenges. In December 2001 the Israeli Prime Minister, Ariel Sharon (q.v.), announced that his Government would terminate relations with Arafat as President of the PNA since it considered him irrelevant to the State of Israel. During the course of 2002 and 2003 Israeli forces made numerous incursions into Arafat's compound in Ramallah, effectively keeping him under house arrest for long periods. With a travel ban enforced and the USA joining Israel in its refusal to work with him, Arafat had little choice but to accept constitutional reforms creating the post of Prime Minister, in order for the peace process to be rescued. However, Arafat was reluctant to grant too much of his power, particularly over internal security, to the new premiership, and continued disagreement over competencies of the two positions was considered a major reason for the resignation of the first premier, Mahmud Abbas (q.v.). With his international credibility unlikely to recover, and Israel growing increasingly strident in its dismissal of him, by late 2003 it was difficult to imagine Arafat ever regaining his position as the pre-eminent Palestinian figure on the international stage. *Address:* c/o Palestinian National Authority, Jericho Area, West Bank via Israel.

ABDULLAH IBN ABD AL-AZIZ AS-SA'UD: Crown Prince of Saudi Arabia; b. August 1921, in Riyadh; m. (four wives), with more than 20 c. *Education:* he was educated at the royal court. *Career:* he was groomed for political office, becoming Commander of Saudi Arabia's National Guard in 1962, a post he has held ever since. In the mid-1970s he was appointed to political office as Second Deputy Prime Minister. His interest in Western culture and politics made him an ideal candidate for a role centred on improving the country's international relations, and he was a frequent visitor to the USA. He became Crown Prince and First Deputy Prime Minister in 1982, retaining his role as interlocutor with Western governments and regularly representing Arab frustration at apparent bias towards Israel in the handling of the Arab–Israeli dispute. A devout Muslim, he believed that the cause of Islam, while of paramount importance to his country, could best be furthered by an element of dialogue with the West, and he reluctantly supported the presence of a US military force at an air base in the north of the country following the conflict precipitated by Iraq's invasion of Kuwait in 1990. When his half-brother, King Fahd, was incapacitated by a stroke in 1995, Abdullah assumed the functions of monarch and premier. He was seen as relatively liberal, for a Saudi leader, and refused to accept public and clerical pressure to distance the country from the West. He acknowledged the presence of extreme Islamist elements in Saudi Arabia following the terrorist attacks on the USA of September 2001, and risked unpopularity by co-operating with the US Administration and detaining many suspected terrorists. However, he considered certain Western allegations that his country was a sponsor of religious terrorism to be an insult to both Islam and Saudi Arabia. From this time onwards, he became increasingly interested in the prospect of peace with

Israel. He worked on the drafting of a series of Arab proposals for progress in the peace process, and he presented the plan to the USA in April 2002. Although little came of the proposals, and accusations of links between the Saudi Government and Islamist terrorist organizations continued to emerge, he remained a key Western ally and a focus for negotiations with the Arab world on the Arab–Israeli question. *Address:* Council of Ministers, Murabba, Riyadh 11121.

ABDULLAH IBN AL-HUSSEIN: King of Jordan, 2000–; b. 30 January 1962, Amman, s. of King Hussein ibn Talal (q.v.); m., with one s. and two d. *Education:* he was educated in Amman, the United Kingdom and the USA, before attending the British Royal Military College and the University of Oxford. *Career:* following the completion of his studies he joined the Jordanian military, rising to the rank of Captain, commanding a tank division before transferring to the air force. Following a break, during which he undertook a postgraduate course at Georgetown University (USA), he resumed his military career, rising to the rank of Colonel. His father, who was seriously ill, proclaimed him Crown Prince (a title he had held at birth, before it was bestowed upon his uncle in 1965) in 1995, following reports of the King's dissatisfaction with his brother's performance as regent during his absences from the country. Abdullah acceded to the throne upon his father's death in February 1999. Although his involvement with the Arab–Israeli peace process was initially less high-profile than had been his father's, it remained a priority for him, not least because the activities of militant Islamist Palestinian groups represented the greatest threat to the country's political stability, and any progress would tend to diminish those groups' willingness to use force against a moderate Arab regime. In the early 2000s, a time of particular disagreement between the USA and much of the Arab world, Abdullah sought (as had his father) to maintain close relations, despite domestic criticism, insisting that to do so was in the best interests of Jordan and of the peace process. The fact that his wife is Palestinian earned him support among much of Jordan's Palestinian community, despite criticism of his perceived conciliatory attitude towards Israel and the USA. While it appeared unlikely that the Hashemite monarchy would ever regain its position as perhaps the key Arab party in the peace process, Abdullah's continuation of his father's moderate policies suggested that the Jordanian leader would always have a role. *Address:* Royal Hashemite Court, Amman, Jordan.

ANNAN, Kofi: Ghanaian international civil servant, UN Secretary-General, 1997–; b. 8 April 1938, in Kumasi; m., with one s. and two d. *Education:* he studied economics at the University of Kumasi, Macalester University, MN, USA, Massachusetts Institute of Technology and the Institut des Hautes Etudes, Geneva (Switzerland). *Career:* he entered the service of the UN in 1962, as an economist with the World Health Organization. Successful in positions with a number of UN bodies, he became a Deputy Secretary-General in 1987. Following Iraq's invasion of Kuwait in 1990 he oversaw the repatriation of UN staff from Iraq, and he subsequently led the early negotiations for what became known as the 'oil-for-food' programme in that country. He was appointed Under Secretary-General in 1993, and was charged with overseeing events in the former Yugoslavia, following the signing of peace agreements in the conflict there. He became Secretary-General in 1997, stating that his priorities were to promote peace and to change the UN in response to a changing world. Direct UN involvement in the Arab–Israeli dispute was relatively slight in the initial stages of his term of office, but following the escalation in violence in 2000 Annan became closely personally identified with the search for a solution to the conflict. He repeatedly urged all sides to abandon violence and resume negotiations. He swiftly became unpopular with the Israeli media, however, which perceived his criticisms of Israeli violence as excessive compared with those of violence against Israel. This unpopularity spread to diplomatic circles in March 2002 when he urged Israel's abandonment of what he termed its 'illegal occupation of Palestinian areas', an unusually strong choice of words for the holder of his position. Although he still carried considerable weight in the peace process, the UN being one of the members of the Quartet of 'roadmap' sponsors, by this time his comments were rarely well received by the Israeli public. This was exacerbated following the events at the Jenin refugee camp in April 2002—Israel perceived that Annan's call for an investigation by a special commission amounted to a prejudgement of the case and an acceptance of a partial, Palestinian version of events. While much of the world continued to perceive him as an honourable, capable diplomat, he was all but totally discredited in Israel. However, he refused to reduce his involvement in the issue, reiterating that his central point was that both sides must end violence in order for peace to be viable. He accepted the Nobel Peace Prize on behalf of the UN in 2001. *Address:* Office of the Secretary General, United Nations, United Nations Plaza, New York, NY 10017, USA.

ASHRAWI, Hanan: Palestinian politician and academic; b. 1946, m. Emil Ashrawi, with two d. *Education:* she studied at the American University of Beirut, Lebanon and the University of Virginia, USA. *Career:* A Christian Palestinian, before entering politics Ashrawi held the position of Dean of Arts and Chair. of the English Department at Birzeit University in the West Bank from 1973–90. It was, however, her participation in a US-televised debate between four Israelis and four Palestinians regarding the Middle East Peace Process in April 1988 that established her reputation for eloquently voicing Palestinian concerns. In 1991 she was appointed by the leader of the PLO, Yasser Arafat (q.v.), as a spokeswoman for the Palestinian delegation at the Madrid Peace Conference. She resigned from this position in 1993, following the concluding of the Declaration of Principles on Palestinian Self-Rule by the PLO and Israel at Washington, DC, USA, claiming that the agreement conceded too much to Israel. On her return to the West Bank, Ashrawi founded the Palestinian Independent Commission for Citizens' Rights in 1993. Following the establishment of the Palestinian National Authority, she was elected as an independent candidate to the Palestinian Legislative Council. Arafat appointed her Minister of Higher Education, a position which she held until August 1998 when, together with several other prominent politicians, she resigned in protest at corruption in the Cabinet—Ashrawi had also been critical of the PLO's human rights record. Wounded during Israeli military actions near her home in March 2001, in July the League of Arab States (Arab League) appointed her as their official spokeswoman. *Address:* c/o Arab League, POB 11642, Arab League Building, Tahrir Sq., Cairo, Egypt.

ASSAD, Lt-Gen. Bashar al-: President of Syria 2000–; b. 11 September 1965, Damascus, s. of Hafiz al-Assad (q.v.); m.; *Education:* he studied medicine in Damascus and in London. *Career:* he practised ophthalmology in the United Kingdom, and married the daughter of a prominent figure in London's Syrian community. He returned to Syria in 1994 following the death of his elder brother, Basil, who was widely understood to have been groomed to succeed to the presidency after his father's eventual departure from office. Bashar al-Assad became the 'heir apparent', a role for which he was, at the time, completely unprepared. He enrolled in the country's military academy, eventually reaching the rank of Colonel, before leaving to oversee a number of modernization and information technology programmes. After his father's death in June 2000 he was immediately claimed as the next President, although he had not reached the constitutionally required age of 35 years—the country's legislature swiftly amended the Constitution to permit his election to the office, and elected him immediately. His time spent living in the United Kingdom and his stated interest in information technology led to hopes of an outlook more friendly to the West than that of his father, and of an enthusiasm for peace in the region. However, despite some moves towards allowing a free press and ending political detentions, many of his domestic and foreign policies proved very similar to those of his father. Initial public statements of enthusiasm for peace with Israel amounted to little, and the prospect of any progress on the Syrian track of Arab–Israeli peace receded. However, following severe and sustained criticism from the USA, before, during and after that country led a military intervention in Syria's neighbour, Iraq (Syria was accused of supporting terrorism, of assisting the regime of Saddam Hussain in Iraq and of developing its own weapons of mass destruction, among other allegations), Assad, who fiercely criticized the US action, exhibited renewed enthusiasm for dialogue with Israel. He proposed negotiations on numerous issues, including the status of the Golan Heights, the most important issue for many Syrians; Israel responded by inviting him to Jerusalem for talks. Although Assad declined the offer, stating that some of the attached conditions were unacceptable, by the end of 2003 it appeared that Syria was more open to the idea of some form of diplomatic contact with Israel than it had been for some time. *Address:* Office of the President, Damascus, Syria.

ASSAD, Lt-Gen. Hafiz al-: President of Syria, 1971–2000; b. 1928, in Qardaha; m., with four s. (one deceased) and one d. *Education:* he studied at a number of military institutions. *Career:* Assad pursued a successful career in the Syrian army, culminating in his appointment as Minister of Defence and Commander-in-Chief of the Air Force in 1965. In 1971 he led a *coup d'état* against the President of Syria, Dr Nur ad-Din al-Atassi, and assumed the office himself. A strong anti-Zionist, the main aims of his foreign policy were to establish Syria as a leading guardian of Arab interests in the Middle East and recover the Golan Heights region lost to Israel in the 1967 Arab–Israeli war. Consequently, in the 1970s he sought to secure close relations with Syria's Arab neighbours, assisting Egypt with attacks on Israeli territory in October 1973 and forming a Supreme

Command Council with King Hussein (q.v.) of Jordan, to co-ordinate military operations against Israel. President Assad also intervened in the Lebanese civil war in 1976 on the side of the mainly Muslim Lebanese National movement in order to establish Syrian influence in the country and guard against potential Israeli attacks. In May 1983 Assad attempted to gain control of the PLO by supporting a revolt against the leader, Yasser Arafat (q.v.), but was unsuccessful. Assad was also among the first of the Arab leaders to terminate diplomatic relations with Egypt and condemn its President, Anwar Sadat (q.v.), for attending peace negotiations with the Israeli Government in 1977. Sadat's eventual success in reducing Egypt's diplomatic isolation in the Arab world began to threaten Assad's aims of leading the Arab resistance against Israel in the Middle East. Instead, Assad concentrated on increasing Syria's influence in Lebanon, urging its Government to abrogate a treaty it made with Israel in 1984, while ensuring that Syrian troops remained stationed there. However, the restoration of diplomatic relations between Syria and Egypt in 1989 indicated a new direction in Assad's policy on Israel. In 1991 he attended a regional peace conference in Madrid, Spain; despite being critical of the Oslo Peace Accords concluded by Arafat and the Israeli Government in 1993, in 1995 Assad's Government agreed with Israel to a 'framework understanding' on security arrangements in the Golan Heights. Subsequent peace negotiations with the Israeli Government were hampered, however, by Israel's disputing of Assad's claim that before his assassination, Prime Minister Itzhak Rabin (q.v.) had agreed to a full Israeli withdrawal from the Golan Heights. The last attempt by the US President, Bill Clinton (q.v.), to persuade Assad to resume negotiations with Israel at talks in Switzerland in March 2000, failed. Assad died on 10 June 2000.

BARAK, Ehud: Prime Minister of Israel, 1999–2001; b. 2 February 1942, Israel; m. Nava Cohen, with three d. *Education:* he studied at the Hebrew University in Jerusalem and at Stanford University, USA. *Career:* Before entering politics, Barak pursued a distinguished military career, culminating in his appointment as Director of Military Intelligence of the IDF from 1982–86 and as Chief of General Staff from 1991–94. During the Six-Day War he commanded a reconnaissance group and, in the Yom Kippur conflict, led the campaign on the Sinai Front. He also co-ordinated the IDF withdrawal from Jericho and the Gaza Strip in 1994. On his retirement from the military in 1995, he was elected to the Knesset, representing Labour, and was appointed Minister of the Interior by the Prime Minister, Itzhak Rabin (q.v.). As Minister of Foreign Affairs in Shimon Peres' (q.v.) administration in 1995–96, he was instrumental in negotiating the Israeli-Palestinian Interim Peace Agreement in Oslo and the separate peace with Syria. In 1997 he was elected to replace Peres as Chairman of the Labour Party. His centrist policies helped him to secure victory in the prime-ministerial elections held in May 1999, defeating the incumbent, Binyamin Netanyahu (q.v.), whose handling of the peace process had been blamed for the deterioration of the Israeli economy. Barak's newly formed Labour alliance, One Israel, also won the largest number of seats in the Knesset. Despite a favourable start to his term in office, in which he exchanged words of mutual respect with President Hafiz al-Assad (q.v.) of Syria and held a series of summit meetings with Arab and European leaders, the peace process was to cause problems for Barak. In July 1999 the Palestinian delegation rejected Barak's proposal to postpone the implementation of the terms of the Wye Memorandum to combine it with discussions on the final status negotiations. The following month Barak accused the Palestinians of refusing to compromise, prompting them to abandon the talks. Although he concluded a revised version of the Wye Memorandum with the Palestinian leader, Yasser Arafat (q.v.), in September 1999, he failed to implement its provisions. Barak's last year in office was overshadowed by violence on the West Bank and Gaza Strip, known as the al-Aqsa *intifada*. He resigned from the premiership in January 2001 and was defeated in the consequent election to the post by the Likud candidate, Ariel Sharon (q.v.). *Address:* Israeli Labour Party, 110 Ha'yarkon St, Tel-Aviv 61032, Israel; tel: 3-5630666; fax: 3-5282901.

BEGIN, Menahem Wolfovitch: Prime Minister of Israel 1977–83; b. 16 August 1913, in Brest-Litovsk, Russia (now Brest, Belarus); m. Aliza Arnold, with one s. and two d. *Education:* He studied law at the University of Warsaw. *Career:* Begin was appointed head of the activities of the Zionist organization, Betar, in Czechoslovakia, being promoted to leader of Betar Poland in 1938. Following a period of detention in a Soviet prison camp in Siberia during the early years of the Second World War, he joined the Free Polish Army and was dispatched to Palestine for training. In 1942 he helped to found the Zvai Leumi Irgun movement, which campaigned against the British Mandate. Irgun was disbanded on the independence of the state of Israel and Begin was appointed Chairman of the newly formed Herut party. As the leader of the opposition in the Knesset he in particular protested against the Government's conclusion, in 1952, of an agreement with the Federal Republic of Germany concerning war reparations. From 1967–70, he served as a minister without portfolio in the Government of Golda Meir (q.v.), before leaving to form the Likud bloc. In 1977, Likud defeated Labour to win the largest number of seats in an election to the Knesset and Begin was appointed Prime Minister, leading a coalition Government. In December he became the first Israeli Prime Minister to visit Egypt and, in the following year, he concluded with the Egyptian President, Anwar Sadat (q.v.), two agreements which provided a framework for a peace treaty between the two countries in March 1979. In October 1978, Begin and Sadat were jointly awarded the Nobel Peace Prize. He retained the premiership following the legislative election held in 1981. In June 1982 his defence minister, Ariel Sharon (q.v.), ordered the invasion of Lebanon by Israeli troops, ostensibly to destroy bases of the PLO in the country's territory. Following the death of his wife, Begin experienced depression, thought to be exacerbated by the unforeseen length and difficulty of the Lebanese war. He resigned from the position of Prime Minister in September 1983. He died on 9 March 1992 in Tel-Aviv.

BEN-GURION, David: Prime Minister and Minister of Defence of Israel, 1948–53, 1955–63; b. David Grün, 16 October 1886, in Plonsk, Russia (now Poland); m. Paula Monbaz. *Education:* he graduated from the University of Constantinople (now İstanbul, Turkey) in 1914 with a degree in law. *Career:* Having migrated to Palestine in 1906, he became a member of the central committee of the Po'alei Zion (Workers of Zion) movement. Following a brief period of exile, he returned in 1917 to assist the British military in expelling the Ottoman forces from Palestine and subsequently helped to found the Israeli Labour Party. From 1935–48, Ben-Gurion acted as chairman of the executive committee of the Jewish Agency of Israel, advising the British Government on the establishment of a Jewish homeland in Palestine. However, the issue of legislation ('The White Paper') by the British Government in 1939, which included measures to restrict Jewish immigration and land purchase in Palestine, prompted him to argue that while Zionists should fight alongside the British in the Second World War, they should also fight the British White Paper as if there were no war. He was instrumental in the drafting of the Biltmore Programme of 1942, which included a demand for the formation of a Jewish state, and in the same year assumed the defence portfolio of the Jewish Agency Executive. On the declaration of Israel's independence on 14 May 1948 he was appointed to the post of Prime Minister. During his tenure he sought to consolidate the Jewish state, creating the Israeli Defence Force and encouraging Jewish immigration. In an attempt to secure the economic future of Israel, in 1952 he concluded a reparations agreement with the Government of the Federal Republic of Germany, attracting severe criticism from opposition groups. In 1953 he retired to the Sede Boker kibbutz. He returned to politics in 1955 to assume the defence portfolio and, later in the same year, he resumed the office of Prime Minister. In 1956 Ben-Gurion ordered the military occupation of the Gaza Strip and the Sinai Peninsula. Divisions within his party, principally over the imposition of military government in Arab-inhabited areas, forced him to resign as Prime Minister in June 1963. Having retained his position in the Knesset, he was a founder member of the Rafi party in 1965 and established the Hareshima Hamalachit in 1968, although he achieved little success with these parties and in 1970, retired from politics. He died on 1 December 1973 at Sede Boker.

BERNADOTTE, Folke, Count of Wisborg: UN Mediator; b. 2 January 1895, Stockholm, Sweden; m. 1928, Estelle Romaine, with two s. *Education:* Karlberg military school and Stromsholm military riding school. *Career:* A nephew of King Gustavus V, Bernadotte served in the Swedish armed forces, obtaining the rank of Major in 1941. As Vice-Chairman of the Swedish Red Cross Society during the Second World War, he supervised the evacuation of Norwegian and Danish inmates from German prison camps and acted as a mediator in peace negotiations between the German Government and the British and US authorities. Following the outbreak of the first Arab–Israeli War, the UN appointed him as mediator on 20 May 1948, charged with seeking a solution to the conflict. He arranged a conference between Arab and Jewish leaders in Palestine, which resulted in a four-week cease-fire beginning in June. Bernadotte's peace plan required Israel to surrender the Negev to an Arab state in exchange for West Galilee, the limitation or suspension of immigration to Israel after two years and envisaged an economic and military union between the two states. The plan was rejected by both parties. Bernadotte was assassinated shortly afterwards, on 17 September 1948, by agents of the extreme Zionist organization, Stern (in 1950 the Israeli Government paid a sum in excess of US $50,000 to the UN, in reparation for his death).

BUSH, George Walker: President of the USA, 2001–; b. 6 July 1946, son of George Herbert Bush (US President 1989–93); m., with two d. *Education:* he studied at Yale and Harvard Universities. *Career:* he worked in the petroleum industry, founding Spectrum 7 Energy Corpn. Following a merger with Harken Energy Corpn in 1986 he became a director of the latter. He led a consortium that took control of the Texas Rangers Major League Baseball franchise in the early 1990s. His interest in politics had been heightened by his father's victory in the presidential election held in 1988, and following the sale of the Rangers he announced that he would contest the governorship of Texas in 1994. He won, but resigned the position in 2000 upon securing the Republican nomination for the presidential election. Despite numerous complaints and legal actions from his opponents, he was adjudged the winner in the state of Florida (where his brother was Governor), and that state proved decisive in the national election.

As President, his early policy towards the Middle East was less interventionist than that of his immediate predecessor, Bill Clinton (q.v.), preferring to observe the process, rather than drive it. This led many Arab politicians and commentators to accuse him of showing undue favour towards the status quo and, therefore, Israel—an accusation which had been levelled at his father and the previous Republican Presidents, Ronald Reagan and Richard Nixon (qq.v.). However, following the resumption of violence in 2000 his Administration began to acknowledge that the USA had a role to play in the dispute. The terrorist attacks on the USA of September 2001 and the roughly contemporary escalation in hostilities between Israel and the Palestinians hardened this view. In the prelude to the US-led intervention in Iraq in 2003 Bush began to state his belief that a just peace in the region was of prime importance. It became clear that Israel would not go uncriticized if the US Administration considered its actions excessive, and a number of military interventions in the Palestinian areas drew rebukes from Bush and his Secretary of State, Colin Powell (q.v.). Settlement activity was also termed as unhelpful on several occasions. However, he remained fiercely critical of Palestinian attacks on Israeli targets and joined the Israeli Government in refusing to deal directly with the Palestinian President, Yasser Arafat (q.v.).

By early 2003 Bush was in a position to sponsor the so-called 'roadmap' peace proposals, drawn up by the Quartet of the EU, Russia, the UN and the USA. However, following the failure in August of an initial cease-fire negotiated by members of Bush's Administration, the US profile in the faltering negotiations was again lowered. As he prepared to campaign for re-election, Bush was accused by some commentators of having a confused position on US involvement in the peace process. The military interventions in Afghanistan and Iraq had left him highly unpopular in most of the Arab world, and any successful personal involvement appeared unlikely in the short term. *Address:* The White House, Washington, DC 20500, USA. *Internet:* www.whitehouse.gov.

CLINTON, Bill (William Jefferson): President of the USA, 1993–2001; b. 19 August 1946, Hope, AR; m. Hillary Rodham 1975, one d. *Education:* Georgetown University, University College, Oxford, United Kingdom, Yale Law School; Professor, University of Arkansas Law School, 1974. *Career:* Before his election to the presidency in 1993, Clinton had held a number of state government offices in Arkansas, including that of Attorney-General and State Governor. Having inherited the US role at the series of bilateral talks that followed the Madrid Peace Conference in 1991, Clinton presided over the negotiations between the Palestinian leader, Yasser Arafat (q.v.), and the Israeli Prime Minister, Itzhak Rabin (q.v.), leading to the conclusion of the Oslo Accords in September 1993. The Declaration of Principles on Palestinian Self-Rule included in the Accords was signed at a ceremony at the White House in Washington, DC, at which the two leaders symbolically shook hands. When Arab–Israeli relations deteriorated following the Israeli Government's decision to open an archaeological tunnel close to the al-Aqsa mosque in September 1996, Clinton again mediated in crisis talks between Arafat and the Israeli Prime Minister, Binyamin Netanyahu (q.v.). While Clinton had supported the Israeli Government in its military campaign 'Operation Grapes of Wrath' against Hezbollah targets in Lebanon in 1996, he criticized the actions of Netanyahu's administration in support of the construction of a Jewish settlement at Har Homa, East Jerusalem, affecting a number of Arab towns. Nevertheless, together with King Hussein of Jordan (q.v.), he witnessed the signature of the Wye River Memorandum between Arafat and Netanyahu in October 1998, which provided for the redeployment of Israeli troops in the Occupied Territories and a series of talks on 'final status' issues (those concerning Jerusalem, Palestinian refugees and Jewish settlements). Clinton hosted the first of these discussions at the Erez check-point between Israel and Gaza the following December, and subsequently a further round in Ramallah in November 2000. At the same time, Clinton increased efforts to improve relations between Israel and its Arab neighbours. Having already been instrumental in the reconciliation between Israel and Jordan in 1994, in December 1999 he mediated in discussions between the Israeli Government and President Hafiz al-Assad of Syria (q.v.). However, these and further discussions in March 2000 achieved little progress. In the last six months of his presidency, Clinton invested a substantial amount of time in the Middle East peace process, beginning with discussions between Arafat and the Israeli Prime Minister, Ehud Barak (q.v.) at Camp David, USA, in July 2000. The outbreak of violence in the West Bank and Gaza in September following the visit of the Likud leader, Ariel Sharon (q.v.), to the disputed sacred site known as Temple Mount by the Jews and Haram ash-Sharif by Muslims prompted Clinton to lead a 'summit' meeting under the auspices of the UN in Sharm esh-Sheikh in Egypt. The meeting achieved some success in persuading both parties to agree to end the violence. In December 2000 Clinton made his final effort to mediate an agreement on the 'final status' issues between the Israeli Government and the Palestinian leadership. He is believed to have proposed that in return for the creation of a Palestinian state, comprising the Gaza Strip and 95% of the West Bank, the Palestinians relinquish their demand for the right of return for Palestinian refugees who were forced to leave their homes in 1948. Arafat rejected the plan. Clinton left the presidency upon the expiry of his second term of office in January 2001, his tenure being remembered as much for a number of financial and sexual scandals as for his efforts to mediate peace in the Middle East and in other major world disputes. *Address:* 55 W. 125th St, New York, NY; tel. (212) 348-8882; internet: www.clintonpresidentialcenter.com.

EBAN, Abba (Aubrey Solomon Meir): Israeli politician and diplomatist; b. 2 February, 1915, in Cape Town, South Africa. *Education:* he studied at the University of Cambridge, United Kingdom. *Career:* having moved to the United Kingdom with his family in childhood, Eban served in the British military during the Second World War. Towards the end of that conflict he served as the Allies' representative to the Jewish community in Palestine, and he represented the same community to the British Government after the end of the war, before deciding to return to what would shortly become the State of Israel. He became Israel's representative at the UN, negotiating the resolution approving the partition of Palestine, and serving as the country's Ambassador to the organization for more than 10 years (during much of which time he was also Ambassador to the USA). He returned to Israel and became a member of the Knesset, representing the Labour Party, in 1959. After three years as Deputy Prime Minister, in 1966 he was appointed Minister of Foreign Affairs, serving until 1974, throughout perhaps the most turbulent period of his country's short history. Seen by many Israelis as excessively moderate and conciliatory, he was the major negotiator of the text of Security Council Resolution 242, which has remained the framework for a peace settlement for more than 35 years. However, he later admitted that the conditions allowing for progress on the basis of Resolution 242 were never achieved. He remained in the Knesset during the Likud governments of the 1970s and 1980s, becoming Chairman of the influential Foreign Affairs and Security Committee in 1984, until quarrels with party leaders caused his departure from politics in 1988. He became a broadcaster and author and taught at several US universities. Although he was considered 'dovish' by many, he remained a respected figure in Israeli life, and was awarded the country's highest honour, the Israel prize, in 2001, the year before his death. A skilled speaker in several languages, he is credited with coining one of the best-known sayings used in the context of the Arab–Israeli dispute—that the Palestinians 'never miss an opportunity to miss an opportunity'.

EREKAT, Saeb: Palestinian Chief Negotiator, Palestinian National Authority Minister of Local Government; b. 1955, Jerusalem. *Education:* San Francisco State University, USA, University of Bradford, United Kingdom. *Career:* Erekat lectured on political science at the An-Najah University in Nablus and wrote for the *Al-Quds* newspaper before taking a prominent role in the negotiations leading to the Oslo Accords in 1993. Together with other senior negotiators, Hanan Ashrawi and Faisal Husseini (qq.v.), Erekat threatened to resign over Yasser Arafat's (q.v.) handling of the negotiations with the Israeli delegation, which he considered too autocratic. In 1996 Arafat appointed him head of the Palestinian Negotiation Steering and Monitoring Committee. In the same year he was elected to the Palestinian Legislative Council and appointed Minister of Local Government. Erekat led the negotiations for the implementation of the Arab-Israeli Interim Peace Agreement and in 1997 he was successful in securing a protocol from the Israeli Government for the redeployment of Israeli troops from the West Bank by 1998. The following year, however, amid rumours that Arafat would unilaterally declare an independent Palestinian state, Erekat again expressed dissatisfaction with the Palestinian leadership's attitude towards negotiations. Indignant that the speaker of the Palestinian Legislative Council, Ahmed Korai, had held direct talks with the

Israeli Prime Minister, Binyamin Netanyahu (q.v.), and his aides, Erekat resigned as Chief Negotiator in September. Erekat returned to the post in 1999, to lead the negotiations for the implementation of the terms of the Wye River Memorandum. His frustration at Israel's delay in releasing Palestinian prisoners and redeploying troops from the West Bank became apparent when he requested the US Secretary State, Madeleine Albright, to intervene in August. The following February he took the unusual step of issuing the Israeli delegation with a series of questions regarding its position on redeployment and other issues, stating that the Palestinians were prepared to resume discussions only after the receipt of the Israeli answers. He continued to pursue a strict line of negotiation, immediately dismissing an Israeli government pledge in May 2001 to halt any further construction in Arab areas on the condition that existing Jewish settlements be allowed to develop internally. The stalling of the peace process proved particularly frustrating for a negotiator such as Erekat. An Arafat loyalist, he was appointed Minister for Negotiations in the Government formed by Mahmud Abbas (q.v.) in April 2003. He resigned the post after being excluded from the delegation for the first meeting between Abbas and the Israeli Prime Minister, Ariel Sharon (q.v.). However, following Abbas' resignation, he was reappointed chief negotiator. *Address:* Palestine Liberation Organization, Negotiation Affairs Department, POB 22445, Ramallah, West Bank via Israel.

ESHKOL, Levi: Prime Minister of Israel, 1963–69; b. 1895, in Ukraine. *Education:* he attended the Hebrew Gymnasium, Vilna, Poland. *Career:* Eshkol emigrated to Palestine in 1914 and began working as an agricultural labourer. Following the expulsion of the Ottoman forces from Palestine by the British, he served in the Jewish Legion of the British army from 1918–20. As a representative of the Assembly of the Palestinian Jewry, in 1935 he succeeded in securing an agreement with the German National Socialist Government for the transfer of German-Jewish property to Palestine. In 1944 he became Secretary of Mapai and a member of the Executive of Histadruth. He proceeded to the position of Head of the World Zionist Organization in 1948 and began to work for the Settlement Department of the Jewish Agency. In the administration of David Ben-Gurion (q.v.) he served as Minister of Agriculture and Development (1951–52) and Minister of Finance (1952–63). When Ben-Gurion resigned as Prime Minister in June 1963, Eshkol was appointed as his replacement. He worked to develop Israel's diplomatic relations, making the first visit of an Israeli Prime Minister to the USA in 1964 and concluding negotiations begun by Ben-Gurion for the re-establishment of diplomatic relations with the Federal Republic of Germany. Domestically, he succeeded in merging the rival Labour factions to form the Labour Alignment, which was victorious in the 1965 legislative election. Despite his own conviction that the Government's policy towards the Arabs should be conciliatory rather than aggressive, as war with Egypt and Syria appeared increasingly likely in 1967, Eshkol appointed his adversary within the movement, Moshe Dayan, as Minister of Defence. He also formed the first Government of National Unity, which included the opposition leader, Menachem Begin (q.v.). Following Israel's victory in the Six-Day War, he began talks with Palestinian leaders in the newly captured territories, in the hope of promoting peace. He died in office on 26 February 1969, following a heart attack.

GEMAYEL, Bachir: Lebanese military commander and politician; b. 10 November 1947, Beirut. *Education:* he studied at St Joseph's University, Beirut and in the USA. *Career:* he briefly practised law, before becoming a senior figure in Kataab, a right-wing political party founded by his father and popular among Lebanese Christians. As the political situation in Lebanon deteriorated in the mid-1970s, he formed a militia, which most observers now believe was financed by Israel. Gemayel's various groupings, known as the Christian Phalangists, fought against numerous Muslim factions in Lebanon, including the PLO, most of whose members were in exile there. Collaboration with Israel, though never admitted at the time, was increasingly close. Although the Phalangists had their own ends, it is believed that Gemayel considered them to be linked with those of Israel, especially following the latter's invasion of Lebanon in June 1982. In August of that year, Gemayel was elected President by the National Assembly (most Muslim members abstained in protest at the expulsion of the PLO from the country). However, before he could take office, as scheduled, one month later, he was assassinated at the Kataab headquarters. His principal significance to the Arab–Israeli dispute is that, in response to his death (among other factors), the Phalangists, protected by Israeli forces, attacked Palestinian refugee camps at Sabra and Chatila, in an operation alleged to have been approved by the Israeli defence minister, now Prime Minister, Ariel Sharon (q.v.). The action provoked highly emotional responses, Palestinians terming it a 'massacre'. The International Committee of the Red Cross estimated that 2,750 people were killed in the camps. Sharon's alleged involvement in the affair caused the extreme nature of his unpopularity with Palestinians, resulting in the controversy that surrounded his visit to Temple Mount/Haram ash-Sharif in September 2000, the event that proved the spark for the al-Aqsa *intifada*.

HUSSEIN IBN TALAL AL-HASHIMI: King of Jordan; b. 14 November 1935, Amman, Jordan; m. Princess Dina (marriage dissolved), one d.; m. Antoinette Gardiner (assumed the name Muna el-Hussein, divorced 1972), two s., two d.; m. Alia Baha Eddin Toukan (died 1977), one d., one s.; m. 1978 Lisa Najib Halaby (assumed the name Queen Noor), two d., two s. *Education:* he studied at Victoria College, Alexandria, Egypt, Harrow School and the Royal Military Academy, Sandhurst, United Kingdom. *Career:* When he formally acceded to the throne in 1953 at the age of 18 years, Hussein was required to contend with several issues relating to Israel, most notably the increasing influx of Palestinian refugees into Jordan, the use of the waters of the River Jordan, the definition of the border between the two countries and the status of Jerusalem. He sought security among his Arab neighbours, making a defence alliance with Egypt as war appeared imminent in 1967 and assisting the Syrian army in the Golan Heights during the Yom Kippur War of 1973. Despite conflict between his army and Palestinian guerrillas at the end of the 1960s, Hussein also joined the members of the Arab League in recognizing the PLO as the sole legitimate representative of the Palestinian people at the Rabat conference in 1974. In February 1985, he and the leader of the PLO, Yasser Arafat (q.v.), concluded an agreement on a joint peace intiative. Following the PLO's refusal to accept the resolutions of the UN as the basis for negotiations, however, the intiative failed and Hussein briefly attempted to increase Jordanian influence in the Occupied Territories by passing legislation which provided for greater West Bank representation in Jordan's House of Representatives and announcing a plan for investment in the area, although this was withdrawn in the late 1980s. Jordan's economic reliance on Iraq prompted Hussein to support the Iraqi invasion of Kuwait in 1990, describing the intervention of US forces and their allies as a war against all Arabs and Muslims. In the 1990s Hussein began to develop his role as a representative of the Palestinians in negotiations with the Israeli Government, undeterred by opposition both within the House of Representatives and among the Jordanian public. In 1994 he concluded both an agreement for economic co-operation between his Government and the PLO in the Occupied Territories and a peace treaty with Israel. The Washington Declaration, which was signed by Hussein and the Israeli Prime Minister, Itzhak Rabin (q.v.) in July 1994, ended the state of war between the two countries and appointed Hussein as the guardian of the Muslim holy places in Jerusalem. Diagnosed with lymphatic cancer in 1998, King Hussein continued to work towards peace in the Middle East as his health deteriorated. In October of that year he truncated a pro-gramme of chemotherapy treatment he was receiving in the USA in order to mediate between Arafat and the Israeli Prime Minister, Binyamin Netanyahu (q.v.), in negotiations for the Wye River Memorandum. Hussein died on 7 February 1999; the number of heads of state and prominent politicians from both Arab and Western nations who attended his funeral bore witness to the respect held for him throughout the world.

HUSSEINI, Faisal: Palestinian politician and negotiator; b. Baghdad, Iraq, 1940; m. Najat Husseini, one s. and one d. *Education:* University of Cairo, Military College, Syria. *Career:* Husseini was born into a highly respected Palestinian family in exile. His great uncle was the Grand Mufti of Jerusalem and his father died fighting for the Palestinian army during the 1948 Arab–Israeli war. It was as a student in Cairo that he first became involved in Palestinian causes by helping to establish the General Union of Palestinian Students. He soon abandoned his studies in favour of political campaigning for the Arab National Movement. In 1964 he moved to East Jerusalem and joined the PLO. It was during the 1987 *intifada* against Jordan, however, that his role as a Palestinian spokesman became apparent. Throughout the 1980s, he was imprisoned several times by Israel, during which time he opted to learn Hebrew, which he believed was essential for communicating to the Israelis the plight of the Palestinian people. Husseini subsequently acted as unofficial diplomat for the PLO, most importantly restoring relations with the USA following the Organization's decision to support the Iraqi leader, Saddam Hussain, during the conflict following Iraq's invasion of Kuwait in 1991. Although his work had facilitated the organization of the Madrid Peace Conference in October 1991, the Israeli Government objected to his inclusion in the Palestinian delegation since he resided in East Jerusalem. Husseini managed to maintain his involvement in the peace process, however, by his appointment to a PLO advisory committee. His residency in East Jerusalem similarly prevented him from candidacy in the 1996 Palestinian National

Authority elections. Nevertheless, he was appointed as Minister Without Portfolio by the Executive President, Yasser Arafat (q.v.), with special responsibility for Jerusalem affairs. Husseini continued with his diplomatic work, receiving foreign dignitaries at Orient House, the PLO offices in East Jerusalem. During a diplomatic mission to Kuwait on 31 May 2001, he suffered a heart attack and died.

JARRING, Gunnar: Special Envoy of the UN Secretary-General on the Middle East, 1967–91; b. 12 October 1907, Brunnby, Sweden; m. Agnes Charlier 1932, one d. *Education:* Lund University, Associate Professor of Turkic languages, Lund University, 1933–40. Jarring began his diplomatic career as Sweden's Attaché to Turkey 1940–41. He subsequently occupied diplomatic positions in Iran, Iraq, Ethiopia, Ceylon (now Sri Lanka), India and Pakistan before being appointed Sweden's Permanent Representative to the UN in 1956. He served on the UN Security Council from 1956–58, before returning to direct diplomatic service, as Ambassador to the USA in 1958. Subsequent ambassadorial postings included the USSR and Mongolia. Following the Six-Day War of 1967, Jarring was chosen as the Special Envoy of the UN Secretary-General on the Middle East with the mission of obtaining a peaceful solution to the conflict on the basis of UN Security Council Resolution 242, which condemned the acquisition of territory through war and recommended that Israeli troops withdraw from the Occupied Territories. His attempts to implement the Resolution were hampered by the refusal of Egypt and Israel to attend direct negotiations. However, in 1970 the newly elected President of Egypt, Anwar Sadat (q.v.), stated his willingness to pursue discussions with Israel, prompting Jarring again to propose that Israel and Egypt accept their obligations according to Resolution 242 in order to further peace negotiations. Israel again rejected Jarring's proposals. He left his diplomatic posts in 1973 and continued, albeit with a lower international profile, to represent UN peace initiatives in the Middle East until his retirement in 1991. *Address:* Pontus Ols vaeg 7, 26040 Viken, Sweden.

KISSINGER, Henry Alfred: US Secretary of State, 1973–77; b. 27 May 1923, Fürth, Germany; m. 1st Anne Fleisher 1949 (divorced 1964), one s. one d., m. 2nd Nancy Maginnes 1974. *Education:* Harvard University. *Career:* Following service in the US military he pursued an academic career at Harvard, in the Department of Government. He became a member of a number of state bodies in the fields of governance, defence and international relations, and was appointed consultant to the US Department of State in 1965. He accepted the appointment to the post of Assistant for National Security Affairs upon the election to the US presidency of Richard M. Nixon in 1968, assuming the post in the following year. During this period he began active involvement in the Arab–Israeli dispute, in addition to his role in negotiating the end to US military involvement in Viet Nam (for which he was awarded the Nobel Peace Prize in 1973). In September 1973 Kissinger was appointed Secretary of State, maintaining his previous position, and his involvement in the Middle East expanded. Almost immediately, he was active in the attempts to negotiate a cease-fire in the Yom Kippur War. He again animated efforts for peace in the Suez-Sinai region, through a series of visits to Middle Eastern leaders in February–March 1975 (known as 'shuttle diplomacy'); he later attributed the failure of this mission to

Israeli obstinacy. The consequent threat of a reassessment of US policy towards Israel prompted a further round of negotiations in August, and a limited agreement was signed in September. Although at times unpopular with all parties in the Arab–Israeli dispute, Kissinger formalized the USA's position as the most significant intermediary between the two groups. He remained Secretary of State until January 1977, when President Gerald Ford, who had succeeded Nixon, left office. Kissinger subsequently became a consultant on international affairs and an adviser to a number of companies and governments, most notably as a member of the US President's Foreign Intelligence Advisory Board from 1984–90. He remained a respected, if controversial, figure in the field of international relations into the 2000s. *Address:* 1800 K St NW, Suite 400, Washington, DC 20006, USA.

MEIR, Golda: Israeli Minister of Foreign Affairs 1956–66, Prime Minister 1969–74; b. Golda Mabovitz, 3 May 1898, in Kiev, Russia (now Ukraine); m. Morris Meyerson 1917 (separated 1956), one s. and one d. *Education:* Milwaukee Teachers' Seminary, Wisconsin, USA. *Career:* Meir first became active in Zionist organizations in Wisconsin, USA, to where her family had emigrated in 1906. In 1921 she and her husband migrated to Palestine, where she became involved in the Histadruth (General Federation of Labour) organization, serving as the secretary of its Women's Council of Labour in 1928. Following her membership of the Executive and Secretariat Federation of Labour from 1929–46, she was appointed Head of the Political Department of the Jewish Agency for Palestine in 1946. A signatory of Israel's Declaration of Independence in May 1948, she was subsequently appointed Ambassador to the USSR. In the same month, she travelled to Transjordan (now Jordan), disguised as an Arab woman, where she undertook to persuade King Abdullah not to attack Israel, but was unsuccessful. In 1949 she won a seat in an election to the Knesset, representing Mapai, and was appointed Minister of Labour and National Insurance. It was not until she took up the post of Minister of Foreign Affairs, in 1956, that she was persuaded to hebraize her name to Meir. In that year she was involved in the planning of the Israeli-French-British invasion of the Sinai Peninsula in response to the Egyptian nationalization of the Suez Canal and proceeded to strengthen Israel's relations with the USA and cultivate new connections with countries in Africa and Latin America. She relinquished the foreign-affairs portfolio in 1966 and subsequently served as General-Secretary of Mapai until 1968. On the death of the Prime Minister, Levi Eshkol (q.v.), the members of the Israel Labour Party (to which Mapai now belonged), elected Meir as Prime Minister in June 1969, a position she consolidated by leading the party to victory in legislative elections held in October of that year. Her term as Prime Minister came to be dominated by a series of disputes between right-wing and moderate factions within the party regarding the territories gained in the Six-Day War of 1967. These disagreements were widely considered to have contributed to Israel's lack of preparation for the Egyptian and Syrian attacks which began the Yom Kippur War in 1973. Despite the party's victory in the December 1973 elections, demands for a new leader persisted, and prompted her to resign in April 1974. Having suffered from leukaemia since 1966, she died on 8 March 1978.

MESHAAL, Khalid: Palestinian paramilitary leader; b. 1956, in the West Bank, Jordan. *Education:* he trained as a physics teacher. *Career:* A Jordanian Palestinian, he sought work elsewhere in the Arab world, and taught in Kuwait in the 1980s. He was believed to be a member of a number of Islamist groups at this time. Following Iraq's invasion of Kuwait in 1990 Meshaal, along with many other Palestinians fleeing from Kuwait, returned to Jordan. He developed closer links with the militant Islamist Palestinian organization Hamas, which, under leaders including Sheikh Ahmad Yassin (q.v.) and Abd al-Aziz ar-Rantisi (q.v.), had attracted much popular support during the *intifada*. Meshaal operated a fund-raising office in the Jordanian capital, Amman. It was here that, in 1997, Israeli agents poisoned him—his life was only saved after the Jordanian monarch, King Hussein ibn Talal (q.v.), demanded the antidote from Israel. However, the presence of such a prominent figure on Jordan's territory left many uncomfortable, and after his accession to the throne, Hussein's son, Abdullah ibn-al-Hussein (q.v.), ordered that the operation in Amman be closed and Meshaal deported. He relocated to Syria, effectively becoming the head of Hamas' international operations. Bitterly opposed to the peace process with Israel (whose legitimacy he refuses to recognise), that country's Government has held him responsible for planning and financing numerous suicide bombings. He is thought to represent Hamas at meetings of Palestinian factions that take place outside Israel or the Occupied Territories.

MOSKOWITZ, Irving I.: American entrepreneur and philanthropist; b. 1928, New York City, USA. *Career:* The son of Polish-Jewish immigrants, Moskowitz trained as a doctor before establishing a successful business in the construction of small hospitals. In 1968 he founded the Irving I. Moskowitz Foundation, whose remit included charitable work in the state of California in addition to the funding of Jewish settlement projects in the Occupied Territories—before and after this time he served as leader of a number of US Jewish organizations. Moskowitz's opening of a gaming hall in Los Angeles in 1988 increased the foundation's income considerably; however, it increased opposition to his activities in the USA. In 1997 he caused controversy by installing four Jewish families in apartments he had bought in the Arab neighbourhood in Ras al-Amud at a time when the Israeli Government was under pressure from the UN to cease the construction of Jewish settlements in East Jerusalem. Following public demonstrations and unrest, Moskowitz agreed with the Israeli Prime Minister, Binyamin Netanyahu (q.v.), to remove the settlers on the condition that they were replaced with 10 students to act as security guards. In May 1999, following the election of Ehud Barak (q.v.) as Prime Minister, Moskowitz announced that he was determined to construct 132 houses for Jewish families in Ras al-Amud. As well as settlement projects, he provided funds for the reopening of an archaeological tunnel close to the al-Aqsa mosque by the Israeli Government, which precipitated violence in the Gaza Strip and the West Bank. Moskowitz was also alleged to have made large donations to political parties and leading Israeli politicians, and was seen as an important link between Israel's settler community and the US Jewish community. Despite a relatively low personal public profile he remained a highly controversial figure, who attracted the opprobrium of many pro-peace groups, who saw his policies as obstructive to the Middle East peace process. *Address:* c/o The Irving I. Moskowitz Foundation, Hawaiian Gardens, CA, USA.

MUBARAK, (Muhammad) Hosni: President of Egypt, 1981–; b. 4 May 1928, in Kafr El-Moseilha, Minuffrya Governate; m. Susan Sabet, two s. *Education:* he graduated from the Military Academy and Air Force Academy, before attending Frunze General Staff Academy, Moscow (then USSR, now Russia). *Career:* Mubarak held a number of senior positions in the Egyptian army before being appointed Commander of the Air Force and Deputy Minister for Military Affairs in the administration of Anwar Sadat (q.v.) in 1972. The following year he was promoted to the rank of Lt-Gen. and the office of Vice-President. Following the assassination of Sadat in October 1981 Mubarak succeeded him in the presidency. He began his first term by completing negotiations begun by Sadat with Israel for the return of the Sinai Peninsula. Having demonstrated his commitment to the maintenance of good relations with Israel, Mubarak sought to end Egypt's consequent diplomatic isolation among the Arab nations. Through his support for Yasser Arafat (q.v.) during a rebellion against his leadership of the PLO in September 1983, Mubarak was able to effect a reconciliation between Egypt and the Palestinian leaders. He also secured Egypt's readmission to the OIC in March 1984 and negotiated with King Hassan of Morocco to end the country's suspension from the Arab League. His meeting with Shimon Peres (q.v.) in September of that year, during which the two leaders discussed ways of reviving the peace process, marked the beginning of Mubarak's role as an intermediary between the Arabs and Israelis. In September 1989 he announced a series of proposals, which he maintained the Israeli Government should accept to allow progress in its negotiations with the Palestinians, and subsequently negotiated with the USA regarding proposals for elections in the Occupied Territories. Mubarak also helped to mediate the Gaza Strip-West Bank Israeli–Palestinian Interim Agreement in September 1985. During the 1990s Mubarak became increasingly concerned that the lack of progress in the peace process would strengthen the cause of militant Islamist groups in his country. He aimed to secure a position as a major Arab leader with whom Israel could negotiate but, despite his role in the international diplomatic attempts to end the violence which escalated in the Gaza Strip and West Bank in September 2000, Mubarak concurred with the Arab League's decision in November, that the Israeli Government's policies were responsible for the unrest. Mubarak remained keen to seek solutions that could move the peace process forward, and Egypt regularly hosted cease-fire discussions among the Palestinian factions. *Address:* Office of the President, Al-Etehadia Bldg, Heliopolis, Cairo, Egypt.

NASRALLAH, Sheikh Hasan: Lebanese cleric, paramilitary and politician; b. 1960, Beirut. *Education:* he attended school in Beirut and in Tyre. *Career:* a Shi'a Muslim, he became especially devout in his mid-teens, and joined the Amal movement. He studied at the seminary in Najaf (Iraq), but was forced to leave that country in 1978 when its leader, Saddam Hussain, severely restricted the activities of Shi'a organizations. Amal had transformed into a secular movement, allowing the returned Nasrallah (who was teaching theology in Baalbek) and other young, militant clerics to fill the religious void in the movement's followers with their own ideology. Supporters of militant Islam became more numerous after the Israeli invasion of Lebanon in 1982, and the presence of an élite force from Shi'a Iran, sent to fight the Israeli forces, meant that they had military backing. The group organized attacks on Israeli forces, including suicide bombings, and by 1985 it had become known as Hezbollah (Party of God). Nasrallah served as its military commander in Beirut, and scored some notable victories over Amal forces. In 1992 he was appointed the organization's leader after Israeli security forces killed his mentor, Abbas Moussawi. Attacks on Israeli targets grew in frequency and success, and financial support continued to flow from Iran and, by the mid-1990s, Syria. Israel unilaterally withdrew its forces from Lebanon in 2000. Although this was hailed as a victory for Hezbollah, Nasrallah declared that the war with Israel was not (and would never be) over, and skirmishes continue in the border area. Hezbollah initially struggled to transform itself into a constitutional party in post-war Lebanon, but Nasrallah adapted to the changes required, and the movement continues to operate military and political wings. Although the focal point of Israel's clash with Islamist paramilitaries has moved to the West Bank and Gaza, Hezbollah remains a significant threat to the country's interests, owing to its ability to conduct large-scale operations. Nasrallah's commitment to the twin tracks of political and military Islamism appears unlikely to wane, especially while his popularity among Arabs across the region remains so high.

NASSER, Gamal Abd an-: Egyptian army officer and President of Egypt 1956–70; b. 15 January 1918, in Alexandria. *Education:* he attended the El-Masira Secondary School, Cairo, and the Military Academy, Cairo. *Career:* As a boy, Nasser was allegedly expelled from school for organizing an anti-British demonstration. Seventeen years later, in 1952, his secret revolutionary group, the Free Officers, staged a *coup d'état,* forcing the British to withdraw completely from Egypt. After initially taking a less prominent role in the Revolutionary Command Council, in November 1954 Nasser deposed the President of the Republic of Egypt and assumed the office himself. His position was consolidated in a new Constitution approved by plebiscite in 1956. Through his policies of land ownership reform and programmes of economic and social development, which became known as 'Arab socialism', he gained great popularity among Egyptians. In order to fund these programmes, Nasser announced in July 1956 that the Suez Canal Company had been nationalized. France and the United Kingdom contested this and, with the assistance of Israeli troops, occupied the Sinai Peninsula and carried out air raids in the region. The intervention of the UN in favour of Egypt and the subsequent establishment of a UN Emergency Force in the border area between Egypt and Israel caused Nasser to gain great popularity in the Arab world. Although he had earlier espoused a policy of Non-Alignment, under Nasser's rule Egypt's relations with the West deteriorated and the country concluded economic and arms agreements with the USSR. Nasser became President of the United Arab Republic upon the union of Egypt and Syria in 1958 (dissolved 1961); his personal style of leadership proved popular, but was frequently criticized as authoritarian. Following the Six-Day War with Israel in June 1967, in which the Arab participants were heavily defeated, discontent towards Nasser increased within Egypt, as some accused him of provoking the Israeli attacks. However, significant public demonstrations of support persuaded him to withdraw an offer of resignation. Although Nasser failed to secure a peace agreement with Israel, he was able to overcome his disapproval of the Palestinian guerrillas' rejections of US peace proposals and hijackings of Western aircraft to mediate a reconciliation between their leader, Yasser Arafat (q.v.), and King Hussein of Jordan (q.v.), confirmed shortly before his death from a heart attack, on 28 September 1970.

NETANYAHU, Binyamin: Prime Minister of Israel, 1996–99; b. 21 October 1949, Israel; m. Sara, with three c. *Education:* he graduated from Massachusetts Institute of Technology, and Harvard University, USA. *Career:* Following a period of service in the IDF, Netanyahu pursued a successful business career, managing companies in the USA and Israel, before entering politics. He worked for the Israeli embassy in Washington, DC, and, from 1984–88, served as the Israeli Permanent Ambassador to the UN. During his tenure of this office, he successfully campaigned for the UN Nazi War Crimes Archives to be opened in 1987. Having joined Likud, he was elected to the Knesset in 1988 and was appointed to the positions of Deputy Minister of Foreign Affairs and, subsequently, Deputy Minister in the Prime Minister's Office. Netanyahu was elected leader of Likud in 1993 and he worked to restore morale and support for the party following its electoral defeat in 1992. He was criticized, however, for appearing to cultivate right-wing support, following the assassination of the Prime Minister, Itzhak Rabin (q.v.). In May 1996 Netanyahu unexpectedly defeated Shimon Peres (q.v.) in the first direct elections to the premiership. His Government declared that it would never accept the formation of a Palestinian state, prompting violence on the West Bank. The situation worsened when Netanyahu authorized the opening of a tunnel near the al-Aqsa mosque. In 1997 Netanyahu suffered from a domestic political crisis, arising from allegations of corruption surrounding his appointment of an undistinguished lawyer, Roni Bar-On, as Attorney-General. Although Netanyahu was subsequently acquitted of fraud and breach of trust, his Government was defeated in a motion of 'no confidence', surviving only because the vote in favour did not achieve the absolute majority required. The following year, he concluded the Wye River Memorandum with the Palestinian leader, Yasser Arafat (q.v.), under the mediation of the US President, Bill Clinton (q.v.). His attempts to ratify the agreement in the Knesset, however, made apparent the divisions within his Government and he was forced to resign and arrange a general election. During the election campaign Netanyahu's leadership of Likud was challenged and when exit polls indicated his defeat, he resigned from both the leadership of the party and from the Knesset less than one hour after voting had closed. In March 2000 the police recommended that charges be brought against him and his wife for accepting free services during his term in office and keeping official gifts when he left. These were abandoned in September, however, and in December he announced his candidacy for forthcoming elections to the premiership, providing that the Knesset could either enact legislation removing the requirement for candidates to be members of the legislature or vote to dissolve itself. The Knesset refused to adopt either of these measures and he withdrew from the contest. His return to government came in December 2002 when, following the collapse of the previous coalition, Ariel Sharon awarded him the foreign affairs portfolio in the interim government. Netanyahu then aimed to complete his political rehabilitation by winning the Likud nomination for the general election scheduled for January 2003 (which the party was widely expected to win). Sharon defeated him easily, however, and duly won the election. Netanyahu was offered the post of economy minister. While this was commonly perceived as a demotion, Netanyahu later revealed that he had only accepted the position after receiving guarantees that he would have total control over economic policy. His return led commentators to suggest that Sharon might seem 'dovish' in comparison to a Netanyahu revived in enthusiasm, reputation and popularity—even some pro-Palestinian commentators stated that they considered Sharon preferable. *Address:* c/o Likud, 38 Rehar King George, Tel-Aviv 61231, Israel.

OLMERT, Ehud: Israeli politician, Mayor of Jerusalem 1993–2003; b. 30 September 1945, Binyamina; m., with four c. *Education:* he studied psychology and law at the Hebrew University of Jerusalem. *Career:* he qualified to practise law, but swiftly entered professional politics, securing election to the Knesset, representing Likud, in 1973 at the age of 28 years (he was, at the time, the legislature's youngest member). A popular and respected politician, he served on the Knesset's foreign affairs committee, and became its senior member in 1984. Despite seats on this committee being regarded by certain commentators as more prestigious than some ministries, he accepted the post of Minister of Minorities in the Government of Itzhak Shamir (q.v.) in 1988. He was appointed Minister of Health two years later. He left ministerial office (although he remained in the Knesset) when Likud lost power in 1992, and sought the party's nomination for the mayoral election in Jerusalem to be held the following year. He defeated the incumbent Mayor in November 1993, following a campaign dominated by the status of Jerusalem, an issue brought to prominence by the signing of the Oslo Accords two months earlier. Olmert was a firm advocate of the city's remaining undivided under Israeli control, although he acknowledged that its position as a holy place of Islam presented practical and moral difficulties. His decision to allow the opening of a tunnel beneath a sacred Islamic site in 1996 was blamed for causing significant civil unrest. He was re-elected in November 1998, resigning his Knesset seat (as required by new legislation) following his confirmation in office. The outbreak of the al-Aqsa *intifada* in September 2000 provoked renewed criticism of Olmert's handling of Palestinian public order. Olmert decided to return to the national political stage, and was again elected to the Knesset in February 2003. Ariel Sharon (q.v.), whose visit to Temple Mount/Haram ash-Sharif had sparked the 2000 violence, and who was now Prime Minister, appointed Olmert as one of his deputies, and assigned to him the trade and industry portfolio. Later in that year, Olmert, a fluent English-speaker who was popular with international politicians and broadcasters, began to advocate what had hitherto been unthinkable for many Israelis, particularly for Likud—the unilateral withdrawal from the Occupied Territories in order to secure a unified, Jewish-majority Israel. It was widely considered that Olmert's rhetorical skill had made him the ideal candidate to test public and international opinion on this controversial issue, which eventually drew more explicit support from Sharon. *Address:* Ministry of Trade and Industry, POB 299, Jerusalem 91002.

PERES, Shimon: Prime Minister of Israel, 1977, 1984–86 and 1995–96, Minister of Foreign Affairs, March 2001–; b. Shimon Persky, August 1923 in Vishneva, Poland (now Belarus); m. Sonia Gelman; two s. and one d. *Education:* he studied at New York University and Harvard University, USA. *Career:* Peres emigrated to Palestine with his family in 1934 and became involved with Zionist activities from an early age, being elected to the Secretariat of Hanoar Haved, a youth group connected to the General Federation of Labour. During the period of the British Mandate, he joined the clandestine opposition movement, Haganah. As Director-General of the Ministry of Defence (1953–59), he developed Israel's nuclear-weapons programme with the assistance of France. In 1959 he was elected to the Knesset representing the Mapai party, and was duly appointed Deputy Minister of Defence, a post he held until 1965. When David Ben-Gurion (q.v.) formed the Rafi party (Israeli Labour List) in 1965, Peres was appointed Secretary-General and did much to solicit support for the movement. In 1968, however, he was instrumental in reuniting Rafi with Mapai to form the Labour Party; although the party was narrowly defeated in legislative elections in 1974, Peres was appointed as Minister of Defence in the Government of National Unity led by Itzhak Rabin (q.v.). In this position he sought to restore morale in the armed forces following the Yom Kippur War of 1973. In 1977 the central committee of Labour unanimously elected him as Chairman and he briefly served as Prime Minister in an interim administration prior to the general election held in June, in which Labour was defeated. He retained the Labour leadership throughout the premiership of Menachem Begin (q.v.), however, and led the party to a narrow victory in the general election held in 1984. As Prime Minister he oversaw the withdrawal of most of the Israeli troops from Lebanon and secured a large loan from the USA with which to stablilize the Israeli economy. Following a defeat in the Knesset, Peres resigned and a Likud-dominated administration took office. In February 1992 Peres lost the leadership of the Labour Party to Rabin. Following Labour's victory in the legislative elections held in June, Rabin appointed Peres as Minister of Foreign Affairs and he helped to negotiate an agreement with the PLO, providing for a degree of autonomy in the Gaza Strip and Jericho. For his efforts he was awarded the Nobel Peace Prize, together with Rabin and Yasser Arafat (q.v., the leader of the PLO), in 1994. Following the assassination of Rabin in November 1995, Peres was once again elected Labour leader. As Prime Minister he authorized 'Operation Grapes of Wrath', a military campaign against alleged members and installations of Hezbollah in Lebanon in 1996. His reputation as a conciliatory figure was exploited by Likud prior to the country's first direct election to the premiership in May of that year, in which he was unexpectedly defeated by Binyamin Netanyahu (q.v.). With the return of Labour to power in 1999, Peres joined the Government led by Ehud Barak (q.v.) as Minister of Regional Co-operation and, the following June, sought election to the presidency, being defeated by the Likud candidate, Moshe Katsav. Despite the two men's differing reputations with regard to the peace process, Peres unexpectedly agreed to serve as Minister of Foreign Affairs in the coalition administration led by Ariel Sharon (q.v.) in March 2001, becoming the member of the Israeli political establishment with whom the Palestinians, including Arafat, could most successfully negotiate. Following Labour's withdrawal from the governing coalition in November 2002, it appeared that Peres would gradually retire from political life. However, following Labour's poor performance in the general election held in January 2003, he was approached with the idea that he might become interim leader of the party, while a new generation of politicians and a new set of policies was prepared. He agreed, and defeated two younger rivals to win the post, but stated that he would not remain leader beyond mid-2004. *Address:* Israeli Labour Party, 110 Ha'yarkon St, Tel-Aviv 61032, Israel; tel: 3-5630666; fax: 3-5282901.

POWELL, Colin Luther: US soldier and politician; b. 5 April, 1937, New York; m., with one s. and two d. *Education:* he studied at City College of New York and at George Washington University. *Career:* The son of Jamaican immigrants, he entered the US Army as a Lieutenant upon graduating from college, and became a career soldier. He rose to the rank of General, and received numerous decorations, before being appointed Chairman of the Joint Chiefs of Staff by President George H. Bush in 1989. During his period in this office he oversaw the US-led military action following Iraq's invasion of Kuwait in 1990. Following his retirement from the military in 1993, it was widely suspected that he would eventually enter politics, although he had never made overt political statements—indeed his party affiliation was far from certain. Rumours of possible presidential candidacies in both 1996 and 2000 were unfounded, but following the election of George W. Bush to the presidency in the latter year, he accepted the nomination to the post of Secretary of State, becoming the most senior African-American in the country's political history. Initially an internationally recognizable and popular figure, he was soon portrayed as rather more reserved and conciliatory in matters of foreign policy than the rest of the Administration, particularly with regard to Iraq, and rumours of disenchantment and a possible resignation began to emerge. However, he remained in office throughout the conflict and beyond. Powell, who retained an element of international popularity even among fierce opponents of the Bush Administration, then began a mission to revive the stalled Arab-Israeli peace process. While any hint of possible variation from the position of the Administration as a whole was keenly awaited, Powell proved rather more acceptable a mediator to the Palestinian side than many had expected, electing to meet Yasser Arafat (q.v.) in 2002, at a time when Israel insisted that the Palestinian leader was not a partner for peace, and anyone negotiating with him would not be welcomed. Although he subsequently accepted the Israeli position and advocated Arafat's removal from a negotiating position, he refused to alienate the Palestinians completely. Despite the competing attentions of the US-led 'war on terrorism', Powell was a constant figure in the peace process, even as he represented an Administration whose policy on Arab–Israeli relations was sometimes regarded as rather confused. *Address:* Department of State, 2201 C St, NW, Washington, DC 20520, USA. *Internet:* www.state.gov/secretary.

QURAY, Ahmed ('Abu Ala'): Palestinian Prime Minister, 2003–; b. 1937, Jerusalem. *Career:* a banker by profession, he joined Fatah in the 1960s. He became a senior, if low-profile, figure in the PLO during the 1970s, eventually becoming head of its commercial operations. Always regarded as a moderate within the PLO, he became a member of Fatah's central council in 1989, and was a member of the Palestinian delegation to the secret peace talks leading to the Oslo Accords in the early 1990s. Although a cerebral, undemonstrative figure, he enjoyed considerable personal popularity as his profile grew, and received the most votes in the Jerusalem area in the elections to the PLC in 1996. He was elected Speaker of that body at its first meeting, and retained that post until, in September 2003, he accepted the offer of the Palestinian leader, Yasser Arafat (q.v.), to succeed another long-time ally, Mahmud Abbas (q.v.), in the still-developing role of Prime Minister of the Palestinian Authority. The formation of his Government was delayed by reported quarrels with Arafat, said to be the main reason for his predecessor's departure, but he was confirmed in office in late November. A strong supporter of the 'roadmap' and a long-term opponent of violence against Israel, he was considered an acceptable negotiating partner by the Israelis. *Address:* Palestinian Authority, Ramallah, West Bank.

RABIN, Itzhak: Prime Minister of Israel, 1974–77, 1992–95; b. 1 March 1922, Jerusalem; m. Leah Schlossberg, 1948, one s. and one d. *Education:* he attended Kadoorie Agricultural School, Kfar Tabor and the military Staff College, United Kingdom. *Career:* Rabin began a distinguished military career in 1940, when he fought against British rule in the Jewish militia, Haganah. He commanded a force in the Arab-Israeli War in 1948 on the Jerusalem front and in 1964 was appointed Chief of Staff of the IDF. In 1967 he led the IDF in the Six-Day War, capturing large areas of Arab land. In 1968 he retired from the army and was appointed Ambassador to the USA; during his tenure he succeeded in securing US support for Israel and pledged to protect Western interests in the Middle East. Following his election to the Knesset representing Labour, in April 1974 he was appointed Minister of Labour, only to be promoted to the premiership when Golda Meir (q.v.) resigned two months later. During his term in office he worked to improve Israel's economy and strengthen the IDF. Rabin resigned as leader of the Labour Party following its defeat in the general election held in 1977. He returned to the government in 1984 to serve in the Labour-Likud coalition Cabinet in a number of ministries, including that of defence during the period of the Palestinian *intifada* on the West Bank in the late 1980s. In February 1992 Rabin was elected Chairman of Labour and, following the party's victory in the general election held in July, began a second term as Prime Minister. Amid continuing unrest on the West Bank and the Gaza Strip, he negotiated an agreement with the PLO in May 1994, providing for Palestinian autonomy in those areas; for which he received the Nobel Prize for Peace jointly with the Israeli Minister of Foreign Affairs, Shimon Peres (q.v.), and the leader of the PLO, Yasser Arafat (q.v.). However, on 4 November 1995 he was assassinated by a right-wing Israeli opposed to the peace process. His death became seen as a symbol of the difficult nature of the peace process, his memorial being a focal point for pro-peace groups.

RANTISI, Abd-al-Aziz ar-: Palestinian paramilitary leader and doctor; b. 23 October 1947, Yubna. *Education:* he studied medicine at the University of Alexandria. *Career:* while a student in Egypt he came under the influence of the Muslim Brotherhood, a proscribed Islamist organization. He qualified as a paediatrician, and practised for several years upon his return to Gaza (to where his family had moved in his infancy, following the establishment of the State of Israel). He made numerous attempts to transfer the ideology of the Muslim Brotherhood into an Islamist Palestinian opposition to Israel, although none of the groups gained momentum until the beginning of the *intifada*. At this time, he joined with numerous other Islamist militants, including Sheikh Ahmad Yassin (q.v.), and formed an organization that became the Islamic Resistance Movement of Palestine, more commonly known by its Arabic acronym, Hamas. The length and frequency of his periods of detention increased during the *intifada*, and in March 1988 he was detained indefinitely by the Israeli security forces. Apart from a brief period of release in 1990, he remained in custody until December 1992, whereupon he was expelled to Lebanon. Following the creation of the Palestinian Authority (PA) he felt able to return to the areas under its control, but the PA, fearing his impact on public opinion and the effects of Islamist violence on the peace process, chose to detain him, although he was never incarcerated for more than a few weeks at a time. By 1999 he was the effective political leader of Hamas, while Yassin was the organization's spiritual head. Both men were implacable opponents of Arab recognition of the legitimacy of the State of Israel and, following the outbreak of the al-Aqsa *intifada*, the violence of Hamas' actions increased. Under Rantisi's leadership, the organization became the prime exponent of the suicide bombing against Israeli targets. His opposition to any peace process with Israel also brought him into conflict with Yasser Arafat (q.v.) and, later, the two Palestinian premiers. Following a spate of suicide bombings in May and June 2003, he became a high-profile objective for the Israeli military's programme of 'targeted killings', surviving one such attempt on his life in June. As the peace process stalled, Rantisi's leadership of Hamas remained constant in its support of violence against Israel and in its view of those negotiating with Israel as traitors to Islam and to the Palestinian cause.

ROGERS, William Pierce: US Secretary of State, 1969–73; b. 23 June 1913, Norfolk, NY, USA; m. Adele Langston 1933, with three s. and one d. *Education:* Colgate University, Cornell University Law School. *Career:* Following a brief period in private law practice, Rogers joined the public justice-administration system. Having served as US Attorney-General from 1957–61 and, following a return to private practice as a civil-rights lawyer, US Representative in the UN General Assembly from 1965–69, Rogers was appointed Secretary of State by President Richard M. Nixon in 1969. One of his major tasks was to construct US Middle East policy following the Arab–Israeli conflict of 1967. In December 1969 he issued a set of proposals which became known as the Rogers Plan. Among the document'ss 10 points was the assertion that there should only be a minor modification of Israel's pre-1967 boundaries, causing it to be rejected by the Israeli Government. He was successful, however, in mediating a cease-fire between Egypt and Israel following an exchange of bombing raids in 1970, and at this time he attempted to persuade the two parties to reconsider his plan. However, subsequent conflict between the Jordanian Government—which was in favour of the plan—and PLO guerrillas, combined with increasing tensions between Israel and Syria, caused the US Government to abandon the proposals. Tensions between Rogers and Nixon's national security adviser, Dr Henry

Kissinger (q.v.), prompted Rogers to resign in 1973, upon which he again entered private law practice. He died in January 2001.

ROSS, Dennis B.: US Special Middle East Co-ordinator. *Education:* he studied at the University of California, Los Angeles. *Career:* Ross entered US government service in 1977, serving on the National Security Council as Director of Near East and South Asian affairs during the presidency of Ronald Reagan. In the Administration of George Bush he became Director of the State Department's Policy Planning Office, co-ordinating US policy on the USSR, the reunification of Germany and the conflict with Iraq in 1991. President Bill Clinton (q.v.) promoted Ross to the office of Special Middle East Co-ordinator and he first began to take a prominent role in mediating negotiations following the secret draft agreement between the PLO and Israel in August 1993. Described by a senior Palestinian official as a 'postman' between the two sides, he was instrumental in the US-led peace initiatives of the 1990s, assisting with the Israeli-Jordanian peace treaty in 1994, the Interim Peace Agreement between Israel and the PLO the following year and the Wye River negotiations in 1998–99. In February 2000 he reacted to criticism of his country's intervention in Middle Eastern affairs with the assertion that the role of the USA was to support and facilitate the peace process rather than act as guarantor. He left the position of US envoy following the inauguration to the US presidency of George W. Bush in January 2001, his final attempt in December 2000 to persuade the PLO leader, Yasser Arafat (q.v.), to accept President Clinton's proposals for the creation of a Palestinian state on the condition that the PNA relinquish its demand that Palestinian refugees be allowed to return to areas they had left in 1948, having been unsuccessful. He subsequently joined the Washington Institute for Near East Policy as a Distinguished Fellow and Counsellor. *Address:* c/o The Washington Institute for Near East Policy, 1828 L St NW, Suite 1050, Washington, DC 20036, USA; *e-mail* dennisr@washingtoninstitute.org.

SADAT, Muhammad Anwar al-: President of Egypt 1970–1981, Prime Minister 1973–74, 1980–81; b. 25 December 1918, Mit Abu al-Kawm; m. Jihan Sadat, one s. and three d. *Education:* he graduated from Abbasia Military College. *Career:* As a member of Col Gamal Abd an-Nasser's (q.v.) revolutionary Free Officers, Sadat was imprisoned twice during the Second World War. He escaped from his second period of detention and rejoined Nasser's group to take part in the *coup d'état* of 1952, which forced King Farouk to abdicate and led to the withdrawal of the British from Egypt. During the early period of the Egyptian Republic and the United Arab Republic (initially, from 1958–61, a union with Syria), he held various government posts, including Minister of State from 1955–56, Chairman of the National Assembly from 1957–60 and Vice-President from 1964–66 and from 1969–70. Following the death of Nasser during this last period, Sadat assumed the presidency on a temporary basis, before being formally elected to the position in October 1970. He broke with Nasser's policy of receiving aid from the USSR and, in July 1972, expelled several thousand Soviet advisers from the country. He also aborted earlier plans to form an Arab federation with Sudan and Libya. The Egyptian army's successful penetration of the Bar-Lev line on 6 October 1973 and invasion of the Sinai peninsula caused Sadat to be regarded as a hero in the Arab world, despite the Israeli army's recapture of the territory. Following the war, he began a campaign to secure the return of the peninsula to Egypt. In June 1974 he held discussions in Cairo with the US President, Richard M. Nixon, leading to a *rapprochement* with the USA. In November 1977 he addressed the Israeli Knesset; during the speech he recognized the existence of the State of Israel, but warned that peace in the Middle East depended on Israel's withdrawal from the Sinai. Knowing that this would provoke criticism from Egypt's Arab neighbours, he terminated diplomatic relations with Algeria, Iraq, Libya, Syria and Yemen in December. Following negotiations in the USA with the Israeli Prime Minister, Menachem Begin (q.v.), Sadat signed the Camp David Agreements in September 1978, which led to the conclusion of a peace treaty by the two governments and Israel's withdrawal from the Sinai. Sadat received the Nobel Peace Prize jointly with Begin in October 1978. However, this accommodation with Israel further angered other Arab states, and Egypt was effectively isolated by the Arab world. The withdrawal of diplomatic contacts and economic aid from the petroleum-producing countries greatly weakened his position. Following several months of unrest caused by militant Islamists, Sadat was assassinated by the right-wing Lt Khaled Islambouli on 6 October 1981.

SHAATH, Nabil: Palestinian/Egyptian administrator, industrialist and politician; b. 1938, Safad. *Education:* he studied at the Universities of Alexandria and Pennsylvania (USA). *Career:* After taking Egyptian citizenship upon his return to Egypt from his postgraduate studies in the USA in 1965, he took up a teaching post at the American University in Beirut. He subsequently became an industrial development consultant, overseeing infrastructure and personnel projects throughout the Arab world. He became involved in Palestinian politics in the early 1970s, and quickly became a senior political adviser to the leader of the PLO, Yasser Arafat (q.v.). He has represented both the PLO and the Palestinian Authority (PA) at the UN. A skilled negotiator, he was the PLO's representative at its first official meeting with an Israeli minister in 1983. He was subsequently a senior member of the negotiating teams in the Oslo and Madrid processes, and was once dubbed 'Washington's favourite Palestinian'. He became the PA's Minister of Planning and International Cooperation in 1994, and was elected to the Palestinian Legislative Council in 1996. A man of significant personal wealth but scant domestic popularity, allegations of corruption were directed at him in 1997, and an official investigation the following year suggested that there was incriminating evidence against him. He refused to resign, however, and was reappointed to his post when the weight of numerous corruption scandals eventually brought down the entire PA Government in September 2002. Following the appointment of Mahmud Abbas (q.v.) to the newly-created post of Prime Minister in April 2003, Shaath accepted the foreign affairs portfolio. He had for some time acted as the international proxy of Arafat during the latter's period of confinement to Ramallah, and the new post appeared to be a logical extension of this role. He retained the position after Abbas' replacement by Ahmed Quray (q.v.) in October 2003. *Address:* Palestinian Authority, Ramallah, West Bank.

SHAMIR, Itzhak: Prime Minister of Israel, 1983–1984, 1986–1992; b. Yitzhak Yernitsky, 15 October 1915 in Ruzinoy, Poland; m. with one s. and one d. *Education:* University of Warsaw and the Hebrew University of Jerusalem. *Career:* Having left the University of Warsaw without completing his law degree, Shamir emigrated to Palestine in 1935, where he joined the clandestine Irgun Zvai Leumi organization. He subsequently helped to found and lead the independence movement, Lohamei Herut Israel, in 1941. He was arrested twice by the British Mandatory Authority for separatist activities, once in 1941 and again in 1946, when he was exiled to Eritrea. From there, he escaped to French Somaliland (Djibouti) and was granted political asylum by France. Shamir returned to the Middle East after the foundation of the State of Israel in 1948 and found employment in the civil service. Following success in several commercial enterprises, he became a member of Herut in 1970 and served as the Chairman of its Executive Committee from 1975–92. In 1973 he was elected to the Knesset and occupied the post of Speaker from 1977–80. As Minister of Foreign Affairs from 1980–83, Shamir worked to improve relations with the USA and African countries. Following the Israeli incursions into Lebanon in the early 1980s, he also led the negotiations for peace with Lebanon, culminating in a peace agreement in May 1983. He was subsequently elected leader of Likud (the alliance to which Herut now belonged), following the resignation of Menachem Begin (q.v.), and assumed the post of interim Prime Minister, until the general elections of July 1984. Likud and Labour formed a Government of National Unity—in accordance with the coalition agreement between the two parties, Shamir served as Minister of Foreign Affairs and Deputy Prime Minister, assuming the position of Prime Minister in October 1986. His proposal to hold Palestinian elections in the Occupied Territories in 1989 divided the Government. Although it was approved in the Knesset, Ariel Sharon (q.v.), then Minister of Trade and Industry, attempted to have the proposals amended. Following his defeat in a vote of 'no confidence' in his leadership in the Knesset, Shamir was forced to resign. The failure of his successor, Shimon Peres (q.v.), to form a coalition government caused Shamir to be reinstated as Prime Minister for a further two years, until Likud's defeat by Labour in June 1992. Shamir remained a member of the Knesset until his retirement in 1996. Address: Beit Amot Mishpat, 8 Shaul Hamelech Boulevard, Tel-Aviv 64733, Israel.

SHARON, Ariel: Israeli politician and army officer, Prime Minister of Israel, 2001–; b. 1928, Ariel Sheinerman, Kfar Malal, Palestinian Mandated Territory (now Israel); m. with two s. *Education:* Hebrew University, Tel-Aviv, Staff College, United Kingdom. *Career:* Sharon began a military career which was to last 25 years, fighting in the Sinai Campaign of 1956 and in 1967 led a Brigade group in the Six-Day War. In 1973 he was recalled from retirement to command a regiment on the Sinai Front in the Yom Kippur War. Shortly after the end of that conflict, he was involved in the foundation of the Likud bloc and was elected to the Knesset in the same year. However, he resigned his position shortly after his election in order to act as special security adviser to Itzhak Rabin (q.v.) during his term as Prime Minister. As Minister of Agriculture and Chairman of the Ministerial Committee for Settlements during the administration of Menachem Begin (q.v.), he oversaw the expansion of Israeli settlements in the Occupied Territories and rejected proposals for their return to Arab sovereignty.

In 1981 he was promoted to the position of Minister of Defence and, in the following year, he ordered the IDF to invade southern Lebanon in a campaign to destroy military positions maintained by the PLO, led by Yasser Arafat (q.v.). 'Operation Peace for Galilee' was conducted without the explicit approval of Begin and violence escalated when IDF soldiers did not prevent Lebanese Christian militias from killing several hundred Palestinian refugees in the Sabra and Chatila refugee camps. Sharon was forced to resign following a government inquiry, which held him indirectly responsible for the killings, although he remained in the Government as Minister Without Portfolio. Subsequent ministerial appointments included trade and industry, construction and housing and (from 1996–99) foreign affairs and national infrastructure portfolios. Following the electoral defeat of Binyamin Netanyahu (q.v.) in the prime-ministerial election held in May 1999, Sharon was elected leader of Likud. In September 2000 he caused further controversy by visiting the disputed site known as Temple Mount by Jews and Haram ash-Sharif by Muslims. Protests by Palestinians objecting to the visit to the holy Muslim site by the man they held responsible for the Sabra and Chatila massacres escalated into violent unrest, which became known as the al-Aqsa *intifada*. Following the resignation from the premiership of Ehud Barak (q.v.), Sharon made a central feature of his electoral campaign his opposition to any peace agreements that, as he perceived it, endangered Israel's security by conceding land to the Palestinians. He was elected Prime Minister in February 2001, obtaining 62.4% of the votes cast. His election was widely perceived among international observers as detrimental to the peace process and, as the al-Aqsa *intifada* continued, his administration withdrew many of the concessions offered by previous governments and, on numerous occasions, reimposed military control over certain areas administered by the PNA in response to acts of terrorism perpetrated by militant Palestinian groups. In December 2001 he termed the President of the PNA, Arafat, as 'irrelevant' to Israeli–Palestinian relations, following what Sharon perceived as Arafat's failure to act sufficiently against Palestinian individuals and groups held responsible for acts of violence committed in Israel. His robust style won him few admirers outside Israel and the USA and, together with his controversial past, ensured that he would always remain newsworthy. The allegations of his complicity in the attacks on the Sabra and Chatila refugee camps in 1982, while far from new, gained new prominence in 2001 when a Palestinian living in Belgium brought legal action for war crimes against Sharon in that country's court (the Belgian parliament had earlier introduced legislation enabling the country's courts to have global jurisdiction in cases of crimes against humanity). Following the presentation of action against numerous other world leaders, the Belgian Government came under pressure to repeal the legislation permitting non-Belgians to be tried in the country for offences that took place outside the country, and it assented. Sharon's Government fell in November 2002, following the withdrawal of Labour members, and he was forced to appoint his fiercest Likud rival, Netanyahu, to the foreign ministry in an interim administration, thus opening the way for him to challenge for the leadership prior to the general election to be held in January 2003. Netanyahu was easily defeated, however, and the party performed strongly at the poll, enabling Sharon to form a new Government, in which Netanyahu was 'demoted' to the finance portfolio. While the country's economic performance and allegations of malpractice worried many Israelis, security was the paramount issue, and Sharon appeared as strong as ever. However, in late 2003 he suggested, following preliminary public statements by his deputy, Ehud Olmert (q.v.), that Israel might be best served by a unilateral withdrawal from some Palestinian territories. The proposed policy drew criticism from across the political spectrum, although this, as always, is a position in which Sharon has thrived. *Address:* Likud Party, 38 Rehov King George, Tel-Aviv, 62131 Israel; Office of the Prime Minister, POB 187, 3 Rehar Kaplan, Kiryat Ben Gurion, Jerusalem 91919, Israel; tel 3-5630666; fax 3-5282901; *internet:* www.pmo.gov.il.

WAZIR, Khalil Ibrahim al- ('Abu Jihad'): Deputy Commander of the Palestinian Liberation Army; b. 10 October 1935, Ramla. *Education:* he studied at the University of Cairo. *Career:* Wazir fled Ramla with his family during the 1948 Arab-Israeli War and settled in the Gaza Strip, where he finished his secondary education at a school established by UN relief funds. After a brief period of study at the University of Cairo, which he left without completing his degree, Wazir met Yasser Arafat (q.v.) during a military training course. In 1956 they founded the clandestine Palestinian opposition movement, Fatah, which was later to become a major group in the PLO. Wazir, who adopted the *nom de guerre* of Abu Jihad, was given particular responsibility for military training and recruitment and in 1963 established the Organization's offices in Algeria. However, it was after the Arab armies' defeat in the 1967 Six-Day War that Abu Jihad's profile in the PLO was raised as he was promoted to key positions on the Palestinian National Council and the Supreme Military Council of the PLO. It is believed that he directed the PLO's military campaigns in Israel, including the Occupied Territories, and operations during the conflict in Jordan in 1970–71. It is also thought that he played a major role in developing the Palestinian resistance network in the West Bank and the Gaza Strip and helped to secure supplies of arms from Communist countries during the 1980s. He was assassinated by Israeli forces on 16 April 1988 at his office in Tunis, Tunisia.

YASSIN, Sheikh Ahmad: Palestinian religious leader, founder of Hamas movement; b. 1938, in the Palestinian Mandated Territory. *Education:* he attended the Al-Azhar University in Cairo, Egypt. *Career:* At the time of the creation of the state of Israel in 1948, Yassin fled with his family to the Gaza Strip. A childhood accident rendered him quadriplegic and partially blind. While pursuing Islamic studies in Egypt, he formed the belief that Palestine was an Islamic land 'consecrated for future Muslim generations until Judgement Day'. At this time he also became a member of the religious organization, the Muslim Brotherhood, for which he was later imprisoned by the Israeli authorities. In the Palestinian *intifada* of 1987 he gained prominence as a spiritual leader, establishing the Islamic Resistance Movement, known as Hamas. Two years later he was again arrested and sentenced to life imprisonment for ordering the killing of Palestinians accused of collaborating with the Israeli army. Yassin was released in October 1997 in exchange for the return of two Israeli secret-service agents who had been detained in Jordan. In the years following his release, Yassin worked to secure financial support from Arab regimes for a welfare programme for displaced Palestinians. He remained implacably opposed to the peace process, which he maintained was no substitute for *jihad* (holy war) as a means of removing Israel from the 'consecrated land'. Hamas' policy of suicide-bombings received the explicit and public approval of its leader on a number of occasions throughout the al-Aqsa *intifada*, most notably in November 2001 after two attacks which killed a combined total of 25 Israelis. Yassin was also highly critical of the leader of the PLO and President of the PNA, Yasser Arafat (q.v.), claiming that his policies had sought to appease Israel at the expense of Palestinian and Muslim unity. His extreme Islamism increased in appeal to many Palestinians throughout the al-Aqsa *intifada*, and the perceived threat to regional security of even greater popularity, should Arafat lose or relinquish power in Palestine, was keenly felt by the international community. He survived at least one 'targeted killing' attempt by Israeli forces in 2003 and, despite his physical frailty, continued to preach his vehemently anti-Israeli message as the suicide bombings and Israeli reprisals multiplied.

Select Bibliography

Abdel Malek, A. *La pensée politique arabe contemporaine.* Paris, Editions du Seuil, 1970.

Abed, George T. (Ed.). *The Palestinian Economy: Studies in Development under Prolonged Occupation.* London, Routledge, 1988.
  The Economic Viability of a Palestinian State. Washington, DC, Institute for Palestine State, 1990.

Abu Jaber, Kamel S. *The Arab Baath Socialist Party.* New York, Syracuse University Press, 1966.

Abu-Lughod, Ibrahim (Ed.). *The Transformation of Palestine: Essays on the Development of the Arab-Israeli Conflict.* Evanston, IL, Northwestern University Press, 1971.

Aburish, Said. *Cry Palestine: Inside the West Bank.* London, Bloomsbury, 1991.

Adams, Michael, and Mayhew, Christopher. *Publish it Not ... the Middle East Cover-up.* London, Longman, 1975.

Ajami, Fouad. *The Arab Predicament: Arab Political Thought and Practice since 1967.* Cambridge University Press, 2nd edition, 1992.

Algosaibi, Ghazi al-. *The Gulf crisis—an attempt to understand.* London, Kegan Paul International, 1993.

Allan, Tony. *The Middle East Water Question: Hydropolitics and the Global Economy.* London, I. B. Tauris, 2001.

Allen, Richard. *Imperialism and Nationalism in the Fertile Crescent: Sources and Prospects of the Arab-Israeli Conflict.* London, Oxford University Press, 1975.

Alterman, Jon B. *New Media, New Politics? From Satellite Television to the Internet in the Arab World.* Washington Institute for Near East Policy, 1998.

Anderson, Jack, and Boyd, James. *Oil: The Real Story Behind the World Energy Crisis.* London, Sidgwick and Jackson, 1984.

Aurur, Naseer, and Shuraydi Muhammad A. (Eds). *Revising Culture, Reinventing Peace: The Influence of Edward W. Said.* Ithaca, NY, Olive Branch Press, 2001.

Ashkenasi, Abraham (Ed.). *The Future of Jerusalem.* Frankfurt-am-Main, Peter Lang, 1999.

Ateek, Nairn, and Prior, Michael (Eds). *Holy Land Hollow Jubilee: God, Justice and the Palestinians*. London, Melisende, 1999.

Ayoob, M. (Ed.). *The Middle East in World Politics*. London, Croom Helm, 1981.

Ayubi, Nazih N. *Over-Stating the Arab State: Politics and Society in the Middle East*. London, I. B. Tauris, 1995.

Bailey, Sydney. *Four Arab-Israeli wars and the Peace Process*. London, Macmillan, 1990.

Barnaby, Frank. *The Invisible Bomb: The Nuclear Arms Race in the Middle East*. London, I. B. Tauris, 1989.

Beinin, J., and Stork, J. *Political Islam*. London and New York, I. B. Tauris, 1997.

Bell, J. Bowyer. *The Long War, Israel and the Arabs since 1946*. Englewood Cliffs, NJ, 1969.

Ben-Zvi, Abraham. *Decade of Transition: Eisenhower, Kennedy, and the Origins of American-Israeli Alliance*. New York, Columbia University Press, 1999.

Bennis, Phyllis, and Moushabeck, Michael (Eds). *Beyond the Storm: A Gulf Crisis Reader*. Edinburgh, Canongate Press, 1992.

Berberoglu, Berch (Ed.). *Power and Stability in the Middle East*. London, Zed Books, 1989.

Bethell, Nicholas. *The Palestine Triangle*. London, André Deutsch, 1979.

Bidwell, Robin (Ed.). *Dictionary of Modern Arab History*. London, Kegan Paul International, 1998.

Bill, J., and Springborg, R. *Politics in the Middle East*. London, HarperCollins, 4th Edition, 1994.

Binder, Leonard. *The Ideological Revolution in the Middle East*. New York, 1964.

Biswas, Asit K. (Ed.). *Core and Periphery: A Comprehensive Approach to Middle Eastern Water*. Oxford University Press, 1998.

Blake, Gerald H., and Drysdale, Alasdair. *The Middle East and North Africa: A Political Geography*. Oxford University Press, 1985.

Bonine, Michael E. (Ed.). *Population, poverty and politics in Middle Eastern cities*. Gainesville, FL, University Press of Florida, 1997.

Bregman, Ahron, and El-Tahri, Jihan. *The Fifty Years War: Israel and the Arabs*. London, Penguin and BBC Books, 1998.

Brenchley, Frank. *Britain and the Middle East: an economic history, 1945–1987*. London, Lester Crook Academic Publishing, 1989.

Breslauer, George W. (Ed.). *Soviet Strategy in the Middle East*. London, Routledge, 1989.

Brown, L. Carl. *Diplomacy in the Middle East*. London, I. B. Tauris, 2001.

Buchanan, Andrew S. *Peace with Justice: A History of the Israeli-Palestinian Declaration of Principles on Interim Self-Government Arrangements*. Basingstoke, St Martin's Press, 2000.

Bull, Gen. Odd. *War and Peace in the Middle East: the Experience and Views of a UN Observer*. London, Leo Cooper, 1976.

Bullard, Sir R. *Britain and the Middle East from the earliest times until 1952*. London, 1952.

Bulloch, John. *The Making of a War: The Middle East from 1967–1973*. London, Longman, 1974.

Burke, Edmond. *Struggle for Survival in the Modern Middle East*. London, I. B. Tauris, 1994.

Burrows, Bernard. *Footnotes in the Sand: the Gulf in Transition*. London, Michael Russell, 1991.

Butt, Gerald. *A Rock and a Hard Place: origins of Arab-Western conflict in the Middle East*. London, HarperCollins, 1994.

   The Arabs: Myth and Reality. London, I. B. Tauris, 1998.

Butterworth, Charles E., and Zartman, I. William (Eds). *Between the State and Islam*. Cambridge University Press, 2001.

Carré, Olivier. *L'Idéologie palestinienne de résistance*. Paris, Armand Colin, 1972.

   Mystique et Politique. Paris, Presses de la Fondation nationale des sciences politiques and Editions du Cerf, 1984.

Carrère d'Encausse, Hélène. *La politique soviétique au Moyen-Orient, 1955–1975*. Paris, Presses de la Fondation Nationale des Sciences Politiques, 1976.

Cattan, Henry. *Palestine and International Law: The Legal Aspects of the Arab-Israeli Conflict*. London, Longman, 1973.

   Jerusalem. London, Croom Helm, 1981 (Reissued, Gregg Revivals, 1994).

Chomsky, Noam. *Peace in the Middle East?: Reflections on Justice and Nationhood*. London, Collins, 1976.

   The Fateful Triangle: The United States, Israel and the Palestinians. London, Pluto Press, 1983.

   Pirates and Emperors: International Terrorism in the Real World. Armana Books, USA, 1990.

Cleveland, William L. *A History of the Modern Middle East*. Oxford, Westview Press, 1994.

Cobban, Helena. *The Palestinian Liberation Organization: People, Power and Politics*. Cambridge University Press, 1984.

Cohen, Michael J. *Palestine: Retreat from the Mandate*. London, Elek Books, 1978.

Conrad, Lawrence J. (Ed.). *The Formation and Perception of the Modern Arab World, Studies by Marwan R. Buheiry*. Princeton, NJ, The Darwin Press, 1989.

Cooley, John K. *Green March, Black September: The Story of the Palestinian Arabs*. London, Frank Cass, 1973.

   Payback: America's Long War in the Middle East. London, Brassey's, 1992.

Cordesman, Anthony. *Weapons of mass destruction in the Middle East*. London, Brassey's, 1991.

Corm, Georges. *Fragmentation of the Middle East: the last thirty years.* London, Unwin Hyman, 1988.

Curtiss, Richard H. *Stealth PACs: how Israel's American lobby took control of US-Middle East policy.* Washington, DC, American Educational Trust, 1990.

Dekmejian, R. H. *Islam in Revolution: fundamentalism in the Arab World.* New York, Syracuse University Press, 1995.

De Vore, Ronald M. (Ed.). *The Arab-Israeli Conflict: A Historical, Political, Social and Military Bibliography.* Oxford, Clio Press, 1977.

Dimbleby, Jonathan, and McCullin, Donald. *The Palestinians.* London, Quartet, 1970.

Dowek, Ephraim. *Israeli–Egyptian Relations, 1980–2000.* London, Frank Cass, 2001.

Dupuy, Trevor N. *Elusive Victory: The Arab-Israeli Wars 1947–1974.* London, MacDonald and Jane's, 1979.

Easterman, Daniel. *New Jerusalems—reflections on Islam, fundamentalism and the Rushdie affair.* London, Grafton Books, 1992.

Efrat, Moshe, and Bercovitch, Jacob. *Superpowers and Client States in the Middle East: The Imbalance of Influence.* London, Routledge, 1991.

Ehteshami, Anoushiravan, and Hinnebusch, Raymond. *Syria and Iran: Middle Powers in a Penetrated Regional System.* London, Routledge, 1997.

Elon, Amos. *A Blood-Dimmed Tide: Dispatches from the Middle East.* London, Allen Lane, 2000.

Ettinghausen, Richard. *Books and Periodicals in Western Languages dealing with the Near and Middle East.* Washington, DC, Middle East Institute, 1952.

Field, Henry. *Bibliography on Southwestern Asia: VII, A Seventh Compilation.* University of Miami, 1962.

Fisher, S. N. *The Middle East: A History.* New York, McGraw-Hill, 4th edition, 1990.

Fisher, W. B. *The Middle East—a Physical, Social and Regional Geography.* London, 7th edition, 1978.

Frangi, Abdallah. *The PLO and Palestine.* London, Zed Press, 1984.

Freedman, Robert O. *Soviet Policy toward the Middle East since 1970.* New York, Praeger, 3rd edition, 1983.

Friedman, Thomas. *From Beirut to Jerusalem.* New York, Farrar, Straus and Giroux, 1989.

Frye, R. N. (Ed.). *The Near East and the Great Powers.* Cambridge, MA, Harvard University Press, 1951; London, New York and Toronto, Oxford University Press, 1952.

Gallagher, Nancy Elizabeth (Ed.). *Approaches to the History of the Middle East: Interviews with leading Middle East historians.* Reading, Garnet, 1995.

Gee, John. *Unequal Conflict.* London, Pluto Press, 1998.

Gelber, Yoav. *Palestine 1948: War, Escape and the Emergence of the Palestinian Refugee Problem.* Brighton, Sussex Academic Press, 2001.

Gerner, Deborah J. *Understanding the Contemporary Middle East.* Boulder, CO, Lynne Rienner, 2000.

Gershoni, Israel and Jankowski, James (Eds). *Rethinking Nationalism in the Arab Middle East.* New York, Columbia University Press, 1998.

Giacaman, George, and Dag, Jrund Lonning. *After Oslo: New Realities, Old Problems.* Pluto Press, 1998.

Gilbert, Martin. *The Arab-Israeli Conflict: Its History in Maps.* London, Weidenfeld and Nicolson, 1974 (reissued, Dent: International Publishing Services, 1993).

Gilmour, David. *The Dispossessed: The Ordeal of the Palestinians 1917–80.* London, Sidgwick Jackson, 1980.

Golan, Galia. *The Soviet Union and the Middle East Crisis.* Cambridge University Press, 1977.

Gomaa, Ahmed M. *The Foundation of the League of Arab States.* London, Longman, 1977.

Gowers, Andrew, and Walter, Tony. *Behind the Myth: Yasir Arafat and the Palestinian revolution.* London, W.H. Allen, 1990.

Gresh, Alain, and Vidal, Dominique. *A–Z of the Middle East.* London, Zed Books, 1991.

Guazzone, Laura. *The Islamist Dilemma.* Reading, Ithaca Press, 1995.

Guyatt, Nicholas. *The Absence of Peace: Understanding The Israeli-Palestinian Conflict.* London, Zed Press, 1998.

Halliday, Fred. *Islam and the Myth of Confrontation: Religion and Politics in the Middle East.* London, I. B. Tauris, 1995.

Nation and Religion in the Middle East. Boulder, CO, Lynne Rienner, 2000.

Hansen, Birte. *Unipolarity and the Middle East.* Richmond, Curzon Press, 1999.

Hare, William. *The Struggle for the Holy Land.* London, Madison Publishing, 1998.

Harris, Lillian Craig. *China Considers the Middle East.* London, I. B. Tauris, 1994.

Hart, Alan. *Arafat—Terrorist or Peacemaker?* London, Sidgwick and Jackson, 2nd edition, 1994.

Hassan bin Talal, Crown Prince of Jordan. *A Study on Jerusalem.* London, Longman, 1980.

Hatem, M. Abdel-Kader. *Information and the Arab Cause.* London, Longman, 1974.

Herzog, Maj.-Gen. Chaim. *The War of Atonement.* London, Weidenfeld and Nicolson, 1975.

The Arab-Israeli Wars. London, Arms and Armour Press, 1982.

Hewedy, Amin. *Militarisation and Security in the Middle East.* London, Pinter, 1989.

Higgins, Rosalyn. *United Nations Peacekeeping 1946–67: Documents and Commentary*, Volume I, *The Middle East.* Oxford University Press, 1969.

Hiro, Dilip. *Inside the Middle East*. London, Routledge and Kegan Paul, 1981.

Islamic Fundamentalism. London, Paladin, 1988.

The Longest War. London, Grafton Books, 1990.

Dictionary of the Middle East. London, Macmillan, 1996.

Sharing the Promised Land. An Interwoven Tale of Israelis and Palestinians. London, Hodder Stoughton, 1996.

Hirst, David. *Oil and Public Opinion in the Middle East*. New York, Praeger, 1966.

The Gun and the Olive Branch: the Roots of Violence in the Middle East. London, Faber, 1977.

Hirszowicz, Lukasz. A Short History of the Near East. New York, 1966.

Hoare, Ian, and Tayar, Graham (Eds). *The Arabs. A handbook on the politics and economics of the contemporary Arab world*. London, BBC Publications, 1971.

Hourani, A. H. *Minorities in the Arab World*. London, 1947.

A Vision of History. Beirut, 1961.

Europe and the Middle East. London, Macmillan, 1980.

The Emergence of the Modern Middle East. London, Macmillan, 1981.

Hoveyda, Fereydoun. *Que veulent les arabes?* Paris, Editions First, 1991.

Hudson, Michael C. *Arab Politics: The Search for Legitimacy*. New Haven, CT, and London, Yale University Press, 1977/78.

Hurewitz, J. C. *Unity and Disunity in the Middle East*. New York, Carnegie Endowment for International Peace, 1952.

Middle East Dilemmas. New York, 1953.

Diplomacy in the Near and Middle East. Vol. I, *1535–1914*; Vol. II, *1914–56*. Van Nostrand, 1956.

(Ed.) *Soviet-American Rivalry in the Middle East*. London, Pall Mall Press, and New York, Praeger, 1969.

Middle East Politics: The Military Dimension. London, Pall Mall Press, 1969.

International Institute for Strategic Studies. *Sources of Conflict in the Middle East*. London, Adelphi Papers, International Institute for Strategic Studies, 1966.

Domestic Politics and Regional Security: Jordan, Syria and Israel. London, Gower, International Institute for Strategic Studies, 1989.

Ionides, Michael. *Divide and Lose: the Arab Revolt 1955–58*. London, Bles, 1960.

Jansen, G. H. *Non-Alignment and the Afro-Asian States*. New York, Praeger, 1966.

Militant Islam. London, Pan Books, 1979.

Jansen, Johannes J. G. *The Dual Nature of Islamic Fundamentalism*. Ithaca, NY, Cornell University Press, 1997.

Jawad, Haifaa A. *The Middle East in the New World Order*. London, Macmillan, 1996.

Jerichow, A., and Simonsen, J. B. (Eds). *Islam in a Changing World and the Middle East*. Richmond, Curzon Press, 1997.

Johnson, Nels. *Islam and the Politics of Meaning in Palestinian Nationalism*. Henley-on-Thames, Kegan Paul International, 1983.

Kaye, Dalia Dassa. *Beyond the Handshake: Multilateral Cooperation in the Arab-Israeli Peace Process, 1991–96*. New York, Columbia University Press, 2001.

Kemp, Geoffrey, and Harkavy, Robert. *The Strategic Geography of the Changing Middle East*. Washington, DC, The Brookings Institution, 1996.

Kemp, Geoffrey, and Pressman, Jeremy. *Point of No Return: The Deadly Struggle for Middle East Peace*. Washington, DC, The Brookings Institution, 1997.

Kerr, Malcolm. *The Arab Cold War 1958–1964*. Oxford University Press, 1965.

Khadouri, M. *Political Trends in the Arab World*. Baltimore, MD, Johns Hopkins Press, 1970.

Khalil, Muhammad. *The Arab States and the Arab League* (historical documents). Beirut, Khayats.

Khouri, Fred J. *The Arab-Israeli Dilemma*. Syracuse, NY, 1968.

Kingsbury, R. C., and Pounds, N. J. G. *An Atlas of Middle Eastern Affairs*. New York, 1963.

Kingston, Paul W. T. *Britain and the Politics of Modernization in the Middle East, 1945–1958*. Cambridge University Press, 1996.

Kirk, George E. A Short History of the Middle East: from the Rise of Islam to Modern Times. New York, 1955.

Klein, Menachem. *Jerusalem: The Contested City*. New York University Press, 2001.

Kliot, Norit. *Water Resources and Conflict in the Middle East*. London, Routledge, 1994.

Kreutz, Andrej. *Vatican Policy on the Palestinian—Israeli Conflict: the struggle for the Holy Land*. London, Greenwood Press, 1990.

Kurzman, Dan. *Genesis 1948: The First Arab/Israeli War*. London, Vallentine, Mitchell, 1972.

La Guardia, Anton. *Holy Land, Unholy War: Israel and Palestinians*. London, John Murray, 2001.

Lall, Arthur. *The UN and the Middle East Crisis*. London and New York, 1968.

Laqueur, W. Z. *Communism and Nationalism in the Middle East*. London and New York, 1957.

A History of Zionism. London, Weidenfeld and Nicolson, 1972.

The Struggle for the Middle East: The Soviet Union and the Middle East 1958–68. London, Routledge and Kegan Paul, 1969.

Confrontation: The Middle-East War and World Politics. London, Wildwood, 1974.

(Ed.) *The Middle East in Transition*. London, Routledge and Kegan Paul, 1958.

(Ed.) *The Israel-Arab Reader*. London and New York, Penguin Books, 4th edition, 1984.

Lemarchand, Philippe (Ed.). *The Crescent of Crises: A Geopolitical Atlas of the Middle East and the Arab World*. Paris, Editions Complexe, 1995.

Lenczowski, George. *The Middle East in World Affairs*. Ithaca, NY, Cornell University Press, 4th Edition, 1980.

Oil and State in the Middle East. Cornell University Press, 1960.

Lesch, David W. (Ed.). *The Middle East and the United States: A Historical and Political Reassessment*. Boulder, CO, Westview Press, 1996.

Lloyd, Selwyn. *Suez 1956: A Personal Account*. London, Jonathan Cape, 1978.

Logan, William S., and White, Paul J. (Eds). *Remaking the Middle East*. Oxford, Berg, 1997.

Longrigg, S. H. *Oil in the Middle East*. London, 1954, 3rd edition, London 1968.

The Middle East: a Social Geography. London, 2nd revised edition, 1970.

Louis, William Roger. *The British Empire in the Middle East 1945–51*. Oxford University Press, 1984.

McCarthy, Justin. *The Population of Palestine*. New York, Columbia University Press, 1991.

Macdonald, Robert W. *The League of Arab States*. Princeton, NJ, Princeton University Press, 1965.

Maddy-Weitzmann, Bruce, and Inbar, Efraim (Eds). *Religious Radicalism in the Greater Middle East*. London, Frank Cass, 1997.

Mallat, Chibli. *The Middle East into the Twenty-First Century: The Japan Lectures and other studies on the Arab-Israeli conflict, the Gulf crisis and political Islam*. Reading, Ithaca Press, 1996.

Mendelsohn, Everett. *A Compassionate Peace: a future for Israel, Palestine and the Middle East*. New York, The Noonday Press, 1989.

Meskell, Lynn. *Archaeology Under Fire: Nationalism, politics and heritage in the Eastern Mediterranean and Middle East*. London, Routledge, 1998.

Monroe, Elizabeth. *Britain's Moment in the Middle East 1914–71*. London, Chatto and Windus, new edition 1981.

Moore, John Norton. *The Arab-Israeli Conflict*. 4 vols. Princeton, NJ, Readings and Documents, 1976–92.

Morris, Benny. *Righteous Victims: A History of the Zionist–Arab Conflict, 1881–1999*. New York, Knopf, 1999.

Morris, Claud. *The Last Inch: A Middle East Odyssey*. London, Kegan Paul International, 1996.

Mortimer, Edward. *Faith and Power: The Politics of Islam*. London, Faber, 1982.

Morzellec, Joëlle Le. *La question de Jérusalem devant l'Organisation des Nations Unies*. Brussels, Emile Bruylant, S.A., 1979.

Mosley, Leonard. *Power Play: The Tumultuous World of Middle East Oil 1890–1973*. London, Weidenfeld and Nicolson, 1973.

Munson, Henry, Jr. *Islam and Revolution in the Middle East*. New Haven, CT, and London, Yale University Press, 1988.

Murakami, Masahiro. *Managing Water for Peace in the Middle East: Alternative Strategies*. Tokyo, United Nations University Press, 1996.

Nasr, Seyyed Hossein. *Science and Civilization in Islam*. Harvard (1968), revised edition, 1987.

Navias, Martin. *Going Ballistic: the build-up of missiles in the Middle East*. London, Brassey's, 1993.

Niblock, Tim. *Pariah' States and Sanctions in the Middle East: Iraq, Libya, Sudan*. Boulder, CO, Lynne Rienner, 2001.

Niblock, Tim, and Murphy, Emma. *Economic and Political Liberalism in the Middle East*. London, British Academic Press, 1993.

Nizameddin, Talal. *Russia and the Middle East*. London, C. Hurst Co, 1999.

Nonneman, Gerd. *Development, Administration and Aid in the Middle East*. London, Routledge, 1988.

(Ed.) *The Middle East and Europe: The Search for Stability and Integration*. London, Federal Trust, 1993.

Nutting, Anthony. *The Arabs*. London, Hollis and Carter, 1965.

No End of a Lesson, The Story of Suez. London, Constable, 1967.

Nydell, Margaret K. *Understanding Arabs: A Guide for Westerners*. Yarmouth, ME, Intercultural Press, 1992.

O'Ballance, Edgar. *The Third Arab-Israeli War*. London, Faber and Faber, 1972.

The Gulf War. London, Brassey's Defence Publishers, 1990.

Odell, Peter. *Oil and World Power*. London, Penguin, 1983.

Owen, Roger. *The Middle East in the World Economy 1800–1914*. London, I. B. Tauris (1972), revised edition, 1993.

State, Power and Politics in the Making of the Modern Middle East. London, Routledge, 2nd edition, 2000.

A History of Middle East Economies in the 20th Century. London, I. B. Tauris, 1998.

Palumbo, Michael. *The Palestinian Catastrophe*. London, Faber, 1987.

Parker, Richard B. *The October War—A Retrospective*. Gainesville, FL, University Press of Florida, 2001.

Persson, Magnus. *Great Britain, the United States and the Security of the Middle East: The Formation of the Baghdad Pact*. Lund University Press (Sweden), 1998.

Piscatori, James P. (Ed.). *Islam in the Political Process*. Cambridge University Press, 1983.

Islam in a World of Nation-States. Cambridge University Press, 1986.

Polk, W. R. *The Arab World Today*. Harvard University Press, 1991.

The Elusive Peace: The Middle East in the Twentieth Century. London, Frank Cass, 1980.

Rikhye, Maj.-Gen. I. J. *The Sinai Blunder*. London, Frank Cass, 1980.

Rivlin, B., and Szyliowicz, J. S. (Eds). *The Contemporary Middle East— Tradition and Innovation*. New York, Random House, 1965.

Rodinson, Maxime. *Israel and the Arabs*. London, Penguin, 1982.

Rogan, Eugene L., and Shlaim, Avi (Eds). *The War for Palestine: Rewriting the History of 1948*. Cambridge University Press, 2001.

Ro'i, Ya'acov. *The Limits of Power: Soviet Policy in the Middle East*. London, Croom Helm, 1978.

Rondot, Pierre. *The Destiny of the Middle East*. London, Chatto Windus, 1960.

Roy, Olivier. *The Failure of Political Islam*. London, I. B. Tauris, 1995.

Rubin, Barry M. *The Arab States and the Palestine Conflict*. New York, Syracuse University Press, 1981.

Sachar, Howard M. *Europe Leaves the Middle East 1936–1954*. London, Allen Lane, 1973.

Said, Edward W. *The Question of Palestine*. London, Routledge, 1979 (reissued, Vintage, 1992).

Covering Islam. London, Routledge, 1982.

The End of the Peace Process: Oslo and After. New York, Pantheon Books, 2000.

Salame, G. *Democracy without Democrats? The Renewal of Politics in the Muslim World*. London and New York, I. B. Tauris, 1994.

Salem, Paul (Ed.). *Conflict Resolution in the Arab World: Selected Essays*. American University of Beirut, 1997.

Scott Appleby, R. (Ed.). *Spokesmen for the Despised: Fundamentalist Leaders of the Middle East*. University of Chicago Press, 1997.

Seale, Patrick. *Abu Nidal: A Gun for Hire*. London, Hutchinson, 1992.

Searight, Sarah. *The British in the Middle East*. London, Weidenfeld and Nicolson, 1969.

Shadid, Muhammad K. *The United States and the Palestinians*. London, Croom Helm, 1981.

Shapland, Gregory. *Rivers of Discord: International Water Disputes in the Middle East*. London, C. Hurst and Co, 1997.

Sharabi, H. B. *Governments and Politics of the Middle East in the Twentieth Century*. London, Greenwood Press (1962), revised edition, 1987.

Nationalism and Revolution in the Arab World. New York, Van Nostrand, 1966.

Palestine and Israel: The Lethal Dilemma. New York, Pegasus Press, 1969.

Shlaim, Avi. *War and Peace in the Middle East*. New York/London, Penguin Books, 1995.

Shlaim, Avi, and Sayigh, Y. (Eds). *The Cold War and The Middle East*. Oxford University Press, 1998.

Smith, W. Cantwell. *Islam and Modern History*. Toronto, 1957.

Stevens, Georgina G. (Ed.). *The United States and the Middle East*. Englewood Cliffs, NJ, Prentice-Hall, 1964.

Stewart, Desmond. *The Middle East: Temple of Janus*. London, Hamish Hamilton, 1972.

Susser, Asher, and Shmuelevitz, Aryeh (Eds). *The Hashemites in the Modern Arab World: essays in honour of the late Professor Uriel Dann*. London, Frank Cass, 1995.

Taylor, Alan R. *The Arab Balance of Power*. New York, Syracuse University Press, 1982.

Taylor, Trevor. *The Middle East in the International System: Lessons from Europe and Implications for Europe*. London, Royal Institute of International Affairs, 1997.

Tessler, Mark A. *A History of the Israeli–Palestinian Conflict*. Bloomington, IN, Indiana University Press, 1994.

Thayer, P. W. (Ed.). *Tensions in the Middle East*. Baltimore, MD, 1958.

Tillman, Seth P. *The United States in the Middle East*. Hemel Hempstead, Indiana University Press, 1982.

Trevelyan, Humphrey (Lord). *The Middle East in Revolution*. London, Macmillan, 1970.

Tschirgi, Dan. *The American Search for Mideast Peace*. New York, Praeger, 1989.

Usher, Graham. *Dispatches from Palestine*. London, Pluto Press, 1999.

Vassiliev, Alexei. *Russian Policy in the Middle East: from messianism to pragmatism*. Reading, Ithaca Press, 1993.

Vatikiotis, P. J. *Conflict in the Middle East*. London, George Allen and Unwin, 1971.

   Islam and the State. London, Routledge, 1991.

Viorst, Milton. *Reaching for the Olive Branch: UNRWA and peace in the Middle East*. Washington, DC, Middle East Institute, 1989.

Wadsman, P., and Teissedre, R.-F. *Nos politiciens face au conflict israélo arabe*. Paris, 1969.

Waines, David. *The Unholy War*. Wilmette, IL, Medina Press, 1971.

Wasserstein, Bernard. *Divided Jerusalem: The Struggle for the Holy City*. London, Profile, 2001.

Wolf, Aaron T. *Hydropolitics Along the Jordan River: Scarce Water and its Impact on the Arab-Israeli Conflict*. Tokyo, United Nations University Press, 1996.

Woolfson, Marion. *Prophets in Babylon: Jews in the Arab World*. London, Faber, 1980.

Wright, Clifford A. *Facts and Fables: the Arab Israeli conflict.* London, Kegan Paul International, 1989.

Wright, J. W., Jr (Ed.). *The Political Economy of Middle East Peace: The Impact of Competing Arab and Israeli Trade.* London, Routledge, 1999.

Wright, J. W., Jr, and Drake, Laura (Eds). *Economic and Political Impediments to Middle East Peace: Critical Questions and Alternative Scenarios.* New York, St. Martin's Press, 1999.

Yapp, M. E. *The Near East since the First World War.* London, Longman, 1991.

Yergin, Daniel. *The Prize: the Epic Quest for Oil, Money and Power.* New York, Simon and Schuster (1990), revised edition, 1993.

Zeine, Z. N. *The Struggle for Arab Independence.* Beirut, 1960.